Rothschild

Also by Derek Wilson

East Africa Through a Thousand Years: A History

England in the Age of Thomas More

The People and The Book:
The Revolutionary Impact of the English Bible, 1380-1611

Sweet Robin: A Biography of Robert Dudley, Earl of Leicester, 1533-1588

The Tower, 1078-1978

A Tudor Tapestry: Men, Women and Society in Reformation England

White Gold: The Story of African Ivory

The World Encompassed: Drake's Great Voyage, 1577-1580

Rothschild

The Wealth and Power
of a Dynasty

DEREK WILSON

CHARLES SCRIBNER'S SONS
New York

Charles Scribner's Sons
Macmillan Publishing Company
866 Third Avenue, New York, NY 10022

Library of Congress Cataloging-in-Publication Data
Wilson, Derek A.
Rothschild : the wealth and power of a dynasty / Derek Wilson. —
1st American ed.
p. cm.
Bibliography: p.
Includes index.
ISBN 0-684-19018-4
1. Rothschild family.   2. Bankers—Europe—Biography.
3. Businessmen—Europe—Biography.   4. Europe—Politics and
government—1789–1900.   I. Title.
HG1552.R8W56 1988
332.1′092′2—dc19   88-19736   CIP
[B]

Macmillan books are available at special discounts for bulk
purchases for sales promotions, premiums, fund-raising, or
educational use. For details, contact:

Special Sales Director
Macmillan Publishing Company
866 Third Avenue
New York, NY 10022

10 9 8 7 6 5 4 3 2 1

Printed in the United States of America

CONTENTS

LIST OF ILLUSTRATIONS

Illustrations can be found between pages
118–119
246–247
374–375

ACKNOWLEDGEMENTS

I could never have written this book without the generous help of several members of the Rothschild family. At this point I must make it quite clear that the present work is, in no way, an *official* history of the Rothschilds. Material has been readily given by members of the family and I have endeavoured to reproduce it as accurately as possible. But the interpretation placed on it is entirely my own, as is the responsibility for any errors which may have crept into the narrative.

Mr Lionel de Rothschild provided me with introductions to his family and also enabled me to up-date the family tree. In addition, I am grateful to all the following who, by personal interview, letter or telephone, provided information and helped me check my facts: Lord Rothschild, Mrs James de Rothschild, Dr Miriam Rothschild, Baron Guy de Rothschild, Baron Elie de Rothschild, Mme Batsheva de Rothschild, Mr Edmund de Rothschild, Mr Evelyn de Rothschild, Baron Edmond de Rothschild, Baronne Philippine de Rothschild, the Hon. Jacob Rothschild, Mrs Bettina Looram, Mr Lionel de Rothschild, Miss Charlotte de Rothschild.

I have much reason to be grateful to the staffs of various public archives and libraries, especially those of the Archives Nationales in Paris, the Museen der Stadt, Nationalbibliothek, Staatsarchiv and Österreichisches Finanzarchiv in Vienna, the Historisches Museum in Frankfurt, the British Library, British Museum Print Room and Manuscript Department, Kent County Library and Cambridge University Library. A number of individuals and picture libraries provided me with illustrations which I acknowledge *in situ*.

My research has involved considerable travel and indebtedness to several people. My German publishers, Messrs Zolnay, provided hospitality on my visits to Vienna and Fräulein Ariane Engelhorn devoted weeks of patient endeavour helping me track down and translate documents in the Staatsarchiv and Finanzarchiv, as well as books and old newspapers in the university and municipal libraries. She also undertook a considerable amount of translation work. Professor Edouard März and Dr Dieter Stiefel helped me to an understanding of the history of the Creditanstalt and, in particular, of the 1931 banking crisis. In Paris, Baron Elie de Rothschild provided me with monographs on the art bequests and charitable activities of the French family and arranged a tour of the Fondations Rothschild on the Rue Picpus. By one of those rare strokes of good fortune which occasionally befall a researcher, a mutual friend acquired from Mrs Sylvia Anderson the unpublished memoirs of Baron George de Worms, a direct descendant of Mayer Amschel Rothschild, which provided a fascinating nineteenth-century chronical parallel to that of the Rothschilds. Mr M.B Cullen generously shared with me the result of his researches into his family history, and Mr Michael Hall drew my attention to some little known aspects of Rothschild art collections.

The brunt of the editorial work has been borne by Mrs Sara Mengüç of Messrs André Deutsch Ltd. Her enthusiasm and perception have delivered the author from a number of errors and inconsistencies. Several versions of this book have passed through the mysterious workings of my word processor. Every single syllable of them was entered by my uncomplaining wife.

Finally, I must include a word of thanks to my friend Anthony Wilkinson, who suggested the writing of this book in the first place.

Derek Wilson, May 1988

Part I
1560–1836

CHAPTER 1
"A civilised life, amidst barbarism"

Nothing now remains of the place in which this story begins. An Allied bombing raid in March 1944 made sure of that.[1] Today the visitor to Frankfurt-am-Main will find that amid the criss-cross of modern roads only a single fragment of the medieval city's north-eastern wall survives to help him gain his historical bearings. Immediately beyond that wall, cut off by it from Christian habitation, lay a curving, squalid half-mile of over-crowded tenements — Judengasse, Jew Street.

Something else that has disappeared with the centuries is the painting that adorned the Brückenturm, the main gateway to the old city. It depicted the devil watching with approval as a rabbi sat astride a pig and held its tail up so that another rabbi could eat its dung. Underneath the sow Jewish children were drinking its milk. The message was plain: "Jews and pigs not admitted." In the proud, free city of Frankfurt, one of the great entrepôts of Europe, Jews and Christians lived rigidly segregated lives. They were separated by centuries of hatred, jealousy and suspicion, which sporadically flared up into outbreaks of looting, arson and mob murder when the Jew-baiting cry of "Hepp! Hepp!"* sounded along Judengasse and the inmates hurried to drag their children inside and bolt their doors. They were separated by cultural barriers, maintained with equal determination by rabbis and Catholic priests. They were separated by Gentile insistence that people who lived amid the squalor and the stench of the overcrowded Jewish quarter were less than human.

Not that the ghetto had been designed to be overcrowded. The word itself derives from the Italian "borghetto", meaning simply a "little borough", a "township". When, in 1460, the city fathers moved the only eleven Jewish families into their own quarter there was plenty of space for them. It was an exercise in separate development, not human degradation. But apartheid never was an enlightened philosophy. It was, and is, born of prejudice and fear; and its inevitable consequences are

---

*An exclamation with no specific meaning; a call to others to join in. The English equivalent is "Hip!" as in "Hip, hip, hurrah".

violence, squalor and contempt for human dignity. The Jewish population increased. The size of the ghetto did not. Its inhabitants were only allowed into the city on business. They were not permitted there at all on Sundays. Their wives could not use the Frankfurt shops, nor their children play in the Frankfurt squares.

By 1750 three thousand men, women and children were crammed, cheek-by-jowl, into less than two hundred houses. Forty-five years later a foreign visitor noted: "Up to the roof every nook and cranny was filled with narrow rooms whose inhabitants consider themselves lucky when they can leave their dingy hole and get a breath of fresh air out on their dirty and damp street."[2] The broad-fronted residences of the fifteenth-century mercantile community had been subdivided again and again. The spaces between had been filled. Backyards had been built over. When most of the ground on either side of the street was covered, building had come to a halt. From time to time groups of houses collapsed, their foundations no longer able to bear the weight above. In 1711 an appalling fire destroyed the entire street but even after that the *Rat*, the city council, did not take the opportunity to improve conditions in the ghetto.

Frankfurt grew but the Jewish quarter did not. Instead, it became engulfed by the commodious dwellings of the Gentile city. A map of 1678 shows Judengasse sandwiched between the narrow streets of old Frankfurt and a new, more spacious residential quarter which stretched as far as the new fortifications. Nor could the Jews even look out on these pleasant suburbs. The "Building Regulations for Jews" of 1702 decreed: "So that it will be impossible to see into the houses of Christians [the side windows of the Jews] shall be walled in and pasted over."[3] The inhabitants' view was thus confined to the market stalls and open sewer of their own introverted cosmos, to Judengasse itself, thronged by women in blue-black striped veils and men wearing the hats and kaftans prescribed by law. The street was closed at its northern end by the Bornheimer Pforte and to the south by the Monchsturm. Access was controlled both by the *Rat*, and also by the leaders of the Jewish community, for restrictions on comings and goings served to protect the inhabitants as much as to prevent defilement of the Gentile population.

For the inhabitants of the ghetto anti-Semitism was a fact of everyday life. A fact which was also taken for granted in the world beyond the narrow confines of Judengasse. For example, it was a "well-known fact" that Jews kidnapped children because they needed their blood to mix with their Passover bread dough. The smell of the ghetto which hung around its inhabitants' clothing was often identified by clergy as the stench of hell. The very poverty and degradation of most Jews seemed proof to their Christian neighbours that these people belonged to a lower level of animal existence and for the minority who prospered things were no better. Kept from all other professions by the restrictive practices of the craft guilds, the Jews had no option but to engage in money lending and trading, and that only because the medieval church placed restrictions on the practice of usury. Yet their very success in these pursuits only roused resentment, greed and envy. For if a Jew prospered to the point where his wealth rivalled that of the leading burghers, it was simply taken as proof that he was in league with the devil, at whose behest he was bleeding honest Christians of their hard-earned cash.

Nor was anti-Semitism only manifested in ignorant superstition and mob prejudice. It was given intellectual respectability by philosophers of the stature of Immanuel Kant:

The Palestinians living amongst us are, since their exile, because of their usurious spirit not unjustifiably renowned for their deceitfulness, so far as the great majority is concerned. It does not indeed seem disconcerting to conceive of a *nation* of usurers ... by far the largest part of which is bound together by a superstition recognised by the state in which they live and do not seek any civic honour. But they try to compensate for this lack by the advantages of outwitting the people amongst whom they find shelter and even by deceiving each other. Now this cannot be otherwise in a whole nation of pure merchants [who are] non-productive members of society.

And it was one of Kant's disciples, J.G. Fichte, who roundly rejected any improvement of the Jews' lot: " ... to give them civic rights — I see no means to do that except, one night, to cut off all their heads and give them new ones in which there would not be one Jewish idea".[4] German society at all levels was shot through with race-hatred and the leaders of the Jewish community had every reason to be careful that their people should be locked in at night or whenever trouble brewed.

Persecution, like other forms of pressure, serves to compact and solidify the object to which it is applied. Under the impress of centuries, even millennia, of persecution, the Jewish communities had become the closest-knit groups of people in Europe. The men and women of the ghetto were united by a religion, a language and a sense of historic destiny older, far older, than the faith or culture of the people among whom they lived. Persecution intensified their sense of identity, the warmth of their fellowship, their commitment to life. One nineteenth-century writer, a child of the Frankfurt ghetto, expressed it like this: "More ingenuity, more spirit was expended in one day in the Jews' street in Frankfurt than in all the rest of Germany in a year ... for centuries this street represented a

5

civilised life, amidst barbarism, where in an oppressed society, faith, charity and justice reigned . . . "[5] It was an exaggeration, of course. There were many Jews who resented the sordid restrictions of the ghetto. In every generation some escaped to freer societies, such as that of England. But it would certainly be a mistake to overemphasise the negative aspect of life in Judengasse. The women kept their houses clean, their menfolk well turned out, their children educated. Neighbours cared for one another in times of sickness or hardship. The affairs of the community were regulated by a council, in theory elected, but in practice controlled by the wealthier families. The chairman of the council, who was also the judge, religious leader and educational supervisor, was the rabbi. The whole of life in the ghetto revolved around the synagogue, an impressive building with three onion-shaped cupolas, rebuilt after the fire in 1711. Private and public conduct was minutely regulated by the Torah and the great feasts and festivals marked the high points in the life of the community, whose affairs were administered by a small group of paid officials including, in addition to the rabbi, the ritual butcher, the cantor, the beadles and the guardian of the cemetery.

Even death did not free Frankfurt's Jews from overcrowding. The small burial ground allocated to the Jews in 1241 was never enlarged, despite frequent appeals by the community. Since handling old corpses involved ritual defilement, new graves could only be prepared by covering the cemetery with further layers of earth. When the burial place was closed in 1828 it contained 5930 headstones. One of those simple slabs of granite marked the passing in 1585 of Isaak Elchanan, the first Rothschild. Sometime in the 1560s this man, about whom nothing else is known, acquired a house somewhere on Judengasse which had the distinguishing feature of a red signboard or shield, a *rot Schild*. Jews were not allowed patronymics, and Isaak's descendants were known by a variety of names — Bacharach, Hahn, Waag, Bauer. But some called themselves after the house where they lived and, though later generations moved their place of residence, the soubriquet "Rothschild" stuck.

In the century following Isaak's death, his family seems to have prospered in a modest sort of way. In 1690 the head of the family was taxed on a disposable income of six thousand florins.[6] Bearing in mind the enforced frugality of his life, he would have been able to keep his family decently and hold his head high in the synagogue. Steadily, in that tiny ghetto world where differences of wealth and status were keenly observed, the Rothschilds advanced their fortunes, generation by generation.

By the fifth decade of the eighteenth century the head of the family was a certain Amschel Moses, who dealt in a variety of merchandise including silk cloth, despite a city ordinance forbidding Jews to trade in this luxury product. He had also inherited from his father a money-changing business.

At this time Germany was a bewildering patchwork of 235 principalities and duchies and fifty-one free cities, each of which issued its own coinage. There was therefore a need, especially in a great commercial centre like Frankfurt, for dealers who knew the comparative purity and worth of Austrian dollars, Saxon thalers, Westphalian ducats and the hundreds of other coins. But Amschel Moses not only continued the money-changing business, he went further and ventured cautiously into the far more dangerous territory of the banker. In taking this step he was following a path pioneered by another native of Judengasse, Josef Süss Oppenheim.

Oppenheim's career illustrates one way (perhaps the only way) an enterprising Jew could escape the degradation of the ghetto. He was born in Frankfurt, but moved to Hanover where his family had a banking business. There, making the most of his family's wealthy contacts, he entered the service of the Duke of Württemberg and rose to be his Minister of Finance. Wealthy magnates needed skilled financiers and many of them hired Jews for this purpose. The successful career of his erstwhile neighbour provided an opportunity which Amschel Moses was quick to grasp. He cultivated Oppenheim and the latter channelled some business his way.

But the life of a "court Jew", though privileged, was also precarious. He enjoyed considerable freedom of movement, was exempted from the Jewish poll tax and from degrading regulations concerning residence and dress. Against this had to be set the insecurity that arose from his total dependence on his prince. It was this dependence which made the relationship so attractive from the ruler's point of view. He could safely put one of the despised sons of Abraham in charge of his finances, for the man would never dare to cheat him. Furthermore, when taxes and levies proved onerous the Jew would be blamed rather than his master. This was the fate that befell Oppenheim in 1737. In that year the Duke of Württemberg died and the protectorless Oppenheim was exposed to the wrath of his enemies. He was dismissed from office, tried and executed on 4 February 1738.

Rothschild seems to have shrugged off this setback. Certainly he continued to apply himself to his buying and selling with sufficient success to get married within the next few years, for his first son was born on 23 February 1744*. He was named Mayer Amschel. Amschel Moses' ambitions for the boy became clear as soon as he was ready for formal education. The synagogue, where most of the boys from Judengasse received such instruction as their parents considered necessary, was not good enough for Rothschild's heir. He was sent to a rabbinical school two hundred kilometres away at Fürth. There he was taught German and

*1743 in some sources.

7

Hebrew, civilised languages far superior to the mongrel Yiddish which Christians found so amusing.[7] This obviously bright lad was destined by his father to become a rabbi.

It may have been at Fürth that he acquired the passion for collecting which was to be so important in the development of his own business and which was to become one of the more remarkable traits inherited by subsequent generations of Rothschilds. Certainly, his years at Fürth would have made him aware of the large world outside Judengasse and, perhaps, of some of the disturbing ideas permeating that world. For he had been born into a period of ferment and innovation such as Europe had not seen since the Reformation — an age later historians would call the "Enlightenment".

During Mayer Amschel's lifetime the Enlightenment would transform the intellectual climate of Europe and the Jews would be among those most profoundly affected. An early omen of the changes to come appeared when he was just four years old. *Die Juden*, a new play by the dramatist and philosopher Gotthold Lessing, was performed in a Leipzig theatre and caused a sensation. Lessing portrayed his central character, not as a villain or an object of ridicule, but as a man of culture and natural nobility. The spirit of toleration and anti-racism which informed Lessing's play appealed to many intellectual radicals.

In 1755 Lessing himself met and became a close friend of Moses Mendelssohn, the frail, totally unprepossessing little hunchback Jew who was one of the most remarkable intellects of the age. His books were widely read by students of philosophy and many flocked to the Berlin silk factory where he lived, to imbibe his wisdom. The coming together of Mendelssohn and Lessing was an important turning point in the history of western thought. The Jewish philosopher went on to develop Hashkalah, the enlightenment within Judaism. It sought to synthesise Jewish religion and law with reason, to remove the barriers of exclusivity erected by Christian and Jewish theologians, to encourage cross-cultural influences, and to establish the belief in the equality of all men before God.

> Surely, the Christian who seriously desires to discover light and right will not challenge the Jew to a fight when their respective truths seem to clash or scripture seems to contradict reason. On the contrary, he will join him in an effort to discover the baselessness of the contradiction. For this is their joint concern. The discussion of their doctrinal differences ought to be postponed until later. Their most important task right now is to join forces to ward off the danger that threatens both of them. They must either discover the fallaciousness of their reasoning or demonstrate that they had merely been troubled by an apparent contradiction.[8]

Such ideas were resisted as vigorously by orthodox rabbis as they were by conservative Christians and by reactionary upholders of the *ancien régime* — and with as little long-term effect. A new spirit was abroad in Europe, a spirit which would create undreamed-of opportunities for Mayer Amschel Rothschild and his five sons, yet unborn.

In the year that Mendelssohn and Lessing first met, the young Rothschild lost his father. Within eight months his mother was also dead, a victim of one of those smallpox outbreaks which readily assumed epidemic proportions in the cramped and overcrowded Judengasse. The plans made for the eleven-year-old boy on whom, by now, the hopes of four brothers and sisters rested, had to be changed. Mayer Amschel was sent north to Hanover by his new guardians and lodged with Amschel Moses' old friends, the Oppenheims, who had survived their reversal of fortune and had agreed to take the lad on as a trainee in their banking business.

In the six years Mayer Amschel spent in Hanover he saw many wealthy and powerful men and their agents. The boy from the ghetto must have studied these magnates with their magnificent coaches, their elaborate wigs, their braided and embroidered clothes and have realised that the way to wealth and modest luxury lay in serving such men and winning their confidence. How, he must have asked himself, did they use their money? What did they spend it on? How could he divert some of it through his own hands?

One craze that afflicted many of them was the collecting mania. Art and antiquities were madly in fashion. Grand dukes, archbishops and princes vied with each other in their acquisition of antique statuary, Renaissance paintings, books, jewels, coins, bronzes — anything that would adorn their palaces and enhance their prestige. The young Rothschild had already developed an interest in curios. Now he set himself to study, to build up a modest collection of his own, and to become an expert in the field.

His speciality was old coins. In the days when he had helped his parents run their business he had learned to identify specimens which were unusual because of their fine moulding or antiquity. At Hanover, according to tradition, he made the acquaintance of General von Estorff, a keen collector and adviser to William of Hesse, Count of Hanau, the heir to the principality of Hesse-Kassel. Certainly, sometime in the 1760s, he began supplying coins to the young prince, always at bargain prices, sometimes at less than cost. He was not interested in immediate profit. He was building a relationship. If he was successful he would become court Jew to the wealthiest and shrewdest ruler in Europe.

Prince William's forebears had grown rich on war. Not waging it; furnishing it. From 1618 onwards there was scarcely a conflict in Europe

9

or overseas in which Hessian mercenaries were not involved. Every soldier hired to England, Prussia, Sweden or other Continental power brought money to the coffers of the Landgrave of Hesse-Kassel. Every soldier killed earned him a special premium. The profits from this trade in death, augmented by advantageous dynastic marriages, enabled successive landgraves to transform Kassel into one of the most elegant capitals of northern Europe, resplendent with parks, town houses and a picture gallery. The palace of Wilhelmshöhe was the envy of princes who ruled larger and more prestigious states. But, like the good businessmen they were, the Landgraves did not squander all their income. Some was invested. The residue was loaned to other governments at handsome rates of interest. No country has ever been run more like a commercial enterprise than was the Landgravate of Hesse-Kassel.

The heir to the managing directorship of this concern – the man whom Rothschild was carefully cultivating – was admirably suited to fill that position. William of Hanau, one year older than Mayer Amschel, was energetic, self-willed, licentious and avaricious. As he grew to manhood he threw himself with enthusiasm into everything he did, whether whoring (he sired over seventy illegitimate children), studying classical antiquity or drilling his troops (he was a martinet who personally checked soldiers' buttons for polish and measured the length of their pigtails with a special ruler he carried for the purpose). And coin collecting was no exception. In 1761 Prince William took up residence in his palace at Hanau, twenty kilometres from Frankfurt. A few months later, Mayer Amschel went home to Judengasse, determined to build on the modest business relationship he had already established with the Prince.

But such ambitions were for the long term. In the meantime he set up in business as a general trader. The eighteen-year-old head of the family dealt in all kinds of cloth, in wine and skins, in anything brought by merchants to the fairs and markets of Frankfurt which might yield a profit, while at the same time continuing to act as a money-changer. But the boy whose mind had been stretched by travel could not now be confined to the traditional trading patterns of the ghetto. He had developed a taste for and a knowledge of luxury items affordable only by a discerning and wealthy clientele. So, year by year, he ploughed surplus cash into his side-line. Year by year he produced a catalogue for his customers, describing the rare and beautiful objects which he could offer. And, year by year, these increased in variety and value.

By 1783 he was able to offer besides coins, medals and prints, "several figurines, stone sculptures and framed pictures set with diamonds. If any art lover wishes to examine these items we will deliver them and arrange the lowest possible prices."[9] These catalogues were distributed to noble courts within a wide radius of Frankfurt, and Mayer Amschel often left his brothers to look after the Judengasse ship while he sat in the anterooms of distant palaces, striking bargains with minor officials. Patiently he built up vital contacts not only with the house of Hesse-Kassel but with other leaders of the social and political life of Germany.

At some point he added to his clientele the family of Thurn and Taxis who filled a curious, but vital role in central Europe: they operated the only official postal system in the Holy Roman Empire. From their office at Frankfurt they had, for several generations, organised a service of mounted couriers who sped with despatches over the abominable, brigand-infested roads of Germany and Austria. They were licensed by the Emperor and their duties to their master often went beyond collection and delivery: they included opening, copying and resealing any letters whose contents might be of interest to Vienna.

Services to the house of Thurn and Taxis brought Rothschild into contact — albeit distant contact — with the imperial court. More importantly, perhaps, they brought home to him the importance of an efficient communications system. It was a vital lesson — or, maybe, vivid confirmation of a lesson already learned — the lesson that information creates wealth. Certainly Mayer Amschel took it to heart, for when, a few years later, he and his sons set about building up financial operations on an international scale their success owed everything to their incomparable courier service. They prospered because they received before their rivals news of market trends, commodity prices and major political events.

For the moment, however, the key to Mayer Amschel's ambitions lay closer to home. True, his circle of influential clients grew wider and wider, but it was the patronage of Prince William which was to prove crucial to the Rothschild fortunes. In 1769 the twenty-five-year-old merchant believed that the time was right to seek a favour of the Prince. It was, in itself, a small thing and it cost William nothing, but it took the house of Rothschild another rung up the ladder of professional prestige. The humble petition was granted and Mayer Amschel proudly displayed a fresh-painted sign on his house front declaring that he was, by appointment, a supplier to the Principality of Hesse-Hanau.

The following year the up-and-coming young merchant married. Gutle, the seventeen-year-old daughter of Salomon Baruch Schnapper, another Judengasse tradesman, brought with her a modest dowry of 2400 florins, a warmth of personality and an industriousness which made her an ideal consort for the ambitious Mayer Amschel. Over the first twenty-two years of their married life she bore him children at the rate of one every sixteen months. Ten of those nineteen babies survived infancy — five boys and five girls.

The house with the sign of a cooking pot where they all lived served them as both living and business premises. It must have been crowded and noisy, always ringing to the sound of childish laughter and tantrums. Yet there is no reason to suppose that the household it contained was less happy than any other in Judengasse. The family business prospered. Both parents were pious and brought their children up within the secure faith of the Chosen People. Life at home was punctuated by the age-hallowed festivals of Pesach, Shabuoth, Sukkoth, Rosh Hashan and Yom Kippur. Beyond the front door was the enveloping warmth of the Jewish community, knit together by suffering and by the regular worship of the synagogue.

But even into this inward-looking, tradition-dominated little world the first glimmerings of the Enlightenment had penetrated. Mayer Amschel was among a minority in the ghetto who found themselves attracted to the new, radical ideas which were stirring hope among some Jews, suspicion and fear among others. Moses Mendelssohn's disciples, who called themselves Maskilim, were now spreading their message among the ranks of educated Jewry by publishing pamphlets and a regular journal, *Hameasef (The Collector)*. They wrote in Hebrew, and not Yiddish, urging Jews to broaden their minds by studying the culture of those among whom they lived.

There was encouragement, too, from a different direction. In 1782, the Emperor Joseph II issued an Edict of Toleration aimed at integrating his Jewish subjects into society and making their wealth and talents more readily available outside the ghettos. Irksome restrictions, such as the wearing of distinctive dress and the paying of a racial poll tax, were lifted and educational advancement was encouraged. The reverse side of the coin was the abolition of Yiddish and the inclusion of Jewish men on the list of citizens available for military service. These regulations were not applicable within the free city of Frankfurt but the stirrings of liberalism in Vienna, as well as the ideas of the Maskilim, must have been constant subjects of debate in the synagogue and the shops of Judengasse.

They certainly seem to have made an impact on Mayer Amschel who, quite apart from welcoming movements towards racial tolerance, could see the commercial advantage of a more open society. In 1792 he attempted to found a Jewish school, the Philanthropin, in conscious imitation of Mendelssohn's Freischule, established in Berlin in 1778, where the new values would be taught. It was opposed by conservative elements within the community, led by Rabbi Horwitz.* Perhaps this was the Rothschilds' first experience of Jewish conservative opposition. It would not be their

*The new Gymnasium was eventually opened in 1804.

last. Over the ensuing decades, as Mayer Amschel and his sons took maximum advantage of the revolutionary shifts of power in European society and politics, they would frequently find themselves caught in the crossfire between the forces of assimilation and exclusivism.

But in the 1770s and 1780s Mayer Amschel's first priority was to build up his own business by enlarging the foothold which he had established in the Gentile world. He concentrated in particular on developing a close relationship with Prince William's principal financial agent, Karl Friedrich Buderus, and took every opportunity of impressing on the courtier his own financial standing and his eagerness to serve the Prince in other ways. What he wanted was to become a banker to the court of Hanau and thus, in course of time, to the court of Hesse-Kassel. The prestige gained by such dealings would bring in business from other wealthy clients, and slowly but surely, Rothschild would have followed in the footsteps of the Oppenheims and other Jews who had climbed laboriously out of the ghetto.

The principal function of the bankers, whose ranks Mayer Amschel aspired to join, was the discounting of bills of exchange. A bill of exchange was a kind of promissory note, a document which made major transactions possible without the transporting of large quantities of gold. The person drawing the bill promised to pay a specified sum on a certain date to whoever presented the bill for payment. Any bill drawn by an individual or institution (such as a government, bank or business house) of good financial standing could be changed for cash by the drawee with a third party. What happened in practice was that bills were presented to on-the-spot bankers or merchants, who bought them at a discount, and made their profit from the fee they charged for their service and the difference between what they paid for the bills and the face value which they subsequently collected from the drawer.

Let us take an imaginary example: suppose King George III received a regiment of mercenaries from Hanau (as indeed he did in 1776 for service against the rebellious American colonists) for an agreed payment of a hundred thousand pounds. His government would issue a bill of exchange for the sum in triplicate (to guard against one or more copy being lost), promising to pay the bearer of the bill on 1 January 1777. This bill, with others, would find its way to Hanau where a whole department was constantly employed in the task of getting them discounted by bankers or merchants. This was a complex and sensitive operation. The bills had to be released on to the market in such a way as not to upset the discount rate and they had to be offered to bankers and merchants who would not charge too high a commission for cashing them. All manner of commercial and political crises could, of course, affect both discount and commission rates. The royal agents, therefore, sought to spread the business around among as many financiers as possible.

Fortunately, there was no shortage of bankers and merchants eager to buy their way into the Prince's favour. Once a goldsmith, a furrier or a dealer in coins had proved his ability to pay and his good commercial standing, he might reasonably hope for a share of the discount business, which, in addition to the profit involved, added enormously to his prestige.

Let us suppose that our imaginary bill is bought by a leading Hanau banker for ninety-five thousand pounds less commission. He would then send two copies separately to London, via his own agents, to be cashed. The British Treasury would pay out on the first copy received on or after 1 January 1777.

Probably Rothschild had been favoured with a number of small financial transactions by William of Hanau before 1785. He had certainly prospered. By sheer hard work and persistence he had increased his fortune appreciably, if not dramatically. In that year he could afford to move his large family into a bigger house. The residence, marked with his sign of a red shield, was mean by any modern standards. There was a room for business, a sitting room, a kitchen, a bedroom for Mayer Amschel and Gutle and another bedroom for the seven children the couple already had. The house boasted a small courtyard, a tiny roof garden; and – luxury of luxuries – its own water pump. Had Gutle not brought her children up strictly and kept her house scrupulously clean, the place would have been a shambles. Yet, for the family, it represented a distinct improvement in living conditions.

However, before they had been installed a few months in the new premises, Mayer Amschel may have regretted the move. In October 1785 something happened which threatened to affect his fortunes very seriously. In distant Kassel, the Landgrave died suddenly and unexpectedly. Prince William immediately left Hanau to take up his inheritance. If Rothschild had already established himself firmly in the new Landgrave's confidence, this would have been excellent news. But for all his endeavours, he was still only a minor figure in the commercial life of the Hanau court, and that court had now departed, with its bags and baggage, along the valley road leading via Fulda to Kassel.

Rothschild now had to redouble his efforts to improve his standing with his principal patron. He spent months getting together a very fine collection of coins, medals and *objets d'art*, then set off with them to Kassel. The Landgrave was impressed but not sufficiently so to elevate the dealer to an important position in his business organisation. However, some jobs did come Rothschild's way. He helped to negotiate a loan of three hundred thousand florins from Hesse-Kassel to the Principality of Salm in 1786 and another of a hundred and fifty thousand florins to the Prince of Thurn and Taxis the following year.

Yet still a share in the lucrative trade of discounting bills of exchange eluded him. In 1789 he wrote to the Landgrave reminding him of his long service and assuring his royal master that he could handle bills on more advantageous terms than those offered by the major Kassel banks. The only immediate result was a raising of his credit rating at court from a thousand to two thousand florins.

Rothschild might have gone on patiently for years, slowly climbing higher in the Landgrave's favour, swallowing disappointments, snubs and frustration, had it not been for another event in that year of 1789; an event which changed millions of lives, though none more dramatically than those of Mayer Amschel and his five sons.

On 14 July, a Paris mob overthrew the royal fortress-prison of the Bastille. As the French Revolution pursued its turbulent course it not only unleashed a chain of violence that would engulf Europe for a generation, but ideas which would change the world, not least the world of Jewry, for ever. In 1791 a new law was promulgated in Paris:

> The National Assembly, considering that the conditions requisite to be a French citizen . . . are fixed by the constitution, and that every man who, being duly qualified, takes the civic oath and engages to fulfil all the duties prescribed by the constitution, has a right to all the advantages it ensures; annuls all adjournments, restrictions, and exceptions, contained in the preceding decrees, affecting individuals of the Jewish persuasion, who shall take the civic oath . . .

The full citizenship granted to Jews in France made no difference to the inhabitants of Frankfurt's Judengasse — yet. But within a very short time the new radical ideas were being exported in the baggage trains of the armies of the Republic. The strong wine of *liberté, egalité et fraternité* became freely available, even in the ghetto. Some Jews relished it. Others feared its effects. Some grasped the opportunity to leave the narrow, smelly street and make their mark in the world. Others remained mentally in Judengasse, barricading their culture behind walls of tradition and conservatism. Inevitably families were split. None more so than the Rothschilds.

CHAPTER 2

"There was not room enough for all of us in Frankfurt"

Ironically, it was the enemies of the French Revolution, rather than the revolutionaries themselves, who took the first, fatal step which was to change the face of Europe beyond all recognition. In April 1792 the new Austrian Emperor, Francis, in alliance with the King of Prussia, provoked a war which would, he hoped, quickly bring the republican rabble to its senses and restore the divinely ordained authority of Louis XVI.

The consequences were dramatic: in Paris the extremists under Danton seized power, imprisoned the King and Queen and summoned the convention which was to declare a republic. The French forces, which at first fell back in face of the invading Prussians, rallied and, on 20 August, won a resounding victory at Valmy.

Now the tide turned with a vengeance. In the autumn of 1792 one French army swept into Nice and Savoy, another seized the Austrian Netherlands, while a third, under the brilliant Adam Philippe de Custine, crossed the Rhine and captured Speyer, Worms and Mainz. On 22 October, the Frankfurt *Rat*, in order to avoid pointless bloodshed, opened the gates of their city to Custine.

Earlier in that year, Gutle had given birth to her last child, a boy named Jacob, who would later prefer to be called James. The uncomprehending infant may well have been held up at a window to watch some passing troops of French soldiers but neither his anxious parents nor his excited brothers and sisters could possibly have guessed the implications this invasion would have for them all. The new baby would be twenty-three before lasting peace was finally restored to Europe. The family would be scattered far and wide from Frankfurt. And James himself would not only be living in the French capital, he would also be among its wealthiest and most respected inhabitants.

But, for the moment, Mayer Amschel and the other leaders of the Jewish community in Frankfurt must have regarded the invaders with mixed feelings. These strangely garbed and ill-equipped soldiers were free men, fighting for a cause they believed in. They were quite unlike Landgrave William's immaculate, well-drilled cannon fodder, who were pressed into service solely to enrich their royal master. Moreover, they represented a government which was, in theory at least, attempting to realise the ideals of brotherhood and equality, regardless of race or creed. Mayer Amschel with a capital of at least a hundred thousand florins and an annual income of between ten and fifteen thousand florins,[1] was now one of the wealthiest members of the Frankfurt bourgeoisie, but as a Jew he had no place whatsoever in the social and political life of the city. The cause which inspired the French and which was rapidly gaining the support of radical thinkers throughout Europe must have had its appeal for him.

Yet, as a shrewd and ambitious businessman, Mayer Amschel must have recognised that, for the moment at least, his interests still lay with the representatives of the established order. There was no role for a court Jew in the republican scheme of things, and although Mayer Amschel may not have relished the need to ingratiate himself with men who affected to despise his race, he was nothing if not a realist. He would have clearly appreciated that his own fortunes were inextricably tied up with those of his clients. It is, therefore, likely that considerable relief was felt in the Rothschild household when Frankfurt was liberated by Hessian and Prussian troops on 2 December after a skirmish around the Bockenheimer Tor.[2]

Yet the relationship between the Jews and their patrons was changing. Thanks to the war, William IX of Hesse-Kassel needed his bankers more than ever before. He was raising and equipping troops on an unprecedented scale for the allied cause. For this he had to have cash. But much of his capital was tied up in English investments, and one of the immediate effects of the war in Europe was that it had become extremely difficult to raise money. Wealthy landowners and merchants hid or expatriated their gold and valuables. The French invasion of Holland in 1795 led to the closing of the Amsterdam Bourse, the leading Continental exchange. The Jacobin government tried to seal France's borders to international commerce. As a result, many merchants and bankers were hard pressed to carry on their business and in no position to oblige the Landgrave with large, short-term credits.

Thus when William approached his usual financiers in 1794 for a hundred and fifty thousand florins against monies being repatriated from England, four of them (Metzler, Bethmann, Gontard and d'Orville) had to decline. Instead the business was carried out by a consortium of Ruppel, Jordis — and Rothschild.

This was the point at which Mayer Amschel's patient cultivation of Buderus finally paid off. For it was thanks to the courtier's recommendation that he at last gained entry to the select circle of agents handling large sums of money on behalf of the wealthiest prince in Europe. As a result he had now the opportunity to apply his acumen and his personal fortune to the business of making money on a really large scale. And, as he faced up to this new challenge, he could now look to his sons for help.

From the birth of James until the marriage of the eldest daughter in 1795 Mayer Amschel and Gutle had all their children around them. In 1792 these were: Jeanette (21), Amschel (19), Salomon (18), Nathan (15), Isabella (11), Babette (8), Carl (4), Julie (2), Henriette (1) and baby James. It was a bustling household in which all the children were expected to take on a responsibility at an early age. Responsibility for helping mother, for looking after younger brothers and sisters, and, above all, for learning the business. By 1792 the three older boys were already fully involved and there was probably little they did not understand about their father's complex commercial operation.

Day in and day out Mayer Amschel trained his sons rigorously in the ardent pursuit of success. He consciously founded a financial dynasty. In 1796 he took his two older boys formally into partnership and their brothers were, one by one, brought in as they reached maturity. He allowed his daughters no share in the management of the family concern. There was nothing unusual in that. But he was equally firm in excluding all male relatives. Jeanette's husband, Benedict Moses Worms, was permitted no stake in Rothschild business nor were Mayer Amschel's cousins and nephews, despite the fact that there was plenty of work to do. The head of the family was determined only to involve those on whose commitment and discretion he could completely rely — his sons.

These were the young men who became known to posterity as the "Frankfurt Five". They were very different in character, and by no means equally talented. In fact, while two were undoubted financial geniuses, the other three, had they been born into any other family, might well have lived quite unremarkable lives. They also differed markedly in personality, and, as there were many matters on which they did not see eye to eye, they squabbled frequently. Yet, it was these brothers, dispersed to the leading capitals of Europe, who built up, in the space of two decades, the greatest international banking syndicate in the world. We must, therefore, run a little ahead of our story to describe each of these men.

Amschel, the eldest, always remained a son of the ghetto. Pious and orthodox in religion, ultra-conservative in everything, he was the closest in outlook to his father, while lacking Mayer Amschel's commercial flair and independence of outlook. He grew up as the Rothschild second in command, a task for which his dependability and lack of imagination fitted him admirably. He was his father's deputy in the synagogue and the Judengasse council where he would one day take his place. That was the extent of his expectations and his ambition.

Amschel, thin, pinch-faced and wrinkle-browed, was a worrier. He worried about the risks his partners took. He worried when business was bad. And, when business was good, he worried that it might be bad tomorrow. Above all else he worried that his brothers and their families were erring from the path of Jewish orthodoxy. He himself had no family. His marriage to the daughter of another prominent Judengasse resident was one of duty and was destined to be loveless and childless. He brought Eva, his wife, to his parental home and it was several years before they moved to a house of their own, commensurate with their immense wealth. Amschel was never happy away from Frankfurt and, apart from journeys necessitated by business, he remained there to the end of his long life.

Salomon was the diplomat of the family. Genial, sympathetic, self-effacing, he was equally effective at gaining the favour of princes and courtiers and keeping the peace between his brothers. Indeed, it was to Salomon that the others instinctively turned when they found themselves outraged by the innuendoes or accusations of one of their partners. Although not robust in health, Salomon undertook most of the frenetic travelling that the rapid business expansion of the war years involved. If he had a fault it was that he was too easy-going not to be taken advantage of. This sometimes had a bad effect on business. Yet without Salomon's talent for smoothing ruffled feathers it is doubtful whether the partnership of the Frankfurt Five would have survived its early years.

The third son, Nathan Mayer (or "N.M." as he was often called), was cast in a very different mould. This red-headed, stocky, bustling, impatient, often ill-tempered man could not tolerate the restrictions of ghetto life. Neither his ambition nor his imagination could be caged. To his creative mind the troubled state of Europe suggested exciting possibilities for business expansion. At the earliest opportunity he would leave Frankfurt and seek a new base where his dynamic spirit of enterprise could find freer expression.

Carl, eleven years younger than Nathan, was pulled in different directions by his elder brothers. He idolised N.M. for his vigour and brilliance and longed to escape from Frankfurt and to emulate his exploits. But his impatience sprang, not from frustrated talent, but from a lack of self-confidence. And although he forever complained that Amschel's conservative and hide-bound attitudes restricted him, he seems also to have sensed that he could not survive without the support of his family, his religion and his community. Carl would eventually set himself up in Naples but he would never commit himself to life in a foreign land and would spend as much time in Frankfurt as in his adopted city.

By the time James grew to manhood his father and brothers had established the family fortune. He had travelled widely, tasted the luxuries of foreign capitals, experienced the freer atmosphere of France and England and turned his back on the ghetto for good. He learned readily and had a precocious talent for business. He appreciated the good things of life and was prepared to work to achieve them. He drove himself and his subordinates hard and could be brusquely intolerant of inefficiency and stupidity. Although the youngest son, he was the second to establish permanent residence abroad, and proved himself almost as talented as N.M. in running and building an independent business.

At the point where we resume the narrative, all the Rothschilds were still in Judengasse and, in that year of 1796, Judengasse was an even less healthy place to be than usual. Prussia had been forced to withdraw from the war and to conclude the Treaty of Basle (April 1795). Left to carry on the war alone, Austria found herself hard pressed, largely due to the activities of a young general called Bonaparte, and unable to defend her German provinces against the armies of France. By July Frankfurt was once more under siege. This time Austrian troops retreated to a position within the walls and forced the *Rat* to resist a call for surrender.

As a result, on the night of 14 July the attackers bombarded the city. Several fires broke out, but were all quickly brought under control – except for one which started in Judengasse. The citizens were much more interested in saving their own homes than in helping the occupants of the ghetto and the Jews were left to cope as best they could. By morning the synagogue and one hundred and forty houses at the northern end of the street had been burned to the ground. The house of the red shield was damaged but escaped destruction. For the Rothschilds, however, this was not an unmitigated disaster. While rebuilding was in progress on Judengasse the limitations on Jewish residence were lifted and Mayer Amschel was able to rent part of a leather trader's premises on Schnurrgasse, in the city centre, as a warehouse and office.

There were plenty of fresh opportunities for him to exploit. After the Treaty of Basle, Hesse-Kassel withdrew from the war, but on the financial front, Landgrave William redoubled his efforts and quickly became the biggest money-lender in Europe. Almost every authority, from the Frankfurt *Rat* to the Emperor of Austria, seems to have borrowed from Hesse-Kassel. These dealings could not, of course, be conducted openly for fear of French reprisals. William therefore used intermediaries, among them the Rothschilds, who handled a large amount of the business.[3]

Nor was William the only prince who had cause to be grateful to Mayer Amschel for the prompt and efficient handling of their affairs. This is evident if only because some showed their gratitude by conferring honours and titles upon the elderly Jew. Rothschild encouraged them to do so. Royal endorsements were good for business, and he proudly publicised such decorations as the German Order of St John.

But there were other titles that were even more prestigious and also carried tangible benefits. In 1799 he appealed to the Emperor of Austria, in the most flowery language, for the honour of being appointed Imperial Crown Agent. He stressed his financial services to Francis II's servants and allies, particularly to the house of Thurn and Taxis. The favour was granted under a patent dated 29 January 1800. It carried with it various privileges such as the right to bear arms, exemption from certain taxes and freedom of movement throughout the imperial domains.

Thus Mayer Amschel Rothschild became one of the first of a new breed of businessmen – the truly international merchant banker. For centuries Jews had played a prominent part in long-distance commerce. Their sense of racial identity, their centuries of ghetto existence, the contempt of their Christian neighbours, forged close links between the European Jewish communities and created a commercial sub-culture. In 1712 the London *Spectator* had likened the business world to a framework of which the Jews were the pegs and nails. But always the sons of the Dispersion had needed the patronage and protection of kings, princes and nobles if they were to operate effectively in a basically hostile environment.

Now the focus of economic power was shifting. The Industrial Revolution and radical political ideas were creating an entrepreneurial class whose status rested securely on money and not on ancestry. Tradition was not swept away by Napoleon. It would, indeed, be an unconscionable time dying. In 1800 a century of uprisings and radical reform still lay ahead. But because Mayer Amschel's toughness and resilience had been proved in the fire of the revolutionary years, his sons were able to take their place among the leaders of the new class. Seldom in the political limelight, always discreet in its professional dealings, the house of Rothschild won for itself an independence, a strength and a dignity that no Jewish family could have hoped to achieve under the old dispensation.

The first, and the most important, break with the past came in 1798, when the first Rothschild left Judengasse. Nathan, scarcely waiting to attain his majority, quitted Frankfurt and set up business on his own account in England. He seldom returned to the Continent, becoming a naturalised Englishman in 1806, and, as far as can be ascertained, saw his father only once more before his death. The break from the ghetto was abrupt and complete. The only explanation of what lay behind this decision comes from an account of the story told by N.M. at a dinner party over thirty years later:

21

There was not room enough for all of us in Frankfurt. I dealt in English goods. One great trader came there who had the market to himself: he was quite the great man, and did us a favour if he sold us goods. Somehow I offended him, and he refused to show me his patterns. This was on a Tuesday; I said to my father "I will go to England." I could speak nothing but German. On the Thursday I started.[4]

This account should not be taken wholly at face value. In his later years Nathan was an audacious raconteur and this has all the marks of an oft-told, tongue-in-cheek story, one that he trotted out on the frequent occasions when he was asked how he had embarked on the accumulation of his immense fortune. But, if we fillet it rather carefully and add other snippets of information, we can probably arrive at least at an approximation of the truth.

The most telling sentence of Nathan's version is the first. "There was not room enough for all of us in Frankfurt." N.M. was a young man with big ideas. He felt stifled by the ghetto and was constantly at odds with his less imaginative father and elder brothers. He could never suffer fools gladly and, in his estimation, a fool was anyone who lacked his clear and quick grasp of financial matters. Arguments were, therefore, frequent in the claustrophobic atmosphere of Mayer Amschel's house. They continued in later years. "My dear Nathan, you must not be angry with your father",[5] wrote Mayer Amschel in 1805, and his brothers constantly complained about N.M.'s insults and castigations:

Your letters make me feel ill. It is impossible for me to send such letters to Frankfurt. I cannot for one believe that even if I were "the learned Nathan Rothschild" the other four brothers would all be stupid boys and I would be the only wise one. Let us however forget all this. I do not wish to be upset any more than I already am . . . I am therefore returning all these letters to you . . . The English mail day is a regular terror for me. Every night I dream of these letters.[6]

No wonder there was "not room" for this quick-tempered visionary in his father's counting house. Nathan knew that he had to leave. Eventually he won the support of his brother-in-law, Benedict Worms, in his bid to get away. The two men set up a textile importing business, Worms to look after the German end and Nathan to move to Manchester.[7] So with, as he later claimed, twenty thousand pounds capital, N.M. set off on one of the most momentous journeys in the commercial history of Europe.

There was nothing unique about the step which Nathan took. Several German-Jewish commercial houses had established representatives in England, attracted by its growing commercial importance and its tolerant attitude towards their race. This was, moreover, part of a more general pattern of Jewish immigration. During the course of the eighteenth century thousands of Jews travelled to Britain to escape persecution and the appalling conditions of the ghettoes. In the absence of accurate census figures it is difficult to assess the numbers of Jews living in England at this time but the population around the end of the century has been put somewhere between twelve and twenty-five thousand.[8] Most of the immigrants were poor and settled as pedlars and small traders in London and other seaport towns. But a few were very wealthy, active in the colonial trade, the stock exchange and banking. At the head of the community were a handful of financiers who enjoyed the confidence of the government and furnished loans for war purposes and other extraordinary expenditure. Men like Aaron Hart, who travelled to Canada as commissary officer with General Amherst's army in 1760, and Abraham Franco, a City merchant, who, in 1777, died leaving a fortune rumoured to be a staggering nine hundred thousand pounds.*

England at the end of the eighteenth century was, therefore, very much the land of promise and must have attracted Nathan for some time before he decided to go there. Although he was essentially entering into business for himself, it was certainly understood that he would also be an agent for his father and Mayer Amschel must have seen the very clear advantages that might be gained from having a permanent presence in England. In order to fund their growing banking enterprise the Rothschilds had to have maximum liquidity and their day-to-day cash income came from trade. Most of the goods entering Frankfurt, the warehouse of free Europe, either originated in England, or came from the colonies via English intermediaries. Cotton and woollen cloth, sugar, indigo, coffee, tobacco and wine were the staples of Mayer Amschel's commercial business. The frustrating fact was that the Frankfurt merchants were virtually at the mercy of their English suppliers who could, and did, exaggerate the difficulties caused by the war as an excuse for upping their prices. The desirability of cutting out the middle man was obvious and Mayer Amschel eventually bowed to the inescapable logic of his impatient son's arguments.

Earlier histories of the family created the myth of a far-sighted Mayer Amschel despatching his sons to major European capitals as part of a grand design to establish a financial empire. It has long been realised that the growth of the Rothschild business was more haphazard. Yet, even among serious historians something of the old legend persists. They have

---

*To achieve an approximate modern equivalent this should be multiplied by at least fifty.

assumed that Nathan was "sent" to England by his father to set up a foreign branch of M.A. Rothschild and Sons. In fact the greater integration of Nathan's activities with the family business did not come about until a few years later, and then combined operations were very much run from London, not Frankfurt. In 1796, Nathan was, first and foremost, escaping from the claustrophobia of the ghetto to a more open society. Thereafter, although he occasionally drew on Mayer Amschel's credit in London, he was, from a commercial point of view, a distinct entity. When his father and brothers drew up a partnership agreement in 1810, N.M. was excluded from it. Nathan's first objective was to concentrate on the enormous task of breaking into the Manchester textile business — far from easy for a foreigner with a poor grasp of English. He spent a few months in London with L.B. Cohen and Levi Salomons (whose son would become the first Jewish Lord Mayor of the city), with whom his father regularly did business, in order to learn the language and the commercial customs of the British.[9]

The young man from Frankfurt was warmly welcomed by the leaders of the Jewish community — or, rather, by the leaders of Ashkenazim. British Jewry was divided into two groups, the Sephardim, who originated in Spain and the Mediterranean seaboard, and the Ashkenazim of France and Germany. Until recent years, the former group, who were rigorist in matters of faith and practice, had been in the majority but immigration from northern Europe had evened up the balance. The rivalry between the two communities was symbolised by their separate London places of worship. The Sephardim attended the Bevis Marks synagogue, close by Houndsditch, on the edge of the City, and the Ashkenazi synagogue was just along the road in Duke's Place. Both groups were represented on the Joint Board of Deputies, the body which looked after Jewish interests, but they were frequently at loggerheads. However, Nathan had no time to get caught up in these disputes for, in about May 1799, he moved north, to the fastest-growing industrial city in Europe.

The small, stout, red-headed Jew with his heavy German accent who now burst upon the Manchester exchange soon became the butt of jokes among the blunt-spoken local traders (just as he would later become an irresistible target for cartoonists). Some of them were very soon laughing on the other side of their faces.

I soon found out that there were three profits — the raw material, the dyeing, and the manufacturing. I said to the manufacturer, "I will supply you with material and dye, and you supply me with the manufactured goods." So I got three profits instead of one, and I could sell goods cheaper than anybody . . . My success all turned on one maxim. I said, I can do what another man can do, and so I am a match for the man with the patterns, and for all the rest of them.[10]

N.M. succeeded because he worked harder than his rivals, because he gave his customers value for money and because he was always on the lookout for new markets, new ideas, new ways of doing business. As a foreigner he had one advantage over the cotton kings of Manchester: he was not bound by tradition. He gathered into his own hands as many stages of the business as possible and he made himself popular with the cloth suppliers by prompt payment.

Weaving was still mainly a cottage industry and the artisans were largely at the mercy of the dealers who would only take goods on credit, frequently not paying for two to six months. Nathan went into the market with ready cash and thereby obtained all the pieces he needed at a lower price. Having cut his production costs to the bone, he could sell cheaply. He kept a close watch on the war situation so that, by changing his cross-Channel routes as necessary, he could ensure the promptest possible delivery. But he was far too clever just to provide a cold, efficient service and leave it at that; in his father's shop he had learned the cardinal salesman's rule, "Make the customer feel important." His business letters were larded with compliments and offers of special treatment: a little present for this customer's wife; a "secret" offer to provide goods on the same terms as those he normally only offered to leading Frankfurt houses, etc., etc.[11]

But Nathan's business expansion certainly did not pursue a smooth and uninterrupted course. He encountered many difficulties and failures. The complications created by the war imposed strains on his resources and his temper. More and more of Britain's trading partners were either conquered by Napoleon or drawn into alliance with him. More and more ports were closed to English shipping. N.M. had to keep himself informed about Continental roads and harbours which might be blocked by French action. Selecting the best routes and ships was a constant headache. But it did force him and his agents to hone their communications system to a fine edge. They employed an increasing number of couriers and Nathan never begrudged money spent chartering fast ships to cross the Channel carrying important news.

As soon as conditions eased in 1802-3 following the Peace of Amiens, Nathan was off to the Continent in search of additional customers but he soon concluded that his new clientele was not worth the trouble: "I cannot possibly understand the reason why all these French houses make so much noise and trouble, as I am certain that all the goods are very cheap and that no house in Manchester purchases goods cheaper . . . than

I do."[12] Another pressure Nathan was under was his constant need for ready cash. His way of doing business obliged him to be incessantly laying out money for goods. Nor did he want his reputation as a man of means to be called in question by any temporary embarrassment. He was, thus, frequently obliged to borrow wherever he could. "Being just now short of money," he wrote to the Hanau and Company office in Amsterdam, "your brother, when he was in town, told me ... I might draw upon you."[13] Such requests were frequent. When news of them reached Frankfurt it did nothing to ease relationships within the family. Mayer Amschel watched anxiously the progress of his prodigal son, by no means convinced that N.M.'s daring methods would pay off.

But after the first few turbulent years, Nathan prospered and, because his business was expanding, Benedict Worms and his father prospered also. He dealt in a steadily increasing range of merchandise. British, Colonial, American and Oriental goods reached markets all over Europe via the Rothschild commercial network. More importantly, N.M. was also establishing himself as a financier. He forced his way into the discounting business by taking a commission of one per cent on Continental bills when the established banks charged one and a half or two per cent.

Overall, the picture we have of the young Nathan Rothschild is that of a man of enormous energy and self-confidence, brimming over with ideas and eager to put them into practice. A man ready to take risks and cut corners. A man too impatient for success to bother with the petty details of book keeping and business administration. A man intolerant of those incapable of sharing his vision or carrying out his behests. In the relentless pursuit of success he drove himself hard and demanded high standards of subordinates and colleagues. He undoubtedly needed not only his energy and courage, but also his thick skin in order to succeed and stay a step ahead of his rivals, for he was making his way in a very hard world, a world in which many well-established merchants went bankrupt. But N.M. did not go bankrupt. As the new century got under way his fortunes perceptibly improved. By 1806 he was ready to marry: he chose Hannah Cohen.

The marriage marked his acceptance by the cream of Anglo-Jewish society. Hannah was the eldest daughter of Levi Barent Cohen, the leading London financier. Six years later Cohen married another daughter to Moses Montefiore, destined to become the most celebrated Jew in England. He was a captain in the Surrey Militia and a prominent member of the Exchange (a privilege for which his father had paid twelve hundred pounds). In 1815 relations between the two families were more firmly cemented when Moses' brother married Nathan's sister, Henriette. The new liaison also connected N.M. to the Salomons, Goldsmids and other prominent families. His bride was in many ways an ideal comple- ment. As well as love, beauty and business expertise, she possessed the elegance and social graces Nathan so patently lacked. Twenty years later a discerning German nobleman, comparing Hannah with the wife of a rival banker, remarked on "how far the Jewish golden queen surpassed the Christian one in cordial amiability and external dignity and good breeding". According to this reporter, she excelled her husband in "tact and knowledge of the world, though not perhaps in acuteness and talents for business".[14] Hannah Cohen might not be able to turn Nathan Rothschild, with his imperfect grasp of the language and his abrupt manner, into an English gentleman, but she could ensure that his sons would be English gentlemen.

For his part, N.M. associated totally with his adopted country. He became an English citizen and made many friends among the London business community. Like many immigrants, he became passionately con- cerned about matters of national interest. In 1806 it was the war with "Bony" which dominated public concern. And that war had entered a critical phase.

CHAPTER 3
"God, how things have changed"

By the end of 1806 Napoleon Bonaparte had made himself undisputed master of the mainland of Europe. Austria had been defeated decisively at Ulm and Austerlitz the previous year and Prussia had now been punished at Jena and Auerstadt for re-entering the conflict. Napoleon was left with but a single adversary, Great Britain. But the British, unlike the Continental powers, could not be defeated by a single, dramatic military campaign. For the battle of Trafalgar, fought on 20 October 1805, had confirmed the Royal Navy's command of the sea and there was now no chance that a French army of invasion would embark at Dunkirk and Boulogne for the conquest of England.

There was, however, still one weapon with which Bonaparte might bring the obstinate islanders to their knees: he could block their trade with the Continent. To achieve this goal his control of Europe's ports and of its system of internal commerce had to be complete. The great international market of Frankfurt particularly attracted his attention. He could not allow it to retain its status as a free city. It now became the headquarters of a new client state, the Confederation of the Rhine, and its citizens found themselves bound by new laws enforced by officials of the French Empire.

This changed situation was clearly one fraught with dangers for the Rothschilds and their trade. Like other bankers and merchants, they could have cut their losses and come to terms with the new regime. There was plenty of business to be done with the French rulers and their puppet princelings. Indeed, to do otherwise, to continue their association with exiled monarchs and to trade with France's enemies would, it seemed likely, only be to invite police searches, intercepted correspondence, confiscation of goods, brutal interrogations and, perhaps, imprisonment or even death.

Moreover, there were many aspects of the new regime which the Rothschilds and their co-religionists welcomed. The liberal laws prevailing in the French Empire, which were promulgated throughout the Confederation by the *Organizations-patent* of 16 August 1810, were greatly

28

to the advantage of the Jews. They now enjoyed complete equality and could become citizens (although they had to pay for the privilege). In 1811 they were liberated from the ghetto, though Mayer Amschel and Gutle continued to live there. Given that Jewish emancipation was to be a subject of intense interest to the family in every generation and that, as we have seen, Rothschild money had already helped to found a school where the revolutionary principles of equality and tolerance were taught, these changes must have been welcomed by the family.

But there were other factors Mayer Amschel and his sons had to take into consideration. One was the state of affairs in Frankfurt, where not all changes were for the better. The citizens were obliged to provide billets for foreign troops and heavy taxes were levied (a total of eight million florins over the fourteen years of occupation). Then, there were their relationships with the Landgrave of Hesse-Kassel and other rulers hostile to the French. Buderus was very anxious to retain their services and pointed out that, though helping his master was a hazardous occupation, the change in Prince William's circumstances offered unprecedented opportunities for bankers who remained loyal to him.

Buderus's entreaties were mild compared with the urgent promptings of Nathan. During the course of the war the value of imported goods had steadily increased. So had the profit margins of Benedict Worms and the Rothschilds, and they were reluctant to abandon a system that was working very well. But they had to operate with increasing determination and cunning, for Napoleon was determined to make his policies bite. In November 1806 the Emperor imposed the Continental System.

He decreed that "no ship which comes directly from England or the English colonies ... shall enter any of our harbours".[1] During the following year he forced Russia and his other Continental allies to join him in this campaign of economic sanctions against his one unconquered foe. By early in 1808 all ports from the Baltic to the Mediterranean were, in theory at least, closed to British merchandise. The government in London retaliated by declaring a blockade on all coastal towns participating in the Continental System and threatened to confiscate ships attempting to unload their cargoes in them.

On balance, the German Rothschilds decided to continue their clandestine trade with Britain and their support for other enemies of Napoleon. Of course, they kept up a front of allegiance to the Emperor. For example, they obliged their new masters with low-interest loans and established good relations with the administration in Frankfurt, which was, in fact, not too oppressive. The Prince Primate of the Confederation of the Rhine, Archbishop Carl von Dalberg, was a German patriot of ancient family who had thrown in his lot with Napoleon because he saw

29

the Emperor as the only man who could unite the country. He was personally well disposed towards the Landgrave of Hesse-Kassel and turned a blind eye to the Rothschilds' business activities on his behalf.

Some of Napoleon's agents had little enthusiasm for their master's grand designs. Others were simply corrupt. It was thus not all that difficult for the Frankfurt Rothschilds to play a double game. Their relationship with the court of Hesse-Kassel shows this quite clearly.

Now that he was master of Europe, Napoleon was in a position to settle old scores. None was more pressing than his grudge against the Prince of Hesse-Kassel (upon whom the dignity of 'Elector' had been conferred by the Austrian Emperor in 1803). Napoleon knew, of course, that William had for years been aiding his enemies, while feigning neutrality. Now the time had come to exact a swift and total revenge. The Emperor sent an order to his field commander, Marshal Mortier:

> You will seal up all treasures and stores and appoint General Lagrange as Governor of the country. You will raise taxes and pronounce judgements in my name. Secrecy and speed will be the means through which you will ensure complete success. My object is to remove the House of Hesse-Kassel from rulership and to strike it out of the list of powers.[2]

But Napoleon's agents had no monopoly of "secrecy and speed". William had foreseen the danger and for weeks his servants had been engaged in the mammoth task of shipping or concealing chests of bullion along with the ledgers, bundles of bills and mortgage documents that would, if they fell into the hands of the conquerors, allow the elector's complex business affairs to be unravelled.

In the event, the Prince's efforts were only partially successful. For this he had no one to blame but himself. Mean and suspicious to the point of paranoia, he could not bring himself wholly to trust his agents even at such a moment of dire crisis. As a result, the bulk of his silver was stranded in Kassel because he could not agree a price with a boat captain hired to take it by river and sea to England. The amount in dispute was fifty thalers. The bullion that fell into French hands was valued at millions of thalers. Indeed, William's reluctance to be separated from his treasure almost cost him his freedom. His coach and six left the capital, Kassel, by one gate as Napoleon's troops were entering at another.

Amschel Rothschild had departed only a few days earlier. He had taken up residence in Kassel in 1803 to guard the interests of the firm and to counter the activities of rivals who were jealous of the Frankfurt bankers' growing influence. But if he hoped to take advantage of the elector's predicament in 1806, he was disappointed. Neither the Rothschilds nor their competitors were entrusted with William's assets, most of which were concealed about the castle or buried in the grounds.

But the following spring the Prince, now living in exile, had to call on Mayer Amschel's help. He urgently needed someone to take care of his important business documents. So, one day, a coach drew up at the end of Judengasse and four chests were carried to the Rothschilds' front door. This single event gave rise to one of the most persistent legends about the origins of the family's wealth. As early as 1836 the story was well-enough established to appear in an English newspaper (a fact which was, of course, no guarantee of its truth). The writer affirmed that Prince William had begged the old banker to take charge of his money and jewels but that Rothschild, realising the risk involved, allowed himself to be persuaded only with great reluctance.

> The French army was actually entering Frankfurt at the moment when Rothschild succeeded in burying the prince's treasures in a corner of his little garden.
>
> His own property, which in goods and money was worth about 40,000 thalers, he did not hide, well knowing that, if he did so, a strict search would be made and that not only his own but the prince's hoard would be discovered and plundered.
>
> The Republicans who, like the Philistines of old, fell upon Rothschild, left him not one thaler's value of his own money or property. In truth, he was, like all the other Jews and citizens, reduced to utter poverty but the prince's treasure was safe and some time after the French army marched out from Frankfurt, Rothschild commenced again in a small way, as a banker, increasing his business cautiously, by means of the prince's money . . .

The report goes on to tell how, on William's return, Mayer Amschel offered him his property back with interest but that the Prince declared,

> "I will neither receive the interest which your honesty offers nor yet take my money out of your hands. The interest is not sufficient to replace what you lost to save mine; and further my money shall be at your service for 20 years to come and at no more than two per cent interest." [3]

This romanticised and oversimplified account of the origin of the Rothschild fortune was for many years generally accepted. Almost certainly it originated with Nathan. It is the sort of humorous tale he loved to tell when he wanted to have fun at the expense of gullible companions and to conceal the real secrets of his success. It is not dissimilar to an account he gave Sir Thomas Fowell in 1834:

31

"The Prince of Hesse Cassel", said Rothschild, "gave my father his money; there was no time to be lost; he sent it to me. I had £600,000 arrive unexpectedly by the post [approximately £30,000,000 in modern terms]; and I put it to such good use, that the prince made me a present of all his wine and his linen."[4]

What actually happened was both more prosaic and less flattering to human nature. When the French general, Lagrange, gazed on the contents of William's hastily concealed coffers he became greedy, and, when Buderus offered him money to allow William's servants to convey various chests of papers out of the city, he readily accepted the bribe. Thus it was that four chests of bonds, bills and ledgers containing vital information about the Prince's business activities found their way to the Frankfurt ghetto. In the courtyard of the Rothschild house there was a hidden entrance to a cellar connected by an underground passage with the next building. Judengasse was riddled with these subterranean hideaways, originally constructed as refuges in times of persecution. That was one reason why some of the houses were unsafe and prone to collapse. In the secret cellar old Rothschild kept reserves of cash and all his most highly confidential documents. To these were now added the Elector's coffers.

But as the year progressed William soon required other services which, if no less dangerous, were a good deal more profitable. Exiled to the Danish town of Gotlorp and unable to exercise direct control over his remaining assets, he found himself in desperate financial straits. A letter from Buderus to an agent in London conveys the urgency of the situation: "We are in the greatest misery here. Please help us to get some money soon, because we do not know what we shall do otherwise, as we are not getting a farthing from Kassel. God, how things have changed."[5] Mayer Amschel did all he could to aid his patron. He received on William's behalf interest paid on his loans to the Austrian Emperor. He despatched his sons to England and Holland to trace and appropriate monies owing to the Elector. Amschel and, later, Carl paid frequent visits to Prague, where the exiled Prince took up residence late in 1807.

During the Elector's enforced absence from Germany, three banking houses were charged with calling in as many debts as possible before the French could lay hands on the money. These were Lennap at Kassel, Lawätz at Hamburg and Rothschild at Frankfurt. Buderus was in overall charge of the operation and he channelled more and more of the transactions in the Rothschilds' direction. "Frankfurt is the central point of all my business", he informed the Elector as early as March 1807.[6]

32

But soon the Rothschilds became involved in something much more important than debt collection. They began to manage the Elector's investments. William had money piling up in England and he wanted it put to good use. But he was reluctant to trust anyone else with the administration of his fortune. Eventually Buderus persuaded the miserly Prince to allow Nathan Rothschild to handle a modest portion of his funds. In 1808 N.M. bought, on the Landgrave's behalf, a hundred and fifty thousand pounds' worth of British government three per cent stock.

The Rothschilds' reputation for handling — confidentially and efficiently — delicate negotiations across the borders of the empire rapidly reached the ears of other beleaguered princelings. Mayer and his sons were increasingly employed in sending coded messages around Europe, conveying money in the secret compartments of coaches, and concealing in the tunnels of Judengasse all manner of documents that would have been of enormous interest to the enemy.

Meanwhile, Nathan was responding with his usual vigour and ingenuity to the challenge of the Continental System. It is probably no coincidence that the year in which he became an investment broker to the court of Hesse-Kassel (1808) was the same year that he completely reorganised and expanded his business activities. He left the provinces for the capital and opened an office at 12 Great St Helen's Street in the financial quarter of London. The Manchester business continued under the name of Rothschild Brothers. The plan was that Carl should join his brother and run the northern office. He had visited England in 1804 and was anxious to return, though Mayer Amschel had hitherto been unable to spare him. Carl, as well as travelling frequently to the Elector's court, looked after the Frankfurt end of the English trade. He came of age in 1809 and was the obvious brother to succeed Nathan in the day-to-day running of the textile business. [7] But the dislocation of trade forced Nathan to abandon any such plans and to shift the emphasis of his commercial operation. He ran down his textile business and worked solely in London from where he could concentrate all his energies on breaking the Continental System. It was probably at about this time that N.M. bought out his brother-in-law and partner, for nothing is heard about any continued involvement by Benedict Worms. The nature of Nathan's activities was changing from commerce to finance and that involved working more closely with his father's business and clients. His London office had the name "N.M. Rothschild and Brothers" on the door. Nathan applied himself energetically to the business of blockade-running or, as the French saw it, smuggling. He hired a group of audacious captains, most of them working out of the Kent coast around Folkestone, men who knew the Dutch and

Baltic ports well and were prepared to sail in all weathers. With their help, and that of the family's invaluable information network, he sent cargo after cargo across the North Sea to small, unguarded harbours where his agents waited to unload them and convey them rapidly inland.

By now the nerve centre of Rothschild operations had shifted from Frankfurt to London. Nathan took the initiative because he was a financial genius who saw clearly the unique opportunities offered by the war and because living in England provided a very different perspective on international events than living in Germany. The British were solid in their determination to defeat "Bony". Hannah's relatives and N.M.'s colleagues were unflinching in their determination to break the Continental System. Their motives were, of course, primarily commercial but, as with Nathan himself, there was a patriotic element in their thinking. By defying Napoleon's blockade they were playing their part in the war effort. So, from London Nathan planned and controlled the complex operations necessary to maintain the flow of trade.

Two factors worked in his favour: there was a considerable demand for British and Colonial goods which made it worthwhile for shippers, carriers and merchants to take risks. At the same time the Continental System was impossible to enforce effectively. With accurate, up-to-date information, daring, the use of forged papers and the occasional bribe to a corrupt official, it was always possible to find a gap in the wall Napoleon had tried to build around Europe.

Secrecy was vital, especially for the protection of Nathan's relatives. Everyone at the Frankfurt end was under great pressure and frequently under suspicion. They were constantly travelling: Carl to and from Prague; Amschel much occupied in Kassel; Salomon dashing off on trips to Amsterdam, Hamburg and the northern ports; and young James already making visits to France. And there was always risk of discovery. The imperial authorities knew that the Rothschilds were crown agents to the Elector and suspected them of dealing in contraband. So they spied on the family and intercepted their letters. For the residents of the house of the red shield danger was a fact of day-to-day life and the strain was intense. Napoleon's agents were only waiting for an excuse to search the premises and force the inhabitants to yield up their secrets.

In the spring of 1809 William IX handed them that opportunity on a plate. He financed an ill-prepared rising in Hesse-Kassel. Immediately after its suppression Buderus was arrested and cross-examined. On 10 May the commissioner of police led a party of constables along Judengasse and hammered on Mayer Amschel's door.

Fortunately, the Rothschilds had been forewarned by Dalberg. Their first thought had been for the Elector's chests, which they tried to carry through the tunnel to the next house. But they were too wide. In a bustle of hectic activity the cases were opened and the documents dispersed to a variety of other hiding places. When the police arrived all they found was a crowded household, each member apparently involved in what seemed to be a legitimate trading enterprise.

They examined Mayer Amschel's ledgers but could find no fault with them. That was hardly surprising since the old man had for years kept two sets of books, one for public scrutiny, the other decidedly not.

The police searched the house thoroughly. They interrogated every member of the family currently in Frankfurt but could find no flaw in their previously rehearsed stories. The head of the household they judged to be a respectful, sick old man (there was no pretence here; Mayer Amschel had undergone an operation in 1808 and had been sufficiently ill to make a will) who pleaded a failing memory, particularly over those transactions which were of special interest to his examiners. At last, the commissioner left to make his report that the Rothschilds were "exceedingly wise and cunning" and the family breathed a sigh of relief.[8]

But the crisis was far from over. Buderus was known to be the linchpin of the Elector's clandestine operation and was frequently brought in for questioning. In 1810 Mayer Amschel managed to help his old friend by persuading Dalberg to appoint Buderus to public office. But before the year was out the two men and their associates were in trouble again. Napoleon ordered a clampdown on contraband. The unpalatable fact he had to face was that his Continental System had failed. It had done little damage to the British and it had caused inflation, shortages and economic difficulties within his own dominions. As a result, in 1810, he was obliged to relax the restrictions on foreign goods and to introduce a system of import licences which virtually amounted to legalised smuggling. The result was a surge in the importation of British and Colonial goods which, despite being highly priced, were eagerly sought after. But the relaxing of regulations, instead of giving Napoleon's officials more control of the import trade, merely enabled bold merchants like Nathan Rothschild to find more loopholes.

Unable to control the suppliers of contraband, the Emperor decided to intimidate the receivers. Police, informers and the military were used in a vigorous campaign aimed at seeking out and making an example of all dealers in prohibited merchandise. Buderus graphically reported to his master the situation in Frankfurt:

Several French regiments with artillery have come into the town, as well as a host of Customs officials. All the gates have been occupied and nobody is allowed to pass out without being closely inspected; all warehouses have been sealed, and an extensive search for English and colonial goods has been instituted, severe penalties being inflicted when such goods have been discovered. The extent of the general confusion and distress which this has caused beggars description . . . the number of spies and traitors under every guise is so great that it is impossible now to trust anyone.[9]

It seems that Napoleon had decided to make a special example of Frankfurt. Soldiers and officials searched the houses and business premises of all the merchants, looking for concealed illicit merchandise. When goods were discovered the traders involved were forced to pay duty. The items were then confiscated and publicly burned. The bill for merchandise discovered on Rothschild premises was 19,348 francs, a modest share of the nine and a quarter million francs collected from the city as a whole. Doubtless clever concealment and "sweetening" of officials played their part in enabling the family to get off so lightly. In his reports to the Elector, Buderus had nothing but praise for the diligence, courage and cunning of old Rothschild and his sons.

Mayer Amschel was now an old man of sixty-six and in poor health. The anxieties of the last few years must have weighed heavily upon him. Yet looking back over his long and eventful life, he can only have had cause for satisfaction. He had built up the family business from modest beginnings to the point where it had a declared capital of eight hundred thousand gulden. He was principal banker to the richest prince in Europe and had performed valuable services for other rulers including the Emperor of Austria. He had established a wide network of commercial and political contacts, skilful use of which should enable his sons to achieve even greater success. Despite their squabbles the boys were dutiful and united. Provided they remained so, there was no limit to what they could do. But he would no longer be there to witness their triumphs. The time had come to put everything in order for them.

In September 1810 a new partnership agreement was drawn up for the firm of M.A. Rothschild and Sons. In it, the business capital was divided into equal shares and apportioned as follows: fifty for Mayer Amschel, twelve for Amschel, twelve for Salomon and one for Carl. James, who was not yet a partner, was also to receive one share, "instead of a salary and in return for his tiring trips on company business". Rules were laid down for the reapportionment of shares on the marriages of the two younger sons and for the preventing of money being alienated from the business. For example, any marriage settlement Mayer Amschel might make upon Carl and James was immediately to be ploughed into the company. Any claim by any other member of the family was specifically rejected in advance.

This clearly included daughters and in-laws and also N.M.[10] Nathan's was still on paper a separate business, and, though he now played the leading role in Rothschild commerce, it was vital to distance the Frankfurt house from the activities of a merchant ensconced in the territory of an enemy. Therefore, the growing fiction of Nathan's independent operation was maintained.

But that operation was about to enter a new and much more grandiose phase. N.M. not only expanded into areas that involved his brothers, whether they liked it or not; he also undertook a series of breathtaking ventures which, within a mere five years, would dramatically change the scale of the family business. Whatever Mayer Amschel may have foreseen in 1810, he could scarcely have imagined that his thirty-three-year-old son was about to transform the enterprise he had founded into the world's leading banking house.

CHAPTER 4

"The Kurfurst made our fortune"

The transformation which came over Rothschild fortunes in a few brief years was quite staggering. It may well be unique in the annals of commercial history. In 1810 Nathan Rothschild was one among several London entrepreneurs. By 1815 he had become principal financier to the British government, the man behind Wellington's successful Peninsular campaign, the man who provided the money which made possible the greatest of all British victories — Waterloo.

The gulf between a general merchant and blockade-runner, and an official banker to His Majesty's Government was immense — and yet Nathan bridged it in little more than five years. It is small wonder that the most improbable stories were invented to explain how the family from the Frankfurt ghetto had, with a single bound, not only created a success which was the envy of every business house in Europe, but also established for themselves a status that would never be successfully challenged. The remarkable coup could only have been achieved by a complex series of dealings, many of which were encased in a secrecy which cannot now be penetrated. What is clear, however, is that the action of those five years falls naturally into three stages, like the acts of a tense drama.

Act I centres upon the funds which Elector William of Hesse-Kassel placed in the Rothschilds' hands for investment. The Prince's money was the rock on which the family fortune was built, as Carl acknowledged in 1814: "The *Kurfurst* [Prince] made our fortune. If Nathan had not had the elector's £300,000 in hand he would have got nowhere."[1] Carl, for several years the messenger between Frankfurt and Prague, knew better than anyone how important the management of the miser Prince's money was and how difficult it had been to secure.

After the hundred and fifty thousand pounds N.M. had been entrusted with in 1808, he had immediately urged his relatives to ask the Elector for more. But the old man had other London agents and was unwilling to spread his trust too widely. However, at the end of 1809 William relented and allowed N.M. to invest a second instalment of a hundred and fifty thousand pounds in London and Buderus was soon negotiating on the family's behalf for a third sum.

But the Elector was worried. He had not yet received the documentary proof that his money had been safely invested in British bonds. Buderus hastened to assure him that the papers would be sent from London as soon as a safe method could be found. To overcome his master's hesitation, he offered an inducement which he knew William would be unable to resist: "After long arguments, and as the result of great efforts, I have persuaded the Crown Agent Rothschild, in effecting the third investment of £150,000 sterling, to charge a quarter per cent less commission, so that he will deliver the stock for 73¾ per cent, involving a saving of £4,521."[2] That did the trick. The Elector not only agreed to the transaction, he promised to follow it up with a further hundred thousand pounds, paid in instalments. But he was still fussing about the paperwork: ". . . you are to see that the document regarding the first investment reaches me as soon as possible and that I receive the others shortly afterwards."[3] (It seems likely that the Elector was here referring to the second payment, sent to London in 1809. It may be that Nathan had accounted more promptly for the original hundred and fifty thousand pounds, handed over in 1808, as a means of gaining the confidence of his valuable client.)

What Prince William suspected, of course, was that Nathan was using this capital for his own purposes and making the war an excuse for delaying the rendering of accounts. The suspicion was undoubtedly justified. Indeed, it was the temporary diversion of the immense sums of money originating in Hesse-Kassel which enabled N.M. to launch his banking operation, providing him with both liquidity and prestige. Although the money eventually found its way to the British Treasury, the route it followed was circuitous. N.M. was often credited with having a "nose" for the money market. It was said that he could remember the prices of all stocks quoted on the Exchange and knew instinctively which way they were going to move. This may have been an exaggeration, but he did rapidly become a phenomenon in the City and the way he multiplied the money from the Elector by a number of short-term transactions was absolutely remarkable. His dealings must have been complex and cannot now be completely reconstructed, but he was certainly speculating heavily in gold, a commodity which rose considerably in value during the latter years of the war.

But it was not only the Elector's money for which Nathan had cause to be grateful. The Prince's extreme caution also played into his hands. William, naturally, did not want it known just how heavily he was financing Napoleon's enemies. Therefore, he insisted that all his investments were to be made in Nathan's name. The result was that this newcomer suddenly appeared to be taking the City by storm. Within a few months he was buying and selling bonds on such a scale that he had become one of the major government loan contractors. Rivals and colleagues who did not know where Rothschild's money had come from could only look on with amazement at this new financial phenomenon. Other men of affairs hastened to put business his way. Soon Nathan was moving in the highest political and commercial circles.

But while Nathan was busy building up his fortune, it was his brothers and Buderus who had to bear the brunt of the Elector's anger and suspicion. Months passed and still the Prince had not received his certificates. He threatened to remove his support from the Rothschilds:

> I am exceedingly worried about this matter and am most eagerly waiting to hear what you have to say. In the meantime you are to cease making any further payments in respect of these stocks, neither are you to invest in them any further English interest payments. I am still waiting in vain for the documents regarding the capital which I have invested; and, in spite of all the confidence which I have in Rothschild, I cannot tolerate this delay any longer . . . [4]

The Elector had to be pacified with a reiteration of the difficulties of communication and a further cut in the Rothschilds' commission. Carl was immediately despatched to England and returned with a certificate for £189,500.

Now that he had access to large amounts of cash, Nathan was coming to rely more and more on financial and share transactions, rather than blockade-running which, despite the inherent weaknesses of the Continental System, was becoming increasingly hazardous. For all the efforts of Nathan and other ingenious merchants, Britain's balance of trade was looking distinctly unhealthy. In 1810-11 the value of exports and re-exports fell from sixty-two to forty-four million pounds.

It is no wonder, therefore, that Nathan, like many other merchants and financiers, turned his attention increasingly to dealing in bullion and government securities. For those who understood the market there were considerable profits to be made. Britain was in the grip of inflation brought about by the cost of the war, the effects of blockade and a run of bad harvests. The government had abandoned the gold standard and (in July 1811) made banknotes legal tender. This action had the effect of pushing up still further the value of specie. At the same time the administration's determination to continue the war meant that its borrowing grew steadily, year by year, and the market in government bonds flourished accordingly.

The situation was, however, far from stable. Britain could not carry on the war forever with no effective allies and around the middle of 1810 she reached the nadir of her fortunes. The military and economic situations were, alike, bleak. One by one, Napoleon had picked off all his Continental enemies. Only Portugal resisted incorporation in the empire, and bolstering her independence had already cost Britain millions in gold and thousands of soldiers since 1808. In the Peninsula, the British army, led by Wellington, recently created a viscount, was committed to supporting Spanish nationalist guerrillas, but the struggle dragged on, consuming more and more treasure to little effect. Supremacy at sea had thwarted France's attack on Colonial trade, but with diminishing markets in Europe Britain ran the risk of becoming a warehouse of unsaleable goods. Public protests over high bread prices and Whig demands for disengagement put severe pressure on the administration led by Spencer Perceval, an administration which was already weak and divided. To make matters worse, George III subsided into insanity and the Prince Regent, who now took his place, detested his Prime Minister. Nathan, along with other financial leaders in the City, watched the political manoeuvrings of the summer and autumn, daily expecting the government to fall.

But Perceval survived as Prime Minister. A plot to supplant him failed, and he obtained the grudging support of the Prince Regent. Urged on by Lord Liverpool, Secretary of State for War and the Colonies, he pushed through parliament a fresh budget for the army. By February 1811 it was clear to most observers that the administration would continue and that, despite Wellington's complaint that the ministry lacked "the power or the inclination or the nerves to do all that ought to be done to carry on the contest", it would push the conflict with Bonaparte to a military conclusion if at all possible.

On 5 March, five thousand fresh English troops landed at Lisbon. Within a month Wellington had driven the French out of Portugal. This triumph was rapturously received in Britain and the government hailed it as a vindication of their policy. Napoleon, already heading for a breach with Russia, could not commit more men to the Peninsula. Those with the political acumen to grasp the significance of these events realised that the tide of war had turned. Nathan Rothschild was such a man. Through his family and his large network of agents and couriers he was better informed about European affairs than any man in London – including members of the government. And he was anxious to place his knowledge, his contacts and his skills at the disposal of his adopted country.

By now there was an enormous difference between Nathan and his elder brothers. Their thinking was still cast in the traditional Jewish mould.

This was especially true of Amschel. The stirring events through which he lived were quite secondary to the affairs of his own community and the strict maintenance of the dietary and Sabbath laws. This fussy, punctilious unimaginative man filled the place left by his infirm father in the Frankfurt ghetto, indulged himself in few luxuries and worried about his brothers' close contacts with Gentile society. For Amschel "patriotism" was a word with little meaning apart from loyalty and responsibility to the Chosen People. He was content to play the rôle of the dutiful eldest son. He and his childless wife continued to live in Judengasse with his parents and they would remain there long after Mayer Amschel's death.

But Nathan was a new breed of Jew, an assimilationist who took all the opportunities offered by the freer atmosphere of England. In 1809 he and his family moved from Great St Helen's Street, on the edge of the City, where there was a flourishing Jewish business community, to 2 New Court, St Swithin's Lane,* a stone's throw from the Bank of England and the Exchange. There was symbolism as well as good business sense in this relocation of his premises. N.M. was now at the centre of English financial affairs. He was not yet a part of the establishment. Indeed, he affected disdain for the airs and graces of the aristocracy and enjoyed the reputation of being a gruff, no-nonsense businessman. If he was not yet ready to buy his way into polite society it was not religious scruples which held him back. He was just too busy to bother.

Day and night Nathan Rothschild pored over his ledgers and the letters from his brothers which gave him minute information about gold, commodity and security prices in European markets. For double security, these were written both in Judendeutsch and code. He was frank with his family about his total obsession: "I am reading through your letters not just once but maybe a hundred times ... After dinner, I have nothing to do. I do not read books, I do not play cards, I do not go to the theatre. My only pleasure is business and in this way, I read Amschel's, Salomon's, [James's] and Carl's letters."[5] In his replies Nathan's tone became increasingly peremptory. He had come to England partly to act as an agent for his father. Now the situation was reversed. It was the Frankfurt Rothschilds who received their instructions from N.M. – a state of affairs they did not always relish.

One reason why Nathan's letters were often so tetchy is that he was taking more and more risks. He was heavily involved in illicit bullion dealings. For this lucrative but hazardous trade he used a group of Kent coast mariners. The name Rothschild still looms large in the folklore of

*The premises of N.M. Rothschild and Sons still occupy the same site.

42

that region. One story tells how a certain Mr Cullen of Folkestone and his wife were about to retire for the night when there came a tapping at the window. The head of the household discovered in the gloom a man "enveloped in a huge cloak and wearing a big slouch hat, which prevented his face from being seen". The stranger motioned Cullen to silence, slipped in at the open door and only when it had been securely bolted, revealed his identity. It was none other than the head of the house of Rothschild. Nathan, it transpired, had an illicit consignment of a hundred thousand guineas which he had to conceal until a ship bound for France was ready to receive it on board. Cullen agreed to act as caretaker. The bags of gold were brought in and laid on his own bed between the frame and the mattress. The august caller left and the Cullens retired to spend "the uneasiest night of their lives". Next evening Nathan was back and his gold was conveyed to the harbour under cover of darkness.[6]

The kernel of truth at the centre of this doubtless exaggerated story is that Nathan was closely involved with several members of the maritime community along the Kent coast whose way of life included, as well as fishing and normal mercantile pursuits, smuggling, blockade-running, privateering and, perhaps, occasional piracy. These contacts were undoubtedly established in the early days of N.M.'s residence in England when he was setting up a fast and efficient cross-Channel service for couriers and cargo. At that time he became well known along the coast as a man who wanted the best service and was prepared to pay for it — handsomely. Generous bonuses were always available when Mr Rothschild urgently needed a brave captain to put to sea in bad weather. Thus was forged the last, vital link in the astonishing chain of communication which linked Manchester and London with Paris, Frankfurt and scores of Continental business centres.

The Cullens were one of the most important families involved in cross-Channel trade. Richard Cullen was a self-made man, a mariner and shipowner of Folkestone. By 1810 he controlled, perhaps in part-ownership, a little fleet of ships of between seventy-five and two hundred and fifty tons burthen. He operated the Folkestone packet under licence from the Post Office, hired the *Rover* to the navy as an armed lugger, and certainly used other vessels, from time to time, as privateers. He also specialised in the high-risk business of bullion transportation. Fluctuations in the bullion market made coin-smuggling a very profitable operation in which several south-east coast captains were involved on behalf of wealthy clients. In local legend the name of Rothschild is clearly connected with these clandestine activities.

The detailed truth will never be known. What *is* clear is that the Rothschilds' connection with the Folkestone area and its people was both

43

close and long. For example, several generations of the Cullen family served the London bank in various capacities and when, in the middle of the nineteenth century, one of Nathan's sons was a popular MP for Hythe and Folkestone his election agent was one Thomas Cullen.[7]

Nathan reposed considerable trust in these Kentish mariners and they were prepared to risk tempest and enemy action for him. But not only for him. These same shipowners and sailors were a vital part of Britain's war effort. The Narrow Seas were kept open by the navy, but it was men like the Cullens who were employed to make holes in the Continental System and also to convey supplies to Wellington's army in Spain. It seems likely that throughout much of the campaign Rothschild money was also involved in helping to provision the Peninsular force.

It was Nathan's varied involvement in the economic aspects of the war which suggested to him a dramatic expansion of his activities in ways which would be profitable to himself and beneficial to his adopted nation. His plans developed as a result of the French government's decision, in 1810, to relax their regulations on the illicit trade in goods and money. To control imports they established a special customs post at Gravelines, between Calais and Dunkirk, for the official reception of contraband. N.M.'s captains took full advantage of this arrangement for "licensed smuggling" and, to look after the Continental end of the business, Salomon and James made frequent visits to the French town. Indeed, from the autumn of 1810 James was scarcely ever absent from there. But the scheme which their English brother now proposed involved a *permanent* Rothschild presence in France, and Nathan wrote to his father asking him to arrange this.

It was not difficult for Mayer Amschel to sort out the necessary formalities. Dalberg, as Grand Duke of Frankfurt and Primate of the Confederation of the Rhine, was planning a trip to Paris to be present at the sumptuous christening of Napoleon's long-awaited son and heir and he urgently needed cash for himself and his entourage. Once more he turned to old Rothschild. Mayer Amschel happily obliged and, in return, asked for the favour of a passsport for his nineteen-year-old son. That favour was granted, and with James's departure for Paris, Act I of the drama draws to a close.

CHAPTER 5

"Employ that gentleman in the most secret and confidential manner"

James's arrival in Paris was the signal for the entire Rothschild family to embark upon a burst of even more frenetic activity. From the handsome house in the Rue Napoléon (now the Rue de la Paix) where he established his base, James, and often Salomon as well, travelled frequently to Gravelines, Dunkirk and Amsterdam, with occasional forays across the Channel. As for Nathan, scarcely a day passed without his despatching an agent, a message or a consignment to one of the other brothers. Amschel and Carl, engaged in the normal business of the Frankfurt house, often had to drop everything to comply with some urgent instruction from London.

Those secret, frenzied, anxious toings and froings, which were to continue throughout Act II of the drama, were necessitated by a bewildering series of deals involving coins, bills and bonds and, above all, gold. For Nathan now dramatically stepped up his speculation in bullion and specie.[1] Soon it reached massive proportions. With the capital they now had at their disposal the Rothschilds were ideally placed to profit from the nervous Continental money markets. In fact, they increased their wealth tenfold in the space of a few years.

As the fortunes of war swung back and forth, so prices on the stock and bullion markets rose and fell. It was the sort of situation in which fortunes are lost and made. Those men were likely to be most successful who possessed a cool head, an ability to make bold decisions, and an excellent information service. Such a man was Nathan Rothschild who, in a remarkably short space of time, was recognised as the "wonder" of the City. In 1813, writing about N.M.'s brother-in-law, Moses Montefiore, a contemporary observed that he was in "constant intercourse with Mr N.M. Rothschild, through whose prudence and judicious recommendations with regard to the Bullion Market and Foreign Exchanges he is enabled not only to avoid hazardous monetary transactions, but also to make successful ventures in these difficult times."[2]

It is impossible to reconstruct the pattern of Rothschild financial dealings at this time but the main element in that pattern seems clear.

45

The price of gold in London was high, as we have seen, and restrictions on its export further boosted its value. Anyone who could find a way of conveying it to the Continent and of regulating its flow so as not to depress the market stood to make a fortune. Nathan found a way.[3] The Frankfurt house (all business was done in the name of the parent house in order to conceal the involvement of the English Rothschild) opened large credits with two Dunkirk merchant bankers, Veuve Dominique Morel et Fils and R. Faber and Co. Nathan's captains conveyed gold (usually English guineas) across the Channel to Gravelines. James received it and paid for it with bills drawn on London houses. Through their Paris connections, Morel and Faber placed the specie with leading banks in the capital. From there James and his brothers could use the money to buy bills drawn on any Continental bank. There were various charges and expenses involved in this enterprise but gross profit on the exchange could be as much as thirty-three per cent.

The French authorities, of course, knew what was happening. The police had greeted James with considerable suspicion when he presented himself to them upon his first arrival in Paris, and it would, in any case, have been impossible to conceal such large movements of precious metal. So James made no attempt to conceal his activities. On the contrary, he explained the nature of his business soon after his arrival. It was sufficiently important for Count von Mollien, the Finance Minister, to describe it in a memorandum to the Emperor Napoleon on 26 March:

> I can today state with certainty that a citizen of Frankfurt, now in Paris with a passport issued in Frankfurt, who goes by the name of Rothschild is chiefly engaged in bringing guineas from the English coast to Dunkirk and that in a single month he has brought over 100,000 guineas (2,400,000 francs). He is involved with the leading Paris bankers, such as the houses of Mallet, Charles Davillier and Hottinguer, who make over to him bills drawn on London. The same man states that he has just received letters from London, dated the 20th of this month, and that these letters reveal that there is speculation in England that, in order to prevent the export of gold and silver specie, the value of the crown will be raised from five shillings to five and a half shillings and the value of the guinea from twenty-one to thirty shillings ...[4]

Mollien was delighted with this information. He regarded this run on gold as evidence that Britain was on the verge of economic collapse, and that her trading partners were rushing to get their capital out before the crash. This was little more than wishful thinking. There was no significant depreciation of the British currency and the inflow of bullion from

America and the Colonies more than balanced the drain to the Continent. In any case, the flow of gold across the Channel was by no means one way. James and Nathan (and the same must have been true of other bankers) sent money in both directions in order to profit from small shifts in the exchange rate and also to prevent wild fluctuations which would have created instability. So, for the time being at least, neither side exerted itself to prevent the bankers making a "killing". The French government was happy to tolerate a trade which seemed so much to their advantage. As for the English government, it was not as alarmed as some rumours suggested; indeed, as we shall see shortly, it had its own reasons for turning a blind eye to what was afoot.

But for the Rothschilds the whole process was an exhausting and nerve-racking experience, involving constant diligence and attention to detail. The four Continental brothers, as they raced their carriages around Europe, worked long hours, went without sleep and endured vituperative letters from London, must sometimes have wondered if the game was worth the candle.

As for Nathan, it is hardly surprising that he was so impatient and ill-tempered. He was masterminding one of the most protracted and complex programmes of financial speculation ever conceived. When he stopped to reflect on just what was at stake, as he must have done frequently, the reality was frightening. He was handling ever greater sums of money for extremely prestigious clients throughout a war-torn continent in which currency and share values fluctuated wildly. A miscalculation could destroy the delicate structure of trust he was patiently creating with statesmen, merchants and bankers. Though the family was amassing money as never before, a sudden loss of confidence could spell ruin. In August 1811 Nathan sold up his Manchester concern and premises in order to devote all his time and resources to his Continental operations. He was now risking everything.

The biggest single worry was the need for secrecy. It was vital that the imperial authorities should not discover that the traffic flowed both ways — if they were delighted to see gold being smuggled out of England, they would, by the same token, have been furious to find that some of it was being smuggled back again. It was also essential to conceal the real nature of the relationship between London and Frankfurt. For this reason all the activities had to be cloaked under the mantle of legitimate commerce.

But the greatest need for secrecy arose from the fact that some of the Rothschilds' business was connected with the British government. Once the brothers had bought British bonds for the Elector of Hesse-Kassel. Now they were buying them on their own account. Much of the profit gained from their bullion dealings went into taking up government loan stock in London. As we have seen, the determination of Perceval's administration to maintain the war effort led to a massive increase in borrowing. The sum raised through the City in 1811 was twenty-three and a half million pounds. In 1812 this increased to thirty-two and a quarter. A considerable slice of this was provided by the Rothschilds. And they were also buying up bills drawn on the government and officials. This was especially risky since, if such pieces of paper turned up in Paris or Frankfurt and were discovered by the authorities, James or Amschel (now in charge of the day-to-day running of M.A. Rothschild and Sons) would be very hard put to it to explain them away.

But if popular legend is to be believed, the Rothschilds went far beyond these purely banking activities. Romantic myths would have us believe that they were smuggling gold directly to Wellington's commissariat. Some tales tell of the younger Rothschilds scurrying about Europe in coaches with secret compartments stuffed with bullion.[5]

How much truth lies in these stories? By the end of 1813 Nathan was certainly discounting Wellington's bills in London and he may well have been doing so before then. Ever since 1809 Wellington had been complaining of an acute shortage of cash to pay his troops and he had been obliged to borrow at exorbitant rates from Spanish and Maltese bankers. The angry despatches from the Peninsula were the common stock of daily discussion in the commercial and political circles where Nathan moved. He would therefore have known all about the general's bitter complaints and probably shared the conviction (voiced in one of Wellington's despatches to Lord Liverpool) that Britain's only choice lay between fighting Napoleon in Spain and fighting him at home. But on 1 October 1811 Nathan established an even closer link with the military action in Spain.

On that day John Charles Herries was appointed Commissary in Chief, which meant that he was responsible for financing and equipping the British armies in the field. Herries came from a London mercantile family and was an almost exact contemporary of Nathan. He had gained part of his education in Leipzig (where he had a mistress, of whom more anon) and had returned to England in 1798, the same year that N.M. took up residence in Manchester. While the young man from Frankfurt had been emerging as a formidable personality in the commercial arena, Herries had been enjoying a no less spectacular (and thoroughly deserved) rise in government circles. It is inconceivable that the two men, both prominent figures in the small world of London politics and finance, did not know each other and know each other well.

Two years later, as we shall see, John Herries and Nathan Rothschild put together a plan for financing the latter stages of the Peninsular War.

Taking all the circumstantial evidence into account it seems extremely likely that N.M.'s involvement in this highly important business was a sequel to earlier, unofficial, activities on Wellington's behalf.

Unfortunately, this conclusion does not enable us to accept the romantic picture of N.M.'s brothers racing their carriages over the roads of southern France to clandestine rendezvous at which chests of guineas were handed over to agents who conveyed them by narrow Pyrenean passes to the British army. The Rothschilds were not strangers to such activity, but there was no need to provide these sort of services for Wellington. All that Nathan and James had to do was obtain bills drawn on the Paris banks holding the gold they had exported from Britain. These bills were conveyed to Wellington either by bank or government courier for presentation to Spanish houses. Moreover, the sheer quantity of coin necessary, weighing several tons, would have been quite impossible to conceal in a gentleman's carriage, or even a fleet of such carriages.

While their menfolk were scurrying around Europe, the Rothschild wives were not just keeping the home fires burning. In early nineteenth-century Europe the Jewish attitude to women was quite distinct from that prevailing elsewhere. The wife was a helpmeet to her husband behind the shop counter and desk. She was expected to understand and participate in his business. She was often as well educated as her brothers. When it came to emancipation and participation in a man's world she had a head start over her Gentile sisters. Thus, for example, Salomon's wife, Caroline, as well as looking after her own home and her two children, Betty and Anselm, would have run her husband's office during his frequent absences and worried about his health. Constant travel exacerbated a rheumatic condition to which Salomon was prone and he was also affected by migraines which business anxieties and constant squabbles with his brothers did nothing to improve.

Salomon spent a great deal of time in Paris helping James, who was the pivotal point of so many negotiations. The strain on the youngest Rothschild was enormous. He was constantly besieged from both London and Frankfurt for money, bills, bonds and up-to-date accounts. He had to carry on the daily business with Morel and Faber as well as agents farther afield. He had to keep constant watch on the Paris exchange rate, deciding when to sell and when to hold tight. And all the time he had to be on his guard against raising the suspicions of the French. He was up at five o'clock every morning and seldom in bed before midnight. It was a great deal to ask of a young man, isolated in a foreign country without family or friends. It was a baptism by fire and, in the long term, it would turn James into a tough, resilient financier.

External pressures were mounting on all the Rothschilds. In the early weeks of 1812 Napoleon's recruiting gangs were out conscripting men, and even fourteen-year-old boys, into the largest army Europe had ever seen. The Emperor was preparing for his Russian campaign and was squeezing his dominions hard to provide the manpower for his Grande Armée of 612,000 soldiers. Two-thirds of this force came from France's satellite states and there was only one way that young, able-bodied men could avoid the draft. Mayer Amschel, like other wealthy fathers, would have had to pay a considerable sum to secure his sons' immunity from military service. Had James and Carl not avoided the march to Moscow the story of the family and, indeed, of Europe would have been different. Of the 612,000 men who entered Russia in June only 110,000 returned in December.

Meanwhile, in Spain, French troops had been driven out of all the territory south of the Tagus. Even after such savage reverses no wise commentator would write off Napoleon Bonaparte but Britain's dogged opposition could now be seen to be paying off. Those who had supported her lone stand might begin to look forward to a share of the glory and the spoils of victory.

But Mayer Amschel Rothschild would not live to see the downfall of the dictator. His life came to a close in a darkened room of that house in Judengasse where he and Gutle had lived for twenty-seven years and from which they had launched the most remarkable financial dynasty in history. On 16 September Mayer Amschel, now sixty-eight, was taken ill after attending prayers in the synagogue. Though in declining health he had not spared himself. His body was worn out and the next day he summoned his lawyer to draw up a revised will.

It was a sensible and sensitive document. A generous settlement was provided for Gutle for life, there were bequests to his daughters and their children and marriage endowments were set aside for Carl and James. A codicil allowed Amschel to use part of 148 Judengasse as a home for himself and his wife. All the old man's other sons, except unmarried Carl (who, in any case, spent much of his time travelling), had left the ghetto but Amschel had remained at his elbow, his devoted partner in business and in the affairs of the synagogue. All the rest of Mayer Amschel's fortune, except a hundred gulden bequeathed to various Jewish charities, was to remain in the business, his share now divided among his other partners. The dying head of the family strongly reaffirmed the exclusion of his daughters and sons-in-law and their heirs from the business of M.A. Rothschild and Sons. They were not entitled to have access to any business transactions, account books or documents nor to make any claim against the bank. The old man concluded: "I could never forgive any of my children if, in defiance of my paternal wishes, it transpired that my sons were not allowed to continue to exercise their business interests . . . in tranquility."

Any of his children who questioned this arrangement were to lose their entitlements under the will and Mayer Amschel took this final oportunity to exhort them all to live in unity. "I urge my dear children to regard each other always with mutual love and friendship, and to obey as dutiful children my . . . testamentary dispositions."[6]

The dying Mayer Amschel impressed on his sons the need for unity because their financial success had only been bought at the price of strained relationships. They were all, with the possible exception of Salomon, strong and determined personalities. Up till now they had been held together by their reverence for him but he must have known the different forces which impelled each one of his sons and feared that they might have been driven apart. He would have recognised Amschel's religious zeal and his anxiety that his brothers were becoming contaminated by close contact with the Gentile world. As for Nathan, ambition had driven him far from home and might yet lead him into total independence. Carl and James were both impatient young men who felt overshadowed by N.M.'s success. So, the patriarch instilled into the men who inherited his business as well as his fortune a pride in the name of Rothschild, and he so ordered the commercial affairs of the family firm that self-interest might reinforce unity if brotherly affection failed. History has proved how shrewd and far-sighted he was.

Mayer Amschel died on 19 September 1812 with only two of his sons, Amschel and Carl, at his bedside. The end had come too suddenly for the others to be summoned but even had it been otherwise the old man would probably not have wished Nathan, Salomon and James to be brought for a final blessing. He knew how crucial was the work they were doing and how difficult it was for them to be away from their desks even for a few days in such troubled times. So, this remarkable man quietly passed to his ancestors in the ghetto where they had all lived and where his wife would continue to live for another thirty-seven years.

As well as his remarkable commercial achievements in the half-century he had devoted to building a family business, he had been instrumental in liberating the Jews of Frankfurt from the shackles that had bound them for generations. One of his last acts had been to conclude a deal with Dalberg whereby the Frankfurt Jews were granted full citizenship rights. Prior to this agreement their position had been somewhat ambivalent.

Napoleon had implemented the liberal reforms of the Revolution not out of humanitarian concern but as a means of giving unity and cohesion to his empire. As far as the Jews were concerned he wanted two things: effective control of their business activities and wealth, and their speedy assimilation into French civilisation. He had set up a centralised organisation governing the activities of all the synagogues and in what came to be called the "Infamous Decree" of 1808 he regulated Jewish settlement throughout his Germanic dominions, attempting to break up ancient communities by restricting the populations of the ghettoes. Beyond such limitations, the Jews were "free" but it was up to the leaders of the various communities to negotiate with local authorities the precise details of Jewish emancipation.

In Frankfurt it was M.A. Rothschild and J.J. Gumprecht who took this responsibility on themselves. They persuaded the Grand Duke to cancel the annual tax on the Jewish community in return for a once-for-all payment of 440,000 gulden, of which Mayer Amschel personally provided a hundred thousand. This removed the last official distinction between the Jew and his Christian neighbour with whom he now became an equal citizen before the law. The old Frankfurt ruling families were furious. Rumours soon circulated as to how Rothschild had "bribed" Dalberg's officials and the Jews were left in no doubt that their new privileges would be swiftly curtailed once their protector was removed from office. The struggle was by no means over but it must have given Mayer Amschel no small satisfaction to know that he had done everything in his power for his people. With his passing Act II of the drama comes to an end.

Napoleon's disastrous retreat from Moscow in 1812 put heart into his reluctant allies. Supported once more by British subsidies, Austria and Prussia joined forces with Russia and the campaign of 1813 ended in a decisive defeat for Napoleon at Leipzig on 18 October in the Battle of the Nations. Immediately the Confederation of the Rhine fell apart. Dalberg left Frankfurt. Within weeks, the exiled princes, including the Elector of Hesse-Kassel, returned to their capitals. Meanwhile, Wellington had driven the last of the French armies out of Spain and was securely established north of the Pyrenees. For the first time in twenty years the French were fighting on their own territory.

But the war was not over. The final defeat of Napoleon would require more men and money. It was against this background that Act III of the drama was played out, and the Rothschilds' success culminated in their becoming official bankers to the allies.

By now Nathan and his brothers had given ample proof of their loyalty, their discretion and their ability to move large sums of money efficiently around the Continent. So it was to Nathan that J.C. Herries turned when he needed help with a major logistical problem. If Wellington's troops were to advance unhindered from the south they had to have a continuous and reliable supply of French gold. No other currency would do. The soldiers had no use for English guineas and crowns; they wanted money they could spend on the spot. Herries presumed that there were large quantities of French coin in the recently abandoned territories of the empire. Could the Rothschilds and their agents gather it up in sufficiently large amounts, transfer it to the Dutch coast at Helvoetsluys and see it safely aboard English ships? Nathan assured him that they could.

Herries reported this to his superiors and on 11 January 1814 received a confidential memo from Nicholas Vansittart, Chancellor of the Exchequer:

It being the utmost importance to the public Service [sic] at the present moment that the commander of His Majesty's forces in the South of France should speedily be supplied with a large sum in specie, applicable to his expenditure in that country, than it has found practicable to produce through the Bank of England or any other usual channel, it has been judged expedient by Lord Liverpool [now Prime Minister] and myself, upon consideration of your report to me of the substance of the conferences, which you have had with Mr Rothschild, to authorize you to employ that gentleman in the most secret and confidential manner to collect in Germany, France and Holland the largest quantity of French gold and silver coins, not exceeding in value six hundred thousand pounds sterling, which he may be able to produce within two months from the present time. We are aware, however, that Mr Rothschild cannot be expected precisely to estimate the sums which his different agents may be able to procure in various and distant places and that it may therefore be reasonable not to consider the sum I have mentioned as the strict limit of his commission, but you will express to him our expectation that he will endeavour to confine himself as nearly as possible to that amount ... and you will take care that it will be distinctly understood by Mr Rothschild, not only that he is to take upon himself all risks and losses, which may occur, prior to the delivery on board His Majesty's ships, but that he will be held responsible for any deficiencies which may be discovered upon the final delivery and inspection of the packages to the consignee ... Upon consideration of the magnitude of the object in view of the dispatch and secrecy which it requires and of the risks which may be incurred, it is not thought unreasonable to allow Mr Rothschild a commission of 2% with all charges necessarily incurred on the sum actually delivered . . . [7]

For the Rothschilds this was the opportunity not only of a lifetime but of a century. Its consequences would be immeasurable. If the family failed, they would seriously embarrass the English government, perhaps affect the outcome of the war and certainly put a stop to their own commercial expansion. If they succeeded, the door would lie open to lucrative state business, not only with Britain but with other nations in Europe and overseas. Nathan therefore embarked on the new commission with more than his usual degree of manic energy.

The task was daunting. The difficulties of finding sufficient quantities of napoléons d'or in lands ravaged by war can easily be imagined. The Emperor's troops certainly left little cash behind them and citizens who had managed to hoard gold, as the only commodity certain to retain its value, were unwilling to part with it. But once again the Rothschild machine went into action. Once again, Nathan's brothers and Continental agents were flayed by his impatient demands for results. Soon the holders of French specie were being persuaded to part with it in exchange for gold bars brought over from England or for bills drawn on London banks.

And carts were lumbering over the roads of northern Europe towards the Dutch port of Helvoetsluys where their precious cargo was loaded on to English warships bound for St Jean de Luz near Biarritz. Herries and his superiors were delighted. So well did the operation work that as Herries later reported:

> The Chest [sic] in the South of France was furnished with French gold from Holland by shipments at Helvoetsluys so rapidly and completely that the Commissary General was abundantly supplied for all his wants without having to negotiate a bill; and from that time no Military Debt, the source of so much loss and embarrassment [in the Peninsula] was created on the Continent. [8]

Even more remarkable than the quantities of gold handled, running to tens of millions of pounds, was the fact that the complex negotiations were carried out in total secrecy. No one suspected that the British government was the beneficiary of the frenzied transactions being pushed through by Nathan and his brothers. For all that Napoleon's agents could discover, the Rothschilds were simply continuing their personal speculation in bullion. And that was precisely what Herries and his superiors wanted them to think. Throughout the tumultuous months of 1814, he and Nathan were in almost daily contact and, as he saw for himself how the London banker worked, any anxiety he may have had about entrusting such a vast enterprise to the "Frankfurt Five" completely evaporated and he was soon contemplating putting other government business in N.M.'s hands.

The Commissary in Chief certainly had had his reservations at the beginning of the business. With so much at stake — including his own career — he had to keep a close personal watch on N.M.'s movements and had also appointed an agent to represent him in Frankfurt, to cooperate with the German Rothschilds and to supervise their activities. This was the Chevalier de Limburger, a Leipzig Jew who was by trade a tobacco dealer but who was, more importantly, an old and trusted friend of Herries. Their close relationship probably went back to student days and Herries had at least one child by Mme de Limburger (presumably before her marriage). This close companion immediately made discreet enquiries about the Rothschilds' standing, then became intimate with the Frankfurt brothers. Amschel, Carl and Salomon, for their part, made sure that Herries' friend was well looked after and that Mme de Limburger also benefitted from their financial expertise. [9]

The Rothschilds were adept at using influential connections but they also worked hard for their success and never harder than during the months following the abdication of Napoleon on 13 April. Allied troops entered Paris on the last day of March. The Emperor resisted the inevitable as long as possible but finally accepted the generous offer of sovereignty over the tiny island of Elba and, on 20 April, departed into exile. Louis XVIII, who had lived in England since 1807, made immediate plans to return to his country. But he had no money to pay for a stylish and triumphant entry to Paris, so he appealed to the British Treasury. Herries was put in charge of the negotiations and Herries called in N.M. Thus, when the Bourbon monarch drove back to his palace amidst the none-too-enthusiastic acclamation of his Parisian subjects, it was by courtesy of the Rothschilds, who had advanced two hundred thousand pounds to cover his immediate needs.

Peace brought no slackening of the European governments' desire for money. Although the war was, seemingly, over, the needs of the allies were still numerous. For a start there were the troops quartered all over Europe. They had to be paid and, as it would be some weeks before the allied armies could be disbanded, the specie collection had to continue throughout the summer. Nathan went on organising the complex operation from London and despatching couriers daily to the east coast ports. The payment of troops was concluded at the end of August. But then there were subsidies to be paid to the Continental allies so that they could finally send their soldiers home. There was a twenty-five million francs indemnity levied on the French government. And, as the various European nations set about rebuilding their war-battered economies, there were state loans to be funded. The Rothschild banks in Frankfurt, Paris and London had now accumulated immense capital assets and established between them a unique clearing house system for international bills of exchange. They might therefore, reasonably, have expected to enjoy a large share of the new banking opportunities now opening up. Nathan organised New Court to cope with a steady expansion of business. In doing so he remembered the obligation he owed to his original partner, Benedict Worms. He brought Solomon, the old man's eldest son and N.M.'s nephew, over from Frankfurt and established him as a broker in his firm and a member of the Exchange, where he made good progress under his uncle's expert tuition.[10]

But if the Rothschilds imagined that new business would now come pouring in from grateful governments, they reckoned without human nature. The jubilant royal and noble families who now returned to their palaces were intent on a full restoration of the *ancien régime*. Everything Napoleon and his revolutionary predecessors had stood for was to be buried and forgotten. That included Jewish emancipation. A spirit of violent reaction was abroad. In Frankfurt and other cities the old patrician families were determined to re-assert their supremacy. Princes who had eagerly courted Mayer Amschel in the dark days of the war now shunned his sons. Jealous rival bankers who had watched the meteoric rise of the Rothschilds now determined to oust them from the major markets. The result of all this was that the family had to fight hard for every major piece of business. Amschel was particularly anxious to be retained by Austria to handle her subsidy and share of the indemnity. But, despite numerous letters to leading court officials and despite the support of Herries and Limburger, the negotiations were entrusted to Viennese banks. Though Nathan and James did secure important contracts from the Russian government, they were refused negotiation of the indemnity payments to Belgium.

Then, while everyone's attention — including the Rothschilds'— was elsewhere, something happened which threatened to throw everything back into the melting pot. At five o'clock on the morning of 2 March 1815 Moses Montefiore was rudely roused from sleep by a pounding at his front door. It was his brother-in-law, Nathan, calling with startling news: Napoleon had left Elba and was back in France. The bank courier had arrived with the information not minutes since. It was hours before the Prime Minister was officially informed by his own messenger.[11]

Napoleon marched northwards, rapidly gathering support from thousands of Frenchmen who resented the imposition of a king who had arrived "in the allies' baggage train". This unexpected crisis gave Nathan the opportunity to establish his financial supremacy beyond any doubt. The Herries-Rothschild machine went once more into high gear. Again there were subsidies to be paid. Again there were armies to be financed. The Austrians once again demurred at contracting business with the Frankfurt Jews. But this time there was a greater urgency. When Herries approached the embassy in London with the following polite but firm request, it did not fail of its effect:

> Sir, the English Government has requested me most particularly to commend to Your Excellency's consideration the House of Roths-child at Frankfurt which carries out the transfer of our subsidies. The firm is represented by several brothers, one of whom is established here, and is employed by the British Government in connection with all their principal financial operations on the Continent ... I ... have to ask Your Excellency to grant that firm every help and protection that lies in your power.[12]

The Rothschilds handled virtually all the subsidy payments of 1815.

The problem of raising enough French coinage for the fighting could not be solved in the same way as before. Now there was definitely not enough specie in circulation. So Nathan proposed to Herries that they should melt down bullion and other money and strike new gold and silver coins. To this day there survives at New Court a velvet-lined case containing what appear to be used coins of the type provided by Nathan for the British government. The case bears the date "April-October 1815". No explanatory records exist but there seems no reason to doubt that these are from the consignment of coin which enabled an army of 209,000 English, Dutch and Prussian soldiers to assemble in Belgium, and to confront Napoleon Bonaparte on the battlefield of Waterloo; coin provided by the Rothschilds.[13]

In mid-June 1815 all Europe awaited the outcome of what was expected to be the climax of a war which had been raging on and off for almost a quarter of a century. The first news to reach the Continental capitals told of a Prussian defeat at Ligny. Then came word that Napoleon had confronted the allied army under Wellington on 18 June. Early reports reaching London spoke of severe British reverses at La Haye Sainte. At eleven o'clock on the night of 21 June Major the Hon. Henry Percy arrived at the War Office and delivered to Lord Bathurst a despatch from Wellington announcing a great victory at Waterloo. The exhausted officer had left immediately after the battle and not stopped to take rest. Yet Nathan Rothschild had received the information a full twenty-four hours before.

Many legends have grown up about the way N.M. received the news and the use to which he put it.[14] Most of them are quite bizarre. One has the corpulent banker prancing about the battlefield on an Indian horse. Another, an anti-Semitic tract, records the profit made by Nathan and his brothers from the advance information as 135,000,000 frs. Various versions of the legend have it that the carrier was: a Jew who came upon the news almost by accident; an English yachtsman who happened to be cruising off the French coast; the engineer Isambard Kingdom Brunel (aged nine at the time); a Kentish clairvoyant; and a Rothschild employee named John Roworth, who was reputedly an eyewitness of the battle.

It is only natural that tales and speculations should have accumulated around one of the stranger aspects of the most celebrated of all English land victories. Yet the truth is, at the same time, more prosaic and more remarkable, for it is the greatest possible testimony to the efficiency of the by then well-established Rothschild courier service. There is no need to look for exotic messengers. Davidson, the Rothschild's Amsterdam agent, will have made sure that someone was on hand — if not actually on the battlefield, at least in Brussels or Ghent. That someone may have been Roworth. It may have been any one of the regular Rothschild couriers. The news of the victory reached the Belgian capital around midnight on 18 June. A messenger, equipped with fresh post horses, could have been at Dunkirk or Ostend in about eight or nine hours, where he would have known that a ship, perhaps skippered by one of the Cullen brothers, was waiting.

By whatever means he received the information, Nathan's first impulse was, naturally, to report the magnificent news to the Prime Minister and, despite the late hour, he hastened to Downing Street, only to be confronted by an imperious butler who informed him that Lord Liverpool had retired for the night and was not to be disturbed. Even in the morning, when the Rothschild message was delivered, his lordship declined to believe something which ran counter to all his official intelligence. N.M., meanwhile, had obeyed his second impulse — to go down to the Exchange and invest heavily in government stock. It was a sound business move but by no stretch of the imagination can he be said to have made a "killing". The increase in share values brought about by the news of Waterloo and the amount of stock actually available for purchase indicate that Nathan's profit may have been measured in thousands but certainly not millions.[15] And, undoubtedly, any short-term financial gain was insignificant when compared with the fact that the house of Rothschild had proved to the leading governments of Europe its ability to handle vast sums of money with discretion, integrity and despatch.

These, then, were the three stages or acts in the establishment of the Rothschild fortune during the closing years of the Napoleonic Wars. They make up one of the most dramatic success stories of all time.

CHAPTER 6
"The richest people in Europe"

The Rothschilds emerged from the war as millionaires and celebrities. But they did not yet indulge that taste for an exuberant life style for which they later became famous. In fact, their very wealth posed problems for them. The brothers from Judengasse were not like the hundreds of other entrepreneurs who had joined the ranks of the *nouveaux riches* as a result of the war. These *arrivistes* lost no time in aping the manners of the aristocracy, acquiring extravagant clothes, fine carriages, *objets d'art*, splendid town houses and country estates and buying their way into polite society. Some of the Rothschilds had similar ambitions: but for them life was not so simple. There were two important restraints upon their acquisitiveness: they were Jews and they were engaged in confidential government business.

The close connection between the administration and the Jewish bankers had inevitably attracted unfavourable comment. Accusations of collusion and bribery were common. Nathan was widely believed to have made extortionate profit from official contracts. It was even said that certain ministers were "in his pocket". It is, therefore, not surprising that he and Herries were sensitive to anything that might attract criticism. Nathan and his family lived fairly modestly for some years and it was not until the last months of his life that he indulged the luxury of acquiring a country estate.

There were few things N.M. abhorred more than publicity. As we have seen, he liked to think of himself as a straightforward, simple businessman, without any inclination for the socialising and personal extravagance by means of which the leaders of London society courted attention. But anonymity was impossible for the banker who had played so prominent a part in the overthrow of Napoleon and who had, in the process, become one of England's wealthiest citizens. Nathan and his brothers were marked men, written about in the newspapers, gossiped about in the salons and frequently lampooned by cartoonists. Yet he found it very hard to come to terms with being a public figure.

It was, in a way, flattering to be noticed by popular commentators; it was a good barometer of the Rothschilds' importance. But Nathan found distasteful even the mildest lampoon such as *A View from the Royal Exchange* by Richard Dighton. N.M.'s portly frame, thick lips and heavy German accent made him an easy target for satire but Dighton's sketch is a not unkind portrayal of a man who had by now become an established "landmark" of the Exchange. However, it displeased Nathan and gentle Salomon had to soothe him by pointing out that such was the lot of all public figures. "I hope that our beloved children . . . will find themselves so caricatured when, with God's help they have achieved some position in society." [1]

As Dighton's picture suggests, N.M. was regularly to be found in the south-east corner, which was the area of the Exchange reserved for the Jews not licensed as brokers, and always standing against his favourite Doric pillar. The scene was described by an American visitor:

> [Rothschild] was leaning against one of the columns, with his face towards the courtyard giving audience to a crowd of suppliants. He was a very common looking person, with heavy features, flabby pendent lips, and a projected fish eye. His figure, which was stout, awkward and ungainly, was enveloped in the loose folds of an ample surtout. Yet there was something commanding in his air and manner, and the deferential respect which seemed voluntarily rendered him by those who approached him, showed that he was no ordinary person. [2]

This position from which N.M. regularly held court was also captured by Thomas Jones in his 1829 caricature *A Pillar of the Exchange* (see illustration). Inevitably there were members of the financial fraternity who resented Nathan's semi-regal posture. On 1 December 1833 *The Observer* reported a "CURIOUS SCENE IN THE ROYAL EXCHANGE":

> A strong sensation was created in the Royal Exchange on Tuesday in consequence of Mr N.M. Rothschild, the eminent capitalist, being prevented from taking his usual station, with his back leaning against one of the pillars of the building at the south-east corner of the Royal Exchange. A Mr Rose, of Trinity Square, placed himself in this spot just as Mr Rothschild entered the Change to conduct his transactions in the Foreign Exchanges. In vain did Mr Rothschild courteously remonstrate with the intruder — in vain did the Exchange porters exert themselves — Mr Rose would not stir from the pillar, and Mr Rothschild was ultimately compelled to retreat to the benches in the rear . . . he was so excited by being displaced that it was some time before he could compose himself and commence business.

Pranks and caricatures such as these were harmless enough. Yet the racialism and resentments from which they sprang sometimes assumed more sinister forms. This was another reason why the Rothschilds were circumspect about displaying their new wealth. In Frankfurt, Amschel received threatening letters from a secret society pledged to the expulsion of Jews. In Austria, the attitude of the ancient nobility towards the *nouveaux riches* Rothschilds was summed up by Prince Metternich's right-hand man, Friedrich von Gentz: "The Rothschilds are vulgar, ignorant Jews, outwardly presentable, without the remotest inkling of any higher relationship. But they are endowed with a remarkable instinct which causes them always to choose the right. Their enormous wealth (they are the richest people in Europe) is entirely the result of this instinct."[3] Even in liberal England Nathan had to live with hatred and tension. Once he alarmed a group of small-time bankers who had called upon him by suddenly flinging books and ornaments at them and calling at the top of his voice for help. The reason for his outburst was that he had, that very morning, received an assassination threat. Seeing the group of strangers fumble in their pockets for their letters of introduction, the nervous financier assumed they had gone for their guns.

But it was in the German states that anti-Semitism assumed its ugliest forms. The region was in the grip of post-war depression and, as usual, the Jews were at the top of everyone's list of scapegoats. It was in 1819 that emotions spilled over into violence. Anti-Semitic riots broke out in various parts of southern Germany and, in August, Frankfurt experienced yet another outburst of the old prejudice and hatred. On the 10th a mob of young men swaggered through Judengasse and adjoining areas shouting out the old Jew-baiting slogan "*Hepp! Hepp!*", and scrawling obscene graffiti on walls and doors.

From that point "urban confrontation" developed in a way still all too familiar to us. Jewish youths responded to the taunts. There were scuffles. Men and boys grabbed up stones and other makeshift weapons. Some citizens ran away from the fighting but others hurried to join in. Confrontation, arson and looting continued late into the night. By dawn the streets were scattered with debris, blood and broken bodies. The only crumb of comfort the Jews could find in the situation was that for the first time ever the city militia turned out to help protect them. It was the soldiery who prevented Amschel's bank being sacked. Nor were James and his co-religionists in Paris altogether safe. There were several minor outbursts of anti-Jewish sentiment in the French capital.[4]

Often it was the Rothschilds who were singled out for attack. Their position within Jewry had changed dramatically. As the richest and most famous Jews in Christendom they had assumed, whether they liked it or not, a symbolic role and were widely thought of as representatives of their people. An anti-Semitic pamphlet in circulation a few years later was entitled "Rothschild I, King of the Jews", and the words accurately reflect the popular image of the family. As we shall see, the brothers were quite prepared to use their eminence to campaign for Jewish rights, but in other respects their main concern was to keep a low profile. Cultivated by prospective clients, despised by others, the Rothschilds were not deceived by the ambivalence of their position.

Another influence on the lives of the Frankfurt Five was their mother. Gutle Rothschild, despite a few little luxuries which she permitted herself, set her face firmly against ostentation. She refused to move from the house she had shared with her husband, a house which still had lodged in the wall a ball from the French bombardment of 1796, despite attempts by her sons to persuade her to take up residence in a safer and more comfortable home. It would have needed more than a few broken windows and painted slogans to drive her from Judengasse. She remained there, until her death at the age of ninety-five, living the simple life of a typical pious Jewish widow — determined, warm-hearted and dictatorial. The poet, philosopher and satirist Heinrich Heine painted a touching word picture of her:

> The old Mother Rothschild could tell the Germans a thing or two about real patriotism. Look over there on the left, there's a small house — she lives there; she is called Laetitia, mother of so many financial wizards, the family of money lenders, and in spite of her sons' world famous reputations and wealth, she does not want to leave her tiny family stronghold in the Judengasse. Today she's decorated her window with white curtains to note this festival of joy. How lovely it is to see the tiny candelabra which she lights herself when celebrating a festival ... Whenever this dear old lady looks at the candelabra, tears glisten in her eyes, as she remembers with melancholic delight all the times in her youth when Mayer Amschel celebrated the Festival of the Maccabees with her, when her sons were mere babies — when they put little candles on the floor, which shed lively shadows capturing the children's enthusiasm for the festival.[5]

Gutle followed the careers of her sons with interest and pride, exchanging gifts, giving sage advice, always urging upon them the importance of holy and simple living. But never would she visit them to see for herself what great men they had become. Her children, grandchildren and great-grandchildren always had to come to her, even though that meant leaving their carriages at the end of narrow Judengasse and picking their fastidious way along the grimy street. One great-granddaughter recalled the pilgrimage she made as a child to the house in the ghetto and to the old lady who had become a phenomenon to her descendants, and one held in both affection and awe:

I remember being ushered into a room by two maids, who led me up to a couch on which reposed the tiny form of a little old lady wearing a big cap that framed her face and hid her hair. She raised herself up a little and said some words to me in German. I shrank back somewhat alarmed, but the two maids proceeded to offer me cakes and fruit, after which I was led from the room.

Years afterwards I realised that I had been admitted into the presence of a remarkable personality, the mother of nineteen children, ten of whom had grown to adult estate. Born long before the French Revolution that convulsed and changed the face of Europe, my great-grandmother would never leave her old home ... She lived in the simplest conditions, constantly visited by her children and grandchildren, who were devoted to her.[6]

Avoiding unnecessary ostentation was one thing; securing marks of re-cognition for their services was quite another. The Continental brothers, facing snobbery and prejudice ingrained into society over several centuries, eagerly cultivated the political leaders of Europe and hoped to gain by so doing not only new business but also those tangible honours which would bring increased dignity to themselves and the Jewish com-munity. In such activities they were quite unstinting in their expenditure. They began to attract important guests to their table and proved themselves generous and accomplished in the art of entertaining. Christian bankers and businessmen might not ask them to dinner but that did not prevent the Rothschilds from issuing invitations to their own sumptuously spread tables. As time went by more and more such invita-tions were accepted, especially when the Jews' guests were known to include foreign dignitaries. One such was Friedrich von Gentz, Metternich's secretary, who arrived in Frankfurt in the autumn of 1818 and was immediately made much of by the Rothschilds. It was not just food and drink that the brothers offered the Austrian official; they did not hesitate to buy his friendship and favours with gifts of money and loan stock. As a result Gentz became a vital ally. He helped to cement the relationship the Rothschilds had already formed (see p.66) with his master, the most influential statesman in Europe. This was, of course, a time when financial inducements were among the recognised perks of office. Gentz was quite open about the sums of money he received from the Rothschilds.

While on the subject of Rothschild hospitality, it is amusing to note that it could sometimes be very far from lavish. When Prince von Metternich visited Frankfurt in 1821, Amschel diffidently issued him an invitation. Perhaps the banker did not wish to appear too opulent. Whatever the reason, all he offered the greatest statesman in Europe was "soup at noon".[7]

The family's first major coup after the war was made in the very country which had hitherto held the Rothschilds at arm's length. The extensive Austrian Empire was desperately in need of funds. Metternich, the Chancellor, and Count Stadion, his Finance Minister, were determined to set the state finances back on an even keel. Their experiences over the subsidy and French indemnity payments made it clear that only one banking concern in the whole of Europe could advance the necessary sums at attractive rates of interest, with efficiency and despatch. The enormous amounts of money handled by the five brothers and the remarkable expansion of the house of Rothschild clearly put it in a different league from the major Viennese banks which had hitherto handled all imperial business. Stadion was a realist. Whatever his personal feelings about German Jews, he knew that Austria needed the Rothschilds. He also knew that the Rothschilds needed Austria. There was something Amschel and Salomon desired that only the Hapsburg emperor could give. They had for several months been hinting to Austrian officials that some form of official recognition for their services might be appropriate.

In class-ridden, nineteenth-century society, titles were important. They were the proofs of royal patronage, the badges of respectability and the passports to bigger and better business opportunities. The Rothschilds were no different to their rivals in seeking to acquire honours, a quest which invariably involved the payment of *douceurs* to court officials.

We do not know the details of the financial transactions which passed between Frankfurt and Viennese government departments. Stadion certainly discussed with several colleagues the most appropriate way of honouring the Rothschilds. Various medals and minor titles were considered. The court had to take into account not only what the Frankfurt brothers deserved but what other groups and individuals would tolerate. By June 1816 Stadion was ready to make his report to Francis II. He said that he felt it

his duty to recommend that the services of the Frankfort banking firm, Meyer [sic] Amschel Rothschild & Sons, should be recognised, as the efforts of that firm contributed in a special degree to securing the prompt payment of the English subsidy moneys, and in the present circumstances it may be necessary to have further recourse to the good offices of that firm. The firm has very considerable resources and enjoys an even more ample credit; it can carry through transactions that appear enormous to a private person on the Continent, because the British Government employs it in the most extensive operations, and therefore supports it with the necesary funds ...

Having carefully considered all the possibilities, the Finance Minister had concluded that nothing less would do than to raise the two elder brothers to the Austrian nobility. He realised that such an honour might "excite the envy of Christian banking firms and ... create a particular sensation at the present time, as the rights of citizenship of the Jewish community at Frankfort are the subject of negotiations". But, he respectfully suggested, there was no acceptable alternative to someone as wealthy and important as Amschel Rothschild.

... the civilian medal would hardly come up to his expectations. In view of his very considerable wealth, a reward in money or money's worth ... would be even less appropriate. In the opinion of Count Stadion, orders are more suitable as a reward for officials, and as Rothschild has already many officials under his direction, an order is not likely to impress him. Count Stadion therefore requests that, as a public mark of Your Majesty's satisfaction with the services rendered by the Frankfort firm, Mayer [sic] Amschel Rothschild & Sons, Your Majesty will graciously confer on the two brothers of this firm resident here the German hereditary title of nobility, free of all dues, and will authorise him, Count Stadion, to convey to the firm, in a special letter, Your Majesty's satisfaction.[8]

This recommendation was passed through the proper channels – and a very rough ride it had. The privy councillor, Baron von Lederer, rejected it on two counts. Jews, he argued, did not enjoy full citizenship rights and hereditary titles should, therefore, only be conferred on them in exceptional circumstances. Furthermore, the Rothschilds were merely businessmen. Any services they had performed had been undertaken purely for profit and not out of loyalty to the Austrian Emperor. If some kind of reward were thought appropriate, "I consider that the most suitable thing would be that Your Majesty should make a gift to each of the two brothers Rothschild of a gold snuff-box bearing Your Majesty's monogram in diamonds. Count Stadion might be consulted as to the monetary value of such a gift."[9] In the face of such conflicting advice, Francis referred the matter to Metternich. The Prince was a pragmatist. He knew that it was more important to please wealthy financiers than haughty aristocrats. Besides, he had already established close relations with Salomon Rothschild — relations which would eventually grow into friendship. On 25 September 1816 the patent for Amschel's and Salomon's ennoblement was issued. On 21 October the names of Carl and James were added to the patent, since it was felt that they had played a valuable part in the financial negotiations of 1815.

The new honour admitted the Rothschilds to the ranks of the minor nobility, entitled the recipients to add "von" to their names ("de" in French-speaking countries) and to apply for a grant of arms. They were not slow in taking up all these privileges. The heraldic escutcheon approved for the family incorporated the device of a hand grasping four arrows to symbolise Rothschild unity. The fifth arrow was conspicuous by its absence. Though Amschel and Salomon asked for all five brothers to be represented, the Heralds' College insisted that it would be improper to make any reference to a foreign national. Thus, Nathan, who had masterminded the complex sequence of transactions for which the family was being rewarded, was the one member of the family deliberately excluded from honours.

He did not care. Or, at least, he affected not to care. If Amschel and the others wanted fancy titles that was their business. As for him, plain "Mr Rothschild" would suit well enough.

His devotion to business remained total. Years later, he responded quickly to an acquaintance who suggested that surely he would not wish his children to devote themselves to money to the exclusion of more important things. "I am sure I should wish that. I wish them to give mind, and soul, and body, and heart and everything to business; that is the way to be happy. It requires a great deal of boldness, and a great deal of caution to make a great fortune."[10] Yet Nathan's very simplicity was a kind of inverted ostentation. It declared, in effect, "I am wealthy and influential: important people court me. I don't need to put on airs and graces." Certainly many stories illustrating his contempt for affectation have attached themselves to the biography of this remarkable man. Some are, doubtless, apocryphal, such as the one concerning a German prince who arrived at New Court to present his letters of credit. He was shown into N.M.'s office while the banker was working on some papers. The banker, without lifting his head, said, "Take a chair." After a minute or two's silence the visitor, annoyed at this incivility, exclaimed, "Did you not hear, Sir, who I am?" and he repeated his impressive name and titles. Nathan deigned to offer his guest a glance and then said, laconically, "Oh, very well, take two chairs then."[11]

That anecdote did not appear in print until thirty-five years after Nathan's death. But other stories are well documented, including an incident recorded by the Prussian Ambassador, William von Humboldt:

> Yesterday, Rothschild dined with me. He is quite crude and uneducated, but he has a great deal of intelligence and a positive genius for money. He scored off Major Martins beautifully once or twice. Martins was dining with me, too, and kept on praising everything French. He was being fatuously sentimental about the horrors of the war and the large numbers who had been killed. 'Well," said Rothschild, "if they had not all died, major, you would probably still be a drummer." You ought to have seen Martins's face.[12]

Yet even stolid Nathan was not immune to human vanity as we know from the most vivid existing word picture of Nathan Rothschild at work and at home. This came from the pen of Prince Hermann von Pückler-Muskau, an impecunious German magnate who, having come to England in search of a rich marriage and failed in his quest, turned instead to authorship and published a very popular account of his travels. He first met the banker in October 1826. A tour of the great financial centre of the world, he recorded, could not be considered complete without a visit to the City's "real lion ... it's ruler − in a word Rothschild". He was somewhat surprised to find Nathan living in an "insignificant" dwelling beside his counting house but less astonished to discover access to it blocked by a waggon filled with silver ingots.

The Prince's arrival coincided with that of the Russian Consul, "a distinguished and intelligent man, who knew perfectly how to play the rôle of the humble debtor, while retaining the proper air of dignity". It was a dignity neither visitor found easy to maintain when confronted by N.M.'s gruff brusqueries, delivered "in a language peculiarly his own, half English, half German, the English with an entirely German accent. Yet all declaimed with an imposing self-possession which seemed to find such trifles beneath his notice." Russians and Germans were always begging money off him, Rothschild grumbled. It was all very well for rich people who could travel about and amuse themselves, "while on him, poor man, there rested the cares of the world".

Pückler-Muskau tried to soften his host with a compliment about the valuable services he performed for the governments of Europe. N.M. modestly disclaimed such praise: "Oh no, you are only jesting; I am but a servant whom people are pleased with because he manages their affairs well, and to whom they let some crumbs fall as an acknowledgement."[13] However, the interview went well and ended with the Prince's being invited to dine with N.M. in his house at Stoke Newington.

This residence also surprised the visitor by its modesty. He had expected something "ducal" but discovered no more than a "pretty villa". The company similarly was not drawn from the higher echelons of fashionable society but from Nathan's business colleagues – other Jewish financiers and some directors of the East India Company. Their host was in good form and kept them amused by telling scurrilous tales about some of his titled clients.

> Mr R[othschild] was in a high good-humour, amusing, and talkative. It was diverting to hear him explain to us the pictures around his dining-room, (all portraits of the sovereigns of Europe, presented through their ministers,) and talk of the originals as his very good friends, and, in a certain sense, his equals. "Yes," said he, "the –––– once pressed me for a loan, and in the same week in which I received his autograph letter, his father wrote to me also with his own hand from Rome to beg me for Heaven's sake not to have any concern in it, for that I could not have to do with a more dishonest man than his son. 'C'était sans doute très Catholique;' probably, however, the letter was written by the old –––– who hated her own son to such a degree, that she used to say of him, – everybody knows how unjustly, – 'He has the heart of a t–– with the face of an a–––'" [14]

Nathan could afford to laugh at the world's great and powerful who were obliged to sue for financial services but he was at pains to point out to his guests that he honoured all crowned heads equally, whatever their politics, for he never liked to "quarrel with my bread and butter".

Pückler-Muskau seems to have become, if not a Rothschild intimate, at least an habitué of Rothschild circles and a frequent guest at New Court and Stoke Newington. Indeed, Nathan and his wife appear to have quite taken to their hearts this sojourner in a strange land. The Prince attended some of their impressive banquets, such as that held on 26 May 1827, when he was one of a distinguished company, eating from a fine dinner service of silver and vermillion, admiring the banker's treasures, and entertained by leading musicians of the day. Yet he was also admitted to intimate family gatherings, such as that on 26 March 1827, at which the great man let his hair down even more than usual.

> . . . [Rothschild] ordered the servant to bring his new Austrian consular uniform, which "his friend Metternich", as he said, had sent him from Vienna; showed it to us, and even suffered himself to be persuaded to try it on before the looking-glass, and to walk about in it. And, as virtuosi when they have once begun never know when to stop, he now sent for other magnificent Court dresses, and changed

his toilette several times, as if he had been on the stage . . .

It was . . . rather droll to see how this otherwise serious tradesman-like man tried to assume the various bendings and bowings, and the light and gracious air, of a courtier, and, not in the least disconcerted by our laughing, assured us, with as much confidence as joviality that N[athan] M[ayer] R[othschild], if he liked, could act any part; and, with the help of five or six glasses of wine extra, could make as good a figure at Court as the best of them.[15]

But on yet another occasion Pückler-Muskau found Nathan ready to engage in a long, private discussion about religion. On this subject he showed himself to be highly orthodox and conservative, being what the German called "of the ancient nobility in matters of faith".[16]

N.M. Rothschild obviously made a considerable impression on this German visitor who was, by no means, easily moved to admiration and could be caustic in his comments about respectable English society. Months after he had left London, Pückler-Muskau wrote his last observation about Nathan. He was reflecting in poetic vein on how great events can spring from insignificant beginnings. He considered Napoleon who, "born incognito in Ajaccio, made all the thrones of the earth quake; I then thought of the avalanche, which launches itself under the claw of a starling and five minutes later buries a village — and of Rothschild, whose father sold ribbons, and without whom no power in Europe today seems able to make war."[17] It was a fanciful exaggeration but the comparisons were far from inapt.

Nathan Rothschild's awesome wealth and power constantly drew forth comment from his contemporaries in their letters, diaries and published works. Heinrich Heine, travelling in Italy in 1828, claimed to have met a flowery tongued chiropodist who boasted of once having ministered to "the great Nathan Rothschild, to whom the Emperor of Brazil pawned his diamond crown". Heine related his acquaintance's account of the incident in words heavy with irony:

It took place in his cabinet. He sat there in his green arm-chair like a king, with his courtiers standing around, and he all the while was a-sending expresses to all the kings. And while I was cutting his corns I thought in my heart, "Now, you've got in your hands the foot of the man who holds all the world in his hands, and you too are a man that's somebody, for if you cut too deep he'll be angry, and cut the kings himself more cruelly." It was the happiest moment of my life.[18]

The Stoke Newington house where N.M. entertained Pückler-Muskau had been acquired by Nathan in 1816 to provide space and fresh air for his growing family. It was a rented property — Nathan rigidly eschewed the image of the country landowner — but here he did lavish on his four sons and three daughters some of the luxuries he denied himself. The children had a tiny carriage drawn by four white goats. Lionel, the eldest son, later graduated to horses and his father bought him the finest thoroughbreds — even, on one occasion, acquiring an Arab from the Sultan of Morocco. The boys were educated at a Jewish boarding school in Peckham, later toured the Continent with a private tutor and completed their studies at university (Lionel, Anthony and Nathaniel at Göttingen; Mayer at Cambridge).

It was, in fact, in their attitude to their children's upbringing that the Rothschilds revealed their real appreciation of emancipation. They might be ambivalent about luxuries and social graces, but they made sure that their sons and daughters had the best and were equipped to take their place among the noblest and richest and finest in Europe. The older among the next generation were Salomon's children, Anselm and Betty, who were just into their teens at the end of the war against Napoleon. Anselm studied at the Philanthropin, Frankfurt's best Jewish school which his grandfather had helped to found, and his sister was educated by private tutors. Sometimes Salomon took one or other of them on his foreign trips and encouraged them to absorb European culture. At home they learned both the practicalities of business and the ways of cultivated society. They were thus expertly and successfully groomed for their future roles in life — Anselm as an international financier and Betty as an accomplished hostess.

Amschel meanwhile was delighted with his new title. He saw the honour as a victory won for German Jewry and a useful tool for improving business prospects. The two most important things in his life were "our fortune and the honour of our community".[19] But prudence and religious scruples still caused him to eschew ostentation. He moved the bank to impressive premises on Berkheimerstrasse but his own life style remained unchanged.

Young James reacted very differently. Living in Europe's most fashionable capital, he was impatient to cut a dash. He found it irksome to deny himself luxuries he could well afford, just because his elder brothers counselled sobriety and a simple life style. By and large he ignored their admonitions. He had his clothes made by the best London tailors. He learned to dance and to ride. The latter was not an entirely successful experiment. It resulted in a bad fall and a broken ankle — an accident which brought him no sympathy at all from Nathan. Sometimes he was driven to making ingenuous excuses for behaviour which the family might consider frivolous: "Dear, good Nathan, don't be bad tempered ... I think of nothing except business; if I attend a society party, I go there to become acquainted with people who might be useful for the business ... "[20]

But what annoyed James more than the disapproval of his brothers was the snobbery and anti-Semitism of the Parisian *haut monde*. He longed for social acceptance and felt keenly his exclusion from the world of smart salons, clubs and glittering parties. "Laffitte gave a great ball. I was not invited. From envy, they don't want us to become bigger than we are",[21] he complained in March 1817. But James did not accept such snubs lying down. Only a few days before his exclusion from Laffitte's ball he had entertained the Duke of Wellington to dinner and thereby, as he claimed, "created a sensation".[22] He won the patronage of the King's favourite, Elie Decazes, Minister of Police and the most powerful man in France. And a coup of even greater long-term significance was that which won the Duc d'Orléans as a client of the bank, for the Duke, better known as Louis Phillippe, would become the next King of France.

In fact, despite the difficulties which he felt so keenly, the entry of the red-haired, stocky, squat-faced young man to the *haut monde* of the capital was assured and rapid. It was punctuated by two changes of residence. In 1817 he moved to the Rue de Provence, the financial heart of Paris. Then, at the end of 1818, he transferred his household to the Rue d'Artois (later renamed Rue Laffitte). Here he occupied an impressive *hôtel* which had once belonged to Hortense, daughter of the Empress Josephine (these premises remained the headquarters of the French Rothschild bank until its nationalisation, a century and a half later). This now became the home where he entertained politicians, courtiers, artists and musicians, and from which he rode out to visit the theatre, the opera and the fashionable salons. The young Rothschild's eagerness to ingratiate himself in Gentile society became something of a joke, since it was noticed that fellow Jews were seldom seen at his table. The story is still told in the family of an Austrian nobleman who arrived at one of James's soirées and greeted his host with the words, "What are you doing here?"[23]

His mother and brothers thought it was time that James got married and negotiations were set in hand for an alliance with the von Eskeles. They were one of the very few ennobled Austrian-Jewish families and as such fulfilled the demanding criteria the Rothschilds felt they must now insist upon when choosing a bride. Any woman to be brought into the family must share the same faith, be of the same rank and command a substantial fortune. In the end, nothing came of these proposals. Perhaps James was determined to hang on to his bachelor existence a little longer. He was the only brother still unmarried. Carl at the age of thirty, in 1818, took as his wife the beautiful, eighteen-year-old Adelheid Hertz, daughter of a Jewish Frankfurt merchant.

Between 1816 and 1818 the brothers took stock of their business relationship. Now that their activities were no longer dominated by the need for frantic haste and total secrecy, affairs could be placed on a regular footing which distributed profits equitably and allowed all the participants to be kept fully aware of what each was doing. In 1816 the Paris bank was refounded as Rothschild Frères. The three houses remained quite distinct business entities but the balanced accounts of each were regularly circulated to the others and profits were aggregated. It was this flexible interdependence which was to prove so powerful in all the commercial challenges of the nineteenth century.

Nathan's leadership was now formally recognised. His brothers realised that all their prosperity was due to his energy and vision. They agreed, therefore, to allow him a bigger share of profits. The division of capital in the family business over the next decade was as follows (in French francs):

	1818	1825	1828
Amschel	7,776,000	18,943,750	19,693,750
Salomon	7,776,000	18,943,750	19,693,750
Nathan	12,000,000	26,875,000	28,200,000
Carl	7,488,000	18,643,750	19,393,750
James	7,488,000	18,643,750	19,393,750[24]

The other brothers were very conscious that the one who had founded their fortunes was denied the recognition they now enjoyed. They were determined that the English Channel should represent no rift between them. They wanted to see those four heraldic arrows increased to five and Nathan enjoying some honour from the Austrian Emperor. It took months of hard negotiation to achieve this end. It also involved another major trial of commercial strength.

In September 1818 the leaders of Europe met in congress at Aix-la-Chapelle (Aachen) to discuss the rehabilitation of France, the removal of foreign troops from her soil and general matters pertaining to the preservation of peace among the nations. As in 1918 and 1945 international statesmen believed that issues of potential conflict could be settled in some kind of "talking shop" (in this case the Congress System) without recourse to the devastation of war. There were also important financial arrangements to be discussed and all the leading bankers clustered around the congress like importunate suitors, anxious to display their eligibility.

The most important piece of business on the agenda was the floating of a second instalment of a French loan designed to help the restored government pay off its war indemnity. The Rothschilds had not been involved in the first instalment but were hoping for a substantial share of the new one. Salomon and Carl hastened to Aix to argue their case. Carl's bride, Adelheid, went with them. Though married scarcely more than a few hours she had to learn that Rothschild women, like Rothschild men, were expected to subordinate everything to business. Adelheid's beauty and charm proved considerable assets at the balls and dinners which filled most evenings, but they were inadequate to counter the firmness with which the Rothschilds' rivals resisted sharing their business with "Jewish upstarts".

The main beneficiaries of the first French loan had been Ouvrards of Paris, Hopes, the ancient Anglo-Dutch banking house, and Barings of London. They had seen the value of their French stock rise dramatically in two years and they were determined that they and their associates would take up the lion's share of the new issue. Each of these houses had good commercial reasons for wanting to keep the Rothschilds out. In some cases personal animosity added salt to their business interests. Alexander Baring, particularly, resented the Herries-Rothschild alliance. His father, Sir Francis, had built Baring Brothers and Company up from almost nothing. By the time of his death in 1810 he was recognised as "unquestionably the first merchant in Europe; first in knowledge and talents, and first in character and opulence".[25] The bank had been the principal financial supporter of the English government throughout the greater part of the war, only to find its position usurped by the Rothschilds in 1814-15. Baring had attacked Herries in parliament and was N.M.'s bitter opponent in the City. He and his colleagues now successfully saw off the Rothschild bid — but not for long.

Salomon and Carl despatched couriers to Frankfurt, Paris and London. Within days the powerful Rothschild financial machine was in action. The first the businessmen gathered in Aix knew about it was that French loan stock, after a sharp rise, was falling on the exchanges. Suddenly, the new issue they had heavily invested in was losing its value. There seemed to be no rhyme or reason for this dramatic downturn in the market. The bankers met in urgent conclave, comparing notes and scraps of information brought in by their own couriers. Gradually, the truth emerged. The Rothschilds and their agents had bought up every parcel of loan stock that came on the market. As the price had risen more investors had hastened to sell and the Rothschilds had gone on buying. Then, at a prearranged time, they dumped all their shares, simultaneously. It was an unprecedented demonstration of commercial muscle and it had the desired effect: the other bankers were obliged to allow the Rothschilds an appropriate share of the business.

Nothing illustrates more dramatically the astonishingly powerful position the three Rothschild houses now occupied. Their main business was dealing in government stocks and arranging state loans and cash transfers. They consistently won contracts from their rivals in these important deals on the basis of their past record. They had acquired a name not only for efficiency and confidentiality but also for fairness. They habitually charged small fees and low interest rates. In 1818, for example, when the Prussian government urgently needed a loan, they found Berlin banks ready to do business but eager to cash in on the country's desperate need for funds by demanding high rates. When application was made to Nathan Rothschild, it must have been a distinct relief to learn from Humboldt that the English house would handle the business at reasonable rates. However, as the Ambassador pointed out, N.M. only transacted deals on his own terms:

> . . . Rothschild is now easily the most enterprising businessman in this country . . . He is moreover a man upon whom one can rely, and with whom the Government here does considerable business. He is also, as far as I know, just, exceedingly honest, and intelligent. On the other hand, I must add that if business is given to him to carry out, it will be necessary to fall in with his ideas, for he has acquired the independent habit of mind developed by riches and a fairly long sojourn in this country, and he is now engaged in such a constant number of financial transactions that it will not greatly affect him if one of them fails to come his way. He wants to take over the whole loan himself; on this point he is likely to be exceedingly firm, and he has asked in advance that the Prussian Consul here, against whom he is prejudiced, shall not be allowed to interfere in the matter in any way.[26]

There was no lack of people who wanted to share in the Rothschilds' good fortune and the brothers had to be constantly on their guard against spies. Rivals would go to any lengths to gain inside information. One story is uncorroborated but, as the present Lord Rothschild has commented, "it deserves a place in the apocrypha of family history".[27] It concerns a stockbroker named Lucas who was a neighbour of Nathan's at Stoke Newington and longed to be a party to the great man's secrets. Observing N.M. depart in haste for the City late one evening,

He jumped into his carriage and followed Rothschild who made a gallop for New Court, his town residence. A few moments later, Lucas, apparently drunk, staggered through the doorway and, in spite of the protests of the servants, entered Rothschild's study, where he fell to the ground like a heavy sack. Rothschild and his friends, not a little disturbed by this unexpected visit, sprang upon the apparently unconscious man, and lifted him on the couch, sprinkled him with cold water and perfume, and rubbed his limbs to bring the blood back to them. It was all in vain; and, as the conversation which had been interrupted by the appearance of Lucas was extremely important, and the quiet and regular breathing of the man seemed to show that he had fallen into a healthy sleep, they continued the discussion. It was a matter of great urgency, as important news had come from Spain and provided an opening for some good business, if they could buy up certain stock at once without attracting attention. They drew up a plan of campaign and went their various ways, intending to enter upon the business the following morning. They did not, of course, forget the sick man, and Rothschild told the servants to take him home as soon as he recovered.

There was no need to do this. As soon as Rothschild had gone Lucas left the house, in spite of the clamour of the servants, though he still seemed to be very weak, and his gait was uncertain and staggering. He had, of course, no idea of returning home; he hurried to his office, and made arrangements to snatch up the stock in question before Rothschild could get them. He completely succeeded, and made an enormous profit. It was the last time that Rothschild sprinkled Lucas's forehead with perfume.[28]

After the Congress of Aix-la-Chapelle no one could seriously doubt the Rothschilds' financial supremacy. Princes, ambassadors and ministers assiduously courted the brothers; none more persistently than those representing the Emperor Francis II. Thus it was that the importunate requests from Frankfurt for still further honours were always given careful consideration, and in March 1820 Amschel succeeded in winning some recognition of Nathan's services. Mr N.M. Rothschild was appointed Austrian Consul General in London. Membership of the diplomatic corps enhanced Nathan's social standing considerably. It carried certain valuable immunities and privileges, such as the use of the diplomatic bag for private and business correspondence (though he knew well that letters sent in this way would be opened by imperial agents). And it gave the family greater standing in European political circles. The government in Vienna also benefitted from the arrangement, since the Consul was obliged to convey to the London embassy any information likely to be of interest to the imperial government. As Salomon had suggested, a consulship was offered to James a year later.

These close ties with the imperial government, and especially the negotiating of an enormous new loan, involved Salomon (who specialised in Austrian business) in frequent visits to Vienna. He always stayed at the leading hotel, the Römischer Kaiser in Renngasse. It was the hostelry where visiting royalty and nobility lodged. It was the only hotel in the musical capital of Europe which boasted its own small concert hall, a chamber famed for its acoustics. Here fashionable Viennese society gathered regularly to hear performances by the celebrated Schuppanzigh Quartet and sometimes the "lion", Beethoven, graced the establishment. For example, on 11 April 1814 the deaf genius played the piano part in his Trio Op. 97 and the following year he conducted a performance of his oratorio *Christus am Ölberge* for the Viennese élite gathered in the Römischer Kaiser.

As Salomon's stays in this famous hotel became more and more protracted he rented the best suite on a permanent basis. Soon he was spending more time in the Austrian capital than in Frankfurt. He took more rooms at the Römischer Kaiser and installed his wife and his two teenage children. At last, the ardent wish of Salomon and Caroline had been granted: the years of hectic, often painful, travel were over. They were able to spend more time together in their own home. But not in their own house. The Jewish population of Austria had experienced none of the enlightened, liberating laws of the Napoleonic regime. They could not own property. They were excluded from politics, administration and most professions. They could not buy army commissions. They had to pay a per capita tax. Their movements and even their right to marriage were severely restricted. And foreign Jews were only given brief residence permits. This latter provision was waived in Salomon's case as were some of the other more humiliating legal requirements, but his request to buy business and residential premises was rejected. It must have seemed like a step back in time for Salomon and Caroline. Rights which had been at least partially ceded in Frankfurt had not begun to appear in Vienna.

Salomon decided to stage a restrained protest. He could, undoubtedly, have rented suitable accommodation in the city. He did not do so. Instead, he took over the Römischer Kaiser. All the chambers and all the public rooms were converted into business offices and living accommodation for his family. As a hotel, the building ceased to exist. VIPs who habitually stayed at the Römischer Kaiser had to go elsewhere. This little inconvenience was a constant reminder to the authorities of Salomon's presence and his opinion of the anti-Jewish laws.

It was at this ex-hotel that Salomon also ingratiated himself with the Austrian nobility by inviting its luminaries to dinners, banquets and balls which rapidly became the talk of the town. No scion of an ancient house could excel the sumptuousness of the Jewish banker's hospitality. Even when Salomon gave a children's fancy dress party it served as a display of Rothschild wealth – and an opportunity for political propaganda. A guest at one such function, a junior *bal masqué*, described how the boys and girls were richly decked out as kings and queens, and played an elaborate charade.

> ... one of the biggest was dressed precisely like old Nathan Rothschild. He acted his part very well, kept both his hands in his breeches pockets, shook his money, shook his head, as if vexed when any of the little kings wanted to borrow anything, and only showed favour to the little one with the white coat and red pantaloons (the "Emperor of Austria"). This fellow he patted on the cheeks and praised him, "You're my boy, my pet, my pride ... "[29]

Metternich was delighted that Salomon had settled in Vienna. The banker was a wise and shrewd adviser on matters of economic policy, he gave the Austrian government access to the incomparable Rothschild information service, and he was always on hand to negotiate funds for the imperial coffers and for Hapsburg client states. But, above all, Metternich found the gentle, deferential Jew a congenial companion.

Within the family the Imperial Chancellor was known as "Uncle" Metternich. The creation of a close bond between Salomon and the most powerful man in Europe was a major coup for the Rothschilds. Metternich was the arbiter of Europe throughout the first decade of peace and his influence was considerable for several years thereafter. He was pledged to stability, the settlement of disputes around the conference table, the balance of power between legitimate governments and the suppression of revolutionary elements. This maintenance of international order suited the Rothschilds well during a period when they were consolidating their position as state financiers and expanding into industrial markets (see pp.128f.). Metternich's patronage brought them not only immense prestige and new business opportunities, it gave them a means of influencing policy in ways favourable to commercial expansion. The Rothschilds rapidly developed a taste for covert political influence.

Metternich, for his part, was not reluctant to enhance the standing of his financial allies. When Salomon approached him with a request for promotion beyond the minor nobility there was no hesitation, no interdepartmental debate. On 29 September 1822 all five brothers and their male descendants were raised to the rank of baron. The new coat of arms they were granted incorporated the Austrian eagle and a lion representing Hesse-Kassel. It bore the motto *Concordia Integritas Industria* (Harmony, Honesty and Diligence). It also showed a hand grasping *five* arrows. But once again the fifth "arrow" declined to avail himself of the honour. Still sensitive to public opinion, Nathan did make tentative enquiries in government circles about whether there would be any objection to his using a foreign title but, before the replies came in, he had probably decided to go on being known as plain *Mr* Nathan Rothschild.

CHAPTER 7
"Lord and master of the money-market of the world"

In 1822 Prince Metternich banned the sale of *Allgemeine Zeitung* throughout all Austrian dominions. He made no bones about the nature of the newspaper's offence: it had dared to criticise the Rothschilds for being the financial prop of the reactionary imperial regime. As a letter from the Prince's secretary, Gentz, to the editor made clear, the reputation of Metternich's government and that of their Jewish bankers stood or fell together.

> The constant attacks upon the House of Rothschild invariably, and sometimes in the most outrageous manner, reflect upon the Austrian Government by necessary implication, since, as everybody knows, it is transacting important financial matters with that house, which is not only unimpeachable but honourable and thoroughly respectable. The persistent rumours respecting new loans are invented simply and solely in order to undermine the confidence which our public securities have won and which they deserve.[1]

The protection afforded by Metternich indicates just how valuable the Rothschilds were to Austria. And not only to Austria. Throughout the 1820s and 1830s the brothers conducted important government tran sactions for England, France, Prussia, Austria, Belgium, Spain, Naples, Portugal, Brazil, various German states and other smaller countries. They acted as bankers to many of the crowned heads of Europe and a taunt that was often made had some foundation: "In ancient times the Jews had one king; now the kings have one Jew." In their rôle as credit bankers, they enjoyed the custom of the wealthiest people in the world and they financed several mercantile and industrial ventures. They handled the financial arrangements of the American consular service and they were active, through agents, in markets as distant as the USA, India, Cuba and Australia.

But Europe was and would remain the principal sphere of Rothschild activity. In 1821 the fifth bank was set up. Carl became the last of the Frankfurt Five to leave his home town and establish himself in a foreign capital. His original mission to the Italian Kingdom of Naples was expected to be a short-term one but the complexities of the international situation, coupled with Carl's own desire to escape permanently from Amschel's suffocating influence, lengthened his stay indefinitely.

The crisis which caused the move was a popular rising in the Kingdom of the Two Sicilies. Italy, like Germany, was a jigsaw puzzle of small states. Unrest in one could rapidly spread to another and if that happened the Austrian Empire, itself a ragbag of nationalities and races, would be extremely vulnerable. Metternich therefore sent troops to the aid of Ferdinand I in his southern Italian kingdom. Armies have to be paid, and the Prince had no intention of saddling Austria with extra debt. So he called in Salomon and arranged a loan which would be repaid by the Neapolitan government. It was to organise the Italian end of this deal that Carl took up residence in Naples.

Within months the royal government had to apply to Carl for more funds. The financial burden of the army of "liberation" was simply more than the Neapolitans could bear. Thus, little by little, the Kingdom of Naples became totally dependent on the Rothschilds.

Nominally at least, Carl and Adelheid and their family of four sons and one daughter settled in southern Italy. But "settle" is, in this case, too strong a word. For Carl and his children never identified themselves with their country of residence in the way that James (although he never became a French citizen), Nathan and, to a lesser extent, Salomon did. The Neapolitan Rothschilds showed very little initiative in developing local commercial opportunities. They frequently returned to Frankfurt, and in their thinking and beliefs remained close to the orthodoxy and piety of the ghetto. When childless Amschel died it would be one of Carl's sons who took over the running of the parent house.

But that was still far in the future. The next major event to excite the family was the marriage of James. In 1824, at the age of thirty-two, the youngest brother at last succumbed to the pressure of his elders to select a wife and settle to the serious task of perpetuating the dynasty. His choice of bride was to have enormous consequences, not only for his own success and that of his descendants, but for the future of the entire Rothschild enterprise. James offered his hand and fortune to his nineteen-year-old niece, Betty.

Betty had grown into a young woman who, if no great beauty, was socially accomplished, intelligent, vivacious and charming. Under the careful tutelage of her parents, she had acquired that confident ease of manner which James did not possess. She spoke French with scarcely a trace of foreign accent, had acquired the skills — piano playing, needlework and drawing — considered important for young ladies, was much travelled and well read, and could converse upon a wide range of topics from philosophy and art to contemporary politics. She was thus an ideal consort for an up-and-coming leader of Paris's social and business world.

She was also a Rothschild and her marriage to her uncle created a precedent which was followed by most of her younger relatives until, by the third quarter of the century, the Rothschilds had become one of the most inbred families in Europe. Endogamy was not unusual in aristocratic and wealthy circles but no other family was to practise it to the same extent as the Rothschilds. In the generation of Mayer Amschel's grandchildren, where the tendency was most marked, there were fourteen marriages of which only four involved outsiders. The end result was a highly complex series of relationships. For example, when, in 1867, Carl's granddaughter, Emma Louisa, married Nathan's grandson, Natty, her Aunt Charlotte became her mother-in-law.

This web of intermarriage had obvious business advantages. It played a vital part in holding together the five banks and maintaining Mayer Amschel's vision of a united financial operation. The next generation of Rothschilds would be Austrians, Frenchmen, Englishmen, Italians and Germans, living in and, to a greater or lesser extent, identifying with nations which were often at odds, and sometimes at war with each other. It would have been easy for the banks to have drifted apart. It remains one of the more remarkable aspects of the Rothschild phenomenon that this did not happen. Each house developed its own quite distinct style, its own business operations and international contacts, but at the same time it kept up almost daily communication with its sister banks, with whom it did considerable business, and with whom, when the need arose, it could combine in a most formidable way. The intricate network of intermarriage throughout the nineteenth century constantly reinforced the family ties and helped achieve that *Concordia* of which the Rothschild motto boasted.

It also, of course, kept the maximum amount of money in the family. Fathers could afford to be generous in the matter of dowries when they knew that the cash was not falling into the hands of strangers. Salomon, for example, settled on Betty a million and a half francs. Marriage within the family also protected the Rothschild girls. There were many potential suitors for their hands, most of whom were unacceptable – fortune-hunters, Gentiles, men with poor business contacts. On the rare occasions when stubborn Rothschild daughters insisted on following their hearts rather than their heads, it was at the cost of much bitterness among their relatives.

As Lady Battersea, a member of the family,* later pointed out, the Rothschilds' unique position made frequent intermarriage almost inevitable:

*Constance, daughter of Anthony and Louisa.

At that time the Rothschild family had attained a very remarkable position in England, France, Germany, Austria, and Italy ... Their vast financial undertakings in the five European capitals brought them into close touch with the rulers and statesmen of those countries; no other Jewish financiers had before that time attained to such a position, or if they had, they had ceased to be Jews. But the Rothschilds were strict adherents to the Faith and deeply interested in the affairs of their Community. They were looked upon as the leaders of the Jews wherever they lived, and deserved such appreciation. From all these causes they were on a different social plane from their co-religionists, and gradually became habitués of a world still closed to many of their own Jewish friends and connections. But as orthodox Jews they were strongly opposed to mixed marriages; thus the frequent intermarriages amongst relations became the only way out of a difficulty which was the result of circumstances. [2]

That suggests a degree of calculation in matrimonial transactions which in the Rothschilds' case is an exaggeration. Nineteenth-century marriages were arranged, especially in the circles in which the family now moved. What well-to-do parents looked for in a prospective daughter-in-law was a girl capable of running a genteel household and producing healthy heirs, and one who also brought with her a good dowry and social connections. If deep affection could be found and sustained within the nuptial bond, well and good. If not, it might be sought — discreetly — elsewhere. Such were the conventions and everyone accepted them. But the Rothschilds did not ignore romantic love. Indeed, it might be said that their daughters fared better than many of their contemporaries who, for dynastic reasons, were disposed of to husbands whom they scarcely knew or, in some cases, had never even met before the wedding. The Rothschilds were both more subtle and more considerate of their daughters' dignity. They did not arrange the inter-family marriages, they simply brought their offspring together, especially when they were at their most susceptible age, in the hope that mutual passions would develop. The practice worked surprisingly often.

And for at least one obvious reason. As Baron Elie, a senior member of the French family, succinctly put it: "For a Rothschild girl, a Rothschild boy was often the best possible catch." Throughout childhood and adolescence these young ladies had grown up in close contact with their male cousins. They found them cultured and cosmopolitan, well travelled and fluent in at least three European languages. They knew them to be amusing and intelligent companions. Since they accepted the absolute necessity of marrying rich, Jewish husbands, there can have been very few young men who could compete with their own relatives.

So, the family remained physically united in a way that old Mayer Amschel may not have envisaged but which would certainly have delighted him. Neither he, nor his sons, nor even his grandsons, knew anything about the consequences of inbreeding and could not have realised that the concentration of genes, generation after generation, would produce some quite remarkable results.

James and his young bride were married in 1824 and Betty immediately assumed the demanding rôle of managing her uncle-husband's magnificent household. Her success was never in doubt. One appreciative English guest, Lady Granville, wife of the English Ambassador in Paris, wrote to her sister: "On Saturday we dined at a sumptuous feast at Rothschild's. He has married his niece, a pretty little Jewess, née coiffée [born with a silver spoon in her mouth], a very good thing at Paris, for just out of her nursery she does the honours of her house as if she never had done anything else."[3] Betty's easy grace impressed all who were fortunate enough to be invited to her husband's table. According to another visitor, she possessed "that noble indifference which gives the most sumptuous luxury an air of everyday habit".[4]

With his new wife at his side James finally achieved the social success he had so long craved. But even Betty could not have made up, by herself, for her husband's all-too-apparent limitations. An English journalist had him principally in mind when he wrote: "The manners of the Rothschilds are blunt and by no means polished, nor have they much that is persuasive in speech."[5]

James had no social refinement, nor were his tastes in art and literature well developed. He was, in most respects, a typical *nouveau riche* bourgeois, seeking to hide a lack of refinement behind a façade of vulgar, ostentatious display. What saved him, and what also contributed largely towards his professional success, was his unerring judgement of other men's talents. He was not a natural connoisseur of paintings, furniture, silver, porcelain or *objets d'art*, but he was a superlative connoisseur of men, and he surrounded himself only with the best.

The lavishness of his ménage might have given courtiers and aristocrats something to scoff at had it not been for the people he selected to oversee it. His carriage, trimmed and monogrammed in gold, might have appeared too lavish had bystanders not been impressed with the way the Baron's stable had polished it and groomed the four immaculate greys which pulled it. The gilded furniture and décor of his town house and the residence at Boulogne-sur-Seine which he bought soon after his marriage were selected and arranged by a leading architect of the day. His kitchen was supervised by one of the great master chefs of all time, Carême, who had served the English Prince Regent and the Russian Tsar before joining the Baron's employ. No French or foreign gourmet, whatever his opinion of upstart Jews, could resist an invitation to the best table in Europe. The extent of the Baron's hospitality was prodigious. He regularly entertained more than thirty people to lunch and sixty to dinner and his guests included diplomats, statesmen, royalty and the cream of the artistic world.

Paris in the heyday of the Romantic movement was rich in talent. Victor Hugo, Alfred de Musset, Honoré de Balzac, George Sand, Alexandre Dumas, Heinrich Heine, Franz Liszt, Gioacchino Rossini, Eugène Delacroix, Jean Ingres — seldom has there been such a concentration of creative genius in one place at one time. Artists need patrons, and patrons, for reasons of prestige, need artists. So it was that many great writers, painters and musicians of the age became the intimates of the Rothschilds.

Legend tells how a young composer came to Paris in 1831 intent on establishing his reputation. After several months of frustration, his savings all but spent, he was on the point of emigrating to America. One evening, an aristocrat friend, Prince Valentin Radziwill, took him to the Rothschilds' house, where he had been invited to dinner. The young foreigner played the piano for his hostess who was so enraptured that she immediately engaged him to give her lessons. Thus did Frédéric Chopin gain entry to Parisian society — and he never looked back.

Alas, as is so often the case with entertaining stories, the provenance of this romantic tale is questionable. What is certain, however, is that Chopin did gain the patronage of Baron James during his early years in Paris and became a frequent visitor to the Rothschild household. He taught Betty and, later, her eldest daughter, Charlotte, and was very fond of both ladies. Towards the end of his life the composer confided to a friend that he "loved the house of Rothschild and the house of Rothschild loved him".[6]

The undoubted ruler of the Paris music scene between 1824 and 1836 was Rossini. He was musical director of the Théâtre Italien and composer to the King. He, too, was a frequent Rothschild guest, as well as a client of the bank. Relations between patron and artist are inevitably double-edged and it is difficult to know just how close the bonds were between James and the men who relied upon him for financial support or influence. Heinrich Heine probably came as close as any man of letters to being a confidant of the Baron. The two men were united by nationality and race (though Heine had converted to Christianity — purely for reasons of preferment, as he openly admitted) and James enjoyed talking with the poet. Heine noted in his memoirs:

Once, when I told Herr — that I had lunched *en famille* with Baron James in the chambers of his bank, he clapped his hands together in astonishment and told me that I had enjoyed an honour which had hitherto been granted only to those of Rothschild's blood or to certain reigning princes, an honour for which he would sell half his nose. I will say that the nose of Herr —, even if it were shortened by half would still be of a prodigious length.[7]

But neither such moments of intimacy nor the generous subsidies he received from his patron inhibited Heine from satirising his benefactor:

. . . one must have some respect for this man, if only for the respect which he inspires in most people. I like best to visit him at the offices of his bank, where I can observe as a philosopher how the people, and not only God's people, but also all others bow and scrape before him. They do such a twisting and turning of their spines as would make the best of acrobats be hard put to it. I saw people who shivered when they approached the great Baron as though they had touched a Voltaic pile. At the very door of his office many of them were seized by an awful shuddering, such as Moses felt when he stood on the holy ground of Horeb. And just as Moses then took off his shoes, so many a broker or *agent de change* would take off his boots before daring to enter the private office of Herr von Rothschild, if he were not afraid that his feet would smell and so incommode the Herr Baron. That private office is, indeed, a remarkable place which excites noble thoughts and sentiments, like the sight of the ocean or the starry heavens: we see in that office how small is man, and how great is God! For money is the God of our time, and Rothschild is his prophet . . . Once, when I wanted to see Herr Rothschild, a liveried servant carried his chamber pot across the corridor, and a speculator who happened to pass at the same moment took off his hat reverently to the mighty pot. So far, I say it with all respect, goes the respect of certain people. I made a note of the name of that devout man, and I am convinced that in time he will be a millionaire.[8]

The poet was particularly quick to react if he thought that James was treating him as a paid entertainer for the amusement of his friends. When he received an invitation to join the Rothschilds and their guests for coffee one evening, he sent a note by way of reply saying that he was accustomed to taking his coffee where he had taken his dinner. Rossini, too, could be sharp if he felt his patron was being less than generous. Once he received a gift of grapes from the Baron's hothouse. His thank-you letter ran thus: "Excellent though your grapes were, I am not accustomed to taking my wine in tablet form."

The days had now passed when the Rothschilds had to regulate their expenditure carefully for fear of creating an unfavourable impression. They had learned that, however they lived, political enemies and Jew-baiters would pillory them as blood-sucking usurers. There was, therefore, no reason for them not to enjoy their wealth. In 1825 Nathan decided that New Court was too small to serve as both home and business premises. He bought the sumptuous 107 Piccadilly in the heart of fashionable London.* This magnificent residence overlooked Green Park and was only a short step from the Duke of Wellington's Apsley House. Ten years later he exchanged his Stoke Newington residence for a fully fledged country estate — but one within easy reach of the City. Gunnersbury Park, close to the villages of Acton and Ealing, was one of the finest houses on the periphery of London. In the eighteenth century it had been the home of Princess Amelia, one of George II's daughters. During the Napoleonic Wars the estate was acquired by Alexander Copland, a builder who had made a fortune constructing army barracks. He erected a fine, new house and it was this that Nathan bought in 1835. But it was not good enough for the banker. As soon as he obtained title, he had architects, builders, landscape artists and painters at work enlarging and improving the property. Only the best was now good enough for London's richest citizen — the man who, in 1825, had rescued the Bank of England and the British government from disaster.

This episode put the seal on N.M.'s relationship with his adopted country and conclusively demonstrated the extent of the Rothschilds' financial power. In the ten years since Waterloo commercial activity at home and abroad had grown fast and, as a result, there had been a vast increase in credit transactions. This had led to the floating of hundreds of small banks, many of whom became overextended partly as a result of rash speculation (particularly in South America). The situation was so brittle that a sudden decline of public confidence could easily have triggered a run on gold. That would have threatened the country with economic crisis. That is exactly what happened in November 1825. Within a matter of days nearly seventy banks collapsed, leading immediately to pressure upon the Bank of England itself. The bank's supply of sovereigns quickly

*It remained in the family until well into the present century, by which time so many other nearby properties had been acquired by Rothschilds that Piccadilly was popularly known as "Rothschild Row".

shrank to a mere hundred thousand pounds and it became clear that it would soon be unable to meet its commitments. The governors applied to the government for permission to suspend payment till they had time to build up the bank's reserves. Lord Liverpool refused. To associate his administration with the crisis would lead to demands for his resignation and would only exacerbate the situation. Angry meetings took place in the City and at Westminster while *The Times* inveighed against a government which had encouraged speculation in "hollow, fraudulent and destructive enterprises" and diverted capital from its "proper" function, the fuelling of industry and agriculture.[9] Banks continued to fail. In all, about 145 went to the wall in 1825 and 1826. But the Bank of England did not close its doors. It maintained a public façade of rocklike dependability. It honoured all its obligations. The crisis was kept within bounds and general panic was averted.

The engineer of this financial "miracle" was Nathan Rothschild. Around the middle of November he was taken into the government's confidence, probably by Herries. His immediate gruff response was that if they had come to him earlier he could have prevented the crisis in the first place. He immediately set about supplying the Bank of England with sovereigns from New Court and Rue Laffitte. But this did not produce enough coin to supply the shortfall between the production of the Mint and the customers' demands. Over the next year N.M. had to organise shipments from Austria, Turkey, Russia and other countries. The total extent of his rescue operation amounted to around ten million pounds. It was a mammoth task. Only Rothschilds could have done it.[10]

Nathan's nephew, Solomon Worms, told a story of another incident which occurred at the height of this crisis, as a result of which a severe fall of government securities was averted. Here it is, as set down later by his son: One morning N.M. said, brusquely,

> "Solomon, come a mal (an expression of his, really *einmal*, 'with me') to the Duke of Wellington. I will set this panic all right." [Though only a junior member of the cabinet, Wellington carried more weight than the Prime Minister, Lord Liverpool.]
> Off they drove in a hackney coach to Apsley House. The servant said the duke did not receive so early — it was about ten o'clock in the morning — except by appointment. To this Rothschild answered, "Tell him Mr Rothschild wants to see him on important business." In a minute or two Mr Rothschild and his nephew were ushered into [Wellington's] presence. The duke was in a flannel dressing gown, and said, "Well, Mr Rothschild, what is the news . . ."
> "Well, fine doings in the City," said Rothschild.

"What is to be done?" answered the duke.

"Send in Cole."

"Cole? Mr Rothschild, I do not understand you."

"I mean, send in Cole, the government broker, with an order to buy Exchequer bills without limit, and you see it will stop the panic."

"Very well, Mr Rothschild, you go home and I will do it."

In the course of the afternoon, Cole went into the Stock Exchange, bought Exchequer bills, and the panic subsided.

On another occasion Nathan stopped a run on Masterman's Bank by the simple expedient of going down to the bank's premises in St Nicholas Lane, fighting his way through the crowd of anxious customers, tossing a large bundle of notes on to the counter and shouting, so that all could hear, "Put that to the credit of my account."[11]

By 1830 a new generation of Rothschild bankers had begun to appear. There was no question of any of them following any other career. All of them were specifically trained to follow their fathers and uncles. The eldest and most accomplished was Salomon's son, Anselm, who was totally dedicated to the business. It was just as well that this was so because, for several years, he had to assist in both Frankfurt and Vienna, where Amschel and Salomon, respectively, were operating single-handed. Anselm shared some of his father's characteristics. He was genial and good natured, and often acted as the family's trouble shooter. But he was altogether tougher than Salomon, a hard-edged businessman, not hampered by an over-trusting nature.

In 1826 Anselm married Charlotte, the eldest daughter of his uncle Nathan, a sweetly pretty young woman with ringlets of dark hair framing a placid face. She had a genuine feeling for music and art and at her Frankfurt house presided over the only salon in the city worthy of the name. At her splendid table Mendelssohn, Liszt, Rossini and other visiting artists frequently sat alongside her husband's business associates and distinguished clients. Anselm acquired a fine collection of great masters but only with the aid of expert dealers and advisers. It was Charlotte who really appreciated the pictures and taught her children, as one of them recalled, to distinguish "a Teniers from an Ostade or a Wouvermans [sic] from a Both". Charlotte bore and raised three sons and four daughters who survived infancy, all of whom loved her dearly. Years later, one of her sons still cherished glowing memories of his childhood.

All my love went to my mother, who indeed sacrificed the whole of her short life to the care and tuition of her young family. I could hardly bear to be out of her sight; my happiest moments were when I was recovering from an illness and she nursed me and stayed at my bedside, telling me stories of which I never tired. My mother was my guardian angel, the one being around whom my existence revolved . . .

. . . we resided in Frankfurt, spending the winters in the town and the summer at a villa close by. As soon as the swallows made their appearance my father's curiosities were packed and stored away in a strong-room, where they remained until the cold drove us back again from the country. It was my privilege on these occasions to place some of the smaller articles in their old leather cases, and then again in the winter to assist in unpacking them and rearranging them in their places. Merely to touch them sent a thrill of delight through my small frame. [12]

It is not surprising that three of Charlotte's children became art collectors of international repute, while a fourth grew into an extremely accomplished musical composer and performer. Artistic sensibility was a characteristic not only of Mayer Amschel's Frankfurt grandchildren but of most of their generation. They had a greater sympathy with and understanding of creative talent than their fathers had possessed. For example, Chopin and Rossini were closer to James's daughter, Charlotte, than they ever were to James, and Rossini struck up a deep and lasting friendship with N.M.'s son, Lionel. They were brought up in homes where superb works of art and craftsmanship were familiar, everyday objects. The collections might be accumulated and enlarged by their acquisitive fathers; but it was from their mothers that they discovered the significance and worth of these artefacts, and learned the appreciation of beauty.

While Charlotte settled to the life of an elegant hostess in Germany, her brothers were, one by one, completing their education and, as a matter of course, going into the family business. Lionel, a reserved young man with a sardonic sense of humour went straight from university to New Court. Having learned the basics of business, he was sent to Paris for four years to help his Uncle James. Nathaniel, always known as "Nat", spent his apprenticeship with Carl in Naples. When Lionel returned to England, Nat took his place at De Rothschild Frères. James, two of whose sons were children and the other two as yet unborn, relied heavily upon his nephews. Anselm from Vienna and the four English boys did long terms of service at Rue Laffitte.

Nat, in fact, never escaped. He would love to have done so. This slim, elegant, fashion-conscious young man liked Paris, but over the years his disdain for the French steadily deepened. He was an Englishman through and through, avidly reading *The Times* every day, feeding on gossip from his visiting countrymen and crossing the Channel on the slightest pretext. For a while he hoped that his stay in France would not be permanent and that, when James's sons were grown up, he would be able to return home. But his Uncle James relied upon him more and more and, being a Rothschild, Nat did his duty by the family. It was only after seven years that he accepted the inevitable, and asked for his most treasured possessions to be removed from New Court and shipped across to Paris.

Travel played a large part in the education of all Nathan's sons. As we have seen, the third boy, Anthony, studied at Göttingen and Strasbourg, and made an extensive tour of the Continent with his tutor, before being deposited in Frankfurt to learn the rudiments of financial affairs. Anthony's journeyings did not end in Frankfurt. After a year, this jovial, roly-poly figure, known affectionately in the family as "Billy", came home to do a stint at New Court and was then sent to Vienna.

Serving an apprenticeship in each of the five banks was part of the standard training for the rising generation of young Rothschilds. For the most part it was a training they welcomed. It brought the excitements of travel and freedom from parental restraint. They could see new places, meet new people, learn new business practices, become proficient in the languages in which their tutors had imperfectly instructed them. They could become men of the world, and taste its varied pleasures. Paris, Naples, Vienna, London — they all had delightful prospects to offer. But not Frankfurt.

Frankfurt meant rigid, pious Uncle Amschel, and his unhappy, childless wife. Frankfurt meant kosher food and strict observance of the Sabbath. Frankfurt meant cultural starvation and dull company. Frankfurt even meant antiquated business practices.

> A bill falling due was presented at the office of the acceptor and paid entirely in silver coins — thalers, florins, etc. — and these were put in sacks and the sacks into a wheelbarrow and taken through the streets to the office of the payee by two or more of his employés and there to be recounted . . . the most primitive arrangement possible. Cheques and banking accounts as in London being totally unknown.[13]

But there was more to it than that. Frankfurt was not just a dreary backwater. In the minds of the younger Rothschilds it had a dual significance. It was the parent house, to which they all felt allegiance. And it was the ghetto, from which they had all escaped. One or other of those two facts would always be uppermost. Rothschilds would either feel drawn to Frankfurt and all that it represented, or repelled by it. This place of origin was for the Rothschilds a "holy land". Some would return there, like Carl's sons, back from sunny Naples. Others would be the Rothschilds of the Diaspora. And as the decades passed, the differences between these two breeds of Rothschilds would grow more marked.

By giving their sons a broad education Nathan and his brothers were making sure that the future of the banks would be in the hands of a group of polished and cosmopolitan young men who in terms of scholarly and social accomplishments would be the equals of any aristocrat or royal prince in Europe. Nor was it only the efficient running of the business which concerned them. Acquiring good taste and perfect manners was one way of demonstrating to the Gentile world that Jews were not merely money-grabbing tradesmen. For the Rothschilds the battle against anti-Semitism was to be refought in each generation, and it took up much of their time and energy.

CHAPTER 8
"To make ourselves absolute masters"

The Rothschilds had rapidly propelled themselves into a position of immense financial power and political influence. They were an independent force in the life of Europe, accountable to no one and, to a large extent, reliant on no one. Popular lampoons depicted them as the real rulers of Christendom, before whom monarchs and popes were obliged to prostrate themselves in supplication. The five brothers and their sons were fully aware of the responsibilities imposed by their unique position. The first was always to the family and to business — they strove for even more success and more money. The second was, undoubtedly, to their race.

In the wake of the Napoleonic Wars, it was obvious to the Rothschilds that, as soon as the constitution imposed by the French was overthrown, the authorities in the German states would try to restore the old, oppressive race laws. To forestall this, in 1815 they helped to organise a Jewish delegation to the Congress of Vienna and succeeded in gaining a declaration that all represented states should grant equal citizenship rights to Jews. But, without a superpower to enforce them, any guarantees depended entirely on the good will of individual governments. Most newly restored monarchs were disposed to pursue policies which would enhance their popularity. Promulgating pro-Jewish legislation did not .come in that category. As we have seen, the German states suffered a particularly virulent epidemic of anti-Semitism. The people had just experienced the humiliation of military defeat and enemy occupation. This was followed by economic dislocation and widespread poverty, which led to the anti-Jewish riots of 1819, already described.

When news of them reached Paris, James reacted angrily and energetically. He sent a flurry of letters to relatives and business associates urging rapid and firm action. To David Parish, a Rothschild agent, who was at Carlsbad in Bohemia where the ministers of the new German Confederation (formed after the war) were meeting, he stressed that, if nothing else moved the authorities, self-interest should stir them to ensure that such outbreaks never occurred again.

What can be the result of such disturbances? Surely they can only have the effect of causing all the rich people of our nation to leave Germany and transfer their property to France and England; I myself have advised my brother at Frankfurt to shut up his house and to come here. If we make a start, I am convinced that all well-to-do people will follow our example, and I question whether the Sovereigns of Germany will be pleased with a development which will make it necessary for them to apply to France or England when they are in need of funds.

Who buys State bonds in Germany, and who has endeavoured to raise the rate of exchange, if it be not our nation? Has not our example engendered a certain confidence in State loans, so that Christian firms have also taken heart and invested part of their money in all kinds of securities? . . .

. . . if the peace of the rich in Germany be disturbed, they will find themselves forced to emigrate for their safety, and they will certainly not take any interest in the funds of a country where their very life has been endangered. The object of the agitators at Frankfurt seems to have been, as a preliminary, to collect all the Israelites into a single street; if they had succeeded in doing this, might it not have led to a general massacre, and in that case would the public have had many scruples about plundering their houses? I need not point out to you how undesirable such an occurrence would be, especially at a time when our house might be holding large sums for the account of the Austrian or Prussian Court. It seems to me to be really necessary that Austria and Prussia should devise measures to be applied by the Senate at Frankfurt for energetically dealing with occurrences such as those of the 10th of this month, and thus making each man secure in his possessions.

I am sure you will be so good as to speak to His Highness Prince Metternich about this matter, and your friendship for me makes me feel confident that you will appeal to him strongly on behalf of our nation.[1]

There was a great deal of sense in what James said. Frankfurt especially was experiencing a period of dramatic economic decline and could ill afford to lose its wealthier residents. The *Rat*, determined to maintain their city's proud tradition of independence, had refused to join a Prussian-led customs union or Zollverein. The effect on trade was catastrophic: Frankfurt merchants had to pay heavy duties on goods coming from or through member states while their own exports were priced out of neighbouring markets. All the symptoms of depression rapidly appeared:

93

smuggling, a black market, bankruptcies and unemployment. Many tradesmen left the city, most of them settling in neighbouring Offenbach, which was a member of the Customs Union.[2] The last thing the *Rat* wanted was to encourage the emigration of Jewish merchants and bankers by failing to offer them adequate protection. They made a great show of force and determination to seek out the ringleaders of the riot and bring them to account hoping thereby to satisfy the leaders of the Jewish community and those representatives at Koblenz who were calling for firm action.

The Rothschilds did not leave Frankfurt, although it was strongly rumoured that they contemplated doing so. There was even a move by some imperial officials to persuade them to transfer their headquarters to Vienna. But nothing would have induced Amschel to leave his home town. He was never happy away from the warmth and security of the Frankfurt Jewish community. He hated travel, partly because it made difficult the close observance of the ritual and dietary laws which were so important to him. This devout Jew, who always put the Hebrew date on family letters, and dressed in the traditional style of his ghetto ancestors, was unlike his brothers in that he set narrower limits to his ambition. He was all for commercial enterprise and innovation but he was not prepared to pluck up his cultural roots and risk transplanting them to an alien soil.

Even from a business point of view there was little reason to leave Frankfurt. Large-scale financial transactions were not affected by customs duties on merchandise. So Amschel sat out the crisis. But the tension remained and there were other incidents. For example, after the family's ennoblement in 1822 Amschel arrived at his business premises to find the word "Baron" daubed over the walls with various comments in gutter wit. The most telling reason for remaining in Frankfurt was, in fact, that it was the best base from which to fight for Jewish rights. That was where the Federal Diet met and the best way of ensuring the protection of the law in Frankfurt and other states was to make sure that legislation was promulgated at the higher level and not left to individual member governments. The Rothschilds ardently continued the campaign, bringing constant pressure to bear on leading statesmen such as Prince Hardenberg, the Prussian Chancellor:

> After all that Your Highness has done for our community in recent years we cannot but hope that Your Highness will not withdraw your powerful support at this decisive moment. That, and that alone, can secure a tolerable existence to the Frankfurt Jews. Since everything depends upon the Commission nominated by the Federal Diet, proceeding according to just and reasonable principles in dealing

with this matter, and as any influence exerted by Your Highness in that direction cannot but have the most satisfactory result, we beg to submit our most humble and relevant request that you will most graciously convey to the Royal Prussian Ambassador at Frankfurt, as speedily as possible, those general instructions which are ... the only means of salvation left to us.[3]

Such ardent appeals for reform were just as vigorously countered by the Jews' opponents. Goethe, the greatest writer of the century, raged in his old age against the conspiracies of "omnipotent Rothschild" and prophesied that any relaxing of the laws against Jews would have catastrophic results: "The most serious and most disastrous consequences are to be expected ... all ethical feelings within families, feelings which rest entirely on religious principles, will be endangered by these scandalous laws."[4]

Nor was it only Gentiles who hated and resented the Rothschilds. Many critics were to be found among their own people. A savage cartoon appeared in London in 1824 entitled *A King Bestows Favours on a Great Man's Friends*. It depicted N.M. in the basket of a balloon labelled "Money Bags" supported by a bull and bear, preceded by his coachman who was checking off a list of minor donations to poor Jews. These unfortunates, lined up in the street, were expressing such sentiments as, "O Lord, have mercy upon us for we are overwhelmed with contempt; overwhelmed is our souls with the scorn of those who are at ease and with the contempt of the proud." The great majority of Europe's Jews were poor. Many of them looked for relief to the more affluent members of their own nation. This caricature suggests that, in London at least (and beggars queued outside New Court every day to await N.M.'s arrival), they did not meet with a generous response. It may well have been commissioned by a co-religionist intent on shaming him. Similar attacks were made on Nathan's brothers.

It is difficult to know how far such comments were justified because little information has survived about the Rothschilds' charitable giving. Amschel certainly had a reputation for generosity. He gave twenty thousand gulden a year to the poor, and not only the Jewish poor. Carl was associated with his eldest brother in much of this work. It may be that the others, whose primary concern was to become assimilated into the society of their adopted lands, gave Jewish charities a lower priority. James did not associate himself closely with the small Israelite community of Paris and it seems to have been some years before he was subscribing regularly to Jewish charities.[5] Nathan, as Warden of the Great Synagogue, was the proposer of a scheme for alleviating suffering among poor London Jews but his offer of an inaugural loan of five hundred pounds to set the fund going was scarcely generous.[6] He was, however, associated with other philanthropic activities which were not restricted to his own people. For example, for some years he was a governor of the City of London Lying-in Hospital. And he made donations to such diverse institutions as Bath Penitentiary and Lock Hospital. He was also deeply concerned about the suffering of famine-haunted Ireland and in 1826 wrote to the Prime Minister, Lord Liverpool, urging the government to purchase American and East Indian rice at prevailing low prices for the relief of the Irish peasants.

But N.M. made no show of his compassion. Those who saw only the outward man, like those who were conscious only of James's ostentation, or Amshel's piety would, and did, make constant accusations of avarice, parsimony and corruption.

When mud is thrown, it not only hits its mark but may besplatter other people. Those closely associated with Nathan certainly sometimes paid dearly for the privilege. In September 1827 J.C. Herries, at the express wish of George IV, was appointed Chancellor of the Exchequer, a post to which he was eminently well suited. Unfortunately, the administration, led by Viscount Goderich, was weak and beset by personality clashes. In the following January it fell, to be replaced by a coalition led by Wellington. Herries might have expected firm support from the man whose military reputation he had done so much to advance, and he was very distressed when, in the ensuing cabinet reshuffle, he was dismissed from office, receiving as a sop the post of Master of the Mint.

There is no doubt that his enemies made full use of the Rothschild connection in bringing Herries down. His great rival, William Huskisson (President of the Board of Trade), had made several bitter attacks on Nathan, whom he saw as primarily responsible for the growth of financial speculation and the outflow of capital. During the weeks of lobbying and jostling in the anterooms of Westminster, several malicious rumours had been spread about Herries and a campaign was mounted against him in the press. These tactics had their desired effect. It was claimed that he had enriched himself by selling confidential information to the Rothschilds, and also that he and N.M. were in league to provide the King with unlimited funds for his grandiose building projects.

In a debate in the House of Commons on 18 February Herries defended himself against these calumnies, but a greater impact was made by the speech of the radical MP for Hertford, Thomas Duncombe, who, in the course of a swingeing attack, referred to "an invisible, incorporeal person who boasted to be the arbiter of peace and war, who possessed an unbounded credit in financial affairs and upon whom frequently depended

96

the fate of nations, and he trusted that the Duke of Wellington and the Secretary for the Home Dept. would not allow the finances of this great country to be controlled any longer by a Jew".[7]

The incident was lampooned in a Cruikshank cartoon entitled *Secret Influence Behind the Curtain* or *The Jew and the Doctor*, which depicted N.M. as a tubby cherub descending from heaven brandishing bags of gold and Herries as a jumped-up clerk whose ambition had been thwarted. The caricature shows both men as having received consolation prizes to compensate for the loss of influence: Nathan has arranged a loan for Dom Miguel of Portugal, with Wellington's assistance; and Herries is enjoying copious helpings of "mint sauce" — a reference to his appointment to the lucrative post of Master of the Mint (see illustration). By now, Nathan had learned to ignore such public taunts. His passing reference to his old friend's downfall in a letter to Carl is casual to the point of insensitivity: "Our friend Herries is annoyed because he has been given a poor job — he is annoyed, but I cannot help him. He must be patient and perhaps he will get another job . . . "[8]

Popular dislike of Herries was influenced by a growing disenchantment with Wellington and this, in turn, reflected opposition to the reactionary governments controlling Europe. The Tories were ousted from office in 1830 and the most popular member of the new Whig administration was Foreign Secretary, Lord Palmerston, known as "Lord Pummicestone" for his abrasive and outspoken attitude towards the "old woman" of Austria and other absolutist regimes. Nathan had no party affiliation but he and his sons were naturally drawn towards the Whigs and, later, the Liberals, the party of nonconformity and new money. They had no reason to support the old landed aristocracy and the politics of privilege, and every reason to favour a moderate reform which would place more power in the hands of the commercial and professional middle class. Like other minority groups such as Roman Catholics and Nonconformists, British Jews had recently been campaigning for emancipation from certain political and social disabilities. The Rothschilds had played a prominent part in this agitation and were indignant when Wellington abruptly and decisively dashed their hopes in 1830 by declining support for reforming legislation.

1830 was a year of revolutions throughout Europe. Safe in England, Nathan's eldest boy, Lionel, welcomed the upsurge of democratic sentiment. Like many of his generation, he believed he was witnessing the dawn of a new age. For others like Baron James, whose family and business were put at risk by the disorders, the issues were not quite so clear cut. He had for some time been worried about the ultra-conservative stance of the French King, Charles X, but had continued to serve the regime and was on confidential terms with Prime Minister Polignac.

When, in July 1830, the King suspended the constitution and attempted to restore pre-revolutionary autocracy, James was taken completely by surprise. He (and Salomon who had come to Paris to report on the situation to Metternich) watched, horrified, as the barricades went up in the streets of the capital and fighting broke out between the people and royalist troops. For a few anxious days, he and other prominent citizens feared a return of 1789, but this time the crisis passed rapidly with the abdication of Charles X. The man now crowned and popularly called the "Citizen King" was none other than James's old friend and client, Louis Philippe. The Baron wasted no time in seeking the favour of the liberal regime: he made a very public donation of fifteen thousand francs "for the pitifully wounded and the widows and children of those who had fallen in the last days of July".[9]

The change of government greatly enhanced the Rothschilds' standing in Paris. The proclamation of Louis Philippe as "King of the French by the grace of God and the will of the people" marked the triumph of the bourgeoisie — and James de Rothschild was the archetypal bourgeois. The new ruler, faced with concerted and persistent opposition from legitimist, Bonapartist and republican factions, deliberately made the middle class his power base. Baron James was among those admitted to his inner councils and now enjoyed unprecedented political power. As an unofficial adviser with unrestricted access to the court, he had even greater influence than that enjoyed in Vienna by his brother and father-in-law. For example, he successfully campaigned on behalf of Casimir Pérrier, to get him appointed Premier in March 1831. Pérrier was a fellow banker and friend with whom James had worked closely for many years. He established the new administration on a sound basis before his tragic death in the cholera epidemic of 1832. Soon the wife of the Russian Foreign Minister, Count Nesselrode, could write to Moscow with a sarcasm which came close to the truth, "Do you know who is Viceroy or even King of France? It is Rothschild."[10]

Those who lampooned or vilified the Rothschilds for their "sinister" influence had a considerable amount of justification for their anger and anxiety. The banking community had always constituted a "fifth estate", whose members were able, by their control of royal purse strings, to affect important events. But the house of Rothschild was immensely more powerful than any financial empire that had ever preceded it. It commanded vast wealth. It was international. It was independent. Royal governments were nervous of it because they could not control it. Popular movements hated it because it was not answerable to the people. Constitutionalists resented it because its influence was exercised behind the scenes — secretly.

Clandestinity was and remained a feature of Rothschild political activity. Seldom were they to be seen engaging in open public debate on important issues. Never did they seek government office. Even when, in later years, some of them entered parliament, they did not feature prominently in the assembly chambers of London, Paris or Berlin. Yet all the while they were helping to shape the major events of the day: by granting or withholding funds; by providing statesmen with an unofficial diplomatic service; by influencing appointments to high office; and by an almost daily intercourse with the great decision makers.

There were, of course, good reasons for secrecy, although, as we shall see, it was to become an unjustifiable obsession with some members of the family. As bankers the Rothschilds were pledged to confidentiality. As businessmen they were wary of rivals. As leading Jews, constantly under attack, they had every reason to maintain maximum privacy in their dealings with kings and ministers. Prominent figures who are frequently misunderstood or deliberately misrepresented by the press can react in one of two ways: they can explain themselves publicly or they can maintain a disdainful silence. The Rothschilds have unerringly, and almost without exception, chosen the latter course.

But it would be a mistake to believe, as some contemporaries believed, that the nineteenth-century Rothschilds were omnipotent. They were not kingmakers. Their fortunes lay in maintaining good relations with whoever happened to be in power — of whatever political complexion. It was not in their interests to court hostility by engaging in subversive plots. Like the Vicar of Bray, they kept their political convictions to themselves and served both reactionary and reformist regimes. On the Continent, at least, they were never party activists. Thus, though they strove mightily to influence the day-to-day decisions of governments, the claim which they frequently made, to be apolitical, had a certain — limited — truth. This we have to understand if we are to unravel successfully the family's activities in the turbulent middle period of the century.

The eventful year of 1830 saw uprisings in Poland, Belgium and the northern Italian states of Parma, Modena and Romagna as well as minor disturbances in several other countries. The governments in Vienna, Berlin and St Petersburg responded nervously to every outbreak. They were restrained by the more liberal powers. But they were also restrained by the Rothschilds. Armed intervention meant money. Money meant applying to "the five brothers of Europe". And the brothers now began to attach political strings to their loans. Salomon was quite open about this:

"These gentlemen should not count on us unless they decide to follow a line of prudence and moderation . . . Our goodwill does not yet extend to the point of putting clubs into the hands that would beat us, that is, lending money to make war and ruin the credit that we sustain with all our efforts and all our means."[11]

This comment, referring to the leaders of the Belgian uprising against their Dutch masters, reflected a fundamental of Rothschild policy. As far as it was in their power to control such things, they would maintain peace and stability, denying to reactionary and radical governments alike the financial sinews of war. It was, for them, a policy of stark survival. The fortune which had been created by revolution could be destroyed by revolution. If Europe were to return to chaos, if states were tempted to renege on loan repayments and security values began to plummet, the Rothschilds would be ruined. Salomon's firm message to the insurgents certainly had its effect. The Belgian revolutionaries, denied weapons, relied more than they would otherwise have done on negotiation and their nation's independence was eventually settled by international congress. After the revolution, the Rothschilds were ready to help the new kingdom to establish a stable economy but, as James explained bluntly to his agent in Brussels, loans were no longer purely a matter of business: "Now is the moment of which we should take advantage to make ourselves absolute masters of that country's finances. The first step will be to establish ourselves on an intimate footing with Belgium's new Finance Minister, to gain his confidence . . . and to take all the treasury bonds he may offer us."[12]

Once a government had become dependent on the Rothschilds, it was caught between the Scylla of bankruptcy and the Charybdis of creeping liberalism. James and Salomon, now the confidants of powerful leaders, were not slow to exploit their position — though always very respectfully. Salomon reported to Metternich from Paris:

> The King assured me that he was opposing revolutionaries in all countries as far as his position as a constitutional monarch allowed him to do, but he stated that he was compelled in his position to show a certain regard to liberal aspirations. "I would be exceedingly glad," he said to James, "if you could possibly be the means of communicating my views to His Highness Prince von Metternich and request him in his wisdom to make urgent representations to the Court of Naples, so that it may be moved to make a few concessions in the general interests of the country, and in accordance with the progress of contemporary ideas".[13]

To all knowledgeable observers Rothschild power was awesome. In

1835 Anton Apponyi, Metternich's Ambassador in Paris, wrote to explain the bankers' activities in troubled Spain, a country in the grip of civil war. Nathan had committed the four houses to a sixteen million franc advance to the Madrid government and had also provided the Minister of Finance with considerable *douceurs*. When the administration abrogated the terms of the loan, Salomon and James took the affront personally. They were "cut to the heart" by such bad faith and ingratitude and resolved to teach the Spaniards a lesson. They and their brothers allocated eighteen hundred thousand pounds to speculation in Spanish government stock, and engineered a dramatic fall in its value. "What power the house of Rothschild has", the writer exclaimed. "What misfortune and, at the same time, what stupidity to expose oneself to their vengeance!" [14]

The public at large reacted to this phenomenon with jealousy, scorn and suspicion, which were easily provoked by hostile press comment. In France James was nicknamed the "High Priest of Judaism". When, after arranging a Vatican loan, he was received in audience by the Pope, one journalist poured out a torrent of sarcastic prose: "Rothschild has kissed the hand of the Pope ... Order has at last been re-established ... If Rothschild had been able to obtain his Roman loan at sixty per cent, instead of sixty-five. ... He would have been permitted to embrace St Peter. Wouldn't the world be happier if all Kings were deposed and the Rothschild family placed on their thrones?" [15] Whether couched in terms of wonder or bitterness, such contemporary comments are ample confirmation of the degree of influence now wielded by the five brothers. The myth and the reality of Rothschild power were converging.

In 1836 there was another family wedding. These occasions were becoming almost commonplace. But this one was destined to be very different: an historic event attended by sorrow. It was the union of Lionel to his seventeen-year-old cousin, another Charlotte, daughter of Neapolitan Carl. The ceremony was fixed for 15 June and, in early summer, most of the members of the family started out from their various homes to meet in Frankfurt for the celebrations.

Lionel himself took the opportunity of making a leisurely journey through Belgium and the Rhineland with his old friend Rossini to show the composer the sights. His companion enjoyed the holiday enormously:

I have made a trip to Frankfurt, passing through Brussels, Antwerp, Aix-la-Chapelle, Cologne, Coblenz [sic], Mainz, etc and I assure you that nothing in the world is more beautiful than the banks of the Rhine. What richness, what vegetation, what cathedrals, what objects from olden times! I do not speak of the pictures by Rubens and Vandyke, as I should want to have twenty pages to describe their beauties and number to you. I am truly satisfied with this little trip, the entire purpose of which was to attend at Frankfurt, the marriage of Lionel Rothschild, my very dear friend.[16]

The city was *en fête* for the great occasion, its hotels filling not only with Rothschilds but many of their important friends from the worlds of finance, politics and art. Only one shadow fell across the happy preparations. On the journey from England Nathan had been inflicted with an extremely painful inflammation at the base of the spine. On 11 June a leading German surgeon was summoned. He diagnosed a boil and prescribed patience. Nathan got up for the wedding and forced himself to be cheerful throughout the proceedings. But his condition did not improve and now his English physician was urgently summoned. The German doctor operated on the "boil" (in fact an ischio-rectal abscess) to no effect and the poison spread through the patient's bloodstream. Despite his discomfort Nathan, who nowadays would be dubbed a "workaholic", kept his wife and sons busy with an unending stream of instructions and dictated letters. Anxiously his family watched for the crisis to pass, but as day succeeded sleepless night N.M. grew weaker. After a month it became obvious to all that Nathan was dying. The end came on 28 July. The life of Nathan Rothschild ceased in the city where it had begun fifty-nine eventful years before. And carrier pigeons were sent winging across the Channel carrying the simple message *"Il est mort"*.

In anticipation of the news, the value of government securities on the London market had been dropping for some days. But when the fact was known, prices revived — probably, as *The Times* suggested, "on account of the understanding there is that his business, under the management of his sons,* will go on as usual".[17] The long obituary published by the newspaper acknowledged the death of N.M. as "one of the most important events for the city, and perhaps for Europe, which has occurred for a very long time".[18]

A lithograph was published depicting Nathan's pillar at the Exchange with a bulky figure beside it in grey silhouette and a legend which read *"The Shadow of a Great Man"*. But the most eloquent and long-lasting memorial came from the pen of Benjamin Disraeli who, eight years later, transformed Nathan Rothschild into the elder Sidonia in his novel *Coningsby*, thereby ensuring that the great man's obituary would, albeit

*N.M. Rothschild and Brothers had, by now, become N.M. Rothschild and Sons.

unwittingly and with a few alterations necessitated by the novel's plot, be read by generations to come:

> During the long disorders of the Peninsular war, when so many openings were offered to talent, and so many opportunities seized by the adventurous, a cadet of a younger branch of this family made a large fortune by military contracts, and supplying the commissariat of the different armies. At the peace, prescient of the great financial future of Europe, confident in the fertility of his own genius, in his original views of fiscal subjects, and his knowledge of national resources, this Sidonia ... resolved to emigrate to England, with which he had, in the course of years, formed considerable commercial connections. He arrived here after the peace of Paris, with his large capital. He staked all that he was worth on the Waterloo loan; and the event made him one of the greatest capitalists in Europe ...
>
> Sidonia had foreseen ... that, after the exhaustion of a war of twenty-five years, Europe must require capital to carry on peace. He reaped the due reward of his sagacity. Europe did require money, and Sidonia was ready to lend it to Europe. France wanted some; Austria more; Prussia a little; Russia a few millions. Sidonia could furnish them all ...
>
> It is not difficult to conceive that, after having pursued the career we have intimated for about ten years, Sidonia had become one of the most considerable personages in Europe. He had established a brother, or a near relative, in whom he could confide, in most of the principal capitals. He was lord and master of the money-market of the world, and of course virtually lord and master of everything else. He literally held the revenues of Southern Italy in pawn; and monarchs and ministers of all countries courted his advice and were guided by his suggestions. He was still in the vigour of life, and was not a mere money-making machine. He had a general intelligence equal to his position, and looked forward to the period when some relaxation from his vast enterprises and exertions might enable him to direct his energies to great objects of public benefit. But in the height of his vast prosperity he suddenly died. [19]

Part II
1836–1870

CHAPTER 9
"The Great Baron"

Nathan's sudden and unexpected death left the Rothschilds temporarily leaderless. For although Amschel, as the eldest brother, had been titular head of the family for the previous twenty-four years, N.M., as the strongest and most talented of Mayer Amschel's sons, had assumed the role of "first among equals", at least where business was concerned. Now, long before anyone had given thought to the question of an heir presumptive, that great man had suddenly been taken away.

Fortunately the gap was quickly filled. By common, if tacit, consent James assumed the mantle of leadership. Although the youngest of the Frankfurt Five (he was forty-four when Nathan died) he had already established his predominance over the remaining brothers. Like Nathan before him, James owed his position to the fact that he was both a more forceful character and a more innovative and successful businessman. Even before Nathan's death there had been some signs that Paris was beginning to challenge London's pre-eminence in the family's financial affairs. In part this was due to James's intimacy with Louis Philippe. But it was also because the French house had been the first to respond positively to the changing economic realities of the 1830s. This was an age of explosive industrial expansion. British entrepreneurs were exploiting to the full the possibilities of steam power and had opened up a lead of several years over Continental counterparts. Now the latter were scrambling to catch up. Everywhere in western Europe new mines, steel foundries, railways, textile mills and light industrial complexes were being established. And they all needed financing. Nathan had been wary of the speculative investments which had brought down many joint-stock banks in Britain and had declined to involve himself heavily in the industrial sector. James was more adventurous. He led the family firmly into this new area of business and, by a combination of imagination and ruthlessness, proved immensely successful.

Like Nathan, James was not a man to suffer fools gladly, and this category, in his view, often included other family members. In middle age he became truculent and dictatorial. The younger Rothschilds, who affected amusement at his larger-than-life antics, referred to their uncle as "the Great Baron". While the title was often used ironically, it also implied considerable respect. Both in the family and the bank he was regarded with awe and sometimes fear. One subordinate recorded:

> It was incredible how everything in this immense banking house was ruled with a rod of iron. What amazing order everywhere! Such willing employees and so intelligent! Such submissive sons! Such a sense of hierarchy! Such respect! . . . I do not think it is possible to find anywhere in the world a bank where everything is so organised, correct and respectable. The atmosphere is one of important business and of a solid fortune laboriously acquired . . . [1]

Perhaps because he had lived so long in N.M.'s shadow, James now became self-assertive to the point of rudeness and assumed a confidence that bordered on arrogance. He had endured Nathan's often brutal criticism for a quarter of a century. Although it had been some years since he had had to scurry around Europe at his elder brother's behest, he must have always felt that bulky presence looming over his shoulder every time he made a decision. With Nathan gone, James must have felt that now, at last, he was wholly his own man, free to pursue the affairs of Rue Laffitte with a single-mindedness that brooked no opposition.

He was subject to moods, frequently of violent anger, that scared his subordinates and earned the respect of colleagues. Ernest Feydeau, father of the famous playwright, worked for some years in the bank and left a vivid picture of his irascible employer:

> "Vat a pest you are! Vat do you know about dat? Get de defil out from here," were the civilities he addressed to me or to others whenever we took it upon ourselves to make some observation concerning an order . . . And it would have been ungracious of me to resent his rudeness, since his behaviour was even more uncouth towards others: "Ah! Der you are, damned teefing Cherman Chew," he said one day to a co-religionist . . . The poor man stood there, crushed, without voice or expression. He may even have taken it as a compliment.[2]

Not unnaturally, such behaviour created enemies, several of whom longed to bring down this "insufferable Jew". Some tried. They lived to regret their rashness.

Members of the family, who experienced Uncle James's warmth and generosity as well as his bad temper, were more understanding. They knew that he felt a patriarchal responsibility for all his nephews and nieces and that this burden in addition to the long hours he spent at his desk weighed heavily upon him.

In public the Great Baron lived up to his title. He looked on no man as his superior and was in the habit of giving even the most exalted personages the benefit of his advice. Perhaps because of his undoubted influence in French politics between 1830 and 1848, James fell into the habit of proffering his opinion even when it was not called for. Certainly he sometimes embarrassed his relatives in London and Vienna by giving the benefit of his experience to foreign diplomats and visiting ministers. If other Rothschilds protested about his tactlessness James remained impervious. What did they know about world events? Had they forgotten that he, James, had helped defeat Napoleon? Everything about Baron James, except his physical appearance, was "big". His Paris house contained, in the words of Heine, "everything the sixteenth-century mind could conceive of and the nineteenth-century purse could buy . . . it is the Versailles of the absolute monarchy of money".[3] For James, collecting was an obsession. Long after he had filled his houses in the Rue Laffitte, at Ferrières and at Boulogne-sur-Seine with old masters, French furniture of the finest eighteenth-century *ébénistes* and all manner of antiquities and *objets d'art*, he continued to buy — continuously and compulsively. One of his nephews, accompanying the Great Baron on a visit to Heinrichsbad, reported:

> You have no idea what an interest our good uncle takes in running after the productions of classic antiquity. As soon as he hears of anything that is to be sold he immediately orders a carriage and does not mind in the least the distance or the weather. In this way we went to Constance which is at least 40 miles from here and all that was worth seeing consisted of a couple of dozen . . . cracked, painted window-glasses. His fancy or mania has become so known that all the peasants from the surrounding country bring their ornaments. However, he has managed to pick up a very handsome cup and dish, for which he had to pay a good, cosy price . . .[4]

No major European auction sale was complete without the presence of James or one of his agents. He bought from royalty as readily as from the peasants, acquiring items from the collections of George IV, Christian VIII of Denmark, William I of the Netherlands and several European nobles.

James's taste in art was catholic, almost indiscriminate. The reception room walls of his Paris house were hung with works by Rembrandt, Velázquez, Frans Hals, Van Eyck, Rubens, Murillo and Van Dyck; all recognised old masters approved by the nineteenth-century art establishment. The point was, of course, that what was approved was also valuable. For as much as anything else, the collection represented a safe investment, and was insured for ten million francs. In themselves, the exquisite possessions which James amassed seem to have meant little to him — it is significant, for example, that in his private chambers, where a connoisseur might be expected to keep those treasures with which he felt a special intimate rapport, the main items were family portraits and a sentimental *Moses in the Bulrushes.*

One type of "masterpiece" James did appreciate was good wine. He was especially fond of claret, notably the produce of Château Lafite, generally recognised as the leading vineyard of the Haut Médoc. When, in 1847, he offered to undertake his favourite nephew's oenological education there could, in his opinion, only be one way to begin the process: " . . . you are going to get 50 bottles of good Château Lafite . . . if you like my choice and are ready to trust me, I will be happy . . . to take charge of stocking your wine cellar . . . " [5]

Seventeen years earlier, anxious to secure an unlimited supply of the best, James had tried to buy this celebrated vineyard from its nominal owner, the English banker, Sir Samuel Scott. [6] The offer was declined. But the Great Baron's interest did not wane. He could afford to wait. And wait he did, for thirty-eight years (see p. 200).

James may have been foiled in that first attempt to buy his favourite vineyard, but he could console himself with the thought that he now owned a fine ten-thousand-acre sporting estate. On his recently acquired land at Ferrières to the east of Paris he could entertain important clients and friends in as grand a style as any offered by a French aristocrat on his inherited property. His English relations enjoyed its amenities but were not unstinting in their praise. It seemed to their more reserved taste a little too opulent, too exuberant, too . . . everything.

Like all James's younger relatives, N.M.'s sons were at his beck and call. They were almost a generation older than his own children and, as we have seen, the Great Baron frequently demanded the presence of one or other of his nephews at Rue Laffitte to help cope with the rapidly expanding business. Nor was it for business purposes alone that these young Englishmen were obliged to cross the Channel. James and his wife often travelled to one or other of the fashionable European spas, convinced, as were most of their contemporaries, that taking the water would ease their various ailments. For his nephews an invitation to accompany the Baron on one of these trips was clearly a familiar hazard of family life. But so strong was their sense of obligation that they tolerated the dreary weeks spent among elderly people obsessed by their health.

Despite his ready assumption that members of other branches of the family would leave their own affairs and hurry to obey his every summons, James was very possessive where his own children were concerned. Thus, when his only daughter was married to her English cousin, Nat, it was the groom who had to make his permanent home in Paris. James would not allow his beloved Charlotte to take up residence in a foreign capital. His was a close family bound by ties of real affection and, if James was strict, he could also be indulgent. Besides Charlotte, the eldest, he and Betty had four sons — Alphonse, Gustave, Salomon and Edmond — who were, as a matter of course, provided with the widest and best education that parental love could contrive and money could buy. They travelled extensively, learned from gifted tutors (one of them was paid a thousand francs per month, this at a time when a university professor's salary was about five hundred francs) and were instructed in the civilised pursuits of dancing, drawing and gymnastics. Nor was their religious training neglected; for although James was not punctilious in matters of the faith, his wife made up this deficiency just as she also compensated for his lack of social graces. "My good lady never drives on the Sabbath", he would explain to friends and colleagues, or "My good lady would not go out today, but I must do such-and-such things." Clearly, he enjoyed Betty's respectable orthodoxy without being personally inconvenienced by it.[7]

Like her husband, the Baronne grew into her rôle, becoming a re-markably accomplished and a truly formidable woman. Not only did she speak French exquisitely, she also wrote it with verve and style. Her circle of close friends, embracing the leading literary, artistic and political figures of the day, included Marie Amélie, Louis Philippe's queen. Her knowledge covered a wide range of subjects and she was a fluent conversationalist. Add to all this a strong will and an enquiring mind and it is scarcely surprising that some of her relatives found her overpowering. A typical encounter with the Baronne was reported by one of the English Rothschild women in 1849:

> Yesterday we went to St Leonards to see Betty . . . [She] was as usual fascinating, eloquent — *tant soit peu exagérée et grande dame*. I found the afternoon's visit long enough and was not sorry to regain the comparative quiet of the steam carriage, for Betty's torrent of words and thoughts rather stunned me and made me feel even more stupid than usual . . . [8]

At home in Paris during the 1840s Betty presided over a salon which made her the envy of every hostess in the capital. The Rothschilds' intimacy with the Orléans court enabled her to attract the cream of society, and her own interests ensured that the company was well leavened with talent and aspiring artists. The guests at Rue Laffitte might be treated to a duet by Liszt and Paganini; invited to hear Chopin play, together with Karl Filtsch, an arrangement for two pianos of his E minor Concerto; or to listen to readings by Balzac; or be kept amused by Heine's wickedly clever wit. There were few of Europe's artistic luminaries who, at one time or another, did not shed a little of their light in Baroness Betty's superbly appointed chambers. But that in itself did not put her soirées in a class apart. What really distinguished Rue Laffitte from its rivals was the rapport between the hostess and the musicians, writers and painters who surrounded her.

The Rothschilds' Jewishness had always set them somewhat apart from the blue-blooded *habitués* of the Faubourg Saint-Germain, and this enabled the Baronne and, to some extent, the Baron to enjoy a greater casualness and freedom in their relationships with the Bohemian *demi-monde*. In 1842, for example, Chopin and George Sand set up a ménage in the Place d'Orléans and the house became a regular meeting place for all their talented friends. Among the company who might be found there, enjoying an evening of impromptu music making and poetry reading, were James and Betty de Rothschild.[9] Similarly, James particularly valued, even courted, the friendship of Honoré de Balzac. "You completely forget your friends," he once chided, "and don't come to see us. Won't you choose a day to come and dine with us? . . . I should be truly charmed to see you at my house . . ."[10] Balzac dedicated one of his novels, *L'Enfant Maudit*, to Betty and another, *Un Homme d'Affaires*, perhaps more appropriately to the Great Baron.

Yet James's relationship with Balzac, as with Heine and Rossini and, perhaps, other great artists, never had the degree of intimacy he may have wished for. Like the Gentile aristocracy, though for different reasons, theirs was a world in which he could never feel at home. They had different values. They affected an indifference to, or even a contempt for, the commodity he spent all his professional life amassing − money. They were fiercely independent. Take Jean Auguste Dominique Ingres, for example. This "court painter" to the Parisian bourgeoisie was in frenzied demand by the *haut monde*. Yet he affected to disdain portraiture and was highly selective when accepting commissions. The Great Baron actually had to go cap-in-hand to persuade the master to paint his wife.

James, the patron, freely handed out gifts and "loans". But James, the banker, could not help but be shocked at his protégés' importunity and imprudence. Yet, at the same time, he envied their simple, easy-come-easy-go existence. Heine told a story which, though doubtless coloured by the writer's own bitterness, gives us a rare glimpse of the private thoughts of James de Rothschild:

"How are you?" a German poet once asked the Herr Baron. "I am mad," he answered. "Until you throw money out of the window," said the Poet, "I won't believe it." But the Baron said with a sigh, "That *is* my madness, that I do not throw money out of the window."[11]

If James's feelings towards the artistic world were always to remain equivocal, the same was not true of some of his children. Alphonse may well have been an artist *manqué* (see pp. 246ff.) and Charlotte was very gifted. She was a talented watercolourist whose topographical drawings are now sought after by collectors. There are two portraits of her at Château Lafite. One depicts her as a little girl of about seven. The other shows her in the full beauty of young womanhood. Yet both artists have caught the same expression, a wistful, half-sad, faraway look, as though the sitter was not aware of her surroundings, but concentrating upon her inner world. Charlotte was sensitive both to beauty and to the needs of others and seems to have been universally adored. She was one of Chopin's best pupils and a member of his circle of close friends. In 1849, the last year of his life, when the composer's body was wasting away with consumption and he was obliged to restrict his lessons to those of his more advanced students who were understanding of last-minute cancellations and altered arrangements, Charlotte was among those who called to receive tuition and to give comfort.

Chopin spent that last summer on the cool heights of Chaillot, outside the city, and there, in July, Charlotte and some of his other friends arranged a special treat for the dying master. They brought the celebrated soprano, Jenny Lind, to sing for him. After his death a little cushion worked for him by Charlotte when she was a young girl was found among his most treasured effects. Little wonder, then, that Chopin dedicated no less than three works to his young friend — two waltzes (the C sharp minor, Op. 64 No. 2 and the A flat major, Op. 69 No. 1 – the "Farewell"), and his magnificent, moving Ballade in F minor, Op. 52 No. 4. Charlotte was also the dedicatee of a little work by Rossini. An unnamed piano solo which the composer presented to her personally bore this inscription: *"Petit Souvenir, offert à Madame la Baronne Charlotte Nathaniel de Rothschild par son très devoué G. Rossini. Paris 10 Sept. 1843".*[12]

Charlotte had, as already mentioned, married her English cousin, Nat, in 1842, thus fulfilling her duty as a Rothschild daughter. The marriage must have been especially welcome to her father because it had become apparent, just three years earlier, that not all the new generation would necessarily fall in with their elders' wishes and expectations in this respect. It was in matters of the heart that the young men and women found family loyalty most stifling. Their amours were watched closely by their uncles and aunts and they received firm lectures if they seemed to be drifting into "unsuitable" liaisons. What the elders feared above all things was that one of these emancipated youngsters might form an attachment for a Christian.

Predictably, it was Amschel, in particular, who frequently pointed out this danger; and when Anthony was rumoured to be seeing rather too much of a non-Jewish young lady the news threw him into a panic. In fact, the young man had probably only sown a few wild oats. Certainly he had already established a reputation where ladies were concerned; some of his companions had even been known to turn up at the bank demanding payment for "services rendered".

To a certain extent Amschel's brothers shared his concern that the new life style might engender a contempt for traditional customs and for the Jewish faith. As early as 1817 plans to send Salomon's fourteen-year-old son, Anselm, to Paris were cancelled on the grounds that the gaiety of the French capital might distract him from religion and business. The brothers' worries were not unfounded. This was a period during which many old Jewish families converted to Christianity, and their numbers increased with the passing of the years.

Then, in 1839, the unthinkable happened. A Rothschild girl married out of the faith. The culprit was Anthony's sister, Hannah. 'H.M.' (Hannah Mayer) as she was known in the family, perhaps in acknowledgement of the fact that she had much of her father in her, was Nathan's fifth child, born in the year of Waterloo, and was the inheritrix of her father's iron will and stubborn spirit. She had been a withdrawn child, given to outbursts of temper, and her independent spirit hardened as she came to marriageable age and saw the manner in which her elder sister and her female cousins were being packed off to foreign capitals to grace the bridal beds of their relatives. Lionel's wife, Charlotte, was very unhappy in London.

With such an object lesson before her eyes, it is scarcely surprising that at the age of twenty-four, by which time Rothschild girls were usually wives and mothers, H.M. was still a spinster. A spinster who had, it seems, decided that if she were to marry it would be for love; certainly if "suitable" family matches for her were ever discussed, she rejected them. But then she met Henry Fitzroy, eight years her senior, the second son of Baron Southampton and MP for Lewes. Fitzroy's town house in Great Stanhope Street was only a stone's throw from 107 Piccadilly and he was a member of the political set with which Lionel was becoming increasingly involved. It therefore seems likely that the couple met at one of the many fashionable balls and parties the Rothschilds regularly attended.

However emotional the family discussions that took place as the relationship blossomed (and there must have been several) they only strengthened Hannah's resolve. She accepted Henry's proposal of marriage and agreed to the ceremony being performed in church. The date and place were fixed: 29 April 1839 at St George's, Hanover Square. The anguish her decision caused within the close and happy family circle where orthodoxy was taken for granted, can scarcely be imagined by people who live in a more tolerant and open society. For Hannah, her mother, the conflict between affection and pride must have been intense, and both she and her sons would have known that they faced a deluge of Rothschild indignation if they could not talk H.M. out of her resolve.

Anthony and the youngest boy, Mayer, were both away from home — the former on the Continent and the latter completing his studies at Cambridge. The remaining brothers, Lionel and Nat, adopted characteristic, and very different attitudes towards the crisis. Lionel, the taciturn head of the family, was angry at the upset his sister was causing and, perhaps, angry with himself for being unable to exercise control over her. Nat's feelings were determined by his love for and sympathy with his sister, and he was prepared to stand by Hannah Mayer, and plead with his relatives to exercise a mature tolerance. But he could not prevent the rift.

When the day came, Lionel said not a word. He spent his usual hours in the bank. Nat regarded this as unfeeling and stupid. He was at his sister's side as she left her old home for the last time. He drove with her to St George's and was the only member of the family to attend the service. Their mother went as far as she could: she accompanied them in the carriage but left them at the door of the church and returned home, her thoughts and emotions in a state which we can only guess at.

When the news reached the Great Baron, he was furious. For a while, he suffered in silence. The task of pacifying him was left to Nat, who wrote from London, and Anthony, who joined his uncle on his tour of health resorts. Nat's careful explanation brought, after some delay, a broadside from James in Heinrichsbad. The news, he said, had made him ill. Young Hannah's offence was quite unforgivable. She had

> robbed our whole family of its pride . . . You write to me that she has found everything but religion [in her marriage]. But that means everything. Our luck, our blessings depend upon it. However, we shall have to forget her and cut her out of our memory . . . We just wish her happiness and in future we shall just look upon the whole matter as though she had never existed . . . [13]

This outright rejection was too much for Nat. He replied with some heat

115

that all his sister had done was marry a Christian in a Christian country. For that she did not deserve to be ostracised. James was unmoved. Ever since she was fifteen, he retorted, H.M. had been attracted to the Christian religion. This had now led her to flout the wishes of her family. He reiterated his ban on any contact between his household and the newlyweds and he spelled out his reasons.

> What sort of example for our children would a girl be who says, "I marry against the wishes of my family"? . . . Why should my children or my children's children obey my wishes if there is no punishment [for disobeying]? . . . we have striven always to keep up the love of [and] attachment to the family, so that children . . . would never think of marrying outside the family, so that the fortune may stay in the family . . . [14]

In a long, passionate and rambling letter James went on to stress that this appalling liaison had done what he had so much feared: it had outraged that most sacred of principles – Rothschild unity. If a strong stand was not taken now, he concluded, somewhat hysterically, other daughters would not be contented until they, too, had married into the Christian nobility.

James's attitude reveals how closely religion, money, tradition and family pride had been bound together in the minds of the generation that created the Rothschild phenomenon. As we have already seen, James was no religious purist like Amschel; his attitude to his co-religionists was, to say the least, ambivalent. But when it came to those things which ensured the continued unity and wealth of the family there could be no compromise. For Nat the problems were very different. He and his brothers and sisters were popular in London society. Their friends were liberal, tolerant Englishmen who did not take their own religion very seriously and could not understand why sophisticated Jews should be slavishly devoted to theirs. Ostracising H.M. had, in fact, had a worse effect on Nat than on his sister. All their friends had rallied round Henry Fitzroy and his new bride: it was the Rothschilds who found themselves isolated in the eyes of society.

Before Nat could take up his pen for another angry riposte, he received a letter from his brother, who was doing his best to calm the situation. Anthony, perhaps encouraged by the fact that his own matrimonial intentions were still the subject of suspicion, tried to see both sides of the argument and urged Nat to make allowances for his French relatives. Uncle James, he pointed out, had really been very ill. So much so that "the least thing puts him out and when it does he is not well for days and months together". He went on to urge patience and caution:

116

I have requested uncle James as well as Betty to write to you in friendly terms upon that subject, as I said it would, I am sure, have a greater effect than all the quarrelsome letters in the world ... I advise you ... not to receive H.M. for the present so as to keep the union of the family ... when all is forgotten one can do what one likes ... I told them that Mama would follow her own feelings; but it would be better if she did not invite H.M. for the present.[15]

The problem which thus came home to the Rothschilds so poignantly was an inevitable consequence of assimilation. It was indeed creating, throughout European Jewry, what one modern authority has described as

A crisis of the first magnitude ... for the Jewish people, which for the first time in its exile, seemed unable to adapt itself to changed conditions. Unaccustomed as they were after centuries of seclusion to the idea of a full Jewish citizenship in a non-Jewish national state, the problem of adjusting completely their religious loyalty to the new political and social status which they had won appeared to them formidable.[16]

Freed from at least the more blatant forms of oppression, the Jews of Europe now confronted a crisis of identity: were they Jews first and foremost, or Frenchmen, Englishmen and Germans? And what was a Jew? Was he a member of a particular race; an adherent of a unique religion; or part of a historic nation, temporarily living in Diaspora? One solution to the problem, adopted by men such as Karl Marx, was to break completely with Judaism, and seek new loyalties. Thus, out of the political and cultural turmoil of the age, emerged the phenomenon of the Jewish Socialist, the man who had turned his back on the exclusiveness of his upbringing and espoused a new religion of universal brotherhood. In rejecting their past, such men frequently turned upon their own people, calling them money-grubbing capitalists, the enemies of humanity. Thus Marx could write bitterly:

The late Czar Nicholas made Stieglitz a Russian baron, as the late Kaiser Franz made old Rothschild an Austrian baron, while Louis Napoleon has made a cabinet minister of Fould, with a free ticket to the Tuileries for the females of the family. Thus we find every tyrant backed by a Jew, as is every Pope by a Jesuit. In truth, the cravings of oppressors would be hopeless and the practicability of war out of the question, if there were not an army of Jesuits to smother thought and a handful of Jews to ransack pockets.[17]

Others reacted differently and, concluding that assimilation was both impossible and undesirable, turned to Jewish nationalism as the only

117

logical alternative. "A common, native soil is a precondition for intro-ducing healthier relations between capital and labour among Jews,"[18] wrote proto-Zionist Moses Hess.

The followers of the Reform movement, founded by David Friedlander, sought a middle way, insisting that Judaism was *only* a religion and that, in all other ways, Jews should integrate with their Gentile neighbours. Friedlander even applied to the Lutheran Church for conditional mem-bership for himself and his followers. The condition was that they were not asked to subscribe to the divinity of Jesus! But Heinrich Heine, as we have already seen, went the whole distance. His sad story illustrates well the tensions of assimilation. He accepted baptism quite openly in order to qualify for a university post but the position was still denied to him and he spent much of his life as a bitter, disappointed man. It is against this background of controversy and turmoil within Jewry that the family's reactions to Hannah Mayer's marriage must be seen.

Ultimately, as Anthony had hoped, time did heal the breach. H.M. and Henry were not outcasts for long, at least from the English family. Soon they were once more included in the round of social calls in which the Rothschilds were constantly engaged. But, if this was the case, the credit was due much more to Henry Fitzroy than to his wife. He worked very hard to restore good relations, especially with Lionel. H.M. found it much more difficult to forgive and forget. She remained sensitive to the slightest suggestion of a snub. Subsequently, this touchiness would turn to bitterness. Sadly, this marriage was not destined to be long and happy. Her son Arthur was crippled as a result of a fall from his pony and needed constant nursing. He died in 1858 at the age of fifteen. Hannah Mayer's husband, after a long illness, passed away in the following year. The tragedy of her widowhood was deepened by her inability to find consolation in the support of her family, not because they had permanently rejected her, but because she had built – or at least had been unable to break down – a barrier of resentment between herself and her relatives.

Yet it was not only within H.M.'s breast that resentments lingered, resentments capable of poisoning the minds of a generation unborn at the time of the notorious wedding. As late as 1858 Hannah Mayer's niece, Annie (Anthony's daughter), confided in her diary an opinion she had absorbed from the grown-ups: "I cannot help thinking that all the misfortune and distress which have overtaken poor Aunt Hannah Mayer have been a punishment for having deserted the faith of her fathers and for having married without her mother's consent."[19]

Whatever their personal feelings about H.M., all the leaders of the family shared one reaction to the crisis of 1839 – it must not be allowed

Top: *The sitting room in the Judengasse house — the only communal room for Mayer, Gutle and their large family.* (Historisches Museum, Frankfurt)

Middle: *Mayer Amschel's counting house in Judengasse. A desk and a heavy chest for money, bills and ledgers were the only furnishings he needed.* (Historisches Museum, Frankfurt)

Right: *This late nineteenth-century engraving of Judengasse illustrates well how centuries of cramming more and more houses into a small space had led to serious structural defects.* (Historisches Museum, Frankfurt)

Gutle Rothschild
(BBC Hulton Picture Library)

Baron James de Rothschild
(BBC Hulton Picture Library)

Baron Amschel von Rothschild
(BBC Hulton Picture Library)

Baron Carl von Rothschild
(BBC Hulton Picture Library)

Above: A satirical cartoon of
1848 depicts 'Rothschild' pondering
on which of Europe's rulers to
favour with loans, while
revolutionaries challenge the
ancient order he is supporting.
(Historisches Museum, Frankfurt)

Right: A piece of seventeenth-
century propaganda shows one of
the gates of Frankfurt with its anti-
Semitic painting.
(Historisches Museum, Frankfurt)

Below: A nineteenth-century print
illustrating an anti-Jewish riot.
(Historisches Museum, Frankfurt)

The Ashkenazim synagogue in Duke's Place, London, where Nathan and his family worshipped. (Rowland and Ackerman, *Microcosm of London*)

A PILLAR of the EXCHANGE

A caricature of Nathan Rothschild, showing him in his habitual position before one of the pillars in the Exchange.
(British Museum Print Room)

THE SHADOW OF A GREAT MAN.

Another drawing, based on A Pillar of the Exchange, *indicates the gap Nathan's death left in the life of the City.*
(British Museum Print Room)

A Cruikshank cartoon of 1828 depicts N.M. Rothschild as an unlikely, 'incorporial' cherub and J.C. Herries as a failed politician. The two confederates console themselves after Herries' failure to win the Chancellorship. N.M. comforts himself with a loan to the new King of Portugal, Dom Miguel, and Herries is placated with 'mint sauce' — the Mastership of the Mint. (British Museum Print Room)

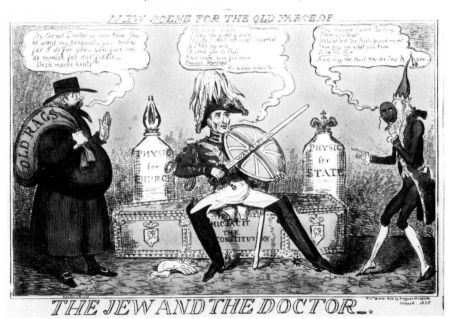

In a House of Commons speech in 1828 Thomas Duncombe, a radical politician, averred that the real power in the land was exercised by Sir William Knighton, the King's physician, and Nathan Rothschild. This Cruikshank cartoon illustrates the point. (British Museum Print Room)

Baron Salomon von Rothschild. (Baron Eric de Rothschild)

Cover of a gold-embossed address presented to Salomon on his seventieth birthday.
(Historisches Museum, Frankfurt)

Left: *Baron James de Rothschild.*
(Baron Eric de Rothschild)

Below: *A cartoon representing the visit made by Napoleon III to James de Rothschild at Ferrières on 17 February 1862.* (Taken from E. Corti, *The Rise of the House of Rothschild*, II)

A drawing room at the Château of Ferrières. (Baron Guy de Rothschild)

*Ingres' magnificent portrait of
Baronne Betty de Rothschild.*
(Baron Guy de Rothschild)

*A portrait of the wistful Charlotte de
Rothschild by Ary Scheffer.*
(Baron Eric de Rothschild)

*A painted panel on leather − The Triumph of David. One of a series by the
seventeenth-century master, Govaert Flinck, which once adorned the walls of
Ferrières and are now in Baron Guy de Rothschild's Paris house.*
(Baron Guy de Rothschild)

to happen again. Marriages must be arranged for the other young Rothschilds as quickly as possible, before any more of them were carried away by "stupid ideas".

That same summer, Hannah took H.M.'s sister, the nineteen-year-old Louise, off to France with her and there presided with satisfaction and relief over her betrothal to Mayer Carl de Rothschild of the Neapolitan house. By the following March Anthony's fate, too, had been settled. He resisted any attempt to get him married off to one of the available Rothschild girls and chose instead a more distant relative, Louisa Montefiore, to whom he felt he could pay court with a sufficient degree of enthusiasm. He did, however, think it prudent to warn his betrothed of what lay in store: "You will perceive, my dearest Louisa, that all the family are complete slaves to business. Therefore, whatever plans we may make or wish for, may be very much changed by circumstances . . . "[20] And the demands of business, as Anthony was only too well aware (after the events of the previous year) were the least of the challenges his wife would face. He also warned her, more than once, that his family could be smothering in its possessive introspection: "You know, my best Lou, what I told you, that we must not be too near any person. Our family is large and it will be requisite for us to live for ourselves."[21] It may well be that Anthony's commonsense, open-eyed attitude contributed a good deal to the happiness of the marriage. For her part, Louisa was a highly intelligent and warm-hearted woman. With Anthony she established a home that friends and relatives loved to visit and one where they always found a warm welcome.

Further cause for celebration came in 1842, with Nat's marriage to James's daughter, the lovely and sensitive Charlotte, which took place amidst much Rothschild pomp and circumstance, and resulted in the establishment of a distinct branch of the family. Nat worked assiduously at the bank, but he never fully identified with the French Rothschilds. Later, his sons' relations with Rue Laffitte became even more tenuous and, by the third generation, Nat's descendants had developed other interests.

Thus, within three years of H.M.'s wedding, Hannah had redeemed the standing of the English branch of the family by finding suitable partners, two of them fellow Rothschilds, for no less than three of her children. As a result her family was now widely scattered. This did not prevent her from continuing to exercise a deep influence over them, for she visited each in turn, quite undeterred by the travelling involved. Indeed, from the time of her bereavement until her own death in 1850 Hannah dominated the lives of her children and their spouses. She continued to live at 107 Piccadilly, an erect, proud woman, with keen blue eyes, who played a major rôle in business, as well as family affairs. In the will which N.M. had dictated on his death-bed he had indicated that Hannah was to have a vote in all major business decisions and that his sons "shall not embark in any transaction of importance without having previously demanded her motherly advice, and that all my children's sons and daughters are to treat her with true love, kind affection and every possible respect, which she deserves in the highest degree, having shared with me joy and sorrow during so great a number of years, as a fond, true and affectionate wife."[22]

Hannah took her business responsibilities very seriously. Her sons were relatively young and inexperienced and, though she was careful not to give the impression of interfering in the day-to-day affairs of the bank, she certainly provided very clear guidance. She discussed with Lionel and her Continental sons-in-law fluctuations in share prices, the impact of crop failures, problems faced by the Bank of England and other issues of importance.

Even in her old age, Hannah was tireless in her care for her children and the family's business. She visited her daughters and daughters-in-law frequently and expected them to call on her with equal faithfulness. But her solicitousness and involvement in the lives of her children were by no means universally appreciated. Lionel's wife, Charlotte, felt suffocated by Hannah. She hated England in any case and for several years after her marriage pined for her Neapolitan home. When Lionel on one occasion made a quite civil enquiry about her movements, he received a very sharp reply. "You ask, dear husband, if I am going to Mentmore [her brother-in-law, Mayer's home. See pp. 159f.]. As your mother wishes to go there for a few days, I have no choice but to go with her. Ever since I became your wife I have had to do what others want, never what I would like to do. Pray that I shall be compensated in Heaven."[23] At the time of writing Charlotte was staying with her mother-in-law at Gunnersbury, where Hannah retired for a few weeks every year together with various female members of the family who were expected to keep her company.

This was an experience the younger generation regarded with a distinct lack of enthusiasm. Louisa's report to her husband, Anthony, was typical: "I felt my usual *chill* creep over me when we advanced through the stately carriage drive to the stately mansion and were received in a rather stately manner . . . Time must pass, however, whether pleasantly or otherwise, and I do not suppose I shall be here longer than a fortnight."[24] Even the Rothschilds, it seems, were not immune to mother-in-law problems. And Rothschild girls, at least of this generation, rarely had their own mothers on hand, as most of them were faced with the prospect of married life in a foreign capital. Inevitably some were happier than others. Hannah's daughters, Charlotte and Louise, did have the consolation of one another's company, for both of them spent most of their time in Frankfurt. Anselm, Charlotte's husband, was the dominant figure in both the

Austrian and German banks. As his father and uncle grew older he spent most of his time shuttling between Frankfurt and Vienna. Mayer Carl, to whom Louise was married, left Naples in the 1840s to help Anselm in the parent house.

Charlotte, if she regarded Frankfurt as a dreary place of exile, certainly made the most of it. She turned her own home into a place of culture and brilliance which sparkled in its dull surroundings like a diamond brooch on the bosom of a plain woman. Old Gutle still lived her simple life in the ghetto; Amschel had, at last, acquired a fine house in its own park outside the city, while still remaining aloof from society "frivolity", but Charlotte gave soirées, dinners and parties which, as we have seen, were the high points in the Frankfurt social calendar. They took place in the delightful villa called Grüneburg which Anselm had acquired on the outskirts of the town, and if they did not compare with the glittering parties given by Betty in fashionable Paris, they nevertheless attracted such luminaries of the Romantic movement as Mendelssohn and Schumann. Charlotte spared no effort in trying to bring the great and the talented to her table, as Anthony reported on one of his visits:

> . . . I have been to two or three parties, all of which I found very dull and uninteresting, with the exception of one that Charlotte gave last Sunday, when my ears and indeed almost all my other senses were rejoiced by the sound of Rubini's sweet voice. This delightful singer, accompanied by Liszt, was here for a few days and Charlotte took the opportunity of giving a soirée to the *beau monde* of Frankfurt. Liszt was unfortunately engaged and could not play. He was replaced by Dohler, who, though not so wonderful, plays beautifully and above all most agreeably. Rubini and his talented companion gave a further concert the evening before last, where I had an excellent opportunity of hearing and seeing the most extraordinary player in the world. I say *seeing* because he is as curious to look at as to hear, with his long hair at times streaming over his face, at others completely thrown back by a violent toss of the head, his wild eyes, which he now and then turns on every side as if to see what kind of impression he is producing, and his frequent smile which has something unnatural in it, seeming to mean sometimes "Am I not wonderful?", at others that he is delighted with his own performance. Dearest, he is an agreeable, talkative man in society and is no doubt a dear and pleasant companion . . . [25]

Much of Charlotte's time was devoted to bringing up her seven children. They were a lively and talented brood, but the one who really shone was the second daughter, Mathilde. She was the most gifted Rothschild of her generation and she responded well to the cultured atmosphere of her home and the encouragement of her sensitive mother. Mathilde possessed an incredible intellectual grasp of a whole range of subjects and a charm that endeared her to all who met her. Dr Miriam Rothschild, who knew Mathilde in the early years of this century (she died in 1924 at the age of ninety-two) remarked that were she alive today, in an age when women have more opportunities, she would either be a Golda Meir or a great concert pianist. Mathilde was musically brilliant. Like James's daughter, Charlotte, she received lessons from Chopin when she was in her teens. The master was so impressed by her that even during his last illness when he took few pupils he found time for "the Rothschild girl".[26] Mathilde went on to become not only a highly accomplished performer but also a composer of merit. She wrote four volumes of songs and a number of piano pieces all well above the usual amateur standard. Of course, she was destined to become a Rothschild wife and mother. She and her elder sister, Julie, both married sons of Neapolitan Carl. But, in the days before they left their father's house, the Grüneburg was a happy, relaxed family home. So relaxed, indeed, that one small visitor was quite astonished by her first meeting with her cousins: "Julie and Mathilde had very graceful, beautiful figures, and were of most distinguished appearance ... The two sisters were the first female smokers that I had ever come across, and my youthful eyes gazed with astonishment at this masculine indulgence – the ladies were smoking cigars, not even cigarettes ... "[27]

CHAPTER 10

"You remain unmoved"

The Rothschild banks had, as we have seen, been born out of one great upheaval in European history. But no sooner had the family consolidated the position which it had won for itself in the era of the revolutionary wars than it had to come to terms with another period of change and turmoil — this time economic as well as political. Between 1830 and 1848 two phenomena dominated the European stage: an unprecedented economic expansion brought about by unfettered, "grimy-fingered capitalism", and an equally unique upsurge of nationalist, ultra-radical discontent. Fifteen years after Waterloo, much of Europe had once more reached a dangerously volatile state. The concessions made by the old absolute monarchies in 1830, left the extremists far from satisfied. Over the following two decades men continued to gather in student clubs and secret societies to dream and talk about representative government. Among them were Karl Marx and Friedrich Engels who first met in Paris during the 1840s, and who, through discussions with other socialists and rev-olutionaries, created the fusion of ideals, policies and "historical prin-ciples" that emerged as the *Manifest der Kommunistischen Partei*. But at the time the two Germans, despite their later eminence, were no more than two voices among many, unable to make themselves heard above the clamour of radicalism that raged across the Continent. In this atmosphere those in power became ever more nervous about the pos-sibility of revolution. The use of informers and *agents provocateurs* was widespread, and force was frequently invoked to suppress any manifes-tation of anti-monarchism.

In Germany the situation was complicated by rivalry between the traditional authority of the Hapsburg Emperor and the rising power of Prussia. Both paid lip service to the independence of the thirty-nine states which made up the new, loose German Confederation. Yet at the same time both struggled to establish their primacy in Germany, where many people looked back to Napoleon's short-lived Confederation of the Rhine and hoped for the day when the German-speaking peoples might be united in a single nation. Not unnaturally the princes who ruled over the mosaic of tiny statelets fiercely rejected this vision. The Emperor sought to bolster Austria's claims by appealing to his authority as hereditary president of the Confederation; meanwhile the Prussian government, adopting a more practical attitude, continued to gather north German states into its customs union. In 1836 Frankfurt deferred to the inevitable and joined this Deutscher Zollverein, thus buying economic recovery at the cost of economic independence.

Even in Britain the combination of Industrial Revolution, poor harvests and a growing resentment of political inequality led to occasional riots and government instability. Between 1827 and 1841 there were eight changes of administration and the excitement over the Reform Bill in 1831-2 split the nation as no issue had divided it since the Civil War.

Inevitably, as bankers to virtually every government in Europe, the Rothschilds were suspected of manipulating their clients' policies to serve their own ends. We have already seen some of the satires "exposing" this supposed backstairs influence, and discussed the "apolitical" Rothschild stance chosen in the interests of international peace on which their fortune depended. Publicly they had no political opinions, though they could hardly have been expected to sympathise with those who took radicalism too far! Heine related the story of a Communist who wrote to James demanding that the Great Baron share with him his fortune, which he estimated at some three hundred million francs. James made some calculations, presumably based on population figures, and sent the young man his portion — nine sous — with the comment: "Now leave me in peace."

Privately, however, the Rothschilds' attitudes were bound to be more equivocal. It could scarcely be otherwise, for their unique position meant that they were pulled in different directions. As bankers, heavily involved with despotic governments, they had a profound interest in preserving the status quo. As members of an underpriviliged minority they were on the side of egalitarian reform.

On one issue, and one issue only, were they prepared to abandon their stance of political neutrality. In the cause of their co-religionists, as we have already seen, they were ready both to declare their interests and to use the power which their position gave them. In carrying out their crusade they took heart from the situation in Britain, where Jewish leaders had a secure platform of past achievement and general acceptance from which to launch their campaigns.

Two important changes came over the British-Jewish community in the first half of the nineteenth century. First of all many Jews prospered and became middle-class citizens. Immigration fell to a mere two hundred or so per year (it would increase again with the European political upheavals, famines and pogroms after 1848), and at the same time many families moved out of the crowded areas of east London into the provinces and the more fashionable suburbs such as Stoke Newington. It is true that there was still considerable poverty. Fagin had many real-life counterparts. Racial and religious barriers to Jewish advancement still existed and would not be dismantled entirely until the 1870s. But British Jews were freer than most of their co-religionists. The career of Moses Montefiore, N.M.'s brother-in-law, who devoted most of a very long life to the welfare of his people, demonstrated that British society had become relatively open to men of talent and patriotism. He was chosen Sheriff of London and knighted in 1837, and received a baronetcy in 1846.

The other significant development during these years was that the leaders of Anglo-Jewry assumed the leadership of the wider Jewish world. And the success of Anglo-Jewry came to be seen as living proof that assimilation without loss of racial or religious identity was a real possibility: that a Jew could prosper without becoming a convert to Christianity and without being despised and resented by his neighbours. The great families — the Montefiores, Rothschilds, Goldsmids, Cohens and Salomons — were not content to form societies for fostering cultural life and education in their community. Rather, they encouraged their fellow Jews to look across the Channel and seek ways of aiding their less fortunate brethren. To take just one example, Moses Montefiore went personally to St Petersburg in order to persuade Tsar Nicholas to revoke some of Russia's harsh anti-Semitic laws.

The Rothschilds, who either lived or had business in every capital of Europe, were naturally especially conscious of the fact that this was a question which transcended frontiers and nationalities. They were also aware that they could exercise a degree of leverage. One city where, inevitably, their co-religionists suffered under a reactionary regime was Rome. Twice the Vatican approached Carl for loans and on both occasions concessions regarding the treatment of the inhabitants of the ghetto featured in the subsequent agreements. In 1847 Salomon made a direct approach from Vienna: he appealed to the Pope to abolish the tax levied on the Jews at the beginning of Lent every year.

Five years later, in Paris, James made an even more magnificent and lasting gesture. Though circumspect in his social contacts with his co-religionists, he accepted enthusiastically his public rôle as a leader of Jewry. This displayed itself tangibly in the building of a hospital and hospice complex for Jews on Rue Picpus, in a working-class district of Paris, opened, according to L'Univers Israelite, with a three-hour ceremony which "was one of the grandest that Judaism has ever celebrated within its midst".[1] The institution that James built still exists, serving five hundred sick and elderly people (no longer exclusively Jewish). But that is not its only significance: it has also become the cornerstone of a veritable empire of Rothschild benefactions. Later generations were to found homes, a remarkable number of orphanages, hospitals, research establishments and housing projects which would be brought together under one administrative umbrella and known as Les Fondations Rothschild (see pp. 441ff.)

On the other side of the Channel, Hannah, too, was actively involved in many Jewish charities. In particular she maintained her interest in education. N.M. had helped to establish the Jews' Free School, the first of many such seminaries founded in London and the provinces, and his widow maintained the family's interest and support. The community as a whole placed great importance on education. If their young people were to be able to take advantages of the opportunities available to them in Britain it was essential that their minds should be trained. Since virtually all native schools were under the control of the churches, the Jews had no alternative but to create as many places as possible in schools of their own founding. Hannah contributed generously and often to this cause but was not content merely to scatter largesse; she was actively engaged in fund raising. For example, she was an indefatigable organiser of charity concerts and recitals. She approached many celebrated artists to perform at these events, including Jenny Lind, the operatic soprano who made her sensational London début at Her Majesty's Theatre in 1847, and Frédéric Chopin who paid a short visit the following year. But she always expected value for money. "What do you charge?" she asked Chopin. "Twenty-five pounds," the great composer replied. Baroness Rothschild frowned. "Well you certainly play very prettily," she graciously informed him, "but your price is wanting in moderation." And with that she made her exit.[2]

Hannah's heart was readily touched by any human suffering. Like her late husband, she was troubled by the situation in Ireland and when a fund was got up in 1847, the year of the great potato famine, Hannah was among the first to subscribe. It was Lionel and a group of City colleagues who took the initiative in this matter. Appalled by government inaction, they held a meeting at Rothschild's bank on New Year's Day and set up the British Association for the Relief of the Extreme Distress in the Remote Parishes of Ireland and Scotland. The first chairman of the association was Thomas Baring but the real labourers, according to a contemporary, were "Rothschild, Kinnaird [Baron Kinnaird, Whig politician and reformer] and some dozen other merchant princes, meeting every day and working hard".[3] This committee immediately set about gathering information and raising funds. The representative they sent to Ireland soon disposed of any suspicions that the appalling stories reaching London must be exaggerated: "No pen can describe the distress by which I am surrounded. You may now believe anything which you hear and read because what I actually see surpasses what I ever read of past and present calamities."[4]

Within three months, while the British government was still dithering, the association raised £470,000 (two thousand pounds was given by the Queen and a thousand by Rothschilds), and had already distributed £160,000 in the form of food, clothing and fuel. It had also demonstrated a humanitarian concern which crossed all religious barriers, for the committee of the British Association brought together many leading philanthropists including Quakers, Evangelicals and Jews. They all shared a conviction that the wealthy had a responsibility imposed upon them by God for their less fortunate brethren, a responsibility which compelled them to oppose the sort of considerations proffered by one government spokesman: " ... if the Irish once find out that there are any circumstances in which they can get free government grants ... we shall have a system of mendicancy such as the world never saw ... "[5]

At about this time there was in circulation a particularly vicious caricature which, although only repeating an old lie, was grossly unfair in the light of the Rothschilds' ever increasing philanthropic commitments. It shows a figure representing the banking family, sitting on a pile of money sacks and surrounded by the kneeling figures of European kings and princes. Rothschild carefully ponders the problem to whom he will lend money. But the ragged beggars on the fringe of the crowd he ignores completely (see illustration).

In the same year James and his colleagues were doing everything in their power to alleviate suffering in France, another country afflicted by poor harvests. They offered to buy corn and flour abroad and sell it at an uninflated price, bearing any loss themselves. They established a special bakery at Chapelle-St Denis to provide bread for the poor and supplemented this action with a system of bread vouchers for the really destitute. Not that this philanthropy brought the Rothschilds much in the way of public gratitude. James continued to be attacked in the left-wing press for hoarding grain and exploiting the distress of the people for his own devious ends.

However genuine the Rothschilds' concern was for the less fortunate members of society, their principal activity was still finance. In the 1830s and 1840s, under the leadership of the Great Baron, they became bankers on a major scale to the commercial sector. This was the age of the small industrialist and entrepreneur. There was no stopping the proliferation of factories, shops and service trades, the growth of new towns, cities and holiday resorts, or the population shift, which, within two generations, turned an agrarian country like England into a nation of town dwellers. Such developments required finance on a grand scale and they also needed a vast infrastructure: ports, mining areas and centres of production had to be linked by an efficient transport system.

James knew that if the Rothschilds did not take up their share of this business, others would. There was a further consideration: in a time of relative peace, Europe's leading nations had less need of state loans. Ordinary revenue from taxation and customs dues was sufficient to meet government expenditure. Between 1832 and 1839 France issued no public loans and Britain only issued one. If the Rothschild banks were to continue to flourish, it was clear that the emphasis would have to switch from government business to the private sector with its greater risks and longer-term investments.

One day in September 1830 two earnest-looking foreign gentlemen disembarked at Manchester from a carriage of the Liverpool and Manchester Railway Company's train. They made careful notes. They conferred together. They examined the locomotive and the track. They talked with the driver. They attended a long meeting with the directors of the company. They wrote lengthy reports. They then returned to the Continent, one to Paris, the other to Vienna, where their words were studied carefully by James and Salomon de Rothschild. Both brothers realised that, if what the reports said was true, the railway was the transport of the future, and both were anxious to take the lead in introducing it to Europe.

But, at a time when even steam engines were a comparative novelty, building a railway line not only involved financial and technical problems; there were political hurdles to be overcome. In conservative Austria, in particular, the new form of locomotion had been widely ridiculed. The human frame, it was urged, could not stand speeds in excess of fifteen miles per hour. People would suffocate in tunnels. Lives and property would be at risk from out-of-control locomotives. No less terrifying in a Europe increasingly plagued by radical political movements, was the odd but alarming suggestion, seriously canvassed in the press and among courtiers, that these smoke-belching monsters would inflame the passions of the populace — more specifically, that they might help to unite as yet isolated groups of malcontents throughout the large empire.

In France, James was less restricted. Because he was not prepared simply to finance other men's enterprise, he decided to become an industrialist himself. He formed a company to construct an eleven-mile length of track from the Place de l'Europe in Paris to St Germain. Naturally a top-class businessman with some knowledge of engineering would be required to supervise the project. James chose Emile Péreire. Emile and his brother Isaac were great enthusiasts for the "new age" of industrialisation and social progress. In one way they were exactly what James needed and Emile threw himself into the railway project with unstinted zeal.

But there were important differences between the Péreires and the Rothschilds. For one thing, the Péreire family came from Sephardic stock, with basic attitudes that differed fundamentally from those of the Ashkenazi Rothschilds; in addition they were disciples of Claude Henri de Rouvroy, Comte de Saint-Simon, one of the founders of French Socialism. Saint-Simonianism envisaged the abolition of privilege and the creation of a society in which all the means of production – including banking – would be controlled by the state for the common good. Such ideas were anathema to Baron James and, in due course, he would find himself at odds with the Péreires. However, Emile Péreire knew all about railways and, for the present, that was all that mattered.

The line was opened in a ceremony such as only the Rothschilds could mount, on 24 August 1837. The Queen graced the occasion. Marie Amélie and a battalion of notables sat down to a sumptuous luncheon. Crowds gathered to gaze at the incredible iron monster which hurtled towards St Germain at over ten miles per hour. Several of the onlookers had a personal stake in the railway: they had bought many of the five hundred franc shares issued by the company. This was one of the earliest examples in France of small investors being able to acquire part of the equity of a major concern. Since Rothschild held the controlling interest, no one could doubt that his money was safe. Most believed that the prestige of the greatest name in banking assured them of massive profits.

The venture proved a success from the start. France was seized by railway mania. Thousands of people wanted to set up and invest in *chemin de fer* companies. There seemed to be no way that money poured into the new form of transport could fail to realise a handsome profit, and one which would increase year by year as more passengers and freight were carried. Thus, when James and Péreire devised their next scheme – a line from Paris to Versailles along the right bank of the Seine – they found themselves in competition with a company building a similar line on the left bank. The principal of the competing railway was Achille Fould – a converted Jew, a brilliant financier, a member of the Chamber of Deputies and no friend of the Rothschilds. The rivalry between Fould and Baron James was both bitter and personal. From 1836 to 1839, while the competing tracks raced each other to completion along the banks of the Seine, each group of directors did everything in its power to discredit the other. Their weapons were political influence and the press. Both were used freely and with lethal intent.

By this time Salomon, although well advanced in years, had followed his brother's example and taken a pioneering rôle in Austria. As always, he had to reckon with the by now traditional alliance of aristocrats and bankers who did not want to see the Rothschilds become any more powerful than they already were. On the other hand, Salomon had the support of Metternich and others in the government who were determined not to allow Austria to fall further behind the powers who were modernising. He proceeded with his usual caution, first obtaining permission for a freight-carrying railway to bring coal and iron from Galicia into Vienna. Then, after several meetings between financiers and ministers, at which Emile Péreire was among the expert advisers consulted, imperial sanction was given for a complete system of state railways.

Salomon assembled a consortium which successfully applied for a concession to construct the pioneer northern route, the Nordbahn. One member of the company's board was banker Baron George von Sina who put his experience to good use by setting up a rival group which gained the concession for a southern line, to the Adriatic. The two companies were soon engaged in acrimonious competition, each hoping to establish the superiority of its own system and so gain the contract for the rest of the network. First blood went to Salomon when he obtained permission to call his line the Kaiser Ferdinand Nordbahn. Von Sina's counter was vicious but effective. Pamphlets appeared in which it was claimed that Baron von Rothschild was besmirching the imperial dignity. Furthermore, the scurrilous literature claimed his engineers were ignoring safety factors: the Nordbahn would be a death trap. Public concern mounted and the Emperor himself was shaken – perhaps he had been over-eager in lending his name to Rothschild's enterprise. Salomon hit back with a report vindicating the undertaking as the most exciting Austrian venture of the generation.

Von Sina, still a director of the Nordbahn, now demanded a shareholders' meeting at which he challenged Salomon and his supporters to resign. It was a fatal error. Salomon listened in patient silence, then with magisterial calm, a calm born of sixty-five years of combatting hostility and abuse, he played his trump card. If any shareholders were dissatisfied, he told the meeting, he would be more than delighted to buy them out, such was his confidence in the Nordbahn's profit potential. Von Sina suffered a complete and decisive defeat. It was he and his friends, not Salomon, who handed in their resignations.

On 7 July 1839 the Austrian Nordbahn was opened – the Continent's first major railway. But Salomon's ambitions did not stop there. Railway building was, he had discovered, a voracious consumer of iron and steel. So he now sought permission for his company to buy the ironworks at Wittkowitz (modern Vikovice in Czechoslovakia). As soon as this was granted in August 1842, he bought the plant for one and a half million gulden and immediately followed up by seeking the coal and ferrous metal concession throughout a large area of Silesia (a province now bisected by the Polish-Czechoslovak border). This application received the royal assent in December 1842. That same month a major privilege was granted by the Emperor: Salomon was made a citizen of Vienna.* This made the Rothschilds the only Jewish family entitled to own property in the capital. Immediately Salomon bought the old Römischer Kaiser, where he had lived and worked for over twenty years. He completely rebuilt the hotel and the adjoining building and turned them into more suitable business premises. One interesting relic of the old hotel, however, remained. Because of the licence issued to the original establishment, S.M. Rothschild's was the only Viennese bank permitted to sell alcoholic drinks.

Yet still Salomon was not satisfied. In November 1843 he once again addressed himself to the Emperor:

> Since his Royal and Imperial Majesty has graciously given permission to the underwritten humble supplicant to purchase the ironworks of Wittkowitz in Mähren . . . his Royal and Imperial Majesty's devoted servant is emboldened to request permission to buy a private property in Mähren . . . [Should this request be granted] he will undertake the duties of a patron by supporting schools and houses for the poor as he has already demonstrated by building a school at Wittkowitz and providing an endowment for paying the school teacher . . . [6]

Again, the request was granted and Salomon embarked on a veritable spending spree, buying several estates and two castles, one of them the magnificent Schillersdorf in Silesia. Within the space of a few months the Jew whom the Hapsburg establishment had held at arm's length, while gladly making use of the capital he loaned them, became one of the biggest landowners in the empire.

Thus, in the closing years of his life, Salomon's long siege of the court of Vienna was finally concluded. Through exemplary patience, a careful cultivation of his friendship with Metternich and an irresistible spirit of enterprise, he had forced the most reactionary state in Europe to recognise his worth. Through the breach he had made, other Jews would soon follow, thus justifying Salomon's determination to obtain a territorial stake in the empire. For it was a desire to achieve equality of treatment for

---

*The same dignity was conferred on Anselm in 1847.

his people that was his prime motivation. No great stirring of the spirit drew him to beautiful Schillersdorf or cultured Vienna. He spent little time on his country estates and he got away from the Austrian capital whenever possible. He was convinced that the city by the Danube was bad for his rheumatism and other ailments. Whenever he could, he escaped to Paris to be close to James and his beloved Betty. Sometimes other members of the family visited him in his château at Suresnes, on the western edge of the city. A young English Rothschild found Great-Uncle Salomon a curious relic of the past: " . . . we talked German to him and his wife – he calling out *'Gute nacht, Kinderchen'* every night when we went to our beds. He was not long in following us, for his strange habits led him to retire at 8 o'clock in the evening, to go out driving at 5 A.M. in the summer, and at 7 A.M. in the winter."[7]

In September 1844 Salomon attained the age of threescore years and ten. The accomplishment was marked, among other celebrations, by the presentation of a superb, ornate illuminated address from the city of Frankfurt. The cover made for this document (now on display in the Historisches Museum in Frankfurt) is a magnificent example of the gold-smith's art, displaying in immaculate detail the Rothschild coat of arms and various symbols representing Salomon's activities in trade, industry and railways. It was a deserved tribute. Although Salomon had been over-shadowed by his more flamboyant brothers, his achievements were, in some ways, even more remarkable. Nathan and James had established their banks in the capitals of liberal and enlightened states. Salomon's successes, by contrast, had been gained only by steady, persistent pressure against the laws, customs and prejudices of an empire whose attitude towards the Jews was as antiquated as it was unyielding.

The London house had missed the opportunity of taking part in the British railway boom. It was, therefore, obliged to look further afield and become involved in several foreign railway ventures. One such was of particular significance. The Belgian system was probably the best conceived and executed of all the early railways. Here, the government planned the entire network, thus avoiding the piecemeal private development and frantic commercial rivalry which occurred in Britain and elsewhere. The venture was capitalised by a state loan of a hundred and fifty million francs, and because of the government's earlier happy relationship with N.M. Rothschild and Sons it was that bank which received a major part of the business. By 1850 Belgium's railway system, like that of England, was almost complete, while most of France's was still in the planning stage.

With the London bank deeply involved on one side of the frontier and James's railway companies active on the other, it was natural that Rothschild eyes should have alighted on one of the most glaring gaps in the burgeoning system of railways that were spreading across Europe. James and Lionel had in fact long had their eyes on the rich mining areas of northern France and the valleys of the Sambre and the Meuse in neighbouring Belgium. They had financed several concerns which were beginning to realise the industrial potential of the region, including the Sambre-Oise canal, which made Belgian coal much more readily available in Paris, the Société Charbonnière et de Navigation Franco-Belge and various coal mines.

The success of these ventures pointed towards the need for a railway and the Rothschilds were early approached by the Société Générale de Belgique, one of the great pioneer merchant banks, to set up a consortium. Opposition from vested interests and a financial crisis in 1838 caused these plans to be set aside but the northern railway was such an obvious scheme that it could not remain pigeon-holed for long. Other financiers and industrialists were, of course, interested but everyone shrank before the immensity of the task and the uncertainty of the cost. The Rothschilds were certainly not prepared to commit themselves without government involvement and guarantees. For months James lobbied influential members of the administration and so did his rivals. Ministers were divided about whether French railways should be controlled by the state or private enterprise. Not so the Rothschilds. The bankers, who would once have been content to underwrite a government loan for the development, realised that there was much more profit to be derived from a major permanent stake in the enterprise that would manage it.

Various items of piecemeal legislation culminated, in 1842, in a scheme for a complete system of major lines radiating from Paris. The land and property would belong to the state, which would finance all the necessary compulsory purchases and initial costs. The new lines would be exploited for the good of the nation, though sections of the system would be leased to private companies who would be expected to lay track, provide and maintain rolling stock and run an efficient service.

It was agreed that the first railway to be put out to tender would be a Paris-Lille-Valenciennes line with a spur from Lille to the coast at Dunkirk and Calais. Competition for the concession was intense, and James threw himself into the fray with an energy that aroused accusations of sharp practice, bribery and every kind of deceit. But in the end most of his rivals concluded that his financial "muscle" and his influence at court rendered him invincible, and they hastened to join his consortium. In September 1845 the contract was awarded, on a forty-one-year lease, to

133

the Compagnie du Chemin de Fer du Nord. Twenty-five per cent of the capital was held by the Paris and London houses and James, Lionel and Nat were members of the board.

The Chemin de Fer du Nord was to be for several years the brightest jewel in the Rothschilds' commercial crown. It grew into a well-run and immensely profitable railway. But it also brought its headaches. For the first time, members of the family found themselves running a major industrial concern. The experience was not always a happy one.

Much of the work in the early years fell upon Anthony's shoulders and a real burden it proved to be. He had no engineering training and was, therefore, in the hands of experts. Of course, he hired the best — including George Stephenson — but even the best can make mistakes. Sometimes there were accidents. Men were killed. Apart from Anthony's genuine distress, he also had the problem of dealing with shareholders made nervous by such calamities. Then there were large gangs of navvies to employ, qualified engine drivers to be found, land to be bought, and a hundred and one other specialist problems all completely new to the harassed Englishman.

As if these practical problems were not enough, Anthony and Nat had the Great Baron to deal with. James constantly fretted and fumed over the railway. He was obsessed with the Chemin de Fer du Nord. He looked upon it as the crowning achievement of his career. So, while his nephews took care of the nitty-gritty of daily administration, he was constantly overseeing progress and fighting its battles in the political and financial arenas. All this did little to sweeten his temper. But James's worries about "his" railway were soon to be overtaken by even more important concerns. Perhaps because he had been so bound up in the *chemin de fer* boom and in other major industrial commitments, or, perhaps, because he was too close to the Orléans monarchy of Louis Philippe, he failed to see that the advancing storm was about to break. In 1848 the liberal and nationalist aspirations which had been suppressed for over thirty years burst out all over Europe. The Metternich system of alliances which had kept reactionary governments in power collapsed. In the years which followed this year of tumult the institutions which had underwritten that system were shaken to their foundations. Foremost among those institutions were the Rothschild banks of Paris, Vienna, Frankfurt and Naples.

The crisis hit Paris in February 1848 with great suddenness. On the 22nd barricades went up in the streets. On the 23rd royal troops fired on a crowd of demonstrators. On the 24th the elderly King fled to England with his family. Within a week a republic had been declared. In the troubled days that followed, the Rothschilds were, inevitably, among those who received threats to their personal safety and their property. James immediately sent

Betty, Charlotte and three-year-old Edmond, his youngest son, to London, where they stayed with Anthony and Louisa. A few days later their elder brothers were despatched in their wake. But James himself remained to ride out the storm with Nat by his side. Or perhaps it would be more accurate to say that he "ran before the storm" for, as in 1830, James's sole concern was the preservation of his business, and he hastened to welcome the new regime. Ernest Feydeau reported an incident which occurred at the height of the unrest when the revolutionaries

having ransacked the private apartments in the Tuileries, were strutting about in the garden, grotesquely decked out in the shawls and cloaks of the princesses ... and amusing themselves by firing shots in all directions ... Bullets whistled down the Rues de Rivoli and Castiglione and through the Place Vendôme ... Around noon ... I saw two gentlemen, arm in arm, calmly appear out of the Rue de la Paix and move towards the Tuileries, and I recognised one of them as the Baron de Rothschild. I quickly went up to him.

"M. le Baron," I said, "you would seem not to have chosen a very good day for taking a walk. I think it would be better if you returned home rather than expose yourself to bullets whizzing in every direction."

"My young frient," he replied, "I tank you for your hatfice. Put tell me, vy are you here? Isn't it your duty? Vell, I too, de Baron de Rothschild, haf gome for de zame reason. Your duty is to shtand harmt vatch und hassure de zafety of goot zitizens; mine is to go to de Ministry of Finance, to zee vedder dey may not neet my hexperience und my gounzel," and with this he left.[8]

The Baron was interested in the rapid restoration of calm and the resumption of business. His only hope of continuing to play a leading rôle in the financial life of the Republic was to assume a confidence in it which he did not feel and to ingratiate himself with its leaders. Just as in 1830, so in 1848, he contributed generously and publicly to the fund opened for wounded heroes. This time it cost him not fifteen thousand but fifty thousand francs. The new administration was as anxious as the business community to see a speedy return to stability and James soon became involved in talks with ministers, pledging his support in getting the wheels of finance turning again.

But the sang-froid he displayed outwardly covered deep fears and anxieties as is shown in his reply, dated 4 March, to his wife's plea to let her return.

My beloved angel,

I received a letter, my dear angel, that is very dear to me, dated the 2nd, in which you insist upon coming here for a few days. I admit that my heart beats faster, and I'm happy to consent to your promise . . . One never knows what to expect with a republican government. I feel much calmer now. I view the situation as still dangerous. All that we can do here is meet our obligations. I'm taking on new business . . . All that I ask of you is that you obtain a passport under a different name for a round trip. If you bring Alphonse, he too should have a supplementary passport with another name, because I don't want the newspapers to print a headline saying "Madame de Rothschild has returned to London", if you decide to go back there. That would give rise to idle gossip . . . My good Betty, I think we should rent a small house and live in peace . . . Do as your heart dictates. Come, and bring Alphonse, although I wonder whether we shouldn't keep him out of politics. If they see him, he'll be required to enlist in the National Guard. He may come if he lies low . . . [9]

Well might James talk of going into humble retirement. In those heady, egalitarian days there were wild rumours of banks and railways being nationalised and property shared. A measure of calm was soon restored to the capital, but gangs of ruffians and looters still roamed the provinces and the family looked on with horror and foreboding as violence spread across national frontiers.

But not all members of the family regarded the disturbance with unalloyed dismay. In liberal — and relatively safe — England, Anthony's wife could write in her diary, "It is impossible to think of or occupy oneself with anything but this wonderful revolution." She shared her husband's concern for his family but confessed to a "simple indifference, or, rather, dislike to grandeur and display". If the success of democratic revolution called upon her to adopt a simple life style she would, she said, be perfectly content. "I feel that I could bear up very well with a change of fortune, but Anthony's distress takes away all my courage." [10] However, as the year rolled on and reports of fresh outrages reached her from all over Europe she, too, joined the chorus of despair: "The description of the fury and cruelty of these new revolutionists is appalling and seems to show that civilisation — that civilisation of the nineteenth century of which we were so proud — was only on the surface of society and had left untouched the fierce, rugged hearts of the lower classes." [11]

The men of the family could not be so detached. They spent the remainder of the year travelling from house to house, conferring, transferring funds, holding talks with the new politicians thrown up by the mob, preserving whatever they could from the chaos and praying for better days.

In mid-March the revolution spread to Austria and Germany. On the 13th Metternich was sacrificed in the hope of preserving the regime. He fled Vienna in disguise, having first had to borrow from Salomon the money he and his family needed for their flight to England. The Baron was happy to oblige his old friend; a thousand ducats loaned to the fallen Chancellor was a small matter. But in terms of major finance the Viennese house was in a mess. It was caught up in a banking crisis of major proportions and was in danger of collapsing as suddenly and completely as the Metternich ministry. Salomon, perhaps a victim of his own good nature, had helped other financiers and, as a result, now found himself over-extended.

Anselm hurried back to Vienna to try to resolve the problems. By dint of patient effort and close liaison with London he managed to bring order out of chaos. The effect of all this financial and political upheaval on Salomon and Amschel was catastrophic. Everything they had worked so hard to build seemed to be collapsing back into the revolutionary morass from which it had emerged in their distant youth. Salomon was intensely depressed. Amschel, who never needed a crisis to panic, was in a frenzy. Financially, the situation of the Frankfurt house was not desperate. Widespread alarm had, inevitably, brought the value of securities tumbling and caused a run on gold. Amschel was hard-pressed* and responded with bitter recriminations against the other Rothschild houses for not coming to his aid with funds. But he and his brothers had ridden out such crises before and, as Anselm doubtless argued, there was no reason why they should not ride out this one, as long as they all kept their heads.

Yet a mob on the rampage is an ugly sight. In those troubled March days, and the worse riots which followed in May, old Amschel might well have seriously feared that the establishment must collapse before the forces of revolution. A relative, visiting from England, vividly described the atmosphere in a letter home:

---

*He was not too preoccupied, however, to help out two young nephews who had speculated unwisely. George and Anthony Worms had bought five hundred pounds' worth of nominal Spanish International Stock, planning to sell at a profit on a rising market before account day. But the market fell and they could not pay. In desperation they appealed to Uncle Amschel. "I went to his house on the Ziel and told him the whole story," George noted. "He laughed at our dilemma. He said, 'You draw a bill for the whole amount wanted on your father. I will give you the money for it. You pay for the Spanish stock and send the bond by registered letter to your father.' We did and the affair was settled." [12]

On Saturday a deputation of respectable persons went to the Senate, assembled in the Romer, with a petition signed by upwards of 20 thousand persons *requesting* (they said if you don't give what we ask we will take it) the 8 following articles: liberty of the press, pardon for all political offenders, trial by jury, German parliament, civil and religious liberty, open Courts of Law, and permission to carry arms. A crowd of at least 7 to 8 thousand persons followed, shouting tremendously. They assembled before the Palais de Justice at 4 p.m. making an awful noise, at five o'clock the Senate granted the two first articles but refused the others until they had consulted with the other states of the Confederation. The people refused to allow the Senate to depart unless they gave them all they wanted, and about 6 a large body rushed into the building and actually entered the Council Chamber but were repulsed by the National Guard. The alarm was then sounded and all the soldiers turned out. A body of about 400 of the National Guard marched in front of the palace and 500 of the line, and 100 cavalry behind it in order of battle. The people climbed up and planted the republican flag — red, black and gold — in front of the edifice. It was instantly pulled down. The mob remained till 1 in the morning there, when it came to a crisis. They were charged with the bayonettes and 2 or 3 wounded and 40 made prisoners. Yesterday at 6 a.m. *all* the citizens of F'furt were under arms, making 15 or 16,000 armed men. A body of National Guards took possession of the Romerberg, planted 5 field pieces there and held it in their power. More than 1000 men were there all day. Bodies of men paraded the streets with guns and swords. All the gates closed and nobody permitted to enter (but citizens) without being examined; all those who had weapons about them instantly imprisoned; at every corner of the streets 2 sentinels with loaded guns and the Senate issued a request that all citizens or foreigners wishing to shew their desire to keep the peace should wear on their left arm a white and red band. (I and Tony of course wore them). At night every street was guarded by troops and nobody save those who wore such bands could pass under any pretence; all persons shouting or howling instantly arrested and those who resisted shot on the spot (only one man was shot). In the evening it was the most beautiful sight I ever beheld, torches everywhere and nothing but soldiers, foot and horse, passing and repassing everywhere. The Senate wanted to have 5000 Austrians but the Citizens undertook to defend the town and well they did it. I assure you, everything remained quiet. The reason of all these precautions was that on Saturday, when some one asked what they wanted with their *Freiheit* they answered, *Geld, Blut.*

Had such severe measures not been taken we should have certainly had here worse scenes than in Paris, every house would have been plundered and burnt and God knows what, but, thank God, all is now right ... [13]

Such relief was premature. The rebels kept up their pressure in the main German centres. Berlin was the first to crack. Frederick William IV of Prussia granted a liberal constitution and promised to put himself at the head of a united German nation. There were fresh riots in many places, including Frankfurt, where Amschel suffered no worse indignity than having his windows broken (smashing "Old Rothschild's" windows seems to have been a ritual reaction whenever there was unrest in the city). A meeting of the Federal Diet was fixed for 18 June to draw up a constitution for the new Germany, whereupon Amschel, like James, hastened to associate himself with the country's new masters.

Once again, the pragmatic Rothschilds were able to divorce their actions from their feelings. Privately, they had nothing but contempt for the undisciplined egalitarians. This contempt was reinforced when a mob armed with hatchets and other crude weapons broke into Salomon's Paris château, broke up the furniture, slashed the old masters, then set fire to the wreckage. Patrician sensibilities, particularly those of the younger men, were outraged by the demagogues and uncouth leaders who were the heroes of the hour. But, as James's eldest son, Alphonse, observed with cynical resignation, "The workers are our masters; we might as well get used to it."[14]

Though outwardly calm, the Great Baron lacked the twenty-one-year-old's resilience. He was still desperately concerned for his family. Alphonse had calmly taken his place in the National Guard, and Gustave (nineteen) was eligible for service whenever he returned to France. Their father spent sleepless nights worrying about them. Eventually, he decided to act:

> I don't want to wait until the National Guard may be obliged to go into action, with Alphonse having to fight other young men. As a father, I want to avoid all these uproars. What's more, I'm not all that much of a republican. This is why I've decided to send him to America; all the more willingly since Nathaniel thinks it could be useful for our business. The only problem is that he's still a bit young, and I think someone as resolute and efficient as Mayer ought to accompany him ... I want Alphonse to leave Paris quickly, and I also want him to begin working seriously and to become a man.[15]

In fact it was another five months before Alphonse took ship for America (see pp. 180ff.). In the meantime he and his brother were sent to Frankfurt out of harm's way.

From the business point of view things continued to look black. Serious plans were made to nationalise the railways, and James combined with several banking colleagues to oppose them firmly. But this proved to be the last attack on property in France. Everyone was growing tired of the extremists, and their brief exercise of power was almost over. In June the army and the National Guard were turned out against the rabble. The result was a blood bath known to history as the "June Days". The lower orders and their Socialist leaders were put in their place. Schemes for nationalisation and wealth redistribution were buried, and James's optimism returned:

> If order can be restored permanently, confidence will revive. The Chamber of Deputies and the government will at last understand that power can be exercised only with force. I think that will do a lot of good for all governments . . . It will no longer be possible to seize the railways . . . I think the whole world will benefit from what has happened here. Everything, everywhere, will change for the better . . . [16]

Certainly it seemed that the aspirations of liberals, embryo-Communists and nationalists had been frustrated, largely by their inability to agree among themselves. At Frankfurt rival factions squabbled and threw away the initiative they had grasped. Risings in several parts of Italy failed, and Austria, despite its own political problems, laboured to strengthen the resolve of all the monarchical governments which came under threat. But there were serious alarms at the centre of the empire before the crisis passed. It was in Vienna that the last outburst of savagery occurred, in the autumn. It created the worst situation any of the houses faced and it drove Salomon finally from the scene of his triumphs. An army mutiny on 6 October led to an attack on the War Office where the War Minister, Count Latour, had taken refuge. The unfortunate man was dragged out and murdered. The court and the government fled and the rebels were left in command of the city. It was twenty-five days before imperial forces reasserted control. During that time the mob went on the rampage, seizing and ransacking, among other buildings, Salomon's headquarters in Renngasse. The Baron and his son hid and, as soon as they could escape, took carriage for Frankfurt. Anselm only returned four weeks later when order had been restored. Salomon eventually settled permanently in Paris, where he spent his few remaining years.

In all their centres, the Rothschilds survived. "In Paris everyone is ruined", an English observer reported. "The bankers are tumbling one after the other. Rothschild alone stands erect, albeit bled white."[17] There were two reasons why the family survived yet another major crisis. The first was that combination of huge financial resources, solidarity and flexibility which had always undergirded their position. The gold and the brains of London, Paris, Naples, Frankfurt and Vienna were pooled to ensure that those banks under pressure received all the help they needed. The other reason was that the new regimes could not allow the Rothschilds to go under, for such a widespread collapse would only lead to financial catastrophe. Thus, for example, at the height of the crisis the republican ministers in Paris renegotiated with James a recent government loan.

The prospect of Rothschild wealth and power standing rock-like while the waves of revolution beat vainly against it filled many observers with awe. Throughout the upheavals of 1848 few public figures had stood so outwardly calm and resolute as the Great Baron — James de Rothschild. Little wonder that he was widely regarded as a phenomenon of the age. Those who had always admired him now had fresh cause to do so. Those who hated him henceforth did so with a more concentrated vigour. Many looked at him with frank amazement. Even the radical editor of the *Tocsin des Travailleurs* could not prevent his sarcasm being tinged with reluctant respect:

> You [James] are a wonder, sir. Louis Philippe has fallen, Guizot has disappeared, the constitutional monarchy and parliamentary methods have gone by the board; you, however, are unmoved! . . . Where are Arago and Lamartine? They are finished, but you have survived. The banking princes are going into liquidation and their offices are closed. The great captains of industry and the railway companies totter. Shareholders, merchants, manufacturers, and bankers are ruined *en masse*; big men and little men are alike overwhelmed; you alone amongst all these ruins remain unaffected. Although your House felt the first violence of the shock in Paris, although the effects of revolution pursue you from Naples to Vienna and Berlin, you remain unmoved in the face of a movement that has affected the whole of Europe.[18]

But those who looked deeper saw that significant changes had taken place, changes from which not even the Great Baron was immune.

CHAPTER 11

"If they admitted Jews, where would they stop?"

Life in Britain during the 1830s and 1840s was more tranquil than on the Continent. For Nathan's successors at New Court it was as well that this was so. Lionel and his brothers lacked their father's flair for business and his total dedication to it. Lionel, Anthony and Nat were certainly thrown in at the deep end as a result of Nathan's early death, and their frequent summonses to Paris did little to help the smooth running of New Court. Yet, over the years, they and their younger brother Mayer, known as "Muffy", came to exercise an influence in Britain even greater than that of N.M. It was a different kind of influence, based not on sheer financial strength and force of character, but on their political and social standing as English gentlemen, a standing which they were specifically urged by their mother to make their paramount objective.

Hannah was as English as she was Jewish and she inculcated into Nathan's children a real sense of national identity and pride. She was also extremely ambitious for her sons. She it was who encouraged them to mix with the *haut monde* and to use the title of "Baron" their father had shunned, who entered Muffy at Cambridge, who advised her sons to acquire country estates, who urged them to play an active rôle in politics and generally to take up their "birthright" as members of a British élite.

In some respects her efforts to ensure that her children were assimilated into English society, succeeded almost too well. Hannah Mayer, as we have seen, caused a family scandal by marrying into the Gentile aristocracy. Nat, and to a lesser extent, Charlotte and Louise, never really settled in their foreign homes. Charlotte even transmitted her love of her motherland to her family: two of her children (Ferdinand and Alice) moved permanently to their mother's country when they grew up (see pp. 225ff.).

They were not alone in regarding Britain as a haven of peace and toleration. On the Continent, where minorities had to resort to intrigue, violent demonstration and periodic revolution to achieve a greater say in the running of their own lives, many people looked enviously at Britain as the home of liberalism and a model of gradual evolution towards a politically free society.

But, of course, much of this was an illusion; Britain was no utopia. Social and religious distinctions divided the nation and minority groups, including the Jews, still had many battles to fight for the attainmemt of equal rights. For example, entry to the professions, higher education and political life was controlled by the established church. For almost 170 years all positions of power and influence had been closed to any who were not communicant members of the Church of England, or would not subscribe to its Thirty-Nine Articles of Religion or were by conscience debarred from swearing an oath to uphold the Christian faith "in the form by law established". In the era of the Reform Bill there was a liberal ground swell against such anomalies. Protestant Dissenters gained emancipation in 1828 and their Roman Catholic counterparts the following year (partly, it must be admitted, as a result of the government's fear of revolt in Ireland if the reform was denied).

So, when the Jews sought similar privileges, few of them could have envisaged a long-drawn-out struggle against entrenched forces of reaction. Initially all seemed set fair and when, in the spring of 1830, Jewish communities throughout the country organised support for a Jewish disabilities bill, they received considerable backing from Gentile friends and neighbours. For example, a petition in London attracted fourteen thousand signatures and another in Liverpool secured twenty thousand. There was considerable respect for the thirty-five thousand Jews living in Britain. As we have already seen, many of them had prospered and joined the ranks of the middle class, thanks, in some part, to the newly established Jewish schools. To many Englishmen it seemed self-evident that such responsible citizens deserved the same rights as their Christian neighbours.

But when the bill reached Westminster the going became harder. It was first introduced by Robert Grant, a prominent Whig MP, as a private member's bill; but Wellington, the Prime Minister, refused to give it government backing and this resulted in it being defeated on its second reading. Undeterred, Grant brought the measure back into the house in 1834 during the Whig administration led by Lord Grey. It passed with a huge majority in the Commons but was thrown out by the predominantly Tory House of Lords. A similar fate befell bills introduced in 1835 and 1836. Unfortunately, the Jews lost their leading parliamentary champions when Grant took up his appointment as Governor of Bombay in 1835 and the veteran Whig peer, Baron Holland, died in 1840. Yet it was not only Whigs and radicals who supported the concept of Jewish political freedom. Nor was it only clergy and reactionary aristocrats who opposed it. Among those who rejected the suggested reform were leading progressives such as Lord Shaftesbury, the great reformer, and Thomas Arnold, radical headmaster of Rugby. The latter wrote to a friend in 1836:

143

I want to take my stand on my favourite principle, that the world is made up of Christians and non-Christians; with all the former we should be one, with none of the latter. I would pray that distinctions be kept up between Christians and non-Christians. Then I think that the Jews have no claim whatever to political right . . . the Jews are strangers in England, and have no more claim to legislate for it than a lodger has to share with the landlord in the management of his house.[1]

There were other levels than the national one at which progress for the Jews came more easily. One involved the government of the City of London. Here the protagonists were helped by the liberal sentiments prevalent within the business community and the emergence of several Jewish men of outstanding ability who were held in considerable esteem. The first barricade to be stormed was the office of Sheriff of London. In 1835 David Salomons, a founder governor of the London and Westminster Bank, was elected to that office. This led to a head-on confrontation with Jewish disability because the new incumbent was required to take a Christian oath. To escape an absurd situation a sheriff's declaration act was quickly passed through parliament. Salomons thus became the first English Jew to hold a political office. Round One to the reformers.

Round Two went to the establishment. Salomons' request to take his seat as newly elected Alderman for Aldgate ward without the traditional oath was rejected on appeal. Over the next few years Jews were elected to serve on several provincial corporations and in many cases the local authorities ignored the law which would have prevented them from taking their seats. In 1841 the Jewish lobby secured the presentation of a bill which would have allowed such councillors to swear an amended oath. When this was defeated, feelings in the London business community ran high, particularly as it prevented Jews sitting on the Common Council, the City's elected administrative body. In the general election of the same year the elder Rothschild brothers and their friends campaigned on behalf of the Whigs (or Liberals as they were now coming to be called). The Conservatives, led by Sir Robert Peel, were successful but, as J.C. Herries (whose recent defeat at the hustings had removed him from the political arena for the first time in forty years) warned the new Chancellor of the Exchequer, the party had alienated a powerful group of men.

It may be as well to bear in mind that the said gentry may not be so propitious to you as in former times. The part which Jones, Lloyd, Sam Gurney and the Rothschilds, etc., took in the City elections indicates no kind feeling towards the Conservative party.[2]

The point was well taken. When a fresh attempt was made to introduce legislation in 1845 it had government support and was successful. Immediately Jews took their place on the governing bodies of the City, Salomons becoming an alderman in 1847 and Lord Mayor in 1855. "Thank goodness," a bishop is supposed to have observed to the Prince Consort, "we've got a gentleman in the civic chamber, at last." "Yes," Albert replied, "but you had to go beyond the pale of Christianity to find him."[3]

In August 1847 there was another general election and the campaign leaders decided to apply to parliament the same tactics that had proved so successful when applied to other representative bodies. They encouraged prominent Jews to enter the contest. David Salomons stood as a Liberal for Greenwich. It was his third appearance on the hustings. The electors of Shoreham (1837) and Maidstone (1841) had presumably concluded that it was pointless giving their votes to a candidate who would be unable to take his seat. At Beverley in Yorkshire, Sir Isaac Goldsmid, an elderly London financier much of whose life had been devoted to the cause of Jewish emancipation, occupied the Liberal platform. Two Rothschilds joined the fray. Mayer stood for the Kent seat of Hythe and Folkestone and in the City of London one of the Liberal candidates was the head of the family, Lionel de Rothschild.

Lionel and his brothers had for many years been active in the cause of political emancipation but hitherto they had worked behind the scenes. Yet, the idea of standing for parliament was not a new one in the family. In 1841 Anselm had written from Vienna commenting on the English political scene, "I hope in a year or two to be able to congratulate one of you on a seat in parliament".[4] "A seat in parliament" — that was what Lionel and Mayer now wanted *for its own sake.* "A seat in parliament" was part of the birthright of the wealthy English gentleman and they were determined that wealthy Jewish gentlemen should share it. Just as Salomon had recently won landowning rights for Austrian Jews, so his English relatives were determined to achieve political rights for Anglo-Jewry. Neither Lionel nor Muffy was an avid party member. They sought no forum for the advancement of passionately held political convictions. As for their responsibilities to society, they discharged them already as landowners, employers, patrons and generous supporters of charity. They did not need a public arena in which to air their views. Indeed, Lionel shunned publicity as far as he could.

This does not mean, of course, that they had no political opinions. Like all leading Jews, they were Liberals, because the Liberal party was the party of constitutional reform and minority rights. Muffy (sometimes also called "Tup", a reference to his virility — "tup" is northern dialect for a ram) was the more ardent of the two. His political convictions had, probably, been forged during his Cambridge days and he was regarded as

145

the "radical" of the family. It is interesting that in 1841, long before his own experience of the Paris mob, Nat commented about his twenty-three-year-old brother, "I never was much of a Vig, like old Tup, and I must say that I am now rather more of a Tory than when I was in London. I don't like levellers and destructives."[5]

In 1847 Mayer was only twenty-nine but already he was stocky of build, and jovial with it. Indeed, he might have modelled for a painting of John Bull. That would have been appropriate for he was, in many ways, the most English member of the family and spent the greater part of his life as a gentleman farmer, breeding pedigree cattle, hunting and horse racing. "Muffy" was the most amiable of men and was universally liked. He was a born diplomat, with a gift for understanding how other people felt and responding accordingly. He was one of the few younger Rothschilds who could handle the Great Baron, and was something of a favourite with the old man. As we have already seen, it was Mayer whom James regarded as a suitably "resolute and efficient" person to accompany Alphonse to America. The connections established by his father with the Cullens and other families of the Kent coast were maintained by Mayer. In 1847, for example, he helped to negotiate a loan for the improvement of Dover harbour. It is, therefore, not surprising that the electors of Hythe and Folkestone should have invited him to contest their seat, even though it would have been impossible for him to take his place in parliament if he had been successful. Mayer lost the contest, but Lionel fared differently and it was upon him alone that the hopes of British Jewry were now pinned.*

Lord John Russell, the Liberal leader, knew what was in Lionel's mind. It may have been to encourage him that, soon after becoming Prime Minister in 1846, he recommended the banker for a baronetcy. To the dismay of Lionel's friends and many members of his family, he turned the honour down. His mother was alarmed. "A personal compliment from the highest personage should be esteemed and may lead to other advantages, but to repudiate it might create anger."[6] If Lionel was anxious to improve the lot of his fellow Jews, he did not seem to be going the right way about it. Such arguments were urged upon him, but Lionel was a proud and stubborn man and the more insistent his critics became the more rigorous grew his resolve.

He seems to have had two motives for declining a title. First, he was already an Austrian baron and felt that he could not accept a mere baronetcy. There could be no question of an English peerage. Even if the government had taken the unprecedented step of admitting a Jew to the

*David Salomons and Sir Isaac Goldsmid were also unsuccessful.

aristocracy, Lionel would have had to decline the offer, for the ceremony of installation involved swearing a Christian oath and this, clearly, Lionel would not do. If Lionel had accepted the lesser honour he would, in his own eyes at least, have been acquiescing in a system which discriminated against Jews. The second reason was that the other Jewish baronetcies had been created in recent years for men Lionel appears to have considered his inferiors. Lionel canvassed the opinions of the family. His mother counselled, "The previous granting to the two other gentlemen, I think, has nothing to do with yours and decidedly does not reduce the compliment. This is my opinion. Excuse my candour."[7] And Cousin Anselm urged, "it does not at all matter that others, not so worthy of it, were favoured with it before you".[8]

Who, then, were these men who were so base that Lionel would not lower himself to be associated with them? The fact is that they were the two most distinguished "elder statesmen" in the ranks of English Jewry and had given years of devoted service to their community. Sir Isaac Goldsmid was sixty-nine, a founder of University College, London (the only establishment where Jews could obtain a degree until 1871), the prime mover of the first Jewish disabilities bill, a generous supporter of charities and a reformer who numbered Elizabeth Fry and Robert Owen among his friends and fellow workers. His extensive financial operations on behalf of the Portugese government had recently won him the title of Baron de Palmeira. The other recent baronet was Sir Moses Montefiore (sixty-three) Lionel's own uncle. He had been a business partner with Nathan Rothschild in many ventures, most notably the Alliance Insurance Company. Sir Moses had travelled widely on missions to improve the lot of Jews in Russia and the Levant. He served with Lionel on the Board of Jewish Deputies, the body which represented the interests of all British Jews. What objections could thirty-eight-year-old Lionel possibly have had to these two old and respected leaders?

The answer is to be found in the divisions within Anglo-Jewry. The process of assimilation created tensions within Jewish society. Some welcomed it. Some feared it. We have already seen the different attitudes taken by members of the Rothschild family. It is not surprising, then, that the issue of political emancipation split English Jews into rival camps and that feelings within those camps were, at times, very bitter. Broadly speaking, there were three factions: radicals, moderates and reactionaries.

The radicals were for all-out assimilation, as a people. Anything less than complete equality they regarded as a slur on their race. They dismissed objections based on religious and cultural arguments as obscurantist, and generally tended to play down Jewish distinctiveness. The more extreme radicals were prepared to use a wide range of tactics to

147

achieve their objective — rallies, demonstrations, political lobbying and, if necessary, unconstitutional action.

The reactionaries wanted to preserve purity of faith and tradition by remaining separate from Gentile society. They would have agreed with Thomas Arnold that Jews and Christians were different and that any attempt to interfere with this arrangement was flying in the face of providence. Assimilation could only mean compromise and was, therefore, to be resisted. For example, how could a devout Jew assume a public office which would involve attending public functions on the Sabbath or sitting at meal tables where non-kosher food was served?

Between these two extremes lay the moderate majority which, like all majorities, was pragmatic rather than doctrinaire. While in no way rejecting the basic tenets of their faith or their valued traditions, members of this group believed that concessions could be gradually won by persuading the establishment that the emancipation cause was a just one. They rejected, on the one hand, extremist tactics which would tend to alienate public opinion and, on the other, exclusivism which might also have that effect.

The English Rothschilds belonged, quite definitely, to this last group. Goldsmid and Montefiore did not. Sir Isaac was a radical who consorted with Socialists like Robert Owen and other extremists. Sir Moses was a member of the strict Sephardic sect which disapproved strongly of any laxity or compromise where orthodox beliefs and practices were concerned, and who had even become estranged from his own brother following an argument over religion. Lionel probably felt that each man, in his own quite different way, reflected undesirable aspects of Anglo-Jewry and that they certainly did not merit public recognition by the Crown. To accept a baronetcy would, inevitably, be to associate himself with Goldsmid and Montefiore and to constitute with them a kind of triumvirate of Jewish leadership. This idea was so repugnant to him that, despite the almost unanimous urgings of the family, he would not be moved. He did, however, eventually yield to Anthony's suggested compromise: if the head of the family would not accept the honour why not let one of his brothers do so? Thus it was that the second of N.M.'s sons became Sir Anthony de Rothschild Bart., with reversion of the title to Lionel's male descendants.

For his part, Lionel was soon preoccupied with the parliamentary contest. He was not an enthusiastic public speaker, but he took electioneering seriously and addressed his audience, not just on the subject of Jewish civil rights, but on justice for all minorities and a whole range of Liberal policies. On the hustings, of course, he had to take his fair share of heckling, some of which could be cruel. On one occasion Lionel boasted

148

to the crowd that he stood as the free choice of the people. From somewhere in the sea of faces before him came the gruff comment, "So stood Barabbas."[9] In the City of London there were four parliamentary seats and Lionel's fellow Liberals included the Prime Minister himself, Lord Russell. When the votes were counted Russell's men came out clearly in the lead over their rivals and Lionel de Rothschild was placed third in the poll with 6792 votes. The first British Jew had been elected to the House of Commons. Congratulations poured in from the family and community leaders at home and abroad. In her excitement, Aunt Betty abandoned her usual elegance of expression for a welter of mixed metaphor: "Hope is lighting up all Europe and from every corner the echo sounds, carrying far the seed of this new era now approaching on a wider horizon."[10]

Salomon wrote from Vienna to convey the congratulations of many friends, including "Uncle" Metternich. He passed on the Prince's opinion that parliament would not hesitate to ratify Lionel's election.[11]

Many English observers probably shared Metternich's optimistic assessment. A Jew, having been constitutionally elected by the good burgesses of the capital city, and enjoying the personal support of the Prime Minister, could surely not be barred from taking his seat. But those who moved in influential circles in Britain knew the strength of the anti-Semitic lobby and the phobias and prejudices it nursed. The magazine *Punch* lampooned the opponents of Jewish representation by informing its readers of certain rumours supposedly current in Westminster. These suggested that Baron Rothschild, if admitted, would immediately introduce bills prohibiting the importation of German ham, restricting the marketing of pigs, and limiting private commercial enterprise.[12]

Ridicule aside, there was one serious obstacle to Lionel entering the House of Commons. This was the procedure for admission, which involved the swearing of Christian oaths. To deal with this difficulty the Prime Minister personally introduced a new disabilities bill in December. It was designed to allow Jews to swear a different form of the oath. In these memorable Commons debates Gladstone, Disraeli and Peel were among those who spoke in favour of the motion. Meanwhile public demonstrations of support were organised by a subcommittee of the Board of Deputies gathered in Lionel's office at New Court. Meetings were held throughout the country and a petition containing a quarter of a million signatures was presented to the government. The bill passed its second reading in the Commons in February.

But the real opposition, as everyone knew, was in the upper chamber. Lionel and his supporters were desperately concerned with the outcome of the Lords debate. For weeks Lionel could think of little else. So desirable

149

was the end for which he was contending that he was prepared to consider any means to achieve it — including bribery. He wrote anxiously to Paris asking for advice. Did they approve? Would they help finance the stratagem or should he look to friends and well-wishers? Nat and James discussed the matter very carefully. Lionel's brother, appalled at the corruption in French political life, hated the thought of Westminster going the same way. However,

> on this occasion our worthy uncle and your servant are of opinion
> that we must not be too scrupulous, and if it be necessary to ensure
> the success of the measure we must not mind a sacrifice. We cannot
> fix the *amount*; you must know better what is required than we do. I
> hope that, as you say, half the amount will suffice. At all events our
> good uncle has authorised me to write that he will take it upon
> himself to satisfy all the family that whatever you do is for the best
> and that you may put down the *sum* to the house. I . . . do not see
> how you can propose a subscription to your friends. On what plea?
> And what do you suppose they will give? If only a trifle it will not be
> worthwhile. If, on the other hand, they will cash up and not ask for
> particulars, of course, I would take their money . . . [13]

If the Rothschilds did indeed resort to this "sacrifice" of cash and principle it availed them nothing. The alliance of bishops and Tories, who had already seen the interrelation of Church and State weakened by the admission of "dissenters" and "papists", unhesitatingly drew the line at opening parliament to the unbaptised. As the Bishop of London declaimed, "If you destroy the groundwork of Christianity upon which the legislature is based, in order to gratify for a time a handful of ambitious men, you will destroy Christian England." [14] Their lordships threw out the bill by 163 votes to 125.

The emancipation campaigners were stunned. *The Jewish Chronicle* compared Bishop Wilberforce to a Spanish inquisitor whose words savoured "more of the superstition and a spirit of persecution than of true religion". [15] The City electors stood by Rothschild, content for the sake of principle, to disfranchise themselves. When there was another by-election the following summer the Tory candidate was received at the hustings with shouts and catcalls, while Lionel, speaking for the Liberal candidate, was cheered to the echo. This support strengthened the Baron for the fray. He now determined to fight to the end, though he can hardly have foreseen that that end was still a whole decade away.

In 1849 Russell tried to get another form of oaths bill through parliament. Louisa, Lady de Rothschild, watched the debate.

Lord John made a very clear, earnest speech, and Mr Gladstone delivered a fine, silvery-toned one in our favour. Seven oppositionists attacked it, but not very brilliantly and *Disi* [Disraeli] was silent. Mrs Disi was right when she spoke of the changes that friendship undergo. Last year he was our warmest champion — and now!*[16]

This bill met the same fate as its predecessor. Following its defeat Lionel resigned his seat and then immediately contested the resulting by-election. The City electors entered into the spirit of the thing. They re-elected Lionel by 6017 votes to 2814, throwing down the gauntlet in no uncertain fashion to the House of Lords.

This decision may need some explanation, for no body of freeborn Englishmen ever disenfranchised themselves without good reason. Doubtless the national predilection for supporting the underdog has something to do with it, but there were other more important reasons for the encouragement the Liberal candidate received. For the City electors Lionel de Rothschild stood as a symbol of all that was best in English society. As a businessman his reputation for integrity and reliability was unimpeachable. He had taken over from his brilliant but maverick father and turned N.M. Rothschild and Sons into a solid, conservative financial institution. But he was also a national figure. The memory of his inauguration of the fund for the relief of Ireland was still fresh in people's minds. More recent was the support that he and his family had given to the Great Exhibition project. The scheme, under the active patronage of Prince Albert, to put the technical achievements of Britain and her empire on proud display to the world needed a guarantee of £180,000. Rothschilds had not hesitated to pledge fifty thousand. The Jewish family had become a national institution. The thought of the head of this family being debarred from parliament was monstrous.

In July 1850 Lionel decided to see what would happen if he presented himself to take his seat. In correct manner he approached the table bearing the Commons mace. The clerk rose to administer the oath. Members on both sides waited eagerly for the outcome. People in the packed gallery leaned forward. They heard Lionel's grave, distinct voice. "I wish to be sworn upon the Old Testament." Uproar. Lionel was asked to withdraw and quietly did so. A heated debate ensued at the end of which it was agreed to let Lionel swear as he wished. There were in fact three oaths to be sworn and it was the third which contained the phrase "upon the true faith of a Christian". Slowly, deliberately, Lionel repeated the words of the clerk — until the offending affirmation was reached. "I

*See p. 157ff. for Disraeli's relationship with the Rothschilds.

151

omit these words", the new member stated, "as not binding on my conscience." The Speaker once more asked Mr de Rothschild to withdraw. He had no option. And this time the Commons could not agree to amend their rules.

The following year was marked by the defeat of yet another disabilities bill in the Lords and, paradoxically, the first speech by a Jew in the Commons. David Salomons had won a by-election in Greenwich and duly presented himself in the House. He took the same stance as Lionel on the oaths and was asked to withdraw. At this point an MP stood and demanded to know whether the government would prosecute Salomons if he took his seat. The question caused some confusion on the Treasury Bench and did not receive an answer until the debate was resumed three days later. Then Russell calmly replied that the government would not contemplate legal action if such an unlikely incident occurred. Thereupon, amidst scenes of uproar such as even the Commons has rarely seen, Salomons marched in and took up a place in the opposition back-benches. During the heated and confused debate which ensued he was actually called upon by the Speaker to address the House, and did so. His behaviour cost him a fine of five hundred pounds and lost him his seat at the next election,* but it added useful publicity to the emancipation campaign.

The general election of 1852 found Lionel back at the hustings to defend a seat he had held for five years without spending a single moment on the Commons benches. This proved to be the crisis point of the campaign. There was a swing of opinion towards the Tories and many City voters had tired of being unrepresented. Lionel was fearful of the result but, at the count, it was discovered that he had been returned though with a greatly reduced majority.

Between 1853 and 1856 four separate attempts were made to get legislation through parliament but the upper house continued to block it. It seemed that there was no way out of the impasse. But Lionel still persisted. In the 1857 general election he again appeared before his electorate and again he was voted into office. When, a few months later, the Lords once more refused consent to a bill, Lionel took the initiative by resigning a second time and offering himself for re-election. This time the Conservatives, heartily sick of the whole matter, did not put up a candidate and Rothschild was returned unopposed.

The "Jewish Question" was now making the House of Peers a laughing stock. Their lordships were frequently held up to ridicule in the press. For instance, when Earl Nelson (descendant of the great admiral) spoke against the bill in 1851, *Punch* had great fun at his expense:

*He was re-elected in 1859 and represented Greenwich from then until his death in 1873.

We have a NELSON still who fights for our homes and altars; for the gallant and reverend earl ennobled by Trafalgar has led the van against the Hebrew host, now thundering at the gates of Parliament . . . Heroically beautiful was NELSON, "flaming on the quarter" of the Spanish three-decker; no less . . . dreadful was the NELSON still spared to us, boarding the Synagogue! . . . When shall white-robed virgins sing his praises — when shall rejoicing elders chant his name?[17]

According to the sarcastic columnist, the Earl was to be praised for warning parliament of a dreadful fate into which it was rushing: "If they admitted Jews, where would they stop?"

Lionel and his supporters knew that, whatever happened in the upper chamber, they had won the popular debate. It was a considerable cause of satisfaction to realise that most right-thinking Englishmen were on their side. Sensitive parliamentarians now made serious efforts to find a face-saving compromise. It was Lord Lucan, whose military ineptitude had resulted in the loss of the Light Brigade at Balaclava, who now scored a notable triumph on the political battlefield. He suggested a simple bill empowering each house to select the wording of oaths administered to new members. With relief Lords and Commons accepted the escape route the Earl had opened for them. On 26 July 1858 Lionel de Rothschild once more walked the length of the Commons chamber to take the oath. After what was now no more than a brief formality he took that place on the Liberal benches to which he had been elected almost exactly eleven years before.

The news of final victory was sent by telegram to all the other banks and the congratulations poured in. It was quite obvious all Lionel's relatives shared the conviction that this was the Rothschilds' most important contribution to the cause of emancipation.

The battle had been won, and for Lionel that was what mattered. He continued to represent his constituency almost to the end of his life, but he never made a single speech in the chamber. Though Lionel had many friends in parliament, they were chosen for personal and not party reasons. His attendance at the Commons seems to have been equally casual. There is no evidence that he ever made a point of being present for a crucial vote or that he avidly attended a debate on a subject which passionately concerned him. He simply fitted his parliamentary duties into the intervals of his business life.

His more enthusiastic brother was not slow to take advantage of the opportunity now available to him. In the following February, Muffy contested a by-election at Hythe and Folkestone, the seat he had failed to take in 1847. The circumstances which caused the vacancy were unusual and suggest an arrangement. The sitting Liberal, Sir John Ramsden, resigned in order to become the candidate for a Yorkshire constituency. Muffy was returned unopposed and thus became the second Jew to take his seat, using the new, acceptable form of oath. However, within weeks, he had to defend it at a general election. A letter he wrote to his agent, Thomas Cullen (whose father had ferried gold across the Channel for N.M.) suggests that he had already begun to take his parliamentary duties very seriously:

> ... I agree with you it is necessary for me to visit the electors and shall come down on Wednesday early. You can fix a public meeting at Folkestone for that day. Let it be early in the afternoon so that I may return the same night. But you are on no account to fix any public meetings for the following days, either at Hythe or Sandgate, as there are most important questions coming on in the House which require my attendance. As I have the whole day on Wednesday, I might on that day meet the various committees in the morning at the different towns; but, at all events, you can assemble a public meeting for Wednesday at Folkestone ... [18]

Mayer was much more committed than his brother to the principle of extending the franchise. In the 1860s Russell and Disraeli were kicking parliamentary reform around like a party political football, and Muffy was present at every crucial debate, hoping that the Liberals would be the ones to give the vote to the urban proletariat and become the party of the working man. He ran a decided political risk in adopting this commitment, representing, as he did, a rural constituency. The proposed reform involved a shift of political power as between town and country, so that Muffy's vigorous campaign of 1865 found him rushing around his constituency explaining the issues to farmers who mistrusted the changes.

However, his own popularity saved him from defeat. As well as being personally well liked he had the advantage of being a Rothschild. His commercial connections at home and abroad enabled him to be of service to the maritime and trading communities of the Kent coast. Moreover, in the days when votes were quite unashamedly bought (the secret ballot did not appear until 1884), Rothschild guineas must have played their part in his continued electoral success.

But by no means did he rely simply on the family's name and wealth. Quite unlike his eldest brother, Muffy loved the rough and tumble of the hustings. This genial extrovert was a master of popular oratory, as a speech of 1868 (an election which produced a Liberal landslide), reported in the local press, illustrates:

Baron Rothschild was received with the greatest enthusiasm, the assemblage rising almost to a man to wave their hats and cheer him. He said, "I have to make my excuses to you for having been away from you several days and absent from my canvass but it was a long pending engagement and I thought I was bound to keep it (hear, hear). It was no other than an engagement with the Prime Minister of England [Disraeli] to accompany him to Newmarket races (loud cheers), to witness that which we as Englishmen so cordially and enthusiastically support (cheers). The result of your races and regattas induced me so to do, and I trust it will receive your approbation (loud cheers) . . . "[19]

Mayer went on, in an amusing and vigorous tirade, to uphold the Gladstonian principles of "Peace, Retrenchment and Reform". Yet public bombast was the only form of political oratory in which Mayer indulged. Like his brother, he managed to complete a long parliamentary career without once addressing the House.

British political activity was not, of course, confined to the hustings and the debating chambers. Some of the more important events went on in Westminster offices, gentlemen's clubs and the town houses of ministers and MPs. These were the places where the Rothschilds exercised a significant and increasing influence. Lionel set the pattern other members of the family would follow. He did not bother to speak in the Commons largely because it was easier to achieve his ends in other ways. He deliberately cultivated the leading political figures. Immediately after his admittance to parliament he acquired 147 Piccadilly and began a massive rebuilding programme to create a magnificent town mansion rivalling next-door Apsley House, originally the residence of the Duke of Wellington. While the work was being done he rented Kingston House in Knightsbridge where Charlotte presided over dinner parties and other social occasions which never failed to impress. In 1859 the veteran Whig parliamentarian, Thomas Babington Macaulay, was among her first honoured guests. The distinguished politician and historian, who died suddenly a few months later, was a passionate champion of social justice who had supported the cause of Jewish emancipation ever since his maiden speech upon the subject in 1830. Though not an intimate of the Rothschilds (few men could claim close friendship with Macaulay), he was a man to whom they had reason to be grateful and one of those whom they wished to impress. One of Macaulay's letters suggests that they succeeded:

Yesterday I dined with Baron Rothschild. What a paradise he lives in. I had no notion of the beauty and extent of the gardens . . . The dinner was a curiosity, seeing that pork in all its forms, was excluded.

There was however some compensation as you will see from the bill of fare which I enclose. Send it back that I may show it to Lady Trevelyan. Surely this is the land flowing with milk and honey. I do not believe Solomon in all his glory ever dined on *Ortolans farcis à la Talleyrand*. I may observe in passing that the little birds were accompanied by some Johannisberg which was beyond all praise.[20]

Making contacts, obtaining information, providing finance, quietly exerting pressure — these were the aspects of political activity at which the Rothschilds excelled, and they were to be seen in action, not only at their own dinner tables, but in frequent meetings of Liberal leaders at the Reform Club and Brook's.

Sir Anthony, who never himself stood for parliament, was often present at these gatherings, and enjoyed the world of political intrigue, a fascination not shared by his wife. She noted in her diary on 3 July 1852: "Anthony much excited about the coming elections. I do not feel as much interest about it as I ought and should wish to do. On Charlotte's account principally, I hope ... that Lionel may be returned ... on *national* grounds, I fear I do not care much about it ..."[21] In 1858 Anthony eased Lionel's burden by taking over the Austrian Consul Generalship which his brother had inherited, somewhat unwillingly, from his father and which he had always regarded as a chore. In the country he supported the Liberal cause with his personal prestige and his "tin" (as he frequently referred to money). But it was probably as a host at Aston Clinton, his Buckinghamshire home, that Anthony performed his best services to the party: a convivial man, described by his daughter as "Of a naturally bright and cheerful disposition, ready to make the best of everything, satisfied with his round of daily duties and the enjoyments that his love of social life and his country pursuits brought him,"[22] he welcomed all the political leaders of the day, put them at their ease and created an atmosphere in which they could discuss matters of national interest away from the pressures of Westminster.

One of the most frequent guests was no Liberal. He was a man whose life for several years was closely bound up with the Rothschilds and with whom they had a curious relationship. His name was Benjamin Disraeli.

CHAPTER 12

"It is absolutely vital that you free yourself from the tutelage of the Rothschilds"

The Rothschilds' friendship with Disraeli and his wife began during the 1840s, by which time the dandified and exotic young politician had already made his mark in the Tory party. Common cultural origins must go a long way towards explaining the bond between them, for they disagreed on most things and, although "Dizzy" professed deep and abiding affection for his friends, they were often highly critical of him. Lionel, for example, found his philosophical theorising on racial and religious matters faintly absurd and was frankly sceptical of his sincerity. During the long battle for Jewish political equality, Disraeli, a baptised Christian, who had married a Christian and who strove hard to put his Jewish past behind him, blew hot and cold, sometimes supporting, occasionally opposing, mostly remaining silent. The Rothschilds suspected, not without reason, that the calculating *enfant terrible* of British politics was using the emancipation issue for his own ends and found such cynicism contemptible. After sitting next to Disraeli at a dinner party given by her parents and finding the politician depressed as the result of a reverse in the House, Anthony's wife, Louisa, commented:

> Had Disraeli ever wished to carry out any great principle, or to bring forward some truly useful measures, he would not be so cast down; he would feel that, in or out of office, he had high and noble duties to perform and that his talents need never be unused. But, his own elevation having been his only aim, he has nothing now to sweeten the bitter cup of ill success. The Duchess of Somerset desperately in love with him. What could have fascinated her in him?[1]

The Disraelis, nevertheless, were regular recipients of the Rothschilds' hospitality, which had become legendary for its lavish generosity, and Disraeli regarded them as being among his intimate friends. To be called "friend" by one of the two great parliamentary giants of the Victorian era was certainly flattering, but the relationship, for all its superficial warmth, remained an arm's-length one, at least in its early years. The next generation of Rothschilds, however, was completely won over, for Dizzy and his wife, Mary Anne, whose own marriage was childless, really loved children and formed close bonds with the Rothschild boys and girls when they were small. These ties lasted until the end of the statesman's days, when, as a lonely widower, he relied heavily on the sympathy and support of Lionel's children (see p. 234). Nor did the family's reservations about Disraeli himself extend to his wife. One of Anthony's daughters remembered her very affectionately: "Dear, fond woman! If foolish, and perhaps at times even ridiculous, she was a splendid wife; one could smile at her absurdities and love her all the same, or all the better."[2]

One story related in a letter from Charlotte (Lionel's wife) to Lady Rothschild dated 10 September 1845, is irresistible, both for the picture it provides of Mrs Disraeli and the evidence it gives of her attachment to the Rothschild children.

> . . . I'll tell you a secret that will astonish you, if aught relating to our excellent and eccentric friend Mrs Disraeli can possibly produce an impression, a feeling of that kind. About a week after Hannah Mayer had been pronounced out of danger and the clock had struck six there was a visitor ringing and pulling at the bell, and into the room, and presently into my reluctant arms rushed Mrs. Disi.
> "I am quite out of breath, my dear, I have been running so fast, we have no horses, no carriage, no servants, we are going abroad, I have been so busy correcting proof-sheets, the publishers are so tiresome, we ought to have been gone a month ago; I should have called upon you long ere now, I have been so nervous, so excited, so agitated, poor Dis' has been sitting up the whole night writing; I want to speak to you on business, pray send the darling children away" etc., etc., for it would without any exaggeration, take more than ten pages to put down conscientiously all the lady's words, not noting exclamations and gestures and tears. You know, dear Louisa, that I am easily terrified and almost speechless. I had never seen her in such a state of excitement before, and all I could do was to gasp out — "Has anything happened?"
> Mrs Disraeli heaved a deep sigh and said; "This is a farewell visit, I may never see you again — life is so uncertain, poor Mrs Fitzroy has been so very, very ill, Disi and I may be blown up on the rail-road or in the steamer, there is not a human body that loves me in this world, and besides my adored husband I care for no one on earth, but I love your glorious race, I am rich, I am prosperous, I think it right to entertain serious thoughts, to look calmly upon one's end" etc., etc.

Mrs Disraeli's conversation is not exactly remarkable for clearness of thought, precision of language, or for a proper concatenation of images, ideas and phrases, nevertheless, I had always been able to comprehend and to reply, but on that memorable Friday, I was quite at a loss to understand her meaning . . . I tried to calm and quiet my visitor who, after having enumerated her goods and chattels to me, took a paper out of her pocket saying:

"This is my Will and you must read it, show it to the dear Baron [Lionel] and take care of it for me." I answered that she must be aware of my feelings, that I should ever truly be grateful for such a proof of confidence, but could not accept such a great responsibility. "But you must listen," replied the inexorable lady: she opened the paper and read aloud:

"In the event of my beloved Husband preceding me to the grave, I leave and bequeath to Evelina de Rothschild [Baroness Lionel's daughter, aged six] all my personal property."

I leave you to picture to yourself my amazement and embarrassment. Mrs Disraeli rose and would hear no answer, no objection.

"I love the Jews — I have attached myself to your children and she is my favourite, she shall, she must wear the [diamond] butterfly." Away rushed the testatrix, leaving the testament in my unworthy hands . . .

The next morning I breakfasted in a hurry, walked in a hurry to the abode of genius and his wife, to whom I returned the Will. There was a scene, a very disagreeable one, and then all was over . . . [3]

During the 1840s and 1850s much of the entertaining and socialising which the English Rothschilds regarded as both necessary and enjoyable was transferred to a new setting. Lionel and his brothers had long been familiar with Buckinghamshire, and the Vale of Aylesbury in particular. The area was attractive for several reasons. The countryside was strikingly beautiful, it was easily accessible from the City, and it offered excellent sport in the hunting field. A foothold was established in 1839 when the family formed their own pack of staghounds and kept them in rented accommodation at Tring Park. But the conventions of elegant society demanded more. Persons of the Rothschilds' standing were expected to have "country seats", and as, one by one, the brothers bowed to these conventions, it was only natural that they should look for estates and houses around Aylesbury.

Mayer was the first to move. In a sense he was freer than the others to make such a decision. Because of his political responsibilities, Muffy played little part in the running of the bank. He loved country life and when not in the Commons wanted to invest his time, energies and capital in land, farming and stockbreeding. In 1842 he bought the nucleus of an estate at Mentmore and Wing and immediately set about acquiring neighbouring lands, eventually building up a five thousand acre holding. So rapidly did he settle into the rôle of "Squire of Mentmore", as Nat called him with a mixture of teasing humour and envy, that in 1847 he was appointed Sheriff of Buckinghamshire.

In 1850, at the age of thirty-two, Muffy married his nineteen-year-old cousin, Juliana Cohen and in the same year began the first of the great Rothschild houses. To design it, he turned to Joseph Paxton, architect and gardener to the Duke of Devonshire, whose novel plan for a glass palace to house the Great Exhibition had recently been selected in preference to 233 other entries. For Baron Mayer, however, Paxton stuck to the accepted orthodoxies of the day, designing a magnificent mansion in the prevailing Jacobean style. There, for his remaining twenty-four years Muffy lived the life of a traditional English country gentleman, with his hounds, his racehorses and his herd of pedigree Jerseys.

Anthony and Louisa longed to follow Muffy's example, but it was not until 1853 that the demands of the London and Paris houses relaxed sufficiently to allow them to spend the summer months in Buckinghamshire. At nearby Aston Clinton, they bought an eighteenth-century house which Louisa considered "too small to be very comfortable", [4] and set about enlarging it at whim. It spread in a ramshackle way, which contrasted totally with the drawing-board symmetry of Mentmore, and became a country home which Anthony and Louisa and their two daughters loved dearly.

Lionel, however, did not immediately follow his brothers. Although he acquired farms and properties around Halton as investments, he was largely content with Gunnersbury Park as a rural retreat. The City and Westminster made great demands on his time and since, after his mother's death in 1850, he and Charlotte had the Acton property to themselves, there was no reason for him to move farther out of town. Only in 1872, when Tring Park came unexpectedly on to the market, did Lionel buy a substantial Buckinghamshire house, and then it was not for himself, but for his eldest son, Natty, who had been Liberal MP for Aylesbury for seven years. In the next generation more members of the family moved into the area, but by 1870 the extent of their property holding and their social standing were such that the Vale of Aylesbury was already known as "Rothschildshire". With estates, mansions, packs of hounds and racing studs, Lionel and his brothers were part of the landed establishment *par excellence*. They had successfully claimed a stake in that timeless social order rooted in the soil of England and their position was secure.

* * *

Across the Channel life was very different, as Lionel's daughter, Leonora, (Laury) discovered. In 1857 she married her cousin, Alphonse, the eldest son of James and Betty. The wedding was, of course, magnificent. It provided the society columnists with their best opportunity of the year for eulogistic prose. The Disraelis, Lord John Russell and the Duchess of Wellington headed a guest list which included the cream of the nobility, the diplomatic corps and the business and political communities. "The assembled company presented a *coup d'oeil* the most brilliant in beauty and costume that can be conceived," the *Illustrated London News* enthused. Even more splendid than the company was the display of wedding gifts, "rivalling the wealth of the Indies", according to the journalist. The Great Baron's offering of jewels alone was worth thirty thousand pounds. The banquet — "such as an epicure would not forget" — was laid out in a specially constructed pavilion built on to the dining-room at Gunnersbury Park. Candelabra and mirrors provided points of light which scintillated against drapes of white and rose and "the choicest exotics in all the bloom and perfume of Oriental nature". Music was provided by the band of the First Life Guards. As darkness fell the whole house was illuminated within and without and the guests stayed on to enjoy a ball which continued until after two in the morning. The bride's trousseau, "admirable for its exquisite taste, as well as its extensiveness, had engaged the entire skill and almost exhausted the elegant fancy, of Madame Roger, of Paris, 'dressmaker to the Empress'". The recorder of this glittering occasion noted, with approval, that, "Amid the hospitalities of the day the host and hostess had not forgotten their humbler and poorer friends, who were generously feasted; and the feeling of the neighbourhood was shown in the numerous flags hung out at the houses along the road, and the festive appearance assumed by the whole vicinity."[5]

After a brief honeymoon the couple returned to Paris. Although Laury had paid many visits to her uncle's home, taking up permanent residence across the Channel was a new experience. The atmosphere in France was very different from the well-ordered stability of her homeland. The political situation was volatile. Beneath the superficial splendour of the Second Empire, with which Prince Louis Napoleon had replaced the short-lived republic of 1848, powerful forces were stirring — forces intent on changing the existing social order. Elsewhere in Europe, too, there were rumblings of discontent and upheaval and, in the decade that followed Laury's wedding, yet another succession of crises would put an end to the Naples bank and come close to detroying the Paris and Vienna houses also.

There were also tensions in Laury's marriage. On the face of it, the match was one which would have pleased any young woman, even a

Rothschild. Alphonse was a talented young man. In his preparation for leadership of the Paris bank he travelled extensively, even spending several months in America (see pp. 180ff.). He had a good head for business and slipped easily into the place allotted to him at Rue Laffitte. He was an accomplished amateur artist and became one of Europe's most knowledgeable and enthusiastic patrons of painters (see pp. 246ff.). In his youth he had also been a keen sportsman, until an accident in the shooting field curtailed his athletic activities.

This incident, which happened at Ferrières, vividly illustrates one aspect of Alphonse's character. Apparently, an inexperienced member of a shooting party discharged a shotgun too close to his host, who received some pieces of shot in the face. Despite the ministrations of the finest doctors, he lost the sight of one eye. It is recorded that, although Alphonse knew who had inflicted this terrible injury on him he never revealed the man's identity, or reproached him or withdrew his friendship from him. For Alphonse was a patrician: stoical in matters concerning his own destiny; impelled by a strong sense of duty; and possessing a deep concern for and obligation towards social inferiors, which sometimes expressed itself in spontaneous ways. Once when he was travelling abroad on important business, a fanatic delivered a parcel bomb at Rue Laffitte. It exploded in the face of a subordinate who opened it, causing severe injuries. As soon as the news was telegraphed to him, Alphonse hurried back to Paris to pay several visits to the unfortunate employee's bedside and to ensure personally that he received the best treatment available.

At the same time, however, Alphonse often found it difficult to express affection for those closest to him. When he was courting Laury, his future mother-in-law described him as "a man who perhaps for ten or fifteen years has run the round of the world [and] is completely blasé, can neither admire nor love".[6] Moreover, as his colleagues knew, he was given to putting his opinions across strongly and often sarcastically, and with the passage of time he became quite irascible. Someone who knew both Alphonse and his younger brother, Gustave, when they were mature men, described the latter as "more religious and less vindictive" than Alphonse.

Alphonse also had a strong streak of chauvinism. Unlike his father, he became a French citizen and his national pride often led him to disparage things foreign — especially those of English origin. His wife did little to soften his attitude towards the British. Laury was a lively wit, an enthusiastic sportswoman and an acknowledged beauty — when she was presented at court in 1856, the year before her wedding, Queen Victoria noted in her diary that the young Jewess was "extremely handsome". She was also, and remained to the end of her days, intensely English. She returned to her own family once or twice a year, and seldom missed a few weeks hunting in Buckinghamshire during the season — a passion shared by another English exile, her Uncle Nat, though a riding accident had left him permanently lamed and deprived him of this pleasure. She established her own pack of staghounds at Ferrières under the command of a huntsman who was, naturally, English. Laury's attitude towards the French never seems to have risen above the level of amused (or sometimes exasperated) tolerance. She despised the artificiality of Parisian society. She was completely incapable of understanding Gallic aspirations and the French preoccupation with *la gloire*. She was, therefore, unable to sympathise with the natives of her adopted country throughout the troubled half-century during which she lived in their midst. In her will Laury gave instructions that her remains were to be interred in the country of her birth (instructions which were faithfully carried out when her long life came to an end in 1911).

It was only natural that Laury should make common cause with her Uncle Nat, who had already spent the best part of twenty years in Paris at the time of her marriage. Nat, too, must have been a source of irritation to Alphonse. This cousin, who was also his father's right-hand man, constantly extolled all things English. The frequent sight of him and Laury with their heads together laughing over the latest gossip about their family and friends in London cannot have greatly pleased Alphonse.

In 1853 Nat took a step calculated to irritate his French relatives even further and, in so doing, laid the foundation for still greater rivalry in the future: he bought one of the most cherished of all French institutions, a leading Bordeaux vineyard. It was not Château Lafite, which James had tried in vain to acquire, but it was the next best. In fact, it was next door. Château Brane Mouton, now renamed Mouton Rothschild, bordered Lafite and shared with it that indefinable combination of soil, situation and drainage which enabled both vineyards to produce, year after year, the finest clarets. Rivalry between the two establishments of Pauillac parish had raged for decades. It was made worse in 1855, the year of the Paris Exhibition, when the wines of the region were classified and Lafite was placed first among the four vineyards which received the coveted title *premier cru*. The grading, naturally, did not meet with approval from all the other growers, but the man most annoyed by the new "league table" was Nat who was furious when Mouton was designated as a mere *deuxième cru*. He immediately expressed his defiance by adapting an old jingle:

> Premier ne puis
> Second ne daigne,
> Mouton suis*

*First I cannot be. Second I do not choose to be, Mouton I am.

Nat's pride in Mouton was immense, and he took very seriously the production and selling of its wine. Every year, when the price for the vintage had to be decided, Lafite and Mouton competed to see which would obtain the higher. The rivalry, more a matter of prestige than profit, was treated in deadly earnest by both sides. "Rely on me to uphold the honour of the flag", Emile Goudal, the manager of Lafite, boasted to his principal in 1857 when he had outsmarted the Baron by forcing him to put his Mouton wine on the market first and then, subsequently, capping the price.[7] When the owner contemplated selling part of the property, known as Les Carruades, Goudal was beside himself with worry that it might fall into Rothschild hands.

> The sale of the Carruades to M. Rothschild would be very improper and could have for you the most disastrous consequences. *This is very serious.* If M. Rothschild would buy the Carruades, which are appreciated by everybody as vineyards of the highest quality, which can do good to any wine it will be mixed with, M. Rothschild, having great wealth, will try to get Mouton made a first growth. Do you realise the consequence this will have for you? Mouton as a first growth could only depreciate Lafite . . . it would be better to sell the Carruades for 50,000 francs to a stranger than for 50,000 more than that to M. Rothschild.[8]

Nat entered into the spirit of the contest, for he was completely caught up in the mystique and rivalry of viniculture. He also relished the fact that he, a "mere Englishman", could offer his guests a superlative wine with his own name on the label. More practically, he regarded the purchase as a good investment. He was not alone in this view. The early 1850s had seen a run of bad harvests and a number of Médoc landowners were, as a result, forced to sell their estates cheaply. This allowed several Paris-based financiers to add good farming land to their portfolios. Among the other vineyards which changed hands at this time was Château Palmer. The purchaser was Emile Péreire – the man who had done so much to establish the fortunes of Rue Laffitte, but who had now associated himself with Achille Fould – deadly enemy of the French Rothschilds and determined to remove the Great Baron from his throne in French money markets.

Péreire's rise had been as rapid as James's fall from favour. He was one of the new men – men of ideals, talent, enthusiasm and exciting plans – chosen by a new ruler to carry out a wide-ranging social and economic revolution. Louis Napoleon was a man of modest ability saddled with a great name which he desperately tried to live up to. Elected President of the Republic in 1848, he abolished the constitution three years later and had himself proclaimed, first, Prince-President and then, after a plebiscite, Emperor. In his campaign he had appealed directly to the working class, promising the people a new era of progress, material prosperity and social justice, an era when poverty and exploitation would be done away with and all would share the benefits of an expanding economy. The Saint-Simonian and free trade principles Napoleon warmly espoused were a direct challenge to the financial and industrial establishment. The government turned elsewhere for money, advice and enterprise. Above all, they pledged themselves to extend the ownership of the means of production and give ordinary citizens a financial stake in the business sector.

In order to implement the promised reforms and organise the ambitious programme of public works he had promised, Napoleon turned to a radical group of experts and politicians, high priests of Saint-Simonianism, who combined technical competence with an evangelistic zeal for the gospel of humanitarianism. Typical of the breed was Emile Péreire's brother, Isaac, who, as a young man, had written:

> We rely mainly on the *conversion* of men; above all it is on the arousing of their sympathies for the less fortunate classes that we base our greatest hopes ... we have devoted the riches which the accident of birth has bestowed upon us to improving the lot of the poorest and largest class ... We hope that our efforts will inspire you to follow our example. *We are waiting.*[9]

Isaac Péreire and his brother were involved in the planning and execution of several of the splendid schemes of public works now set in hand by the administration — rebuilding the centre of Paris, laying new railways, reclaiming wasteland and staging the great Paris Exhibition of 1855. Their particular responsibility was to raise the immense sums of money needed for these impressive undertakings and needed also for the industrial expansion the government wished to encourage.

But the man singled out to be the leading architect of the new order and who now became Napoleon's economic adviser was that old enemy of the Great Baron, the converted Jew, Achille Fould. He became Finance Minister in 1848 and was seldom out of ministerial office throughout the next twenty years. It was he who advised his master, "It is absolutely vital that you free yourself from the tutelage of the Rothschilds."[10]

For the Great Baron it was a shock to find himself, after eighteen years of enormous political influence, suddenly excluded from the intimate group of imperial advisers. It was also galling to know that he and his ilk, who had pioneered French industrial expansion, were now regarded as the enemies of progress. James felt keenly those little rebuffs, such as not being invited to some court functions, which subtly indicated to Parisian society his change of status. But he did not show it. He affected a supreme aloofness to the new government, as if to say, "republics may come and emperors may go, but De Rothschild Frères goes on forever". Baroness Betty was less restrained in demonstrating her disdain for the new order. With typically feminine consistency she refused to abandon her Orléanist friends or pretend a respect for Louis Napoleon which she did not feel. She declined to be presented to the President or to attend state functions. And her husband certainly put no pressure upon her to conform.

It was partly to show defiance to rivals who exulted in his partial exclusion from court circles that James espoused the cause of Eugénie de Montijo. At the age of twenty-two this Spanish beauty had won the heart of the new head of state. Those close to Napoleon considered her quite unsuitable as a consort; and the lady herself did not deign to be a mistress. Impasse. Eugénie was snubbed by leading ministers and society hostesses – but not by the Rothschilds. Betty invited her to the salon at Rue Laffitte and several of her friends followed suit. The climax of this little farce came during a Tuileries ball in 1853. Feeling somewhat tired after several dances, Eugénie wanted to rest. No seats could be found until James escorted her to an empty sofa. Immediately, a self-important *belle dame* flounced up to her. "Those seats are reserved for ministers' wives," she announced, plonking her bulky frame upon the silken cushions. But the triumph was short-lived. Louis Napoleon stepped briskly to Eugénie's side, offered his arm and escorted her to the room set aside for his own party. Eleven days later the couple announced their engagement. But such little skirmishes, however interesting, were of little consequence for the real war, which was being fought elsewhere and in deadly earnest.

The terrain over which the combatants marched and countermarched was the financing of the government's programme of economic expansion. Normally it would have been the leading private banks which provided the necessary funds. The Rothschilds and their colleagues were well experienced in forming consortiums, often referred to as *haute banque*, for just such a purpose. But this was not at all what the Saint-Simonians had in mind. They were insistent that France must free herself from the apron strings of the *haute banque*. How then was the regime to finance the ambitious programme to which it was committed? Fould and the Péreires had no doubts about the answer: since existing financial institutions could not be used, it would be necessary to create a new one. They were clear, too, about the form which this new institution would take. It would be a people's credit bank, financed by the savings of the public at large and directed by the state.

Napoleon's ministers lost no time in putting their plans into effect. On 15 November 1852 the Crédit Mobilier was established by imperial decree. Headed by the Péreire brothers, it had a capital of sixty million francs, and shares were available to the public at five hundred francs each. To the small investor the Crédit Mobilier seemed to offer a foolproof opportunity for making money. It was lending to the government and to government-backed consortiums. It could not fail. Citizens all over the country rushed to put their savings into the new bank. This was nothing less than a declaration of financial warfare. State Socialism had thrown down a gauntlet before the feet of private enterprise; idealism was confronting pragmatism; new money was challenging old money. Thus began the celebrated *lutte bancaire*, the battle of the banks. From the start it was a struggle in which both sides used, without hesitation, whatever weapons came to hand; and it would be a fight to the death, for the Péreires aimed at nothing less than toppling the Rothschilds from their position of financial power and taking control of the exchange, the banks and major industrial undertakings.

To dislodge the Rothschilds from their deeply entrenched positions, the Péreires employed the impressive siege pieces of imperial support and massive public backing. They also launched an all-out assault on several fronts: on the Bourse, in the boardrooms of industrial companies, and in the courts and chancelleries of Europe. The Péreires, who knew better than most people just how the Rothschild system worked, challenged them all over the Continent by competing for business and driving commission rates down. Moreover, during the early years of the struggle, at least, they had virtually limitless resources. The Crédit Mobilier was such a success that money poured into the new bank. Its share values rose steadily. Ironically, this encouraged that very speculation on the exchange for which the Saint-Simonians had criticised the old private banks. It also provided the Crédit Mobilier with more funds than its promoters had expected.

Soon the Péreires were financing railways – this was to be the main battleground on which they engaged the Rothschilds (see p.174) – and other industries on a continental scale, from Spain in the west to Turkey in the east, Italy in the south to Germany in the north.

The financial zealots actively encouraged and assisted the formation of credit banks in other countries, where governments often welcomed the idea as a means of financing the transportation systems and factories they had to build if they were not to fall even further behind the major industrial powers.

In the face of this attack, Baron James could rely on the help of powerful allies and the immense resources of the family. He barricaded himself behind fortifications of solid gold and regularly sallied forth to confront the Crédit Mobilier on battlefields both at home and abroad. From the start he planned a war of attrition. Accepting that he could not defeat the enemy in a single decisive battle, he hoped to lure the Péreires into greater commitment. He knew that, if they became overextended, they would forfeit public confidence and those who had supported them would turn against them.

In the meantime, there were plenty of skirmishes to be fought, and James plunged into the fray with vigour. The most obvious and easy place for him to confront the Péreires was on the exchange. Crédit Mobilier shares were too secure for him to be able to undermine them but he could do the next best thing. Ernest Feydeau recounted how one day the Great Baron ordered him to buy a thousand Crédit Mobilier shares. The clerk was surprised but did not question his master's instructions. However, when James repeated the purchase every day for five days, Feydeau could restrain himself no longer. Was the Baron, he respectfully suggested, not running the risk of appearing rather foolish? James flared up in angry, sarcastic rebuttal:

"Vat are you saying, my yonk frient? I am not at all making a fool of myself. I haf ze greatest confidence in ze genius of Messrs Péreires. Zay are ze greatest financiers in ze worlt. I who am ze fazer of a family, I must invest part of my liddle fortune in zeir pisnesss. Ze only zing I rergret is zat I cannot entrust all my capital to zese highly intelligent men."[11]

But a few days later James sold his entire Crédit Mobilier holding. The operation had, of course, been simply a minor manoeuvre in the war. Rothschild's purchases had forced a rapid rise in share values. When he came to sell he gained, according to Feydeau, between ten and twenty times the value of his investment and his friends on the Bourse had a good laugh at the Péreires' expense.

Preserving a front of insouciance was part of the Great Baron's strategy. In conversation he affected to regard the Crédit Mobilier as an insignificant upstart and he gave the impression that nothing disturbed the even tenor of Rue Laffitte. Perhaps it was this unshakeable bravado which prompted James to undertake a project which was, even by his standards, both ambitious and expensive. Sometime in 1852 he saw the plans for Muffy's new mansion at Mentmore. Probably the thought of being outdone by a nephew – even his favourite nephew – was too much for him. He summoned Muffy's architect, Joseph Paxton, to Paris and issued him with a simple instruction: "Build me a Mentmore, only bigger." Soon hundreds of workmen and thousands of cartloads of stone and builders' supplies were converging on Ferrières to create the new château which would be France's most magnificent example of nineteenth-century domestic architecture.

The design which Paxton produced and, by 1859, executed was a square-plan, Victorian-Jacobean mansion in the same style as Mayer's house but on a far vaster scale, with rooms for dozens of guests, a hundred servants, and stables for eighty horses. Inside, although the décor was masterminded by the painter Eugène Lami, there was a profusion (or, perhaps, a confusion) of styles and tastes – tapestries in one room, hangings of painted leather in another, wainscot in a third. There were painted ceilings, marble busts, Louis Seize furniture, bronzes, cabinets stuffed with porcelain, books and *objets d'art* – everything that a wealthy and acquisitive man could accumulate to beautify his house and impress upon the world that he and his dynasty were here to stay. Ferrières had every modern convenience, including a separately housed kitchen and an underground railway to convey hot food to the dining room. Somewhat surprisingly perhaps, it was a comfortable and pleasant house to live in, at least according to Baron Guy de Rothschild's childhood memories.

> The main hall was a truly magical place. Its vast dimensions and the soft light falling through the glass roof suggested the nave of a cathedral, and its height permitted two different décors: on the upper level, the walls were covered with emerald green velvet and hung with a series of tapestries . . . On the lower half, at eye level, were a number of paintings, including some of the most beautiful from my grandfather's collection: Ingres' famous portrait of my great-grandmother Betty; *The Marquise Doria* by Van Dyck, later donated to the Louvre; a charming portrait of a woman by Gainsborough; and Franz Hals' *Woman with a Rose*. Busts of Roman emperors stood guard while a woman generously bared her bosom above the great marble mantelpiece. The two large doors opening onto the principal entrance were flanked by a pair of Blackamoors several metres high, who seemed to bear all the weight of the ceiling on their shoulders. A billiard table in one corner, a piano in another, Italian Renaissance cabinets delicately carved and inlaid with ebony, ivory, marble, onyx and semi-precious stones, an assortment of sofas, armchairs, benches, sideboards and tables laden with precious objects, all served to define different areas where one could be alone to read or, alternatively, gather together for conversation and games. [12]

But not all early visitors to Paxton's masterpiece were favourably impressed. Among the hundreds of visitors James proudly conducted round his palace and its ever-growing collection of treasures, opinions varied between those who concluded, "everything is in good taste and

169

quite magnificent" and those who indignantly dismissed Ferrières as "an idiotic and ridiculous extravagance, a pudding of every style, the fruit of a stupid ambition to have all monuments in one". Evelina, Lionel's lively, twenty-five-year-old daughter, was tactful on her first visit to Uncle James's palace.

> ... Mama has already given you a description of all its treasures and magnificence, so I will not trouble you with a second edition, but I own I was quite astonished and *éblouie*. I had never seen Ferrières in foliage and, besides, the Great Baron is always bringing new treasures. ... We ... were shown all over the palace, estate and gardens and when we came back I pleased Uncle James by telling him that I could find only one fault — the place was too royal to be without sentinels ... [13]

Evelina felt, but was too polite to say, that Ferrières was overdone and that seems to have been an impression shared by many visitors, including those who admired it. Even by the standards of the mid-nineteenth century, an age given to "fussiness" in internal décor, the mélange of beautiful, grandiose and curious objects with which James stuffed his new château was excessive. The modern visitor must use his imagination to recreate the lavishness of a bygone era. The great house today stands empty and monumentally forlorn, an architectural shell forever stripped of the furniture, paintings, tapestries and statuary which originally proclaimed its creator's wealth (see p. 428).

Of course, the main function of the whole Ferrières phenomenon was to make a statement about Rothschild power and affluence. Yet even here, the Baron's enemies scored a minor triumph in a war which, as well as being wide-reaching in scope, was also intensely personal. The Péreires succeeded in buying the forest of Armainvilliers bordering the estate and thereby thwarted James's plans to extend his domain. Naturally, they made sure that everyone knew about it. But this was only a diversionary tactic to cover their next major offensive.

On 1 January 1855 the Crédit Mobilier bought the Austrian State Railways. Austrian government finances had been in a mess for years and by 1854 had reached a crisis which could only be resolved by placing the entire railway network on the market. Since the Rothschilds had done so much to create it, it possessed a symbolic as well as a financial value, and the success of the Péreires' bid was a blow to Rothschild morale as well as a defeat for the banks. Yet the year that had begun so badly would also prove the turning point in the *lutte bancaire*, beginning in defeat and ending in a spectacular victory.

But before the tide of war turned in James's favour, he had to take a succession of blows which were not of the Péreires' making. One after another within a period of a few months his three surviving brothers died.

Salomon had already retired from business and had been living in Paris since 1848. His death was a double loss to James and Betty, depriving the one of a brother, the other of a father. Unlike Salomon, Amschel and Carl remained active in their counting houses right to the end. Perhaps it might have been better had they, too, made way for younger men.

Under Amschel the Frankfurt house had remained a German bank, largely existing to contract loans with the states and great princes of the Confederation. While Paris, London and Vienna had become involved in industrial and foreign enterprises, Amschel had stuck to the business he knew. In banking and politics, as in religion, he opposed progressive ideas as contrary to the will of God. He was a firm supporter of Rabbi Sampson Raphael Hirsch, leader of the orthodox Frankfurt Jews. In 1852 he generously endowed a synagogue for Hirsch's congregation. The rabbi was an advocate of *Austritt* or separatism. He vehemently urged his disciples not only to refuse unnecessary contamination with Gentiles, but to distance themselves from all progressive Jews. It was typical of Amschel that he should be the follower of such a man. His mind had never left the ghetto and he was not really at home in the fine house and garden he had bought for himself. Bismarck described him as " . . . but a poor man in his palace . . . a childless widower who is cheated by his servants and despised by conceited Frenchified and Anglicised nephews and nieces who will inherit his wealth without any love or gratitude . . . "[14] It was a harsh judgement but one that rings true. The gulf was still widening not only between Amschel and his "progressive" relatives, but between the Rothschilds of Paris, London and Vienna, on the one hand, and those of Frankfurt on the other.

It is difficult to say whether more dynamic leadership would have kept the parent bank on a par with the other houses. Frankfurt was falling increasingly under Prussian domination and, in 1866, finally lost its "free city" status. Much of northern Germany was an industrial backwater until Bismarck's aggressive leadership of the united nation dramatically changed things in the later decades of the century. By then the focus on financial activity had moved to Berlin. There was some suggestion that Mayer Carl, who took over after the death of his uncle, might set up a branch in the new capital but nothing came of it. The two brothers certainly ingratiated themselves with the Prussians but made no serious attempt to establish a permanent presence in their country. Perhaps they disliked the ever-present undercurrent of anti-Semitism in Berlin. Perhaps, having no male heirs, they saw little point in making future plans. For it is a curious fact that Wilhelm Carl and Mayer Carl sired ten daughters and not a single son.

171

For whatever reason, the Rothschilds' German business remained in the Frankfurt bank and continued to decline in importance.

In Naples, too, things were far from well and when the founder of the Neapolitan bank, Carl von Rothschild, died at the age of sixty-seven, he had still not really established its identity as a separate house. He had continued to divide his time between Frankfurt and Naples and deferred to his brothers in most major policy decisions. Unlike them, Carl had never used his independence creatively. The plain fact is that he lacked the financial genius possessed, in varying degrees, by Nathan, James and Salomon. He had opportunities in plenty. Like Germany, Italy was a confusion of insecure little states whose governments were in constant need of money, both for defence and for that industrial modernisation which, they hoped, would create wealth and stave off demands for political change. But Carl was unable to take advantage of this situation. For example, when Piedmont, the most progressive Italian state, wanted money it negotiated with the Rothschild house in Paris. And when governments did approach Carl, he dithered. Twice (in 1832 and 1849), the Pope appealed to him for loans. Twice, serious negotiations were set in motion. Twice, the Neapolitan Rothschild backed out and left the business to Baron James. When, in 1853, Carl's beloved Adelheid died, the widower lost what little enthusiasm he still had for business.

To be fair, Carl lacked the advantage of living in an important capital city, where he could enjoy daily contact with a stable government and major commercial investors. As official banker to the Kingdom of the Two Sicilies, he was supporting a reactionary monarchy which owed its existence to the diplomatic and, when necessary, the military support of Austria. The passage of the years brought a steady growth of national and liberal sentiment and occasionally threw up men who were more than a match for the Rothschilds. For example, Camillo Cavour, who became Prime Minister of Piedmont in 1852, played so skilfully on the rivalry between James and the Crédit Mobilier that he was able to say to the Great Baron, "If you want to do business in my country, you do it on my terms." Whereas the French, British and Austrian houses had thrived on major challenges, those in charge of the Neapolitan house lacked the necessary determination and flair. It was this underlying weakness which, within a few years, brought the firm of C.M. Rothschild and Sons to an end (see p. 192).

The triple loss sustained by James in 1855 added to his worries — and, despite his outward calm, he was very concerned. In October the French Ambassador in London reported to his Emperor on a recent visit he had received from James, Lionel and Anthony. They had complained about the activities and growing power of the Crédit Mobilier: "Mr de

Rothschild delivered himself of the most lively and contradictory recriminations against the Crédit Mobilier. Soon that establishment would jeopardise the public wealth; soon it would become so rich and powerful that it would dictate new laws to the government."[15] James had every reason to be anxious. The Péreires were planning to set up a sister bank in Vienna. If it was successful, it would suck Austrian capital away from the Rothschilds just as the Crédit Mobilier had already absorbed much French capital. Baron von Bruck, the Finance Minister, had decided that the establishment of a credit bank was the only way to reorganise the imperial state finances and regenerate private industry. In August he gained government approval for the scheme. It now only remained to allocate the concession to the right financial group. The Péreires were confident that, with their experience and the major stake they already had in the country, they would be favoured. Furthermore, they were in alliance with another old Rothschild enemy, von Sina. But they had reckoned without the resident Rothschild — Anselm.

The head of the Viennese bank had no intention of allowing his family's rivals to establish themselves in the Hapsburg Empire. But he had already been thinking deeply about the country's problems and come to the conclusion that the private banking system simply could not cope with the degree of investment needed. He agreed with Bruck that a state credit bank was the only answer. So he had discussions with James and presented him with the unpalatable truth that the only way to keep the Péreires out of Austria was to take a leaf from their own book and set up a Rothschild credit bank. Thus it was that Anselm and a group of aristocratic colleagues put forward a rival scheme for an institution to be called the Österreichischen Creditanstalt für Handel und Gewerbe. Anselm worked closely with Bruck and there was never really any doubt which proposal the government would accept. The Creditanstalt was tailored much more carefully to Austria's needs. Unlike the Crédit Mobilier, its investments were confined within the limits of the Hapsburg Empire and it was much more heavily capitalised.

The new bank received its charter on 31 October 1855. On 12 December fifteen million guldens' worth of shares was made available for public subscription. On the evening of the 11th a long queue had formed on the pavement of the Renngasse outside the premises of S.M. Rothschild and Son. Hundreds of people, careless of the flurrying snow, had come, determined to obtain shares at the opening price. Anselm sent bank servants out to keep them supplied with hot soup throughout their nocturnal vigil. The fortitude of those pioneers was richly rewarded. The new stock was heavily oversubscribed and share values trebled within days. The first meeting of the board of directors of the Creditanstalt, with

Anselm as vice-president, took place on 30 December 1855.[16] It had been quite a year.

But the longest campaign in the *lutte bancaire*, and the one which proved decisive, was the battle of the railways. The Péreires had first joined the railway boom in April 1853, when they formed a consortium, called Le Grand Central, to exploit a major concession extending from the Rhône Valley to the Limousin Plateau, a large area of central France. This cut across territory already being worked by other railway companies, Paris-Lyon, Paris-Orleans and La Mediterranée. The objective of Grand Central was simply to force its rivals out of business and control the entire network south of the capital. Towards the end of 1855 Baron James drew the directors of the three threatened companies into a syndicate of his own, the Réunion Financière. This group would create a massive private industrial credit bank which would deploy its capital to enable companies to resist the pressures of the Crédit Mobilier. The Péreires were alarmed and appealed to their friends in government. The Réunion Financière application for a charter was turned down. James was furious. With the Emperor behind them there seemed no way to block the advance of the Péreires' financial machine in France.

Yet it was stopped — not by any masterstroke of the Great Baron's, but by a combination of his dogged opposition and changed economic circumstance. The year 1856 saw the start of a depression. Share prices fell. Government demands for finance increased. The Crédit Mobilier found itself overextended, as James had always believed — or hoped — it would. In 1857 it was obliged to put Grand Central into liquidation. Its stock and concessions were quickly gobbled up by the rival railway companies. Investors were soon selling Crédit Mobilier shares heavily. In 1858, in an attempt to arrest the decline, the Péreires paid a dividend out of capital. It was the beginning of the end. The Saint-Simonian dream of state-controlled credit had faded before the cold reality of *haute banque* finance. The Crédit Mobilier survived for another nine years, but it had failed to unseat the great private bankers and that meant that the Péreires' challenge had failed. The Rothschilds, and all that they stood for, had proved invincible.

CHAPTER 13

"There is not a people or government in Christendom in which the paws . . . of the Rothschilds are not plunged to the very heart of the treasury"

The Rothschilds were a European phenomenon. They remained so throughout the rest of the nineteenth century and well beyond. Europe was then the commercial centre of the world. Into it poured the vegetable and mineral wealth of America and the Colonies. From it went textiles, manufactured goods, railway locomotives and engineering expertise. The banking, insurance and other skills which lubricated international trade were located in London and Paris and, to a lesser extent, in the other capital cities of the Old World. From their counting houses, the Rothschilds could control an ever widening network of activity.

But the world was changing. As the decades slipped past, European supremacy began to be challenged. Almost imperceptibly at first, hitherto undeveloped countries gained ground on the leaders in the commercial race. The vast North American continent grew rich — and powerful — on southern cotton, Californian gold and the grain of the prairies. Australia and South Africa boomed after the discovery of gold and (in the latter) diamonds. By the end of the century even Japan was making a bid to be taken seriously as an industrial nation.

The Rothschilds had up till now been models of flexibility and resilience. They had defeated the Péreires, just as they had defeated Napoleon, by a combination of family solidarity and adaptability to change. But they were essentially Europeans. Could they continue to combine the properties of the willow and the oak in the face of new challenges which, though more gradual, were in the long run, more powerful than any which had confronted them before?

Up until the mid-century the Rothschilds entrusted to agents their business in distant lands. These might be on-the-spot financiers or merchants, or trusted bank employees sent abroad after years at New Court or Rue Laffitte. Whoever they were, their positions carried enormous responsibility and prestige, as well as the potential for considerable personal profit.

Rothschilds were in the vanguard of overseas development. As new colonies were opened up in Africa, and the newly created nations of South America sought to expand their economies, the agents of the Paris or London house were there to buy up mining concessions, finance railway building or provide state loans. They owned or had major shareholdings in Central American ironworks, North American canal construction companies and a multiplicity of other concerns. They became the major importers of bullion from the newly discovered goldfields; in 1855 the London bank established its own gold refinery on Tower Hill in premises recently vacated by the Royal Mint. In the same year De Rothschild Frères helped the Banque de France out of a severe monetary crisis by providing it with large consignments of gold.

The name "Rothschild" was, thus, beginning to be heard in places far removed from sophisticated London and Paris. But the connection with the great bankers was sometimes tenuous. In 1841 Maurice Worms went out to Ceylon and set up the Rothschild Coffee Estate. Writing of this event, his nephew explained:

> It has been thought that this name was given to the property because the Rothschilds themselves were interested in it. This is totally erroneous; it belonged solely to Maurice Worms and his brother Gabriel who came out and joined him in 1842. The name of "Rothschild" was given to the property at the express request of Messrs Worms' uncles, the Baron Anselm von Rothschild of Frankfurt and Baron James de Rothschild of Paris.[1]

We can only assume that the reason for this strange request was to enhance the reputation of Rothschilds as an international commercial concern (though the Worms brothers' prestige would also have been increased by the arrangement).

However, in many of the developing lands the name meant exactly what it said — that the world's leading private bankers had a man on the spot. The appointing of such agents always posed a problem of trust. The Rothschild representative in New York, Mexico City, Havana, Cape Town, Melbourne, Singapore or some other faraway capital, had considerable freedom in handling negotiations running into thousands, sometimes millions. It took weeks for instructions and reports to travel to and fro across the oceans, so the men *in situ* had to be allowed considerable latitude and encouraged to use their initiative for the firm rather than for their own advantage. The Rothschilds' policy was to appoint only men they could trust — and then to check up on them whenever possible.

Of all the overseas capitals, New York was, of course, the most important. The Rothschild representative there was a remarkable man and one about whom the family could never make up their minds.

In 1829 a fifteen-year-old Jewish boy called August Schönberg arrived in Frankfurt and talked his way into a menial job in Amschel's bank. He was good at talking. When it suited him, he could be very charming and he knew, quite clearly, what he wanted. It could be expressed in one word – "money". That was why, after a wild, unruly childhood, he had left home with the fixed intention of attaching himself to the fabulously wealthy and successful Rothschilds. This thrusting, aggressive youth combined some of the qualities of Nathan and James. He was brusque, impatient, single-minded and possessed an insatiable appetite for the finer things in life. He was also a financial genius. Amschel and Carl were not slow to recognise this talent, and young August earned rapid promotion. In 1832 he was transferred to Naples to widen his experience. By the time he was twenty-three, he had mastered the intricacies of international banking and become fluent in English, French and Italian. Then came his lucky "break". In 1837 the Rothschilds needed someone to go to Cuba where their interests were being seriously affected by the spread of revolt against Spanish rule. They chose their brilliant young protégé and despatched him without delay. A few months later they had a shock.

August Schönberg set off for the Caribbean. But August Belmont arrived in New York. With scant regard for his employers, he grabbed the opportunity to establish himself as a virtually independent financier. America was the land of promise – not Cuba. So, he simply disembarked in the commercial capital of the United States. And, because that capital was swarming with German Jews, August transliterated his name into French and changed his religion.

He could not have chosen better the moment of his arrival. He walked into one of the greatest financial and political crises in American history. The Bank of the United States, which had been set up to finance the government of the Union and provide a measure of economic stability, had never been popular with the leaders of the various states who regarded it as a weapon of the central power, nor with the more adventurous businessmen who resented the restrictions it imposed on commercial development. The nation was booming. Impatient farmers, railroad builders and industrialists looked elsewhere for sources of capital, and speculators in Europe and America fell over themselves to oblige. State banks did brisk business. Rothschilds and other European financiers supported major projects. Small banks sprang up all over America, especially after President Andrew Jackson, siding with the radicals, made it clear that the central bank's charter would not be renewed after 1836. In that year, when the last restraints were removed, there was a frantic rush of investors into the market looking for quick profits. Within months the inevitable happened: the overheated economy burned itself out. Investors now hurried to cash in their shares. Companies went bankrupt. Banks stopped paying out specie. Several crashed. Trapped in the middle of all this confusion were millions of dollars' worth of Rothschild investment. Seven weeks before Belmont's arrival the Rothschild agents, J.L. and S.I. Joseph and Company, had gone bankrupt. Belmont simply took their place. He rented an office on Wall Street and, almost as an afterthought, he wrote to his superiors for authentication. Without waiting for a reply, he began using his employers' prestigious name and their money to acquire shares in a depressed market.[2]

If the Great Baron and his brothers were angered by such audacity, they may have reflected that Belmont was only doing with their resources what Nathan had done with the Elector's gold a generation before. In any case, they could scarcely afford not to back Belmont. It would take months to appoint, brief and despatch a new agent. But the banking crisis demanded urgent attention and there was a great deal of other pressing business to be attended to. Over the years since N.M., the Manchester textile manufacturer, had bought cotton from the southern states, Rothschilds had developed heavy American commitments. Nathan had been very impressed by the opening of the Midwest and the development of agriculture and industry, and had acquired a considerable stake in the future of the continent. He had made loans to various states of the Union, had been, for a time, the official European banker for the US government and was a pledged supporter of the Bank of the United States. Thus, the London house, although far from happy at being presented with a *fait accompli* by Belmont, had little choice but to accept his offer.

Belmont — now August Belmont and Company — set about salvaging what he could from the wreckage. He wrote letters to every client demanding to see accounts, calling in loans, arranging repayments. He dealt reasonably effectively with a very difficult situation, but stubborn doubts about the agent's trustworthiness remained lodged in his principals' minds. As soon as possible, Lionel sent out a senior member of the bank to supervise Belmont and find out just what he was up to. The report which came back was generally favourable. Yet New Court and Rue Laffitte continued to be nervous about the amount of their business the agent was handling. Belmont, for his part, resented their lack of trust. The transatlantic bickering went on year after year; and while the Rothschilds grumbled about their all-too-independent representative, Belmont established himself as a highly successful banker. Indeed, he went further: by rapid degrees he became the leading figure in the social and political life of New York.

There is more than a hint of Baron James's technique in the way that the young Belmont took the city by storm. It was a "new" city — bustling, thriving, growing. Unlike more established communities such as Boston and Charleston, it was not under the fusty influence of old settler families. A man with personality and money could make his mark. Belmont was physically unprepossessing but he had enormous magnetism. He was deliberately reticent about his past. When rumours of delicious scandals circulated (it was even hinted that he was an illegitimate Rothschild), he did nothing to stop them. He gave large dinner parties at Delmonico's. He served the best French wines. He sprinkled his conversation with Europeanisms and appointed himself an arbiter of taste. Women found him irresistible. Men accorded great respect to the representative of the world's greatest private bankers.

As soon as his income allowed, he bought an impressive house on Manhattan Island and gave such lavish parties and entertainments that the leaders of society were soon clamouring for invitations. His more sedate dinner parties brought resident and visiting celebrities flocking to his table.[3] Belmont understood well the importance of public display: the appearance of wealth creates confidence. Thus, when he drove through the streets of New York, it was in one of the finest carriages in town. He kept a string of racehorses and was a joint founder of the Jerome Park racecourse. He would do anything to be the focus of attention. When his close friendship with a certain lady attracted unfavourable comment from a jealous rival, Belmont "called out" the offender and let it be widely known that he had challenged the man to a duel for impugning the lady's honour. It was a risky thing to do, for Belmont was not a practised shot. In the event, the assignation was, like most duels, something of an anti-climax. Both pistols were discharged. Both missed their mark. But honour was satisfied and Belmont's fame was enhanced. His entertainments became increasingly lavish. He enjoyed giving fancy dress balls and always had to outdo his guests in the magnificence of his costume. It is even reported that he attended one such function in a full suit of gold-inlaid armour which cost ten thousand dollars. There was, to be sure, a section of New York society which resented this brash upstart, and kept him at arm's length. But, before long, Belmont was able to deal with this clique in true Rothschild fashion. Finding himself not invited to a prestigious ball, he called upon the organisers and intimated that if his name did not appear upon the guest list they would awake the following morning to find themselves seriously embarrassed financially. Like the great N.M., Belmont became a legend in his own time; a man around whose name the most unlikely stories gathered.

Within eight years Belmont had built a sizeable personal fortune and was able to take up a large portion of a federal government loan at the time of the Mexican War. He also purchased this and other state stock for his principals. The Rothschilds learned to recognise that they were getting an excellent service from their US agent, despite frequent disagreements with him and their constant suspicion that he was making huge profits at their expense. Belmont found plenty of business for London and Paris in this exciting, expanding land and kept them extremely well informed of transatlantic events. Year in and year out the New York office maintained an almost daily flow of correspondence, so that the parent houses would remain up to date with their investments in bullion, cotton, tobacco, federal bonds, state bonds, railways, state banks and a wide range of industrial companies.

And Belmont provided an excellent service for the government in Washington, giving them access to Rothschild funding throughout a period when adequate cash supply was a constant headache. His usefulness took on a new dimension in 1844, when he successfully negotiated for the Austrian Consul Generalship, and joined the Democratic party, rapidly rising to a prominent position in its ranks.

In Europe the superlative courier service developed by the Rothschilds had been instrumental in shaping their political rôle: it was because they could provide superior information that they had been taken into the confidence of princes and ministers, and had become advisers on policy. History now repeated itself. Politicians at Westminster and in the Elysée Palace wanted information about America, and the Rothschilds were the best people to provide it. From there it was but a short step to governments on both sides of the Atlantic using the bankers as an unofficial channel of communication. Periodically the Rothschilds planned to send a member of the family to check personally on Belmont. In 1840 Nat proposed a visit but nothing came of it. In the spring of 1848, as we have seen, James decided to despatch Alphonse to get him out of revolutionary France. This plan, too, failed to materialise. But later that year Alphonse did go. He had a specific brief: in view of the volume of business they were now doing through New York, should the Rothschilds continue with Belmont or set up their own bank?

Since the European bankers were contemplating removing their agency from August Belmont and Company, Alphonse can scarcely have expected a warm welcome. He certainly did not receive one. The New York agent's behaviour was haughty and churlish. "The day I set foot on American soil," Alphonse reported, "Belmont realised that his reign was at an end."[4] And he was soon pouring out his complaints: the Rothschilds treated him more as a correspondent than an agent; they did not trust him; they were always ready to let hard-won American business drop if it

180

did not suit them. Despite his cool reception, Alphonse really did try to understand Belmont's position. After twelve years of virtual independence, he suggested, it was difficult to expect the man to submit to firm control, and perhaps there were faults on both sides.[5] But the psychological gulf between the two men remained as wide as the Atlantic.

Throughout the six months that Alphonse spent in America he and Belmont were very wary of each other. But the young Frenchman had other things to do. He toured extensively, familiarised himself thoroughly with the present state of Rothschild business in America and assessed the future potential of the continent. It impressed him enormously.

> Without the slightest doubt, this is the cradle of a new civilisation
> ... The settlement of California is an event of enormous potential
> for America, not only because of the more or less fabulous seams of
> gold she conceals in her depths, but above all because of her geo-
> graphical position. In a few years from now America will have
> attracted to itself the greater part of trade with China and the Indies
> and will be enthroned between the two oceans ... the country
> possesses such elements of prosperity that one would have to be blind
> not to recognise them, and one cannot but admire the intelligence
> and energy with which the people know how to exploit them. In
> Europe there are many prejudices about America, but they dissolve
> when confronted by the facts.[6]

He was in no doubt about the implications for his family:

> I have no hesitation in saying that a Rothschild house, and not just
> an agency should be established in America ... Today we are
> presented with a fine opportunity. Later on, difficulties will of
> necessity arise as a result of competition from all sides. Since you
> have decided to put your American business on another footing, you
> should make a complete change.[7]

As far as the chauvinistic Alphonse was concerned, there could be no question of continuing to trust Belmont, who was "an American in the full sense of the word". By this he meant that the agent was touchy, suspicious, excitable and too independent.[8] Alphonse offered to take charge of the new office, "although it would be painful to me to remain separated for a long time from my family and friends".[9]

All seemed set for what would have been one of the most momentous developments in Rothschild history and an event of great significance in the economic history of the western world. Then, suddenly, the whole idea was dropped. Alphonse was summoned home and Belmont was confirmed in his position.

This was the greatest opportunity the Rothschilds ever lost. Had they established a bank in New York at this early stage in the nation's growth, there can be little doubt that the wealth derived from that one source would have dwarfed, within a generation, all that they had amassed so far in Europe. It is difficult to understand why James and Lionel ignored Alphonse's powerful advocacy. It may be that family ties were too strong, and that the Great Baron was not prepared to send his eldest son into semi-permanent exile from Paris. Probably, there was a strong element of prejudice in the decision to avoid greater involvement in the turbulent young nation. At the end of his life James was convinced that "America is a country that defies all calculation".[10]

What is certain is that Belmont did all in his power to prevent himself being displaced. He was working hard to consolidate his social position in New York and, within months of Alphonse's departure, he achieved his greatest coup. This was his engagement to Miss Caroline Perry, daughter of Commodore Perry of the United States Navy. Caroline came from one of the leading Democrat families and this eased Belmont's own political career. His future father-in-law was already a distinguished officer and later he won a place in history when, with only four ships, he forced Japan to end centuries of isolation and open diplomatic relations with the United States. Belmont's engagement to the palely beautiful Caroline earned him the supreme social accolade – he was admitted to membership of the exclusive Union Club.

The couple were duly married, set up home on newly fashionable Fifth Avenue and eventually acquired the street's most imposing mansion. The house became the social focal point of the city. It was the first residence to have its own ballroom, used on one evening a year only for the principal event of the season. The couple's dinner parties were, it goes without saying, the ultimate in elegance. Epicurean dishes prepared by a chef trained by Carême, were served on gold plates by a battalion of wigged and liveried footmen. August Belmont, it was confidently whispered in New York salons and counting houses, spent two thousand dollars a month on wine alone. James and Lionel may well have concluded ruefully that the man's position was now impregnable and that it would have been folly to set up against him a member of the family who was still little more than a boy.

For the next decade Belmont continued to handle the family's growing interests in New York with considerable success. Then crisis struck once more at American commerce, as North and South began to drift towards civil war. Back in Europe, the bankers avidly read their agent's reports about mounting tension and the disruption of trade. As open conflict became inevitable they were faced with the question of which side to support. From a professional point of view, the decision had to be a pragmatic one: it was necessary, above all, that they should back the winning side.

As in Europe, so in America, the clash of ideologies confronted the Rothschilds with moral choices. As members of a despised minority they sympathised with the cause of emancipation. On the other hand they had a considerable stake in the slave-owning south and a greater understanding of its paternalistic society. Moreover, they were, as ever, suspicious of "revolutionary" movements which threatened to upset public order. Belmont, by contrast, had no such doubts. He was one of the northern Democrats who had come out in support of the Union, and in his letters he urged James and Lionel to use their influence to gain political support in Europe for the North. But the Barons decided that the issue was too important for them simply to follow their agent's advice. Once again they sent a member of the family.

The man chosen for the job was Salomon, the third son of James and Betty. One of his cousins described him as "brilliantly gifted but less addicted to steady work than his brothers".[11] Some delightful early photographs at Château Lafite bear out this opinion. They show Salomon practising "levitation" and other high-spirited pranks. Certainly he was a strong, lively character, and it was therefore inevitable that either he would follow his father and become an aggressive, creative *homme d'affaires*, or that he would rebel. There could be no other outcome because James did not contemplate the possibility of his sons' choosing any career other than the bank. Salomon did not want to go into the bank. Nor could he take being a Rothschild very seriously. This infuriated James.

Had he been allowed to go his own way, Salomon might have made something of his life. He was a young man with a keen eye for detail and a cool head for appraising a situation. But, as the odd man out in the immediate family and business circle ruled by Baron James, Salomon could only seek to play down the tension by masquerading as the clown of the family. Finally, according to contemporary gossip, he committed what was, for a Rothschild, the unforgivable sin; he speculated wildly and unsuccessfully on the Bourse. This led to an almost complete breach with his father and he was packed off to Frankfurt for a couple of years. So furious was James with Salomon's whole attitude that for a time he not only turned the young man out of his house, he actually forbade him to stay in Paris. It is not surprising, therefore, that, in the autumn of 1859

183

James grasped the opportunity of killing two birds with one stone. He despatched the twenty-four-year-old rebel to America where he could gather important information and, perhaps, grow up a little.

Salomon formed decidedly strong opinions about the American situation. In his extensive travels on both sides of the future divide, he conceived a profound dislike of the northern cities and of Union political activists. While taking the waters at Saratoga Springs, NY, he reported:

> ... there was a big meeting in favour of Douglas [Stephen Douglas, northern Democrat presidential candidate], in which the speakers called the people of the South a rabble, traitors, etc. To show still more enthusiasm, the partisans of the "little giant" put a barrel of tar and resin in the street and set fire to it. The flames were going splendidly when up came a stage-coach driven by a coachman of a different political party ... [He] drove his carriage straight at the barrel, which he knocked over and broke to pieces. In a second the inflammable material spread, causing a fire that the people at the "meeting" had to put out themselves. What scum all these people are!! ..." [12]

Belmont was Democratic National Chairman and one of Douglas's leading supporters, so Salomon doubtless felt obliged to attend such gatherings, however deeply they offended his patrician sensibilities:

> The meeting was opened not by a banquet nor even by a meal, but by a veritable wallow of food on which the famished mob leaped like a pack of wild animals. The orgy over, they gathered around the platform. I will spare you the political part and tell you only that Belmont, a friend of Douglas and president of the "meeting", gave a "speech" to the crowd that was nicely done, although improvised. [13]

Salomon also gave the Republicans a hearing. He found them even less to his taste:

> The next day, Thursday, was the Republicans' turn. Beginning at eight in the morning, traffic was blocked by a great demonstration. From all parts of the city, bands headed towards Cooper Institute, where the "meeting" was held. When the speeches were finished, the audience formed squads, each carrying a torch and most of them dressed in red. They went through the most densely populated sections of the city in perfect order, but with the most infernal shouting. I cannot tell you what an impression this scene, worthy of Dante, made on me. It reminded me of the sad days of '48; it made me think of the dangers that constantly hang over our heads and made me foresee for this country an era of revolutions and civil wars. [14]

The election of Abraham Lincoln in November 1860 was seen by Salomon as merely one step closer to the abyss, and he had nothing but contempt for the new President.

> ... he is not up to his position and the Republicans themselves regret having nominated him. He rejects all forms of compromise and thinks only of repression by force of arms. He has the appearance of a peasant and can only tell bar-room stories. The other day I saw one of his supporters, who had been to see him at Springfield to chat with him about the situation. He found him seated, legs on the mantlepiece, in shirtsleeves, hat on his head, amusing himself by spitting great gobs of tobacco juice that he extracted from his quid. After conversation which shed no light on the way Mr. Lincoln viewed things, the visitor − who is one of the Republican leaders − went away very disappointed in the future president. In this country, people do not take umbrage at nonentities; the greatest claim to public favour is to be unknown.[15]

By contrast, Salomon found everything about the South appealing. Society was well ordered, and its political leaders were courteous, educated and intelligent. His final conclusion, written in a long letter of 28 April 1861, shortly before his departure, was that Europe should hasten to recognise the Confederacy and thus halt the Civil War.

In his advice regarding the family business, Salomon was quite unequivocal. He disagreed completely with his elder brother's earlier assessment of America's economic potential. It was, in his view, a country in turmoil, a country in which investment could never be regarded as safe, a country to which the Rothschilds would be unwise to increase their commitment.

Belmont was seriously alarmed by Salomon's assessment of the situation, which he could only regard as wrong in every particular. In his view, everything depended on preserving the Union. That meant *more* investment by the Rothschilds, not less. Belmont knew that if they did not help finance the North, their rivals would. After the war the government would certainly remember who their real friends were. It was, therefore, in some desperation that he travelled to Europe in 1861 to persuade the Rothschilds to his point of view. He discovered that the attitude of the Old World towards the American conflict was mixed. The French were inclined to favour the South but the British were divided − a state of affairs summed up in the *Punch* jingle:

> Though with the North we sympathise,
> It must not be forgotten,

That with the South we've stronger ties,
Which are composed of cotton.

Everyone was agreed in wanting to see the conflict, and the consequent disruption of trade, brought to an end as swiftly as possible. The suggestion was made in London that the European powers might be able to mediate a peace between the two sides. But Belmont was vehemently against this. He insisted that his fellow countrymen would regard any such intervention as interference.

Belmont was in a very difficult position. In fact, he was at a crisis point in his business and political career. The Rothschilds had refrained from financial commitment to the rebels but they persistently urged the need for a speedy peace and a compromise on the slavery issue which would not impoverish plantation owners in the South. Furthermore, they had become decidedly reserved about providing funds to the government in Washington. As a result Belmont's influence in official circles suffered a setback. His political enemies in the North were not slow to attack what they saw as unprincipled mercenary attitudes. "Will we have a dishonourable peace, in order to enrich Belmont, the Rothschilds, and the whole tribe of Jews . . . or an honourable peace won by Grant and Sherman at the cannon's mouth?" *The Chigaco Tribune* demanded. And a political opponent entertained a rally with soap-box oratory:

> The agent of the Rothschilds is the chief manager of the Democratic Party! . . . There is not a people or government in Christendom in which the paws, or fangs, or claws of the Rothschilds are not plunged to the very heart of the treasury . . . and they would like to do the same here . . . We [Americans] did not want to borrow [from the Rothschilds], and the Jews have got mad, and have been mad ever since. (Cheers). But they and Jeff Davis and the devil are not going to conquer us. (Prolonged applause).[16]

Events, of course, justified Belmont: permanent peace was only possible in the wake of victory by the North and the restoration of the Union.

The Rothschild bankers ended by endorsing neither his suggestions nor Salomon's. They compromised. Probably, there had never really been much chance of Salomon exercising a creative influence on their policy. In sending him across the Atlantic, James's main aim, as we have seen, had been to provide him with the time and opportunity to grow out of his youthful rebelliousness. The experiment failed. Far from returning a reformed character, Salomon only managed to blacken the family name in a distant land. His extravagances and womanising became the talk of New Orleans and he was thrown out of the elegant New York Club for telling risqué jokes and showing around nude photographs. After his return he continued to be a trial to his family. In 1862 they got him married off to one of Mayer Carl's serious daughters, Adèle. But if that was meant to calm him down, it, too, failed. A relative who met the honeymooning couple in Venice found Salomon "genial, brilliant and somewhat dare-devil".[17] A year later he became the father of a daughter, who was named Hélène.

It is possible that responsibilities and middle age might have induced a more sober outlook on life. Salomon did have a serious side to his character. He was an active member of the Jewish Charity Committee and gave generously to the poor. He felt deeply about the sufferings of his people. At the age of twenty-three he had paid a personal visit to Jewish refugees in Tangier who had been rendered homeless by the war between Spain and Morocco, and made provision for their medical needs. Sadly, he had no time to display his true worth. He died suddenly on 14 May 1864 at the age of twenty-nine. Gossips said his unexpected collapse was the result of overexcitement while gambling on the Bourse. It might be truer to say that what killed him was the attempt to force this very unusual peg into a conventional Rothschild hole. The pressures of being a Rothschild could be intolerable and lead to disastrous consequences. Hannah Mayer had discovered this. So had Salomon. The ensuing decades would produce others whose spirits were either cramped by family expectations or broke out in exuberant extravagance.

Among those who had been most devoted to Salomon – and he was a great favourite with many of his younger relatives – was his young widow, now alone at the age of twenty-one. She preserved her husband's memory by remaining single for the rest of her long life and by keeping their house on the Rue Berryer exactly as it had been on the day Salomon died. Within its walls she became a semi-recluse. She had many friends whom she entertained with charm and style, but she refused to return their visits. She was a considerable patroness of artists and authors, but she did not go to galleries and ateliers to see their work. Whenever she heard of a young painter or poet or sculptor who seemed worthy of note she had her carriage and four prepared. This was sent to the appropriate address and returned to Rue Berryer bearing the man and examples of his work. Apart from visits to her country properties, the Baronne Salomon continued to live in this way for fifty-eight years. But tragedy was not finished with her. When her daughter, Hélène, was twenty-four she married a Christian. Adèle, a devout, orthodox Jewess, banished the girl from her presence and cut her out of her life. When she died, in 1922, the bulk of her estate was bequeathed to the city of Paris. This included the house in the Rue Berryer, in which nothing had ever been changed since the day that the madcap Salomon had died.

Meanwhile, Rothschild representation in New York remained on its traditional footing. That meant that, in real terms, Rothschild power and influence declined in the Union. As Belmont had feared, other bankers emerged from the Civil War crisis able to challenge the Rothschild-Belmont ascendancy. Particularly influential were J. and W. Seligman and Company. They had been the main financial stay of Lincoln's administration during the war and they reaped the benefits afterwards. They became major contractors in the government bond market and, by the mid-1870s, were regularly linked in consortiums with Rothschilds, Morgans and other great finance houses. But they did not stop there. In deliberate emulation of the Frankfurt Five, the Seligmans set up branches in London, Paris and Frankfurt as well as the major centres in the USA. They were soon being talked about as the "American Rothschilds".

Secure in their European bastions, the true bearers of that august name could afford to be patronising towards the new money men. When, in 1874, Isaac Seligman wanted to discuss a share deal with Baron Lionel, the latter consented to give him a few minutes at his town house on a Saturday morning. When the nervous Isaac entered, his host greeted him with the taunt "I am a better Jew than you; I don't go to business on the Sabbath." Gazing at the document-strewn table in Lionel's library, Isaac quickly replied, "Baron, I think you do more work here on a Saturday than I do in a whole week at my office." Lionel's expression thawed into a smile and the two men became friends. Isaac's brother, Henry, did not have the same success in Frankfurt. At a large reception he saw Wilhelm Carl on the other side of the room and asked to be introduced. Baron Rothschild acceded to the request. But the two men never met: neither would demean himself to cross the floor to the other. Small wonder that the head of the firm referred in a letter to the difficulty of dealing with "so haughty and purse-proud a people as the Rothschilds".

But Lionel and his cousins had miscalculated. A century after the Civil War the Rothschilds would have to fight their way back into the American market and it would not be easy.

CHAPTER 14

"A very serious and dangerous situation"

During the 1860s the concept of a European balance of power, maintained by mutual agreement between the leading nations, suffered a terminal illness. It had been something of a popular fiction for years and had almost received its *coup de grâce* when Russia, Britain and France went to war in the Crimea (1853-6). Yet that conflict *had* been settled in a *congress*, in Paris, at which the Continent's statesmen had also discussed other international problems. But by 1860 it became clear that the powers would pursue their own national interests, without reference to greater issues such as reactionary solidarity or European peace. The potential foci of conflict grew in number: the future of Germany; the unification of Italy; the disintegration of the Ottoman Empire; safeguarding the short route to India. They were brought into sharper relief by the personal ambition of Napoleon III and Otto von Bismarck.

What constantly disturbed the minds of the senior members of the family was the fear that national identity would, like water on a stone, gradually break down Rothschild unity. Assimilation had served them well. It had enabled the Frankfurt Five to win the confidence of statesmen and business leaders in the countries where they settled. But could a man be a completely loyal Englishman, Frenchman, German or Austrian and still put first the interests of his own international family?

Anselm was the most politically independent of all the Rothschilds. Within the Viennese house, he occupied a position similar to James's in Paris: he dominated policy but had by the 1860s relinquished routine administration to his sons, Nathaniel and Salomon Albert (though it was the latter, usually known as "Salbert" by his foreign relatives, who eventually took over sole control). Despite the enormous advances made by Salomon, Anselm and his family were still only recognised as belonging to the second rank in the highly stratified society of the Austrian capital. They were not officially accepted at the court of the autocratic Francis Joseph and still had many enemies among the aristocracy.

Anselm considered it prudent to distance himself as far as possible from imperial policy. Central government was all too often dominated by members of old families, selected more for birth than ability, whose major concerns were maintaining the existing order against creeping radicalism and the steady encroachment of Prussia. Factions and intense rivalries were the stuff of court politics, and scandals were not infrequent. Such distractions effectively prevented the pursuance of a consistent and constructive financial policy, capable of solving the economic problems of the unwieldy empire. Anselm thus saw little advantage and much potential danger in involving himself in politics. He confined himself to banking. But even in that sphere he sometimes found himself walking a tightrope.

This was particularly true of his work for the Creditanstalt. The board of the bank was divided into two factions – aristocrats and financiers. Anselm and his colleagues wanted a greater investment in major private enterprise, especially heavy engineering. They met with constant opposition from the conservative element, who believed that more resources should be channelled into support for the government. In 1859 Austria went to war with Piedmont, which was supported by Napoleon III. The imperial government, at the end of their financial tether, asked the Creditanstalt to fund food supplies to the army. It was probably this that brought matters to a head on the board. Anselm resigned, ostensibly over a disagreement about the filling of a vacancy. It was a wise move. Rumours were soon spreading that the bank directors had bribed army generals for the business. Baron von Bruck, the architect of the Credit-anstalt, was sacked from his post as Finance Minister and committed suicide shortly afterwards. The bank's directors were imprisoned but when the case came to court they were largely cleared (as was Bruck). The effect of this sordid affair within the Creditanstalt was to restrict severely the influence of the aristocratic clique. When the dust had settled (1861), Nathaniel von Rothschild took his father's old place on the board. He was able to bring to fruition several of Anselm's plans.[1] The fact that the Creditanstalt became more of an industrial investment bank than an organ of state policy, like the Crédit Mobilier, represented a quiet triumph for Rothschild principles.

It was an embarrassment to Anselm that, at Frankfurt, the brothers Mayer Carl and Wilhelm Carl were much more open in their support of the Prussian regime which, under Otto von Bismarck's leadership, was rapidly assuming the control of northern Germany. "Your Excellency knows", Mayer Carl wrote to Bismarck in 1863, "my old, proven and un-bounded devotion to your person and knows how attached I have always been to Prussian interests."[2] Mayer Carl was a jovial, extrovert character. He was good company at family parties, where he and his daughters (he had seven) could, with no difficulty whatsoever, be prevailed upon to sing, and he had a fund of funny stories. But his relatives regarded him as rather empty-headed and far too sycophantic. In 1867 he was elected to the north German Bund* and this served only to increase his commitment to the militant regime headed by Bismarck. Prussia pursued steadily more aggressive policies which could only alarm the heads of the other Rothschild banks who had always held the maxim that peace was the soil in which business could flourish best. When the Berlin banker, Gerson von Bleichröder, approached Baron James in 1862 for assistance with a government loan, the head of the Paris house, knowing that the money would be used to advance Prussia's military preparations, firmly declined the offer of participation. "It is a principle of our Houses", he wrote, "not to advance any money for war and even if it is not in our power to prevent war, then our minds at least can be easy that we have not contributed to it."[3]

Religious attitudes also helped to isolate the Frankfurt family from their relatives. They belonged to the strict synagogue financed by Amschel and presided over by the ultra-conservative Rabbi Sampson Raphael Hirsch, whose followers cut themselves off from liberal, "compromising" Jews and followed a path of strict orthodoxy. Hirsch exercised a remarkable degree of control over his own congregation and the Frankfurt Rothschilds were no exception. They stuck strictly to ritual observances, and displayed an intense moral rectitude and a deep sense of social responsibility. This sometimes clashed with their social ambitions. For example, though she esteemed very highly every mark of royal favour, Wilhelm Carl's wife once sat through an entire banquet given by the King without tasting a morsel because there was no kosher food available (history does not relate whether her husband was equally resolute).

Even the marriages, designed to reinforce the links between different branches of the family, did not always achieve the looked-for results. We have already seen how dissatisfied Lionel's wife, Charlotte, was with her lot, at least during the early years of her marriage, and that the differences between Laury and Alphonse did not make for a happy relationship. Nor did Laury's Uncle Nat fare any better in his pursuit of marital bliss with the lovely and talented French Charlotte. As for the clutch of Frankfurt girls, four of whom married within the family, the cultural and religious assumptions they brought with them sometimes created the most appalling tensions. Poor Adèle (Salomon's widow) lived the life of a semi-recluse in Paris, estranged from her only child. Two of her sisters, Emma and Thérèse, lived married lives that could not be said to be normal (see below, pp. 255ff., 269ff.).

*After unification in 1871 he became a member of the Reichstag.

The Rothschilds' sense of national identity would not have been so damaging to family concord if the Congress System had succeeded in containing the rivalries of the major European states. It did not. When, in 1859, France took the field against Austria over Italian unification she completed the breakdown of European order which the Crimean War had begun.

It was the movement to make of Italy one liberal nation which brought about the downfall of the Rothschilds' Neapolitan house. In 1860 a revolt led by Garibaldi and financed by Cavour seized first Sicily, then Naples. King Francis II fled to the promontory stronghold of Gaeta, where he held out for five months. Desperately in need of money to finance his resistance, he turned to Adolph von Rothschild, who had taken over the bank on the death of his father, in 1855. Francis offered the entire royal treasure in return for ready cash. The banker was in a position to drive a hard bargain and he did so. He refused to take any item incorporating Christian symbols. As for the rest, he acquired at a knock-down, all-in price a remarkable collection of regalia, jewellery, and objects of gold, crystal and enamel, some dating to Renaissance times. Adolph was an enthusiastic collector of *objets d'art* and, since the royal family never returned to redeem their valuables, these superb specimens went into his cabinets. In the following February, the King bowed to the inevitable and went into permanent exile.

Adolph had little interest in business and certainly lacked Baron James's skill for choosing the right moment for switching to the winning side. He left Italy soon after the King, and the Naples house was closed for good. He refused to participate in any of the other banks and insisted on cashing up his share. It was the first time that the Rothschilds had been obliged to diminish the capital of the family business. The negotiations were long, complicated and, at times, heated. However, a satisfactory solution was eventually reached.

Adolph, having at last escaped the tedium of banking, was able to devote himself to the enjoyment of a more congenial way of life. For this he needed a suitable setting. He, therefore, followed the family trend of building a magnificent new house. Moreover, like his cousins, he offered the commission to Joseph Paxton. The mansion which the architect now designed for Adolph and his wife, Julie (Anselm's daughter), was beautiful both in itself and its setting. Adolph and Julie chose a hillside site close to Geneva and there the soft, French-classical lines of the Château de Pregny still rise imperiously from terraces and lawns which slope gently down to Lake Geneva. Here, well away from the tensions of business and politics, the childless couple settled to the care of their collections and their no less magnificent gardens.

Beyond Switzerland's borders the major European powers were behaving like heavyweight boxers exchanging taunts before a contest. Napoleon III, always haunted by the shade of his uncle, was constantly tempted to cut a figure on the international stage and eventually he played into the hands of an equally ambitious, but far abler, rival: Otto von Bismarck. The man of "iron and blood", as he would later be known, was single-minded in his determination to create a new, powerful Germany, united under Prussian leadership. His ruthless creed of *realpolitik* made conflict inevitable. In the summer of 1866 he went to war with Austria. Four years later his victim was France.

In the midst of all these alarms and excursions the Rothschilds suffered a domestic tragedy. It was one of those sad events that all families experience from time to time — events which, because of the personalities involved, profoundly shock members of the immediate circle of relatives and friends, although they make little impact on the wider world.

Lionel's daughter, Evelina — "Evy" as she was usually known — was a bright, vivacious creature, always full of fun, who had usually been the ringleader in childhood and adolescent escapades. One such prank, carried out when Evy was fifteen, was remembered long afterwards by her cousin, Connie (Sir Anthony's daughter). Charlotte, Lionel's wife, had hit upon the notion of taking her daughter and her nieces to see the inside of a convent at Hammersmith. The prospect was scarcely an exciting one for the girls and Evy decided to liven up the expedition. Constance recalls what happened when they assembled to mount the carriages.

> Punctually we appeared — besides our mother and ourselves, my cousin Evelina and her friend Miss Probyn . . . also a *young lady* who had not been seen by us before. She had large dark eyes, and walked very bashfully, holding her skirts rather tightly round her knees. Who could this be? Tishy Probyn was giggling, so was Evelina — the *young lady* was Leo [Evy's youngest brother] in feminine attire. "She" got into one of the carriages, to our astonishment, and off we all drove to the said convent. There we dismounted and were very kindly received by the Mother Superior, who took us over her domain, not having an idea that we were not all of the feminine sex. I remember one awful moment when Leo caught his skirt on a banister, and a good-natured nun stooped down to set it right for him, and another still worse time when Father Heneage, priest and confessor at the convent, insisted upon receiving us in his parlour . . . As he passed us in review he said to my aunt: "And this a niece,

and this another niece, daughters of dear Anthony?" and then pointing at Leo: "And this yet another niece?"

Oh! how relieved we were when we got safely back into the carriage, and how my aunt scolded and cried, and said she never thought that Leo would have followed us into the convent! . . . but as he was only nine years of age no great harm had been done.[4]

Quite early in her life Evelina was marked out for marriage to her cousin Ferdinand ("Ferdy") in Vienna, who was exactly the same age. But despite being the result of blatant family scheming, theirs was a relationship of genuine affection which, certainly on Ferdinand's side, blossomed into a profound love. It is a sad irony that, at a time when several arranged Rothschild marriages were far from happy, the union of Ferdinand and Evelina, which had the prospect of being really successful, should be destined to end tragically. Unlike some of their cousins, neither of the betrothed faced the prospect of settling in an alien land.

Ferdy had always had a love of England, a love inherited from his English mother to whom he was very close. His interests, moreover, lay in art rather than banking and Baron Anselm seems to have made no attempt to force the square peg into a round hole, doubtless satisfied that he had two other sons to carry on the Vienna house. So, after the death of his mother in 1859, Ferdinand moved to London and took out British citizenship. Six years later, at a ceremony graced by Disraeli and other notables, he and Evelina were wed.

They immediately set off on a journey which was part honeymoon and part family tour, and which eventually led them, in a leisurely fashion, to Baron Anselm's estate at Schillersdorf. They returned at the end of the year and settled to the serious business of establishing a home in Piccadilly. By the spring Evy was pregnant. August found them holidaying at Scarborough where, among other things, they enjoyed the company of some members of what Ferdy proudly referred to as "*our* royal family". The Rothschild women were now eagerly awaiting news of the expected event. The holiday was, according to Ferdinand, only slightly marred by the "little indispositions" attendant on his wife's condition, and, in mid-September, he left her at Gunnersbury while he paid a visit to Austria. In November Evy returned to her own home for her *accouchement*, the child being expected around the middle of the month. It was late. When a boy was finally delivered on 4 December, it was stillborn. Evelina herself did not survive the birth.

The totally unexpected news was an intense shock to the whole family. Letters of stunned condolence arrived from relatives and friends all over Europe, and Connie wrote in her diary:

December 4th, 1866. Evy's death. O shocking, sad day! It seems almost impossible to write about it. And yet it took place. We were happy, merry, even joking, without the slightest thought of such a terrible event. It almost now seems to me impossible.

December 5th: Sadder even than the day before. Coming up to London and reading that terrible message in the paper. It was enough to arrive all trembling with fear and anguish. The house, all dark and shut up, confirmed our unhappy fear. And then, the sight of the mourners — oh, it went to my heart. Saw the bedroom, that gay, bright room with the motionless form on the bed, with the poor, tiny baby on the sofa. Oh, what a sight.[5]

It was the second time in seven years that death had deprived Ferdy of the person closest to him in the world. He made a protracted tour of the Continent in the company of Evy's favourite brother, Leo, in an attempt to rise above his grief. But even the magnificent treasures of St Petersburg failed to console him. Time partially healed the wound and he certainly found many tasks to occupy his mind, but he always remained a melancholy, rather touchy man who was never to remarry.

He did, however, channel his grief in a positive direction. In cramped and overcrowded Southwark he built, equipped and endowed the Evelina Hospital for Children, a hundred-bed hospital which, at that time, was the most advanced such institution in England. He also interested himself in, and became a generous benefactor to, other medical establishments such as the Hospital for Consumptives in Brompton Road and St George's Hospital at Hyde Park Corner.

Ferdy also found solace in the companionship of his youngest sister, Alice. She came to London, took the house next to his in Piccadilly, and had a communicating door built between them. At the age of twenty-one she had good reasons of her own for wanting to escape to England. The last few years had not been happy ones for her, and she had emerged from adolescence an introverted young woman who found human relationships difficult. She had been twelve years old when her much-loved mother died and thereafter she had been looked after by her sister Mathilde, the wife of Willy Carl of Frankfurt. The warm-hearted and highly gifted Mathilde doubtless lavished tenderness and sensitive care on the lonely girl, but for Alice the move from the relaxed atmosphere of Vienna to the rigid piety of her brother-in-law's household was a traumatic experience. She was older than her nieces and, though intellectually gifted, she patently lacked their social graces. The shy adolescent was also exceedingly plain. It is therefore little wonder that she withdrew from family life and became a lover of solitary pastimes. She thus welcomed the opportunity to leave oppressive Frankfurt and move to London in order to look after her equally lonely brother. Like Ferdinand, she was delighted to settle in their mother's country, the scene of the happiest interludes in Alice's youth when she had holidayed at Aston Clinton and greatly enjoyed riding with Annie and Connie, and generally taking part in their open-air life.

Though they shared his distress, Ferdinand's family had more important affairs on their minds at the time. Matters had come to a head between Austria and Prussia in the previous summer. The two countries had gone to war and within seven weeks Austria had been crushed at the battle of Sadowa. The Rothschilds had exerted all their influence to prevent a military confrontation but were powerless in the face of Prussian determination and Austrian pride. Baron James was reduced to expressing his annoyance and frustration by bouncing a five-thousand-franc cheque drawn by the Austrian Ambassador (who responded by shunning a ball given by Alphonse).

In Vienna the political and financial consequences of defeat were serious, and it was to help shoulder the increased burden placed on the bank that Ferdinand had been summoned home in September 1866. There were various payments arising from the war to be made and a new state loan to be negotiated, and all against a background of ministerial incompetence and growing public dissatisfaction. The drop in value in Austrian securities made recovery particularly difficult. At one stage these fell so low that there was a move to suspend dealings on the Paris Exchange. It was the intervention of Baron James, in response to an appeal from the Austrian government, which averted a crisis. The Rothschilds steadied the market and made it possible for Austria's finances to recover their stability.

That recovery came too late for the Rothschilds' great rivals. The Crédit Mobilier had invested heavily in Austrian securities. Following the Seven Weeks War the value of their shares fell from over 800 frs to 140 frs in less than a year. In January 1867 Achille Fould resigned as Finance Minister and within nine months he was dead. The Péreires were forced out of business and retired completely from the banking scene. So, finally, the battle of the banks came to an end.

The Rothschilds did not waste much time in gloating. The collapse of the Crédit Mobilier, though largely brought about by bad management and over-speculation, was a reminder of how easily the market could be upset by political rivalries and conflicts, and in an atmosphere of rising European tension the dangers grew ever greater. Bismarck's ambition of welding Germany together into a modern state and winning her a place among the great powers involved the cynical manipulation of rivalries and alliances and the creation of the best modern army. In the atmosphere of anxiety and mistrust which this created, the chancelleries of Europe needed more than ever a reliable, up-to-date information service. And the Rothschilds' was still the best. They had built up an extensive and labyrinthine network of sources and informants. They had business, social and political contacts in all the major Continental cities. Their couriers had priority access to the main railways. It would be quite impossible to unravel just how this formidable private intelligence service worked. Much of it, of course, operated in total secrecy. But an examination of two of Lionel's agents who were of vital importance in the crucial years 1867-71, will give some understanding of the breadth and depth of the unique Rothschild system.

The first was a French political informant who used the pseudonym "C. de B." His real name was Alexandre Guyard de Saint-Chéron, a legitimist (i.e. supporter of the Bourbon claim to the French throne, currently represented by the Comte de Chambord, acknowledged by his followers as King Henry V). An intimate of many courtiers and politicians, M. de Saint-Chéron seems to have made a successful living for over thirty years from supplying private clients and newspapers with daily bulletins about the deliberations of the great and powerful. He may well have been part of a royalist information network whose aim was to infiltrate and embarrass the imperial regime.[6] He was, then, something of a cross between a journalist and a spy — certainly he did not report exclusively to the Rothschilds. Nevertheless, the information he sent proved extremely valuable, not so much because he was privy to the secrets of the French government, but because he cast light, sometimes by relating seemingly trivial incidents, upon the prevailing mood of Napoleon III and his intimates. True, C. de B.'s bulletins were anti-government, but even after making allowances for bias, they must have given Lionel a convincing picture of the fears, even the fatalism, which pervaded government circles in France.

> Prussia is determined to make war rather than to halt in her movement of infiltrations. Napoleon admits when talking to his intimate friends that he is passing through a most difficult moment, both in home and in foreign politics, and that he cannot yet see how he is going to get out of the wood . . .
> A striking incident took place at the agricultural exhibition at Billancourt, showing quite clearly Prussia's intentions.
> The Prussian commissary at the International Tournament of Draught Horses was praising the superior merits of his country's horses. When the French commissary put forward the qualities of

197

French horses, the Prussian officer lost his temper and ended by saying: "It matters little whether or not you appreciate our German horses, for we shall be bringing them to drink in the river Seine in a few months' time!"[7]

Lionel had quite another kind of secret correspondent in Germany. Gerson von Bleichröder served as the head of the Berlin banking house bearing the same name. As such, he was a leading international financier, with his own network of commercial and political contacts throughout Europe and the Levant. He had for many years been a close business associate of the Rothschilds who, because of the growing importance of Berlin, found it particularly useful to have a colleague there with whom they enjoyed a good relationship. When Bleichröder became Bismarck's financial agent for raising state loans and other transactions, this relationship became even more important.

Lionel placed much more reliance on a man who was both highly intelligent and also intimate with Bismarck than he did on his Frankfurt cousins. Mayer Carl and Wilhelm Carl were, as we have seen, far too uncritically devoted to the cause of Prussian expansionism. From the viewpoint of London, Paris and Vienna, the Frankfurt brothers now appeared more Prussian than the King. They could no longer be relied on for impartial information nor be fully taken into the confidence of the other Rothschild bankers.

The existence of an unofficial diplomatic channel between London and Berlin was often valuable to ministers, not only for providing information, but also for smoothing the path for major negotiations. In 1867, for example, the British government led by Lord Derby and Disraeli was trying to heal the breach between Bismarck and Napoleon III. In formal discussions, the British negotiators took a firm line over certain territorial adjustments and guarantees but when they had pushed the Prussians as far as they could, they had to find a way of retreating without losing face. The answer was the Rothschild-Bleichröder "hot line". Primed by the Foreign Minister, Lord Stanley, Lionel sent a telegram to his friend in Berlin and followed it up with a letter: " . . . our government is inclined to accept the conference under the conditions as suggested. Your friend will like it but please don't mention our name and tell nobody that we give you political news."[8] This time oil was poured and the troubled waters subsided. But there was no way to avoid the impending clash between France and a North German Federation under Bismarck's control, which James, for one, had long predicted.

*   *   *

The Great Baron, now in his seventies and frequently in pain, was anxious about the future he would not live to see. Nothing had caused him to change his opinion of the government in Paris. He regarded Napoleon III's idealistic liberalism with disapproval and apprehension. Three times he had seen France dislocated by revolutionary fervour. He feared a fourth.

> I believe that there must be freedom in the sense that the press have the right to publish straightforward articles and that one is allowed to speak frankly about things that concern everyone, but it is a long way from that to all those liberties that the Emperor longs to bestow. I tell you frankly that we are in a very serious and dangerous situation; whether we want it or not we are going to be forced into war, not by external threats but above all by liberties given too soon and too quickly.[9]

James now exercised no caution about such forthright statements. He had triumphed over all his political and business enemies. On 17 February 1862 that triumph was symbolised by a formal visit to Ferrières made by the Emperor and his court. James had not sought the honour; the initiative came from Napoleon himself. He was, no doubt, interested to see the most celebrated modern building in France: but it was more than mere curiosity which drove the Emperor, who was notoriously conscious of his own dignity, to solicit an invitation from his old political adversary. The fact was that he needed the support of the great banker. The financial revolution planned by Fould and the Péreires had fizzled out and, though Fould had recently been restored as Minister of Finance, the administration had no choice but to offer an olive branch to the *haute banque*.

Most of the family had gathered at the château to witness this little Canossa. From the four towers the imperial standards flew side by side with those of Rothschild. James, mounted upon a platform carpeted in green velvet embroidered with gold bees, received his sovereign in regal style. There followed a magnificent luncheon in the great hall to the accompaniment of music by Rossini, then a tour of the palace. Napoleon planted a tree to commemorate his visit, before his host led him out into the park for a shoot. James had brought in an abundance of every kind of game from Germany to ensure that the imperial party had a good "bag".

Dusk was falling as the hunters returned to discover the château brilliantly illuminated and the tenors, baritones and basses of the Paris Opera Chorus assembled under Rossini's baton. To a percussion accompaniment they sang an "allegro brilliante" — written by the composer for the occasion. It was a heavily allegorical item called *A Chorus of Democratic Huntsmen* and it swelled to a mighty "fortissimo" on

199

its closing phrase, "Friends! The stag is at bay!"[10] The imperial party finally departed after a farewell speech in which James assured the Emperor that he and his family would always treasure the memory of that great day.

From that time the Rothschilds regained something of their old influence but not all. Alphonse and Leonora were for the first time received at the imperial court, but Betty refused to go and James no longer courted or cared for recognition. He did not need it and, besides, he was a sick man. Many years of travelling around the spas of Europe had brought him no permanent relief from gout. His eyesight was failing rapidly and he was afflicted with the added misery of gallstones. He now spent most of his time in health resorts – Gadstein, Carlsbad, Nice. But even when he was at home amid the splendours of Ferrières, the Great Baron now cut a rather sorry figure, as Evelina had once noticed. "We did not see much of uncle James. He was suffering from great pain, so one hour he walked in the gardens and the next he went to bed, he was wheeled about in a little chair, ditto aunt Betty and they each had three attendants, a pair to carry the bread and chestnuts for their deer, fish and birds."[11]

The Great Baron who had dominated the family for more than three decades; the "scoundrel" who had outsmarted and outmanoeuvred so many powerful rivals; the political survivor who had maintained his financial pre-eminence through monarchist, republican and imperial regimes, was approaching the end of his life.

Before his death, however, James opened up one more chapter in the Rothschild story. During the last months of his life he made his last great purchase and, in doing so, fulfilled his one remaining ambition. He bought the vineyard of Château Lafite, which he had coveted for almost half a lifetime. In 1866 the owner, M. Aimé-Eugène Vanlerberghe died and it was his London bank which, in the process of settling the estate, put Lafite up for auction in Bordeaux on 20 July 1868. A group of local merchants, determined to stop yet another vineyard falling into the hands of Parisian financiers, formed a syndicate to bid for the property. Yet, for some unexplained reason, they lost their opportunity and Lafite was withdrawn from sale, having failed to reach its reserve of 4,750,000 frs. On 8 August the auctioneers tried again, this time in Paris, with a lower reserve. The Bordeaux men turned up to bid at the Palais de Justice and soon became aware that the opposition included Baron James de Rothschild's agent. The bidding started off briskly. The new reserve of 3,250,000 frs, was soon passed. The merchants hung in as long as possible but when the price reached 4,440,000 frs, they had passed their limit. That was the figure at which the Great Baron became the very proud owner of what henceforth was known as Château Lafite-Rothschild.[12]

James's pleasure in this last great triumph had about it more than a hint of Anglo-French rivalry. Again he had proved his superiority over his London nephews. He already had a country house bigger and better than Muffy's. Now he had a vineyard better than Nat's. Once installed as the new owner he quickly learned the cat-and-mouse Bordeaux price game, as his nephew ruefully reported in mid-October. "I sold my wine the other day at Mouton at a famous high price of 5,000 the *tonneau*. The quality must be extraordinarily good this year as the merchants are buying it all up. Our worthy Uncle has not yet disposed of his Lafite. He expects a further rise." [13]

But the Lafite purchase proved to be the Great Baron's last big deal. At the end of October he took to his bed. An attack of jaundice finally immobilised his body and undermined his stubborn will. On 15 November 1868 he died. One story, soon circulating the European exchanges, was a macabre — and probably spurious — compliment to James's undiminished business acumen: foreseeing that his death would have a depressing effect upon shares in Lombard Company, of which he was president and chief shareholder, the wily banker is supposed to have speculated largely for the fall during his last days, thus securing immense profits for his heirs. [14]

Alphonse and his brothers inherited the bank, Ferrières and the other houses and, of course, Lafite. In 1870 Nat died and his sons became the owners of Château Mouton. From that time on one has to think of two French Rothschild families, distinct and experiencing a keen rivalry, sometimes friendly, sometimes decidedly not.

The death of Baron James marks a watershed in Rothschild history, not just because he was the last of the "Frankfurt Five", but because he was the last Rothschild to be generally acknowledged as the head of the family. From this point on, as the Rothschilds became more numerous and more widespread, the decentralising forces became irresistible. The new generations were more definitely Germans, Austrians, Frenchmen and Englishmen. More of them married out of the faith. Most of them married out of the family. After 1868 only three Rothschild men found brides among their own cousins. The forces which Nathan, Amschel, James and even old Mayer Amschel had seen at work and tried hard to resist eventually proved too powerful.

But James had done enough. Neither the family nor the business would break up into its constituent parts. The future would bring diffusion and diversification, but not disintegration. The foundations had been too well laid for that.

Part III
1870–1918

CHAPTER 15

"War and warlike talk the order of the day"

Within months of James's death his sons had to face the crisis he had feared. Diplomatic relations between France and Germany continued to deteriorate and, with popular feeling running high on both sides of the Rhine, both countries openly prepared for war.

By the summer of 1870 Europe was tense with expectation, waiting only to see where and when the conflict would begin. In the event the spark was inadvertently provided by the Spanish government, which secretly offered the country's vacant throne to Prince Leopold, a member of the Prussian royal family. Urged on by Bismarck, Leopold accepted on 19 June. When, on 3 July, the news finally leaked out, it provoked the French to universal outrage. Emperor and people were united in opposition to a covert deal which would , the politicians somewhat hysterically claimed, leave them encircled by the might of Prussia.

Napoleon's immediate response was to send protest messages not only to Berlin but to all the other European capitals. His message to London went via the Rothschilds. On 5 July the Emperor summoned Alphonse to St Cloud, and asked him to convey a message to Prime Minister Gladstone via his cousin. It was Lionel's son, Natty, who received and decoded Alphonse's telegram. He reported it to his father who sent him, post-haste, to the Prime Minister. He found Gladstone just about to leave for an audience with the Queen at Windsor, and was invited to share the leader's carriage as far as the railway station. The news was a shock and caught Gladstone completely off guard. Lord Granville had only taken over as Foreign Secretary a matter of days before, on the death of the previous minister, and had actually observed to a colleague that there appeared to be no cloud obscuring the prospect of peace. Gladstone's immediate reaction was one of caution. He agreed that the Hohenzollern candidature was highly undesirable but indicated that Britain could not intervene in the internal affairs of a foreign country.

Lionel was infuriated with what he considered a head-in-the-sand attitude. Alphonse, appalled at the thought of all-out war, urged his father-in-law to do everything he could to avert a crisis and, within days, the English Rothschilds were closeted with Disraeli, leader of the opposition, impressing upon him the urgency of the situation and begging him to challenge the government's non-interventionist attitude.

This may well have been the issue which set Lionel (and, later, his son) and the Liberal leadership on divergent paths. At the beginning of 1868 Gladstone and Disraeli assumed control of their respective parties and British politics was dominated by their personal animosity for the next thirteen years. It was inevitable that others, inside and outside parliament, would take sides. There is no record of Lionel's opinion, but Natty conceived an intense dislike for Gladstone and especially disapproved of almost every aspect of his foreign policy.

For his part, the Prime Minister clearly harboured no animosity towards the Rothschilds. In August 1869, within months of taking office, he presented the Queen with his first prospective honours list. One of the men recommended for a peerage was Lionel. Victoria accepted all Gladstone's nominees — except Lionel. For two months, the Premier argued with his sovereign. He pointed out that there was no one in the commercial sector who came anywhere near to Rothschild as deserving of honour. The Queen was adamant; she refused to ennoble a Jew. Perhaps she was still annoyed that Lionel had declined a baronetcy twenty years before. Gladstone grumbled to Lord Granville, "Her argument is null and void. If it be sound, she has been wrong in consenting to emancipate the Jews."[1] In the end, he had to give way. On at least two more occasions he mooted the possibility of Lionel's peerage. His comments on the second of these occasions, in 1873, suggest that the Prime Minister found himself confronted by the obstacle of Rothschild disdain as well as royal intransigence: "Rothschild is one of the best I know, and if I could but get from him a Mem. of certain services of his father as to money during the war I think it wd carry the case over all difficulty. But though I have begged and they have promised for about 4 years, I have never been able to get this in an available form."[2]

The Hohenzollern candidature put everyone on edge. The French government over-reacted. So did the Rothschilds. When Gladstone and Granville had had time to consider the situation carefully the latter made representations to Madrid and Berlin (where, in any case, the Prussian King, embarrassed by the whole affair, was already reconsidering his position). On 12 July the Foreign Secretary was relieved to be able to rush off a note to his chief, "The Rothschilds have recd a telegram. The Prince has given up his candidature. The French are satisfied."[3]

But any rejoicing was premature. Bismarck was not to be cheated of his war. Despite the disappearance of an immediate *casus belli*, he managed to manoeuvre France into actually declaring war on the 19th. By this time, thanks to the efficient railway systems, hundreds of thousands of troops were already massed on both sides of the frontier.

The Parisian Rothschilds were as anxious as all their fellow citizens and better informed than most of them. They knew that resistance to the Prussian military machine was virtually futile. Alphonse, the patriotic Frenchman, threw his support behind the government which had rushed into a war of which he so much disapproved. He helped to fund and set up a committee to organise proper care for the wounded. Like his father in 1848, he stayed in Paris through the darkest days of the crisis. Laury and her children took refuge in England. It was, therefore, in her parents' house in Piccadilly that she heard of the collapse of the Second Empire. On 1 September Napoleon III and his army suffered a humiliating defeat at Sedan. Even to Laury, who affected a disdain for the destiny of France, and who shared the general Rothschild dislike of the imperial regime, the news of such an unexpected, dramatic and decisive defeat came as a shock. Cousin Constance, who was present on the occasion, recorded it graphically in her journal.

> When we entered the breakfast room we saw a look of astonishment and partly dismay depicted upon the three faces of Uncle Lionel, Aunt Lionel and Laury. A fourth person, Mr Bauer, looking gloomy and dark, stood at the table with a telegram in his hand. These were the words of the dispatch: "The Emperor has surrendered himself to the King, and the army of forty thousand men has capitulated." Poor Laury felt humiliated like a French-woman. Then came the fear of revolution. She was dark crimson with excitement, and her voice trembled so that she could hardly speak . . . War and warlike talk the order of the day, nothing but that . . . It is very awful and horrid and sickening and how will it be averted? How will the end come?[4]

In Paris a republic was proclaimed and the new government resolved to continue the war. By mid-September the Prussians had surrounded the French capital and begun the process of pounding and starving it into submission. As if that were not enough, revolutionaries were soon active, attempting to wrest control of the government from the moderate republicans and make a separate peace with the invader.

Meanwhile, King William of Prussia arrived at Ferrières, where he had decided to establish his headquarters. Seeing the splendours of the château for the first time, he is reputed to have exclaimed, "It is too magnificent for a king; it could only belong to a Rothschild." The seventy-three-year-old monarch, though an aggressive autocrat, was a stickler for etiquette. He gave strict instructions to his staff that the house and grounds were not to be damaged or looted. His own personal conduct was a model of scrupulous propriety. Although he commandeered Leonora's suite, he would not sleep beneath the coverlet of her very feminine *chambre à coucher*. Instead he had his own campaign bed set up. In other respects, also, the King behaved well, as the Rothschild butler, Monsieur Bergman, reported: " . . . he had his own servants and kitchen, the domain supplied everything he needed: game, fruit and flowers; he gave us two thousand francs, but his retinue was very large, 3,000 men and 1,200 horses, divided up between us and the peasants. I myself had 4 officers and 6 soldiers, who were very well behaved . . ."[5] But William's subordinates were not all so restrained. General Gordon, who arrived two days before the royal party, was dissatisfied with the food served to his staff and took out his anger on the Rothschilds' elderly steward:

> . . . he ordered Monsieur Charles to prepare a dinner for fifteen. In the end, they were 32 at table, and very dissatisfied with the dinner. The General summoned M. Saint-Ange and told him that this was impossible, that in Madame de Rothschild's home one should be treated in a manner befitting the name and the style of the château; nevertheless, they drank 65 bottles of wine, including 32 of champagne, but it wasn't enough. The General had M. Saint-Ange taken off to the guard room escorted by four soldiers, and he had to spend the night on a bed of straw. It was sad to see this nice 75-year-old man in such a position; the next morning he was to have left with the army, but at 5 o'clock, Madame Saint-Ange went to see the General, and after much pleading obtained his pardon. I accompanied M. and Mme Saint-Ange throughout the whole sorry affair . . . [6]

Bergman, himself, fell foul of the Prussian bullies on another occasion.

> . . . The soldiers billeted at La Tafarette fished all the ponds, but that wasn't enough for them, so they decided one night to open the sluice-gates in order to find lots of fish stranded the next morning. When I was given warning of this, I went with several of my men and a locksmith to close the gates, but at that very moment the cavalryman arrived to water the horses. Terrible disappointment, no water! The soldiers thought it was I who had had the water drained, and they dragged me to the General, who was billeted with Madame Vavasseur. I explained what had happened, but he didn't believe me; he called the guards to take me prisoner, and I was ordered to have the ponds refilled at once. And this was impossible, and as none of it was my fault, they finally let me go after a few hours . . . [7]

After the King left for Versailles on 5 October, Bergman reported a pronounced decline in the behaviour of the Prussian officers:

... the 6th and 7th, looting of several houses in Ferrières; looting of the château wine cellars, requisitioning of blankets and mattresses for the field hospitals in the area. The King had taken care to request a written statement attesting that nothing was missing from the château at the moment of his departure, and he left behind 75 men on guard, but the officers claimed that this did not prevent requisitions for the field hospitals.

The château was visited by all the officers passing through. I assigned two of my men who speak German to M. Charles to accompany them on their tour but even so several objects have disappeared ... there are several field hospitals, we still have 2,000 invalids; there are no more animals on the farms, we have no more charcoal, but we still have wood. The Prussians and the poachers have killed the game; the grounds are reserved for them, the Commandant has it patrolled at night; the pheasantry and flowers are reserved, the gamekeepers were disarmed the day the Prussians arrived ... there's no money left in our cashbox, we pay with bread coupons, the farms are used as barracks, but the inhabitants still have to lodge a lot of soldiers ... [8]

Bismarck displayed none of his royal master's scruples or sensitivity. If he had had his way, every possible indignity would have been heaped on the French, including the Rothschilds. Having been a guest at Ferrières in happier times and enjoyed its incomparable shooting, he was annoyed to discover that his sovereign had put the game out of bounds. So he simply ignored the prohibition and went off defiantly with his gun into the Ferrières coverts. News of this trespass reached Alphonse in Paris who made a joke about it to a friend. This friend related it by letter to an acquaintance in the country. "The Prussians in the neighbourhood of Paris have a liking for pheasants. Rothschild told me yesterday that they were not satisfied with his pheasants at Ferrières, but had threatened to beat his steward, because the pheasants did not fly about filled with truffles." [9] The letter fell into the hands of the enemy and was eventually shown to Bismarck who was far from pleased at the oblique reference to his actions. During King William's stay at Ferrières, Jules Favre, the French Foreign Minister, spent several days in negotiations there, trying to agree a peace formula with the Germans which would not involve the surrender of Paris. Bismarck would not agree, so the siege went on.

As usual, the Rothschilds of London, Frankfurt and Vienna were better informed on events in the French capital than anyone else in Europe. The bank had its carrier pigeon service (messages were now often photo-graphed to enable the birds to carry more information — the first microfilm). There were also M. de Saint-Chéron's bulletins which left

Paris by balloon. The government authorised a daily service of gas-filled balloons to take mail and occasional passengers over the German lines. As a communications system it was haphazard in the extreme, since the craft were totally at the mercy of the wind and not infrequently within range of the enemy guns. Yet a surprising number of letters got through and from the hundreds of reports Lionel received from C. de B. it is possible to reconstruct an almost day-by-day account of the appalling suffering of the Parisians.

In the early days it was the indiscriminate bombardment which was the hardest to bear.

> The only result has been to kill harmless civilians, old people, women, and children; to destroy buildings and houses, and to kindle amongst Parisians sentiments of vengeance. Last night from 10 p.m. to 4 a.m., the frightened population never went to bed. Women ran out of the houses that were hit, clutching their children in their arms. It was a spectacle of desolation, but also of anger, especially on the part of the women.[10]

Very soon the political extremists were establishing themselves in several quarters:

> The revolutionary clubs, modelled on those of 1789, are already claiming to govern in the name of the Paris Commune, and red posters bearing this title have been placarded in the city this morning calling upon the National Guards to elect members of the Paris municipality. When this election has taken place you will see a display of armed force to set up the Commune.[11]

By early November food was becoming scarce. An inefficient form of rationing was introduced, but this did not stop the appearance of inevitable evils such as hoarding and black-marketeering. In the middle of the month C. de B. calculated:

> We have enough food to last two months, and the issue of a new set of ration books will put a stop to the initial muddling which resulted in far more cards being issued than there were members of families. Unfortunately the mortality has doubled since the beginning of the siege. The consumption of food has gone down in the same proportion.
> The Government's requisition of horses guarantees an adequate meat supply until 25th February. The Paris Cab Company still owns 6,000 horses, the Omnibus Company 6,700.[12]

Hunger, high prices, homelessness, bereavement, disillusionment with

210

the leadership, and a growing sense of frustration exacerbated differences in society and played into the hands of the revolutionaries.

The *Journal des Debats* is exposing the people who still keep luxury horses in spite of the fact that our crack cavalry regiments are obliged to kill their mounts to provide food. This newspaper is unfortunately quite right. I know a wealthy official of the Ministry of Finance who has eight horses, and the fine ladies who have stayed in Paris have nearly all kept theirs. A pretty society woman, who does canteen work, has a mare worth 7,000 francs. This public exposure will probably tighten the regulations.[13]

One of the wealthy Parisian ladies who continued to drive around in their fine equipages was Baronne Betty. Returning home one day at the height of the crisis, she was stopped by an angry mob in the Bois de Boulogne. Some began to unbuckle the carriage harness while others shouted insults. How dare she flaunt her wealth while other citizens starved! But the formidable Baroness, who had outfaced politicians and even scorned an emperor, was more than a match for a bunch of pitiable, hungry Parisians. "Yes," she said, "take my horses if you will have them, but I am as good a patriot as any of you. Come and see my hospital in my own house; and do you not know that I have three sons who are all bearing arms and fighting for our country?" Won over by the force of the old lady's personality, the mob not only stopped molesting her but formed an escort all the way to her gate.[14]

It is doubtful whether Alphonse devoted much time to military service, for his energies were largely expended in organising relief and giving financial advice to the leaders. But Gustave and Edmond played their part as members of the National Guard. Not that that part was, or could be, a very glorious one. The military activities of the French, led by General Trochu, consisted of waiting for help from the provinces which never came and sending a few ill-conceived and disastrous sorties against the German positions.

The attack which I described to you in my last letter developed into the second battle of Le Bourget. It proved as unsuccessful as the first, and this latest failure cost us not only the life of General Blaise, a veteran of our African army, and some 20,000 casualties (less from Prussian bullets than from the intense cold, the temperature suddenly dropping to many degrees below zero), but it has shaken the confidence of Parisians in their leaders, in themselves, and in the future of the war.[15]

It was Gustave's opinion, as stated shortly afterwards to a German diplomat, that firm and imaginative leadership could have achieved a military end to the siege. He probably voiced the complaint of many Parisians when he said, "Whenever there was any sign of trouble, General Trochu was nervous and undecided in dealing with the enemy."[16]

In the end the French were forced to seek peace at the conference table. On 21 February 1871 Favre and veteran statesman Adolphe Thiers (soon to become first President of the Third Republic) went to Versailles to hear the terms Bismarck had decided to impose upon them. The German demands were staggeringly harsh: France was to cede the border territory of Alsace-Lorraine and pay an indemnity of six thousand million francs, before German troops were withdrawn totally from French territory. Bismarck adopted a bluff "take it or leave it" stance but the French representatives said that they would have to call in a financial expert – Baron Alphonse de Rothschild. On 25 March the statesman and the banker (each of whom, in his own very different way wielded immense power) came face to face. Bismarck blustered in German. Alphonse replied in quiet, defiant French. Bismarck insisted on immediate agreement. Alphonse declared that he would have to work out the details with Bleichröder first. The Prussian had no alternative but to yield to further delay. Rothschild had managed to recover a modicum of French dignity.

He did very much more. Organising the payment of the indemnity (eventually agreed at five thousand million francs) proved an immense task, as Bismarck had intended that it should. The unprecedented financial burden was designed to cripple France, complete her humiliation and enable Germany to leave troops on enemy soil as long as possible. But Bismarck had miscalculated. He became the latest in a succession of politicians who underestimated the power of the Rothschilds. Alphonse set about raising the money so speedily and effectively that a rival banker was driven to wonder at the phenomenon: "Rothschild's important European relations and his financial power have created for him a rôle which is absolutely exceptional."[17] First of all, Lionel used his influence on the foreign exchanges to stabilise the French currency. Then he helped Alphonse to bring together a consortium of European bankers. This *haute banque* did two things: it organised a series of state loans and it guaranteed the total sum to the French government in the event of loans being undersubscribed. There was no danger of the latter eventuality. The name of Rothschild worked its old magic and the public clamoured to take up the shares. The five thousand million francs was to be raised by two loans; a two thousand million franc loan launched in March 1871 and another of three thousand million one year later. So massive was the demand that the first issue alone brought in

4,897,000,000 frs by June 1871. The second raised a staggering 43,800,000,000 frs.

The results of this major financial coup were dramatic. It brought huge profits to the participating banks, whose commission ran into tens of millions. They had to risk none of their own money; and they had the short-term use of an immense inflow of funds. Politically and diplomatically, it was a blow for Bismarck. The indemnity was paid within two years and he was obliged to remove his troops. Much more worrying was France's rapid recovery from the war and her new-found solidarity, of which the public response to the loans was just one example. Instead of weakening, humiliating and dividing the nation, as Bismarck intended, the defeat left France proud, united and smarting for revenge. The seeds sown in 1871 would bloom with deadly effect in 1914.

For the Paris Rothschilds, the triumph raised them to a level of prestige in France which they had not enjoyed since 1848. They were partners in the successful foundation of the Third Republic and their political influence was thenceforth guaranteed. But that influence would continue to be exercised behind the scenes. Alphonse was urged to accept nomination for the National Assembly from the constituencies of Paris and Seine et Marne. But he declined the honour on the grounds that political office would inhibit his business activities and that he could serve France better as head of De Rothschild Frères.

While the bankers were organising France's economic recovery, the last bloody episode of the events of 1870-1 was being enacted. The elections of February returned a predominantly royalist parliament, which established itself temporarily at Versailles. This was the signal for the long-threatened revolt of republican extremists to break out in Paris.

18th March 1871. A dreadful day has followed a sorry night. Paris is in the throes of a revolution . . .
The trouble started in Montmartre.
Members of the National Guard started to crack jokes with the regular troops on duty in the streets and squares.
"Those guns and rifles you've got are ours just as much as yours!" said the National Guard. "We all fought together, didn't we? Why don't you come and have a drink?"
A short time afterwards the regular troops, and even a squadron of the Republican Guard, came down into Paris, the butts of their rifles over their shoulders, laughing and joking with the National Guard. A captain who gave an order to his men was shot dead. The guns were left unattended on the Butte-Montmartre. Several battalions of National Guards on their way from the centre of Paris to Montmartre

213

met their fellows coming down and called out to them: "Down with Vinoy!" [General Vinoy was the commanding officer in Paris.] "Down with Paladines!" [General d'Aurelle de Paladines was the officer commanding at Versailles.]

"Long live the Republic!"

"Long live Garibaldi!"

There is no longer any Government in Paris. The National Guard is master of the capital. Perhaps it is a good thing that the National Assembly decided to meet at Versailles, for that august body would certainly have been attacked by the National Guard without being defended by the regular troops.

One general and several officers of the Republican Guard are prisoners at Montmartre.

Several battalions of the National Guard, passing M. Thiers's house in the Place Saint-Georges, cried out:

"Death to Thiers!"

I need hardly add that the red flag has been hoisted again in the Place de la Bastille.[18]

Thus did C. de B. report the beginning of the Paris Commune.

For over two months the revolutionaries created bloody havoc. There were summary executions and widespread looting (sometimes sanctified as expropriation in the name of the people). There were arson attacks on some of the city's most important buildings, including the Tuileries and the Hôtel de Ville. Paris was once again placed in a defensive posture, this time against its own national army. At first the insurgents had the support of many citizens, bitter at the humiliation they had endured at the hands of the Prussians. But soon refugees were streaming out of the capital. Alphonse took up residence at Versailles where he was needed to help organise the government loan, and it is probable that other members of the family joined him there. The Commune came to an end on 28 May and the severity of Thiers' reprisals made it clear that he intended to remove utterly the stain of revolution from the new republic. For it was a republican constitution which eventually emerged from the crisis of 1870-1. Bonapartist and royalist aspirations were, at last, crushed.

The Rothschilds accepted the inevitable with a good grace. Now that the Napoleonic regime had passed, they welcomed the moderate government of Thiers. Perhaps they recalled the words uttered by the Great Baron towards the end of his life: "There are within me on the one side a liberal politician and on the other a financier; unfortunately finance cannot exist without liberty but still less can it exist with too much liberty."[19]

The Paris house had come through forty years of almost continuous storm and stress, and had emerged as undisputed master of the French money markets. Alphonse, who ran the bank with his brother, Gustave, was a worthy successor to the Great Baron but he certainly hoped for a more peaceful reign than his father had enjoyed. For his part, he was determined not to embark on grandiose schemes that might provoke opposition and hostile comment. It was both a tribute to James and an indication of new policies when he told a colleague, "We don't need to make money. Our only desire is to preserve what we have." [20]

A modern historian has said, "the Franco-German war became the first war of nations; the rules of civilised warfare broke down, and the pattern of twentieth-century warfare was created". [21] The shock of 1870-1 gave rise to a new kind of patriotic fervour which, for almost half a century, remained part of the emotional make-up of every citizen of every one of Europe's self-conscious states. Not until the carnage on the Western Front would it be exposed for the stupidity it was.

For the Rothschilds the war both focused and intensified the dilemma they had been aware of for years. For the first time, members of the family found themselves divided — and emotionally divided — by a major conflict. It was not just that the Frankfurt and Paris Rothschilds were committed to opposite sides — though that was serious enough. Tensions also developed between the French and English families. Alphonse was a pronounced anglophobe.* To him Britain's failure to come to his nation's aid against the blatant aggression of Germany was yet another proof of Albion's perfidy. He believed that prompt diplomatic action from London would have halted the armies in their tracks and prevented the horrors of the siege of Paris.

For Lionel and Natty things were not quite that simple. From their vantage point they could see that Alphonse was basically wrong. Napoleon III's *folie de grandeur* was just as much to blame for the war as Bismarck's *realpolitik* and, given two governments hell-bent on confrontation, there was little that Westminster could do to stop them. On the other hand they *were* appalled at the plight of their relatives and they *were* disquieted by the general stance of the Gladstone government.

Basically, what divided Lionel and Natty from the leader of their party was a difference of attitude — even of philosophy. They were pragmatists.

*Nor were the English Rothschilds free of prejudice. Baron Guy tells the story of a visit Robert once paid to London. Afterwards Natty contemptously dismissed his "effete" French relative with the words, "the fellow wore yellow gloves".

Gladstone was an idealist. They believed in decisive action based on political realities. Gladstone took his stand on moral rectitude and carefully weighed the rights and wrongs of every issue. They believed that foreign policy was all about safeguarding the interests of Britain and, where possible, the interests of international commerce. Gladstone submitted every issue to the tribunal of conscience. These irreconcilables became quite evident during the crisis of 1870-1. On two separate occasions in September Gladstone was annoyed because messages passed through Rothschild diplomatic channels had, in his opinion, been distorted.[22] From this point on, the Rothschilds found themselves increasingly distanced from the administration. Early in 1871 Gladstone and Granville hosted an international conference to discuss the current situation. Lionel and Natty hoped − perhaps expected − to be kept informed about the deliberations. They were disappointed. Repeated representations to 10 Downing Street led to their being referred to Granville. The Foreign Minister minuted Gladstone on 9 March: "Lord G[ranville] referred B[aron] R[othschild] to the Statement he had made in the House of Lords on the first night of the session. He stated that the conference had pledged themselves to secrecy till the end of their sittings − that he could give no further information . . . and the Conference would meet again on Monday next."[23]

It was not only the French Rothschilds who had to live with new political realities.

CHAPTER 16
"We were very jolly"

After the tumultuous events of 1870-1, the return of Her Majesty's warship *Galatea* to Portsmouth at the end of a tour in the Far East, occasioned very little interest, even though her captain was Alfred, Duke of Edinburgh, Queen Victoria's second son. The event, however, was destined to have considerable significance for the Rothschilds. For one of the travellers who came ashore, attended by his recently acquired Chinese servant, was the Hon. Eliot Yorke, the Duke's equerry.

This ebullient, fair-haired, blue-eyed young man of twenty-eight was the third son of the Earl of Hardwicke and it was to the family home at Wimpole Hall, near Cambridge, that he now made his way in that summer of 1871. There he found a small house party including Sir Anthony and Lady de Rothschild and their daughters. The Yorkes were a lively family, of whom Disraeli said, "I never met persons who seemed to enjoy life more, or who seemed fonder of each other that the Hardwickes." They had been close to Sir Anthony and his family for some years and the relationship had been strengthened by a shared tragedy when, in 1867, the Earl's second son, Victor, had collapsed and died at the age of twenty-seven while visiting Aston Clinton. The two families also shared a passion for shooting, hunting, sailing, music and amateur dramatics. Indeed, the Yorkes were so devoted to rural life that they seldom left their country estate and, unlike other members of fashionable society, rarely went to London for the season. They were nevertheless members of the intimate circle that surrounded the royal family and Eliot was just one of several Yorkes who occupied positions at court.

However, since his duties had kept him almost continuously abroad for four years, Eliot was a comparative stranger to Sir Anthony's daughters who were immediately taken with their new aquaintance. "On that memorable visit we young ones had a picnic luncheon in the park and were waited upon by the solemn Chinaman. Eliot was full of fun, and kept us all happy and laughing at his jokes. He told us many anecdotes about his Royal master, and was interesting as well as amusing."[1] The description is Connie's but it was her sister who fell in love with the

217

entertaining young man. In so doing she brought tension and unhappiness into a household which had hitherto been one of the most carefree and harmonious in the land. Aston Clinton was the happiest of all the Rothschild homes. Sir Anthony was remembered by his daughter as having "the kindest heart and most generous nature of anyone I have ever known".[2] He loved entertaining, had a passion for dancing, enjoyed music and possessed impeccable taste in art. His wife had a lively mind and was a brilliant conversationalist. She greatly enjoyed the company of young people, and her nephews and nieces seldom missed an oportunity to call upon her. Lady de Rothschild was also widely read and well informed. She especially cultivated friends with religious interests, her own approach being not at all sectarian. Some of her closest friends were Quakers and Anglican clergymen, with whom she enjoyed sharing spiritual experiences and charitable concerns. Louisa and Anthony both loved the country and appreciated it all the more because it was only after thirteen years of married life that they had managed to escape from Paris and London to the relative seclusion of Aston Clinton.

The life style the girls enjoyed thus presents a striking contrast to that of their relatives who were embroiled in the hard world of international banking. Fortunately their journals and reminiscences have been preserved, and these enable us to glimpse something of that other side of Rothschild family life. Rothschild women were, of course, privileged in that they had far greater opportunities than most of their contemporaries: if they wanted to do something, see something or learn something, no obstacles stood in their way. And they took full advantage of this freedom. Most of them learned Hebrew as well as the major European languages, were encouraged to discuss religion, philosophy and politics, studied music with the leading masters, were brought up surrounded by the finest examples of art and craftsmanship, and were able to meet and converse with the cleverest and wittiest men of the day.

In their youth Annie and Connie were enthusiastic travellers and sight-seers. Their journeyings took them all over Europe by rail, carriage and yacht, and they recorded their experiences with unrestrained excitement. "Off by the night train for the South — and the magic of that word, 'South!' It was enough to make the travellers dance with ecstacy."[3]

Thus Constance described the start of a long Continental journey she made with her mother and sister in 1869. It was a trip which brought many excitements to the ladies. In a Rome street, word reached them suddenly that the Pope was coming. They stopped the carriage, jumped out, and curtsied as the papal procession passed by. In a letter to a friend, Annie observed with boisterous irreverence that his holiness was " ... a good-natured, benevolent looking old man. Connie and I were rather disappointed with his attire, which we expected to have been very grand. With the exception of a red hat and red slippers, it is exactly like — what do you think — a certain *negligé* [sic] costume in which you ascend the stairs at Aston Clinton before going to bed."[4] The little party stayed in Rome for Easter and no religious differences could keep the sisters from going to St Peter's Square to hear the Pope's annual message. They were quite overwhelmed by the experience. So much so that what followed could only be an anticlimax. "Alas, we were at Pisa instead of at Rome", Constance complained to her diary a few days later. "What did I care about the Leaning Tower? Sickening object! It only gave me cramp in my legs and a vertigo in my brain. Pisa is a bore, Rome is adorable. Doomed to disappointment. Feel lunatic!!!"[5]

The ladies crossed into Austria where, among the highlights of their tour, was a visit to the great violinist, conductor and composer, Joseph Joachim. They already knew the virtuoso, who had attended several musical evenings at their house in London. Louisa recorded that they

... found him and his wife in a large, old fashioned room with more windows than chairs — overlooking a lovely scene of meadowland, winding river and ranges of mountains.
Joachim was charming: offered us music as simply as another host might have given us coffee — and soon we had a delightful little concert. Joachim played divinely and his wife sang extremely well. A pianist and a painter appeared, then the four little Joachims — and after some conversation we separated — but only to meet an hour later at St Jacob's Village, perched in a green dell high up above Salzburg ... the sun had set and the glow had faded from the face of the rocks — but the scene was beautiful.[6]

Just as their French relatives associated with Rossini, Heine, Victor Hugo, Chopin, George Sand, Honoré de Balzac and other leaders of Parisian cultural life, so Louisa and her daughters numbered many literary and musical giants among their friends. These included Dickens, Matthew Arnold, Joachim, Charles Hallé (the pianist and conductor), Sir Arthur Sullivan and William Makepeace Thackeray. The latter entered the Rothschild circle as the result of a chance meeting with Lady de Rothschild on a Rhine steamer in 1848. The tall novelist made an instant impression on five-year-old Connie, who was travelling with her mother, by carrying her around on his shoulders and telling her fairy stories. Thackeray loved children and was bringing up his own two daughters single-handed, since his mentally ill wife was obliged to live in seclusion. Anne and Harriet Thackeray remained lifelong friends of the Rothschild girls, and their father frequently visited Charlotte (Lionel's wife) and

Louisa. A letter of Charlotte's describes an amusing incident which reveals how intimate the two families were. Seventeen-year-old Evelina had called at the novelist's town house to see his daughters. When she "entered the study of the great writer one sunny morning . . . she found [them] perpetrating a portrait of their slumbering, dreaming sire, who must have had enchanting visions, for he talked of Venus and Cupid . . ."[7] Louisa, especially, was in the habit of engaging her friend in profound conversation:

Yesterday . . . in the afternoon Thackeray called — very agreeable as he always is *en tête à tête*. Singularly enough, he expressed what I had been thinking all the morning, that love is short-lived and that without any apparent reason the being who has inspired us with passionate affection, at whose dear presence our heart has throbbed and our cheek turned pale, becomes perfectly indifferent to us. I had never experienced it, but I felt such might be the case, and with Thackeray it evidently has been the case . . . [8]

But the relationship was essentially a light-hearted and bantering one, as is evidenced by extant letters from Thackeray to the girls:

It has not been Annie's fault but mine that the two most beautiful bon-bon baskets I ever saw have come into the house and given the greatest delight to the children whom you remembered so kindly, and that you have had no word of acknowledgement for such a charming present . . . I hope it's not too late to tell you that I was very pleased when your presents came to think that you were so good as to remember the children. It would have pleased you to have seen their pleasure: and what further pleased me in this pleasant transaction was that the young ones, who thought the two baskets the most beautiful and splendid treasures they ever had in their lives, nevertheless, and with a severe pang, resolved to give one of them away to some little friends of their own who had been very kind to them. This act of self-denial rejoiced the paternal heart, and I like to tell it in confidence to your ladyship, so you see you have made a great number of young folk and a middle-aged gentleman happy. Could bon-bons ever be expected to do more?[9]

The centre of the girls' world was Aston Clinton. There always seemed to be a party going on there. Sometimes it was a dance, such as Anthony loved. At others it was a shooting or hunting party, a fancy dress ball, dinner followed by charades (a great Rothschild favourite) or a musical evening. Most of these events were far less formal than those given by Charlotte at Gunnersbury or Betty in Paris. Even the most celebrated guests found it easy to relax at Aston Clinton.

The musical trio was a capital idea, for they are all great friends and are delighted to play together. Hallé . . . plays whatever he is asked to, and is not a bit fussy.

Before dinner we had a magnificent Fantaisie of Schubert with Hallé and Joachim, which they played twice over . . . artists and common place mortals all got on wonderfully well together, and Count Nesselrode [son of the very celebrated Russian Foreign Minister] lost his heart completely to Joachim — no wonder!

After dinner . . . the music recommenced. Hallé opened the concert by a rapid succession of Chopin, and we are agreed that he surpassed himself. We were such a delighted, enthusiastic audience that we quite roused him into energy and the result was beautiful . . . Then the Hungarian Dances, a kind of wild, diabolical, weird, demon jumping-up effect, at which the violin itself seemed to dance. Joachim played like one possessed, and was most delighted at his dear Brahms, and declares that the Dances cannot be performed too often, that they are some of the finest compositions he has ever heard, and even goes on to say that Brahms is one of the greatest of composers and that he is not appreciated enough . . .

. . . Madame Neruda [the famous violinist] slept in my dressing-room, so we had little chats while we were dressing . . . [10]

By the time they reached womanhood, Annie and Connie were quite at home in any society. In the autumn of 1869 they went with their father to Holkham Hall, the magnificent Palladian home of the Earl of Leicester, where they were to share the splendid hospitality with the Prince and Princess of Wales and their children.

The Rothschilds had entered the small circle of royal intimates a few years earlier. Although some members of the Queen's family had been customers of the bank and acquaintances of N.M. and his sons, it was not until Prince Edward studied with Lionel's eldest boys, Natty and Alfred, at Cambridge that ties of friendship were made. They shared common passions — racing, shooting, hunting, cards and women — and were often seen together at the racecourse and London clubs. The Prince accepted invitations to shoot the Rothschild coverts in Buckinghamshire and the family were reciprocally received at Sandringham. Anthony became His Royal Highness's financial adviser, so it is not surprising to find him among the guests at Holkham. His daughters were certainly not overawed by the occasion.

We were very jolly in the evening, and danced in a charming long gallery. The schoolmaster, a most elegant looking gentleman, played for us, with much success. We danced in a manner which would have

221

delighted Laury, without any of the decorum of which she complained at Mentmore; their R.H.'s like nothing so much as a romp; in more loyal language, they have a great deal of "*entrain*"; Papa was very frisky, and danced so well that the Princess invited him to dance the lancers with her; and under the royal tuition got on very well. There was only one valtz played, but none of the ladies besides ourselves were given to valtzing; the Prince and I had a capital valtz together, during which time I conversed about the smallness of Aston Clinton house. We concluded with a "tempête" which was worthy of its name.

Annie particularly enjoyed the dancing and going for long walks with members of the royal entourage. Connie, who adored children, preferred playing with the Princes: "I had a fearful romp with the little princes, we taught them blind man's bluff and ran races with them. The eldest [the future King George V] is a beautiful child, the image of the Princess, the second has a jolly little face and looks the cleverest. The Princess said to me, 'they are dreadfully wild, but I was just as bad'." [11]

It was into the close, happy, liberal world of Aston Clinton that young Eliot Yorke entered with such devastating effect in 1871. During the following months the mutual affection shared by Annie and the handsome young man deepened. As it did so, Sir Anthony and his wife became increasingly disturbed by a prospect which must have revived painful memories of the trauma surrounding H.M.'s rebellious engagement some thirty years earlier. For their part, the young couple, while sensitive to the problems, became resolutely determined to marry. By the autumn of 1872 the tension was reaching a peak and it was evident that a formal declaration could not long be delayed. The lovers and their families waited like mariners watching storm clouds darken and spread, not knowing how to react or what effect the tempest would have on the fragile craft of their affections. The entries in Connie's journal re-create the atmosphere:

Mamma is in such a miserable state that I had to tell Eliot not to come before Wednesday . . . She still looks ill and white, trembling and sad. She hardly sleeps and her one thought from morning till night is the Marchese [obviously another, parentally approved suitor]. Annie was not in love with him, but she is desperately in love with Eliot.
Poor Eliot! The time is coming nearer and nearer. We none of us sleep or eat, and all feel in a most miserable state.

222

Eliot proposed. I shall never forget this day, the agitation and the pain that we went through. We were almost crazy from morning till night. The gentlemen went out shooting. We met them. Annie and Eliot walked home together. After dinner he spoke to Papa and then came the scene. I shall never forget it.

Papa went away early after a little conversation with me and Joe [her uncle Joseph Montefiore]. Now he has to face New Court . . . Papa came home in the evening quite against it. Eliot left. Annie was miserable.[12]

But things were not the same as they had been thirty years before. The couple were, for example, able to resolve the religious issue in a fashion that was novel at the time: they agreed that each would continue to observe their own beliefs. Unlike H.M., Annie would not be faced with the stark choice of giving up her lover or her family. Attitudes had softened and, if some of the Rothschilds were still bitterly opposed to mixed marriages, there were others who took a more tolerant view, as events soon proved. During October, as Connie records, matters came to a head.

We hardly eat or sleep and lead quite an excitable life. I send little notes to Eliot and we look forward to a happy *dénouement*. Annie is perfectly fearless and hopeful. The feeling is weighing on me that a storm is brewing. Wrote to Eliot to invite him for the 13th. Hope he will come . . . He wrote to say he would and begged of me to speak to Mamma . . .

I advised Annie to speak to Papa and to force a consent from him . . . With her brave, courageous spirit, she actually went to Papa and had it out with him. He gave his consent. Annie is allowed to write to Eliot. Joy![13]

Sir Anthony must have been as relieved as his daughter that the issue was decided. His attitude had never been one of objection on principle. It was the family that was uppermost in his thoughts. Lionel had already opposed the marriage; what would the others say? The engagement was announced at the end of the month. For two or three days everyone at Aston Clinton was tense with apprehension. Then the congratulations began to pour in. Cousin Alfred wrote to assure Louisa of the support of "everyone at Gunnersbury".[14] Charlotte sent her family's good wishes from Paris.[15] A few months later Anselm in Vienna assured Anthony of his reaction towards the happy couple: "When they come here, I will receive them with open arms."[16] On 9 November Queen Victoria at Balmoral ordered one of her ladies-in-waiting to convey her warmest congratulations.[17] Baron Stanley of Alderley, a prominent Tory peer and kinsman of the Yorkes, in conveying his felicitations, noted: " . . . I had before heard Sir Anthony enumerate his large views on the subject of his daughter's marriage and I was not, therefore, surprised. My great admiration for your race and the constant proofs of its most ancient civilization, the great talents of its children now make me rejoice when I see one joined to our younger family."[18] And George Samuel, a close friend of Anselm, complimented Sir Anthony for sticking to his principles. "You have broken a barrier unfitted to our times",[19] he wrote.

But Lionel was not the only one to object to the match. Muffy and Juliana were frigid and for some months there was no word of welcome for Sir Anthony's family at Mentmore. When Connie's father met his brother by accident in a London street, the latter refused to climb into the carriage. This reaction from someone widely renowned for his kindness and geniality must have caused much pain. Certainly it was more hurtful than the predictable response of Baroness Betty, who wrote to Louisa: "The sentiments of sadness fill me more at this moment than I can express. They do not, however, stop me from assuring you of my greatest sympathy in your distress and that of my dear nephew, Sir Anthony . . ."[20]

Of course, the hardliners came round before long. They could hardly fail to do so for in all respects save one this was a highly desirable match. Everyone who had met Eliot liked him. The couple were well suited. They behaved with sensitivity towards their affronted relatives. Above all, the marriage further reinforced the connection between the Rothschilds and the royal family, a link which was already close, as witness an incident which took place in January 1873, a few weeks before the wedding. The Prince of Wales paid a visit to Aston Clinton, intent on personally presenting a gift to the bride. He bounded into the house late in the day when Annie was already changing for dinner. Instead of waiting for a suitable moment after the meal, he insisted, with good-natured impetuosity, on seeing Annie immediately. Down, therefore, she had to come, blushing and embarrassed in a white *peignoir* with her unbrushed hair hanging down her back, to receive the heir to the throne.

The wedding took place in February. A registry office ceremony was followed after a few days by a service in the Yorke family chapel at Wimpole. Once the honeymoon was over, the couple divided their time between a house in Curzon Street, a present from Sir Anthony, and Netley Fort on the Hampshire coast. The attraction of the latter was that it enabled them to indulge their passion for sailing their boat *Garland*. Steam yachting was the latest craze in fashionable society and several of the Rothschilds had taken it up. While Alphonse was living in beleagured Paris in 1870, for example, Leonora spent part of the summer at Cowes, where the activities of the yachting set helped to take her mind off events in France. Among their many sailing friends the English Rothschilds numbered Lord and Lady Brassey who, in 1876-7, accomplished the first circumnavigation of the world by pleasure yacht.[21]

Eliot and Annie's was for a while a carefree life with few responsibilities. But in 1874 Eliot became MP for Cambridgeshire, a seat recently vacated by his elder brother, who had succeeded to the earldom on the death of his father. It was a pure case of *noblesse oblige*, for Eliot had little interest in politics and hated public speaking. His health was not robust and towards the end of 1878 he caught a chill at a public meeting. It turned to pneumonia and he died in December.

Sadly, the loss of a second son in tragic circumstances was not the last misfortune to befall the Yorke family. The new earl, Charles Philip Yorke, was the original "Champagne Charlie", an extravagant, fun-loving dandy, who rapidly dissipated the immaculately kept estate he inherited from his father. "I can see him now," Constance recalled years later, "in faultless attire, with his carefully arranged black satin tie, his beautiful pearl pin, his lustrous hat balanced at a certain angle upon his well-brushed hair, his coat sleeves always showing precisely the same amount of white cuff, his pleased-with-himself-and-the-world expression."[22] Largely as a result of Charlie's carelessness, the red-brick splendours of Wimpole Hall passed into other hands, leaving only memories of the happy days when the irascible old Earl had shooed family and guests about, shouting "Clear the decks! Clear the decks", in preparation for some charade or other home-made entertainment.

In 1874 Anselm of Vienna died. One of the results was that Baron Ferdinand, another tragically widowed Rothschild, came into a considerable inheritance and was, at last, able to consider building a house in which he could display his growing collections of paintings, antiques and *objets d'art*. The style he chose was that of a French Renaissance château and the site was a bare Buckinghamshire hilltop not far from the other Rothschild residences. The project was nothing if not ambitious and several of Ferdinand's relatives were taken aback by his audacity. Constance graphically described her first visit to the site soon after it had been purchased:

> On one cold dark day, in the December of 1874, my cousins, Ferdinand and Alice ... invited me to drive with them to Lodge Hill, six miles beyond Aylesbury, a steep eminence about 600 feet above the level of the sea — really at that time a bare wilderness,

where a farmhouse, a few miserable cottages, and some hedgerow trees were standing. The place under that grey wintery sky did not look attractive, and the roads were certainly not adapted for wheel travelling, excepting for that of farm carts. As we began to mount the hill our horse felt what would be required of him and sagaciously slackened speed, at last refusing to go any further; and this was not astonishing, as the wheels of the carriage were sticking fast in the mud. So we dismounted and, youth being on our side, we managed to struggle on for a while, gaining some idea of the view to be obtained from the top of the hill, without actually arriving at its summit. Tired and somewhat disappointed, I exclaimed at last, "And is it here, Ferdie, that you intend building your palace? Is this to be the site of your future park?"[23]

Ferdinand's architect was a Frenchman, Gabriel-Hippolyte Destailleur, who was a skilled restorer of sixteenth- and seventeenth-century châteaux, and the grounds were designed by M. Lainé, a leading landscape gardener. Between them, they completed the construction of Waddesdon Manor, in the surprisingly short space of ten years (though Ferdinand did make later additions). Even so it seemed very slow to the moody and impatient Ferdinand. So depressed was he at one stage that he left the site almost unvisited for four years.

The problems in a non-mechanised age were enormous. Millions of tons of earth had to be moved. This required an army of workmen and teams of Percheron draught horses brought in specially from Normandy. Ferdinand later recalled that there were frequent landslips. "Cutting into the hill interfered with the natural drainage, and despite the elaborate precautions we had taken, the water often forced its way out of some unexpected place after a spell of wet weather, tearing down great masses of earth. Like Sisyphus, we had repeatedly to take up the same task, though fortunately with more permanent results."[24] To carry the stone and bricks from the nearest railway station, Ferdy had a steam tram installed. At the bottom of the hill the building materials were transferred to trucks drawn up the gradient.

Ferdinand had water brought seven miles from the Chiltern Hills and provided not only to the house, but also to the village. Waddesdon thus became one of the first villages in England to have its own piped supply. In the later stages, as the structure of the mansion neared completion, there was the interior décor to be thought of. Ferdinand scoured Paris and the provinces to find panelling, mirrors, doors, and mantelpieces in ancient houses that were being sold, demolished or rebuilt. When these were installed at Waddesdon, the ceilings were moulded and painted, usually with copies of those in the rooms from which the fittings had been

226

taken. Whenever the Baron could not find suitable originals he had period copies made so that the interiors would be all of a piece. Some of the rooms were specifically designed to display items from his collection. For example the East Gallery was so fashioned to show off two large and splendid Venetian seascapes by Guardi that Ferdinand bought in 1877. It goes without saying that the artefacts with which Ferdinand now filled his treasure house were of the highest possible quality: French furniture by the leading eighteenth-century *ébénistes*; fine gold and enamelled snuffboxes; portraits by Gainsborough, Boucher, Reynolds and Romney; Sèvres porcelain; Savonnerie carpets and tapestries; books in rare and exquisite bindings.*

When all was finished, visitors could only gasp in amazement at both its external aspect and its brilliantly decked interior. A contemporary journal noted approvingly, "There is not a country residence in England which shows more forcibly how much can be done by the combination of unlimited expenditure and perfect taste."[25] But it was David Lindsay, a young aristocrat just down from Oxford, who gave the most perceptive description of Waddesdon and its presiding genius. According to him, the house was "a marvellous creation; a real creation", but he had reservations about its overpowering contents. As for its creator:

Baron Ferdinand whose hands always itch with nervousness, walks about, at times petulantly, while jealously caring for the pleasure of his guests. I failed to gather that his priceless pictures give him true pleasure. His clock for which he gave £25,000, his escritoire for which £30,000 was paid, his statuary, his china, and his superb collection of jewels, enamels and so forth ("gimcracks" he calls them) — all these things give him meagre satisfaction: and I felt that the only pleasure he derives from them is gained when he is showing them to his friends . . . However it is in the gardens and shrubberies that he is happy. He is responsible for the design of the flower beds, for the arrangement of colour, for the transplanting of trees: all these things are under his personal control and I was astonished at the knowledge he displayed . . . It is only among his shrubs and orchids that the nervous hands of Baron Ferdinand are at rest.[26]

Surviving photographs of Ferdinand bear out Lindsay's description. They show a thin, full-bearded, morose-looking man, with anxious eyes. Personal tragedy and his lonely bachelor existence, doubtless go some way towards explaining his reserved nature. But there was another factor.

---

*Fortunately Waddesdon Manor can still be seen in virtually all its splendour. James de Rothschild bequeathed the house and its spectacular contents to the National Trust in 1957.

227

Ferdy was always conscious that he was playing a rôle and was determined to play it to the best of his ability. He was an Austrian-born Jew who had decided to become an English landed gentleman. He studied his part minutely and, like many immigrants, he became *plus anglais que les anglais*. A slightly unkind story told by the English diplomat Henry Ponsonby illustrates the point well. He and Ferdinand were guests at a small dinner party given by Gladstone. The conversation turned to the question of how many books constituted a good gentleman's library. The consensus of opinion was that twenty thousand was the ideal number. Ponsonby was amused to observe that "Rothschild immediately made a note".[27]

Waddesdon, therefore, had to be the country seat, *par excellence*, an estate designed, first and foremost, for entertaining important guests. Over the years there were few Victorian celebrities who did not come to gaze on the splendours of Baron Ferdinand's house and to enjoy its modern comforts. The Queen and most members of her family visited at one time or another, as did foreign royalty. On one occasion the Shah of Persia acutely embarrassed his host. He had expected the Prince of Wales to be among the party. On being told that Edward had been obliged to cancel, he shut himself in his room and sulked, refusing even to come down to dinner. He was only eventually enticed out by the promise of a remarkable conjurer hired by Ferdinand for his entertainment. Most leading politicians of the day, including Gladstone, Disraeli and Randolph Churchill stayed at Waddesdon. Literary and artistic figures on the guest lists included Maupassant, Henry James and Millais.

Ferdinand's hospitality strained after perfection and many good-natured stories about it circulated in society. One concerned the waking ritual. At the appropriate hour, or so it was said, a footman would quietly enter and rouse the recumbent guest. Then the following litany would ensue.

"Tea, coffee, chocolate or cocoa, Sir?"

"Tea, please."

"Yes, Sir. Assam, Souchong or Ceylon?"

"Souchong, please."

'Yes, Sir. Milk, cream or lemon?"

"Milk, please."

"Yes, Sir. Jersey, Hereford or shorthorn?"

The story may be exaggerated, but then again, since Ferdinand took his duties as host extremely seriously and was a man who liked to get everything right, down to the last detail, it may not.

Certainly Mrs James de Rothschild, the last member of the family to reside at Waddesdon, knew a man who, as a boy, had served the Baron as "cake-holder". When elaborate picnic teas were arranged for guests it was his job to stand in the back of a pony trap as it bumped cross-country to a riverside location, carefully guarding all the hampers so that none of the delicate confections within was spoiled.[28]

The owner of Waddesdon was extremely sensitive to criticism of his hospitality and the lavishness of his establishment. For example, he never knew how to respond to the jibes of Richard Haldane, Liberal MP, raconteur and wit. One joke at Ferdy's expense told by this frequent guest concerned his election as MP for Aylesbury: "the rejoicing in the village was such that no less than 143 of his gardeners are reported to have embraced one another in mutual congratulation ... no less than sixty-five other gardeners refused to join the demonstrations of their colleagues". Poor, puzzled Ferdinand, it was reported, could only "twist his black moustache nervously while Haldane developed his witty and mordant attack".[29]

The Baron took his duties as an English magnate no less seriously than his responsibilities as a host and his care for his workers and tenants was legendary. The building of Waddesdon Manor revolutionised the life of the locality. The nearby village, known as "Black Waddesdon" because of its reputation for boorishness and hostility to strangers, was transformed by the new landlord. Ferdy employed ninety per cent of the villagers on his estate and in the 222-roomed mansion. He rebuilt most of the cottages. He provided a village hall and encouraged its use by sponsoring a local orchestra and dramatic society. Elderly residents still remember how the Baron donated instruments for any children who showed musical aptitude, hired costumes from the best agency for performances of Gilbert and Sullivan operettas and then brought his "fancy friends from London" to watch the rustic thespians. He hired a professional coach to teach the Waddesdon lads cricket. The highlight of the year occured on the first Thursday in July which was set aside for "the Baron's Treat". There were sports in which the youngsters competed for generous prizes, a fair, and a sumptuous tea. Little wonder that Baron Ferdinand was a popular landlord.[30]

The person who to some extent shared Ferdinand's country life was his sister, Alice. Theirs was a strange relationship. They were not so much companions as two solitary people living together. Just as Alice lived next door to Ferdy in London, so now she had her own house built four miles away from Waddesdon. It lay beside the Thames at Eythrope and there she spent much of her time. But, at dusk she always drove back to Waddesdon where she dined and slept. Her doctor assured her that the damp nocturnal riverine airs of Eythrope were unhealthy.

Alice, the plain, solitary girl brought up by sister Mathilde, never

229

learned the art of relating comfortably to other people. She did, however, find an outlet for her creativity. She became a gardener. Not just a keen gardener — Rothschilds have scarcely ever been able to indulge their pastimes at the level of mere enthusiasm. For her, the cultivation of the finest outdoor and hothouse blooms became an obsession. Visitors to Waddesdon or Eythrope Pavilion, Alice's house, noted that she never walked in the grounds without a spadelike implement called a spud with which she prised out any weeds that had had the temerity to seed themselves in the herbaceous beds and paths.

Somewhat to everyone's surprise, it was to Alice that Anselm left the old family home of the Grünebrug, just outside Frankfurt. Since Willy Carl and Mathilde had been living there for some years and Alice had no desire to return to Germany, she sold it to her brother-in-law. Years later, when her doctor advised her to avoid English winters, she bought an estate at Grasse in the south of France. There, of course, she established another garden. Everything was laid out with military precision by this horticultural martinet. She created a vision of colour and landscaped harmony. The trouble with visions is that mere mortals cannot enter them. Visitors who came to admire Alice's achievement could, thus, find the experience something of an ordeal. Constance was once walking in the grounds with her hostess when, in a fit of absent-mindedness, she committed the cardinal sin of stepping onto the lawn. This, as she later recorded sent Alice into "a violent passion".[31] Nor was it only thoughtless female relatives who felt the sharp edge of Alice's tongue. Grasse was a favourite stopping place for Queen Victoria. Once she was in the famous garden when, bending forward to inhale the fragrance of a rose, she inadvertently set the royal foot upon a flowerbed. "Come off of there!" bellowed her hostess. The Queen jumped back in alarm and, or so it is said, ever afterwards referred to Alice de Rothschild as "the all-powerful one".

It was not only the men of the family to whom governments and even crowned heads sometimes deferred.

CHAPTER 17
"A close acquaintance with the course of public affairs"

For the Rothschilds, leisure was not completely taken up in socialising with the great and the wealthy. Their sense of responsibility for the less fortunate was deeply ingrained. This genuine humanitarianism undoubtedly had its roots in their religion, but was also a natural response to the constant criticism that Jews in general, and the Rothschilds in particular, were indifferent to the needs of the poor. The Rothschilds would never try to justify their wealth by flamboyant displays of charity or by modifying their life style; but away from the glare of publicity they showed their concern in a thousand ways, by providing practical help where it was needed.

Anselm, for example, was a pattern of the paternalistic squire on his Austrian and German estates. He built over twenty infants' schools in the villages around Schillersdorf and maintained a dozen local churches. His sons, Nathaniel, Ferdinand and Albert, founded a home for orphans in memory of their mother. Anselm, also, long before the days of private and state pension schemes, established a custom (which was enshrined in Austrian law) that every Rothschild worker of twenty or more years standing should in retirement enjoy a perpetual income equivalent to 101% of his salary. And when Alphonse died his will made quite clear the spread of his philanthropic interests. The Baron made the following bequests:

250,000 frs	to the Fondations Rothschild on Rue Picpus
100,000 frs	to be invested to provide dowries for daughters of officials of the Chemin de Fer du Nord
200,000 frs	to the Jewish Charities Committee
60,000 frs	to the poor of Ferrières, Pontcarré and Lagny
1,000 frs	per annum for public works in Ferrières, Pontcarré and Lagny

Anthony maintained his family's interest in the Jews' Free School in Spitalfields, of which he was president for many years. He both supported

231

and took an active part in running scores of charitable institutions at home and overseas. Louisa was as active as her husband but more circumspect. She had an absolute horror of appearing to be an assertive Lady Bountiful. In her diary, she prayed that she would never be carried away by "the indolent luxury of giving". Instead she privately vowed "to try to do real good at our little Aston Clinton . . ." [1]

Louisa's daughters had the same principles instilled into them. And when they were only ten and eleven, they sallied forth armed with reading books, to teach some of the local children. Connie later recalled the development of this educational initiative:

> Our mother soon felt that our youthful attempts at instruction should give place to some method of real education, so my kind and ever-generous father, obedient to her desire, built a beautiful girls' school for the village of Aston Clinton . . . Then we canvassed the village most diligently to secure pupils for the opening day, and proudly counted fifteen girls whose parents were anxious to see their children properly educated. The Rector was most discouraging . . . He did not see the use of education for girls, and thought the Sunday School (which was a very bad one) gave them all the teaching they required. We listened, but inwardly triumphed . . . We really loved that little school, and some of the happiest hours of our lives were spent there. When a few years later it had become too small for the number of scholars, my dear father enlarged it, and later again he was faced by the fact that it could not contain the infants − boys and girls − who were then becoming eligible for school attendance.
>
> It was about that time that, my father asking me what I should like to have for a birthday present, I boldly answered, "An Infants School". My request was granted, and I was allowed to lay the first stone of the new building. [2]

It is easy to fall into the trap of compartmentalising the widely varied activities of the nineteenth-century Rothschilds; to consider separately, for example, their charitable giving, their political activity, their hospitality and their financial affairs. That is certainly not how they would have seen themselves. Most of them shared a profound sense of responsibility with other leading members of Europe's "ruling class". The same sense of public duty motivated them whether they were opening a village school, entertaining foreign ambassadors, trying to influence government decisions or providing capital for a colonial railway. Without doubt, it was in this spirit that Lionel de Rothschild brought off, in 1875, the most celebrated political coup in the family's history — the purchase of the Suez Canal shares.

Egypt, at that time part of the Ottoman Empire, had been in a state of financial chaos for some years past. This was largely due to the grandiose ambitions of the Khedive Ismail who, upon coming to power in 1863, had embarked on a massive building programme aimed at modernising his country and enhancing his own prestige. His most ambitious undertaking was the construction of the Suez Canal, the brainchild of the French engineer Ferdinand de Lesseps. Since the canal, when complete, would halve the passage time from Europe to the Far East, it might have been expected that Britain, with her Indian Empire and her burgeoning colonies in Australia and New Zealand, would have been particularly interested in de Lesseps' plans. But Britain had refused to have anything to do with the enterprise. Successive governments believed, or affected to believe, that a canal linking the Mediterranean with the Red Sea was an engineering impossibility. Their real fear, however, was a disruption of the delicate balance of power in the Levant. Along with France and Russia, Britain watched with concern the weakening of the Turkish Empire. She wanted what Bismarck contemptuously dismissed as "the sick man of Europe" kept alive as long as possible and, whenever the inevitable might happen, she hoped there would be no squabbling over the will. A canal would exacerbate rivalries, since any nation controlling it would enjoy enormous commerical power. For many years diplomatic pressure from London halted progress. But de Lesseps' Suez Canal Company eventually went ahead, financed largely by France and the Khedive, and the canal was opened amidst lavish celebrations in 1869, the Empress Eugénie being the principal guest of honour.

Ismail had had to borrow heavily for the canal and his other schemes, and several European banks had fallen over themselves to provide funds at exorbitant rates of interest. Rothschilds were not among them. They regarded the Khedive as a bad risk and events were to prove them right. But it soon became apparent that the British government's attitude of opposing the project had been short-sighted. Once the canal was open de Lesseps began to raise the dues payable on ships and tonnage and the British were, in effect, held to ransom. This was the situation when, in 1874, there was a general election which ousted the Liberals from office.

That event brought about a dramatic change in the Rothschilds' political influence. Natty retained the Aylesbury seat he had held since 1865 but his father was defeated in the City and retired from the Commons. It is likely that he was not unduly distressed at his removal from the parliamentary scene. His health was poor; he was suffering badly from the rheumatic gout which would eventually deprive him of the use

233

of his legs. Also, his estrangement from the Liberal leadership was growing. He opposed many of his government's policies, not least their taxation proposals. After the election the Liberals were in disarray. Gladstone resigned as leader but remained by far the most effective opposition speaker in the Commons. The rank and file were divided into pro- and anti-Gladstone camps. Disraeli, the new Prime Minister, was not slow to take advantage of this. He used his personal charm to win over all those, of whatever party, who could be useful to him.

This included the Rothschilds, though, in their case, the Prime Minister was not motivated purely by a cynical desire to manipulate people. The death of his dearly loved wife, in 1872, had made him more than ever reliant on the support of his friends. It was about this time that he adopted the habit of frequently inviting himself to dinner at Gunnersbury or 147 Piccadilly. Lionel always gave him a warm welcome. Quite apart from his feelings for Dizzy, the banker was pleased to have regained personal access to the government.

At their intimate meetings, Lionel and the Prime Minister frequently discussed the Egyptian situation. Disraeli was working hard to try to extricate his country from the disadvantageous situation into which it had fallen. At the diplomatic level he was trying to engineer the creation of an international commission which would take over the administration of the canal and prevent the company discriminating against the shipping of any nation. At the financial level he was seeking ways of buying into the company.

It was in connection with the latter possibility that he sought Lionel's help. One result was that Natty was sent to Paris to try to buy shares in the company on behalf of the government. De Lesseps, whose attempts to raise finance in London had been rebuffed, had no reason to be accommodating to the British, and was not interested. A fresh attempt in the summer of 1875 was equally unsuccessful. As time passed the situation became more critical. The Khedive's government could not last much longer. The international community would have to intervene. Britain, it seemed, would find herself in the negotiations without any bargaining counters.

Then, early in November, Ismail, desperately in need of cash, attempted to raise some on his one remaining asset — his forty-four per cent shareholding in the Suez Canal Company. He approached a French banker to arrange a mortgage. The news reached N.M. Rothschild and Sons and H.M. Government simultaneously by different channels. Lord Derby, the Foreign Secretary, telegraphed Cairo for clarification and learned that the Khedive was not committed to a French deal; indeed, he would prefer to sell his shares outright to Britain. This was known by 17 November, on which day it was discussed in cabinet.

234

Disraeli now took a bold initiative, as he reported to the Queen the following day:

> Mr Disraeli with his humble duty to Your Majesty.
>
> The Khedive, on the eve of bankruptcy, appears desirous of parting with his shares in the Suez Canal . . . 'Tis an affair of millions; about four, at least, but would give the possessor an immense, not to say preponderating, influence in the management of the Canal.
>
> It is vital to Her Majesty's authority & power at this critical moment, that the Canal should belong to England. I was so decided and absolute with Lord Derby on this head, that he ultimately adopted my views and brought the matter before the Cabinet yesterday. The Cabinet was unanimous in their decision, that the interest of the Khedive should if possible, be obtained and we telegraphed accordingly . . .
>
> The Khedive now says, that it is absolutely necessary that he should have between three and four millions sterling by the 30th of this month!
>
> Scarcely breathing time! But the thing must be done . . . [3]

The Prime Minister took it upon himself to push the matter to a conclusion and, despite the version of events he gave the Queen, Lord Derby was not the only member of the cabinet who disliked being hustled. But hustled they had to be. If the coup was to be pulled off, speed and secrecy were vital. It was out of the question to approach parliament to vote the necessary funds. The attendant delay and publicity would only invite countermeasures from the French government. There was, in fact, only one way to raise the money. In a private talk with his old friend, he asked Rothschilds for the four million. Lionel requested twenty-four hours to consider. Ironically, it was only because he had been ousted from the Commons that he was able to contemplate the suggestion. The Act of Privilege prevented MPs engineering government contracts from which they would personally profit. That act no longer applied to Lionel. He came back with an offer: his bank would lend the money at five per cent with a two and a half per cent commission. These terms were accepted by the cabinet on 24 November. Within hours Disraeli reported jubilantly to his sovereign:

> It is just settled: you have it, Madam. The French Government has been outgeneraled. They tried too much, offering loans at an usurious rate, and with conditions which would have virtually given them the government of Egypt.
>
> The Khedive, in despair and disgust, offered Your Majesty's

Government to purchase his shares outright — he never would listen to such a proposition before.

Four millions sterling! and almost immediately. There was only one firm that could do it — Rothschilds. They behaved admirably; advanced the money at a low rate, and the entire interest of the Khedive is now yours, Madam.[4]

The deal was pulled off with very little time to spare. French banks and government ministers were rushing telegrams between Paris and Cairo, and de Lesseps offered to buy the Khedive's shares on behalf of the company. Because of Disraeli's purchase the Prime Minister was able to obtain the international commission he had wanted and to guarantee politically unhampered passage through the canal for all nations. The importance of this for the development of international trade over the next century, and particularly for the growth of Britain's African and Asian Empire, cannot be measured.

None of this would have been possible without Lionel de Rothschild's despatch and utter reliability. Probably his response to the Prime Minister's request was never in doubt but, for all that, it was not an easy one to make. He could not do what he would otherwise immediately have done: invite the Paris house to share the burden. As Disraeli shrewdly observed in a letter to the Prince of Wales, "Alphonse is *si francese* that he would have betrayed the whole scheme instantly."[5] Only later, when the news was out, did he offer Alphonse a partnership in the deal. The head of the French Bank pocketed his pride at being "informed" after the event: "We have had the pleasure of receiving your good letters in which you have told us of the operation you have concluded with the English Government. We accept with great pleasure your offer of participation and will keep the money ready at the times you indicate. The news of the acquisition of a part of the Suez Canal shares by England has produced a very strong reaction here . . ."[6] That was an understatement; the French were furious at being presented with a *fait accompli* by Disraeli. They suspected that it was a prelude to a major colonial coup. Such fears became frequent and deep-seated over the next quarter of a century as the two nations repeatedly clashed in the newly exploited lands of Africa and Asia. They inevitably complicated relations between New Court and Rue Laffitte.

This prestigious masterstroke of foreign policy delighted the Queen and cheered most of her subjects. It announced to the world that Britain had a leader as cunning and resolute as Bismarck. That pleased the patriots. But there were those who deplored the extension of great power rivalries into areas far beyond the frontiers of Europe. Foremost among the critics, of course, were Gladstone and his supporters. They complained that such a move should not have been made without consulting parliament. They prophesied future political complications. And they hinted at chicanery. "Is it not possible," Granville suggested, "that Lesseps and the Rothschilds have duped the Govt into giving this great impetus to the value of Suez Canal shares, by threatening them with a purchase by French Capitalists."[7] Disraeli felt it incumbent on him to defend his friends. The Rothschilds, he insisted, "had not made the slightest use of the intelligence, as they considered themselves standing in the position of the government. The world, of course, gives them credit for having made at least ¼ of a million."[8]

The world *did* assume that Rothschilds had made a fortune out of the transaction. In the parliamentary debate on the matter the following February they were attacked for charging a high rate of interest on a loan to which no risk was attached, and also for abusing parliamentary privilege. In a statement to the House, Natty was able to claim exemption from the latter charge on a technicality. Although he and his father were both bankers, Lionel was no longer a member of the Commons and he, himself, was not a partner in N.M. Rothschild and Sons. On the question of interest, the bank's rate was certainly not low (despite Disraeli's claim to the Queen). NMR made about a hundred thousand pounds on the deal. But between the purchase and the parliamentary debate, the unit value of Suez Canal shares had risen from £22.5 to about £35. So the British taxpayer certainly had not got the rough end of the deal.

The fact that Lionel had aided and abetted the Tory administration to achieve something which was anathema to the opposition did nothing to sweeten Rothschild relations with the Gladstonians. By 1875 Natty had abandoned any pretence of support for the party leadership. This became crystal clear the following year. Disraeli was elevated to the House of Lords as Earl of Beaconsfield, and there had to be a by-election in his Buckinghamshire seat. The Liberal managers, not unreasonably, expected the MP for Aylesbury to mobilise his relatives and the Rothschild tenantry and use his considerable local influence in the campaign. Faced with actively helping his party or passively aiding his friend, Natty chose the latter course. Little wonder that an enraged Granville reported to Gladstone, "The Rothschilds are behaving abominably."[9]

Lionel and Natty could ignore such opinions as long as Disraeli remained in power. For the next few years they were in close contact with the government and frequently consulted on matters of foreign policy. Potentially the most threatening issue to European peace was the 'Eastern Question', which now flared up yet again.

The complexities of inter-state rivalries and nationalist aspirations need not concern us; suffice it to say that, in April 1877, Russia invaded European Turkey (which at that time extended from the Bosphorus to the Danube). The Russians anticipated, and all the major powers expected, that they would gain a swift and easy victory over the decadent Ottoman Empire and would be able to claim territorial prizes and free naval access to the Mediterranean as the spoils of war. In the event, the Russian advance was halted for four months at Plevna and by the time their army reached the gates of Constantinople, it lacked the momentum for further conquest. In March 1878 the victors forced upon Turkey the humiliating Treaty of San Stefano. But they had not the remotest chance of making it stick.

Throughout the conflict the diplomatic wires of Europe had been humming, as statesmen tried to prevent a drastic upset of the balance of power. In June 1878 Russia was obliged to submit her territorial ambitions to a congress in Berlin. At that summit meeting Disraeli, aided by the Foreign Secretary, Lord Salisbury, played a magnificent hand of diplomatic poker. Without any court cards, the old, wily statesman managed to dominate play and bluff the other nations into agreeing with most of his suggestions. As the historian A.J.P. Taylor put it: "Great Britain won a bloodless victory with a music-hall song,* a navy of museum pieces . . . no land forces at all . . . [and] without a reliable continental ally."[10]

The Rothschild rôle in this crisis was both crucial and elusive. As ever, this family of financial diplomats wrapped their activities in a veil of secrecy, which cannot be wholly penetrated over a century later. What is quite clear is that Britain's ultimate success was in part due to Lionel de Rothschild's excellent information service. The family was still performing its old function as combined news agency and unofficial diplomatic channel. Bleichröder kept Lionel supplied with almost daily bulletins of information gleaned from correspondence received by himself and Bismarck from St Petersburg, Constantinople and other capitals. And Bleichröder's despatches were now supplemented by those from another Berlin source, the prominent politician, Ludwig Bamberger. C. de B.'s contributions included reports from a close confidant of Midhat Pasha, the Turkish Grand Vizier. Alphonse kept up a running commentary on French political reactions, as well as passing on information from his own foreign sources. Lionel reciprocated with intelligence gleaned from British government circles.

---

*"We don't want to fight, but, by jingo, if we do,/We've got the ships, we've got the men, we've got the money, too./We've fought the Bear before, and while Britain shall be true,/The Russians shall not have Constantinople."

Some of the news gathered by this network was of the utmost importance. Lionel heard the rumour that Russia had fixed on April 1877 for the opening of hostilities at the beginning of January – six weeks before the Foreign Secretary received the news from his representative. In February he knew that, while Russia was ostensibly negotiating a peaceful settlement of her differences with Turkey, she had placed large, secret orders for cannon with the armaments manufacturer, Krupp. He gleaned from Bismarck's private correspondence with his Ambassador in St Petersburg that the Prussian Chancellor, for all his public protestations to the contrary, was, in fact, quite happy to see Russia occupied with Turkey, since this deflected her from potentially anti-Prussian policies in Europe.

The bankers were, like most of the politicians, anxious to prevent war, though not for entirely the same reasons. Apart from any other consideration, the London Rothschilds had five and a half million pounds tied up in Ottoman state loans. Having failed to avert war, Disraeli strove to bring about a peace that would not harm British interests. But would he be in a position to influence the course of events? Lionel was able to reassure him with information provided by Bamberger, that the position of the British Ambassador in Constantinople was now paramount. This knowledge was invaluable to the government.

By April 1878 London had definitely become the diplomatic centre for all matters concerning the Eastern Question. While Bismarck was complaining that he was being kept in the dark, Disraeli and Salisbury were well informed of the attitudes of all the interested parties – what each demanded and what each might be persuaded to accept. Much of this information came via New Court.

Thus it was that the two British statesmen were able to travel to Berlin in June 1878 and bring off one of the greatest coups in diplomatic history; one which enhanced Britain's prestige and secured European peace for thirty-six years. During that journey they may well have reflected on the extent of Rothschild power and influence. Not only did their despatch cases carry valuable information provided by Lionel; the sumptuous railway carriage in which they travelled from Calais had been specially arranged by Alphonse.[11]

The settlement of the Eastern Question was the last major international issue in which Lionel de Rothschild was successfully involved. He died at the beginning of June 1879. The end came suddenly. He had just enjoyed a triumph of a minor kind when his horse, Sir Bevys, won the Derby. On 1 June Natty and his wife crossed to France. They travelled happily on to Paris and there, on the 3rd, were stunned to receive a telegram carrying the stark news that the head of the London house had died of a heart attack. The next morning's issue of *The Times* carried not just an obituary, but a leading article dedicated to the great banker.

Political prospects are intimately involved in the estimate to be formed of any great monetary transaction and to appreciate these, a close acquaintance is requisite with the course of public affairs throughout the world and with the character of public men. Baron Lionel de Rothschild possessed these qualities in a very eminent degree and they combined to render him, not merely a successful manager of his great House, but a very considerable figure in the social and political world . . . [12]

CHAPTER 18
"We are all professionals"

Writing about Baron Mayer (Muffy), *The Graphic* stated that he would be "much better remembered as a patron of art, and as a member of the Turf than as a politician".[1] Since, despite his exuberant advocacy of Liberalism, Muffy never gave the Commons the benefit of his oratory, the argument is difficult to fault. But what was true of the squire of Mentmore was true to a surprising extent of most other members of his family. Only a few Rothschilds in each generation were prominent in national and international affairs but, with very few exceptions, they all shared an interest in animals and field sports and a mania for collecting. Every branch of the family, even the serious-minded Frankfurters, produced a succession of men and women who derived great pleasure from accumulating superb objects of art and craftsmanship, and others whose delight lay in breeding for the show-ring or the racecourse.

Nothing pleased the great bankers of Vienna, Paris and London more than a chance to escape from the city to their great estates of Schillersdorf, Ferrières and Tring. There they could indulge their love of the shoot and the chase. The Great Baron, in particular, had organised the most elaborate sporting weekends at his château for politicians, fellow bankers, and foreign princes and statesmen whom he wished to impress. As we have seen, Bismarck was among those who enjoyed James's hospitality and, though he affected to despise Ferrières, calling its château "an upside-down chest of drawers", he was impressed by the well-stocked coverts which he subsequently returned to plunder, in 1871, during the Franco-Prussian War.

Both Nat and Alphonse, it will be recalled, sustained permanent injuries resulting from their devotion to the ritual slaughter of wild creatures, while the fact that Laury kept her own pack of hounds in France did not prevent her returning across the Channel for some "real" hunting whenever possible. But Muffy was *par excellence* the Rothschild who prided himself on the hospitality and sport he offered his guests. Throughout the third quarter of the century he kept a large stable and could always provide a suitable mount for any lady or gentleman staying

241

in his house. Jonathan Peel, Secretary of State for War (1858-67) and himself a great horseman, once commented that Rothschild's extensive stables included a dozen hunters "any one of which was able to carry sixteen stone across any fox-hunting country in the world".[2] A Mentmore meet, whether of the Bucks Staghounds, of which he was master, or of the local foxhounds, was a major social event.

The high-spirited Connie and Annie loved these occasions. The same could not be said for their father. Anthony was never happy on horseback. An amusing photograph survives of the portly "Billy" astride a very docile skewbald pony and looking as he doubtless felt, very uncomfortable. The girls found it very trying whenever Sir Anthony decided to accompany them to the meet.

> Papa promised not to be nervous and I think he nearly succeeded. We then set off, with a groom behind us and the little boy on Sybile. I wanted to give the ponies a good gallop, but Papa was now and then frightened! and so we rode at a gentle pace to which the horses are very little accustomed . . .
> It took us a whole hour before we arrived at Mentmore. When we approached the terrace we found a very gay scene assembled, more than a hundred redcoats on handsome spirited horses . . .
> Papa went early. We hoped to ride but Mamma would not allow it. How ridiculous to be tied to Edmond's coat-strings, but if Mamma won't allow it I can do nothing and a ride is not really worth putting Mamma in hysterics so I must not think of riding till Wednesday comes, and then I am afraid half the pleasure will be spoilt by Papa's nervousness.[3]

Muffy also went in for the scientific breeding of livestock and had several show successes, most notably with his great Jersey bull named Mentmore. But Baron Mayer's greatest love was the sport of kings. Even while a university undergraduate he was frequently to be found at Newmarket, where his father had a house, rather than among his books at nearby Cambridge. Muffy established his own stud at Newmarket in the 1840s and applied himself to the systematic improvement of his stock. It was a task which absorbed him totally for years. When he felt that all his labours had resulted in a near-perfect horse, a stallion called King Tom, the Baron had a life-size effigy in bronze made and erected it in the park at Mentmore for future generations to admire. He brought to the task the same combination of caution and flair that other Rothschilds devoted to banking. He possessed in full measure the patience necessary to produce winners, and so avoided rash speculations. He bought from the best breeders, employed the best trainers and had, himself, a discerning eye for horseflesh. Muffy's stud produced, over the years, a string of champions. Names like Corisande, Restitution and Hippia still feature among the legends of the turf.

This was one of the reasons for his popularity — a popularity which rubbed off on the rest of the family. The man in the street who liked a flutter on the horses felt, with at least some justification, that "you always get a winner with the Rothschilds". Millions of humble punters put their money on the blue and yellow silks in which all Rothschild jockeys raced. Muffy's own flamboyance also helped to create a popular Rothschild image. People enjoy celebrities. Today they may be pop idols. In the thirties they were Hollywood film stars. In Victorian England they were the "nobs", the gentry and nobility, whose luxurious life style the common man gazed upon with admiration and envy but rarely malice. There were other reasons why the Rothschilds were generally popular. They were good landlords, generous employers and much given to charity. But if they were taken to people's hearts — and, by and large, they were — it was because of the much publicised activities of the more exuberant, not to say eccentric, members of the family.

Muffy's stout figure and genial face, crowned by a topper at a rakish angle, was a familiar sight in the paddocks at Epsom, Ascot and Newmarket. He was usually seen there in the company of the Prince of Wales, Lord Rosebery and other notables of the turf. The climax of his racing career came in 1871, which has gone down in history as "the Baron's Year". His stallion Favonius won the Derby and his great mare Hannah (named in honour of his daughter) carried off three other classic races, the St Leger, the Oaks and the One Thousand Guineas. It was an historic achievement and one which no owner has ever surpassed.

But Muffy was far from being the only devotee of the turf in the family. On both sides of the Channel there were Rothschilds who were scarcely less fanatical about the breeding and racing of thoroughbreds. In France it was James who created the Rothschild stud at Ferrières, where the breeding and training was carried on under the expert eye of a M. Thibault. Nat also kept his own horses and seems to have been one of a comparatively small number of owners regularly racing his animals both in England and France. He was also one of the first Jews to be elected to the French Jockey Club. This was quite an achievement. Although the Great Baron was a founder member of this body (which has more to do with prestige than the actual administration of the sport), it developed decidedly anti-Semitic tendencies. For example, Alphonse only succeeded in getting elected at the third attempt, and in the next generation some Rothschilds failed to win sufficent votes from the aristocratic, exclusionist membership.

In Vienna, it was Anselm's son, Nathaniel, who was the racing enthusiast. He, too, kept his own stud and bred several fine horses, includ-ing three Derby winners.

There is no doubt that all these Rothschilds genuinely enjoyed horse racing; but the social aspect of the sport of kings was obviously important for the family. Most of Europe's men of influence gathered for the major meetings of the season and this provided an opportunity for making useful contacts. The racecourse was a place where business and pleasure could often be combined – and politics, too, on occasions.

But there was one Rothschild activity, perhaps the most remarkable of all, which had no political overtones: collecting. Volumes could be written about the vast and varied collections of exquisite objects that various Rothschilds accumulated. Indeed, over the years very little that was collectable seems to have escaped their attention. Paintings, sculp-tures, books, manuscripts, *têtes de mort*, stuffed animals, lacework, armour, wedding rings, snuffboxes, enamels, jewellery, autographs – the list is virtually endless. And what they collected, they often presented to others. Museums and galleries throughout Europe have become the grateful – if sometimes overwhelmed – recipients of comprehensive Rothschild accumulations.

The family's compulsion to acquire things of beauty and antiquity un-doubtedly originated with Mayer Amschel, whose trade in rare coins and other objects played so vital a part in establishing the family fortunes. The next generation, which had both large houses to fill and the money with which to buy the best, also had the advantage of living at the time when the disruptions of the Napoleonic Wars, and the revolutions of 1830 and 1848 which followed, had led to the break-up of many royal and noble col-lections. The nineteenth century, sandwiched between this artistic "diaspora" and the appearance of the first American millionaire collectors, was the golden age of the European connoisseur. James, Lionel, Nat and other members of the family all made the most of its opportunities. In their frequent travels around the Continent they were constantly on the lookout for bargains, and they employed an army of agents to seek out hidden masterpieces whose owners might be induced to sell.

There was indeed something of the magpie about these early collectors, especially James. The Great Baron accumulated paintings, furnishings, furniture, antiquities and *objets d'art*, with unquenchable enthusiasm and a remarkable lack of discrimination. He was not in the least deterred by the fact that his various houses were already overflowing with treasures. For there was in James a strong element of the parvenu, who bought an abundance of beautiful things because his wealth and status demanded this kind of display.

Much the same could be said of Anselm. His appreciation of art was strictly limited. Dealers naturally clustered around this eager collector who had plenty of money but was obliged to rely on the expertise of others. One such was a certain Professor Oppenheim, who toured the houses of the old nobility, picking up unconsidered trifles such as works by the Renaissance silversmiths of Nuremberg or Augsburg. He would bring these incomparable treasures to Anselm who would select the items which appealed to him and then pay for them — at so much per gram!

His son, Ferdinand, himself a genuine connoisseur, later looked back ruefully at the opportunities Anselm had missed.

> My Father might have formed a matchless collection, as he lived in
> a country where for years old works of art were deemed worthless. But
> his taste was limited to a small range as he cared for minute articles
> only, besides his time was too much occupied with business to devote
> much of it to other pursuits. When I left Vienna for London in 1860,
> I had many opportunities of offering him works of art, but he rarely
> availed himself of them. Many and many a time dealers showed me
> some fine article for which I had not space in my humble lodgings or
> which I had not the means to acquire and which I then offered to my
> Father — but as a rule he declined them.[4]

Ferdinand's attitude was in fact typical of the next generation, who displayed more discrimination than their parents and, as a result, accumulated some of the finest private collections in the world. Their greater sophistication was, no doubt, a product of their upbringing. They had grown up in veritable treasure houses and had come to appreciate beauty and craftsmanship, but they had also become painfully aware that these magnificent objects had been accumulated by bourgeois parents who understood their value more clearly than their worth. The Rothschild men and women of Ferdy's generation inherited not just intelligence and wealth. As we have already suggested, they also felt a sense of responsibility to use both positively. This motivation also lay behind the foundation of the Rothschild collections. They wanted to preserve the best artefacts of past and contemporary artists. They devoted hours of patient and fascinated study to the works they acquired. Several members of the family wrote books and monographs which were acclaimed in academic circles. For all the undoubted temptations of virtually limitless wealth, few of the Rothschilds ever became "dabblers" or empty-headed dilettantes. Their upbringing had trained them against such frivolity. Baron Elie put it to me succinctly when he said, "We are all professionals." Even the playboys of the family, men like Nat's son, Arthur, and his grandson, Henri, Lionel's son, Alfred, and Austrian Nathaniel, became deadly serious when they put on their collecting hats.

245

It was in this spirit that Arthur wrote books about postage stamps and Adolph brought together at Pregny superlative examples of Italian Renaissance craftsmanship. His brother, Willy Carl, assembled what was probably the finest collection of secular medieval silver in private hands. Most of the Rothschild collectors, although they had the best expert advice available, developed their own taste and judgement. But they could make mistakes. Willy Carl's collection contained at least one piece by the celebrated faker Rheinhold Vasters. Vasters worked as restorer to the Aachen Cathedral Treasury during the late nineteenth century. He used his knowledge and his skill as a silversmith to create spectacular pieces of "Gothic" craftsmanship. Baron Rothschild was doubtless thrilled to add to his collection a drinking horn encased in elaborately chased silver set with polished stones and supported on an intricate silver base of gryphons, spires and tracery. Alas, this "fifteenth-century master-piece" was later unmasked as a piece of Vasters' workmanship. In fairness to Wilhelm Carl, however, it should be added that the German forger was only detected by art experts in the 1970s. Clearly, it took a very clever man to deceive the Rothschilds.

One motive for the Rothschild collecting mania was a, perhaps unconscious, desire to be accepted by the *cognoscenti*. They did not always succeed. Some scholars and scions of ancient houses were unimpressed. Where others gaped in wonder, they maintained a patrician reserve. They were faintly amused at Rothschild acquisitiveness and sometimes outraged at what they considered vulgar display. As a young man at the turn of the century David Lindsay, later Earl of Crawford, and himself a considerable connoisseur, visited Tring Park and was repulsed by its showiness and vulgarity. "I told [my wife] that I was so much shocked by the place that I would never again stay in one of the big Jewish houses." Even Waddesdon, as we have seen, did not entirely please Lindsay: " . . . the ostentation was as marked as at Tring, but being a bachelor establishment there was less nonsense and perfumery".[5]

The greatest of all the Rothschild collectors was, undoubtedly, Baron Alphonse. He outshone all his contemporaries as connoisseur, patron and sensitive art lover. If banking was his vocation, art was his passion. If De Rothschild Frères was his wife, the *fraternité des artistes* was his mistress. Alphonse was a true Maecenas, one of those rare and fortunate men who possess not only impeccable taste, wide knowledge and deep understanding, but also the wealth to buy anything that catches their discerning eye.

In a fulsome panegyric published after his death in 1905, a special supplement of the magazine *L'Art* claimed: "The Baron had two families: his own and the arts. If he had not found complete satisfaction in the first (but on that score Fortune always remained faithful to him) he would have

On 29 July 1850 Lionel de Rothschild appeared in the House of Commons to take the oaths of admission. When he refused to repeat the formula 'upon the true faith of a Christian', the Speaker asked him, amidst uproar, to withdraw. A reporter described it as 'one of the most curious episodes of the history of the struggle for . . . civil and religious liberty'. (Illustrated London News Picture Library)

In 1862 Lionel had 147 and 148 Piccadilly demolished to make room for a splendid new town mansion. (Illustrated London News Picture Library)

Baron Lionel de Rothschild. (Dr Miriam Rothschild)

The marriage between Alphonse and Leonora at Gunnersbury Park in March 1857 was one of the most sumptuous social events of the decade. (Illustrated London News *Picture Library*)

*Constance and Annie de Rothschild were elegant and accomplished horsewomen.
They loved riding to hounds . . . their father Sir Anthony did not. (Taken from L.
Cohen,* Lady de Rothschild and her Daughters, 1821–1931)

Ferdinand de Rothschild.
(Mary Evans Picture Library)

Alfred de Rothschild.
(Mary Evans Picture Library)

Lord Rothschild (Natty).
(The Mansell Collection)

Leopold de Rothschild.
(Mary Evans Picture Library)

Vanity Fair *caricatures of the leading members of the English Rothschild family in the 1880s.*

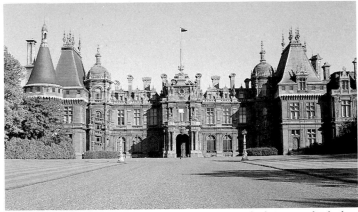

Top: *The superb château overlooking Lake Geneva which Paxton built for Adolph von Rothschild.* (Baron Edmond de Rothschild)

Middle: *This mid-nineteenth-century watercolour illustrates the beautiful view enjoyed from the Château de Pregny.* (Baron Edmond de Rothschild)

Above: *Waddesdon Manor: the elaborate house in the French style built by Baron Ferdinand de Rothschild in Buckinghamshire.*
(The National Trust Photographic Library: Nick Meers)

Baron Alphonse de Rothschild and a draft paying the first instalment of France's indemnity to Germany following her defeat in the war of 1870–71.
(Baron Eric de Rothschild)

Natty and Leo. (Dr Miriam Rothschild)

Natty's wife, Emma, one of the
Frankfurt Rothschilds.
(Dr Miriam Rothschild)

Lord Rothschild with Randolph Churchill, over whom Natty was widely believed to
have exercised considerable influence. (Dr Miriam Rothschild)

Charles Rothschild rides one of the giant turtles at Tring, watched by his elder brother, Walter. (Dr Miriam Rothschild)

The amazing equipage devised by Walter Rothschild, the only man successfully to harness wild zebras as draft animals. (Dr Miriam Rothschild)

been able to console himself with the second, for he admitted it to the same intimacy; he loved it with the same deep and tranquil love; and he gave it the same place in his paternal heart."[6]

It is difficult, perhaps impossible, to envisage the extent and quality of Alphonse's collections; but the anonymous author did describe in loving detail the items in the personal quarters of the Baron's Paris house on the Rue Saint Florentin. In the suite of five rooms were displayed antique marble statues, eighteenth-century bronzes, cabinets gleaming with Renaissance enamels, majolica, faïence and gold figurines, a garniture of clocks and vases by the eighteenth-century master Clodion, a silver repoussé dish by Ascanio (a pupil of Benvenuto Cellini), a monstrance set in gold and enamel which came from the Medici Chapel in Florence, old masters' drawings and watercolours, a magnificient Louis Quinze desk, a whole library of rare and unusual books, clocks, jewels and objects of rock crystal. The paintings crowded into this small space constituted a veritable illustrated guide to the history of European art. They included priceless works by Van Eyck, Jan Steen, Filippino Lippi, Adrien van Ostade, Mabuse, and Sigmund Holbein (brother of Hans Holbein the Elder). The seventeenth-century Dutch masters, whom Alphonse particularly admired, were represented by Hobbema, Wynarts, Wouverman, Van de Velde, Jan van der Heyden and Rembrandt. There was a masterpiece by Watteau which Alphonse had deliberately acquired in England in order to restore to its homeland. Numbered among the later masters featured in the collection were Descamps, Gainsborough, Boucher and Richard Parkes Bonington.

The author grandly concluded: "In the midst of his masterpieces, the Baron forgot all the turmoils of life. Here he refreshed his spirit — always under pressure to find answers to practical problems — in the magnificent nonchalance with which artists occasionally confront the great questions of existence."[7]

Impressive though this list is, it covers only a fraction of the collection Alphonse amassed through inheritance and purchase. It included several of Europe's rarest masterpieces — a narrative series of painted leather panels by Govaert Flinck (a pupil of Rembrandt), which adorned the walls at Ferrières, portraits by Rubens of his wife, hundreds of early engravings (at that time little appreciated), Reynolds' famous portrait of Master Hare and a unique assemblage of the eighteenth-century French masters, Watteau, Boucher and Fragonard.

Little wonder that Alphonse was greatly respected by the art establishment and that his opinion was sometimes canvassed on works of disputed provenance. He was elected as one of the forty members of the French Academy and, in 1904, 163 of France's leading artists subscribed to a

247

bronze which was presented to Alphonse in recognition of his contribution to the creative arts. For the Baron's activity was not confined to buying up the works of dead masters. He was a major patron of contemporary artists. Whenever he saw the work of a painter or sculptor that showed promise he bought it, not to hang on the already crowded walls of Rue Laffitte or Ferrières, but for exhibition in a provincial gallery or museum.

About two hundred such institutions throughout France benefited from Baron de Rothschild's benefactions. This arrangement suited all parties: it brought much-needed cash into the ateliers; it helped curators who were equally hard-pressed for funds; it ensured that the work of promising artists was seen by the public. It also enabled Alphonse to disguise his acts of generosity as businesslike transactions. As we have seen, he was a remote man who kept his emotions well under control. He hated being thanked and, like Anthony's wife, Louisa, he profoundly mistrusted the public image of the benefactor or patron. So he assumed the character of a man who simply bought pictures and then gave them away — quietly, without publicity. Even after death he tried to distance his name from his own charity. He gave two hundred thousand francs to the Academie des Beaux-Arts to provide a biennial prize, but he left the details entirely to the governors.

This shrinking from publicity was a trait Alphonse shared with many of his relatives, notably Lionel and Natty — one developed, as we have seen, out of the demand for discretion placed on the Rothschilds by the positions of trust they occupied as intimates of world leaders. But the growing political polarisation of European society forced them increasingly out into the open. By 1871 adult male suffrage was established in France and Germany, and there was a steady advance towards it in other states (including Britain). The opinions of working-class people therefore assumed a new political importance and, while existing parties vied for their support, new ones came into existence to voice their interests. By the 1880s Socialist parties of varying shades of red existed all over Europe. Some were simply anarchistic; others were dedicated to bringing about change by constitutional means. But all were agreed about their opposition to capitalism. The Rothschilds, most of whom had, until now, occupied the liberal middle ground, found themselves moving more and more to the right in response to these pressures. In the 1868 election, when their kinsman Harry Worms had stood as a Tory for the Sandwich constituency, the English Rothschilds had been outraged and a Liberal journal had published a leader under the title "CAN A JEW BE A CONSERVATIVE?"[8] But the parliamentary heirs of Lionel and Muffy were to take a different stance. Their French cousins, understandably, moved more rapidly to an extreme viewpoint.

Alphonse's political opinions had been forged in reaction to the popular excesses of 1848 and 1870. In 1879 he, uncharacteristically, submitted to a newspaper interview and expressed himself forcefully:

For my part I don't believe in this working-class movement. I am sure that, generally speaking, working people are very satisfied with their lot, that they don't complain at all and that they are not in the least interested in what is called "Socialism". There are, obviously, ring-leaders who try to make a lot of noise and attract a following but such people have neither hold nor influence over honest reasonable, hard-working labourers. We must distinguish between good and bad workers. It is completely mistaken, for example, to say that good workers are demanding an eight hour day; those who are agitating for that are lazy and incompetent fellows . . .

I have never understood what is meant by "Haute-banque" . . . There are richer men and poorer men. That's all! Some are richer today and will be poorer tomorrow . . . Everyone is subject to such variations – everyone, without exception. And no one can boast of being able to escape them. As for these agglomerations of capital, it is money which circulates, works and bears fruit . . . If you frighten it away or threaten it, it will disappear. And, on that day, all will be lost . . . Apart from some unfortunate exceptions . . . each man . . . has that share of the available capital that his intelligence, energy and hard work merits.[9]

There could hardly be a more straightforward exposition of *laissez-faire* capitalism. For Alphonse, economic life was governed by certain immutable laws. Political idealists who ignored these laws were either mis-guided or stupid. And much the same attitude was taken, as we shall see, by his English cousins who found themselves becoming steadily more alienated from Gladstonian Liberalism.

On at least one occasion, however, the laws which brought Alphonse wealth and prestige operated to his disadvantage. The Baron was due to attend a reception in Brussels. He left the Rue St Florentin in rather a hurry to catch the late afternoon express. After his departure, his valet dis-covered that the case carrying his master's dress suit was still standing in the hall. He grabbed it and rushed in a cab to the Gare du Nord only to find that the train had already departed. However, all was not lost; his master was, after all, chairman of the railway company. A hurried word with the appropriate authorities produced a special train which was soon hurtling northwards carrying one passenger and a suitcase. Meanwhile, a telegraph message was sent ahead to clear the track for Baron de Rothschild. Obedient employees diverted every piece of rolling stock that might impede the passage of the special – including the Paris-Brussels express, which was shunted into a siding and remained there while Alphonse and his fellow passengers fretted and checked their watches. The outcome was that Baron de Rothschild's suit arrived in time for the function but Baron de Rothschild did not.

The Baron's weapons against Socialism were the same ones Rothschilds had always used since first acquiring influence. He may have refused election to parliament; he may not have deliberately organised party caucuses; he certainly did not participate in political plots; but because he knew all the leading members of the Assembly and discussed current issues with them; because he was the prime mover in floating state loans; and because few major commerical enterprises could succeed without the backing of one of his banking syndicates, Alphonse de Rothschild was a political power in the land.

Apart from anything else, he was one of the few representatives of stability. The National Assembly was so bedevilled with parties and factions that the first twenty years of the Third Republic saw thirty changes of administration. Much of Alphonse's behind-the-scenes activity was aimed at preventing wild swings on the barometer of economic policy so that the commerical sector could get on with its job. This largely meant trying to counter the activities of the Left which clamoured for greater state control. A valuable ally in this endeavour was Léon Say. A longstanding business colleague, a member of the board of the Chemin de Fer du Nord and of several Rothschild companies, Say entered politics in the early 1860s and rapidly gained a reputation as an expert on economic affairs and a vigorous debater who, often single-handedly, opposed government financial policy during the last years of the Empire. He was fiercely critical of grandiose economic schemes and advocated a policy of bourgeois commonsense in handling the affairs of the nation. He maintained this attitude through the tumultuous early years of the Third Republic, continuing to speak out in favour of private enterprise.

Say was able to put his principles into practice when he became Finance Minister in the administration of Jules Dufaure (December 1877 – January 1879). Inevitably, he was accused of being the Rothschilds' creature. Those who made such accusations failed to understand the subtle mechanism of Rothschild political influence. Alphonse and Léon Say met frequently to discuss current economic issues and they were much in agreement on the resolution of those issues. But, in the delicately balanced state of French politics, Alphonse was too intelligent to be identified with one group. He enjoyed the acquaintance or friendship of men of all shades of opinion.

Much as he disliked the politics of the Left, it would not have occurred to Alphonse to shun Socialist leaders. When, in May 1881, Léon Gambetta was emerging as the man of the hour, the head of the Paris house made a point of getting to know him and trying to reassure him as to what the Baron regarded as the very limited political rôle of the Rothschilds. A contemporary described a dinner at which the two men were present. Before the meal, he says, he observed

... chatting amiably in a window embrasure, the two "kings" – Gambetta, the actual master of France, and Rothschild ... Gambetta wanted to make a naval demonstration against Tunisia [and described his military plans] ... Alphonse de Rothschild then began to speak very knowledgeably about the leading ministers of Italy and England. Gambetta listened with mingled admiration and astonishment: he had not suspected Alphonse de Rothschild of possessing such a well-developed and lively intelligence. Between them, the two men considered Depretis, Caïroli, Sella, Disraeli, Gladstone, Crispi, Hartington, Granville ... Alphonse de Rothschild explained to his fascinated listener the major financial operations in which he had been involved in 1871. He said that he liked M. Thiers even though he (Thiers) unjustly accused him of having been his enemy. For a whole year the two men had not been on speaking terms. Gambetta interrupted, "Thiers told me, 'It was Rothschild who defeated me'"[i.e. in the spring of 1873, when he lost the presidency]. "That isn't true!" Alphonse de Rothschild responded sharply. "I obviously had a certain influence with quite a large number of deputies and I enabled Thiers to hold on for six months longer than he would have been able to do without me. I told my friends in the Chamber, 'Don't overthrow Thiers; that would be a public disaster ... At least let him conclude the important negotiations over the loan; the credibility and fortune of France depend on that.' I never said anything else." Rothschild and Gambetta were obviously agreed [in following] the spirit of Thiers.

But while Alphonse was quite ready to strike up alliances with those on the other side of the political fence, he was far too old a hand to make any rash or irrevocable commitments. The same contemporary reported that when it came to the toasts at the end of the meal,

"To a restored France!" said Gambetta. Alphonse de Rothschild responded "To the man who will restore her!" The words were vague and could be applied to Galliffet [General Gaston Galliffet, currently engaged in occupying Tunisia] equally as well as to Gambetta ... but Gambetta did not hesitate to take them as referring to himself. He searched for some moments for a suitable response, which eluded him, and then replied very simply, "Ah! I would like that very much."[10]

*   *   *

In the financial world, opposition to the Rothschilds came principally from rivals who resented the powerful *haute banque* alliances and formed syndicates of their own to compete for business. The principal mover in these enterprises was the Crédit Lyonnais whose director regarded the *haute banque* as an international conspiracy of private bankers which aimed at excluding the new-style French merchant banks and deposit banks from the market-place:

> . . .faced with this situation, which threatens to remove French establishments from the place they should legitimately occupy in French affairs, these establishments have thought it useful to unite, so as to be able, by collective action, to exercise more influence and bring more pressure to bear on the government. The campaign will be carried on in the press . . . The objective of the syndicate is not so much to remove business from another group as to oblige it to share. We want to gain admittance on an equal footing with our capital, our clientele and the competition that we have a right to bring.[11]

This kind of rivalry could only be healthy. More sinister was the opposition initiated by Eugène Bontoux, a senior employee of the Rothschilds who had risen to be director of their Austrian railway company. Bontoux was a talented engineer, and a highly ambitious and innovative businessman who, with the encouragement of his principals, had introduced many bold schemes for improving the railway. He had also attempted at least one major financial coup — a suggested co-operation between Rothschilds and the Crédit Lyonnais in refloating the failed Wienerbankverein. But he was, at root, an opportunist; for, when the French bank refused to co-operate with Rothschilds, he offered to help them supplant their rivals as loan contractors for Hungary. In 1878 Bontoux and the Rothschilds parted company, and the enterprising engineer launched a new banking consortium called l'Union Générale.

As well as drawing capital from institutional partners, Bontoux hit on an ingenious method of attracting public investment. He represented the Union Générale as a Catholic bank which would wrest control of the money markets from Jews and Protestants. His prospectus contained a message of support from the Pope and he gained the backing, not only of the Roman Catholic hierarchy, but also of the monarchist nobility and other conservative elements. Priests commended the new enterprise to their congregations with all the fervour their medieval ancestors had employed to launch crusades against the infidel. This unleashed an investment rush of Gadarene proportions. Faced with the prospect of striking a blow for the true faith *and* making a profit, ordinary Frenchmen poured their savings into the Union Générale's coffers. The first flotation of four million francs was soon oversubscribed.

The new enterprise made an exceedingly promising start. Using his Austrian connections and his knowledge of Rothschild operations, Bontoux insinuated himself into the counsels of the government at Vienna and usurped something of the position previously enjoyed by his erstwhile employers. In 1880 he was involved in founding the Österreichische Länderbank. The following year the two new institutions combined in a major project for an extension of the Austro-Hungarian railway system to the Turkish frontier. And that was only one of the many bold projects that Bontoux was involved in all over Europe. By the beginning of 1882 Union Générale stock issued at five hundred francs was being quoted at two thousand five hundred.

Then came the crash. There were three main reasons for the sudden downfall of the Union Générale. The established banking syndicates naturally hit back at the upstart and employed their considerable financial muscle. In Vienna, for example, Salomon Albert, head of the Rothschild bank, bought Union Générale shares over several months and then, suddenly, dumped them. Partly as a result of this stratagem, the share value of the Union Générale fell from 2090 frs to 950 frs in a period of just two months. This coincided with a world trade recession, a backlash which followed the enthusiastic boom years of the seventies. The first serious sign of the market turndown came in January 1882 when, for several days, the Paris Bourse was forced to stop trading. But the main reason for the Union Générale's difficulties was Bontoux's own over-speculation. He tried to buttress himself against a run on the bank by investing the reserves to make a quick profit, an expedient which simply accelerated the pace of the impending disaster. The Union Générale went into liquidation and Bontoux was arrested. At the end of a long trial, he was sentenced to five years on various counts of illegal manipulation of funds. He avoided prison by spending the period 1883-8 in Spain. During the hearings and throughout his exile he did everything possible to shift the blame on to others. He was joined in this by thousands of honest Frenchmen who had lost everything in the débâcle, by church leaders, by the forces of reaction and also, ironically, by several Socialist politicians. For the economic crisis had also brought down Gambetta, the darling of the Left. The unleashed fury had one target: the Jewish "conspiracy" and, specifically, the Rothschilds. The *affaire* Bontoux" marked the beginning of a virulent campaign of anti-Semitism which would plague France right up to the start of the Great War.

CHAPTER 19
"Oh, . . . the sense of lavish wealth, thrust up your nose"

After 1881-2 the closing years of the nineteenth century were a period of unprecedented prosperity and confidence. This was the high summer of *laissez-faire* capitalism. It was a time of minimum taxation and maximum opportunity; a time when the rich, if they had any intelligence at all, got richer. This was the age of the music hall and the operettas of Gilbert and Sullivan, of steam yachts and the first motor cars, of holidays on the Riviera and country house parties, of splendidly rebuilt Vienna where two monarchs reigned — the Emperor Francis Joseph and the "Waltz King" Johann Strauss — of an élite for whom, as Oscar Wilde suggested, to be *in* society was "merely a bore, but to be *out* of it simply a tragedy".

There was not the slightest doubt that the Rothschilds were *in*. Many of them pursued the pleasures afforded by their wealth and status with great enthusiasm. For the first time only a minority of the Rothschild men were actively involved in banking. In Paris, Alphonse and Gustave continued to shoulder the burden of Rue Laffitte. In Frankfurt, Mayer Carl and Willy Carl presided over the parent house. But in Vienna, Salbert coped single-handed in the Renngasse and in London, although Lionel's three sons went daily to their New Court offices, Natty was the only one who could be called a dedicated banker. For the first time there was a polarisation of pleasure and responsibility, which, till now, most members of the family had successfully held together. Some Rothschilds gave themselves up with total enthusiasm to public pastimes and private vices, not caring if the world dubbed them eccentrics. Others reacted just as decidedly against the frivolity and moral laxity of the times and devoted themselves almost exclusively to good works.

In London, the brothers who inherited Lionel's fortune and duties were very different in personality. Natty, the oldest of the three, and the undisputed leader, was as outstanding, in his own way, as Nathan and James had been. He had a quick, clear, decisive turn of mind, a remarkable grasp of issues, whether financial or political, and slipped easily into his father's place at New Court, Westminster and within the "corridors of power". In character, too, Natty closely resembled his father. He was a

Rothschilds Living in England 1870-1900

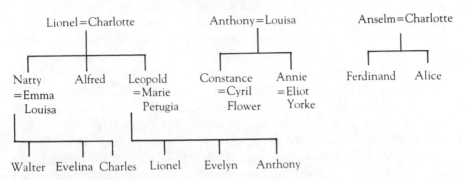

Lionel=Charlotte
- Natty =Emma Louisa
  - Walter
  - Evelina
  - Charles
- Alfred
- Leopold =Marie Perugia
  - Lionel
  - Evelyn
  - Anthony

Anthony=Louisa
- Constance =Cyril Flower
- Annie =Eliot Yorke

Anselm=Charlotte
- Ferdinand
- Alice

reserved and taciturn figure who never found it easy to express his emotions. His immense generosity and kindness were concealed by an obsessive modesty, so that the full extent of his benefactions was discovered only after his death. In particular, he had a keen sense of duty towards those for whom he felt in any way responsible — a category that included his employees, his tenants, British Jews, persecuted foreign Jews, the poor and the thousands of unfortunates who daily appealed to him for help. Balfour, who was a close friend of Natty's for many years, described him as "that self-contained somewhat joyless character. He had a high ideal of public duty and was utterly indifferent to worldly pomps and vanities. Moreover he was perfectly simple."[1]

Natty's wife, Emma Louisa, was one of Mayer Carl's talented daughters. She was an accomplished artist and pianist but forsook these pastimes to devote herself to furthering her husband's career. The self-sacrifice was typical of her. Like most of the Frankfurt family, she had a highly developed religious and moral sense and some of her attitudes struck even her Victorian contemporaries as prudish, not that the opinions of other people would have greatly troubled her. For she was stoical in the face of life's unpleasantness, firm in her opinions and unswerving in her support of Natty. Connie, who was very close to Emma, described her as "reserved", "appreciative", "kindhearted", "intelligent", "ingenious" and "persevering". Her imagination, Connie thought, was "small" and her disposition "not very generous".[2]

After the first few years the marriage was not characterised by outward displays of warmth — with two such restrained people it could not be — but it was marked by mutual respect and admiration. Emma was a perfectionist and performed her public rôle as hostess, benefactress and

255

mistress of a large estate with meticulous care. She supported literally hundreds of charities. One of her granddaughters remembers Emma as a lady with "agonisingly high ideals", whose attitude towards her tenants and servants was not one of grand paternalism but genuine concern.[3]

It is certainly true that the farmers and workers on the estate at Tring regarded themselves as among the most fortunate tenants in the country. Natty and Emma built over four hundred modern cottages, equipped with hygienic sewage arrangements and water supply. They kept farms, farm buildings and even churches in good repair. They provided amenities such as village halls, clubs and schools. They even built a new pub, the Rose and Crown at Tring, in order to provide accommodation for the "servant invasion" which occurred every time they threw a large house party. When they were in residence, they made regular tours of the estate to see that all was running well and to maintain personal contact with their tenants. They operated medical, pension and social benefit schemes that placed them firmly among the most enlightened English landlords.[4] Natty and Emma's care for their agricultural workers was particularly appreciated during the agrarian slump of the 1870s and 1880s when Rothschild money supported the rural economy of the Vale of Aylesbury while, elsewhere, farms were being abandoned and labourers thrown off the land. Their granddaughter Miriam can still vividly recall hearing them agree across the dinner table, some years later, that one of their neighbours was an out-and-out scoundrel. Feeling certain that the man must be at least a bank-robber to have merited such a description, the awe-struck child asked what he had done. "He doesn't look after his tenants' cottages properly", her grandmother replied.[5]

Around Alfred, the second brother, there persists something of an air of mystery. He was the almost perfect antithesis of Natty: a confirmed bachelor, an aesthete, flamboyant to the point of eccentricity, irreverent, at times irresponsible and so unreserved that he was widely regarded as a bit of a buffoon. One contemporary described him as having "a good heart but a mean and miserable little mind".[6] He dutifully played the part that was expected of him in the bank and in public life. Yet, at root, he was one of those Rothschilds who rebelled against family orthodoxies. Like the French Salomon, he all too readily saw the absurdities of his position. While this undoubtedly endeared him to his wide circle of friends, it irritated his more serious relatives. Emma, for example, disapproved so strongly of Alfred's life style that she refused to entertain his intimate friend, Marie Wombwell, under her roof. And his nephew, Charles (Natty's son), was probably not alone in the family in expressing the view that "to be rid of Alfred was cheap at any price".[7]

What was it about Natty's brother that made him such an embarrassment to other Rothschilds? His appearance cannot have helped: he was slim, dapper, sported extravagant side whiskers and often wore a vacant smile. But that expression was no sign of simple-mindedness; Alfred was no fool. He was witty. He spoke fluently several European languages and was genuinely interested in other cultures. As a connoisseur of old masters (and particularly as a collector of eighteenth-century English paintings) he came close to rivalling his brother-in-law, Alphonse, and he put his expertise to good use as a trustee of the National Gallery and the Wallace Collection. It was at his insistence, for example, that the government acquired for the nation the magnificent equestrian portrait of Charles I by Van Dyck, which is now one of the proudest possessions of the National Gallery. He was a well-informed devotee of opera, theatre and music hall (for a time he was a part owner of the celebrated Gaiety Theatre), and interested himself in European politics.

Alfred entered very enthusiastically into the Rothschild responsibility for hospitality. The magazine *Vanity Fair*, perhaps tactfully, suggested that this was his "official" Rothschild role:

> It is his function to represent the great house in Society, and he does it with much thoroughness. He it is who receives the Princes, interviews the Ambassadors, and gives the splendid entertainments to which the chosen smart people of London delight to resort. On these occasions he makes himself the slave and servant of his guests, lavishes upon them all the luxuries that wealth can supply, and sends them away always grateful, if sometimes envious. He knows and is known by everybody in London ... [8]

It was to provide an even grander setting for his lavish entertainments, and also a worthy home for the finer items in his collection, that Alfred built himself a country mansion — and built it with characteristic exuberance. His father had left him land at Halton, near Wendover, and there, in 1881, workmen began on the construction of a remarkable building. Perhaps Alfred intended to rival, or even make gentle mockery of, Ferdinand's house which was nearing completion at Waddesdon; for, like his brother-in-law, he built in the French château style. But there is no real comparison between the two structures. Ferdinand chose a French architect, planned carefully and built slowly. Alfred was less patient. He appointed a leading firm of English builders and paid them well to complete their work in two years. The result was grandiose, spectacular, theatrical — and not to everyone's taste. One aristocratic visitor exclaimed, "Oh but the hideousness of the thing, the showiness! the sense of lavish wealth, thrust up your nose ... Eye hath not seen nor pen can write the ghastly coarseness of the sight." Certainly Halton's exterior does

257

not bear comparison with that of Waddesdon, but the interior provided a magnificient setting for part of Alfred's collection of art treasures.

The completion of Halton in 1883 marked the culmination of a remarkable quarter of a century of building by the Rothschilds. They had carried out no less than eight major architectural projects, beginning with Mentmore and continuing with the country houses of Ferrières, Pregny and Waddesdon, Lionel's London residence at 147-8 Piccadilly, and two town palaces in Vienna (see p. 274). In addition, of course, they had made numerous extensions and improvements to their existing homes. Even in that prosperous and expansionist age, no other family could even begin to rival this achievement. Indeed, this building mania was perhaps the clearest possible demonstration that, as far as wealth was concerned, the Rothschilds were now in a league of their own. If they were to be compared with anyone, it could only be with the great emperors, kings and aristocrats of the past whose palaces were created as marks of permanence and status, as well as settings for personal display and generous hospitality.

Whatever their opinions of Alfred's architectural extravaganza, few people turned down his invitations. For at Halton, Alfred spared neither his own ingenuity nor the labours of his large staff to ensure that his week-end guests had a magical experience. The house itself boasted every comfort and convenience so far invented. It was the first residence to be built with electric lighting, and probably the first to include an indoor swimming pool. The diversions offered were numerous, original and sometimes bizarre. Alfred kept a troupe of performing animals which did their tricks in an open-air circus ring. The performance was not complete until the host himself appeared resplendent in top hat, blue frock coat and lavender gloves, with a ringmaster's long whip. Whatever Alfred took it into his head to do, his indoor and outdoor servants somehow had to carry into effect. "Never say 'No' to Mr Alfred", a new assistant gardener was admonished. "If he tells you to set up a ladder to the moon, at least go and fetch the ladder." Some of the master of Halton's instructions did not fall far short of that. On one occasion rambler roses had to be transplanted to the conservatory and made to twine all around the columns. This was in the middle of the flowering season and the garden staff were given less than a week to accomplish the miracle. When the weekend guests arrived, the conservatory was a mass of blooms. What they did not realise was that the flowers at the tops of the columns were created from wire and paper. One hard winter an even more demanding instruction arrived at Halton – "Make a lake for skating". Miraculously, the next batch of visitors were able to take to the ice. And at the end of a fairy-tale weekend Alfred's departing guests would find their carriages provisioned with boxed

258

orchids, cigars, hampers of cakes and chocolates and baskets of fruit.[9]

Entertaining and entertaining generously was, and remains, a responsibility taken very seriously by most Rothschilds. Yet there was something excessive, almost self-mocking, about Alfred's extravaganzas and his personal theatricality. For Natty and Emma, and Ferdy and Alphonse and Salbert, lavish entertaining had to have some purpose. Alfred felt no need to justify his parties at Seymour Place and Halton. As well as heads of state and prominent *hommes d'affaires,* he habitually brought to his table stage ladies and other persons of dubious reputation. Sometimes he would arrange a dinner in celebration of some prominent actress. Apart from the guest of honour, all the company would be male, come to pay homage to Alfred's latest discovery. The host would preside genially over a sumptuously spread board, eating and drinking sparingly himself because of his "health". Frequently his dinner parties were serenaded by Alfred's personal orchestra, whose members were chosen as much for uniform height as for musical ability. One of his favourite pastimes was conducting and he would often take up the baton himself to direct a post-prandial concert. When any of his friends was ill, Alfred's solicitousness knew no bounds. From his kitchen at Seymour Place, a hamper would immediately be despatched to the invalid, containing soup or a pâté and other nourishing comestibles. Such ostentatious generosity was, perhaps, slightly vulgar but it was good-hearted and harmless enough. We must, therefore, look elsewhere to discover reasons for Alfred's unpopularity with some of his relatives.

One was his disinclination for banking. He habitually arrived late at New Court, left early and took a snooze after lunch. Moreover, this partner in N.M. Rothschild and Sons regarded four days a week as quite sufficient for the discharge of his responsibilities. He never worked on Fridays and legend tells how, in order to get his weekends off to a good start, he always had a thousand pounds sent round from the bank in crisp, new notes. Inevitably, those who shouldered most of the burden of NMR business dealings resented the lack of commitment of one who spent so freely on his friends, his pleasures, on foreign travel, and on charity.

If some of his kinsfolk disapproved of Alfred, the eccentric playboy certainly reciprocated. His dislike of his more censorious relatives expressed itself in practical jokes and witty, often cruel, jibes. Emma was a particular target. "All her children must have been conceived under protest", he once remarked cynically about his strait-laced sister-in-law. Another time, at a dinner party, after having told a particularly risqué joke, he glanced round the table and remarked casually, "Emmie told me that".[10]

Even such behaviour might have been forgiven, but what the family

259

found difficult to overlook was the fact that Alfred broke one of the cardinal Rothschild rules: he was impulsive and indiscreet. One particular scandal caused great embarrassment at New Court. In 1868 he was appointed a director of the Bank of England (the first Jewish director – another Rothschild record) and discharged his responsibilities adequately for twenty-one years. In 1889, however, he became very agitated by rumours that a leading London art dealer with whom he had recently done some business had made an excessive profit. It so happened that the man kept an account at the Bank of England and the temptation to check up on him proved too strong for Alfred. He had a "peek" at the customer's statement. Unfortunately, news of this shocking indiscretion leaked out, arousing a furore in the City, and Alfred was obliged to resign.

Yet still we are not at the heart of the mystery. His lack of "responsibility" and his refusal to take financial matters seriously were certainly irritants to his family. His public eccentricities were an embarrassment and grew more marked as the years passed by. For example, Londoners always knew when "Mr Alfred" was abroad, for his carriage or, in later years, his car was always followed by a second. The nervous little man was always afraid that his vehicle might break down, obliging him to walk or hire a public conveyance. But all these traits together are not sufficient to explain why the familiar smoke screen of Rothschild secrecy blows across the path leading to the *real* Alfred de Rothschild. Why, for instance, is access denied to the Halton visitors' book, which would tell us much more about his circle of close friends? And did he, or did he not, sire an illegitimate daughter? It seems that there was something so shocking about Alfred's sex life that his relatives and even some of his more liberal-minded descendants have kept the facts to themselves.

To penetrate at least part of this mystery we must begin on 12 June 1868. That was the day on which a beautiful French lady, Marie Boyer, was joined in wedlock to Frederick Charles Wombwell, the twenty-three-year-old younger brother of Sir Henry Wombwell, Bart. Within a year the couple had a son, Frederick Adolphus. It was a further eight years before their only other child, a daughter, was born. It was widely believed that Alfred de Rothschild was the father of this girl, christened Almina. Certainly, he did nothing to dispel such stories. He went about openly with Marie for several years and as her daughter grew into a very beautiful and exceedingly wanton young woman, he lavished money upon her. Almina's son later recorded that the doting Alfred could refuse her nothing and that she took full advantage of the fact. It was commonplace for her to ask him for ten or twenty thousand pounds and she was never disappointed.

Why did Frederick Wombwell allow himself to be so openly cuckolded?

He and Marie lived in their Bruton Street home until his death in 1899. In 1895 he presided at Almina's grand society wedding. At no time, apparently, was divorce ever suggested. Probably, he was well compensated for his humiliation out of Alfred's seemingly bottomless coffers. But can money alone explain his endurance of such a painful situation? Or can it be that there were, in fact, no grounds for divorce; that Almina, as her birth certificate stated, was the daughter of Mr and Mrs Frederick Wombwell? Certainly, some living Rothschilds do not accept the story of Almina's illegitimacy.

The next important event in the narrative was that grand society wedding. George Herbert, the young Earl of Carnarvon, was looking for a wealthy bride in order to escape his creditors and sustain his extravagant life style. His choice fell upon the eighteen-year-old Almina and he called upon her "father" to discuss the business arrangements. Alfred agreed to the staggering "dowry" of half a million pounds. Further, he also settled Carnarvon's outstanding debts, which amounted to a further hundred and fifty thousand.[11] Almina and Herbert were duly married and they continued to batten upon Alfred to support a life style consisting of frequent foreign travel, a frenzied social life, raising racehorses and maintaining two large domestic establishments.

It must have irked Alfred's kith and kin to see him lavishing good Rothschild money on a grasping young woman and her husband whose only response to such generosity was to demand more. So why did Alfred do it? Why did he spoil Almina so appallingly? It may be that, like another over indulgent parent, the tragic Lear, he had become, "a very foolish, fond old man . . . not in my perfect mind". That explanation works as long as we accept that Almina was his daughter. If she was not, we must seek the answer elsewhere. Friendship? The relationship Alfred had with the Wombwells cost him millions, and, as we shall see, he left a large part of his estate to Almina (see p. 343). It may be that Alfred found in Marie and her family a warmth and acceptance lacking among his own kindred. Yet that explanation does not entirely satisfy. For one thing, when, after 1899, Alfred and Marie might have come together (either as man and wife or, if religious considerations forbade that, as permanent companions) they did not do so, and Marie's grandson remembers her as a lonely old lady, keeping much to herself in Bruton Street.[12] The smoke persists. Can we disperse any more of it?

According to one family rumour, the reason why Alfred was not Almina's father, and why his name was not romantically linked with any of his theatrical lady friends, was that he was homosexual. Rothschild legend tells of parties at Halton which were far from innocent. This is all conjectural. There is no proof, and perhaps there never will be. But if we

261

accept Alfred's "scandalous" sexual orientation as a hypothesis, everything else does fall into place. His demeanour, his aestheticism, his love of dressing up, his effeminacy, his hypochondria, his close attachment to his friends — all are common marks of men with homosexual tendencies (though, of course, not exclusively so). And nothing would more convincingly explain why he was such an embarrassment to the family.

In the spring of 1895, when the gossip columns were exulting over the details of the Carnarvon wedding, the main story on the front pages concerned the trial of Oscar Wilde and his alleged homosexual acts. Victorian society would not tolerate what it termed "perversion". Any man who found himself attracted to members of his own sex thus had to envelop his desires and his gratification of those desires in secrecy. Involving his friends, the Wombwells, in an elaborate cover of his activities would have been, from Alfred's point of view, an excellent plan and one appealing to his love of theatricality. If Marie, Frederick and Almina were generously recompensed for their part in the deception, the arrangement may well have been satisfactory to all concerned.

Alfred may have squandered money on Almina out of undisciplined affection or a need to buy her silence, or a combination of both. Whatever his motivation, the result was disastrous for Almina. She grew into a grasping, extravagant, vicious, wilful, unprincipled woman. Her son recalled how, at the age of about ten, he made an unfortunate gaffe at a royal garden party. Almina, beside herself with rage, bundled the boy into her carriage and spent the entire homeward journey not only lashing him with her tongue but kicking him on the shins. She then shut him in the attic for two days with nothing but bread and water, and when the King, himself, sent some toys round to cheer the poor lad up she immediately despatched them to a children's hospital.[13]

There was nothing complex or mysterious about the youngest of Lionel's three sons, lovable, genial, Leo. He was a devoted countryman and his special passion was horses. When he finished at university he took over the running of his father's stud at Gunnersbury and subsequently moved it to his own Buckinghamshire house at Ascott where he bred many successful horses, though he had to wait until 1904 for a Derby winner — St Amant. After Muffy's death Leo also took over the mastership of the deerhounds. He moved the pack to Ascott, had new kennels and stables built, and improved the hounds and the deer with the introduction of new stock.

Leo was the most popular of the brothers. He who had shared Evelina's childhood escapades, had grieved deeply at his sister's death and had offered his companionship to the mourning Ferdinand, never lost his sense of fun or his genuine sympathy. This, coupled with his passion for sport, made him one of the most genial of companions.

It is, perhaps, surprising that he did not marry until he was thirty-six but when he did it was to a beautiful young woman half his age. The first the family knew of the attachment was when an Ascott hunt was attended by " . . . an elegant, rather delicate-looking girl, somewhat shy and retiring, simply but very becomingly attired in a dark green cloth dress . . . she was mounted on one of Leo's perfect hunters and rode to the meet with her sister. This was a kind of *baptême de sport* which must have been successful, for within the next few days we were told that Marie Perugia was the fiancée of Leopold."[14] Marie was Austrian by birth and her family had only recently settled in England, but she loved her new country — especially as her marriage gave her an honoured and secure place in the topmost ranks of society. Soon she found herself playing hostess to the Prince of Wales, the Prime Minister, aristocrats, politicians and foreign dignitaries — and loving it.

Muffy died in 1874 and, three years later, his widow, Juliana, passed away aboard her yacht in the Mediterranean. This left her twenty-six-year-old daughter, Hannah, as the sole inheritrix of Mentmore, 107 Piccadilly, a house in Newmarket and estates extending to several thousand acres. The following January fashionable society was stunned by the announcement of her engagement to Archibald Primrose, fifth Earl of Rosebery. The thirty-year-old peer had been a friend of the family for many years. He and Muffy were fellow devotees of the turf and he enjoyed a particularly close relationship with Ferdy. The two young people, therefore, saw a great deal of each other but they had to conceal their real feelings because of the attitude of Hannah's parents to mixed marriages. Any hopes that Muffy and Juliana might be persuaded to take a liberal attitude, must have been dashed by their hostile reaction to Annie's marriage to Eliot Yorke in 1873. So it was not until a decent period of mourning for Juliana had elapsed that Hannah and Archie revealed their plans.

In the event, the news provoked no adverse comment. For the Rothschilds, the times had changed and Rosebery was a remarkably good "catch" by any standards. As well as possessing an ancient title, considerable landed wealth (though not nearly as much as Hannah), a string of racehorses and a prominent place in society, Rosebery was a leading Liberal peer, an outstanding orator and, by common consent, one of the most promising young men in public life. There was thus no trace of reticence about the wedding in March 1878 — on the contrary, it was one of the social events of the year. The Prince of Wales headed a star-studded guest list and the bride was given away by the Prime Minister, Lord Beaconsfield. It was in this fairy-tale atmosphere that the married life of Hannah and Archie began, and for its all-too-brief lease it was to be a happy and fulfilling relationship. Rosebery, supported and inspired by his devoted wife, held with distinction a variety of official posts.

A few months earlier another Rothschild girl had married a Christian. This was Sir Anthony's daughter, Connie. By the time her father died in 1876 Constance was already on close terms with an old Cambridge friend of Leo's, Cyril Flower. Flower was a rather effete, but nonetheless amiable and extremely popular young man who had inherited from his father a sizeable estate in and around Battersea, at that time a suburb of London. The marriage had, apparently, been planned for some time, but the couple may well have decided not to upset Connie's father by announcing their engagement during his last painful months and there could be no question of marriage in the immediate aftermath of his death. The ceremony therefore did not take place until November 1877.

But once married to Connie, Flower was drawn into the Rothschild orbit with a vengeance. So that Connie should not be separated from her widowed mother, the couple lived most of the year at Aston Clinton, spending only the winter months in a house Flower bought at Marble Arch. In both town and country, they continued the tradition of hospitality for which Anthony had been famed. Flower was much involved with the literary and artistic set, and his guests included Burne-Jones, Millais, Tissot, Whistler, Tennyson, Henry James and Alfred Gilbert. Cyril and his wife were both convinced Gladstonians and, soon after the marriage, Cyril was prevailed upon to become Liberal candidate for the safe Tory seat of Brecon. Connie travelled to Wales with him on several occasions to nurse the constituency and she was at his side for the canvassing in 1880. That was the year of Gladstone's celebrated Midlothian campaign which swept his party to an outstanding victory. Flower was carried along on the Liberal tide and took the Brecon seat convincingly. When the result was announced, amidst scenes of great excitement, Constance entered fully into the spirit of the occasion and showed that she, too, could be a politician: "Cyril screamed out a little speech and then returned for more congratulations and handshaking. I was then conducted to the window, and silence was enforced by one of the ministers. I shouted out as loud as I could: 'I must thank you for the great work you have done today, and will only say one word, but that shall be a Welsh one — *Buddigoliaeth* (Victory).' They heard it and applauded vociferously . . ."[15]

Connie enjoyed being an MP's wife. It largely involved entertaining politicians in London and touring the constituency to make speeches and

264

grace official functions with her presence. She was good at all these things. Cyril supported Gladstone staunchly throughout the difficult 1880s and, in 1892, was rewarded with a peerage. Constance was happy enough with her new title of Lady Battersea but was disappointed with her change of rôle. The upper house lacked the excitement of the Commons and she missed the close contact with "ordinary people". There had for some time been tensions in the marriage and this change of pace did not help. The basic problem was that Connie's loyalties were divided between her husband on the one hand, and her mother and sister on the other. There is also a strong possibility that Cyril was bisexual or homosexual, and that he brought to Aston Clinton friends of whom his wife strongly disapproved. Matters came to a head in 1893. On 1 February, Lady Battersea recorded in her diary, " . . . Cyril came home at 6.30, saying, 'I have good news for you.' He flung himself into a chair and said, 'I have been offered the Governorship of New South Wales.' It struck me like a knife . . . "

For Flower, this was a dramatic step forward in his public career. For Constance, it meant only one thing — separation from her beloved mother and sister. No Rothschild woman had ever been taken from her kinsfolk to reside in a distant land. Faced not just with his wife's opposition, but also with that of Louisa and Annie, Flower simply gave in. He declined the governorship and with it all ambitions for high office. He was bitter and angry. The relationship between him and Connie never fully recovered. In her memoirs she could not bring herself to write about the episode but her diaries at the time clearly show that it was on her mind for weeks.

> February 20th: Started for Ireland. Drove up to the castle. Party consists of His Excellency, two sisters, the sister-in-law, and Miss Graham. We all curtsey to His Excellency and are very rigid on all points of etiquette. New South Wales never out of my mind, and I can see Cyril performing the various functions so beautifully and *enjoying* all of it. His Excellency came and sat next to me after dinner, but I felt faint and ill.
> February 21st . . . Dare I say that I most profoundly regret my decision? And yet, had it been otherwise, it might have killed my mother. Oh dear, oh dear! [16]

Another reason why Connie was reluctant to leave Britain was that she could not bring herself to abandon the social work to which she devoted the greater part of her time — a devotion which, as we have already seen, grew out of childhood experiences under the tutelage of her mother:" . . . both my sister and I had been taught to look upon work for others in many a good cause as a privilege and not as a hardship, nor as anything meritorious in itself."[17] The children visited poor Jewish areas in Whitechapel, Bethnal Green and Mile End — areas where life was still very similar to that in the Frankfurt ghetto from which their own grandfather had emerged.

> Many of the men were engaged in tailoring and shoemaking. There were families who only talked Yiddish, which would have made conversation difficult, if not impossible, had it not been for the kind offices of some of the neighbours, who would generally be called in to translate questions and answers. They all belonged to the very orthodox form of Judaism; they all had the "Mezuzah"* on their door-posts.
>
> According to custom, the married women concealed their hair, not under a veil, as they would have done in the East, but under a front of false hair — "Sheitel", as it is called. They still keep a special set of cooking utensils and crockery for the Passover holy days, when a great scrubbing and cleaning takes place, so that it is a pleasure to visit them at that time. An old woman, whom I found reading her Hebrew Prayer-book one Friday evening, assured me that she never looked at a book in any other language on the Sabbath, and I gathered that this was not uncommon in the days of which I am speaking ... I suppose that at times we used to look fagged or worried, for the women would say in compassionate tones, "Poor dears! are you very tired?" and occasionally we might be offered a cup of coffee. Singularly hospitable, friendly, and unceremonious were these women — not respectful, not observers of class distinction, but with a kind of genial familiarity, originating in a strong racial fellow-feeling for their visitors.[18]

From this visiting sprang a mission to prostitutes, the Jewish Ladies' Society for Preventive and Rescue Work (later renamed the Jewish Association for the Protection of Girls and Women), which, over the years, expanded to encompass hostels, homes for unmarried mothers, lodging-houses for working girls, a reformatory school and an orphanage.

In the 1880s the two sisters espoused a new cause, as Connie recorded: "I took the pledge in 1884, and have never had cause to regret my decision or to revoke the words to which I then put my signature. I became president of various temperance societies in the counties of Buckinghamshire and of Bedfordshire, besides doing much active work in London and in other parts of the kingdom, this bringing me into personal touch with

*A case containing a parchment scroll with scripture texts written on it.

266

many remarkable and interesting personages."[19] The movement to combat "the demon drink" was a vigorous one which attracted active participants from all religions and none, so that the Rothschild ladies found themselves sharing public platforms with clergymen, politicians of both parties and foreign adherents to the cause.

As the years passed, more and more of Connie's and Annie's time was devoted to charitable and reforming work, until, eventually, it became a full-time activity. Constance was involved in education and prison visiting and, in 1901, became president of the International Union of Women Workers, a body which co-ordinated all aspects of social philanthropy among women.

The two extremes of indulging pleasures and fulfilling social responsibilities were also manifested among the Rothschilds across the Channel. Nat died in 1870. His wife, the gentle, wistful Charlotte, outlived him by nearly thirty years and was herself predeceased by all but one of her children. Of the three boys and a girl to whom she gave birth, only two sons survived childhood: James and Arthur. In the course of time a marriage was arranged for James with Mayer Carl's daughter Emma,

Descendants of Nat in France

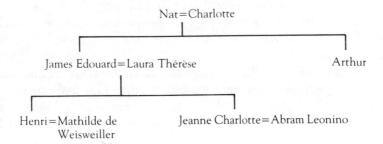

but the engagement was broken off when Emma fell in love with Natty and James had to settle for the younger sister, Laura Thérèse, whom he married in 1871.

James and Arthur both appear to have been victims of two generations of Rothschild inbreeding. Arthur, the younger, was described by his nephew, Henri, as "shy and eccentric or, more precisely, whimsical".[20] It was an understatement. Arthur handled his awesome Rothschild responsibilities largely by ignoring them. He dwelt in bachelor seclusion in an apartment on the Faubourg St Honoré where he lived a life of distracted idleness. He was only marginally involved in the bank. What he lived for was collecting. But in him the family trait became an obsession. He collected the oddest things. There was nothing strange in his devotion to postage stamps, nor in his becoming an expert who wrote learned works on philately. But cigars? And ties? Here is Henri's description of how the collecting mania took his uncle:

> Because he was a mighty smoker before the Lord, he travelled two or three times a year to London and Hamburg in order to obtain supplies of cigars from such well-known importers as Grunbaum, Morriss, Hesse, etc. This veritable expert made his selection with the greatest care and from each voyage he brought back positive cargoes of Coronas, Hupmanns, Henri Clays, etc . . .
> With meticulous care, he arranged his boxes with their multi-coloured covers, in a special room where he had placed two large glass-fronted cabinets, rather like bookcases, but lead-lined and protected against humidity and changes of temperature.
> My uncle had the odd habit of only smoking one cigar from each box. Every morning he made his selection, refilling his cigar-case and taking one specimen from each of six or seven boxes arranged in the right-hand cabinet. He then relegated the depleted boxes, carefully nailed shut once more, to the left-hand cabinet. Around Christmas and New Year he gave presents to friends, to those who had rendered him some service, and to senior staff of Rue Laffitte and the railways. For each one he chose five or six boxes from among those he had sampled. In this way he distributed eight or ten thousand cigars a year.
> One day, a recipient of this bounty came to thank Baron Arthur for his splendid gift. At the same time he informed him that one cigar was missing from each of the boxes he had received. "Obviously a servant is responsible for the crime," the visitor observed, "and I thought it my duty to tell you." My uncle replied, "My dear chap, you are mistaken. It was I who removed them. I could not allow myself to offer you cigars without first sampling them and satisfying myself that they were good enough for you."[21]

It was the same with ties. Arthur bought them by the dozen; ties of every conceivable hue and shade, all arranged in a special wardrobe so that he could, with ease, select the one that suited his mood, or the weather. And, since moods change and clouds pass, so the Baron would alter his neckwear two or three times a day. Once worn, a *cravate* was assigned to another container and would eventually be sent as a gift to some friend or colleague.

Arthur was a harmlessly eccentric playboy. Unfortunately, his elder brother was a sick man. James was prey to a nervous disease and bouts of depression. His condition can hardly have been helped by his wife. Thérèse de Rothschild was one of those women for whom the definition of duty as "stern daughter of the voice of God" might have been written. Just as she never lost her German accent, so, to the end of her days, she retained that devotion to holiness and purity which she had first learned at the feet of Rabbi Hirsch. Thus, despite being the proprietress of one of the country's finest vineyards, she allowed no wine to be drunk in her own household. She enjoyed the company of rabbis and Christian clergy, and she devoted much of her time to charitable works. Like many people who take their religion seriously, she became the butt of family stories that were gleefully passed on down the generations. One such concerns an occasion when the Baroness proposed to observe some festival in her household but discovered that she did not have enough prayer-books. A verbal message was sent to the servants' quarters to go out and buy *sept livres de prières*. The instruction became garbled en route and Thérèse flew into a rage when, later in the day, her maid entered the drawing-room bearing *sept livres de Gruyère* (seven pounds of cheese). She disliked the frivolity of Frenchmen in general, and Parisians in particular.

Her sick husband must have found her a trial. More and more he took refuge in the world of books. The Rothschild collecting obsession had made an ardent bibliophile of James and he had begun amassing a fine library when he was still a child. Eventually it grew to include many thousands of volumes. When, years later, his son presented it to the Bibliothèque Nationale, the catalogue alone filled a cabinet so large that it would not go through the door of the institution. However, there came a time when even his books did not provide James with sufficient solace. He was one of those upon whom the fact of being a Rothschild imposed an immense strain. The tensions involved in being constantly in the public eye, as well as performing the duties and maintaining the standards expected by the family exacerbated his condition. If he had had the support and understanding of a warm, loving wife he might have been able to cope. Denied that, he found nothing to live for. Death, at the early age of thirty-seven, was for him the only release from a life which had become intolerable.

After James's death his widow devoted herself assiduously to the management of his estates, and to the improvement of the material conditions and morals of her dependants. Her grandson, Philippe, graphically related her first visit to Mouton with her children, Henri and Jeanne.

... what she found there must have shocked her to the core. She im-

269

mediately set about building a house for fallen women. No one told her that marriage was not a popular institution among the locals; in fact it was almost unknown. The poverty of the people upset her: the children without boots, the haggard women. She went around the village distributing largesse and good advice. That one visit had such an effect on my father that he never went back. She did, regularly, and her plain little daughter, Jeanne, went with her.[22]

Like any parent with a highly developed sense of moral rectitude, Thérèse tried to inculcate the same virtues into her children. Henri and Jeanne were strictly brought up under the supervision of a succession of governesses who were instructed to fill their charges' time with wholesome pursuits and guard them from worldly temptations. This was particularly hard on Henri, whose childhood was spent in a claustrophobic woman's world, a world dominated not only by his imperious mother, but by his grandmother and even, until her death in 1886, by his great-grandmother, the formidable Baroness Betty. He had few companions of his own age and was driven in upon himself. Inevitably, he turned to collecting, and accumulated a little museum of stuffed animals and birds of which he was justifiably proud. This activity was approved by his mother — until Henri's tutor complained that the taxidermist's chemicals disagreed with him. The specimens were immediately packed up and despatched to the local school, and the disconsolate boy was told to collect something else. He turned his attention to autograph letters and, in true Rothschild style, he accumulated, over fifty years, more than five thousand documents bearing the signatures of kings, queens, statesmen, poets, dramatists and philosophers from the fifteenth century to the nineteenth.

As Henri entered adolescence the restrictive regime if anything increased in rigidity. Thérèse, determined to protect him from sexual adventure and any kind of debauchery, kept him short of money, and filled his time with harmless pursuits. She took him on her visits to the sanatorium for tubercular children which she had founded at Berck, and decreed that her son must become a doctor and devote his life to helping others. Henri was too overwhelmed by his mother to defy her openly, but other members of the family came to his aid. It was with the connivance of Uncle Arthur and another relative, that he provided himself with a mistress, called Anna, and acquired the money to set her up in a Paris apartment.

Henri refused to be denied the attractions of Paris, then in the heyday of its "naughtiness"; here is how he described one of the regular parties thrown by his cousin's mistress:

... during that memorable evening, young bachelors from the best families, husbands estranged from their wives, actresses and fashionable cocottes ... were the guests of the agreeable mistress of the house. Each was assured of finding under her hospitable roof, the best cuisine, excellent wines and cigars imported directly from Havana. After dinner poker and baccarat were openly indulged in by wealthy enthusiasts whose credit-worthiness was beyond reproach, until two or three o'clock in the morning.
The men who resorted to Genevièves were either "boys" looking for experience or those engaged in illicit affairs. The women, so agreeable and easily intimate, gave themselves without restraint to "games of love and chance".[23]

If Thérèse's son frequented such high-class dens of vice she only had herself to blame. The kind of regimen to which she submitted Henri, doubtless with the best intentions, was quite inappropriate for a young man who would become one of the richest and potentially most influential in France. But she persevered nonetheless and, upon finding out about his mistress, promptly put an end to the liaison and packed Henri off on an American tour to forget all about his beloved Anna. Not surprisingly, being deprived of close friends and confidants of his own age, he grew into an introspective man who found communication with other people extremely difficult. Instead, he confided his thoughts, feelings and observations to paper, becoming a compulsive writer. His output was both prodigious and catholic. His published works alone ranged from fiction and stage plays (under the pseudonym "André Pascal") to medical treatises, travelogues, books on collecting and memoirs.

The final result of Thérèse's possessiveness and dominance was predictable: at the age of twenty-three Henri rushed into marriage without any family discussion and in total defiance of the prevailing convention. Although the object of his affection was a young Jewish lady of impeccable pedigree, the engagement was a definite act of revolt and, years later, Henri recorded with satisfaction the moment at which he broke the news to his mother:

About seven o'clock, I tidied myself up and entered my mother's presence. Baronne James was busy writing an important letter and motioned me to take a seat and wait for a few moments. I sat down in a chair and waited quite a while, silent and motionless. I felt weary, emotionally spent. At last my mother raised her eyes.
"Well, what's new?" she asked. "I hope there hasn't been a disaster of some kind."
"Not exactly," I replied. "I've come to bring you some good news — I am engaged."

"Engaged!" my mother spluttered, jumping to her feet. "To whom?"
"A friend of my sister's, Mlle Mathilde de Weisweiller . . ."
My mother seemed bewildered; she could not believe her ears.
"You're joking," she said. "You know I hate being made fun of."
"I'm quite serious," I replied, and I related to my agonised mother
the events which, in less than twenty-four hours, had determined me
upon marriage.
Baronne James's maternal feelings had been knocked for six and she
was quite unable to conceal the fact. Trembling, pale with emotion,
she could not bring herself to put into words the feelings which had
taken possession of her. The unexpected news had stunned her. She
was furious that I had become engaged without her knowledge, hu-
miliated that I had taken this decision without at least asking her
advice, without enabling her to gather information about the family
of the young woman to whom I was about to give my name. My abrupt
decision was scarcely believable, and my poor mother did not know
whether she should indicate satisfaction or disapproval. In her bewilderment she refused to give me the benefit of her initial reaction . . .
Before she could give her consent, Baronne James told me, she would
have to provide herself with complete details [of the Weisweillers].
She would speak to a few people; write to some others . . .
I stopped her short and with a firm voice I said, "It doesn't matter what
the results of your enquiries are. I love this young woman and I am
going to marry her!"
I stayed in my mother's drawing-room until dinner time. My matrimonial plans, and the authority that I had displayed in the course of
our discussion, left the admirable lady utterly prostrate. As for me, I
was glowing with joy. At last the moment announcing my freedom
would soon be here.[24]

In the end, of course, Thérèse reconciled herself to Henri's impulsiveness.

In Vienna, the contrast lay between Salbert and his brother, Nathaniel.
Although eight years younger than Nathaniel and five years younger than
Ferdinand, who was now an English citizen, it was Salbert who, at the age
of thirty, took over the business on his father's death and held court in the
large office in the old Römischer Kaiser, unchanged since Salomon's day.
His granddaughter has an amusing contemporary painting of *Albert von
Rothschild at work*. It depicts a spacious, comfortably furnished chamber
whose occupant, viewed from behind, is just visible sprawled in a deep
armchair. Such a picture belies Salbert's energy. He presided alone over a
complex of enterprises which made up the financial cornerstone of the

Austro-Hungarian Empire. And he was in his element. S.M. Rothschild und Sohne was the largest private bank in Vienna. The Creditanstalt was the largest industrial investment bank. The Bodencreditanstalt, as well as being the leading land bank, managed Emperor Francis Joseph's private fortune, arranged all state loans and drew most of its private clients from among the aristocracy and great landed families. Although Salbert never occupied the presidency of either the Creditanstalt or the Bodencreditanstalt, in practice he exercised a strong influence over both institutions. So important was the Rothschild connection that when, in 1883, he was outvoted on the Creditanstalt board over the replacement of one of its members, the threat of resignation was sufficient to enable him to win his point. No senior appointment could be made in the Creditanstalt without the approval of Baron von Rothschild.

Salbert was a born businessman. He had a cool head and clear vision, and he needed both in the competitive world of Austro-Hungarian finance. In the closing years of the nineteenth century the number of powerful credit banks was increasing steadily and the only way private bankers could hold their own was by forming consortiums to conduct major items of business. When it came to handling these negotiations, Salbert was a master. In 1880 one such syndicate under his leadership handled a vitally important Hungarian government loan conversion; two years later he prevented a disastrous collapse on the Vienna exchange by buying up state debentures. Thereafter, very little happened in the fields of state finance, heavy industry, railway development and trade throughout the Hapsburg territories without Salomon Albert von Rothschild being involved. He was, quite simply, the most important financial figure in Austria.

By nature austere and rather aloof, Salbert was a complete contrast to his bachelor brother Nathaniel, the only other one of Anselm and Charlotte's eight children to remain in Vienna. Nathaniel was good-humoured and easygoing, considerate towards servants and a popular master. The story of how he inaugurated the first Austrian football team is typical of the man. Among his employees was a gardener who had been brought over from England but who found it difficult to settle in a new country among people who spoke a strange tongue, missing the sights and sounds of his native land and, especially, its sport. Reluctant to lose so good a worker, Nathaniel solved the problem by having a football coach sent over from England and starting an estate team. Small wonder that servants got on better with him than with his more formal brother. One senior domestic actually complained to Nathaniel about Baron Albert's haughty manner. "Oh, don't mind him," the older Rothschild replied, with a dismissive wave. "He doesn't matter." [25]

Nathaniel compensated for his lack of interest in business by indulging a passion for beautiful things — both animate and inanimate. He bred racehorses — very successfully. He built himself a magnificent town mansion on the Theresianumgasse, and filled it with rare and beautiful treasures. He had the magnificient Hohe Warte botanical gardens laid out in Vienna and assembled plants from all over the world to fill it. The gardens were Nathaniel's gift to the city, for in indulging himself he did not forget the less fortunate members of society. It was probably experiences within his own family circle (see below) that turned his charitable impulse in a medical direction. He founded a general hospital, institutes for the blind and for deaf-mutes, an orphanage and a neurological clinic. His own health was also something of an obsession with Nathaniel, who cosseted himself and surrounded himself with doctors, though whether this was because he had a weak constitution or because he was a hypochondriac is not altogether clear.

Salbert, too, built himself a mansion. Although he was no connoisseur, there were other things in his life apart from business, and he erected and furnished an establishment on Prinz Eugenstrasse which rivalled his brother's in the splendour and artistic merits of its contents. He was also a keen amateur astronomer and had his own observatory. He enjoyed a good cigar and in the Renngasse strongroom, alongside piles of bullion and the deposits of documents vital to the destiny of nations, were boxes and boxes of Tausenguldenkraut and other smoker's delights brought direct from Havana and arranged according to age and quality. Salbert was also a country lover and, a century before the word became fashionable, something of a conservationist. This was shown most clearly in his activities at Langau.

One result of the rapid growth of Vienna in the mid-nineteenth century was that large areas of forest had been felled for timber, often by consortiums who bought up parcels of land from the old aristocracy and exploited them with no thought for the future. So savage was the spoliation that, by the 1880s, several of these syndicates found that the value of their property had become considerably reduced. It was one such estate that Salbert acquired at Langau, a hundred miles west of Vienna. Immediately he set about reafforestation. That meant introducing a labour force and providing accommodation. The result was Langau Meierhofen, a new village of spacious, well-designed houses with its own post office, shop and other amenities. He restored the original landscape — with improvements such as a changed, more picturesque course for the river — and encouraged a revival of the natural flora and fauna. As time went by Salbert grew increasingly fond of Langau and often stayed in the lodge he built at the centre of the village.

Salbert also had a family life. Seven children were born to him and Bettina (Alphonse's daughter). Of the seven, one died in infancy and another, the youngest girl, Valentine, was born deaf. As often happens in such cases, it was a couple of years before the affliction was diagnosed; parents and nannies assumed that the child was slow or awkward.[26] Otherwise, it was a happy enough existence, with little lacking for the family's comfort − not even that final seal of imperial acceptance which had been denied Anselm. Access to the imperial court was guarded by the most hidebound conventions − conventions which Jews, above all people, could not break through. But in 1887 Salomon Albert and his wife, Bettina, were formally admitted among those who were "received" by the Emperor. This was the coping stone on all that Salomon, Anselm and Salbert had achieved.

Thereafter, by one of those tricks of fate, the lives of Salbert and Francis Joseph were to be strangely and sadly paralleled. Both men lost a wife and a son in tragic circumstances. Both men were to see their dynasties weakened, although they were spared the anguish of witnessing the houses of Hapsburg and Rothschild ceasing to be powers in Austria.

Salbert's brother, Nathaniel, moved in the smart set frequented by the Emperor's children and among his amours was a young, impressionable girl, the Baroness Mary Vetsera. In 1888 she became the mistress of the Emperor's only son, Crown Prince Rudolph, a man driven to frenzied despair by his complete estrangement from his autocratic father. In January 1889 he persuaded Mary to join with him in a suicide pact and their bodies were discovered in the Prince's hunting lodge at Mayerling. The news was sent to Vienna by railway telegraph. Because of its importance, it was conveyed direct to the chairman of the Nordbahn, Salomon Albert von Rothschild. It therefore fell to Salbert to deliver to the imperial palace the terrible news that the heir to the throne had shot himself.

Two and a half years later tragedy struck the banker's family. Salbert's beloved wife, Bettina, only thirty-three years old, was discovered to be suffering from cancer. She died the following March, after months of pain. For Salbert, heavily weighted with responsibility as he was, life was permanently dislocated. He could not bear anything which reminded him of his wife. Above all, that meant the children, from whom he cut himself off completely. While he immersed himself even more thoroughly in his work, they were brought up entirely by tutors and governesses. It is said that on the very rare occasions that he ventured into the nursery, his sons and daughters had to be introduced to him because he could not remember their names.

In 1898 the Emperor Francis Joseph also became a widower in circumstances which, once again, involved the Rothschilds. In the autumn of that year Salbert's sister, Julie (Adolph's wife), received a visitor in her château at Pregny. It was the Empress Elizabeth, with whom she had a longstanding friendship. The sixty-one-year-old consort was a restless woman, who spent much of her time travelling and had never really recovered from the death of her only son. She was not an easy guest to entertain but she seemed to relax during an excellent dinner served amidst the quiet splendours of Pregny, with a concealed orchestra playing soothing music. This was followed by a tour of the conservatories, Julie's pride and joy, where exotic blooms stunned the eye and the air was filled with overwhelming fragrances. It was a relaxed and successful visit — until the Baroness asked her departing friend to sign the guest book. She did so. Then, idly turning back the pages, she saw a name which drove the colour from her cheeks — Rudolf. Elizabeth stayed the night in Geneva and the next morning made her way to the lakeside to catch the steamer for Caux. Suddenly an Italian anarchist, Luigi Luccheni, stepped up and drove a dagger into her chest. She died within hours.

It was about this time that disaster befell Salbert's heir, George. The young man had left Austria to complete his studies at Cambridge. Like many of his relatives who attended the university over the years, he regarded riding to hounds as an important part of the undergraduate curriculum. On one outing he had a bad fall and damaged his head so severely that he had to leave university and return home for treatment. The young man's physical injuries may have been too severe or he may also have suffered from mental problems of a genetic origin. Whichever was the case, his cure was beyond the skill of the leading specialists; he developed schizophrenia and had to be confined for the remainder of his life.

There was still more sadness to come. Oscar, the youngest of the family, was only three when Bettina died. He thus grew up without a mother's love and, thanks to Salbert's remoteness, he also lacked a father's guiding hand. At the age of nineteen he was sent to America to learn something of the business life of that booming land. Suddenly freed from all restraints, he fell passionately in love with the daughter of a Chicago boarding-house keeper. On his return home, he calmly asked his father's permission to marry. Salbert's reaction can easily be imagined. In his eyes the girl was unsuitable in every possible way — a Gentile, a foreigner, uneducated, uncultured, and common — certainly not the sort of woman to hold court in a Rothschild household. There were angry scenes but the old man was quite inflexible. Had he really known Oscar, Salbert might have seen the warning signs of total dejection in the young man's words and demeanour. He did not. The boy simply could not face the loss of the only person who had ever given him deep affection. He shot himself.[27]

Before Francis Joseph's death, in 1916, his nephew and heir, the

Archduke Francis Ferdinand, had been assassinated in Sarajevo and his empire had been plunged into a war which would destroy it. The old man may well have wondered whether there was a curse on his family. It would be fanciful to imagine the same thought occurring to Salbert. Yet, before he died, in 1911, he had seen the once prolific Austrian Rothschilds whittled away by death, childlessness and emigration. He had no grand-children and no Rothschild nephews. The nearest male relative of the next generation was Bettina's French nephew Guy. The only hope for the future of the Austrian house lay in Salbert's, as yet unmarried, children. But the prospect was far from bleak. He left three healthy and intelligent sons to carry on the business and the dynasty. No one could have foreseen that, within two generations, the male line would die out completely.

Austrian Rothschilds 1870-1911

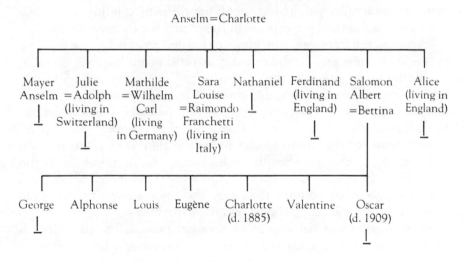

277

CHAPTER 20
"If thy brother be waxen poor . . .
thou shalt uphold him"

To be a European Jew had never been a comfortable experience. To be a European Jew in the final decades of the nineteenth century was both uncomfortable and confusing. Not only was anti-Semitism taking on new and more virulent forms, but several contradictory influences were at work within international Jewry. It was a period of frenzied change both material and intellectual. There was an unprecedented influx of refugees fleeing westwards from persecution in Russia and the Balkans, and Jewish thinkers and agitators were struggling to find and proclaim a rôle for their people in the new age. To the casual observer it might have seemed that the Rothschilds, although the acknowledged lay leaders of worldwide Jewry, were above the struggle; cushioned by their wealth and fully integrated into Gentile society. This was not the case. Not only did the Rothschilds, moved by the suffering of their people, fund relief organisations for the destitute and homeless; they used their political influence to combat anti-Semitism; they were deeply involved in the arguments between Socialists, proto-Zionists, assimilationists and separatists; above all, perhaps, their very Jewishness coloured their whole approach to commercial, political and social problems.

The first major international incident which provoked a united Jewish response had occurred many years before and had brought Baron James to the fore as a spokesman for his people. This was in the celebrated Damascus Affair of 1840. The disappearance of a Roman Catholic priest by the name of Thomas in that city led to a public outcry which focused blame on the local Jews. Some were arrested and, under torture, confessed to ritual murder. It was the sort of incident that sporadically revived the latent anti-Semitism which was still commonplace throughout Europe. The old myth about Jews using Christian blood in their ceremonies was resurrected, provoking a fresh round of public demonstrations, serious government questions and giving rise to the popular joke that it was inadvisable to accept a dinner invitation from a Jew since you might, without realising it, be served a "Father Thomas cutlet". Jewish leaders throughout Europe realised that these calumnies had to be answered and that steps had to be taken to protect their Syrian co-religionists. The Great Baron played his part by stirring his brothers to action in Frankfurt and Vienna, by writing an article in the *Journal des Débats*, and by direct appeal to Thiers and King Louis Philippe. He obtained no support from the Prime Minister and some commentators were quick to connect this rebuff with Thiers' subsequent dismissal.[1]

Year in and year out the Rothschilds watched over Jewish interests both nationally and internationally. More recently, Lionel and Bleichröder had scored a notable success at the Congress of Berlin (1878), where they had succeeded in getting the issue of Jewish rights placed on the agenda, alongside weighty questions of territorial boundaries and access to international waterways. Among the terms that were finally agreed and ratified were the establishment of full citizenship for the Jewish minorities in Rumania, Bulgaria, Serbia and Montenegro.

Because of their official political standing in Britain, the Rothschilds were expected to be the mouthpiece of Anglo-Jewry. Lionel, and Natty after him, took his place on the Board of Deputies and Natty was a member of the Conjoint Foreign Committee, set up in 1878 to co-ordinate action on behalf of overseas Jewish communities. Their French counterparts were likewise members of the Jewish establishment. Alphonse became president of the Consistoire Central (the French counterpart of the Board of Deputies) and Gustave of the Consistoire de Paris. They were major contributors to the building of the splendid new synagogue on the Rue de la Victoire, which was opened in 1875 and became the religious focal point for the Jewish élite of Paris.

Their charitable works for their own community continued. The main focus of the French family's activity was still the Hôpital Israélite on the Rue Picpus but they served on the Comité de Bienfaisance which distributed funds nationally and internationally, and supported Jewish schools, orphanages and social welfare projects. In London, the Rothschilds remained the principal supporters of the Jews' Free School — Lionel's wife, Charlotte, being particularly dedicated to this estabishment. Their involvement with the school, as in the case of other charities, was not confined to sitting on committees and doling out occasional subsidies. Constance recalled:

When we were still in the schoolroom we were taken to the Jews' Free School, of which my father was the honoured President, and my mother a constant visitor as member of committee, and there introduced to the heads of that institution ... We were asked to take a class and to hear the children read, and were permitted to question them upon what they read; this led the way first to frequent and then to regularly-timed visits . . . [2]

Constance and her sister were in their early twenties when together they wrote a book, *The History and Literature of the Israelites*, designed to assist the young pupils in their study of the Jewish scriptures. They and their female relatives started and ran the "Girls' Classes", designed to provide religious education in the evenings for girls working in factories and shops.

The Rothschilds, as we have seen, had the common touch. Something that radicals and social levellers either did not understand or did not wish to acknowledge was that many working-class people did not begrudge such families their riches if they believed these were being used for the common good. By and large, and some more than others, the Rothschilds did use their money responsibly. Fundamentally this was a religious impulse. The Torah and Talmud which fashioned their young minds were clear about the *zedakah* (righteousness) that Yahweh requires. "If thy brother be waxen poor and his hand fail with thee, then thou shalt uphold him." So runs the law of Leviticus (25:35), and the Talmudic gloss explains that "uphold him" implies "provide him with means whereby he can live".

To the Rothschilds, the ways to translate such principles into action appeared self-evident: they supported the hierarchic structure of society, the right of some to rule and the duty of the rest to be ruled; they advanced moderate reform which would extend the franchise and remove obvious social injustice; they upheld strongly the duty of the "haves" to help the "have-nots" but on a purely *laissez-faire* basis; charity was a private matter, a matter of conscience, and not one to be taken over by the state. Like the majority of their aristocratic and bourgeois friends, they felt confident that the existing order could contain the spread of Liberalism and Socialism, working-class suffrage, trades unionism and even the sporadic terrorist outrages of anarchists and nihilists.

Ferdinand probably spoke for most of his relatives at home and abroad when he stated his political creed in a letter to Sir Charles Dilke, leader of the radical wing of the Liberal party, in 1884:

> . . . if I do not call myself a Radical it is [because] I consider it unworthy of great leaders, of men like Chamberlain and yourself, to court popularity with the masses by advocating such trivial measures as the abolition of the game laws . . . and stimulating an unhealthy desire for social and pecuniary equality . . . instead of governing the people on broad principles and leading them into wider issues . . . [3]

But if wealthy Jews like Baron Ferdinand were sanguine about the chances of social revolution, they could not so easily ignore the signs of ferment within international Jewry.

During the last two decades of the nineteenth century the advocates of assimilation found their position under renewed attack from all sides. The forces of orthodoxy and Socialism kept up the sporadic bombardments which the "Old Jewish" families had long since learned to live with. But their ranks were now suddenly swelled by the hordes of destitute immigrants pouring across the eastern frontiers. For the pledges given in Berlin, in 1878, had not put a stop to persecution in Russia and the Balkans (see below). The Rothschilds and their friends were now challenged, as never before, to come to the aid of their brothers, to step down from their positions of privilege, to be "true" to their faith, to share their wealth, to encourage greater democratisation within Europe, and, outside Europe, to support the pioneers of a new creed — Zionism. And, as if that were not enough, the reawakened "Jewish problem", in its turn, roused anti-Semitism from its fitful slumber.

In 1880 there were about five million Jews in the world. Of these only about fifteen per cent lived in western Europe. The vast majority — about seventy-five per cent — were spread throughout Russia, Poland and the Balkans, where they lived for the most part in poverty and degradation. For centuries they had been confined to their own ghettoes and rural settlements, subjected to constant anti-Semitic attacks of a most brutal kind and to occasional pogroms, which reflected official prejudice and indifference. Their situation improved during the reign of the more enlightened Alexander II (1855-81); but the relief was only temporary, for the Tsar was assassinated in the streets of St Petersburg in March 1881 and, worse still, one of his murderers was a Jew. Alexander's successor inaugurated a policy of reactionary terror designed to root out all dis-affection. The old antagonism towards the Jews revived. There were fresh pogroms and anti-Semitic riots. Finally, in 1882, the notorious May Laws were promulgated, viciously restricting Jewish residence and commerce. Hundreds of thousands of families were uprooted and forced into the already overcrowded urban ghettoes.

Things were no better in the areas outside Russian control. The Balkan States had generally disregarded the terms of the Berlin Treaty. Jews in those countries suffered constant arson and looting while their sufferings were ignored by the authorities. It was only in Russia, however, that anti-Semitism was government policy. It was the declared objective of the rulers to squeeze the community so hard that a third of the people would die, a third would be assimilated into the Gentile population and a third would emigrate. The last of these objectives was certainly achieved. Multitudes of men, women and children made their way to Germany, Austria, France, England and the USA, often arriving with nothing more than the clothes they stood up in.

281

Natty immediately set about alerting British opinion to the problem. He gathered together facts and figures about the persecution, interviewed refugees and wrote a series of articles for *The Times* in January. Readers were shocked by these revelations. Protests and offers of help poured in and a meeting at the Mansion House raised a hundred thousand pounds. Similar action in Paris and New York drew forth a similar response. The next task Alphonse, Natty and their supporters undertook was to help co-ordinate relief action. They recognised that it would be pointless simply to throw money at the problem, or to render vague, unplanned assistance; that had never been the Rothschild way. Committees were set up to receive the immigrants and give them whatever assistance they needed in settling (the Paris committee was chaired by no less august a personage than Victor Hugo). As many as possible were encouraged to move on to America which had a greater capacity for absorption. But, inevitably, large numbers settled in the East End of London and the poorer quarters of Paris.

For the Rothschilds this posed a new problem. They were quite prepared to help their co-religionists to settle. What they would not tolerate was the establishment of new ghettoes. If Jews wanted to live in Britain and France, they must integrate with British and French society. Areas of "separate development", especially in the poorer quarters of the cities, would lead to resentment and play into the hands of their racist enemies. That would be bad, not just for the immigrants, but for the whole Jewish community. The complaints the Rothschilds feared were, indeed, soon being voiced. In 1884, for example, the local authorities in Whitechapel complained about "the filthy conditions of the rooms, yards and water closets" in much of their area, a situation "greatly intensified by the arrival within the district of a vast number of foreign Jews".[4]

Charlotte de Rothschild died in this same year (1884) after five years of widowhood. She had never been able to accept Lionel's death. Their relationship had been in many ways stressful to her, but she had come to terms with it and done her duty as hostess, wife and mother. She had lived, above all, for her daughters but death and foreign husbands had taken them from her. Death had also stolen some of her close friends, such as the Disraelis. Now, with Lionel gone, the busy life of arranging dinners and house parties had come to a sudden end. Her sons visited her and wrote regularly when they were away, but the change in her situation was just too much to cope with. She spent her last years at Gunnersbury, her mind in a turmoil, alternating between bouts of lucidity and vague forget-fulness. But in her better moments she was acutely aware of the situation of London's poor Jews and it was her dying wish that Natty should do something about it.

The impatient and direct head of the family scarcely needed such an incentive. Within days of Charlotte's death he called a meeting of interested parties at New Court, which set up the Four Per Cent Industrial Dwellings Company whose aim was "To provide the industrial classes with more commodious and healthy lodgings and dwellings than those which they now inhabit, giving them the maximum of accommodation for the minimum rent . . ."[5] The company was not conceived as a charitable institution. In the staunch tradition of laissez-faire capitalism, the project was designed to attract investors by guaranteeing a return of four per cent. Work began on the first site early the following year and in April 1887 the Charlotte de Rothschild Dwellings were opened. They were followed by the Nathaniel Dwellings in 1892. Their design was not imaginative and the specifications had instructed that costs were to be kept to a minimum. The buildings did provide a place where people could live clean and decent lives, but there was about them a joyless, unimaginative frugality. Nor can we totally excuse their meagreness by saying that they were typical examples of late Victorian working-class housing. Only a few years after these London dwellings were constructed, Natty's French cousins devised blocks of apartments for the Parisian poor. These, as we shall see (see p. 324ff.) were as different from the Rothschild Dwellings as chalk from cheese. Quality of life was a major concern of Alphonse and his brothers when they planned the habitations à bon marché and they took great care in providing for the health and welfare of the tenants.

Social commentators from Victorian times onwards have been hard on Natty's "grim, towering buildings". "These are not HOMES", a contemporary architect averred of a similar tenement. "They entirely rob the beautiful English word of its wonderful charm." These East End blocks of two-, three- and four-roomed flats were examples of social engineering, as Natty and his colleagues would have freely admitted. Together with the Jewish schools and the teaching in the synagogues they were designed, as a modern writer has explained, "to produce a new Anglo-Jewry in the image of the old; to assimilate the immigrants not just within English society — but within middle-class English society". The buildings were not restricted to Jewish occupancy, but in effect a very high proportion of their tenants belonged to the same faith. They did become a kind of ghetto, but not in the sense of being closed, introverted communities. In fact, living conditions were better than that word "ghetto" suggests and many inhabitants developed an affection for the warm, close way of life produced by these small rooms and courtyards. The buildings have been called the "ugly offspring of a reluctant paternalism". Ugly they certainly were and this is only partially excused by the fact that they were a hurried response to a large and pressing problem. But there was nothing reluctant about the paternalism of Natty and his colleagues. They took the initiative because they believed it was incumbent upon them to do so as prominent Jews and leading members of British society. Certainly they lacked breadth of vision, but according to their lights they carried out their function honestly and efficiently. They could not be accused of throwing up jerry-built, insanitary dwellings like some of their catchpenny contemporaries.[6]

For Natty it was not sufficient just to provide for the victims of racial intolerance; there also had to be some effort to stop the persecution. Fortunately, when it came to bringing pressure on the tsarist regime, the Rothschilds were not without resources — they simply stopped doing any business with St Petersburg. This was rapidly and remarkably effective. Taken aback by the Rothschilds' action and by hostile international opinion, the Russian government did relax the enforcement of its anti-Jewish laws — for a while. Eventually New Court and Rue Laffitte resumed business dealings with St Petersburg. But the moment tsarist officials began slipping back into their old ways, the financial taps were turned off.

In their relationship with Russia, the Rothschilds were undoubtedly moved by humanitarian sentiments and outrage at the way their fellow Jews were being treated. But there was also a strain of political realism in their thinking. They genuinely feared another outburst of revolutionary turmoil. When Natty's son, Walter, wrote to Bleichröder in 1890 to ask the German banker to use his influence in St Petersburg, he referred to the Russian laws as "so harsh and oppressive that they may be the cause of many Jews becoming violent Nihilists".[7]

So the Rothschilds continued to monitor the Russian situation closely and to grant or withhold funds as a means of steering the Tsar's government towards more humane policies. Such manipulation of political events, of course, played into the hands of their enemies, who were quite convinced that the Rothschilds devoted a greater part of their energies to such activities; that they were Machiavellian puppet masters, making kings and ministers dance to their tune. An English Socialist, writing in 1891, castigated the Rothschilds as a "blood-sucking crew", constantly stirring up wars. "Wherever there is trouble in Europe," he raged, "wherever rumours of war circulate and men's minds are distraught with fear of change and calamity you may be sure that a hook-nosed Rothschild is at his games."[8] The irony of the situation lies in the fact that when the great bankers *did* try to influence the course of history it was always in the interests of *preventing* change. Their vested interests lay in peace and stability, not in stirring up unnecessary conflict.

Faced with the growing problem of Jewish immigration, the Rothschilds would doubtless have preferred to maintain a degree of emotional detachment, using their funds and influence in a purely paternalistic way. They soon discovered that it was not enough to deal with the problems of European Jewry on the financial level alone. This was principally because the Jews who now arrived in western Europe were very different from the Jews already established there. Although they sprang from a common religious/philosophical stock, the attitudes of the two communities had been formed by radically different experiences. Most of the old families had, to a greater or lesser extent, associated themselves with their adopted countries, become less distinct from their neighbours, and had prospered. Of the newcomers (150,000 of them arrived in London, a city of 4.5 million, between 1881 and 1901 and in the same period 73,600 Jews settled in Vienna among a total population of about 1.6 million) some were ghetto Jews — strict observers of the faith and fluent only in Yiddish. They were natural allies for the conservative elements in the existing Jewish community. But others were men of a new breed, pushed by persecution into bitterness and political extremism. And there was a third group — the Zionists — those determined to create a sovereign Jewish state; a place where they would be their own masters, where the ancient dream expressed in the greeting "Next year in Jerusalem" would become a reality.

The point was that activists from these three elements among the refugees were all, to a greater or lesser extent, inimical to the Rothschilds. They wrote angry letters to New Court and Rue Laffitte. They made impassioned speeches and attacked "comfortable" Jews in the press. Their strident voices merged into the Babel of discontent, along with those of Socialists, revolutionaries, anti-Semites, and others who had simple solutions for changing an unjust world. And while the Rothschilds were eager to improve society, they did not wish to see it changed. Their intuitive response in the face of mounting criticism from so many different directions was to become more and more conservative.

The restrictionism of the immigrant communities challenged, often with prophetic zeal, the position the Rothschilds and older successful families had established by "compromising" their faith. They made demands for more special institutions, such as hospitals and schools, to cater for their increased numbers. They complained that Jewish MPs no longer regarded themselves as spokesmen of their community but sought to make reputations by addressing themselves to wider issues. Around the turn of the century there was a heated debate over the curriculum of Jews' College which trained English rabbis. Some of its supporters rejected the tendency to broaden the base of education to provide students with an understanding of contemporary social and political conditions, and demanded a return to the purer study of Hebrew and Judaism.

The Rothschilds were among those who saw the real dangers of this exclusionist attitude. They realised that it is difficult for a nation to absorb immigrant groups and that those groups increased the difficulty if they constantly drew attention to their cultural, religious and racial distinctness. The British Prime Minister, Arthur Balfour, quietly pointed out the problem in 1904:

> A state of things could easily be imagined in which it would not be to the advantage of the civilisation of the country that there should be an immense body of persons who, however patriotic, able and industrious, however much they throw themselves into the national life, still by their own action, remained a people apart and not merely held a religion different from the vast majority of their fellow-countrymen but only inter-married among themselves.[9]

Intermarriage was, of course, at the heart of the assimilationist controversy and it was an issue which put the Rothschilds firmly over a barrel. Women of their family were known to have allied themselves very publicly with prominent Gentiles. Such unions had created havoc within the family but they had happened, and there was every prospect of their becoming more common. Officially, the Rothschilds frowned upon such matches but, as we have seen, their hearts always overruled their heads in the end. They did, however, draw the line at their menfolk marrying outside the faith. The only occasion on which such a marriage came close to taking place led to the bitter quarrel between Salbert and Oscar, and the latter's tragic suicide. But even where such a terrible outcome was avoided, the prohibition inevitably created stresses and strains. It may well have been that men like Nathaniel and Alfred chose to remain bachelors because they declined to be steered into "suitable" matches with Jewish brides. For the family as a whole, public policy and private conduct clashed at this point and placed them in an unresolvable dilemma. To stay firm was to be accused of that very exclusionism which they detested. To relax their standards would produce a clamour among the orthodox and threaten their position within Jewry. In the event, they accepted the restriction on their marital relationships while at the same time involving themselves with mounting enthusiasm in charitable work of a non-sectarian nature — hospitals, medical research centres, working-class housing, orphanages, and a variety of other worthy institutions. Thus they hoped to show the world that they were good Jews and also good Frenchmen, or Englishmen, or Austrians.

What made this more difficult was the continuing wave of anti-Semitism. It was particularly virulent in France where the principal instigator was Edouard Drumont, a one-time employee of the Crédit

Mobilier, who spent the years that followed the bank's collapse writing a two-volume attack (*La France juive*, published in 1886) on the "conspiracy" of Jewish financiers which he held responsible for the débâcle. That same conspiracy was, he claimed, eating away the very life of the nation; the Jews had wormed their way into every private and public organisation in the name of assimilation. Drumont's fanatical tirades were widely read, and were calculated to arouse fear and hatred: "The dangerous Jew is the shadowy Jew . . . This is the dangerous animal *par excellence* and at the same time the uncatchable animal . . . he is the most powerful trouble-making element the earth has ever produced, and he thus passes through life with the joy which awareness of having, in various ways, harmed Christians, gives Jews." [10] In 1889 Drumont founded the Anti-Semitic League and later provided himself with a regular mouthpiece, *La Libre Parole*.

In the complex political world of France, which over a century had tried several forms of government and found them all wanting, the Jews came under attack from extremists of all kinds. Socialist agitators rounded upon them as part of the privileged and élitist section of the community, though it was not only the Jews who were the objects of their vituperative and often confused oratory. "I call by this despised name of Jew every trader in cash, every unproductive parasite, living off the substance and work of others . . . And when one says Jew it also means Protestant, and it is inevitable that the Englishman, the Dutchman and the Genevan, who learn to read the will of God in the same book as the Jew, profess the same contempt as the Jew for the laws of equity and the rights of the workers." [11] So thundered the Socialist Toussenel, who like many other left-wing Frenchmen was more anti-religious than anti-Jewish. It was not so with the right-wingers, men like Bontoux and Drumont, who allied themselves with the Catholic Church in their efforts to remove Jews from important positions in the state — and particularly the army.

In 1894 they achieved their most celebrated success — the condemnation of Captain Alfred Dreyfus. Dreyfus, a Jewish army officer, was wrongly charged with selling military documents, convicted of treason by a secret tribunal, and sentenced to life imprisonment on Devil's Island. Four years later a vigorous press campaign accused the authorities of forgery and cover-ups and forced a fresh trial. A court martial in 1899 once more found Dreyfus guilty. But during the course of the investigation leading military figures were discredited. In an attempt to sweep the whole sordid business under the carpet, Dreyfus was pardoned and set at liberty. It took the unfortunate officer another seven years to clear his name completely. The long-running Affaire Dreyfus revealed more eloquently than hysterical pamphlets and speeches just how deep-rooted anti-Semitism was in parts of the French establishment.

The public debate had a profound effect upon many Jews in France. One grandson of the Great Baron was so angered by it that he quit his native land and moved to England (see p. 335). And an Austrian journalist living in Paris returned, shocked, to his own country convinced that if Jews were not even accepted as equal citizens in the land of *liberté*, *egalité* and *fraternité* they would be accepted nowhere. The only answer was to establish a Jewish homeland. The journalist's name was Theodor Herzl, the founder of modern Zionism (see pp. 296ff.).

In Germany and Austria anti-Semitism was more blatant. It always had been. Inevitably, therefore, fresh immigration led to new manifestations of hysteria. Many people shared the fears expressed by Richard Wagner in a letter of 1881 to his friend and patron Ludwig II of Bavaria: "I regard the Jewish race as the born enemy of pure humanity and everything that is noble in it; it is certain that we Germans will go under before them, and perhaps I am the last German who knows how to stand up as an art-loving man against the Judaism that is already getting control of everything." [12]

It is an indication of how far Mayer Carl had gone in his servility to the Prussian regime that, despite his own religious orthodoxy, he was prepared to excuse the government and the Gentile population from full responsibility for the latest outburst of anti-Jewish activity: "As for the anti-Semitic feelings," he wrote to Bleichröder, "the Jews themselves are to blame, and the present agitation must be ascribed to their arrogance, vanity and unspeakable insolence." [13]

Even in "liberal" England there persisted, especially among the fashionable élite, a muted anti-Semitism which displayed itself, sometimes in open hostility, but more often in cynicism and frigidity. For all their social success, the Rothschilds always knew that there were some Gentile circles in which they would never be fully welcome. David Lindsay (later Earl of Crawford) was typical of many British aristocrats. On 22 June 1900 he confided to his diary:

> In the afternoon Connie and I went to Hertford House, where a large party invited by Alfred Rothschild and Rosebery assembled to meet the Prince of Wales. The number of Jews in this palace was past belief. I have studied the anti-semite question with some attention, always hoping to stem an ignoble movement: but when confronted by the herd of Ickleheimers, Puppenbergs, Raphaels, Sassoons, and the rest of the breed, my emotions gain the better of logic and justice ... John Burns, by the way, says the Jew is the tapeworm of civilization. [14]

Something that was probably even more disturbing, because it was so difficult to comprehend, was the odd phenomenon of "Jewish anti-

288

Semitism". The maelstrom of left-wing politics which was swirling with a fresh intensity between 1880 and 1895, had caught up many Jewish idealists and intellectuals in its violent current. Writing to a friend in 1890, Friedrich Engels pointed out: "Marx was of purest Jewish blood; Lassalle was a Jew. Many of our best people are Jews. My friend Victor Adler, who is at present paying in prison for his devotion to the cause of the proletariat, Eduard Bernstein, editor of the London *Sozial-Demokrat*, Paul Singer, one of our best men in the Reichstag — people of whose friendship I am proud, are all Jews . . ."[15]

These political activists belonged to Socialist parties and revolutionary groups committed to advancing class struggle and destroying capitalism. But adherence to the international brotherhood of the proletariat created a crisis of identity for these radical Jews. For the most prominent representatives of the detested system they wanted to pull down were their own co-religionists. The impressionable Jewish Socialist, therefore, found himself not only alienated from his own people, but positively attracted by the open racialism of some of the leading Socialist thinkers, men like the French theorist Pierre Proudhon who castigated the Jew as "fraudulent and parasitical", a man who "operates in business as in philosophy, by forging, counterfeiting, sharp practices". "His economic policy", Proudhon thundered, "is always negative; he is the evil element, Satan, Ahriman, incarnated in the race of Shem."[16]

Pulled in two directions by their origins and their political creed, many Jews simply let go of their origins and followed the lead of men like the German Socialist, Ferdinand Lassalle: "I do not like the Jews at all, I even detest them in general. I see in them nothing but the very degenerated sons of a great but vanished past. As a result of centuries of slavery, these people have acquired servile characteristics and that is why I am so unfavourably disposed to them. Besides, I have no contact with them. There is scarcely a single Jew among my friends and in the society which surrounds me here."[17]

This, then, was the other world of the Rothschilds, the world of turbulent European Jewry to which they belonged just as surely as they belonged to the European social élite. No chronicle of the family is complete which depicts their financial power and glittering life style but ignores their commitment to their troubled and troublesome heritage. Nothing was to bring that commitment more into the open than their relationship with Zionism.

Like wealthy Jews throughout the world, the Rothschilds took seriously their obligation to support their orthodox brethren who maintained a Jewish presence in Jerusalem, their historic capital. For example, James and Betty had established a hospital for poor Jews in Jerusalem in the

289

1850s and, a few years later, Lionel and Charlotte endowed a girls' school in memory of Evelina. So, when groups of refugees from eastern Europe arrived in France in the 1880s asking for help to settle in the land of the patriarchs, the men to whom they appealed knew more about the conditions in Palestine than they did.

The country lay under the lax rule of the Ottoman sultans and was divided into three administrative districts, of which the city of Jerusalem was one. The land was worked largely by small-scale Arab farmers, eking out a living from their groves and flocks. For hundreds of years (apart from the occasional excitement such as Napoleon's occupation) it had been a backwater of importance to no one except pilgrims and archaeologists. But the waning authority of Turkey had awakened the concern of the major powers, most of whom, in the middle of the nineteenth century, appointed consular agents, among whose tasks was the encouragement of social and administrative reform.

One result of greater contact with this once-forgotten land was the growth of immigration which raised the Jewish population from about six thousand in 1840 to more than twenty thousand in 1880.[18] Various philanthropic bodies had founded settlements on which men, women and children, fleeing from persecution and degradation, could, theoretically, establish a new and better life. Yet few of these settlements had achieved independent viability. The land was hard to work and could show an adequate return only after several years of capital and labour had been put into it, and most of the settlers were ignorant of the appropriate methods of farming. Deaths from malaria were common. The native population was only too ready to take advantage of the newcomers' naïveté by selling them poor land and overcharging them for supplies. There were occasional conflicts with Muslim leaders, and the immigrants did not always find their own co-religionists very helpful. The orthodox rabbis of Jerusalem feared an influx of foreigners with new ideas and were determined to impose total conformity with the Torah. They insisted, for example, on strict observation of the Levitical injunction which required that the land be left unworked every seventh year, a stricture which poor farmers, scratching a living from the soil, could not comply with. Faced with these difficulties, Palestinian Jews, if they survived at all, only did so with the aid of constant subsidies from the comfortable world of bourgeois western Jewry.

All this the Rothschilds knew. As a result, when they were asked to finance the new surge of migration to the Holy Land which, after 1881, assumed the character of a gold rush, they were, to say the least, cautious in their response. They were anxious to help their persecuted brethren but were not willing to lend the Rothschild name to ventures that could end up being commercial failures or political embarrassments. Nor was it at all clear that Palestine was the best location for Jewish settlements. Rothschilds had little patience with those who romantically believed that they would automatically prosper in a land manifestly *not* flowing with milk and honey. Nor did the concept of a Jewish nation state ever occur to them. When, in the 1890s, Zionism was born, the Rothschilds were unanimous in rejecting it as an ugly, deformed infant which should be mercifully put down.

It is against that background that the career of the Great Baron's youngest son must be seen. When David Ben-Gurion, first Prime Minister of the independent state of Israel, was speaking of the founding fathers of the new nation, he said, "It is doubtful whether throughout the entire period of close on two thousand years which the Jews have spent in exile, any person is to be found who equals or who can compare with the remarkable figure of Baron Edmond de Rothschild."

Edmond was only twenty-three when his father died. As long as he could remember, his much older brothers had been partners at Rue Laffitte. Although he took his appointed place at the bank in the course of time, there was no obvious area of finance in which he excelled. All the important decisions were taken by Alphonse and Gustave. Edmond was thus another of those late-nineteenth-century Rothschilds for whom a career in banking was a far from obvious choice.

He might have become, like some of his cousins, a playboy or a mildly eccentric devotee of expensive hobbies. It goes almost without saying that he was a collector. His particular passion was for old masters' drawings and engravings. The thousands of examples he brought together, and which are now in the Louvre, were only later recognised as being of unsurpassed quality. He had an equally good eye for paintings and accumulated a collection scarcely less impressive than Alphonse's.

But these pursuits came nowhere near to exhausting his energies. Rothschild enterprise, like nature, abhors a vaccum. Edmond had to fill his time interestingly, usefully, productively. He studied archaeology and science. He travelled widely and enjoyed yachting. He was fond of walking, and it was while staying in Zermatt that he undertook a feat which was, in a way, symbolic. He climbed the Matterhorn. Though this peak has been frequently scaled since, it had been first conquered but a few years before, in 1865, and then only at the cost of four lives. It is characteristic of Edmond that, although not an experienced mountaineer, he set himself this considerable challenge. He possessed the family trait of total commitment to whatever he undertook, but as he entered his thirties he had not yet found some serious pursuit to which he could, with conviction, devote his immense capacity for industry.

In 1877 he married one of the Frankfurt girls, Wilhelm Carl's elder daughter, Adelheid. From that moment his life found a new point of balance. Edmond had been brought up by his mother, to whom he was devoted, to take his religion very seriously. But, as we have seen, there was a qualitative difference between the Judaism of easygoing Paris and that of Frankfurt, where Rabbi Hirsch, at sixty-nine, had lost none of his ardour or vigour. Adelheid had no appreciation of the flippancies of Parisian life and, although she performed her function as a Rothschild hostess faith-fully, it was out of duty rather than enthusiasm. Her fervour was reserved for the ritual observances of her faith and for works of charity. And this had its effect on Edmond. He became noticeably more serious, and not just because he had exchanged the rôle of bachelor for that of husband and father (he and Adelheid had three children in the first five years of their marriage).

This was the man who in the early autumn of 1882 was approached to assist with two Palestinian projects. Joseph Feinberg was the ambassador for Rishon Le Zion (First in Zion), a settlement near Jaffa which was on the brink of collapse. The colonists desperately needed money to help them sink their own well and a capital float to keep them out of the hands of local financiers. Shmuel Mohilewer's vision was wider and more vivid. This Russian rabbi brought first-hand reports of the appalling sufferings of Jews under the tsarist regime and told piteous tales about the 225,000 refugee families wandering destitute in Europe. It was not sufficient, he urged, to provide charitably for the homeless or to help them on their way to America. They must be enabled to settle in Palestine, and that would require assistance, both financial and diplomatic. Feinberg and Mohilewer had each approached other potential patrons with little success before coming to Baron Edmond, as the French Rothschild most likely to give them a sympathetic hearing.

Edmond responded positively. He was deeply moved by the eloquence of his visitors. He identified with the plight of his people. He respected the earnest commitment of those seeking a new start in the old homeland. *But*, though he was an ardent Jew, he was also a Rothschild and that meant that in financial matters he was cautious. He told Feinberg that he *would* give Rishon Le Zion the practical aid it needed. His response to Mohilewer was that he would *not* subsidise mass emigration to Palestine.

This scion of a great banking family could see what the fervent rabbi could not. If thousands of Russian peasants converged on Palestine, the result could only be overcrowding and poor land usage. This would result in mass starvation, which no amount of financial aid would be able to al-leviate. None of Mohilewer's projected colonists knew anything about farm management since Jews in Russia were not allowed to own land. But Edmond was not against settlement — far from it. He was, in fact, the only visionary in the family who saw that the recolonisation of Palestine by Jews was both desirable and possible. And he was anxious to realise that vision. Other Rothschilds might use their wealth and influence to counter tsarist oppression and help assimilate immigrants in the West. Only Edmond provided practical help in Palestine. He believed that he could best serve the cause by ensuring that the flow of settlers was controlled and that strong discipline was exercised in the colonies.

Therefore, he told Mohilewer that what he *was* prepared to do was finance an experimental settlement of Polish Jews, provided that they would submit to strict supervision by his agents. Furthermore, he would send an agricultural expert to southern Palestine to report on the viability of farming in the region. He stipulated that his support for the colonists was to be anonymous and he reserved the right to withdraw that support if the settlers refused to obey the instructions of his on-the-spot advisers.

Only when the project leaders had accepted the Baron's conditions and work on the settlements had got into its stride did they discover that Edmond was determined to enforce his agreement to the letter. His agents were intent on imposing a very strict regime: the immigrants were to work on the land, and not to set up as traders and craftsmen. They were not to sell or sub-let their holdings. They were not to hire labour. They were not even allowed to pay their children wages. Many of the colonists deeply re-sented this degree of control. They had not, they said, exercised a holy zeal and sacrificed everything in coming to this barren land merely to find themselves Rothschild tenants governed by a generous but rigid paternal-ism. Edmond's response was quite uncompromising: either they gave him their "unquestioning obedience", rooted out troublemakers and devoted themselves totally to the work in hand, or they would not receive another sou from him.

Inevitably, there were occasional injustices. Some of the overseers may well have behaved like petty tyrants. Just as much as the colonists, they were in a completely new situation. They had no blueprint to guide them in the working out of relationships. Some settlers failed, unable to submit to the hard pioneering life. But there is little doubt that Edmond's tough attitude was the correct one. It put iron in the soul of the new settlement. It replaced escapism and starry-eyed idealism with a hard, practical regimen.

Edmond de Rothschild was, himself, an idealist but one who had his feet firmly planted on the ground. He was aware of the realities of life in Palestine and the potential reaction to the colonies throughout the wider world. "I am not a philanthropist," he told one of the founders of Rishon Le Zion, "I have set out on this enterprise to see whether it is possible to establish Jews on Palestinian soil." [19] Better than most, a Rothschild knew that success — whether in banking, diplomacy, building a spectacular art collection, or colonising barren land — could only be bought with patience, discipline, tenacity and sheer hard work. If the settlers did not develop backbone they would not survive. So if, like Yahweh of old, he dispensed immutable decrees from the invisibility of the mountain top, it was for the good of the struggling farmers and their successors — as he understood it. Thus every new settler was obliged to sign an agreement "to submit myself totally to the orders which the administration shall think necessary in the name of M. le Baron in anything concerning the cultivation of the land and its service and if any action should be taken against me I have no right to oppose it."[20] And Edmond did not hesitate to enforce the terms of the contract.

There was much more at stake than the comfort and the crop yields of the first workers on the land. Edmond, in fact, shared Mohilewer's vision of large-scale settlement because it would make a major contribution towards solving the Jewish Question and because it would show the world in general and anti-Semites in particular that his people could succeed as primary producers and not just as "parasitical intermediaries", as Toussenel and his disciples claimed. He, therefore, added to his colonies as far as, in his judgement, the situation would allow. Fervent nationalists regarded the pace the Baron set as too slow but Edmond knew that Palestinian settlement would be increasingly opposed by the Turks and other interested parties. It was, therefore, all the more vital that the right foundations should be laid by the pioneers and that further advance should be planned as discreetly and cannily as his father had planned his campaigns against Bonaparte and the Péreires. ". . . we must postpone . . . the founding of any new colonies and put all emphasis on those that are already in existence. There must be unity especially in buying land, for if each one acts separately the price of land will rise greatly. In general it is necessary to avoid publicity in such matters. Only if we proceed quietly and cautiously will our work be crowned with success . . ."[21]

Another advantage of setting up what was virtually a personal colony was that Edmond could experiment. At his instigation, the farmers grew not only the indigenous crops — olives, figs, almonds and citrus fruits — but tried out vines, various strains of wheat, flowers for extracting perfume essences and mulberries upon which to breed silkworms. During his travels he kept a lookout for plants that would flourish in Palestinian soil. In this way, for example, the grapefruit was introduced. Because of the success of the Baron's colonies, others already in existence came under his protection and guidance. As the settlements grew he provided for their every need — houses, schools, synagogues, free medical treatment. He may even have attempted to buy the Wailing Wall, the centre of Jewish devotion in Jerusalem.[22]

This happened in the course of an extraordinary tour he made in 1887. By then his patronage of the settlements was undoubtedly an open secret. Yet he persisted in trying to travel incognito. He and his wife journeyed as far as Port Said in their yacht, then made their way less conspicuously to Jaffa, only partially evading the fuss which attended the arrival of a Rothschild. Then they bumped and swayed the fifty dusty miles to Jerusalem in a stifling carriage with the blinds drawn, their servants following at a distance.

In the Holy City, Edmond and Adelheid toured the traditional sites and had talks with Jewish leaders. It was one of them who suggested that the Wailing Wall might be acquired for the community. Negotiations with the Arab owner of the property were begun and a price of seven hundred thousand francs was agreed. At the last moment the Sephardic Chief Rabbi intervened. A divine vision had warned him, he declared, that the purchase would be followed by a terrible massacre instigated by the Muslims. The truth is probably that this leader, perfectly understanding the politico-religious sensibilities of the Jerusalem situation, wanted to head off an action which could only upset his Muslim neighbours. There was, however, no objection to another of the Baron's grand schemes. Profoundly moved by the poverty and illness in the city, he made immediate plans for the building of a new hospital providing free treatment for malaria, yellow fever, trachoma and other endemic diseases.

When the baronial party moved on to the settlements, they were faced with a very muddled picture of success and failure, despair and contentment. At one colony, the people had rebelled against their administrator and turned him out. Edmond and the dispossessed agent had to enter the settlement secretly in the middle of the night. Soon after dawn the Baron had the community assembled and harangued them roundly: "I have tried to prove that the children of Israel are capable of being good colonists and working the land, but all that you have proved instead is that you can create rebellion and be sowers of discord."[23]

However, Edmond was not the sort of man to be discouraged by setbacks. He found much to encourage him on his tour and over the next decade he devoted himself almost exclusively to the well-being of his colonies, acquiring new land, establishing irrigation schemes, commissioning scores of reports, surveys and feasibility studies. Primitive settlements grew into civilised townships. Orange groves and vineyards flourished where once there had only been sunburnt earth. Workshops hummed with activity as the produce of the land was packed or processed. And a new generation of sturdy young boys and girls grew up who would inherit the legacy of the pioneers.

* * *

295

Edmond's attitude towards Palestine was also, in part, conditioned by the responses of his family. Large-scale settlement was supported by his Frankfurt relatives; in particular his father-in-law, Willy Carl. But in Paris and London, Rothschild attitudes were cautious and, in some cases, hostile. It was not just that Edmond's brothers and cousins were anxious about the name of Rothschild being associated with ventures that might fail. What worried them increasingly were the implications of Palestinian colonisation for European Jewry. More and more families were seeking to leave the cramped cities of Germany, France and Britain for the Holy Land. This called in question the whole philosophy of assimilation. "Aha," said the anti-Semites, "you see, we were right: the Jews are, at heart, separatists. They will never truly integrate with us." And the racial purists, particularly in Germany, were not slow to draw the conclusion that settlement in Palestine *or anywhere* was to be encouraged. In fact *all* Jews should be shipped off to their own land, so that they could no longer pollute Europe. With such ideas in the background, it is not surprising that Edmond's relatives were concerned about his support for settlement schemes and positively alarmed when they heard that he had had a meeting with the ardent Jewish nationalist, Theodor Herzl.

Herzl was a Vienna-based journalist of extreme views. In 1896 he published a pamphlet entitled *Der Judenstaat*, an event generally acknowledged as marking the beginning of modern Zionism. In simple, pungent prose, Herzl challenged all that the Rothschilds and the other leading European Jews stood for:

> . . . I consider the Jewish question neither a social nor a religious one, even though it sometimes takes these and other forms. It is a national question . . .
>
> We have sincerely tried everywhere to merge with the national communities in which we live, seeking only to preserve the faith of our fathers. It is not permitted to us. In vain are we loyal patriots, sometimes super-loyal; in vain do we make the same sacrifices of life and property as our fellow citizens; in vain do we strive to enhance the fame of our native land in the arts and sciences, or her wealth by trade and commerce. In our native lands where we have lived for centuries we are still decried as aliens, often by men whose ancestors had not yet come at a time when Jewish sighs had long been heard in the country. The majority decides who the "alien" is; this, and all else in the relations between peoples, is a matter of power . . . In the world as it now is and will probably remain, for an indefinite period, might takes precedence over right. It is without avail, therefore, for us to be loyal patriots, as were the Huguenots, who were forced to

emigrate. If we were left in peace . . . But I think we shall not be left in peace.[24]

Herzl believed that the Ottoman Sultan could and should be persuaded to cede Palestine to the Jews, and he embarked upon a campaign aimed at achieving this objective. His tour of European statesmen and Jewish leaders inevitably brought him before long to Baron Edmond's door. Edmond refused to see him but the journalist persisted.

The meeting, when it took place, was not a success. Herzl harangued the Baron for about two hours. He pointed out that Edmond was to be the cornerstone of his project and virtually threatened that if he declined the honour he (Herzl) would start a Zionist mass movement, using the bludgeon of popular protest instead of the rapier of private persuasion. But he failed to convince, left angrily, and vented his feelings in his diary and his correspondence. In a letter to the Chief Rabbi, Zadok Kahn, he roundly condemned the house of Rothschild as a "national misfortune for the Jews". In his diary he poured contempt on Baron Edmond:

> Edmond is a decent, good-natured, faint-hearted man who absolutely fails to understand the matter and would like to stop it the way a coward tries to stop necessary surgery. I believe he is now aghast at having got himself involved with Palestine and perhaps he will run to Alphonse and say "You were right, I should have gone in for racing horses rather than resettling Jews". And the fate of many millions is to hang on such men![25]

Herzl divided European Jewry. He built up an international Zionist movement, with its own weekly organ, *Die Welt*. In 1897 he summoned the first annual Zionist congress at Basle. As the years passed the numbers and enthusiasm of his supporters grew. His views were received sympathetically by several leading statesmen. But the growth of Herzl's influence within Jewry was matched by the increasing strength of opposition. Many Jews regarded themselves as belonging to a purely religious community. Such was the position of most of the Rothschilds: they would have liked Edmond to denounce Zionism publicly.

He did not do so. But his opposition to what Herzl stood for was as firm as his rejection of Mohilewer's scheme had been. And for the same sort of reason. Too much too soon could ruin everything. A Palestine thronged with Jews — especially Jews displaying an aggressive nationalism — could only provoke a hostile Turkish response, and one against which the settlers would be ill-equipped to retaliate.

In the 1890s Edmond, therefore, was not a Zionist and that for largely practical reasons. However, he was not so naïve as to imagine that the

297

process he was sponsoring, of gradually building a strong Jewish presence within Palestine, would have no influence on the political situation in the Middle East. He doubtless realised that his work and that of Herzl were two rivers destined to converge. At the end of his life he reflected, "Without me Zionism could not have prospered, and without Zionism I could have done nothing." But for the time being he realised that little more could be achieved until the political balance in the area changed. Before the new century was two decades old that balance did change, violently and permanently.

CHAPTER 21

"Have a go at the Grand Old Man
on his own dunghill"

In the closing years of the last century the industrial growth and overseas expansion the Rothschilds had done so much to foster was intensifying politico-economic rivalries and carrying European tensions to distant lands. In Egypt, for example, the setting up of the international commission to administer the Suez Canal — a British initiative in which, as we have seen, Rothschild funds played a vital part — was by no means the end of friction in that arena. Egyptian government finance was in such a mess that by 1876 the Khedive's creditors had forced him to submit control of the economy to an international committee. In effect, this meant control by specialists from Britain and France, the two nations most directly concerned. A *ménage à trois* is seldom a satisfactory arrangement and this one gave rise to constant difficulties.

Because politics and economics were inseparable, the Rothschilds on both sides of the Channel were heavily involved in the Egyptian business. The two banks organised an Egyptian state loan of eight and a half million pounds and were reassured by the appointment of two officials to oversee the financial administration: an Englishman, Charles — later Sir Charles — Rivers Wilson, and a Frenchman, Eugène de Blignières.

Rivers Wilson worked very closely with the Rothschilds in trying to make a complex and sensitive set of relationships work. It was far from easy. The French and British governments mistrusted each other. Their on-the-spot representatives were often at loggerheads. The Khedive exploited these differences for his own ends. And sometimes the Rothschild cousins were infected with the poison of doubt. To make matters worse there were rumblings of nationalist revolt. Pan-Islamic agitators were demanding the expulsion of all foreigners and gaining increasing support, particularly in the army. In 1879 Khedive Ismail made a bid to harness this nationalism to his own ambition. He dismissed the overseers and resumed complete control. Rivers Wilson immediately appealed to Natty. He suggested that Rothschilds should put pressure on the Khedive by calling in the loan. Natty and Alphonse were not prepared to use their financial power directly against the Khedive, but they did join with Rivers Wilson in recommending that the French and British governments should bring pressure to bear on Ismail's overlord, the Turkish Sultan. This was done (though not necessarily because the Rothschilds advocated it). As a direct result Ismail was deposed in favour of his twenty-seven-year-old son, Tewfik.

The Anglo-French Dual Control was re-established and, for a while, everything as seen from London or Paris seemed satisfactory. Then the old complaints began again. The French in Cairo in the person of their overseer, E. de Blignières, were manoeuvring themselves into a position of complete control. Rivalries reasserted themselves. The political situation — and therefore the money markets — were unsettled.

The installation of Tewfik, far from solving the problem, had simply exacerbated it, arousing even greater anger among the nationalist forces who were opposed to all foreign influence. The country rapidly became virtually ungovernable and in 1881 a full-fledged revolt led by Arabi Pasha seemed to threaten both the lives of foreign nationals and the security of the canal.

Meanwhile there had been a change of government in England and one which Natty did not like. In 1880 Disraeli and the Tories had been ousted at a general election by the Liberals. The return of Gladstone to power meant, automatically, the decline of Rothschild influence. "We are not on intimate terms with the present cabinet,"[1] Natty told Bleichröder succinctly. It was not long before he began to find fault with the government's response to the deteriorating situation in Egypt. In his view the administration's policy was characterised by indecisiveness and muddle. Gladstone and Granville certainly hesitated to intervene. They did not want to become involved in a costly military expedition, nor did they wish to upset the Continental powers by taking a unilateral initiative. Eventually, they asked the French to join them in sending an expeditionary force to restore order. The invitation was declined. Meanwhile, the Egyptian state, with no firm hand on the helm, drifted towards the rocks, taking a great deal of Rothschild investment with it.

Natty had no patience with all the shilly-shallying. He believed that Britain should defeat the rebels, gain control of Egypt and the canal, and keep them. Alphonse also favoured action though he doubtless hoped that his own government would share the military initiative.

The English did finally get going in the following September. A force under Sir Garnet Wolseley, without any aid from France, decisively defeated the nationalists at Tel-el-Kebir. From this point on French humiliation and resentment began to be expressed with increasing vigour. The fact that France had rejected the opportunity to share in the campaign did not prevent them protesting at Britain's presence and being

300

highly suspicious of her intentions — suspicions which Bismarck did everything in his power to foster. This put the French Rothschilds in a difficult position. Professionally, they could only view the British occupation with satisfaction. Wolseley had restored order and that was good for business. But Alphonse and his brothers shared the growing anglophobia. Whatever effect this had on relations between London and Paris, in terms of practical financial policy, family unity held firm. In 1885 the two houses jointly organised the loan of £9,424,000 which had been agreed by the major powers to set the Egyptian government on its feet.

In that same year Natty was raised to the British peerage. Gladstone who had unsuccessfully championed Lionel's cause between 1869 and 1873, needed little encouragement to proffer his son's name to the Queen. But the situation had changed significantly in the intervening years. Gladstone had advocated a barony for Lionel purely on merit. His support for Natty had an element of political calculation about it. Several of the Prime Minister's colleagues were worried about Sir Nathaniel Rothschild's coolness towards the Liberal leadership. At a time when a major rift was appearing in the party between pro- and anti-Gladstone factions, they were anxious to keep the support of such an influential man. "He is not a very robust Liberal," one party activist commented to the government chief whip, "but I suppose there is not much object in letting him drift, and still less in driving him over to the Tories."[2] Some overzealous party activists had even canvassed the possibility of ousting Natty from his Aylesbury seat and replacing him with Ferdinand, whom they believed to be more "reliable". Such plotting, the same writer observed, was the height of folly and could only be counterproductive.

> If it is thought that the Rothschilds can be played off one against the other, and that because Ferdinand may be a more acceptable or more pliant colleague, he can be put forward at Natty's expense, a very great mistake is made.
> The Rothschilds have held together for generations, and discipline in their family is differently understood from what it is in that of the Russells. If the Liberal party breaks with Natty, it breaks with the whole clan, and there is I imagine nothing to be gained by such a proceeding.[3]

It was time for the carrot, not the stick.

Yet there was an inevitability about a Rothschild joining the ranks of the English aristocracy and even about a Rothschild being the first practising Jew to take his seat in the House of Lords. Indeed, the only real surprise is that Disraeli had not advanced his friend to this new dignity. Thus, while short-term political advantage may have been the motivation of some of Gladstone's advisers, the creation of the title "Baron Rothschild of Tring" was primarily the formal recognition of a man — and a family — who had done that state some service.

Natty chose to regard the honour not as a personal triumph, but as another great victory for Jewry. He thanked Gladstone for bestowing "for the first time a peerage on a member of our faith" and intimated that, in his eyes, this would "greatly increase the value of the dignity".[4] To underline the point he permanently rejected the convention which would have obliged him, in the manner of the English nobility, to sign himself "Tring"; the simple name "Rothschild" was scrawled at the bottom of all his letters. It announced that he was proud of his Jewish ancestry and that he had gone as far as he would go along the road of assimilation. Alphonse, writing warm congratulations, stated that he did so in the name of all Paris Jews and exulted that the news would outrage the anti-Semitic element.[5]

To no one's surprise, Ferdinand now occupied the parliamentary seat vacated by Natty. As political observers had suggested, he lacked his predecessor's personal animosity towards Gladstone but in matters of policy he took his stand, like Natty, firmly on the right wing of the party. Indeed, he sometimes had to defend himself against the charge of being a covert Tory:

> I am not by nature a Conservative. Conservatism has been the ruin of several foreign countries and liberal policies have been the making of England. To liberalism we — you — owe everything. On no point and in no manner do I incline towards Toryism in any form.
> On the other hand ... I deplore for the sake of the country I have adopted and I love truly, the restricted policy of the present Government, who have sacrificed if not the interests yet the magic power of the English flag and name to the narrower issues of Parliamentary reform. I am perhaps *"plus Catholique que le Pape"* but I would that the Union Jack floated in every island of Polynesia, on every crag of the Himalayas, on every minaret of the East (this is a metaphor).[6]

Ferdinand, of course, came from a country where the word "conservatism" meant something far more extreme than was suggested by its usage in a British political context.

Whatever he may have meant by the disclaimer "this is a metaphor", Ferdinand was clearly infected by the emotional virus of imperialism. This was now spreading through Europe and was reaching pandemic proportions. Under the guise of "taking civilisation to the natives", the agents of the major powers were transferring national rivalries to distant battlegrounds.

> ... youths of England, make your country again a royal throne of kings, a sceptred isle, for all the world a source of light, a centre of peace ... This is what England must do or perish; she must found colonies as far and as fast as she is able ... seizing every piece of fruitful waste ground she can set foot on, and there teaching her colonists that their chief virtue is to be fidelity to their country.[7]

So the aged John Ruskin, Slade Professor of Fine Art at Oxford from 1869 to 1879, had exhorted his students and this nationalistic fervour was shared by millions of his countrymen. It was not shared by Gladstone. He strained every political muscle to pull against the forces of expansionism and to prevent the exacerbation of existing rivalries. This was one reason why Natty disliked him; like Ferdinand, he regarded the government's foreign policy as flabby and injurious to British interests. But Lord Rothschild was not an unbridled expansionist. This is clearly shown by his relationship with a man who *was* an unbridled expansionist — Cecil Rhodes.

In 1867 diamonds were discovered along South Africa's Orange and Vaal rivers. Several mining companies were founded and Rothschilds were naturally to the fore in taking a financial interest in the region. Their on-the-spot agents sent back regular reports on the situation — a situation which was far from satisfactory from a business point of view. The diamond rush at Kimberley had reproduced those conditions the nineteenth century had already witnessed in the boom towns of America and Australia: a mass of claims registered by small operators, many of whom lacked the capital and expertise necessary to develop them properly. To this confusion was added nationalistic rivalry. The English government at the Cape, and the Transvaal Boers, were locked in irreconcilable ideological and territorial conflict. All this caused much concern at New Court. Natty and his brothers agreed with their representative, A. Gansl, that commercial success would only be possible by amalgamating several of the small concerns. Through their major holding in the Anglo-African Diamond Mining Company Limited they participated in the buying out of smaller claim-holders, a process which gathered momentum from about 1882.

Other operators, of course, had the same idea. Eventually the "Amalgamation Stakes" developed into a two-horse race between the Barnato Diamond Mining Company and De Beers. More particularly, it became a contest between two remarkable entrepreneurs: Barney Barnato and Cecil Rhodes. Both had gone from Britain to South Africa as young men. Both had become millionaires while still in their twenties. But there the similarity ends. Rhodes was an Oxford-educated, passionate (perhaps fanatical) imperialist. Perhaps inspired, during his undergraduate days, by Ruskin's oratory, he had become a man with a mission. It became Rhodes' declared aim to create in Africa a "British dominion from the Cape to Cairo", and he devoted a sizeable portion of his fortune to the achievement of this end, both as a businessman and, after 1890, as Prime Minister of Cape Colony. By 1887 his De Beers Mining Company had gobbled up many rivals in the Kimberley area (including Anglo-African).

Barney Barnato was an extrovert Jew with little book learning. He loved prize-fighting and horse-racing. He was born Barnett Isaacs, the son of an Aldgate street trader and, after a few years at the Jews' Free School, had gone to Africa with fifty pounds in his pocket. By far-sightedness and business acumen he had rapidly made a fortune. Barnato was a pure businessman and he actively mistrusted Rhodes' imperialistic dreams.

The contest between these two men for mastery of the diamond fields was keen. By 1887 all the main rival operators except one had been taken over by the Barnato and De Beers conglomerates. The exception was the French Diamond Company, a major concern but one whose mines were only just coming into full production. This did not prevent the value of their shares rising rapidly as Rhodes, Barnato and their colleagues eagerly bought up every company share that became available.

As far as the Rothschilds were concerned, all this activity was making the market too volatile. When, therefore, Rhodes came home in July 1887 and approached Natty personally for financial backing, Lord Rothschild saw the request as a means of restoring a much-needed commerical stability. He guaranteed De Beers one million pounds (three quarters of which was actually taken up) to be used for improving the company's output and, therefore, its profit and bargaining power. He also organised negotiations at the European end and persuaded the directors of the French company to go into voluntary liquidation on very favourable terms. This did not prevent Barnato competing for the company's assets but the combination of De Beers and Rothschilds was too much for him. When he topped his rival's offer by three hundred thousand pounds, Rhodes immediately bid an extra three hundred thousand and made it known that he would go on capping any sum Barnato put up. The Jew could not afford to call his bluff and De Beers emerged triumphant. Soon afterwards the two concerns amalgamated.

One reason why Barnato held out so long was his opposition to expansionism. Rhodes made it clear that the funds of the new company – De

Beers Consolidated Mines Limited – would be used for the northward march of imperialism. There was never any distinction in his mind between making money and carrying the British flag into newly conquered territory. And Rhodes persuaded himself that Lord Rothschild shared his simple idealism.

He was wrong. Lord Rothschild was not an unreserved imperialist, as Rhodes gradually discovered. In 1888 he made a will, nominating Natty to administer the bulk of his estate for financing a sinister secret society for promoting the extension of British power.* Over the next few years Rhodes wrote a stream of letters to New Court on the subject of British politics in southern Africa. He found his correspondent clear-headed, firm and quite unprepared to confuse the roles of banker and politician. In response to Rhodes' suggestion that company funds be used to finance territorial expansion, his banker advised: "if . . . you require money for that purpose, you will have to obtain it from other sources than the cash reserve of the De Beers Company. We have always held that the De Beers Company is simply a diamond mining company."[8] And Rhodes cannot have been very pleased to learn, in 1892, that Rothschilds had floated a loan for the Boer government of the Transvaal. The bank had considerable investments in South African mines, railways and general development. They were, therefore, on the side of peace and stability. Any influence they exercised as the decade wore on was towards the end of preventing Britons and Boers drifting into war. The turbulent Rhodes, by contrast, was implacable in his opposition to the Johannesburg regime and, in 1895, organised an (unsuccessful) uprising to topple it – the notorious Jameson Raid. Rhodes had gone much too far. He was censured by the British government and was forced to resign the premiership. By this time he had long ceased to have close and cordial relations with Natty. Probably he never really grasped the fact that, though the Rothschilds disliked Gladstone's policy of colonial retrenchment, they were not advocates of unbridled imperialism for its own sake.

Put succinctly, what Natty, Ferdinand and others on the right wing of the Liberal party believed was that social reform at home had gone far enough but that in foreign affairs Britain should go very much farther. What the English Rothschilds were concerned about was the preservation, for sound commercial reasons, of Britain's imperial links, maximum freedom of trade, good relations with Germany in order to stabilise European politics,

---

*This later developed into a trust for the establishment of scholarships at Oxford, for which Natty was not responsible.

and resistance to radical demands which threatened domestic social harmony. They opposed the Prime Minister's desire to withdraw troops from Egypt at the earliest opportunity and all other manifestations of "weak" foreign policy. And they were greatly alarmed when Gladstone announced his intention of granting home rule to Ireland. It was because of the government's drift towards a whole range of what he regarded as disastrous commitments that Natty took a progressively more active rôle in party politics.

In the closing years of the century Lord Rothschild played a prominent part in the break-up of the Liberal party. His most straightforward course of action might have been, on the face of it, to transfer his allegiance to the Tories. But the Conservative party were in almost as much disarray as their opponents. Lord Randolph Churchill blazed briefly across the political firmament in the 1880s, his oratory and widespread popularity seeming to mark him as a reincarnated Disraeli (Disraeli died in 1881), determined to create a widely based conservatism, but he was opposed by many of his own party.

In this confused political situation, involving a welter of caucuses, factions, alliances and intrigues, Natty was in his element. Discreetly, he brought his considerable resources to bear and thus influenced the destiny of governments and governed more than the history books will ever be able to tell. With the help of his brothers and cousin Ferdy, he took part in constant meetings and private conversations with Churchill, Lord Rosebery, Joseph Chamberlain and others of both parties who shared his views. "Country house politics" was an activity the Rothschilds had perfected. But no one mastered the art more completely than the first English baron. In the last two decades of the century he presided, amidst the peaceful splendour of Tring Park, over negotiations ranging from the extension of Cecil Rhodes' diamond empire to the reconstitution of London University.[9] Supervising the demolition of old-style Liberalism was undoubtedly the most spectacular accomplishment of this éminence grise. The term "Liberal Unionist" was now coined by those members of the old party who formed part of the Rothschild caucus, for what marked out the new grouping most distinctly was its opposition to Irish home rule and its determination to achieve a majority in parliament opposed to it.

Their moment of triumph came in the summer of 1886. A general election was called and the Irish Question was the burning issue. In a letter to Churchill, Lord Rothschild urged him to take up the cause boldly on the hustings. "Have a go at the Grand Old Man [Gladstone] on his own dunghill",[10] he wrote. The result of the poll was all that Natty could have hoped for. The Tories and their Liberal Unionist supporters (soon to be known as the Unionist party) had a clear majority in the new House.

Lord Salisbury became Prime Minister, and Churchill, as Chancellor of the Exchequer, led the government in the Lower House. For a while it appeared to Lord Rothschild that there had been a return to the halcyon days of Disraelian governments. One observer noted that he and Churchill, "seem to conduct the business of the Empire, in great measure, *together*, in consultation with Chamberlain".[11]

But this state of affairs was short-lived. Within six months the quicksilver Churchill had fallen out with his cabinet colleagues and resigned. He was never again trusted with government office. Within a few years his mental and physical health broke down. He died in 1895 at the age of forty-five.

For all his close contacts with Churchill, Natty seems to have exercised no personal (as opposed to political) influence over him; there was between them no warmth of friendship which might have made it possible for Natty to offer valuable advice. Such relationships were for Lord Rothschild hard, if not impossible. After Churchill's death, Natty was not even above telling discreditable stories about his erstwhile colleague. He revealed to fellow banker Robert Benson how Churchill once used some love letters in an attempt to blackmail the Prince of Wales into using his influence to stop divorce proceedings against his brother Lord Blandford. Natty's passion for secrecy evidently did not always extend to respecting the confidences of others.[12]

But that passion has ensured that Natty's political activitices are and will remain obscure. One student of late Victorian politics complained, "When I get to the bottom of any subject, I find the first Lord Rothschild, and there the trail ends."[13] Those words are quoted by Dr Miriam Rothschild in her biography of her uncle and she devotes a whole chapter to the destruction of private records ordered by Lionel, Natty, Walter and his brother Charles, and other members of the family. She warns that any researchers trying to discover the truth about her ancestors are doomed to "follow a hard and stony path, leading them on inexorably to a very large bonfire".[14] The Rothschild passion for secretiveness had, by the late nineteenth century, become a widespread family trait, affecting some members of the family more than others, but affecting most or all of them to some degree. There were good reasons for the Rothschilds to maintain close confidentiality, as we have already stated, and it is understandable that the family may be sensitive to certain episodes in their history. But there is no denying the fact that, as Miriam points out, for some Rothschilds secrecy became an obsession, something valued for its own sake.

Of no one is this more true than Natty. At his express wish, trunkfuls of letters and documents were destroyed after his death. Only tantalising scraps of information, therefore, survive about his influence on affairs in this formative period of English political life. His opposition to Gladstone, particularly over Ireland, seems to have been total. He eagerly gleaned gossip from every source and passed it on to Lord Randolph. In January 1886, for example, he prised some confidences from Connie's husband, Cyril Flower, who had just returned from visiting Gladstone at Hawarden Castle, the G.O.M's country home. Immediately, this and other information was despatched to Churchill who, in turn, reported to the Tory leader, Lord Salisbury, that Gladstone "is entirely monopolised by the Irish question . . . he confided to C.F. that he was much annoyed with Arthur Balfour . . . Rothschild also saw Brett this morning, who told him that Harcourt and Dilke were yesterday of opinion that Gladstone would abandon Home Rule".[15]

After Churchill's political suicide, Natty seems to have pinned considerable hope on Lord Rosebery, the most outstanding of the younger Gladstonians. Rosebery, who, it will be remembered, was married to Natty's cousin, Hannah, was an original thinker who strove hard to accommodate traditional Liberalism to a form of imperialism shorn of all suggestion of national aggrandisement. Sadly, Rosebery's public career was marked by scarcely less conflict and tragedy than Churchill's. He tried hard to remain loyal to Gladstone under whom he served in various government offices but they differed fundamentally on foreign policy. Rosebery was not diplomatic by temperament and he found the strain of political controversy very taxing. Then, in 1890 something happened which would ultimately drive him to abandon public life altogether: his beloved Hannah died of typhoid fever. She fell ill at Dalmeny, her husband's Scottish estate, and Archie recorded her end in his diary: "She had been delirious for fully a week, only waking up with a wonderful smile whenever I came into the room. 'Archie! This *is* nice', in her old sweet childish way. [About ten o'clock in the evening she said] 'Archie, Archie I am going home.' She probably still thought she was in Paris where she had fancied herself last week. But these were the last words I heard her say."[16] She died just before six o'clock the following morning.

Hannah was buried beside her father in the Jewish cemetery at Willesden and Natty presided over the arrangements. The simple ceremony was attended by Gladstone, several ministers and notables and Sir Henry Ponsonby, representing the Queen. Ponsonby recorded: "Lord Rosebery never spoke but remained close to the coffin till it was lowered into the grave. Lord Rothschild led him back to the chapel but he looked down the whole time."[17] Winston Churchill, who had a fine gift for choosing the right word, described Rosebery as "maimed" by his wife's death. Without the driving force of Hannah's ambition for him, Archie's instinct was to abandon political life completely. It seems he also tried to distance himself from his late wife's connections. David Lindsay noted in his diary that the Earl immediately set about cancelling his subscriptions to Jewish charities.[18] But it must be said that Lindsay loathed Rosebery. Certainly, the Rothschilds remained sufficiently close to the widower to dissuade him from abandoning politics.

In 1892 Gladstone returned to office and Rosebery was urged to become Foreign Secretary. Only when Natty persuaded the Prince of Wales to add his voice to the chorus did the Earl give way to their wishes. What the Rothschilds and their friends wanted, of course, was someone who would stand up to the Prime Minister and pursue a more rigorous policy abroad. The stratagem was successful, though very painful for Rosebery. His disagreement with Gladstone led to him pursuing an independent line of policy sanctioned directly by the Queen. In December 1893 he headed a revolt which led to the G.O.M's final resignation. Victoria sent for her Foreign Secretary and asked him to form a new administration.

Rosebery's sixteen-month premiership was a disaster. He was confronted by a hostile, Tory House of Lords and lacked the ability to unite his own cabinet colleagues. He was never an easy man to get on with and he simply could not cope with the host of personal conflicts thrust upon him while he was still in the midst of his grief. In June 1895 he seized upon a minor Commons defeat as an excuse to resign. How much different things might have been for him, his party and his country if Hannah had lived.

By no means all Rothschilds felt the same way as Natty over Gladstone. Annie and Constance, for example, remained devoted supporters. In 1893 Annie wrote to her elder sister describing a stay at Hawarden as guest of the eighty-three-year-old Prime Minister. It gives a vivid and charming picture of the fiery statesman and his wife in their latter, but by no means declining years:

> I had a delightful dinner listening to literary discussion between the G.O.M. and W. Morley.* The G.O.M. is wonderfully well. He is rather fallen in the face but very lively. Excepting that he is a little deaf, I do not find much change. His old face lights up with vehemence and fire when he talks of the vile Turks and his mouth puckers up with a good-natured little smile at some little joke or nonsense to which he condescends occasionally. He is not very

*A possible mistake. Annie may have meant J. Morley (later Viscount Morley), Liberal MP and staunch supporter of home rule, who, in 1903, published a three-volume biography of Gladstone.

strong about the Vits' [Licensed Victuallers] Bill, which (but this is private) I think he considers should have been a private and not a government bill ... W.G. [Mrs Gladstone] is a wonder. She had driven all the way to Chester in an open carriage to open a bazaar, looked in at the Town Hall at one of the temperance meetings and finished up with our meeting in the evening ... [she is] very dear and kind and thoughtful ... [Greetings] from the G.O.M., G.O.W. and family ... [19]

The Rothschilds were not alone in having a divided attitude towards Gladstonian Liberalism. In Anglo-Jewry as a whole, political unity was a thing of the past. In 1880 three of the ten Jewish candidates at the general election stood on a Tory ticket. In 1900 twenty-two Jews went to the hustings of whom ten were Conservatives. One of the successful Tory candidates in 1880 was the Rothschild's kinsman Henry de Worms. He went on to have a very distinguished political career as Under-Secretary for the Colonies and the first Jewish privy councillor. In 1895 he entered the Lords as Baron Pirbright.

Rothschild political activity was by no means confined to party manoeuvring. Ferdinand, for example, was a more active parliamentarian than his predecessor as MP for Aylesbury. He particularly interested himself in social reform measures. His longest parliamentary battle, which lasted five years, was concerned with better pay and conditions of service for Post Office telegraph clerks. And Natty seems to have taken an active part in the resolution of the dock strike of 1889. The union demanded a wage rise of sixpence − the celebrated "dockers' tanner" − and the employers dug their heels in. Lord Rothschild claimed, according to his granddaughter, that he had been brought in as a mediator and that the resolution of this dispute was his proudest achievement. Unfortunately, there survives absolutely no evidence to back up this claim. The contribution of Cardinal Manning to bringing about a solution is well documented. But one searches official records and contemporary memoirs in vain for any mention of Natty's contribution. Perhaps his love of secrecy did not always work to his advantage. [20]

Whatever the truth of the matter, Lord Rothschild was not only pleased that the men had gone back to work but also that the dispute had been settled without government intervention. He firmly resisted any tendency towards greater state control, especially in the commercial life of the country. What particularly worried him about the wave of industrial unrest was that it was likely to result in just such an increase in government "interference". In politics Lord Rothschild was a man of firm and clear, if unimaginative, views. Few of his contemporaries had a keener sense of social justice. Yet he was convinced that equity could best be achieved by men of goodwill agreeing together, without the supervision of the state. To him there was no need to change the existing order, as long as each man, in his station, fulfilled his duty to those above and below. If all men had shared Natty's deep sense of responsibility, perhaps the seemingly eternal verities of Victorian society might have gone unchallenged. But there *were* landlords who neglected their tenants' cottages. There *were* destitute men and women who had no wealthy patron to turn to. There *were* exploiters and exploited. And there *were* voices in the land, growing now to a clamour, which insisted that injustice was inherent in the very system. Natty could never conceive that those voices might ultimately prevail, nor that they might do so because they had much right on their side.

CHAPTER 22

"Too much Lord Rothschild"

Mayer Carl died in 1886. His brother, Willy Carl, now the only male member of the German family (Adolph, who died in 1900, had long since abandoned banking), took over the running of the Frankfurt house for the next fifteen years. Then, in February 1901 he, too, died. Despite the ties of marriage, there had not, as we have seen, been close business connections between the parent house and the other banks for several years, and, since none of the Rothschild men now expressed any desire to settle in the city of their ancestors, by common family consent, the Frankfurt business was wound up. There was still no suggestion of allowing a son-in-law to take over. Maximilian Goldschmidt, who had married Willy Carl's youngest daughter, Minna Caroline, was a considerable banker in his own right and may well have hoped to take over his father-in-law's business. If so, he was soon disillusioned. The Rothschilds were still determined to exclude strangers from their affairs. But though they could prevent Goldschmidt taking over the bank, they could not stop him taking their name. This is what he promptly did. Henceforth he and his financial operation went under the name of Goldschmidt-Rothschild. He was determined to gain whatever he could of the prestige and business of his wife's family. The reaction is understandable − it must have been very galling for Goldschmidt to have been one of the few non-Rothschilds to come close to gaining a chunk of the family fortune, only to have his hopes dashed. Thus, after more than a century M. A. Rothschild and Sons closed its doors for the last time. In accordance with universal Rothschild practice, all employees received very generous pensions. Those who wished to carry on working were transferred to the Disconts Gesellschaft bank. Then the waggons piled with furniture and chests full of documents trundled away from the now-empty premises in the Berkheimerstrasse. And an era was closed, not only in the life of the Rothschild family, but also in the commercial life of Europe.

There were more changes ahead for the banking Rothschilds. The period 1904-18 saw the passing of all the leading members of the three remaining banking houses. Alphonse died in 1905 and was followed by

Gustave and Salbert in 1911, Natty in 1915, Leo in 1917 and Alfred in 1918. Succession was always a problem for the family. Because outsiders, in-laws and daughters were not accepted into partnership, every generation had to produce sons who were financially gifted and trained to undertake all the responsibilities for which Rothschilds were liable. Since the law of averages decreed that some children would be girls and that some boys would not be interested in banking, it was essential for the Rothschilds to have large families.

The Last of the Frankfurt Rothschilds

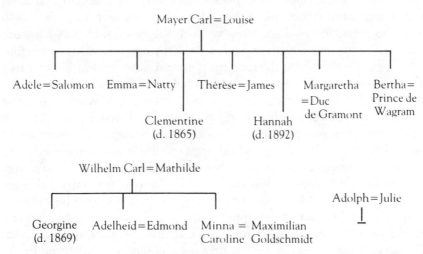

Unfortunately, although they could not have known this, the laws of genetics were working against them. Ironically, the endogamous marriages designed to secure the unity and continuance of the family business came close to destroying it. Two possible results of inbreeding are decreased fertility and a concentration of inherited traits resulting sometimes in genius, sometimes in extreme eccentricity. The Rothschilds had hitherto been fortunate. Every generation of the four families had produced at least one son capable not only of continuing the business but, in most cases, of enhancing it.* It did not matter, therefore, that their brothers developed other interests, whether exotic or philanthropic. They could be indulged, even encouraged, as long as their behaviour did not disgrace the family name. But now luck was running out. The ageing men who had ruled the Rothschild empire during the expansive years of the late nineteenth century now had to hand their crowns on to less gifted

*Apart from the crop of daughters sired by Mayer Carl and Willy Carl.

heirs. Moreover, those heirs would have to operate in a vastly different world, a world such as Natty or Alphonse could not have imagined even in their worst nightmares.

Lord Rothschild and his German-born wife had three children, whose births were spread over nine years. The first was Walter who grew into a very attractive child. After a visit to his brother's family at Tring in 1879, Leo reported that young Walter had shown him his birds and butterflies.[1] Natty's elder son, at that time aged eleven, had already been, for at least six years, a prodigious collector. In his case, the family trait showed itself in a love of and feeling for animals. Birds, butterflies, moths, eggs — he avidly sought all manner of specimens, which he then mounted, studied and catalogued with meticulous care. He read voraciously, wrote letters to various experts, and paid countless visits to the Natural History Museum in London, often exciting the amazement of the curators by his precocious knowledge. By the age of thirteen his personal museum was so extensive that an assistant had to be employed to help him look after it.

It seems that, for many years, Natty did not recognise Walter's interest for what it was, an overmastering passion. Doubtless he thought, or hoped, that the museum was a laudable hobby which his son could combine with banking, just as other members of the family managed to be experts in painting, manuscripts or horses *as well as* finance. Thus Walter was sent to be educated at Bonn and Cambridge (though Natty did allow himself the observation in a letter to Rosebery "to my disgust he wants to study anatomy")[2] and at the appropriate time he was brought into the bank. In 1899 he became MP for Aylesbury in succession to Ferdinand. Like other members of the family, he took a commission with the Bucks Yeomanry. In fact, the first Lord Rothschild did everything possible to force his son and heir into the square hole of family responsibility and obligation, despite all the evidence that he was an irremediably round peg.

For Walter displayed other characteristics to which Natty could not permanently blind himself. First, and most obviously, he suffered from an appalling speech defect. He could not readily form his thoughts into words. This made conversation a slow and embarrassing ordeal, punctuated by extended silences during which Walter stared helplessly into space, struggling for expression. This, allied with his father's disapproval and his own sense of inadequacy, made it difficult for him to sustain relationships and drove him in upon himself. In effect, he became the classic eccentric whose conduct arose, not from a desire to shock, but from an inability to grasp precisely what behaviour was expected of him. Thus he outraged senior members of the House of Commons by appearing in the chamber in a white top hat. His career at Bonn ended abruptly after an affair with his landlord's daughter and he left Cambridge equally suddenly (though the reason is not known). One of his scribbled letters to his mother written during his undergraduate days gives us a fleeting glimpse of his unorthodox mental processes:

> On my return here on Friday I attended the first big dinner I have attended (55 people) and I am quite sure it is the last for I was nearly killed because I would not drink and tried to get out before the toasts began. It ended in my flying home through the streets as hard as I could run without cap or coat or anything except my evening dress. Mr Hugh Smith is here on a visit to his sons. I have no news of any kind.

> Your affec WALTER[3]

In 1894 Walter had some zebras delivered to Tring but instead of turning them loose in the park, along with his father's peacocks and ornamental pheasants and his own ostriches and giant tortoises, he had them installed in the stables. It seemed perfectly reasonable to try to train them as harness animals. For months he worked with patience and ingenuity on these notoriously unbiddable creatures. At last he had them working, although they would obey no one but him, and was able to astonish passers-by with the sight of an extraordinary equipage in The Mall — three zebras and a pony harnessed to a carriage as a four-in-hand. He bowled along right into the courtyard of Buckingham Palace. However, even Walter was alarmed when Princess Alexandra came out to see the remarkable sight and wanted to pat one of the not-wholly-predictable creatures.

Walter was becoming a figure of fun — hardly suitable for the heir of a great banker and an English peer. But worse was to come. For, if Walter was shy and awkward in company, this did not prevent him being a very devil with women. He had a number of affairs with actresses and young socialites, which would not, perhaps, have mattered had he not felt guilty and been very secretive about his liaisons. This gave an appalling opportunity to one of his mistresses, a young and unscrupulous peeress.

This dreadful woman, realising Walter's inherent character defects, set about systematically blackmailing him. Moreover, she kept up this pressure for over forty years. It is difficult for us to understand why Walter submitted to these repeated demands rather than "come clean" about his sexual adventures, which, as far as we can tell, were not outrageously reprehensible. Once again, we have to acknowledge those repeated traits which afflicted generations of Rothschilds. Walter was intimidated by family tradition. He could not bear the thought of his parents discovering his "discreditable" behaviour. Anything was preferable to that. So he resorted to that secrecy which came so naturally to Natty's son. No one must ever know about the blackmailing peeress. He almost succeeded in keeping his guilty secret. Only after his death did his sister-in-law and his niece discover some letters which had accidentally escaped the traditional Rothschild bonfire and which revealed the details of the aristocratic harpy's extortions.

Walter's financial situation, already hopelessly extended, got completely out of control. He was spending enormous sums on his museum (since 1889 housed in a special building covering one and a half acres, and open to the public), sending collectors all over the world for new specimens, buying up collections (a furious row broke out when his father discovered that he had agreed to pay fifteen thousand pounds for a collection of insects) and incurring ever-increasing running costs. So clamorous were his creditors and rival mistresses that he could not bring himself to open his correspondence; letters were thrown into a laundry basket and shut away in a cupboard at Tring. At New Court he was far from pulling his weight. Much of his time was spent writing to scientists and members of the public who inundated him with offers of rare specimens and animal freaks. According to a popular story, Natty was not best pleased to arrive at the bank one day to find his way barred by a man with two brown bears on a leash "for Mr Walter".

It is scarcely to be wondered at that Lord Rothschild was getting near the end of his tether with his elder son. Behaviour that would have been tolerable had Walter been one among several brothers was insupportable in his heir. As this extraordinary man's biographer points out:

> Walter got under his skin. We do not know precisely at what stage of his life Natty, figuratively speaking, threw up his hands in despair and wrote him off; but his mother, his brother, his curators, his sister-in-law, his mistresses, his niece and his valet, who bullied him, sustained him, helped him, loved him, nannied him and regarded him with humourous respect or bewildered affection, all eventually abandoned any serious attempt at understanding Walter – a wayward genius, or rogue elephant, overgrown schoolboy or world-famous zoologist, walking encyclopaedia or half-baked eccentric, romantic lover or figure of fun, into whatever category they mentally placed him. Moreover, no one had previously known anyone remotely like Walter. They were all baffled . . . In fact Walter never confided in anyone, nor was he intimate with a living soul, for he had erected an impregnable defensive wall of awkward unintelligible silence around himself.[4]

The parting of the ways came in 1908 when Natty discovered that, in a desperate effort to recover his financial situation, Walter had been

316

speculating wildly on the Stock Exchange and was even rumoured to have negotiated loans against the security of his "expectations" when his parents died. Poor Walter had become an open scandal, and society gossips relished Natty's discomfiture:

Walter Rothschild is on the verge of bankruptcy. Papa has already paid his debts once or twice: now, he has speculated, he had expended huge sums upon a rather indifferent book about extinct birds, and they say that a lady friend has absorbed many shekels.

Anyhow poor fat Walter has raised money on the post-obits of papa and mamma. The former is furious: most of all that for the first time in history a Rothschild has speculated unsuccessfully. It is a great blow to the acumen of the family. They say that a meeting of the Tribe will be summoned at Frankfurt or Vienna, or wherever the financial headquarters are, so that Walter may be tied up more severely in the future.[5]

There was no meeting of "the Tribe". The miscreant's father simply took the firm action that he probably should have taken years before. He appointed his second son, Charles, to sort out the mess. It took days but eventually the creditors were paid, the young ladies were handsomely compensated and sent away, Walter was relieved of his post at New Court and made an allowance which would enable him to carry on his museum in blissful seclusion. Only the problem of the blackmailing peeress remained. For Walter, in baring his soul to Charles, had not been able to bring himself to confess to that sordid business. Banished to Tring, Walter could now concentrate all his energies on creating the finest private collection of natural history specimens in the world and producing a succession of scholarly studies which would make him one of the leading zoologists of his age.

Charles Rothschild[6] shared his brother's passion for natural history and his thirst for knowledge. He wrote his first published work, *The Lepidoptera of Harrow*, while still a schoolboy, and before the age of twenty-six had been round the world twice and visited several of the planet's remoter regions to indulge his hobbies of butterfly collecting and photography. By that time, also, he owned his own nature reserve. It came about like this: as an undergraduate at Cambridge during the 1890s, he often used to cycle over to Ashton, near Oundle, to visit the untamed woodland, abounding in wild flowers, insects and rare butterflies (including the Chequered Skipper, the search for which first brought him to Ashton). At length, he decided to try to buy some of the acreage to protect it from development (land, especially uncleared woodland, was very cheap at that time). But when he made local enquiries, he was told that the estate belonged to

317

an eccentric peer who would certainly not sell. "What's his name?" Charles asked. "Lord Rothschild", was the answer. Natty, it transpired, had acquired the land in lieu of a debt repayment. He was only too happy to let Charles "do something with it". But he went further. When Charles was away soon afterwards on an extended foreign tour, his father sent some of his workmen from Tring to Ashton. They built a modest manor house in the Elizabethan style and, soon after his return, Charles was able to move into Ashton Wold.

Charles would have loved to have settled at Ashton, pursuing, like his brother, the quiet life of a naturalist, conservationist and research scientist, but that was out of the question. Someone had to shoulder the burden discarded by Walter. Apart from his brother, he was the eldest English Rothschild of his generation and he possessed what Walter did not, a strong sense of family duty.

English Rothschilds 1880-1914

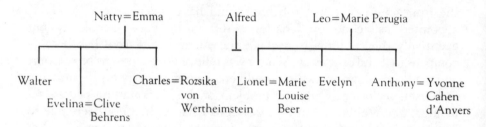

In fact, a sense of responsibility was probably his strongest characteristic. His daughter, Miriam, says: "My father was the most public-spirited man I ever met." He frequently received specimens from other people for identification and comment, and he kept a sign on his laboratory bench which stated "Other People's Property Comes First". He was extremely sensitive. Poverty, misery and injustice affected him deeply, as did the realisation that others did not live up to his high ideals. He was, for example, thunderstruck to learn that Edward Montague had actually bid at auction *against* the British Museum for a collection of butterflies.

Charles, following his father's example, was an exemplary landlord. On taking over his new estate, he found most of the properties in Ashton in a sad state of disrepair. He had all the cottages renovated or rebuilt using local stone and Norfolk reed. The mill was fitted with electric pumping machinery which brought piped water into every home, serving not only the kitchens but the new bathrooms Charles had installed (a real innovation in 1900).

By dint of working an eighteen-hour day, Charles managed to carry out his duties as landowner *and* his scientific studies while also fulfilling his responsibilities at New Court. He collected iris, birds' eggs and various entomological species. But his principal interest was fleas. These parasites had fascinated him since the age of twelve. By the time of his death he had described about five hundred new species and sub-species of fleas, and written a hundred and fifty papers on them. It was a frequent source of amusement that a member of the rich and exalted Rothschild family could devote his time and money to such humble and loathsome creatures. One newspaper columnist reported, quite erroneously, that Mr Rothschild had spent ten thousand pounds on a new flea for his collection. Only professional entomologists can appreciate the true value of Charles's pioneering work in the field but one piece of research was of a more obvious value. This was his discovery of the most important plague-carrying species, a rat-borne flea parasite.

Charles was a pioneer, or perhaps "visionary" would be a better word, in another area: he was virtually the inventor of modern nature conservation. In 1912 he formed the Society for the Promotion of Nature Reserves, the object of which was to conserve important natural habitats, rather than to protect single rare species of animals and plants. His first major undertaking for the society was the compilation of a survey of the most important potential habitat reserves in the British Isles. He listed no less than 284, all of which he had personally selected and surveyed. This was to serve as a basis for all future surveys of this sort executed by the Nature Conservancy when they came into being forty years later.

In politics also he was something of a pioneer, diverging from his father, and, indeed, from the rest of the family (when Lionel, Leo's son, stood for parliament it was on a Conservative ticket). Although he never voted, Charles regarded himself as a "socialist with individualistic tendencies". His attitude was a natural extension of the sensitive social conscience he inherited from his parents. For although Natty was a *laissez-faire* capitalist in theory, he remained in practice a benevolent paternalist with a keen sense of social justice to the end of his days.

It was at the bank that the forward-looking Charles found his ideas and suggested innovations met with least approval. For example, he returned from a trip to Japan convinced of the commercial importance of that country, which had made the transition from feudalism to a modern industrial economy in little more than a generation. But his insistence that a Rothschild branch should be established in Tokyo fell on deaf ears. Similarly, he failed to convince Natty, Alfred and Leo of the growing importance of copper. As to his suggestion that there was a real future in

319

the new invention called the gramophone record – that was dismissed as a very odd idea.[7]

The fact was that, in their commercial dealings, the London Rothschilds had entered upon a very cautious phase. Few of the ventures they were involved in could be dubbed "speculative". They had a large investment in South Africa and helped to pioneer the Transvaal railway. Their traditional links with Brazil carried them into transport and industrial developments there. But very little risk attached to these enterprises. In 1892 NMR gave its support to the first national telephone service but this was only after thirteen years during which various pioneer companies had explored the ground and eventually decided to amalgamate. Sometimes, of course, timidity was justified by events. In 1911 Natty declined an opportunity to share in underwriting the *Titanic*. When asked, after the ship's sinking, if he had had some premonition of disaster, the elderly peer dismissed the suggestion in a typical brief, gruff sentence: "No; she just looked too big to float."[8]

The observation has often been made that the Edwardian era was like a balmy Indian summer. The metaphor may be trite but it seems very apt when applied to the daily, self-assured, tradition-bound routine at New Court. Old members of the staff remember the partners arriving in their motor cars, the way through the City traffic having been cleared for them by respectful police officers, and being greeted in the courtyard by a line of saluting couriers. New Court was a timeless little cosmos with an established hierarchy in which every man knew his place. The mahogany, brass and leather upholstery might have been there since the Creation. Any suggestion of modernising the decor or layout would have been a heresy of Darwinian proportions. Newfangled inventions like the telephone and the typewriter had insinuated themselves into a few corners of the building but they were only accepted on sufferance. No wonder Charles, the visionary, sometimes despaired of dragging the bank into the twentieth century.

Of course, Rothschild paternalism presided over all. Once a year the genial Leopold with gardenia buttonhole and protective handkerchief spread over his waistcoat front, dispensed the annual bonuses from a pile of crisp white banknotes. And cases of special need never failed to evoke a generous response. "One man, suffering from a chest complaint, was sent by Leopold to Switzerland to recuperate and later to Australia for six months; another, distraught by the death of his wife, was given a trip by sea round the world."[9] All staff were pensioned and, as well as the annual bonus, they received numerous payments to mark special occasions, such as Christmas and royal celebrations. When Natty died he bequeathed everyone at New Court a year's salary. Then there were the casual

320

handouts so typical of Rothschild munificence. One employee recalls how this arrangement worked:

> In the prosperous days before 1914, in addition to annual bonuses, called "touchings", presents were often given at Christmas and for summer holidays, and tips were sometimes handed out on birthdays and other anniversaries. A man would announce to the partners that it was his silver wedding, and be rewarded with twenty-five sovereigns; another would mention with an elaborately casual air that he had just completed thirty years' service with the firm and emerge from The Room richer by that number of good pre-war pounds. Some men would contrive by this sort of means to double their basic salaries, which in any case were by the standards of the period not small; and when it is realised that the relatively negligible income tax then levied on their emoluments was also paid by the firm it will be easily understood that our predecessors of sixty and seventy years ago sometimes seem to us to have been on velvet. [10]

To be sure, such reminiscences have about them a nostalgic ring. The "good old days" only exist in our selective memories. For example, although "Mr Leo" was the most popular of the three brothers, and much loved, he was not universally admired. One day in March 1912, as he was driving away from New Court, a would-be assassin, William Tebbitt, stepped forward with a gun. The Rothschild detective immediately grappled with him. There was a shot. The detective was wounded in the neck. But he survived, the criminal was apprehended and Leopold was saved.

Yet, as we have seen, the Rothschilds were, generally, popular and it was precisely their little acts of generosity that stuck in people's minds and coloured their attitudes. They knew that Natty paid for the annual Jews' Free School outing to Crystal Palace and that, whenever there was a procession along Piccadilly, the policemen who lined the route could always pop into 147-8 for a three-course meal. When the 10th Battalion of the Bucks Yeomanry returned from the Boer War Natty provided the officers and men with a "lunch" of which few of them had ever seen the like:

The Menu
Cold Salmon, Sauce Tartare
Surrey Chicken & Tongue
York Ham and Jelly
Pigeon Pie
Sirloin of Beef
Veal and Ham Pie

321

Hind Quarter of Lamb and Mint Sauce
Salad
Fruit Tartlets
Champagne Jelly
Charlotte Russe
Cheese & Biscuits
Strawberries & Cream
Hock Cup Claret Cup Beer
Aerated water

After the meal, Natty gave each man a silver watch.[11]

There is something strange — almost touching — in the prospect of this stern-faced, grey wraith of a man, who found it impossible to give himself to others in warm, human relationships, giving himself so unstintingly to the people. The bank employees, his tenants and thousands of East Enders all knew about Lord Rothschild's building projects, his charitable works, his acts of personal generosity, and they regarded the name "Rothschild" with genuine warmth. Many years later an old Leadenhall market trader still remembered him with affection: "... he had the common touch ... we felt *he was on our side*. We all felt we knew him. Everyone trusted him from the King to the sandwich man."[12]

But Lord Rothschild found himself increasingly out of sympathy with the politicians. In 1895 the Unionists were returned in increased numbers largely because of a pledge to introduce old-age pensions. A committee was set up under Lord Rothschild's chairmanship to work out a suitable system. When they reported that, in their opinion, the idea of state pensions was not practicable, they provoked outraged protest from many parliamentarians, notable among them David Lloyd George. Natty criticised many of the measures brought in by the progressive Campbell-Bannerman and Asquith administrations between 1906 and 1911. He rejected the basic concept of increasing taxation to finance social benefits on the grounds that this removed incentives for the capitalist to employ his money and the indigent worker to apply his labour. Asquith and his Chancellor, Lloyd George, seemed to him guilty of every kind of folly. They were even proposing to give women the vote! The government went on its determined way and Natty came out more and more openly in opposition. In 1909 he chaired a City meeting called to protest at Lloyd George's celebrated budget of that year which raised taxes to pay for a national pension scheme and increased naval spending to counter the threat posed by Germany's massive rearmament. Lloyd George responded with one of his more famous oratorical tirades:

I think we are having too much Lord Rothschild. We are not to have temperance reform in this country. Why not? Because Lord Rothschild has sent a circular to the peers to say so. We must have more dreadnoughts. Why? Because Lord Rothschild said so at a meeting in the City. We must not pay for them when we have them. Why? Because Lord Rothschild said so at another meeting. You must not have estate duties and a super-tax. Why? Because Lord Rothschild signed a protest on behalf of the bankers to say he would not stand it. You must not have a tax on reversions. Why? Because Lord Rothschild as Chairman of an Insurance Company, has said that it would not do. You must not have a tax on undeveloped land. Why? Because Lord Rothschild is Chairman of an Industrial Dwellings Company. You ought not to have old age pensions. Why? Because Lord Rothschild was a member of a committee that said it could not be done. Now, really, I should like to know, is Lord Rothschild the dictator of this country? Are we really to have all the ways of reform, financial and social, blocked simply by a notice-board, "No thoroughfare. By order of Nathaniel Rothschild"?[13]

The French bank was as hidebound as its British counterpart. Edmond, always a reluctant financier, provided the link between his older brothers and the men of the new generation, Edouard and Robert. Their leadership, in the period before the First World War, could not be called dynamic. "The Parisian Rothschilds had grown tired after their long years as international financiers. The several hundred millions they had accumulated were enough for them. From then on they only wanted to manage their capital quietly."[14] That statement from the Viennese newspaper the *Neue Freie Presse*, when shorn of its journalistic hyperbole, is probably not far from the truth. Yet even when they were apparently slumbering, the Rothschilds sometimes found success falling into their lap — as the case of Royal Dutch Shell indicates.

In 1910 Henry Ditterding (of the Royal Dutch Petroleum Company) and Marcus Samuel (of the Shell Transport and Trading Company) began acquiring Caucasian oilfields. Then, in 1912, they made their really "major coup". They approached De Rothschild Frères who owned two oil companies which were stagnating.

Their oil companies had declared no dividends for a couple of years and they were angry about the latest pogroms in Russia. All they wanted was to pull out of the tsar's dominions. Ditterding and

Marcus Samuel acquired this inheritance. They obtained the two big Rothschild companies in the Caucasus — the Banito and the Mazut — for a laughable sum. Rothschilds received 4 million gulden worth of Royal Dutch Shares and £240,000 worth of Shell shares . . . [15]

It was probably Edmond, more than ever involved with his Palestinian settlements, who wanted the bank to shake the Russian dust from its feet but, in purely commercial terms, relinquishing its share of the oil industry at such a time certainly seemed rather hasty. In fact, the deal turned out extremely well. Royal Dutch Shell became the second largest oil company in the world and maintained this position despite difficulties with the post-revolutionary regime in Russia. De Rothschild Frères had been paid for their oilfields with "laughable" Shell shares which increased vastly in value over the years. Furthermore, by selling they had avoided losing millions in a Bolshevik confiscation of their assets after 1917. It had all been a most marvellous piece of good luck. Of course, rivals were convinced that it was just another example of Rothschild cunning.

The French Rothschilds were even more committed to charity and social reform than their English cousins. In the early years of the century they embarked on a prodigious programme of innovative philanthropy. Their various charitable interests continued, especially in the medical field. From 1874 every *arrondissement* of Paris received from a Rothschild fund set up for the purpose a hundred thousand francs annually for distribution to needy families. In 1905 a sixty-two-bed hospital and out-patient centre for the treatment of eye diseases was opened on the Rue Manin (Paris 19ᵉ). The story behind its establishment illustrates the gulf between the Rothschilds and ordinary mortals and how some of them tried to bridge it. Some years before, Adolph had suffered the minor irritation of getting some ash in his eye. Naturally, he had consulted one of the leading specialists of the day. This doctor pointed out to him, perhaps tetchily, that most people suffering far worse ailments could not afford professional attention. In his will, therefore, Adolph provided for the Fondation Ophtalmologique Adolph de Rothschild to provide free surgery and medication for the citizens of Paris.

The French family's most imaginative innovation was the pioneering of public housing. Alphonse, Gustave and Edmond set up the Fondation Rothschild in 1904 to provide economic housing units (*habitations à bon marché* — HBM) in the working-class district of Paris.* This was an event of major importance in the history of social progress in France. As usual,

*This was distinct from the Fondations Rothschild, begun by James, which became an umbrella organisation for a variety of social and medical projects.

the Rothschilds thought big. The building projects they undertook were financed on a quite unprecedented scale. They were planned by some of the leading architects of the day, and only built after extensive research throughout Europe and America into working-class housing units. The apartment blocks were not designed to be purely functional: gardens and courtyards featured prominently and interior communal areas were decorated with murals and coloured tiles. The latest developments in hygienic medicine were built in. The Rothschild tenements were among the first to be equipped with gas and electricity. They incorporated laundry rooms, refuse collection services, fitted cupboards, piped water. The planners tried to consider and make provisions for all the needs of the communities which would occupy the tenements. They provided dispensaries, nurseries and after-school care for children of working parents, grocery stores, and even a scheme for hiring thermometers so that tenants could monitor their own health. Preventive medicine was a built-in feature. Records were kept of every family's births, deaths, marriages, diseases and ailments, with the objective of compiling valuable statistics which could be used to improve living conditions.

As one writer has said, it is not surprising that the first of these new-style apartment blocks was called "the Louvre of working-class habitation". "It was effectively *a museum* which displayed all the theories and technical achievements in the field of popular housing, but it was also a *village* planned to bring together all aspects of life . . . Finally it was a *school* where the workers, freed from their hovels, could learn how to live in the best possible conditions."[16]

It was social engineering. It was paternalistic. It was an attempt to provide by private enterprise what the Rothschilds believed the state could not and should not provide. In conception and execution it was magnificent and, in its way, it marked the apogee of Rothschild influence just as clearly as the gilded palaces they inhabited or the government policies they helped to formulate. But, in reality, it is not possible to divorce the wealth from the social concern and the political influence. All three were still considerable around the turn of the twentieth century. But the times were changing.

CHAPTER 23
"His Majesty's Government view with favour"

The psychological and emotional impact of the First World War was greater than a later generation can probably appreciate. It was not just the sordid carnage of the trenches and the decimation of a continent's youth that shook ordinary men and women and undermined the confidence of nations; it was the reluctant realisation that the old, familiar Europe also lay bleeding to death in the Flanders mud. For the Rothschilds the conflict was even more traumatic than it was for many of their contemporaries.

It was the Armageddon that the older members of the family had warned against and done all in their power to prevent. Most of them would not live to see its conclusion but there was little doubt in their minds what the war would mean for their children and grandchildren: Rothschilds would be fighting on opposite sides for the first (and only) time, forced to choose between country and family. Lives and fortunes would be put at risk and at the end of it all nations would lie exhausted and commerce ruined. Centuries-old royal dynasties would have collapsed or been reduced to political insignificance. The old Europe, the Europe which had made the Rothschilds and which the Rothschilds had helped to make, would be no more. The Continent's affairs would no longer be determined by courts and cabals, nor would wealthy private bankers be able to influence great events by agreeing to lend a few millions here or by dropping a word in the appropriate ear there. Perhaps the old men had no real wish to survive the Europe they had grown up in. There was certainly a fatalism about the way in which they donated their country estates to be trampled by training soldiery and submitted to those heavy taxes they had always rejected as bad economic policy. These were patriotic gestures but they were gestures made by men whose hearts were heavy with foreboding.

On 13 August 1914, nine days after the outbreak of war, Lloyd George wrote to his brother, William, "Just received a letter signed by the Rothschilds congratulating me on the way I had tackled the greatest difficulty that has ever occurred in the finances of this country." [1] True to family tradition, Natty did not allow his personal views to qualify his support of the government in a time of crisis. He hastened to place the resources of himself and the bank at the disposal of Prime Minister Asquith and his cabinet. He was present at a meeting of leading economists, financiers and industrialists summoned by Lloyd George, the Chancellor of the Exchequer, to discuss ways of preventing panic in the City and setting the war effort on a sound footing. The Welshman's comment after the discussion was, "Only the old Jew made sense".[2] Despite their disagreements, the two men had a great respect for each other. Years later, when Lloyd George was asked to name, from among all the men he had known, the members of his ideal cabinet, he said, without hesitation, "Lord Rothschild as Chancellor".[3] Natty was a pragmatist and not a theoretician. His views on government intervention and social reform financed out of revenue were well known; but he was among the first to advocate greatly increased income tax to finance the military conflict.

English Rothschilds 1914-39

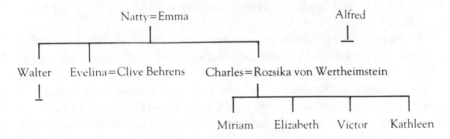

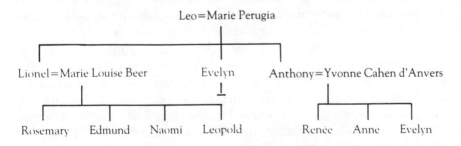

The elderly Lord Rothschild was now in his seventy-fifth year and had only a few months to live. Yet, to the end, and despite failing health, Lord Rothschild did everything in his power to aid his country. At his own expense he had a large consignment of rifles brought over from America because the War Ministry was short of training weapons.[4] Lord Haldane,

327

a close friend of the family, recalled paying a visit to Natty's Piccadilly home early in 1915 to seek the old man's help. He was temporarily in charge of the Foreign Office and was concerned about a ship *en route* from South America which was breaching neutrality by carrying supplies for the Germans. He found Natty lying down and obviously very ill, but he greeted his guest cheerfully. "Haldane, I do not know what you are come for except to see me, but I have said to myself that if Haldane asks me to write a cheque for him for £25,000 and to ask no questions, I will do it on the spot." The minister explained his problem and, immediately, Lord Rothschild sent a message which resulted in the ship being stopped.[5] Days later he died. Tributes arrived by the sackload and glowing obituaries appeared in the newspapers but the most remarkable testimonial of all was an immense crowd of people which thronged the route of his very simple funeral cortège on a bleak April morning in 1915. Lloyd George remarked: "The streets to the cemetery were lined with poor Jews who were there to pay their humble tribute of reverence to the great prince of Israel, who never forgot the poor and wretched amongst his people."[6] But it was not only Natty's co-religionists who turned out to pay their last respects. Thousands of other men and women had cause to be grateful to the first Lord Rothschild.

For Charles, Natty's younger son, the war was disastrous, probably fatal. His health had never been robust. He was one of those people whose moods fluctuate between euphoria and depression. Shouldering those bank and family responsibilities which Walter had proved unable to share proved an immense strain. Then, in 1906, he found Rozsika, and suddenly the world seemed an infinitely brighter place. Rozsika von Wertheimstein came from a Hungarian Jewish family of impressive ancestry and slender resources. Charles met her while he was on holiday in the Carpathians and loved her instantly and deeply. She possessed beauty and athleticism (she was Hungarian ladies' tennis champion and was the first woman to perfect the overarm serve). She also possessed a brilliant intelligence which impressed all who met her. And she was extremely capable. She was seven years older than Charles and strong-willed, a perfect support for a man easily bowed down by anxieties and poor health. Perhaps unconsciously, he recognised in her the mother figure he lacked; for he had always felt, not without cause, that his own mother had lavished all her affection on her "favourite", Walter.

The couple were married in 1907 and, by the outbreak of war, they had had four children. In the summer of 1914 they took their two elder daughters to Hungary to see their uncles and aunts. Charles, who could not bear to contemplate the prospect of armed conflict, took an optimistic view of the international situation, and was happily chasing butterflies in the forest around Oradea (then known as Nagyvarad) when a telegram arrived from his father, warning him of the danger he and his family faced if they did not return immediately. Charles and Rozsika hurried westwards. Travelling partly by train, partly on foot, carrying the tired and bewildered children, it took them a week to reach Dover. They arrived within hours of the outbreak of war.

The next four years added intolerably to Charles's burden of anxiety. He was by conviction both an internationalist and a pacifist, but now Europe was caught up in the most devastating war in its history and his own and his wife's relatives were fighting in rival armies. Charles also had enormous problems at home. After Natty's death, he took over as senior partner of NMR — but only after a row with his uncles. Lionel was kept back from the front to help him (see below) but his other cousins were on active service. The burden he had to shoulder at New Court was, therefore, considerable and it increased when Leo and Alfred died during the war. In addition, Charles had to sort out his late father's estate, which involved, for the first time in the family's history, the payment of heavy death duties. As if all that were not enough, Rozsika had to endure the unreasoning hatred of many British people who were violent in their attitudes towards anyone with Austrian connections.

At the end of 1916 Charles's health broke down completely and he had to go to Switzerland for a rest cure. Yet his absence from England did not distance him from his multifarious concerns. Fortunately, as his daughter points out, Rozsika who stayed at home, was more than equal to the task of deputising for him.

> ... Glancing through his letters from Switzerland one finds him asking her to deal with the following matters: Frohawk who was to make 100 drawings of adult butterflies, a trust deed which Lord Haldane was to look at, the purchase of land in Essex as a Nature Reserve, Sharpe who had ten daughters — and needed a job, the pension problems at New Court, the plans for making small 10 oz gold bars for use in India after the war, the changes in the sale of quicksilver, the payment of Uncle Alfred's death duties, smelting of "sweep" at the Refinery, the separation of the Bullion Department from New Court, cuttings of *Dianthus* from the weed garden at Ashton, the sale of Rio Tinto shares, purchase of the sporting rights at the Reservoir ... There were hundreds of requests and problems to tackle.[7]

Charles returned to England in time to fall a prey to the influenza pandemic of 1918. This appalling scourge, comparable to the Black Death in terms of mortality rate, claimed twenty million lives worldwide and affected fifty times as many people with serious illness. For Charles Rothschild it brought on *encephalitis lethargica*, a disease of the brain marked by profound listlessness, sleepiness and melancholia. As with other forms of encephalitis (multiple sclerosis and rabies, for example), there was no cure but this particular form of the disease was not a killer. So Charles went on from day to day, suffering attacks, varying in severity, which were almost as distressing for his family as they were for himself. Often his wife and children had to engage him in energetic conversation or hammer out music on the piano in order to keep him awake. [8]

Other Rothschilds were more directly involved in the First World War. Charles's cousins, Lionel, Evelyn and Anthony, were the members of the English family most eligible for service. They were all officers in the Bucks Yeomanry and all, in those early days of the war, when it was generally believed that there would be a swift and glorious outcome to the conflict, were anxious to serve. Lionel, the eldest, fully expected to go to the front but he was forbidden to do so — by the highest authority. King George V, an old friend of the family, was concerned that one of the young Rothschilds should remain at the bank throughout the war. In 1914 Lionel's father, Leopold, and his uncles were all old men, and Charles was in poor health. It was a sensible decision but one which had a profound effect on Lionel. The whole country was caught up in a frenzy of blind patriotism. Recruiting officers visited every town and village urging the male population to prove their manhood. And off the brave lads marched — bands playing, wives and sweethearts crying tears of mingled sorrow and pride — determined to "do their bit" for King and Country. Many of those who did not go, for whatever reason, found it difficult to avoid feelings of guilt and shame. Some received anonymous white feathers through the post. All read reproach in the faces of those who had sacrificed loved ones. That was why Lionel resented so deeply the decision which kept him at home while brothers, friends and bank employees went to spill their blood for the homeland. Lionel devoted much time to recruiting but his sense of disappointment had a permanent effect: he became reclusive, turned in upon himself, a man who enjoyed solitude.

What made matters worse was that Lionel's brothers served with great distinction. Evelyn went to the Western Front and was invalided home in November 1915. Within months he was back in action and in March 1916 he was mentioned in despatches by General Sir Charles Monro. Meanwhile, Anthony had been involved in the ill-fated Gallipoli campaign. Allied troops, attempting to force the Dardanelles, spent over eight months of hell on the beaches lining the straits, pinned down by fire from

Turkish forts and gun emplacements. The only successful part of the operation, from the British point of view, was the evacuation of the army in January 1916. By that time Anthony had become one of thousands of casualties who were removed, with difficulty, to hospital ships offshore. The failure of the Gallipoli campaign enabled the Turks to commit forces to the Middle East to threaten the Suez Canal and British oil interests. To forestall this, considerable reinforcements were sent to Sinai and Palestine. It was to this battlefront that the two Rothschilds now went.

The fighting there involved a slow northwards advance, largely through inhospitable desert and scrub, dislodging the enemy laboriously from a succession of strongholds. In one of these engagements Evelyn was killed. He was thirty and unmarried. Beside him fell his friend and relative Neil Primrose, elder son and heir of Lord Rosebery.

It was not only the younger Rothschilds who made sacrifices. Natty and Alfred gave large areas of Buckinghamshire parkland to the military authorities for the duration of the war and Aston Clinton became a divisional headquarters. Thousands of raw recruits were trained on the pleasant acres where once the Rothschilds and their guests had shot pheasants. The avenues, glades and coverts laid out with such care by landscape gardeners disappeared beneath rows of tents and huts, trenches, drill squares, rifle ranges and barbed wire.

For Alfred the outbreak of hostilities was particularly sad. Most of his life he had been a highly strung hypochondriac. He took fastidious care of his health and had his doctor call every day to give him a check-up. Now a nervous, little old man, he found the war quite devastating. He lived in constant dread of being blown to bits in an air raid and had a large wire net erected over his town house in the belief that this would foil the German bombs.

Worse even than the physical fear was the shattering of his dreams. Alfred had, for many years, been convinced that close relationships — even a formal alliance — between Britain and Germany would be the best foundation for the preservation of peace. In the closing years of the nineteenth century, during which the two nations clashed in various colonial arenas, he had taken a personal initiative to disarm rivalries. He had arranged unofficial meetings between government ministers and German ambassadors at Halton and Seymour Place. In 1892 he had even written to von Bülow, the German Chancellor, to protest that Berlin was doing little to ease the tension.

> . . . for some years, the German Press has constantly written against England; indeed . . . I am well aware that the Press in Germany is free, as it is in England, and that it will not have its policy prescribed

331

for it, but when the Press of a country spreads rumours about a friendly Power that are absolutely false, the government could have well taken the first convenient opportunity of stating how much it regrets that such false statements have been given currency.

This has occurred with regard to our Expeditionary Force in South Africa, and such allegations have not merely made the Germans resident in this country indignant . . . people here would have been glad to hear that the caricatures of our Royal Family, which were sold in the streets of Germany, had been confiscated by the police — in a word, of recent years Germany's policy towards England has been a kind of "pinprick" policy, and, although a pin is not a very impressive instrument, repeated pricks may cause a wound.[9]

But few people in high places paid much attention to the faintly absurd figure of Alfred de Rothschild. He lacked the intellectual and moral stature of other members of the family who had, over the years, been listened to with respect in the chancelleries of Europe. Briefly, between January and April 1901, the policy he advocated had come close to being achieved. Alfred had helped to set up meetings between Lord Lansdowne, the Foreign Secretary, Joseph Chamberlain, the leading Liberal Unionist, and German representatives, aimed at concluding a defensive alliance. But the talks had fizzled out. British foreign policy had remained, for the time being, isolationist and public opinion (as in Germany) was hostile. The ensuing years had seen the two countries making pacts with other nations *against* each other, until armed conflict became inevitable.

In his last years, Alfred was sad, lonely and frightened. Many of his old companions were no more (Marie Wombwell died in 1913). His world was gone and, in melancholy despair, he gave up the symbols of it. Halton, the scene of his wildly extravagant and sometimes scandalous revels, he abandoned. Army officers were billeted in the house. Huts and tents studded the lawns. Canadian lumberjacks hacked down the beech woods to make props and duckboards for the trenches.[10]

The loss of family and friends in the war affected him deeply, none more so than the death of Lord Kitchener who had been a frequent guest at Seymour Place and Halton in the "good old days". The Secretary of State for War and the man behind the massive recruiting drive, which increased the army from twenty to seventy divisions, was lost at sea in 1916. Alfred survived him by only eighteen months. In his will he left twenty-five thousand pounds to the memorial fund, "being desirous of doing something to honour the late Lord Kitchener".

Nearby Waddesdon did not suffer the same depredations as Halton. But even there the war made its mark. Miss Alice, the "all-powerful one", she of the immaculate lawns and neat herbaceous borders, had inherited the estate when her brother, Ferdinand, died at the age of fifty-nine in 1898. This martinet ran a very tight ship at Waddesdon. Whenever she went out, six liveried footmen had to line up outside the mansion's impressive entrance to see her into her carriage or motor car. Another servant, apart from the driver, always accompanied her on her excursions in order to open and close the vehicle's door for her. Any maid who had the bad taste to become pregnant faced instant dismissal. Yet she is remembered as a generous and fair employer with amiable eccentricities. She was a crack shot and estate workers still remember her as an old lady sitting in her special chair in the butts, picking off pheasants with the precision of a marksman. They also recall her aviary of parrots, every one of whom was trained by Miss Alice to swear like a trooper.[11] At the manor, she added to Ferdinand's embellishments, her most notable contribution being a fine collection of armour.

But it was the gardens which received her closest attention. In matters horticultural she was an expert with very precise views. She could not build on another's foundation, even her dear brother's. She effected sweeping changes in the formal gardens and the glasshouses. But then came the war and she made what was for her a great sacrifice. She ordered the velvet sward to be grown for hay and the roses to be grubbed up to make room for potatoes.

The French Rothschilds, whose homeland was invaded, remained calm throughout the war, but, then, armed conflict was not a novel experience for them. The family had survived 1830, 1848 and 1870, and the tradition of staying at one's post was a strong one. At the outbreak of hostilities most of the children were sent to their English cousins but once the stalemate of the trenches had become established they returned to Paris. Even towards the end of the war, when the Germans were forty-four miles from the capital and bombing the city from the air, the women and children were only evacuated as far as the Rothschilds' estates near Bordeaux.

Members of the family were actively involved in different ways in the war. Those young enough took part in the fighting. Henri's eldest son, James, was one of the first military aviators and years later his brother vividly recalled his envy at the young hero who returned from the fray and went everywhere with "a flutter of pretty birds around him".[12] Edmond's two sons also donned uniform. James (known as Jimmy), thirty-six at the outbreak of war, and his younger brother, Maurice, were unalike in all

333

respects except one: they were both rebels who declined to adopt those patterns of behaviour which were expected of them as Rothschilds.

French Rothschilds 1914-39

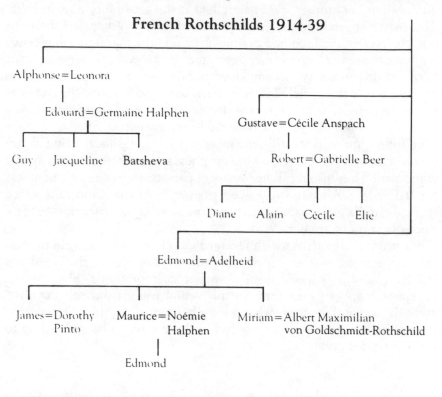

Alphonse=Leonora
Edouard=Germaine Halphen
Guy   Jacqueline   Batsheva
Gustave=Cécile Anspach
Robert=Gabrielle Beer
Diane   Alain   Cécile   Elie
Edmond=Adelheid
James=Dorothy Pinto   Maurice=Noémie Halphen   Miriam=Albert Maximilian von Goldschmidt-Rothschild
Edmond

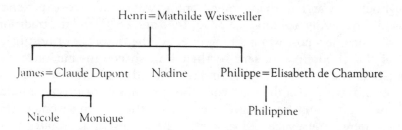

Henri=Mathilde Weisweiller
James=Claude Dupont   Nadine   Philippe=Elisabeth de Chambure
Nicole   Monique   Philippine

Maurice was dubbed, not wholly without cause, the "black sheep of the family". He was only twenty-six years old when, in 1907, he inherited from his second cousin Julie, who died childless, an immense fortune which included the Château de Pregny and all its treasures. He gave himself up to enjoying his wealth and acquiring an excellent collection of modern paintings, recognising, with typical Rothschild flair, the works of artists such as Picasso, Braque and Chagall long before they became fashionable. He was enjoying himself far too much to waste time working,

334

and when his father tried to direct him into the bank, he simply refused. This "irresponsible" attitude did not win the approval of the senior members of the family. Nor did his other escapades. There was an unending succession of women, which continued after his marriage in 1909. It was said in Paris that no young lady was safe with Baron Maurice and one girl cousin remembers being chased around a table by him when she was fifteen — and he was forty-two!

A worse offense, in Rothschild eyes, was his financial speculation. He gambled with his money on the Exchange — usually unsuccessfully. He enjoyed wild parties. His behaviour was unconventional. He was, in short, the sort of rich young man beloved by society gossip columnists. One story reported in the newspapers was about an incident when he was holidaying on the Riviera. He was swimming with a mixed party of friends when, to his annoyance, his newly bought bathing costume began to shrink. Angrily he peeled it off and marched ashore brandishing it aloft, repeating over and over again to the amused crowd which gathered, the name of the tradesman who had sold him the offending garment.

Yet there was much more to Maurice than the rich playboy. His later career was to prove that he possessed in full measure, not only the Rothschilds' sense of social responsibility, but also considerable financial flair. At the outbreak of war in 1914 he volunteered without hesitation, and because of his linguistic gifts and international contacts he was assigned to the British army as a liaison officer.

Jimmy's revolt was of shorter duration but took a much more determined form. After an enjoyable four years at Cambridge, where he spent more time studying racing form than scholarly tomes, he was faced with the — for him — unwelcome prospect of Rue Laffitte. It was not just that he had no taste for finance. He had developed a marked dislike for the land of his birth. France in the 1890s was in the midst of the Dreyfus Affair and many young Jews felt a sense of almost personal outrage at the way anti-Semitism had penetrated the highest circles of society. Jimmy made his views well known quite unequivocally and lost several friends for doing so. Rather than settle in such a reactionary world, he emigrated to Australia under an assumed name. For eighteen months, while his parents made frantic efforts to trace him, he earned his living in a variety of occupations, including bookie's runner and ranch hand. Eventually he was tracked down and returned dutifully to De Rothschild Frères. But his heart was never in it. As often as possible he travelled across the Channel and, in 1913, he married an English girl, Miss Dorothy Pinto. He became the right-hand man in Edmond's Palestinian ventures and developed almost as great a passion as his father for the settlements.

The outbreak of hostilities provided Jimmy with a welcome break from the routine of the bank. He, too, was attached to the British army. After a long spell in hospital because of an accident in which he was pinned beneath an overturned army truck, Jimmy in fact finished his war in Palestine. As the son of the immensely popular Baron Edmond, he was extremely valuable to General Allenby, the British Commander in the Middle East. One of his more spectacular activities was the raising of a battalion from the Jewish settlements, and among the men who served in it was a certain David Ben-Gurion.

Among the older generation, it was Henri and his wife who threw themselves most vigorously into the war effort. The remarkable Baron Henri found a real sense of purpose probably for the first time in his life. After the early years and the birth of three children, the marriage he had embarked on largely to escape from his mother's dominance turned sour. He and his wife lived semi-detached lives. Mathilde enjoyed the world of high Parisian society; her calendar was filled with racing and hunting engagements, balls, dinner parties and visits to the opera. Henri had inherited Rothschild traits which made dedication to such frivolity quite impossible − brilliance, industry and a deep sense of responsibility. He was a man tortured by contradictions. His interests were wide yet he had a passionate desire to excel, which meant limiting his activities. He needed to feel useful to other people yet, because of his upbringing, he found it difficult to relate to other people. He was a doctor who could not bear to be confronted with suffering. He was a paediatrician who did not understand children. He was an inventor with no conception of marketing.

As we have seen, his first impulse was to communicate through his pen. His catholic output included plays − in fact, he concentrated on them. For Henri had developed a passion for the fantasy world of the stage. When he sought company it was among actors, actresses and impresarios. Some of his fifty or so pieces were produced. But the theatrical world valued him as much for his money as his talent. Plays need backers and Baron de Rothschild was generous. And on 18 May 1909 he helped to make history.

Some months before, arrangements had been made to bring a new Russian ballet company to Paris. Then the Tsar had a row with the impresario and withdrew his support at the last moment. Rumours reaching France from St Petersburg indicated that there was something special about the troupe and the manager of the Théâtre du Châtelet was most anxious not to cancel. Henri de Rothschild came to the rescue. With two friends he underwrote the expenses of the tour. The opening performance was one of the turning points in the history of western theatre. The company was Diaghilev's Ballet Russe and the audience was stunned by the choreographic brilliance of Michel Fokine and the dancing genius of Vaslav Nijinsky and Anna Pavlova.

Henri's medical interests covered both his own work and that of other researchers. In his study and his private laboratory at L'Abbaye de Vaulx de Cernay, he performed the experiments and wrote up the notes which resulted in 127 publications on the subject of infant nutrition. He maintained a close personal interest in his own Hôpital Marcadet and made donations to several scientists in other institutions. He was particularly fascinated by the work Professor and Madame Curie were doing on the phenomenon of radioactivity. When the Institut du Radium was set up for the purpose of studying the properties of the newly discovered element, he contributed the first gram of radium bromide and later, in 1919, became one of the founders of the Fondation Curie.

But medicine and the theatre came nowhere near to exhausting this man's energy and talent. He had a passion for motor cars, so he built a factory which turned out vans and taxis under the brand name of "Unic". Other manufacturing enterprises of the Baron's produced soap and mustard. All these companies offered the public high-quality goods but they all failed or were bought up by competitors (Unic, for example, was eventually swallowed up by Renault) because Henri had no interest in day-to-day management. He never attended board meetings himself and never delegated sufficient authority to directors who could make his commercial concerns flourish.

All these projects were, in their various ways, worthwhile but they lacked an overall purpose. That purpose was provided by the war. Henri threw all his gifts into the service of his country. The industrialist turned his Unic factory over to the production of ambulances and the inventor devised a burns unit which could be conveyed by ambulance right up to the battle zone. The inventor was also busy devising airtight tubes which would keep soldiers' rations, such as meat paste and jam, fresh and germ-free. The expert on child nutrition organised a free distribution of pasteurised milk throughout Paris. Meanwhile, his wife, Mathilde, had entered the spirit of the war with no less enthusiasm. She exchanged her silks and furs for a starched nurse's uniform and won the *croix de guerre* for her work among the wounded.

Two of the Austrian Rothschilds — the only two available for service — took up arms in 1914. Of the five sons born to Salbert, the youngest was dead, and the eldest confined to a mental institution. The third son, Louis, had inherited responsibility for the bank and, therefore, could not be spared. This left Alphonse and Eugène, neither of whom was interested in business. Eugène, in fact, was a soldier. He had joined the army in his early twenties and was a lieutenant in the 6th Dragoons. Alphonse, who had married a charming and capable English wife, was of an academic bent. He took a law degree, but never practised. Being a reserve officer in the 6th Dragoons, he was called to the colours at the outbreak of war and was sent as an *Oberst-Leutnant* to the Italian front, where his brother was also serving. Like the battle of the Somme, the Italian campaign also developed into a stalemate. For almost the entire duration of the war the opposing forces confronted each other along the Isonzo river in northern Italy, every attempt at a major breakthrough resulting in little more than heavy casualties. However, the Rothschild brothers emerged from the war unscathed and, though sharing the humiliation of defeat in 1918, were thankful to return to their family.

Austrian Rothschilds 1914-39

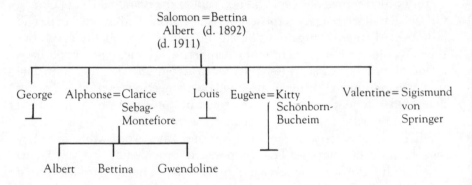

One side-effect of the war was a dramatic change in the prospects of realising the aims of Zionism. The possible — indeed likely — collapse of Turkish power meant that the achievement of a Jewish state in Palestine became, for the first time, a real possibility. For that very reason Rothschild attitudes, on both sides of the argument, hardened.

Edmond had persevered with his settlements and, to ensure their permanence he had, in 1900, transferred administrative power to a body set up for the purpose, the Jewish Colonisation Association, of which he remained president for life. Over the years his own response to Zionist aspirations changed. His original disapproval of nationalism had been partly coloured by his antipathy for the brash journalist Theodor Herzl and his annoyance with the behaviour of some of the settlers. Herzl blazoned abroad his bitter disappointment with the Rothschilds, who, as he saw it, had refused to take up their "historical mission". As for the pioneers who had gone out to Palestine, they were constantly splitting into factions, squabbling among themselves, and squandering the resources he had made available. But, quite apart from his personal frustrations, Edmond was essentially a pragmatist. He did not see how a Jewish political state could be a reality as long as the Ottoman sultans ruled Palestine. But underneath the businessman and the political realist was a deeply religious Jew who shared with the most rabid nationalist the dream of a restored Israel.

When Turkey became embroiled in war with France and Britain in 1914 the whole situation changed, almost overnight: the dream might now become a reality. Few doubted that Britain's Middle East campaign would be victorious. She would, therefore, be in a position to impose terms on the Turks. Thus, if the government in London could be persuaded to establish a protectorate over the Palestinian Jews and incorporate plans for a homeland in the ultimate peace negotiations, such a homeland would have a legal basis backed, if necessary, by force of arms.

Much the same thinking influenced Lord Rothschild, the lay leader of world Jewry. In the last months of his life Natty moved from a firm as-similationist position to one of active pro-Zionism. His continued support for his suffering co-religionists made him more aware than most of his con-temporaries that the overall position was getting worse rather than better. Sporadic persecution continued in Russia and eastern Europe and the problems of re-settlement thus became steadily more acute. In his talks with leading politicians, he found some (notably Balfour and Lloyd George) favourably disposed towards the idea of a strong Jewish presence in the Middle East. In his last months he considered with Herbert Samuel, pre-sident of the Local Government Board, a discussion document the minister was preparing for the cabinet in which he urged his government colleagues to acquire Palestine, "into which the scattered Jews would in time swarm back from all quarters of the globe, and in due course obtain Home Rule". [13] Nothing came of this at the time but the idea of Britain using her imperial rôle to make a historical gesture of epic proportions had its attraction. There was also the practical foreign policy consideration that a friendly state in the Middle East would be a distinct long-term advantage.

The British campaign in Palestine did not go well at first, but by 1917 the tide had turned and in the autumn General Allenby launched a major offensive which carried his forces to Jerusalem by the end of the year. Meanwhile the war cabinet wanted diplomatic and popular support for the Allied cause (especially from the Jewish element in America, which entered the war in April) and, as it became apparent that Britain would play a central rôle in disposing of the former Turkish dominions, they were eager to make use of the bargaining counter which now lay to hand. The conditions thus existed in 1917 for a dialogue with international Jewry. Edmond realised this:

339

When I created my colonies in Palestine I had in view that a time might come when the fate of Palestine could be in the balance, and I desired that the world should have to reckon with the Jews there at such a time. We did a good deal in the last ten to fifteen years; we meant to do still more in the years to come; the present crisis has caught us in the middle of our activities, still one has to reckon with the facts and now we have to use the opportunity which will probably never return again.[14]

But the man whose name is still revered as the father of modern Israel was not personally involved in the bargaining process. His health had been poor for some years and, in any case, he did not regard himself as a political animal. He delegated his elder son Jimmy to represent him.

James de Rothschild, and his new English wife, Dorothy, were ardent enthusiasts for a Jewish homeland. So were the honourable Charles Rothschild and Rozsika. It was Jimmy, however, who, as far as his military commitments allowed, was the main activist. During his recuperation from his accident (see p. 336) the tall, willowy young man with the monocle (a gift to caricaturists) spent much time in England talking with various interested parties. The chief protagonist was Chaim Weizmann, president of the English Federation of Zionists, a gifted research chemist whose important work on explosives had already commended him to Lloyd George. The Rothschilds were also able to win support among leading figures in English society and politics, such as Neil Primrose who, as we have seen, was later killed in Palestine, and his sister, Lady Crewe. But at this juncture another member of the family, rather surprisingly, stepped into the limelight as the very active figurehead of the Zionist movement — Walter Rothschild. This twenty-two-stone human massif emerged from among his glass cases of stuffed animals and drawers of moths and insects, to do his duty as he saw it. His father had been the lay head of Jewry, and Walter, for whom all issues were matters of clear-cut black and white, believed that he had inherited this responsibility as surely as he had inherited Natty's peerage. Like his father and his brother, he was a convinced Zionist and it was, therefore, for him, the most natural thing in the world that he, who had hitherto shown little interest in international politics,* should now conduct a vigorous advocacy with the nation's leaders. This involved several interviews with Balfour, the Foreign Secretary, private and public meetings with Jewish leaders and

---

*In his capacity as MP for Aylesbury, Walter involved himself in debates in which issues of conservation or constituency interests were concerned but his appearances in the Commons during his twelve years as a member were erratic.

340

interest groups, liaising with foreign Zionist bodies, marshalling all the arguments he could muster, counteracting the considerable opposition of anti-Zionist Jews in the press and in private correspondence, and, when the cabinet developed cold feet on the issue, inundating Balfour with urgent letters in his characteristic terse, direct style:

Dear Mr Balfour

There was one point I forgot to mention on Friday and I think you might draw the Prime Minister's attention to this; during the last few weeks the official and semi-official German newspapers have been making many statements, all to the effect that in the Peace Nego-tiations the *Central Powers* must make a condition for Palestine to be a Jewish settlement under *German* protection. I therefore think it important that the British declaration should forestall any such move. If you, as you promised, can arrange the interview I suggested please let Dr Weizmann know as I am going away for a few days on some special business and Dr Weizmann can get at me quicker than if the message is sent to me direct as there will be no responsible person at Tring as my mother is away also.

Yours sincerely,

ROTHSCHILD[15]

The end result of all this activity was the celebrated Balfour Declaration:

Foreign Office,
November 2nd, 1917

Dear Lord Rothschild,

I have much pleasure in conveying to you, on behalf of His Majesty's Government, the following declaration of sympathy with Jewish Zionist aspirations which has been submitted to, and approved by, the Cabinet.

"His Majesty's Government view with favour the establishment in Palestine of a national home for the Jewish people, and will use their best endeavours to facilitate the achievement of this object, it being clearly understood that nothing shall be done which may prejudice the civil and religious rights of existing non-Jewish communities in Palestine, or the rights and political status enjoyed by Jews in any other country."

I should be grateful if you would bring this declaration to the knowledge of the Zionist Federation.

Yours sincerely,

Arthur James Balfour

It was an ambiguous statement — deliberately so. Walter remarked that he would have preferred the word "nation" to "home" but that it was better to have something positive quickly than to bicker over details. Whether or not he was right has been much debated and will, doubtless, continue to be debated. There is no doubt that the declaration was a seminal document. Other powers and subsequently the League of Nations ratified its principles and this widespread moral commitment was, in the fulness of time, decisive in the establishment of the Jewish state.[16]

The development was received rapturously by British Zionists and a packed meeting at London's Royal Opera House heard Jimmy de Rothschild, among others, speak of the challenge of the future. For those unable to be present, the newspapers carried accounts of Jimmy's words:

> The British government representing without any doubt the voice of an enlightened and large-hearted democracy, had ratified the Zionist scheme. What was wanted from the Jewish people was no longer schemes but deeds, and he hoped that in the near future cohorts of modern Maccabees would be fighting their way through the hills of Judea. The Jewish claim was one for justice and that also was the basis of the claims of the Arabs and Armenians, claims which Jews fully endorsed and were pledged to support. Britain stood as the foster-mother of the new-born Jewish nation, and he looked forward to the day when the nation, steeled in adversity but proud in hope, had proved itself by dint of its work to be a real daughter.[17]

The meeting was not without its moments of unscheduled drama; indeed at one point things threatened to get out of hand. The audience in the hall was cheering wildly and more people were trying to press in at the doors. The speakers could not make themselves heard above the din and the chairman, Lord Rothschild, realised that he must restore order. His massive bulk rose up behind the table and, with a voice which rivalled for projection that of any baritone or bass who had ever graced that noble stage, he bellowed, "Silence!" The response was immediate and complete. Having accomplished his purpose, Walter sat down — and the chair splintered beneath him. Yet so commanding was his presence that not one member of that large audience dared to laugh.

But the sudden thrusting of some Rothschilds into the leadership of political Zionism left most of the family unconvinced and prodded a few into active hostility. Leo was strongly opposed to it and, after his death, his widow, Marie, wrote angry letters to Rozsika denouncing Walter as a traitor to the assimilationist principles of the family and of his own father. She apparently had an appalling vision of *all* Jews being shipped off willy-nilly to the proposed new homeland. Immediately after the declaration,

342

her son, Lionel, founded and became president of the League of British Jews, whose object was to resist "the tendency. . . to fix upon the Jews the acceptance of a nationality other than, and in addition to, that of the country of our birth or where we have lived and worked".[18]

Other relatives were less alarmist but the prevailing mood seems to have been one of disquiet. It was felt that the appearance of a politically active international Jewish movement could only provoke the anti-Semites, who, in any case, became more and more vociferous as the troubled years rolled by. Even before the appearance of *Mein Kampf* social theorists and political agitators were nominating "Jewish money men" as the culprits responsible for economic disorder. Some of the Rothschilds were understandably nervous, therefore, about linking the most illustrious Jewish name with Zionism.

These were not the only divisions within the family. Alfred's final gesture was to leave a will (devised many years before his death) which created a considerable stir. When he died, in January 1918, it was found that he had left the bulk of his one-and-a-half-million-pound estate outside the family. The Earl and Countess of Carnarvon were the principal beneficiaries. Almina received fifty thousand pounds and her husband twenty-five thousand. In addition they were bequeathed jointly the house in Seymour Place and its fabulous contents. To each of their two children Alfred left a further twenty-five thousand pounds.

This windfall played an important part in the story of the greatest archaeological discovery of the century. Lord Carnarvon had for some years devoted himself to Egyptology, and particularly to a series of excavations in the Valley of the Kings. With vast funds now at his disposal, he was able to resume the work with unstinted vigour after the war. In 1922 his endeavours were crowned with spectacular success when his colleague Howard Carter uncovered the magnificent treasures of the Tutankhamun tomb. But scarcely less dramatic was Carnarvon's sudden death the following year from an infected mosquito bite. The sensational press made great play with stories of "the curse of the Pharaohs". They might more convincingly have written about "the curse of the Rothschilds". History has shown that few men separate the Rothschilds from their money and survive to enjoy their wealth.

Alfred left the Halton estate and twenty-five thousand pounds to his nephew, Lionel, and another twenty-five thousand to Lionel's brother, Anthony. Apart from these, no member of the family benefited appreciably from Alfred's demise. The testator made various gifts of pictures and china to his relatives and with those they had to be content.

343

One bequest, indeed, was a final joke played from beyond the grave. Alfred left his sister-in-law, Emma, a painting by Greuze called *Le Baiser Envoyé*. It portrays a scantily clad French courtesan blowing a wanton kiss at the viewer. Alfred knew Emma would hate it. She did, and promptly gave it to Rozsika.

Lionel wasted no time in disposing of Halton. What had been Alfred's pride and joy was his headache. He had never liked the house but now, with its denuded parkland and its rows of squalid army huts, it was an exceedingly unattractive proposition. Lionel was eager to sell and the government, with a lack of gratitude which can only be called shabby, took advantage of his impatience. The military tenants had exceeded the terms of their agreement and spread into parts of the estate where they had no right to be. With hostilities about to end, the War Office was in a dilemma. They were obliged to restore the property within six months to the condition in which they had found it. That would be a very costly business. On the other hand, the Royal Air Force, just emerging from the old Royal Flying Corps, needed a training centre, and Halton would suit them very well. But buying the estate would be even more costly. Unless they could get it at a knock-down price.

And, of course, they could. They were in a buyer's market. There was not much of a demand for large estates immediately after the war. And Halton in its existing state was scarcely a desirable property. After a few months of haggling, the government acquired the house, three thousand acres, Halton village, all the farms and cottages and standing timber for £112,000. It would have cost them much more than that just to move their buildings and equipment off the land, and still more to establish the RAF school somewhere else. Not content with this bargain, one of the first acts of the new landlords was to raise rents on the estate. Even then the bureaucrats had not finished with the Rothschilds. In 1919 they announced the compulsory purchase of land from Charles for the building of a sewage works to serve the camp. Protests, even at cabinet level, were of no avail. Such treatment would have been inconceivable in Natty's day. It was almost as if the country's political masters were emphasising that that day was long past and that the Rothschilds were now only ordinary citizens, even in the Vale of Aylesbury.

What a change had come over Rothschildshire in the space of a few years. The sumptuous palaces where kings, statesmen, artists, writers and the great beauties of the age had been entertained in more than regal magnificence were now silent or empty or given over to more mundane uses. Annie and Constance spent only a few weeks a year at Aston Clinton. Mentmore was shut up for long periods. Alice lived in lonely splendour at Waddesdon. Tring Park housed Walter and his animals and his elderly mother. Most of the older generation had gone, leaving their heirs to pay massive death duties. Only two Rothschilds of marriageable age were left to revive the old traditions. And of those two, only Anthony remained in the family home at Ascott. Lionel took the money he had obtained from the sale of Halton and bought himself an estate in Hampshire. However, if legend is to be believed, he at least went out with a bang and not a whimper. Lionel threw one hell of a party before he left. When the new tenants moved into the empty mansion at Halton they found almost every room littered with empty bottles and the indoor swimming pool awash with flat champagne.[19]

That discovery was not without its symbolism.

Part IV
1918–1988

CHAPTER 24

"Caught between two philosophies"

The Great War fractured the social, political and economic order of the old Europe, and the victorious allies put it together again so imperfectly and insecurely that its flaws were obvious to all and could be exploited for their own ends by demagogues, international businessmen and leaders of organised labour. The old convention of a clear distinction between master and servant, employer and employee, was no longer widely accepted and society became a prey to the forces of egalitarianism and social revolution. The old territorial rivalries between nations now became immeasurably complicated by the clash of Communist and Fascist ideologies. The old economic structures were under stress and Europe was plunged into a period of violent instability in which currency values and share prices fluctuated uncontrollably, companies and banks crashed, unemployment rose, inflation soared and governments fell.

For the Rothschilds this was a world in which they no longer exercised their traditional influence. When the hollow-cheeked Jarrow Marchers moved southwards under their defiant banners, Lady Rothschild at Tring refused to eat lunch. It was a private, perhaps pathetic, gesture of solidarity, but it was also a gesture of helplessness by a lady whose husband had helped resolve the Great Dock Strike.

No longer were Rothschilds the automatic confidants and advisers of prime ministers and princes. A new breed of politicians had emerged who, because of their greater accountability to their electorates, were sensitive about their relations with wealthy financiers. Moreover, in the world of international commerce which was now much more complex, Europe's private banking houses, no matter how prestigious, had a changed and reduced rôle to play. America and Japan had emerged as powerful economic centres. Funding the industrial recovery of the post-war period, the reparations payments imposed on the defeated nations, the stability of new — and in many cases non-viable — states, was no longer a matter of raising loans from Rothschild or Baring. The League of Nations, governments, central banks, joint-stock banks and multinational companies might all be involved.

The three Rothschild houses simply failed to come to terms with the changed world of the twenties and thirties. Nor could they fall back on the excuse that the times were out of joint. The fact is that they were in a complacent rut. What had been a tendency towards smug, cosy con-servatism in the pre-war period had, a decade later, become deeply ingrained habit. When twenty-two-year-old Guy entered De Rothschild Frères in 1931 he was appalled at what he saw:

> ... the past clung to everything and everyone. The staff were imbued with the grandeur of "the name" and of the responsibilities it imposed. Vestiges of the previous century were encountered at every moment and in every corner, even some that no longer had any reason for being. The history of the House was as evident in visible relics as in the old stories that everyone loved to tell ...
> Amid all these remnants of an outdated organisation, the telephone introduced a modern note, even though it was largely a decorative accessory because my father used it more often to contact people inside the bank through the switchboard, rather than to make outside calls.[1]

It was exactly the same in the old Renngasse premises in Vienna, as a newspaper reported in 1927: "It is a kind of tradition here that nothing should be changed, and that is why a feeling of the 'good old days' is preserved in the large, old private office of the head of the bank, Louis Baron Rothschild, situated, as it is, overlooking the intimate, cloister-like Schottengarten."[2] Doubtless the very changelessness of the surroundings induced a false sense of security. Within those walls decisions affecting the destinies of kings, nations and great commercial enterprises had been made since the days of the Frankfurt Five. In the long chamber known as The Room (it was the same in all three banks) the partners sat behind the same large, mahogany desks their fathers and grandfathers had sat behind.

What was true of the buildings, the furniture and the daily routine was true of the partners. The new generation of senior Rothschilds included talented, intelligent men and women in plenty. But there was not among them a single imaginative, creative financier. Baron Edouard, the senior partner of De Rothschild Frères, was described by his daughter Batsheva* as "one of the last gentlemen of the century, with a highly developed sense of honour".[3] He was just that: a wealthy gentleman who happened to run a bank. He had no new strategy, no vigorous innovative policies with which to confront new challenges. He was, as his son, Guy, says,

*Mme Batsheva de Rothschild was named Bethsabée by her parents but chose the Hebrew form of her name when she settled in Israel (see p. 405).

a man "caught between two philosophies",[4] those of the old Europe and the new. He was much happier watching his horses race than sitting behind his desk at Rue Laffitte. The same was true of his counterparts: Salbert's son, Louis, in Vienna, was more interested in playing polo and climbing mountains. English Lionel (Leo's son) described himself as "a gardener by profession and a banker by hobby".[5] His brother, Anthony, a Cambridge double first and an expert in Chinese ceramics, would have preferred a secluded, country life (he seldom failed to get in two days hunting a week during the season). These were, we might say, the unfortunate ones, upon whom had fallen the burden of administering the Rothschild empire, from which the whole family derived most of their income but upon which others, like Jimmy, Maurice, Eugène, Alphonse and Walter, had turned their backs.

But, though the Rothschilds made little contribution towards solving the major economic crises of their time, when crisis touched the family directly they could and did spring into action with all the united Rothschild energy of old.

During the late 1920s many western bankers and financial agents behaved like men who walk along a road which steadily becomes narrow, twisty and steep-sided but who go on in the hope that around the next bend it will open out once more into a broad highway. All around them were the signs of economic decline — sluggish markets, rising unemployment, declining industrial output. But, being good *laissez-faire* capitalists, they believed they could invest themselves out of trouble. The only alternatives, after all, were government intervention and international co-operation, and for these concepts the world was not yet completely ready.

The situation was particularly critical in Austria. The mighty Hapsburg Dual Monarchy of Austria-Hungary emerged from the war in 1918 shorn of five-sixths of its territory, its emperor in exile, and its political life dominated by the conflicting aims of Social Democrats and pan-Germanic activists. Many politicians and business leaders clung tenaciously to one grand illusion: that from the debris of the old empire there had been built something almost as splendid — a kind of economic commonwealth of sister states, all autonomous but all looking to Vienna for leadership and financial support. Thus, the major Austrian banks continued to resource industrial and commercial activity throughout the successor nations. Just as they had vigorously lent money in the days when Austria-Hungary was building its industrial base, so they lent money after 1918 to get industry back on its feet. But this "new economic order" *was* an illusion fostered by self-deceived men, seeking national identity and purpose in the aftermath of shocked defeat. It was an alternative to a rival dream — shared by an increasing number of Austrians — union with Germany in a new, powerful, proud central European state.

There were two major flaws in their philosophy: the status of Vienna as an international banking centre was a mirage; and the economies of the small European states into which Austrian banks were pouring money were at best moribund, at worst crumbling. These weaknesses would not necessarily have led to a disastrous outcome if a sound investment policy had been pursued. It was not. In the belief, or hope, or wish, that given sufficient help, industry could be restored to an even keel, bringing in its train full employment and national prosperity, the banks made long-term development loans available to enterprises, many of which only got deeper into debt. In their turn, the lenders were obtaining the bulk of *their* funds from overseas bankers who did not altogether share their optimism, and were, thus, not prepared to make credits available on a long-term basis. In other words, soon after the war the Viennese bankers fell into the fatal habit of borrowing short and lending long.[6]

This was the situation Baron Louis was faced with as he headed S.M. Rothschild und Söhne in the post-war period. His elder brother, Alphonse, had returned from military service to live the life of a gentleman of leisure. He was devoted to philately and classical studies. His daughter remembers him as being hardly ever without a copy of some Greek or Latin text within reach and as often closeted with a visiting scholar or professor, discussing abstruse points of ancient history or literature. His collection of very rare stamps was one of the finest in the world and, as things later turned out, may well have saved his life (see p. 370).

Eugène found his career as a soldier rudely cut short. Part of the price Austria had to pay as a defeated "aggressor nation" was the dismantling of her armed forces. Obliged to seek a civilian occupation, Eugène had contemplated taking over the management of the family's greatest industrial asset, the Wittkowitz complex, now in Czechoslovakia, but he lacked the necessary commercial acumen. So, he settled to the cultivation of his hobbies. Eugène had inherited the Rothschild love of art and took a particular interest in the work of Titian. He wrote an impressive monograph of the great Venetian master, which would have been published had not a rival scholar got into print first with a similar work.

In 1925 he married. He chose as his bride one of the outstanding beauties of the day, an American-born divorcée, Kitty Schönborn-Bucheim. She really was stunning and vivacious. Although she was past her fortieth birthday at the time of her marriage she still turned heads wherever she went. On one occasion, when she was attending the theatre in Paris, she arrived late in her box and the audience stared in her direction. Sacha Guitry, the great comic actor, was in full flow on stage but he immediately stopped his performance with the words, "I will continue when beauty is seated."[7] History does not relate whether the compliment was delivered in sincere admiration or sarcasm.

Eugène and his wife set up permanent residence in Paris, partly, at least, because Kitty was disapproved of by the family and their circle. Being divorced and a spendthrift were not the best qualifications in staid Viennese society. The Austrian capital was no longer the place it had been in the last years of Francis Joseph's long reign. Unemployment and poverty were all too apparent on the streets. A frivolous life style was hardly appropriate in a city which witnessed demonstrations and bread riots.

The responsibility for the Rothschilds' extensive business interests in eastern and central Europe thus devolved upon Louis — handsome, charming, athletic, bachelor Louis. He did not shine as a businessman, but what he *did* possess to a remarkable degree was "style". He was elegant, cool, unflappable, self-assured. The story is told that as a young man Louis visited the New York subway with a view to taking a financial interest in the company. The train he was travelling in got stuck in one of the tunnels and Louis' carriage became unbearably hot and stuffy. But the immaculate Austrian did not show the slightest sign of discomfort. He even declined to remove his overcoat.

Louis kept physically fit and mentally agile. He loved sport of all kinds — mountaineering, shooting at Schillersdorf, hunting, polo. He was a consummate horseman, one of the few allowed the privilege of regularly exercising the magnificent Lippizaners of the Spanish Riding School. In 1937, at the age of fifty-five, he thought nothing of climbing out of a first-floor window of his town house and sidling along a narrow ledge to rescue a stranded cat. One historian described him as a man who "with a regal gesture parried the attacks of an age descending into barbarism".[8] It was Louis' aura of calm confidence and the traditional prestige of his family name that made him a valuable asset to the world of Viennese banking.

Like the sister houses in London and Paris, the establishment over which he presided was in a rut. During the early post-war years the Austrian bank devoted considerable energy to building up a sound industrial base in the new state of Czechoslovakia, but this was their only real initiative.

In July 1921 Louis was prevailed upon to do something which his father and uncle had refused to do for decades. He accepted the chairmanship of the Creditanstalt. Welcoming this decision on behalf of the bank, Philippe Gomperz, the managing director, revealed, inadvertently, just how insubstantial the fabric of Austrian finance had become:

353

Baron Rothschild brings us the glamour of his family name, the international status of his dynasty, and above all the distinction of an outstanding personality. With the dreadful downfall of Austria nothing has survived in the esteem of people abroad other than the firm position of our major banks. By the acceptance of this election Baron Rothschild affirms not only his attachment to our establishment, but likewise fulfils a patriotic duty.[9]

The Rothschilds had always been a major influence within Austria's leading bank and represented on the board. They owned a third of the shares. But ever since Anselm had resigned the vice-presidency, in 1860, they had refused any leadership rôle, preferring not to be openly and irrevocably associated with imperial financial policy. It would have been better for Louis if he had adhered to this practice. But he was under considerable pressure from both bank and government leaders, desperate to secure foreign investment by any means. Thus he harnessed the good name of Rothschild to the lumbering waggon of the Creditanstalt and although this kept the vehicle moving for some years, it could not prevent the eventual breakdown.

The first signs of the disaster became obvious in 1929. That was the year of the Wall Street Crash. One result of that débâcle was that the international money market became even more jittery. Most major banks were henceforth only prepared to make short-term (usually three-month) credits. This squeezed the financial institutions of Vienna even harder.

One of them was already in very great difficulties. The Boden-Creditanstalt, basically a land bank, was on the point of collapse. (Interestingly, when, in 1910, a new managing director, Sieghardt, was appointed, Salbert had laboured with might and main to dissuade the Emperor from ratifying the appointment. His labours had been in vain and it was Sieghardt who had now led the bank to ruin.) The Austrian Chancellor, Johann Schober, sent for Louis but Louis was out of town. He was hunting in a remote and thickly wooded part of the country and had left no directions as to how he was to be found. It was days before an agitated Schober was able to locate him. What happened next has never been very clear. Schober is supposed to have asked − virtually ordered − the Creditanstalt to absorb the ailing bank. And Louis, reputedly, agreed very reluctantly, warning the Chancellor that it was a bad decision and one that he would regret. But if the Baron foresaw the impending gigantic crisis, he certainly did nothing to prevent it. It seems likely that by the time Schober spoke to Baron Louis, the vital decision had been taken and that Louis, patriot that he was, and not having the benefit of sound advice from his own subordinates, supported the government decision. Whoever was responsible for the decision "to take over the corpse of the Boden-Credit-Anstalt" as Professor März, the historian of the Creditanstalt, has called it, it was a blunder of cataclysmic proportions.

The management of the Credit-Anstalt should have perceived this as the proverbial writing on the wall, and either refused to take on the burden of the bankrupt Boden-Credit-Anstalt, or compelled the Austrian government to compensate it far more generously than it actually did for jumping into the breach. Perhaps this was the last opportunity for the Credit-Anstalt to prevent the coming catastrophe by putting its cards on the table in its negotiations with the government.[10]

The opportunity was missed and the financial situation deteriorated steadily over the next eighteen months. On 8 May 1931 the directors of the Creditanstalt had to disclose secretly to the government that the bank's liabilities exceeded its assets and that it was not in a position to continue business. Something had to be done, and done quickly, before the information became public. There could be no question of letting the bank crash: the Creditanstalt was the largest enterprise in the country with a balance almost equal to that of the Austrian state budget. If it collapsed, the national economy would collapse. Baron Louis was among those closeted with the country's leaders over the weekend of 9-10 May to hammer out a rescue plan. S.M. Rothschild und Söhne was, itself, in a far from healthy state at this time. The decline in demand for iron and steel had badly affected Wittkowitz, and Louis had personally underwritten another ailing subsidiary, the Amstel Bank in Holland (which failed the following year). Yet the Baron did not hesitate to commit a sizeable part of his own fortune nor — which must have been more difficult — to appeal to other members of the family for help. In the rescue package, which involved funds from government, banking and private sources, he pledged 16.7 million schillings towards covering the Creditanstalt's losses and thirty million schillings in financial aid.

To meet these commitments, Louis and his brothers had to sell shares, property and family treasures. Alphonse's daughter, Bettina, tells the story that her father was in the bath one day when Louis walked into the room. "By the way," the visitor remarked languidly, "I've agreed to sell off such-and-such an estate of yours." "Really," Alphonse replied, with equal nonchalance, "you might have asked me first."[11] Louis, himself, who met about fifty per cent of the Austrian family's liabilities, moved out of his mansion on the Theresianumgasse into a more modest house nearby and, for the first time, he set about putting his estates on a sound economic footing. Schillersdorf, for example, which had cost millions to keep up,

355

purely for the pleasure of the Rothschilds and their guests, now received a new manager who was under instructions to make the farms and forests pay their way.

Yet, despite these and other examples of thrift, the most striking feature of this episode — the worst financial crisis the Rothschilds had so far faced — is the sheer "style" with which Louis and his relatives comported themselves. Nothing better illustrates Rothschild wealth and unity or the importance they all placed in the family name than the outwardly casual way they met this drain on their resources. The Paris and London houses were completely independent of the Viennese. Shortly before the First World War they had severed formal connections and closed down their joint account. But the honour of the Rothschild name was now at stake: there could be no question of abandoning Baron Louis to his fate.

Quietly, even nonchalantly on the surface, but with frenzied behind-the-scenes activity, the Paris and London houses provided the funds which kept S.M. Rothschild und Söhne from being caught up in the crash. Though all loans were repaid by 1939, the rescue operation cost them dear. The London house, particularly, almost reached exhaustion. De Rothschild Frères had larger reserves but these were heavily ransacked to deal with the emergency. When the Dutch Amstel Bank went bust, it was the French house which indemnified Louis and then went on to make further loans available.

The world, of course, never knew just how hard the great bankers had been hit. No suggestion that the Rothschilds had almost touched rock bottom was ever allowed to circulate. That would have been disastrous for public confidence. Banks may come and banks may go but the Rothschilds are eternal — or so most people believed. If it had ever appeared otherwise, the worldwide shock would have been intense.

Even in Vienna, Louis and Alphonse continued as if nothing had happened. Bettina, who was seven at the time of the Creditanstalt crisis, recalls little in the way of family economies that touched her life in the ensuing years. There were still marvellous holidays at Schillersdorf and Langau. Her parents did close up the Vienna house for one "season" but they were back the following year. Alphonse discussed with his manager at Langau various ways of making the estate more productive but these conversations often ended with some such exchange as:

"But will that upset the deer?"

"Very probably, Sir."

"Then, let's not do it." [12]

And Dr Miriam Rothschild remembers distinctly that as a young woman of twenty-three she was staying with Alphonse and his wife on that fateful weekend in May 1931 and that not once did the Creditanstalt occur in the conversation.[13] It would be an exaggeration to say that the Rothschilds absorbed the Creditanstalt crisis without feeling it but that is certainly the impression they gave – and intended to give – to the outside world.

In fact, it was not Louis but another member of the family who was destined to play the major part in the long and difficult recovery of the Austrian economy. That recovery depended on a continued inflow of foreign capital. So, as Sir Eric Phipps, the British representative in Vienna, expressed it, the Austrian government "put on its velvet gloves to pray to the Rothschilds to appeal to their connections abroad".[14] As a result the major foreign Creditanstalt creditor banks set up the Austrian Creditanstalt International Committee. The chairman of this body was Lionel de Rothschild, senior partner of the London house. Once again a Rothschild was taking the lead in international negotiations which were as much political as they were financial. And the negotiations were tough. The different parties held widely divergent interests. The American bankers wanted to get their money out. The Austrian government were desperate to stave off national collapse (At an early stage of the talks they had underwritten the bank.) The League of Nations (to which Austria had to justify its financial policies) was concerned for the stability of Europe. The French government were opposed to acts of generosity towards one of the aggressor nations in the recent war.

For four and a half years the wheeling and dealing went on, and it was largely due to the patience and tact of Lionel and Sir Robert Kindersley of the Bank of England that a solution emerged satisfactory to all sides. At the end of the day the Creditanstalt was saved, though it emerged as a much slimmer, purely Austrian bank, largely under government control. The International Committee had played a vital part, not only in saving Austria, but in helping Europe recover from the Great Depression.[15]

It is interesting that Lionel is remembered in the family not so much for his activities in the City as for what he did on his Exbury estate (see pp. 362ff.). When he called himself "a gardener by profession and banker by hobby", he played down his very real achievements during the Depression. Even his work for the International Committee is made light of in a story his son Edmund still delights to tell. It was a Friday afternoon, a meeting of the committee was in progress and Lionel was anxious to catch the 4.35 train down to his beloved Hampshire. There were ten complex points on the agenda and Lionel took them at a cracking pace until the representative of Lazard's Bank, a Mr Tyzer, demurred over item ten. The chairman cut him short.

"I say, Tyzer, is that a boil on your neck?"

"Well, yes, as a matter of fact..."

"I have a sovereign remedy for boils." He scribbled some words on his notepad, tore off the sheet and handed it across the table. "There, you get that made up and if it doesn't work, I'll give ten pounds to any charity you care to name. Now then, where were we? Point ten? Not happy with that, Tyzer? Let's strike it out then. Agreed? Good. Then, that appears to be all, gentlemen. Thank you very much. Good afternoon." [16]

Undoubtedly there was an element of bluff in the attitude which Lionel and Louis and others of their generation appeared to take towards banking. If they gave the impression that it was a leisurely, civilised pastime and just one among many to which a gentleman might devote some of his time, it was partly to create confidence and partly to cover their own uncertainties about the world in which they lived.

CHAPTER 25
"One continual party"

The inter-war period might well be described in the words Dickens used of the 1780s — "It was the best of times; it was the worst of times." This was the age of jazz, "flappers" and the Hollywood dream as well as being the age of "Buddy, can you spare a dime?" For those who had the money and leisure to enjoy it, Europe was a gay and exciting place. The Rothschilds certainly came into that category. Members of the family devoted themselves, with their usual wholehearted enthusiasm, to a range of activities, wider and more diverse than ever before.

Walter in the quiet seclusion of Tring Park completed his remarkable life work. For fourteen hours every day this eccentric, totally absorbed zoologist worked in his museum compiling a staggering collection:

General collection for public display
2000 complete mounted mammals (including a Quagga, 13 Gorillas, 228 Marsupials, 24 Echidnas, etc) plus 200 heads and 300 pairs of antlers 2400 mounted birds (including 62 Birds of Paradise, 520 Hummingbirds, 62 Cassowaries, etc)
680 reptiles (including 144 giant tortoises)
914 fishes
A representative collection of Invertebrates

Students' Department
1400 mammal skins and skulls
300,000 bird skins
200,000 birds' eggs
300 dried reptiles
2¼ million set Lepidoptera (thousands of types)
300,000 beetles.[1]

From Walter and his curators there poured forth millions of words, written in books, articles and monographs, based on their study of the collection. The Tring Museum periodical, *Novitates Zooligicae*, alone extended to forty volumes over the forty-five years of its publication.

Walter's principal contribution to science lay in the field of systematic classification. For the acquiring of all those specimens was not just another expression of the Rothschild collecting mania. Only by bringing together large numbers of spiders or moths or birds and submitting each to close scrutiny was it possible to distinguish significant differences between specimens which, to the untrained eye, appeared identical. Walter's pioneer work in zoological classification ensured him a distinguished place in the history of science and his contribution is commemorated in the names of over two hundred and fifty species and subspecies of plants, birds, fish, mammals, amphibians, insects, spiders, etc., which he first recognised and catalogued. Batsheva de Rothschild, who now lives in Tel Aviv and manages a dance company, tells a story of a recent visit to Kenya with her troupe. At a press reception she was being questioned by a local journalist who began by asking her name. "Rothschild," she said. Instantly, the black face broke into a smile, "Ah, yes," he said, "the same as our giraffe."[2] In 1903 Walter had identified a subspecies of giraffe with five horns instead of four, subsequently named in his honour *Giraffa camelopardalis rothschildii*.

The brain housed in Lord Rothschild's massive head was a computer of zoological information and its owner could instantly produce the most obscure detail without having recourse to the thirty thousand volumes in his museum library. Among the many delightful stories recorded by his niece in her biography is an incident which occurred when the sixty-six-year-old Walter was being driven in his Daimler through Hyde Park. He caught a fleeting glimpse of a chauffeur standing by a stationary car with a rug over his arm. "Stop! Stop, Christopher," he shouted to his driver in great agitation, "that rug is made out of the pelts of tree kangaroos!" He then dismounted, accosted the owner of the item in question and eventually persuaded him to sell it.[3]

Walter lived with his mother at Tring Park to the end of her days and did not long survive her. Emma died in 1935 at the age of ninety-one and Walter followed her to the grave thirty-one months later. Nothing disturbed the mother-son relationship between Emma and Walter which, in essence, had changed little since he was a small boy. The point is well illustrated by a story told in Dr Miriam Rothschild's lively prose.

On one occasion Emma — then in her eightieth year — awoke to perceive Walter in the dim, rosy light of her Chinese *veilleuse*, standing at the foot of her bed immaculate in pure silk pyjamas. "Mama," announced Walter in great agitation, "I have been poisoned, Mama."
Emma switched on the light. She always looked rather slight and

sharp in bed — without her *toupé*, without her marvellously realistic false teeth — enveloped and rather lost in a voluminous, old-fashioned flannel nightshirt.

"You look remarkably well to me, Walter — I expect you've had a nightmare."

"Not at all," whispered Walter, "one of the pheasants due at the museum went astray and I've suddenly realized what happened to it — we had pheasant for supper last evening, Mama. The preservative is most toxic — I've got a pain — I'm sure I've been poisoned."

"Then WE have been poisoned," said Emma calmly, "because I had a slice of that bird too, and I'm quite well, thank you, Walter. You will feel better in the morning."

After a long, thoughtful pause he turned on his heel and meekly went back to bed.[4]

In 1923 profound tragedy brought Walter's sister-in-law and her four children into this strange world of Tring. That was the year in which Charles Rothschild, driven well beyond the bounds of sanity by his illness, violently took his own life. For the children, aged between ten and fifteen, the shock was profound. The father whom Miriam remembers as keeping her and her governess in fits of laughter throughout nursery teatimes[5] had long since disappeared, veiled from his family by illness. But the loss in such circumstances was real and deeply felt.

Rozsika, as the only adult member of this branch of the family competent in administration, took over more and more of the organisation of the Tring estate. She and her children spent a large part of every year there, "all boxed up together in a ponderous gilded cage", as Miriam later described the experience.[6] It was an extraordinary setting for youngsters in their formative years, especially for Victor, the only son of Charles and Rozsika, who was twelve when his father died. For him it was a world of women — a deaf grandmother, a mother who never fully recovered from the loss of her husband, his sisters and a succession of nannies and governesses — interspersed with hateful boarding schools, where other children called him a "dirty little Jew".[7] It was also the world of eccentric Uncle Walter, who found it so difficult to communicate with the children yet managed to infect Victor and his sister, Miriam, with his own intense love of science.

In 1931 a profound change came over Walter. The financial demands of the peeress, who had dogged his heels since the 1890s, had never ceased and now were pressed with renewed vigour. Amazingly, Walter could still not bring himself to confide in anyone or seek advice. Now the extortioner turned the screw so ruthlessly that Walter was forced to do the unthinkable — he sold part of his collection. Typically, he conducted the negotiations in secret. Even his mother knew nothing until she read about the sale in the newspapers. Thus, 295,000 birds, painstakingly collected throughout the world over decades and lovingly catalogued at Tring, were crated up and sent to America. The effect on the old man was catastrophic. His biographer records: "Walter seemed to shrink visibly in the period following the sale. His silences were now dull, not pregnant with unspoken turmoil. He felt tired and distrait, and spent only about two hours before lunch in the Museum."[8]

The puzzle of the blackmailing peeress's identity is intriguing and rendered even more so by the fact that the only living person who knows the solution has sworn herself to secrecy. Dr Miriam Rothschild, who revealed the existence of this unscrupulous woman in her biography of Walter, believes that the secret he so persistently kept should never be told. All she will say is that the peeress and her equally unscrupulous husband both suffered greatly in this life and that the ends of natural justice may be deemed to have been served.[9]

Another member of the family who shared Walter's passion for natural history and was also reclusive by nature (though in his case the tendency did not reach eccentric proportions) was his cousin, Lionel. It is tempting to see a symbolism in the fact that this man who was profoundly affected by the First World War — the war in which he was not allowed to participate — dedicated most of his creative energies to flowers. But the truth is that he was a born gardener with a real passion for botany which survived such youthful enthusiasms as motoring (which, Lionel claimed, lost most of its fun after the invention of the shock-absorber). Before 1914 he had acquired a house on the Mitford family's estate at Exbury and the proceeds of the sale of Halton enabled him to buy the whole property.

"Think big" might well be a Rothschild motto and Lionel certainly followed the family tradition at Exbury. He found himself the owner of 250 acres of poor quality, overgrown woodland between the New Forest and the Beaulieu estuary, and he resolved to turn it into one of the most beautiful woodland gardens in the country. It was also to include an arboretum which would contain specimens of every tree which could be grown in Britain (this was the only part of the grand design he failed to complete), decorative lakes and rivers, a rock garden for alpine plants, and, above all, masses and masses of rhododendrons mixed with evergreen and deciduous azaleas, magnolias, camellias, other shrubs and rare trees, growing naturally in a woodland environment yet skilfully arranged to confront the visitor with a kaleidoscope of changing vistas. The first task

362

was to rebuild completely the existing modest house and create a neo-Georgian mansion — the last important example of Rothschild domestic building — where he could entertain in traditional style. Even here bricks and mortar had to give way to nature. When Lionel's architect complained that an elderly magnolia was in his way, he was ordered to build round it.

The work on the house, and subsequently on the estate, necessitated bringing hundreds of craftsmen and labourers into a sparsely inhabited part of Hampshire. Not for a moment did the master of Exbury flinch at the complications involved. He simply built homes for his work-force. The hamlet on the edge of the estate grew into a sizeable village, complete with shop, laundry, bakery, social club and all the other amenities Rothschild landlords considered it their duty to provide. When it came to clearing the ground and laying the garden, nothing was spared that ingenuity could devise and money could buy. Lionel, rushing down from the City every Friday afternoon, supervised the building of a small railway to move rocks, equipment and felled timber. He brought in mature trees for planting and had holes to accommodate them blasted by dynamite. He sank 270-foot bore holes and laid twenty-six miles of irrigation pipes to carry the water all over the garden.

Meanwhile, some remarkable individuals were scouring remote regions to gather specimens of rare species. Lionel's agents included the leading plant-hunters of the day, men who faced discomfort and danger in China, Tibet, Japan, Malaysia and the mountains of Asia, Europe and America, men whose adventures are a story in themselves. Lionel wanted to bring together as many examples of rhododendron and azalea as possible in order to create variety, to extend the flowering season and to experiment in hybridisation. In the two acres of teak-framed glasshouses at Exbury (which still survive after more than sixty years), his gardeners produced seedlings, nurtured plants and cross-fertilised flowers. They developed over 1200 new hybrids, no less than 452 of which were considered worthy of being registered with the Royal Horticultural Society. They were planted out in the gardens where, amidst the background of dense foliage, they stood out in brilliant masses of blossom — red, orange, yellow, pink, white, purple and a host of other subtle hues. Lionel won many awards for his blooms including the one he prized above all others, the Victoria Medal, given for his outstanding original contribution to horticulture. This withdrawn man relished the acclaim of fellow experts. Whenever he received a cup or plaque that had to be returned for the next year's competition, he had a replica made in silver so that he could keep a permanent memento of his triumph.

He was a very private man who communicated through his enthusiasms rather than through his emotions. Many stories are told about his apparent detachment from the world of ordinary mortals. Passing through one of the clerks' rooms at the bank one day, he noticed a handsome canteen of cutlery standing on a side table. On enquiring about it, he was told that one of the senior members of the department was getting married and the cutlery was a gift from his colleagues. He looked at it carefully for a moment and then said, "Well, that's not much good; he'll never be able to have more than twelve people to dinner." [10]

He himself was subject to no such limitations. Reserved Lionel might be, but this did not prevent him and his wife continuing the Rothschild tradition of hospitality. Friends, colleagues, horticulturalists, and members of fashionable society were entertained at Exbury or aboard Lionel's yacht, *Rhodora*. After ten years of prodigious hard work, the gardens were ready ro receive royalty. King George V and Queen Mary came to admire the latest Rothschild wonder. The Prince of Wales flew down in his private plane. The Duke of York (soon to be King George VI) brought his wife to see and admire the beauty of Lionel de Rothschild's earthly paradise. The lavish days of Mr Alfred were past, but Lionel's weekend guests never had cause to complain of the enormous Exbury breakfasts, the exquisite wines from the cellar, the tennis, the shooting, and the colourful tranquillity of the gardens. On Sunday afternoon they were all sent safely on their way and next morning Lionel would drive like a demon to Beaulieu Road station for the London train, carrying in his brief case two fresh eggs for the restaurant car staff to prepare for his breakfast. [11]

Waddesdon, also, continued to perform its rôle as a retreat for the powerful and the famous. In 1922 Jimmy de Rothschild inherited the estate on the death of the formidable Alice. The monocled and impeccably dressed Jimmy, who looked every inch an Englishman and spoke the language without any trace of an accent, had taken up permanent residence in England after the war and become a British citizen. Yet the bequest of Waddesdon came as a surprise and the new mistress, "Mrs James", found the prospect of suddenly having to run a house in the grand Rothschild manner somewhat daunting. But while some economies had to be made (for example the new owners felt they could no longer justify a whole section of the vast greenhouse range being given over to exotic, tropical plants), the Waddesdon tradition was maintained. Jimmy sat as Liberal MP for the Isle of Ely from 1928 to 1945 and, though the fortunes of his party were now waning, many were the political gatherings which took place in Baron Ferdinand's mansion, as Jimmy's widow wryly recalls:

I like to think our friends, including even such dominant personalities as Mr Asquith and Mr Churchill, regarded Waddesdon as a place where they could relax from their labours and indulge in such pastimes as golf, bezique, bridge and Mah-jong — the most popular games at that time. Any political discussion was largely confined to the period at the end of dinner when, in the English fashion, the ladies retired from the dining-room and the men remained, unencumbered by femininity, to settle down, maybe, to serious talk. However useful these masculine exchanges of view may have been to the participants, I chiefly remember them for the unconscionable length of time they seemed to go on.[12]

One addition that Jimmy did make was the establishment of a stud farm at Waddesdon. His passion for racing had continued unabated since his youth. The story he always told to explain his devotion to the turf was that, on his first visit to a racecourse, to witness the Derby of 1898, he had picked, and backed, the hundred-to-one winner. Unfortunately, success rarely seems to have come his way thereafter, either as punter or owner. One cynical friend remarked that, though many people were in the habit of backing outsiders, only James de Rothschild had developed a talent for breeding them.

Interestingly, it was Jimmy's younger brother, Maurice, the "ne'er-do-well", the "scapegrace", the "black sheep", who soon after the war suddenly devoted himself to public service. He entered politics. Until 1925 he served as Deputy for the Hautes-Pyrénées. He was extremely popular and pioneered several important social reforms such as working-class housing projects. After 1926 he represented the Hautes-Alpes in the upper house. During these years the League of Nations headquarters was established in Geneva and Maurice frequently entertained the leading statesmen of the age at nearby Pregny. In the late 1930s the château became a meeting place for the politicians, like Churchill, Paul Reynaud and Léon Blum, who were alarmed at the growth of Nazism and who tried, vainly in an age of appeasement, to organise international opposition to Hitler. During this period Maurice also made his first foray into business. It was highly successful but led to a breach, which turned out to be final, with the senior branch of the French family. What happened was this: Maurice put up the capital for a company, Immeuble Construction de Paris, which was to buy and develop land owned by the city of Paris. Before the company could begin business it was required to put up a bond and this Maurice did in the name of Rothschild. Edouard and his cousin, Robert, were furious. They believed that this was just another of Maurice's crazy schemes and that, when it inevitably failed, it would fall to the bank to honour the bond. They told him that his behaviour had now put him beyond the pale and that he would not be welcome to take up the place at Rue Laffitte occupied by his father, who had recently died. Maurice, therefore, cashed up his share of De Rothschild Frères and went his own way. In fact, Immeuble Construction de Paris proved an excellent venture and though Maurice parted company with his business colleagues after a few years, he had in the meantime made a handsome profit. Soon after the birth of his only son, Edmond, he and his wife were divorced and Maurice lived alone, devoting all his time to his investments and politics.[13]

The senior branch of the French family divided their time between the responsibilities of the bank and the pleasures of wealth. Like Jimmy, they were enthusiastic followers of the sport of kings. Edouard kept a stud at Deauville where he bred some excellent horseflesh. His greatest champion was Brantôme, who was unbeaten as a two- and three-year-old, and won several of the Franch classics including the Prix de l'Arc de Triomphe. Then, suddenly, this magnificent animal went to pieces. One day at Chantilly, before a race, he broke away from his handlers, careered through the town in a frenzy of panic, and only stopped when he was trapped in a cul-de-sac. After this inexplicable incident his nerve went completely and he was withdrawn from racing.

Most of the younger French Rothschild set loved the turf. For them it was an integral part of the social calendar, a calendar which during the 1920s the motor car had extended to include fascinating new possibilities, as Edouard's son, Guy, recalls:

> Then I discovered Biarritz. The month of September was the height of the season. I was twenty, the age for parties, and Biarritz was one continual party from morning until early the following morning, in the midst of a host of Spaniards and South Americans, all very young, passionate, uninhibited.
>
> Every day at noon, in front of the Hôtel du Palais, began the parade of cars, each as shiny as the next: Rolls Royce, Packard, Bentley, Duesenberg, Hispano, driven by arrogant young men accompanied by superb girls with distant, haughty airs. We'd go swimming at the beach called "Chamber of Love" or at the foot of the "Virgin's Rock", before playing golf on the new Chiberta Links, with titled, sun-tanned members of the oldest families of Europe and South America.
>
> As soon as we'd changed out of our golf clothes, there was no question of going anywhere else than to the Basque Bar, to join the

crowd of aristocrats and adventurers, all thirsting for pleasure, champagne and conquests. I believe that I never dined with less than twenty guests, many of whom re-invited themselves each evening; nor ever neglected the tradition of winding up the evening at Sheherazade, a restaurant-nightclub in the open country.[14]

In Paris, Baron Henri embarked on yet another new venture, his most spectacular yet: he built a theatre, the Pigalle. After the war he had returned to his first love, the stage, and was always to be found in the company of actors and actresses, many of whom were frequent guests aboard his motor yacht, appropriately named *Eros*. Then, in 1926, his wife had died. Mathilde had always regarded Henri's obsession with amused contempt. Dr Miriam Rothschild recalls an extremely embarrassing incident on a visit to Paris as a teenager. Mathilde took her to the theatre and promptly fell asleep as soon as the performance began. When the play was well into its stride she awoke with a start as if from a bad dream screeching, "*Je meurs! Je meurs!*" while her companion tried to dissolve into her seat.[15] But now she was gone and there was nothing to distract Henri from his demanding mistress.

The Théâtre Pigalle, built at enormous expense in the very latest, sumptuous style, all chrome and neon, opened in 1929 with a première which attracted the leaders of French society as well as titled visitors from all over Europe. But it proved to be just another of Henri's financial disasters. Even full houses could not pay for the running costs and the extravagant productions. After a couple of years he lost interest in his new toy. In fact, he never wrote another play. Although he did not show it, the Pigalle had probably broken his heart.

His son, Philippe, had been closely associated with him in the design of the theatre. In those years, the young man seemed, like his father, to be a genius looking for a cause. He threw himself enthusiastically into racing. He raced yachts, bob-sleighs, cars, aeroplanes. He made a whirlwind world tour. He was interested in all the new movements in art, theatre and cinema. Then he decided to become a film director. In 1932 he got a company together to make *Lac aux Dames*, one of the first French talking pictures.

But Philippe de Rothschild had already embarked on the career to which he was to apply himself with increasing devotion and which would show him to be the greatest Rothschild businessman of his generation. In the immediately post-war years he fell in love with Mouton, the family's vineyard at Pauillac. Since its purchase by his great-grandfather, no Rothschild had taken a close interest in it. But Philippe did. He liked the place; he liked the people; and he was fascinated by the process of making and selling fine wine. He was convinced that that process could be improved and, after 1922, when his father handed the estate over to him, he set about putting his ideas into practice.

The following years saw the introduction of electricity, running water, properly metalled roads and the rebuilding of the house and *chais*. But the most revolutionary step of all came in 1924. Up till that time each vintage had been shipped off to Bordeaux in cask for the "experts", the *négociants*, to bottle and sell to wholesalers and retailers. Philippe's idea was simply to cut out the middle man: to retain control over the wine throughout its first vital years of development, to bottle it *in situ*, and then sell it direct. The process would be called "château bottling". Nowadays, the best − or at least the most expensive − Bordeaux wines are *mis en bouteille au château*. In 1924 the very idea seemed outrageous. It meant spending a lot of money on bottling plant and storage facilities but money has never deterred the Rothschilds when it comes to implementing a good idea. Thus was built the Grand Chai, the simple, large room where hundreds of barrels are laid out in ideal conditions, and where visitors are still impressed by the rows of sleeping claret and the delicious mingled smell of wine and oak. Other vineyard owners caught on. They could see that château bottling gave a distinction to their product, as well as allowing them a higher profit margin. Soon Philippe, the new boy, had persuaded some of his more august neighbours to join him in what he called the Association des *Premiers Crus*.

But no amount of reorganisation and skilful marketing could ensure a fine harvest. There were good years and bad years. There always had been and there always would be. What was to be done with wine not good enough to be sold under the prestigious Mouton Rothschild label? After various other ideas had been tried, Philippe came up with a new name. Mouton Cadet was born. The impossible had been achieved: a distinguished wine at a modest price. In a very short time Philippe de Rothschild had made his mark on the selling of France's most prestigious product. But he had not finished yet, not by a very long chalk.

The party went on and on. Whether in the frenzied whirl of Riviera resorts or the quiet beauty of an English garden, the Rothschilds and their friends enjoyed their wealth. But only the self-deluded thought that it could continue for ever. Social unrest was everywhere. On the Continent, political rivalries led to assassinations, mob violence and the foundation of frightening, paramilitary units.

In Austria, the resolution of the Creditanstalt crisis did little to ease the political situation. Indeed, if anything, it played into the hands of the German Nationalist party and the Heimwehr (a Fascist politico-military force). The hostility and fear felt by centrist politicians is well illustrated by a speech made by Robert Danneberg to an unruly parliament on 27 October 1931.

We Social Democrats are being dubbed "Rothschild Socialists" because we agreed to legal powers being given to the Finance Minister. *We* are called "Rothschild Socialists" by the same man whose colleagues, Pfrisner and Steidle [Heimwehr leaders], only two years ago, called on Baron Rothschild [to obtain funds for their movement], by the same man whose party is nourished by money obtained from [the Creditanstalt and Boden Creditanstalt] (Cheers from the left) . . . We can't tell this to the people often enough. We have to hammer it home (shouts of "Lies!" and "Sit down!" from the right) . . . I know you don't like this . . . It is no lie . . . Remember the speech of Mr Steidle, when he said he would take money from any source. That was plain speaking! (Uproar). I demand a committee to find out the truth . . . to look into the books of the Creditsanstalt and the Boden-Creditanstalt and see how many thousands have been given to the Heimwehr by Christian and Jewish bankers . . .

We are also called "Rothschild Socialists" by those fly-shit swastika people, by the man [Alfred Freuenfeldt, Austrian Nazi leader] who was an employee of the Boden-Creditanstalt. The man who was a strike breaker in 1923 when all his colleagues came out on strike . . . These are the sort of people who now dare to call us "Rothschilds".[16]

Eighteen months later democratic government in Austria collapsed. For a year Engelbert Dollfuss governed by decree, trying to hold at bay extremists of the Right and Left. In July 1934 he was murdered during an attempted Nazi coup. Although this failed, popular support for union with Germany (Anschluss), where Hitler was in power and had done much to restore national unity and morale, was growing. Nazi forces on both sides of the border used every means to bring about the desired merger. On 9 March 1938 Chancellor Schuschnigg accounced a referendum on the Anschluss. Hitler had no intention of permitting the Austrian people to declare themselves in a free vote and speedily moved troops up to the frontier.

The suddenness of the move took the Rothschilds by surprise. They had grown accustomed to Nazi rhetoric and had persuaded themselves that the threat of invasion was just another piece of propaganda. A few days before the crisis Alphonse and Clarice had gone to London. There was an important philatelic exhibition there and Alphonse had loaned his collection, one of the finest in the world. The Rothschilds had also been invited to dine at Buckingham Palace and, therefore, had a quantity of jewellery with them. This proved to be extremely fortunate. The news from Austria threw them into a panic. They knew well enough what was happening to Jews in Germany and although their sixteen-year-old son, Albert, was with them in London, the girls — Bettina (fourteen) and Gwendoline (eleven) — had been left behind. A very worried Alphonse phoned his brother, urging him to leave Vienna at once and bring the girls with him. But Louis pooh-poohed the whole thing. There was no need for anxiety. Hitler was only posturing again. The supposed emergency would blow over in a few days.

This time cool, calm Louis was taking nonchalance too far. Either he had convinced himself that there was no crisis or he was putting on a front to prevent panic. His instinct as a banker was certainly to play down anything that might create a loss of public confidence. But he also had another motive: that of loyalty to his staff. He felt that he could not abandon them as long as he could do any good by staying at his post. On 12 March Hitler led his army into Austria.

Clarice and Alphonse were frantic with worry. They rushed to Zürich and put through more calls to Vienna. Louis saw his nieces on to a train for Switzerland hours before the invasion. Bettina and Gwendoline got as far as Innsbruck. There, the Nazis took them off the train and held them in custody. It was several hours before two very frightened girls were allowed to cross the frontier and only then because news had arrived of the arrest of their Uncle Louis.[17] There were several prominent citizens on Hitler's wanted list but the name of the country's leading Jewish banker was very near the top. The ultimate confrontation of the forces of virulent anti-Semitism with the ancient house of Rothschild was about to take place.

Baron Louis' handling of that confrontation has become legendary. Not for one moment did he allow his enemies to undermine his dignity or gain any moral ascendancy over him. He carried himself throughout the following unpleasant months with his usual patrician sang-froid and emerged a hero. Within hours of the Anschluss a car arrived at the Baron's Vienna residence. Two Nazi officers emerged and rang the bell. The butler appeared and was peremptorily told that his visitors demanded to see his master. He asked them to wait while he conveyed the message. Soon he returned, polite and impassive. He much regretted that Baron de Rothschild was at dinner and could not be disturbed. Perhaps if the gentlemen would care to make an appointment . . . He held the front door open and, nonplussed, the Nazis left.

For several hours, while his servants, colleagues and friends begged him to leave, Louis had busied himself setting his affairs in order and making financial provision for his domestic and bank employees. He refused to be hurried or flustered. Next morning, when he had done all he could do, he allowed himself to be driven to the airport. He almost made it to the aeroplane but, at the last moment, he was turned back. He was arrested at his home in the early afternoon and, even then, he made his captors wait while he calmly finished his lunch.

For over a year Louis was a prisoner, subjected to a variety of treatment and conditions — now interrogated, now forced to do hard labour, now handled with kid gloves. The fact was that the Nazis did not know what to do with him. They had failed to conquer his spirit or to wear down his very fit body. They were receiving constant demands for his release from Paris and London, and Edouard had organised the best legal brains to negotiate with the Nazis. The Germans' main objective was to lay their hands on as much Rothschild property as possible, and especially the iron and coal complex at Wittkowitz, which they needed to feed their hungry munitions factories. But Louis had forestalled them. In a brilliant manoeuvre he had put the valuable plant beyond confiscation. The resignation of another major shareholder had provided the opportunity for a reorganisation of the corporate structure. In a series of delicate negotiations, he had persuaded both the Czech and Austrian governments that Wittkowitz would be safer if ownership was transferred to a foreign-based company. As a result, the controlling interest went to the Alliance Insurance Company of London, and the major shareholder of the Alliance was still N.M. Rothschild and Sons. Hitler's agents tried all kinds of threats and inducements but Louis simply shrugged them off. The matter was out of his hands. If the Führer wanted Wittkowitz he would have to negotiate with the English owners. And the Führer, who was not yet ready for a confrontation with the British government, was eventually obliged to do just that. The price agreed was two million pounds and Baron Louis' freedom.

At last the arrangements were concluded, the papers signed. In the Vienna prison, Louis' cell door was opened one evening and he was informed that he could leave. But the imperturbable Baron had one more surprise for his guards.

"What time is it?" he asked.

"Just after eight o'clock, Herr Baron."

"Then it's far too late to disturb any of my friends. I will leave in the morning."

And that is precisely what he did.

*　　*　　*

371

But not all members of the family emerged from this troubled period so fortunately. In 1910 Miriam, the youngest daughter of Baron Edmond, had married her first cousin, Albert von Goldschmidt-Rothschild.

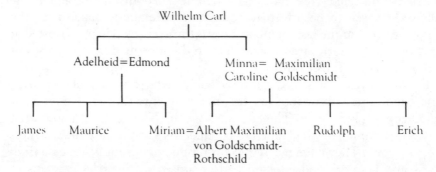

They lived in Paris, a happy couple, very much in love. When the war came in 1914, Albert wanted to return to Germany. Miriam refused to accompany him. They parted but the emotional conflict left its mark upon both of them. Miriam, considered by some to have been the most brilliant Rothschild of her generation, became a recluse. She found some consolation in her magnificent collection of books and paintings, and in amassing an encyclopaedic knowledge of a wide range of subjects. But her grasp of day-to-day reality was as weak as her understanding of art, politics and philosophy was strong. So little care did she take of her own appearance that one day a stranger stopped her in the street and pressed a banknote into her hand with the words "*c'est pour vous, ma pauvre*" (which probably makes her the only Rothschild ever to have been the recipient of casual charity). She was equally vague about matters of security. At the outbreak of the Second World War she decided to have her priceless collection concealed in a sand dune near Dieppe, "for safety". By the end of hostilities it had disappeared without trace.

Albert's reaction to the traumatic separation took the form of partial paralysis which confined him to a wheelchair for some years. The couple were eventually divorced and Albert remarried in 1923. But what one world war had started another finished. In 1939 Albert, like many German Jews, fled to Switzerland. But the government was very jittery about the mass influx. Berlin claimed that harbouring "enemies of the German people" was an unfriendly act and the Swiss were anxious to appear completely neutral. There was, therefore, some talk of repatriating Albert. Rather than face the horrors of Auschwitz or Dachau, the distracted man took his own life.[18]

French Rothschilds 1939-85

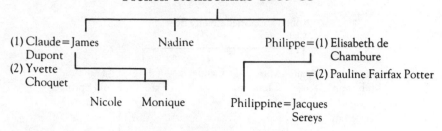

(1) Claude=James | Nadine | Philippe=(1) Elisabeth de
Dupont | | Chambure
(2) Yvette | | =(2) Pauline Fairfax Potter
Choquet |

Nicole   Monique

Philippine=Jacques
Sereys

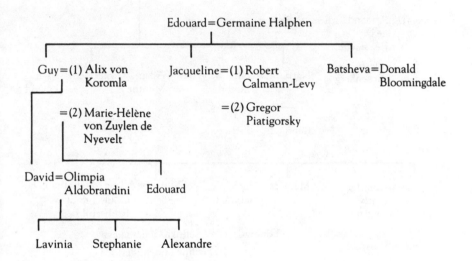

Edouard=Germaine Halphen

Guy=(1) Alix von   Jacqueline=(1) Robert   Batsheva=Donald
Koromla   Calmann-Levy   Bloomingdale

=(2) Marie-Hélène   =(2) Gregor
von Zuylen de   Piatigorsky
Nyevelt

David=Olimpia
Aldobrandini   Edouard

Lavinia   Stephanie   Alexandre

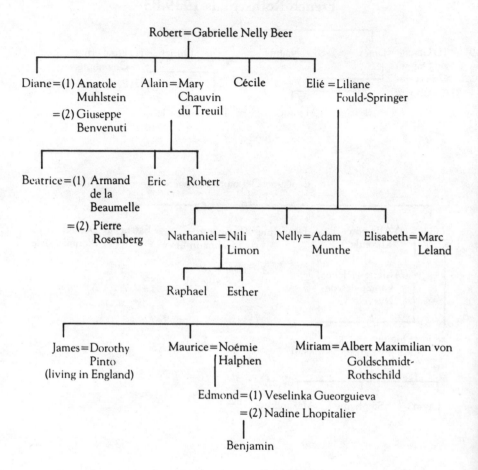

Robert=Gabrielle Nelly Beer

Diane=(1) Anatole
Muhlstein
=(2) Giuseppe
Benvenuti

Alain=Mary
Chauvin
du Treuil

Cécile

Elié =Liliane
Fould-Springer

Beatrice=(1) Armand
de la
Beaumelle
=(2) Pierre
Rosenberg

Eric   Robert

Nathaniel=Nili
Limon

Nelly=Adam
Munthe

Elisabeth=Marc
Leland

Raphael   Esther

James=Dorothy
Pinto
(living in England)

Maurice=Noémie
Halphen

Miriam=Albert Maximilian von
Goldschmidt-
Rothschild

Edmond=(1) Veselinka Gueorguieva
=(2) Nadine Lhopitalier

Benjamin

Left: *'Jimmy' de Rothschild.*
(*Illustrated London News* Picture Library)

Below: *The Hon. Walter Rothschild.*
(*Illustrated London News* Picture Library)

Charles Rothschild photographed on a visit to Japan. (Dr Miriam Rothschild)

The formidable Thérèse . . .
and her troublesome son Henri.
(Mme Philippine de
Rothschild)

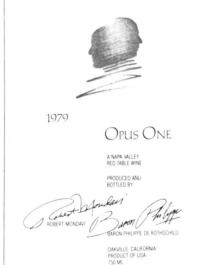

1979

OPUS ONE

A NAPA VALLEY
RED TABLE WINE

PRODUCED AND
BOTTLED BY

ROBERT MONDAVI

BARON PHILIPPE DE ROTHSCHILD

OAKVILLE, CALIFORNIA
PRODUCT OF USA
750 ML

Above: *Baron Philippe de Rothschild at his beloved Mouton.*
(Mme Philippine de Rothschild)

Left: *The label of the first wine produced jointly in California by Baron Philippe and Robert Mondavi.* (Taken from C. Ray, *Robert Mondavi of the Napa Valley*)

Below: *The magnificent museum of wine created at Mouton by Baron Philippe and his wife.*
(Mme Philippine de Rothschild)

Left: *Baron Eric in the cellars at Château Lafite-Rothschild. (Daily Telegraph)*

Below Left: *A nineteenth-century transfer-print plate depicting Château Lafite.* (Baron Eric de Rothschild)

Below Right: *Baron Elie de Rothschild, who restored the fortunes of Château Lafite after the Second World War, seen here showing Queen Elizabeth, the Queen Mother, around the Lafite cellars.* (Château Lafite)

Baron Edmond de Rothschild, 'the Father of Modern Israel'.
(Baron Edmond de Rothschild)

Baron Maurice de Rothschild. (Baron Edmond de Rothschild)

Above: *The world première of* And After..., *22 April 1974. A ballet commissioned by Batsheva de Rothschild's Bat-Dor Company.*
(Mme Batsheva de Rothschild)

Left: *Evelyn de Rothschild, 1963.*
(BBC Hulton Picture Library)

Below: *Guests at the exotic Surrealist Ball held at Ferrières in 1972.*
(Baron Guy de Rothschild)

Above: *Baron Guy de Rothschild, 1975.* (BBC Hulton Picture Library)

Below: *Modern headquarters of the new Rothschild Bank in Paris.*
(Baron Eric de Rothschild)

Dr Miriam Rothschild, 1983.
(Universal Pictorial Press and
Agency Ltd)

Lord Rothschild, 1978.
(BBC Hulton Picture Library)

*The Hon. Jacob Rothschild in 1969, seated before a portrait of his
great-great-grandfather. Nathan would have been proud of Jacob's
business acumen.* (Associated Press Ltd)

CHAPTER 26
"Growing into reality"

The war brought the Rothschilds many distressing experiences. Their homes were looted, their property confiscated, their menfolk experienced front-line fighting and prison camps, friends and relatives disappeared in Auschwitz, Buchenwald and Theresienstadt. Yet two positive results emerged: one was that, for the first time, the Rothschilds made close and prolonged contact with the United States of America. The other was that the years 1939-45 provided an opportunity for what Batsheva calls "growing into reality".[1]

She remembers her childhood and adolescence spent in Paris, Ferrières, Deauville and various luxury resorts, as a time of very little contact with the world of ordinary people, a time when she was indulged by parents who enjoyed being generous. She had a scientific bent and studied biology at university. Her elder sister, Jacqueline, was the artistic member of the family. Like Mathilde, almost a century before, she was musically very talented and took piano lessons from one of the great virtuosi of the day. Her mentor was Alfred Cortot and, though she did not become an international concert performer, she did the next best thing — she married one. Her second husband was Gregor Piatigorsky, one of the finest cellists of the twentieth century. With her new husband, Jacqueline moved to America shortly before the outbreak of war.

Batsheva's brother, Guy, and her second cousins, Alain and Elie, had enlisted on the outbreak of hostilities and were with the French army that was vainly trying to stop Hitler's divisions breaking through the Maginot Line and pouring across the frontier of conquered Belgium. Edouard, now seventy-one, held things together at Rue Laffitte as long as possible but, in June 1940, with German troops advancing on Paris, he conveyed the best of his art collection to Deauville for concealment, then left with his wife and younger daughter. Batsheva (then twenty-six) says that she went along with her parents because she was "not strong enough in mind to make a break". She toyed with the idea of going to England in order to help in some way with the war effort, but eventually yielded to pressure from her mother and father.

There was no question, even for a proud traditionalist like Edouard, of staying at his post as his father and grandfather had done in similar crises. By then many suspected the hideous truth about the concentration camps. The three of them travelled by car, passing other groups of refugees along the road. They reached Spain and then Portugal. Their objective was New York, where Jacqueline was anxiously waiting for news of them. But thousands of other people had the same idea, and all the plane flights were booked. At last, they managed to obtain two seats. It looked as though Batsheva would have to stay in Europe after all. Then a generous American handed over his ticket and the fugitives were soon crossing the Atlantic, together.[2]

New York was to be the meeting place of several exiled Rothschilds. Shortly before the outbreak of war Alain had married Mary Chauvin de Treuil and when he went off to the front he left her in Paris with a daughter less than a year old and another child on the way. There, she received word in March 1940 that her husband had been wounded and captured. While she was waiting, sick with worry and not knowing what to do, a message came from Alain telling her to get out of Europe as quickly as possible. She travelled first to Lafite, accompanied by her English nanny, then crossed into Spain. From there she caught the last ship bound for South America and from Brazil she reached New York in September. There, very shortly afterwards, she was delivered of a son and she called him Eric. It was not a family name but it was a name to which she had every reason to feel grateful. Shortly before Alain went off to war he had been given a pair of binoculars by his old friend, Eric Warburg. He was wearing them on a strap round his neck when he went into battle. A German bullet, aimed at his chest, glanced off them and went into his arm.[3]

Alain and his younger brother, Elie, were both captured in the early days of the war and spent five years in various camps. Alain testified to the fair treatment he received at the hands of his captors. The Wehrmacht officers were, for the most part, soldiers of the old Prussian school who waged war by the book, treated prisoners with the courtesies due to their rank, and were not interested in singling out Jews for special treatment. The only anti-Semitism Alain had to endure was at the hands of other French officers who insisted, usually in vain, on being segregated from their Jewish colleagues. One day when he was on parade in the camp at Lübeck, he later recalled, the order came "All Jews, one pace forward." Alain and his friends complied. But so did a Roman Catholic padré. The commanding officer marched up to him angrily. "I said 'All Jews', Father. You obviously aren't a Jew." "Well now," replied the priest, "one can never be absolutely sure about the honour of one's grandmother."[4] Elie was not so fortunate. Because of his persistent attempts to escape, he ended up in Colditz Castle, the Germans' most secure prison. There, he found his fellow French officers determined on segregation and had to submit to sharing separate quarters with his fellow Jews. He was, however, able to get married. He had become engaged before the war to Liliane Fould-Springer, a childhood sweetheart. She escaped to America with his parents and, in 1942, the couple were wed by proxy — a defiant affirmation of faith in the future at a very bleak time.

Another member of the family, the "renegade" Maurice, was involved in one of the most intriguing and, indeed, historic episodes of the early stages of the war. In May 1940 Winston Churchill became Britain's Prime Minister, charged with the awesome task of trying to stem the Nazi advance. The situation could scarcely have been worse. France was on the point of collapse. The main British and French forces were being driven back towards Dunkirk. It was only a matter of days or weeks before the Germans ruled in Paris. Churchill needed some means of keeping alive a spirit of resistance in France. He discussed the problem with his Secretary of State for War, Anthony Eden. They agreed that an urgent, secret meeting with the French Prime Minister, Paul Reynaud, and his Minister of War, Georges Mandel, was necessary. How could such a meeting be arranged? It was far too risky to use the normal diplomatic channels. Then Eden remembered his friend, Maurice de Rothschild, a member of the Senate who knew all the leading politicians. He made a telephone call to the Baron and explained what he wanted. Within days the British leaders flew to Paris and were conveyed incognito to the Ritz, where Maurice had arranged a private dinner party for the four statesmen. He presided at the table while the others talked. They decided to send to London a man who could act as the focus of "free French" loyalty and aspirations, a charismatic army colonel called Charles de Gaulle. Within a month Reynaud's independent administration had fallen and the tall, abrasive army officer had set up, in London, a French government in exile.

De Gaulle was certainly not the leader Maurice would have chosen. He neither liked nor trusted the man. Of course, his opinion was not asked. His function began and ended with the arrangement of the dinner.[5] Maurice soon found himself in trouble for opposing Marshal Pétain, who succeeded Reynaud in June, and immediately called for an armistice with Hitler.* He planned to settle in England but this was opposed by de Gaulle, who disliked Rothschild as much as Rothschild disliked him. Moreover, the general (as he now was) did not want someone who knew the real circumstances of his summons to London free to tell his story.

*Reynaud spent the war in French and German prisons.

Thanks to de Gaulle's direct intervention Maurice was sent to Nassau in the Bahamas, where he spent a year and a half in "golden" exile supported entirely by funds sent by his brother Jimmy.

In June 1940, when Marshal Pétain came to terms with the invaders and was allowed to remain head of a puppet regime based at Vichy, one of the features of the deal between the Nazis and the collaborators was the confiscation of the property of all "enemies of the state". This, of course, included the Rothschilds. Edouard, Robert and Henri who had proved their opposition to the pro-German regime by flight (Edouard and Robert to America, Henri to Portugal) were stripped of their French nationality and all the assets they had left behind. In their absence, they were sentenced to perpetual imprisonment. The same was true of Maurice, who had made good his escape to the Bahamas.

Flight was not so simple for Maurice's divorced wife and their son. They, too, were proclaimed stateless persons by the Vichy government and it was only a matter of time before they were denounced to the authorities. Noémie decided not to wait. At the end of June 1940, she drove with thirteen-year-old Edmond and a governess into Switzerland. They made for her ex-husband's property at Pregny. But the vast château was shut up and, in any case, was quite unsuitable as a refuge for two ladies and a teenage boy. They installed themselves in a small house on the estate and thanks to a thousand Swiss francs per month sent by Jimmy, they managed to survive. "The local people were not very warm towards us," Edmond recalls. "Not that one can blame them. Harbouring refugees made them very vulnerable. They could not be sure the Nazis would respect their neutrality for ever."[6] Because of this hostility he had to attend an international school in Geneva rather than the local school.

By this time the Austrian Rothschilds had also reached New York. Surprising as it may seem, Alphonse and his family, who had so narrowly escaped the Anschluss, were almost trapped once more on the Continent when war broke out. Alphonse had decided to spend the summer of 1939 in Switzerland. It was part holiday, part rest cure. He had developed a serious heart condition and this had been made worse by two recent tragedies. The first was that of being forced to leave his home and country. The second was the loss of his only son. The sixteen-year-old Albert died in 1938 from what was diagnosed as a septic throat, although it seems likely that he was, in fact, suffering from leukaemia, a disease then little understood. Albert was the last male member of the line descended directly from Salomon. Of the three surviving sons of Salbert, two made no attempt to produce heirs for the Austrian house and Alphonse's other children were daughters. Ever since the death of Anselm, the Viennese Rothschilds had possessed remarkably little dynastic sense, apparently preferring to live their own lives without worrying about the future of the bank. It is almost as if they had resigned themselves to the repeated disasters which fate seemed intent on inflicting upon them. Alphonse's personal sufferings had sapped his zest for life, leaving him melancholy and bemused. Perhaps the old man could not or would not come to terms with the real nature of the cataclysm now sweeping over Europe. He had suffered enough and could not face being harried from his Swiss haven, as he had been driven from Austria.

To be sure, there was still room for optimism. Not much happened during the "phoney war" of 1939-40. But soon thousands of refugees, mainly Jews, were pouring across the border and the Swiss government was growing restive. In the spring of 1940 Alphonse and Clarice decided to try to get back to England. By making a series of short train journeys across France they managed to reach the Channel coast shortly before the retreating British and French forces congregated at Dunkirk. For some months they enjoyed the generous hospitality of their English cousins but there was no question of their staying for the duration of the war. Lionel and Anthony, who had quite enough problems of their own, insisted that the Austrian Rothschilds would be safer in America. Hitler was preparing to invade Britain. Better to move on now than be forced into yet another panic-stricken flight later. So Alphonse and his family packed their bags once more and crossed the Atlantic. Soon after they settled in New York they were joined by Lionel's fourteen-year-old son, Leo, who lived with them until 1945. But Alphonse did not long survive the journey. By now he was very ill and in 1942 he died. His widow faced up to the problems of raising teenage daughters in a strange country, and on a greatly reduced income, with fortitude and strength of character. Bettina recalls that, although the contrast with their old Austrian life style was considerable, they all settled happily and did not really miss the summer palaces and wide parklands of childhood.[7]

The immigrants, especially the younger generation, rapidly put down roots in the land of refuge and promise. Bettina married, in 1943, a young US diplomat, Matthew Looram. Batsheva, her French cousin, studied at Columbia University and afterwards took up factory work and helped to run a woman's welfare group. In 1948 she married into the fashionable Bloomingdale family. Louis settled happily and was much courted in smart society. At the age of sixty-four he threw off bachelorhood to marry another Austrian emigrée, Countess Hildegard Auersperg.

In 1942, after America had entered the war, sixty-one-year-old Maurice managed to reach New York, arriving there via Canada. He had no assets. All he owned had either been confiscated by the Vichy government or was tied up in Switzerland and the only way to avoid a penurious old age was to put his agile mind to work. He began doing what he had done as a young man, speculating on the stock and commodity markets. This time he had more success. He borrowed money at low rates of interest (and banks seldom hesitated to lend to a Rothschild). Then, knowing that the value of raw materials could only rise in a time of conflict and in the period of recovery that would follow, he invested heavily in copper, iron, tin and diamond mines and coffee and sugar plantations. Like a latterday N.M., he used the ebb-and flow of war to his own advantage. With the telephone and the financial press as his only tools and without ever opening an office, he amassed the first Rothschild fortune that had nothing to do with banking.

But not all the family escaped the worst horrors of the war. In June 1940 Philippe, his wife and their daughter, Philippine, made first for Mouton. From there Philippe decided to travel abroad to link up with other non-Vichy Frenchmen. He sent his family to friends in the Dordogne where he hoped that rural obscurity would keep them from harm. But he did not reach his destination. Travelling via Morocco, he was arrested by Vichy agents and returned to France. After eight months he was released and immediately sought out Lili (Elisabeth) and Philippine. He tried to impress on his wife that the war situation was deteriorating rapidly and that she ought to go to England with him. But she refused. She was not Jewish and she believed she had nothing to fear. She did not grasp the fact that anyone connected with the Rothschilds was in danger from the Nazis. In 1942 they even visited their wrath on the Fondations Rothschild. Thirty-five elderly patients (six of them over eighty) were sent to Birkenau camp. Such atrocities did not shake Lili's false sense of security or her patrician hauteur. France was her country and in France she would remain. She did not speak English and had no desire to be left without friends in a foreign country. They parted and Lili took their daughter to Paris where they lived until 1944. To be on the safe side, she reverted to the title she had had before her marriage, the Comtesse de Chambure. Little Philippine was baptised into her mother's Roman Catholic faith – the first Christian Rothschild.

There were no serious alarms until 1944. Then, in the wake of the Normandy Landings, the Nazis began a systematic purge of all "undesirables". Philippine, who was then nine years old, remembers vividly the day, 22 June, when two Gestapo officers called at their house to interview her mother. She was hidden in the cellar by the servants, but the Germans kept demanding to see her and the point was eventually reached when further prevarication was useless. She entered the sitting room and stood by her mother who seemed very calm. The Nazis asked, "Where is your father?" Philippine, who had been well drilled for just such an occasion, replied "I don't know. He's gone away." Lili rose from her seat. Philippine recalls that she was wearing a tartan skirt and a black velvet blazer.

"Well, gentlemen, now you know all there is to know. I presume you are satisfied."

"No. We're taking you in for further questioning." The two men looked at Philippine.

"What about the girl?" one of them asked in German.

"Oh leave her," his colleague replied. "I've got a kid the same age back home."

Lili bent down and kissed her daughter. "Off you go dear. I'll see you later."

She was taken by staff car to the infamous interrogation centre in the Rue de Saussier. She never returned.[8] Lili's last days were later pieced together from eyewitness reports. She was among hundreds of French men and women herded on to the last train from Paris to the death camp at Ravensbrück. There she was savagely beaten and thrown, alive, into the incinerator.

Philippine was taken into the country to the safety of a relative's house. A few days later, a man came to visit her. A strange man, in uniform. It took several seconds for the little girl to recognise the father she had last seen two and a half years before. Lili was not the only member of the family to suffer in the concentration camps. Rozsika lost one sister, hacked to death with meat-hooks, and had a brother who was "lucky" enough to be a Dachau survivor.

Philippe meanwhile had been having a colourful war. After following a circuitous route beset by many adventures, he reached England and spent the next couple of years training with the British army and waiting for the big counter-offensive — D-Day. At the end of June 1944, after the Normandy Landings had established a bridgehead, Philippe's unit crossed the Channel. His tasks were liaison between liberators and liberated, and the establishment of civilian law and order. These were far from easy. Strains and stresses inevitably arose once initial gratitude towards the Tommies had worn off and the realities of Allied occupation began to make themselves felt. Then there was the matter of trying to stop the good citizens of France from lynching every collaborator they could lay hands on. Philippe moved on to Paris with the army and there learned of his wife's arrest. With Lili presumed dead and his house at Mouton (as he discovered) occupied as a command centre by the Luftwaffe, life seemed to be falling apart, but he was overjoyed to discover that little Philippine at least was safe.

One person who did not live to see the post-war recovery was Henri. That diversely gifted man died in 1946 in Lausanne. He had spent the war years in Portugal. Perhaps he had discovered there a refuge not only from armed conflict and persecution but from all the frustration and disappointments of life.

Baron Guy's wartime adventures were as vigorous if not as harrowing as his cousin's. He was among the troops evacuated from Dunkirk, where he won the Croix de Guerre. He returned to France immediately but, when the Armistice was signed, laid down his arms and lived for a while with his wife, Alix, in southern (Vichy) France, where there was no army of occupation. Then came the announcement of the law stripping the Rothschilds of their possessions and their citizenship. There was nothing for it but to follow the example of their relatives. In October 1941 Guy and Alix travelled, via Spain and Portugal, to the USA. They settled in New York surrounded by other members of the family and by friends, old and new.

Soon a son was born to them. And soon Guy had joined with his father and Robert in a small financial venture. It began as little more than a very necessary analysis of all their movable and convertible assets — bonds, shares, foreign currency, overseas properties. Sorting out private and bank possessions and the legalities of what might and might not be "unfrozen", was a long and complex operation. It would only make available a small fraction of the vast Rothschild capital but that was very much better than nothing. Bit by bit, various assets were realised and reinvested and, in a tiny, rented office on Fifth Avenue, a new business came into being. No one could guess, then, what would grow from this commercial mustard seed.

But Guy was not content to sit out the war in transatlantic safety with the women, children and older men. He enlisted with the Free French. On the way to Britain in a convoy, his ship was sunk by a German submarine and he had to be dragged from the sea by the crew of one of the escort vessels. Within days of reaching Scotland Guy was at Waddesdon, sharing a bottle of Lafite 1895 with Cousin Jimmy — there was much that was surreal about the Rothschilds' wartime experiences. In London he was given a job on General de Gaulle's staff, training French officers and assigning them to liaison posts with various Allied units. Then, at last, came D-Day and, weeks later, Guy was back at Rue Laffitte being rapturously welcomed by the remnant of the staff who had been allowed to remain at the bank.

In London, the sister house was faced in 1939 with a similar problem to that which had faced it in 1914. Lionel and Anthony were both past their prime and there was a dearth of younger men able and willing to provide the next generation of Rothschild leadership. Victor, a strong-willed and stubborn young man, had turned his back firmly on New Court. His difficult childhood had bequeathed him an extremely sensitive nature which he protected by building a shell of self-assurance and intellectual brilliance. He had a fine analytical mind which took him with distinction along the established family route of Harrow and Trinity, Cambridge. The feel for scientific research which he had acquired at Ashton and Tring stood him in good stead. But he was no narrow academic. He was a competent pianist, delighting in both Bach and jazz. He was an accomplished cricketer who played as an all-rounder for Northamptonshire between 1929 and 1931, once scored ninety-six off the formidable attack of Voce and Larwood and hit a century in his first game for the university. But he later withdrew from country cricket largely because of his disagreement with bodyline bowling.

He was another Rothschild collector. He brought together a superb assemblage of eighteenth-century books and manuscripts, and was an expert on the works of Jonathan Swift. He numbered many of the fashionable Bloomsbury set of writers and artists among his personal friends. But when it came to the point, he declined to add banking to his activities. He gave New Court a brief try in 1931 — and found it wanting: " . . . it came as rather a shock at the age of twenty-one to learn that I was expected at least to try the life of a banker in the City of London. This I did, but the moment was unfortunate. In 1931 there was a world recession; the City seemed moribund, boring, rather painful. I did not like banking which consists essentially of facilitating the movement of money from Point A, where it is, to Point B where it is needed . . . "[9]

Victor returned to Cambridge to do research and, in 1935, was elected to a fellowship at Trinity. For the next few years he was in his element. He was newly married. He was widely regarded as one of the country's most promising young scientists. His work, studying the movements of sperm and the process of fertilisation and lecturing in the Department of Zoology, was fulfilling. When he was not in the laboratory, he had sport and the company of intelligent friends to amuse him. He was a member of the Apostles, an exclusive debating club open only to the best brains. Intellectually it was an exciting time to be in Cambridge. Political ideas were in a state of ferment. The collapse of the old order was a challenge to thinking men and women. The university was full of eager idealists who believed they had the answers to the world's ills. Some wrote angry poems and articles for the left-wing press. Some went off to fight in the Spanish Civil War. Some were recruited by the Soviet Union to be a secret vanguard of the coming international revolution.

Victor, who became the third Baron Rothschild on Walter's death in

1937, was not a Marxist. Years later he claimed that he was "very ignorant about politics and ideologies in those days, being, so I thought, too busy with my scientific work, sport and social life to have much time for anything else".[10] Yet he was, inescapably, a Socialist and the river of his political thought was fed by two streams: the sense of social responsibility inherited from his forebears and his concern at the serious problems of the day — mass unemployment, the rise of Fascism and the manifest failure of *laissez-faire* capitalism. Perhaps there was also a sense of frustration and helplessness in his outlook on the world. Traditionally Rothschilds had always been active in alleviating the ills of society, bringing their philanthropy and political influence to bear on desperate situations. But, as we have seen, post-1918 Europe had rejected paternalism and the Rothschilds were no longer admitted to the inner councils of the powerful.

But Victor's contemporaries at Cambridge included some young men who felt that they could do something. There was his friend, Anthony Blunt, a fellow occupant of the high table at Trinity, a brilliant art historian and expert on the work of Nicolas Poussin. Rothschild was impressed by the older man's intellect, wit and clever conversation, and also by what he regarded as his "high moral or ethical principles". He felt that Blunt was one of the few people he could turn to for advice.[11] Temperamentally quite different was the flamboyant undergraduate Guy Burgess who threw extravagant parties and was, openly, a Communist and a homosexual. Other contemporaries included Donald Maclean and Kim Philby. With Burgess and Blunt, they made up what would later be known as the notorious Cambridge Four. Maclean, Philby, Burgess and Blunt were all recruited as Soviet agents in the thirties, infiltrated into government service and inflicted considerable damage on British security. Lord Rothschild's social contact with such men in his halcyon Cambridge days would later involve him in much grief.

While Victor was following an academic career, his cousin, Edmund, (usually known as "Eddy") dutifully joined the bank in 1938. Lionel's son was six years Lord Rothschild's junior and the only other member of the family eligible for New Court. But, after only a year, war broke out and Eddy rejoined his regiment, the Royal Bucks Yeomanry. Then, in 1942, his father died. Eddy travelled home to sort out the estate and the suggestion came, from the very office of the Prime Minister, that he should return to New Court. History was repeating itself. But Eddy refused to be trapped as Lionel had been in 1914. He went back to his regiment and Anthony was left alone to see the bank through the war years.

It was a tough and worrying task. During the Blitz Anthony was responsible not only for the maintenance of business, but for the safety of staff and the preservation of valuable records. For much of the war he lived at New Court, on hand day and night to cope with any crisis, a familiar figure to the fire watchers and air-raid wardens who patrolled the premises during the hours of darkness. Many employees were moved out to the relative safety of Tring Park where as much as possible of NMR's business was done.

The uncertainties of war brought home to Anthony the need to consider the future. At such a time family businesses were especially vulnerable. He knew, for example, that if anything happened to himself or his brother, the partnership would cease to exist. This immediate problem was solved, in 1941, by the technical expedient of establishing a company — Rothschilds Continuation — which was appointed a partner in the firm. The wisdom of this move became obvious the following year with Lionel's death. The creation of Rothschilds Continuation was the first step — though probably not conceived as such in 1941 — in transforming NMR from a family partnership into a private company.

However, as far as humanly possible, the bank preserved an atmosphere of "business as usual". After the Blitz the celebrated New Court lunches resumed. Many of the great, the famous and the influential came to Anthony's table. At no other unofficial gatherings in wartime London was there such well-informed conversation ranging over world military, political and economic affairs. For example, on 4 May 1945 John Colville, Churchill's Private Secretary, was among a group of guests which included the Prime Ministers of Canada and Northern Ireland.[12]

Eddy and Victor both saw active service. Eddy was in the British Expeditionary Force which tried to halt the initial German advance. He ended up in charge of five hundred men who were separated from their regiment and evacuated from Cherbourg just after Dunkirk. Later he served as an artillery major in the North African campaign, moved on to the invasion of Italy and ended up in Yugoslavia. He had what he calls "an interesting war". It included being present at the battle of Monte Cassino and being responsible for feeding ten thousand prisoners in North Africa after the surrender of the German forces at Cap Bon, Tunisia. It also included the unsavoury business of witnessing the hand-over to the Red Army of the Uzbeks, Russians who had fought for the Germans. The British government resisted this for some time but when the Soviets refused to release British POWs in their hands the order was sent to comply with Communist demands. Edmund was the powerless witness of hundreds of unfortunate soldiers being loaded into trucks to be transported to the Russian lines — and certain death.

But the war had its lighter moments. He delights to tell the story of his negotiations with a partisan leader over a strip of disputed territory. The Yugoslav knew he was in the wrong but could not lose face by simply admitting the fact, so it was agreed to decide the issue by a football match between Major de Rothschild's men and the patriots. If the English won, the Yugoslavs would cede the territory. If the Yugoslavs were victorious, they would give up the land as a magnanimous gesture. In the event, Edmund recalls, there was such a party and everyone had so much to drink that the result was far from clear to all the participants. However, he is convinced that his men carried the day.

It was inevitable that a man of Lord Rothschild's intellect should spend the war years in Military Intelligence. He was assigned to anti-sabotage activities and was primarily involved in discovering and dismantling bombs, which were usually disguised as innocuous objects such as boxes of vegetables. It was dangerous work for which he received the George Medal. He was also employed as an interrogator. His hard-edged, unemotional brilliance could penetrate the subterfuges of suspected agents and captured enemy officers. He it was who investigated one of the most controversial incidents of the war. In July 1943 General Wladyslaw Sikorski, head of the Polish government in exile, was killed in an air crash near Gibraltar. Sikorski had recently broken off diplomatic relations with the Russians and this was an embarrassment to the Allies at a crucial stage of the war. Several parties certainly had an interest in the removal of this stubborn old soldier from the scene and sabotage was a distinct possibility. It was Lord Rothschild who was charged with ferreting out the truth. The results of his investigations were secret. They have remained so.[13]

Another of his responsibilities was protecting the Prime Minister from possible attack. This meant subjecting to analysis the many cigars that Churchill constantly received from well-wishers. Nor was it only cigars that had to be tested.

> ... On one occasion, when walking across Parliament Square to the House of Commons, the Prime Minister was accosted by a French General who saluted and presented him with a Virginia ham. This greatly pleased Winston who remarked that he would have it for breakfast the next morning. There was panic. How could the ham be tested without his knowing and be ready for breakfast the next morning? An intricate surgical operation was undertaken whereby a very thin slice of ham was removed without disturbing the ham's surface. What could be done with the slice, time being far too short for bacteriological examination? After a high pressure conference a solution was, as usual, found. The slice of ham was fed to the Medical

Research Council cat which was kept under minute examination for many hours. As it survived, the Prime Minister had his Virginia ham for breakfast the next morning.[14]

A similar incident occurred in 1944 when Winston was presented with a case of 1798 Armagnac by a French admirer. Rothschild insisted on having a thirteenth bottle. Testing such exquisite brandy was one of the better perks of an extremely arduous job.[15]

As the Allied armies rolled towards the heart of Germany in 1944-5 the work of intelligence gathering was increasingly important. It was vital to bring the conflict to an end as rapidly as possible to avoid unnecessary loss of life. Rothschild was established in Paris's Avenue de Marigny, as part of a team examining captured enemy officers. Among the notable prisoners who passed through his hands was Otto Skorzeny, a German paratroop commander, whose most notable exploit had been a raid on Campo Imperatore in the Abruzzi Mountains in September 1943. The object of the exercise, successfully achieved, was the rescue of the recently overthrown Italian dictator, Benito Mussolini.[16]

War did not prevent Victor enjoying that social intimacy with the greatest in the land which had become a Rothschild birthright. On 7 February 1944, for instance, he gave a dinner party in a private room at the Savoy for a few friends which included the Prime Minister, his wife and daughter, Brendan Bracken, Minister of Information and a close confidant of Winston's, and John Colville. Colville noted in his journal: "Dinner was excellent and the wine, from the Tring cellars, included Pol Roger 1921, the Rothschild Château Yquem and a remarkable old brandy. There was an extremely good conjuror who appeared at the end of dinner and whom the PM declared to be the best he had ever seen."[17] The Rothschilds were among those who were well cushioned against wartime austerity.

Intelligence work suited Lord Rothschild, not only because he was extremely clever but also because he possessed two other family traits: a desire to be at the centre of things and a love of secretiveness. Other M15 officers have published their wartime memoirs with a greater or lesser regard to their obligations under the Official Secrets Act. Victor has maintained a near-total silence. One benefit the war brought him was a new wife. His assistant throughout was Tessa Mayor, a brave and clever woman whose work earned her the Military MBE. In 1946 Lord Rothschild and his first wife were divorced and he married Tessa.

The war had enabled Victor to demonstrate the power of his intellect in many ways — perhaps too many. By his own admission, he has never been the easiest man to get on with. He described this trait to one interviewer as "a quick anti-reaction".[18] Malcolm Muggeridge, who knew him during his Paris days, formed the opinion that he was a man who had "lost his way", a judgement he elaborated on in these words: "Embedded deep down in him there was something touching and vulnerable and perceptive; at times loveable even. But so overlaid with the bogus certainties of science, and the equally bogus respect, accorded and expected, on account of his wealth and famous name that it was only rarely apparent."[19]

Miriam, Charles Rothschild's eldest daughter, had an intellect scarcely less impressive than her brother Victor's. She was an excellent scientific research worker and also a great lover of nature. She describes herself as the last of an endangered species — the dedicated amateur naturalist. The breadth of her interests is reflected in her three hundred published papers on topics from the measurement of ultraviolet light at an altitude of thirteen thousand metres to the lovelife of snails and the migration of butterflies. Miriam could have followed her brother's example and pursued a university-based career, but Rothschilds are seldom conventional. The combination of brains, independent means and the formidable family name enabled her to pursue her own course. In doing so, she achieved such distinction that professional scientists, most of whom habitually look askance at "pretenders" from outside their narrow, academic world, have been obliged to take her seriously.

It was Miriam's father who set her on this course. Charles told his daughters that there was, in his opinion, nothing to be gained from public examinations, which were a waste of time. Miriam followed this advice. At the age of seventeen she enrolled simultaneously in two degree courses, English literature and zoology, but never offered herself for the degree examinations, despite the fact that her tutors recognised her as more advanced than most of her fellow students. When, years later, Oxford University wished to present her with an honorary doctorate, the authorities were embarrassed to discover that because she possessed no lower degree, she was not eligible for the award. Hurriedly and discreetly they had to change the regulations to meet the situation. The same problem arose when she became visiting professor at the Royal Free Hospital.

Among her other interests, Miriam continued her father's work on fleas. In Charles Rothschild's day, study of these creatures was of immense practical importance because they were vectors of bubonic plague, hence his co-option on to the Plague Commission. In later years these insects sprang into prominence as carriers of myxomatosis, an epidemic disease of rabbits, introduced from South America, which conveniently controlled their numbers. In Australia, however, where the rabbit population reached terrible proportions, they lacked fleas and the disease was carried far less effectively by mosquitoes. The Australian government decided on an attempt to introduce the European rabbit flea into their country in the hope of controlling the plague of rabbits. Miriam was called upon to assist with this experiment. She first solved the problem of breeding fleas on captive rabbits — discovering that the insect's reproduction was controlled by its host's hormones and consequently could itself breed only on pregnant rabbits. She also located a race of the rabbit flea in Spain better adapted to a hot climate and after collecting them established a population on her tame rabbits at Ashton.* These were finally despatched to Australia. But obtaining visas for infested rabbits proved incredibly difficult and telephone messages from the House of Commons were required to get them in and out of India. Eventually the rabbits were delivered to an Australian laboratory but, unfortunately, during a vacation the solitary, overzealous keeper on duty carefully dusted them all with a generous dose of insecticide. Patiently, Miriam organised another collecting expedition to Spain.

Before the outbreak of the Second World War she was working temporarily in the Department of Agriculture in Washington but in 1940 she returned to England to join the Government Information Service at Bletchley (where the celebrated Enigma device was developed). There was a period of waiting during the phoney war, and before moving to Bletchley Miriam filled in time by training as an air-raid warden (she received the Defence Medal at the end of hostilities for her activities as a warden) and also qualified as a dairy maid. Meanwhile a large airfield was installed on her farm at Ashton Wold. After several sessions on a flight-training simulator she had a "brainwave", and designed and fitted the first seat belt (made of saddle girths) to her Austin 10 car. It was over forty years before the invention was made compulsory on all cars in the UK.

The war took an unexpected turn for her in 1942 when she spent a few days leave from Bletchley at the Red Cross convalescent home at Ashton into which her house had been temporarily transformed. The matron announced that there was a patient in the hospital who had nearly lost an arm and who insisted that he had corresponded with Miriam's mother and would like to meet her. Miriam thought this was highly unlikely and said so. But the matron persisted. "I told him your mother had died. He is an Hungarian called George Lanyi." Puzzled, Miriam invited the mysterious young man to tea. She was confronted with a handsome, twenty-six-year-old sergeant who produced a letter from his wallet written on Ashton Wold notepaper and signed "Rozsika Rothschild". It was dated about six months prior to her death and invited Mr Lanyi to contact her. George

---

*Ashton was her home and she inherited it after her mother's death.

explained how he had received it. Shortly before the war he had left Hungary, like many other Jews during the Hitler regime. After his arrival in England he had worked as a writer and journalist. It was an article on refugees arriving at Harwich which had so impressed Miriam's mother that she decided to contact the author. War and Rozsika's death intervened, and it was only by an extraordinary coincidence that he found himself destined, after all, to respond involuntarily to that long-standing invitation to Ashton Wold.

What followed was a typical wartime romance and marriage. But added to the usual circumstances of war was the fact that members of George's family as well as some of Miriam's maternal relatives had perished at the hands of the Nazis and this grim fact united them closely.

Inevitably, the next few years proved very harrowing. George volunteered for an all-Jewish élite fighting troop (of No. 10 Commando) trained in sabotage and hand-to-hand combat, and destined for operations behind enemy lines. Casualties of over fifty per cent were anticipated. These soldiers were trained as individual combatants and not as members of a unit. Thus, they lived with their wives as ordinary citizens. In effect, this meant for Miriam that her husband was often summoned at short notice, usually in the middle of the night, to take part in a raid on the Dutch or French coast. It was always possible that he would not return from such an assignment. Indeed, one night just before D-Day, George landed his speedboat near Calais on a nocturnal reconnaissance – an expedition for which he subsequently received the Military Cross – and did not come back. The British authorities had not granted the men of No.3 Troop British nationality but, fully aware of their added peril if they were captured, they had anglicised their names and thus Miriam's husband was known as George Lane. After six weeks of acute anxiety Miriam, pregnant with her first child, heard George had been captured in France, but knowing that if his real nationality was discovered he would be shot as a traitor, her anxiety was scarcely lessened. In due course, as the first V-2s landed, her child was born, only to die a few days later.

At last, as the Allies surged into Germany, came the good news that George had escaped from Spangenberg. He had been incarcerated there following a spell in a torture camp at Frenned, where he had experienced the dubious distinction of being interrogated by Field Marshal Rommel in person. One day he arrived unexpectedly at Lord Rothschild's office in Paris.

Miriam and George were joyfully united. For fully a year afterwards her first thought on awakening was: "It's true! The war is over!" Meanwhile the authorities decided to give the living remnants of No.3 Troop British nationality.[20]

* * *

Ashton Wold was not the only Rothschild house to be "called up". 148 Piccadilly became an Allied officers' club. It was not, strictly speaking, a Rothschild house for it had been sold in 1937, the disposal of its contents being one of the major events of that year in the art world. (The list of contents for auction filled a 250-page catalogue, with the more important items featured in sixty-four colour plates.) Philippe discovered it when he was in London and had the ironical experience of being entertained as a stranger in the mansion he had stayed in as a child. Tring Park, as we have seen, accommodated several departments of the bank throughout the war, and Exbury House was requisitioned by the navy in 1942. It was here that some of the plans for the Normandy Landings were drawn up. The Rothschilds' temporary tenants looked after Lionel's mansion well but the gardens suffered badly. Without the scores of men who had maintained the illusion of a colourful and well-ordered nature, brambles, ferns and creeping ivy invaded the groves, weed choked the streams, and falling trees blocked the meandering paths. Six local pensioners worked hard to preserve the best specimens and keep the greenhouses tidy but they could not prevent the degeneration of the estate, which was under attack from the enemy as well as nature. In the Blitz fires were lit in the grounds at night in an attempt to decoy German bombers from nearby Southampton. Edmund de Rothschild recalls an evening when he brought his CO down to meet his father. During dinner the butler informed them that a stick of incendiaries had hit the garden, and they all went outside to watch the burning undergrowth and the efforts of the fire-fighters. When Lionel laconically suggested that they return to finish their meal, the officer spluttered his protest, "But I can't drink a man's port while I'm watching his estate burn!"[21]

Lionel's stoicism masked a bewildered sadness. Not only had the pleasant world of his youth degenerated into chaos: that chaos had even penetrated into his beloved Exbury. A weekend guest at the Hampshire estate in October 1939 noted in his diary a conversation with his host as they walked through the lovely autumnal woods. The discussion turned to Hitler's treatment of the Jews. Lionel, making a bitter joke, suggested another version of the "final solution". After the war, the victors should give Germany to the Jews and scatter the "Aryans" among the races of the world.[22]

Jimmy de Rothschild and his wife, Dolly, threw themselves into the war effort in various ways. As we have already seen, they gave considerable financial support to their dispossessed relatives. But there was much more to be done closer to home. Despite failing eyesight, James continued to serve as an MP. One day in 1944 he elicited from the House a rare and solemn tribute. An impromptu speech in which he thanked the British people for giving refuge to many Jews fleeing Nazi persecution brought his fellow members to their feet in a silent gesture of sympathy. A few months later, however, he was received very differently. This was the occasion in March 1945 when he rose to answer questions in his new rôle as Under-Secretary to the Ministry of Supply. The opposition gave him such a rough ride that Churchill commented that if the Commons were ever as rude to Rothschild again, he would make him a privy councillor. [23]

And, of course, there was Waddesdon to be looked after, together with its fabulous contents. At the beginning of the war Jimmy and Dolly crated up the most valuable treasures and stored them in the basement. That nearly proved to be a disastrous mistake. When they checked the pictures after a few weeks to make sure they were all right, they discovered one obscured by a bloom of damp. The Watteaus, Dous, Gainsboroughs and Bouchers had to be hastily rehoused and some were sent off to a Canadian museum for safekeeping. But, they could not regard their large house and estate as an empty museum while others were suffering pain and homelessness. Even before the outbreak of hostilites they were involved in a dramatic rescue of German-Jewish children from the very jaws of the Nazis.

In September 1938 the Philanthropin, the boys' school founded in Frankfurt by the Rothschilds, was attacked by the SS as part of their increasing campaign of intimidation. Hugo and Lilli Steinhardt, who ran the school, realised that worse was to come and tried to find ways of evacuating their charges from Germany. With the help of their two daughters they wrote appeals for help to everyone they could think of. Early in 1939 a letter addressed to "Lord Rothschild, London" was forwarded to Waddesdon. Jimmy immediately sent an agent to Germany to negotiate with the authorities the expatriation of those children whose parents would allow them to leave. During the spring thirty boys made their escape with the Steinhardts and were accommodated in a house on the Waddesdon estate called the Cedars. There they stayed for the duration of the war. Eventually the "Cedar Boys", as they were known locally, dispersed. One later became a high-ranking Israeli diplomat. Another owned his own engineering company in Puerto Rico. None of their friends who remained in Frankfurt have ever been heard of since.

It was not long before more children came to Waddesdon. During the Blitz a hundred infants evacuated from south London to avoid the air raids were billeted in the house. Thus, for most of the war small boys and girls rampaged along the corridors and ran sticky fingers over the silk-covered walls built by childless Ferdinand and cared for so lovingly by spinster

Alice. Outside, the park became an open-air fuel store. Under the screen of trees the army built Nissen huts and filled them with drums of petrol and diesel oil. If ever a stray bomb had come Waddesdon's way the results would have been devastating.

Waddesdon survived the war. Would the Rothschild wealth and solidarity it symbolised be so fortunate?

CHAPTER 27

"The Rothschilds should maintain their traditional rôle"

The death of Lionel de Rothschild, in 1942, came at just about the worst possible time for the English bank. It had survived the Depression and its aftermath but the strains had been considerable and the dislocation of a second war brought NMR close to breaking point. Once again crisis provoked dynastic unity. Just as the London Rothschilds had readily come to the financial aid of their cousins in exile, so members of the family in a position to help rendered assistance to New Court now. Lord Rothschild boosted the bank's capital reserves from his own resources and Rue Laffitte also waded in with funds. In 1947 "Mr Edmund" joined his uncle as what he describes as "a very junior partner". In those days, he recalls, "NMR was still a small outfit; I signed all the cheques and knew all staff at the bank and the refinery — and often their children, too."[1]

It could not remain so. For the banking Rothschilds the moment of truth had arrived. If they were to resume their places as leaders in the world of international finance they would have to expand and modernise, to open the Victorian corridors of New Court to new men and new ideas. But could the old bank reform itself? Anthony, who carried out a holding operation from the time of his brother's death until 1956 when a stroke removed him from New Court, was a strong-minded man set in his ways and he certainly did not appear to colleagues and employees as a bold innovator. One long-time servant of New Court described him as looking askance at the new breed of merchant bankers who sought business by advertising,

> which he thought vulgar, or by dashing constantly about in aeroplanes. He scorned to cultivate men whom he did not part- icularly like for the sake of possibly valuable contacts. He did not travel himself and he did not sit on the boards of the numerous public companies which would have been delighted to have him. "They know where we live," he would say of potential clients; "if they want to do business with us let them come and talk to us." And when they did come, if he did not like their faces or their manners he showed

them the door without hesitation, no matter how profitable the proposed transaction might be.[2]

Yet it was Anthony who began the reorganisation which became the basis for future growth.

It was also the basis for family discord. Immediately before and during the war some of Anthony's relatives had, as we have seen, provided cash "transfusions" from their personal funds to keep New Court alive. Now he proposed that they should do so again but on a new basis. In 1947 the task was completed of transforming N.M. Rothschild and Sons from a partnership into a private company, with Rothschilds Continuation as the holding company. Although Lord Rothschild and Lionel's sons, Eddy and Leopold, all held shares, Anthony retained the largest holding. Effective control of NMR thus passed to him and his heirs. In not dividing the equity and in transferring power to a cadet branch of the family, Anthony, in the words of Victor's son, Jacob, "ignored one and a half centuries of Rothschild history".[3] Nor is it only Jacob who, years after Anthony's death, is unhappy about the way the reorganisation was handled.

At the time, it seems, no such misgivings were voiced. Lord Rothschild, who had no interest in the bank, nor, indeed, in adding substantially to his personal fortune, was content with his twenty per cent holding. Eddy, just back from the war, and Leo, who was only twenty and had not yet joined New Court, went along with what the senior members of the family agreed. Certainly, there was much about the new arrangement which was eminently sensible.

Basically, what it did was separate ownership of the bank from day-to-day administration, thus making it easier for NMR to attract some of the most talented and ambitious men in the City, while retaining control in the hands of the family. As to the distribution of shares, Anthony may have reasoned that the arrangement was just. It was he and his brother who had borne the heat of the battle through the Depression and the war. Victor had opted for an academic life (something which Anthony himself would love to have done) and was manifestly not interested in the decision-making process at New Court. In the new age NMR could not afford the luxury of carrying unproductive partners. As we have seen, some of the problems experienced in the past by all the houses had arisen from the involvement of members of the family who had no interest in or no talent for finance. Anthony may have felt — as the French house had felt, though for different reasons, when it excluded Maurice — that privilege and responsibility should go together. On the other hand, concentrating control in one branch of the family took no account of where the Rothschild banking talent might manifest itself in future generations. Doubtless, this did not seem very significant at the time. No one could have foreseen that the issue would come to a head in a bitter conflict only thirty-three years later.

English Rothschilds 1939-85

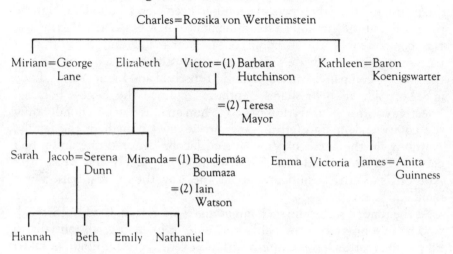

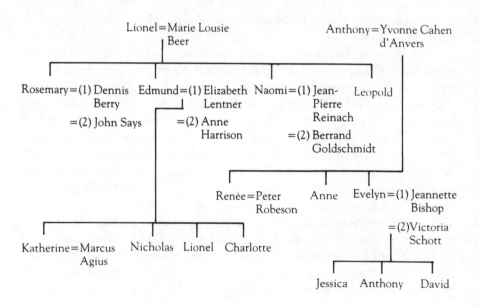

One aspect of Anthony's strategy worked very well: several talented young men were attracted to New Court. Among them was David Colville, the brother of Winston Churchill's Private Secretary. On 1 July 1960 history was made: Colville was admitted as a partner of N.M. Rothschild and Sons. For 148 years the family had remained faithful to the instructions dictated by the dying Mayer Amschel. His guidelines had served the dynasty well. They had also brought it to the brink of disaster. Now Rothschilds took the big step of abandoning them and entrusting bank policy to men chosen for their financial ability rather than their Rothschild blood. As Anthony once remarked to his son, "Your're lucky enough to be able to afford good people; the problem lies in choosing them."[4]

Another new development sanctioned by Anthony was a reappraisal of Rothschild involvement in the USA. After more than a century of regarding North America as an outpost of their commercial empire, the Rothschilds now knew that an active involvement in Wall Street was central to their strategy. The small business, Amsterdam Incorporated, founded on Fifth Avenue during the war, grew steadily, and assumed the character of an important Rothschild subsidiary. In the 1950s it was reformed as an investment bank, under the name of New Court Securities, its share capital being taken up by both the Paris and London houses.

The American operation was just one aspect of Rothschilds' new, deliberate internationalism. The bank's interests had, of course, always been worldwide but for previous generations that had largely meant negotiating loans for foreign governments. The rapid expansion of western commerce and industry in the 1950s demanded a much wider range of skills. They had to organise money movements and credit transfers between countries operating complex and strict currency regulations. They had to advise multinationals setting up new operations. They had to bring together consortiums to undertake major engineering, constructional or mining operations. They had to advise on and execute company mergers. They had to have at their fingertips not only financial expertise, but knowledge of all the new technologies — nuclear power, computers, lasers. This eventually meant establishing subsidiaries all over the world.

In his search for new markets, Edmund became a tireless globetrotter. Soon after the war he realised that defeated Japan would grow into one of the industrial giants of the modern world and took the initiative in rebuilding the commercial bridges between London and Tokyo. He learned the language, paid several visits and in 1962 was asked to lead a delegation from the City of London to Japan to strengthen commercial ties. He eventually went as the number two on the mission which was very well received. Today, visitors to the office he still occupies at New Court are proudly shown the Order of the Sacred Treasure, First Class (equivalent to the KCVO) conferred upon him by Emperor Hirohito – a justifiable pride, as he was the youngest and only the third foreigner ever to receive this honour.

The Rothschilds had certainly not lost their talent for foresight and thinking big. On one occasion Leopold was paying a visit to Brazil. The bank maintained its long-standing links with the country and was instrumental in helping it to liquidate its overseas debts after the war. This time he was coming into Rio de Janeiro by sea when a member of the company pointed to the three-mile straights between the city and Niteroi on the opposite shore, and remarked, "What a pity there isn't a bridge; it would make an enormous difference to the economy." Leopold nodded. "Then let's do it," he said. The result was the bringing together of a consortium to construct one of the world's most impressive spans. The new bridge has cut to a few minutes a journey previously only possible by ferry or sixty miles of road.

But undoubtedly the most impressive scheme Rothschilds initiated in the 1950s was Brinco, the British Newfoundland Corporation. In 1952 Joseph Smallwood, Premier of Newfoundland, called on Sir Winston Churchill, Prime Minister of Great Britain. In the Cabinet Room at 10 Downing Street he unrolled a map of his largely undeveloped country. He waxed eloquent about the immense resources – timber, mineral deposits, hydroelectricity – just waiting to be exploited. What he had in mind, he told his host, was a consortium of private companies based on London and prepared to take over a development concession of fifty thousand square miles in Labrador (out of a total of seventy thousand square miles) and ten thousand square miles in Newfoundland (approximately half the land surface). Churchill was impressed. He remarked "This is a grand imperial concept but not imperialistic", and he promised to do what he could to help. After his guest had departed, the Prime Minister turned to his private secretary, Jock Colville. "Who do we know in the City?" he asked. As it happened, Colville had lunched at New Court that day, so he said, "Rothschilds".

Smallwood went to New Court to explain his scheme to Anthony, whom he found a rather formidable man, "correct, upright, precise and exacting in his insistence upon detail, just as a banker should be".[5] Fortunately, Anthony took a liking to the Canadian statesman. Smallwood was treated to one of the celebrated New Court lunches – delicious but contained within a rigid framework of tradition: the single glass of sherry in The Room, the blind half-drawn at precisely 1.00 p.m. as a signal that the partners had gone to lunch, the principal guest placed at the head of the oval table, the meal abruptly concluded on the stroke of 2.00 p.m. But on this occasion convention faltered. Mr Anthony did not rise from his seat with his accustomed promptness. The meeting went on until three – because the senior partner was fascinated by Smallwood's enthusiastic presentation.

It is probably the greatest storehouse of undeveloped natural wealth left in the world, and it's ours . . . It's British, and we want it to remain British. Here in London you have the headquarters of more companies than anywhere else in the world; companies that have gone out to all the remote corners of the earth, to the jungle, to the frozen wastes, and built railways and opened mines and pioneered . . . My idea is this: we want you to come and develop it. We don't want you to come and sit on it; we're not interested in that – it's been sat on by time for centuries. We want to develop it and we are prepared to be generous. What we would do is begin by giving you twenty, thirty, *sixty* thousand square miles; seventy or *eighty* thousand – there's lots of it.[6]

At last, the Canadian's rhetoric came to a halt. Anthony thanked him quietly and agreed to present the proposition to some of his City friends who might be interested. They were. The general outlines of NMR's involvement were agreed and then Anthony left his junior partner to work out the details.

Over the ensuing years Edmund devoted a considerable amount of his time to this project which, even by Rothschild standards, was breathtaking in its scope. A new company was formed: British Newfoundland Corporation Limited (Brinco). N.M. Rothschild and Sons was one of the founder shareholders, together with Rio Tinto, Bowaters, Anglo-American, English Electric, Frobishers and Anglo-Newfoundland Development Corporation. However, there is no doubt which of these board members was the prime mover of the enterprise. In his memoirs Joseph Smallwood paid this tribute:

The one supremely great name in the whole Brinco-Churchill Falls saga is Rothschild: the House of Rothschild in general, and Edmund de Rothschild in particular. Never was a project, from its first inception, the beneficiary of such endless care and dedication as that given to it by that modest patriotic Englishman.[7]

Within months the immense task began. Logging camps were set up. Mineral prospecting started in earnest. Into the vast emptiness men and trucks moved to build roads, reservoirs, townships. In 1973 the project which was the centrepiece of Brinco's activities was opened. This was the power station which harnessed the spectacular Hamilton Falls (renamed Churchill Falls in memory of Sir Winston), capable of feeding 5,225,000 kilowatts of electricity into the Canadian grid at one powerhouse.[8]

Meanwhile, the French house had also had a concentrated injection of Rothschild creativity. Robert died in 1946 and Edouard was in his late seventies. It was, therefore, the younger generation who took over. Guy, Alain and Elie returned from the war to discover a demoralised bank in a demoralised country. Most of the Rue Laffitte premises had been commandeered by the Nazis for other purposes. Many of the surviving employees were past retiring age. Assets were minimal, clients few, financial expertise almost zero. Guy, who assumed control, admits that he knew virtually nothing about banking despite his pre-war years with De Rothschild Frères. But he did not even consider the possibility of shutting up shop. First, he and his cousins concentrated on getting all the confiscated assets restored. Then they amalgamated as many Rothschild interests as possible, for, though the bank was undercapitalised, various members of the family had important holdings in a variety of commercial companies. So the new generation of leaders charted a new course: De Rothschild Frères would change from being a merchant bank pure and simple to being a financial-commercial conglomerate. It would become a commercial bank with hundreds of branches, utilising the public funds they attracted for a wide portfolio of business and industrial investment. At a time when most French banks were going public, this seemed the obvious path to take. Guy later described the post-war policy thus:

> [It] involved converting the partnership into a larger corporation, opening branch offices in Paris and in other major cities. As we developed the analysis further, other factors emerged, principally the question of size. Below a certain level, a bank is squeezed out by its competitors in a field where volume and power are to a certain extent associated . . . most businesses tended to grow and often to merge in order to create larger and larger units . . . Good management nowadays requires a sophisticated organization, the cost of which must be spread over the largest possible volume of business. For all of us, it went without saying that in a France in full economic expansion, the Rothschilds should maintain their traditional role in the vanguard . . . [9]

That rôle involved a steadily increasing portfolio of interests: oil, mining, cold storage, shipping, hotels, etc., etc. In 1967, on the one hundred and fiftieth anniversary of the founding of De Rothschild Frères, a major change of identity was announced: the bank became a corporation under the name of Banque Rothschild. The new entity was a merger in which the family had a forty per cent shareholding and the remainder was owned by the Rothschilds' other major concern, the Compagnie du Nord (the successor of the Compagnie du Chemin de Fer du Nord).

Like Edmund, Guy could not confine his commercial activities to the bank. The achievement of which he still speaks with considerable pride was the creation of the French mining conglomerate IMETAL. Realising that the post-war demand for raw materials would last well into the foreseeable future, he obtained a seat on the board of the mining company Rio Tinto (by virtue of being a major shareholder, De Rothschild Frères was allocated two seats) and learned, on the job, as he says, far more than he could ever have absorbed at a Harvard Business School course.[10] With this knowledge he reinvigorated two small companies that had been owned by his family since the nineteenth century: Pennaroya, a coal-mining corporation, and Société Le Nickel, formed to exploit nickel deposits in New Caledonia. By obtaining new concessions, improving production methods, and engineering a series of mergers and takeovers, Baron Guy and his associates built a multinational corporation specialising in the mining of nonferrous minerals.

The remarkable Rothschild renaissance was one of the major events in international finance. From virtually nothing, the two remaining banks rebuilt their traditional pre-eminence. The same might have happened in Vienna but Baron Louis made a conscious decision not to refound the Viennese bank. He had put down roots in America and was happily married. He had no sons to inherit. Indeed, with the death of himself and Eugène (also living in America), the male line founded by Salomon at the beginning of the previous century was doomed to extinction. But these were not the only considerations which weighed with him. He returned to Vienna after the war, and was saddened and sickened by what he saw. The news "Rothschild has returned" went like a murmur of hope round the shattered city. Men and women rushed to see him – and to stake a claim to his generosity. Old friends, distant relatives, former employees, acquaintances, even one of his erstwhile prison guards, came with their hard-luck stories and their appeals for money or influence with the authorities or help in emigrating. It was a sorry spectacle, as was the Vienna he had loved. Whole areas lay in ruins, buildings like the Staatsoper and the Burgtheater he had once frequented were badly damaged, and the whole city was divided into occupied zones by the victorious Allied powers. Louis could see no reason to return and less reason to recommence business activities. His main concern was the welfare of old family and bank servants but this was, in fact, covered by the law established by Anselm, and still binding on the family, to provide 101 per cent pensions for all long-serving employees.[11]

There was, however, important work to be done by Louis, Eugène and Aphonse's widow Clarice. This was the recovery of all the property confiscated by the Nazis. It proved a long and difficult business. Locating and identifying most of the works of art was a small problem. They had been stored in a salt mine at Alt Aussee in the Tyrol. This was one of the fabulous caches of looted treasures discovered by the advancing Allied armies in 1945. In the long, cool, dry tunnels were row upon row of crated paintings, sculptures and pieces of furniture; brought from all over Europe, and hoarded by order of Adolf Hitler, the Jackdaw of Linz. A specially appointed tripartite commission had the task of restoring these precious objects to their real owners, if they could be found and could prove title. Fortunately, before the war Louis and Eugène had compiled detailed lists of all the family's valuables and they had no difficulty now in identifying their possessions.[12] Recognising them was one thing; getting them out of the country was quite another. The government staunchly refused to grant export permits. After long argument, a compromise was agreed: the Rothschilds were allowed to remove some works of art as long as they "donated" the remainder to the Austrian people. Thus, several galleries and museums were enriched by involuntary Rothschild generosity. Regaining real estate was even more difficult. Most of the Rothschild land and houses lay in the sector under Russian military occupation and the Soviet authorities regarded them as confiscated "German" property. In vain did the family protest that expropriated Jewish lands could not be called "German". Not until military occupation ended in 1955 were they able to negotiate the return of their estates. The lands, castles and mansions behind the Iron Curtain were, of course, lost for ever. Wittkowitz passed under Communist control. So did magnificent Schillersdorf, which became a jewel in the crown of the Czechoslovakian tourist industry. Today it is a combined hotel and training establishment for catering staff.

The Austrian Rothschilds continued to live abroad. Louis returned to his home on Long Island and remained active to the end of his life. Characteristically, he died while swimming in Montego Bay at the age of seventy-three. Characteristically, also, he left instructions for his body to be returned to Austrian soil and it was buried in Vienna in January 1955. Eugène married for the second time in 1952 when he was sixty-eight (Kitty had died in 1946) to a woman twenty-four years his junior. Jeanne was devoted to him and they lived in England for some years before moving to Monte Carlo, where Eugène died at the age of ninety-two.

But Clarice and her children maintained their links with Austria. Alphonse's widow was heavily embroiled in the battle over the family's property and she kept the estate at Langau. She installed an efficient manager and with the help of local people who had served the Rothschilds for generations, she gradually turned the beautiful forested acres from a sporting estate into a commercial one. For several months of the year she or her daughters and sons-in-law occupied Salbert's old hunting lodge in the centre of the village (now the estate office). They improved the roads and build a sawmill. They constructed a ski lift and turned Langau Meierhofen into a small winter resort, catering for both residents and also day visitors from the capital.

In 1974 the last of the Austrian Rothschilds came home (Gwendoline died in 1972). After a wandering life in the American diplomatic service, Matthew and Bettina Looram decided to retire to Langau. They built a beautiful house high in the mountains overlooking steep, timbered slopes and smoking waterfalls. From this eyrie they managed the estate, enjoying their skiing, fishing and shooting — and paying occasional visits to their wealthier cousins. Bettina laughs at being a Rothschild "reduced" to her last few thousand acres. There is little trace of regret in her voice when she says, "The bank has gone; the iron and coal fields of Wittkowitz have gone; Schillersdorf, the other fine castles, the Viennese town houses, all have gone. Only beautiful Langau is left, the place that Grandfather Albert loved and which still has a high place in the affections of his youngest descendants."[13]

Batsheva, who like Bettina experienced wartime American exile, did not return to France with her brother, Guy. She eventually settled in Israel. But it was not a question of religious or Zionist conviction. Her first visit to the country occurred in 1951, the year her brief marriage came to an end. She was touring the new nation with the famous American dance company led by the remarkable Martha Graham, probably the greatest creative figure in the development of modern dance. Their meeting had been a chance one. Batsheva had for many years been interested in callisthenics. In pre-war Paris, she had studied with a teacher whose method was based on yoga. In New York, she went to a dance school to explore further the interaction of dance and yoga. But at the class someone said to her, "You ought to go up to the next floor and see Martha Graham." The resulting encounter completely changed her life. Martha, then in her fifties, was a dynamic personality who as dancer, choreographer and teacher had made an enormous impact on the world of dance and ballet, freeing it from the restraints of classical formalism and making it a vehicle for the expression of intense emotion. She was one of those magical people who made things happen, whether it was drawing a superlative performance from her troupe, charming money from backers or persuading composers of the stamp of Aaron Copeland to write scores for her. And Batsheva de Rothschild fell under her spell.

"If a Rothschild woman is to succeed, it has to be away from the traditional Rothschild activities. Some of us have had to make our mark despite the family," Batsheva explains.[14] Some of her gifted ancestors in the nineteenth century had felt the same but most of them had been trapped, poured into the mould of Rothschild expectations. By the mid-twentieth century that mould had been broken, but that did not necessarily make it easier for them to discover their destiny. They had money. They had a name which opened most doors. But if "Rothschild" was a key it could also be a millstone for someone who wanted to achieve success in her own right. They also had inherited characteristics which could be just as difficult to bear — impatience to get things done and a prickly perfectionism. Batsheva certainly acknowledges these traits in herself. "Only when something is striving for excellence will I support it. The moment it begins to compromise, I walk out."[15]

In the medium of dance she found the vehicle she had, perhaps unconsciously, been seeking for her energies and talents. She travelled with Martha Graham's company and took on the rôle of wardrobe mistress in order to enjoy a Far East tour, sponsored by the State Department, which terminated in Tehran. She personally organised the next step, a visit to the exciting new state of Israel, a nation in a hurry; a nation consciously developing all the arts and skills of a modern civilisation. The name Rothschild was greatly revered there. In 1954 the bodies of Edmond and his wife Adelheid (who had died in 1934 and 1935 respectively), were brought from France and reinterred at Ramat Hanadiv, in the hills overlooking the excavated port of Caesarea. Their tomb, now a place of pilgrimage, bears the simple epitaph: "Here lie Baron Edmond de Rothschild, 'the Father of the Land' and his wife, the Baroness Adelheid, a woman who revered God."

Three years later their son, James de Rothschild, died, and his will included a bequest of sixteen million Israeli pounds for the construction of the nation's parliament building, the Knesset. It was the last act in a saga of increasing commitment to the Zionist ideal spanning more than sixty years. But if the family name was much respected in Israel, Batsheva discovered, it was also regarded in a much more down-to-earth manner. It was not surrounded with an aura of glamour. And that meant that she could get things done.

From 1958 she spent more and more time in Israel. "People came to ask me for advice and help on a variety of problems from family conflicts to how to help left-handed people," she says.[16] She sponsored a variety of projects from housing improvements to a science foundation. But she did not only provide money — she was too much a Rothschild for that. She sat on committees, helped to draw up plans, did everything possible to liberate the experts whose task it was to execute those plans.

It was that desire to provide resources for talented experts which led to the foundation of the Bat-Dor School in 1967 and the Bat-Dor Dance Company in 1968. Jeannette Ordman, an extremely accomplished exponent of the art of dance, had set up a school in Tel Aviv. It was only a matter of time before she and Batsheva came together. The result was a new professional school, probably the first ever to train dancers with equal emphasis on techniques of classical ballet and modern dance, and a new company with Mme de Rothschild as producer and Jeannette as artistic director and principal dancer. The company soon established a reputation and attracted young artists from all over the world. It has taken its electrifying repertoire on tour all over Europe, Africa and North America. After a performance in Warsaw, for example, the applause and shouts of "*bis*" lasted for a quarter of an hour and, in Gdynia, Ordman was repeatedly called back for twenty-two minutes after her rôle as Edith Piaf. It is an achievement Batsheva is very proud of — but for the troupe's sake, not her own. She has the dislike of personal publicity which characterises many of the family. "In some places," she says, "I got all the credit, and that makes me furious." Eventually she took Israeli nationality. It was then that she abandoned the French form of her name — Bethsabée — in favour of its Hebrew equivalent.

Her sister, Jacqueline, remained in America with her husband (he died in 1976) and finally settled in Los Angeles. She is another example of the remarkable talent which persists in the family. Having not achieved a standard in music which satisfied her, she directed her energies elsewhere. In chess she attained grandmaster status. She won many tennis championships. Later she devoted herself to sculpture. Her work has been widely exhibited, although she has declined the rôle of commercial artist and her pieces are not offered for sale to the public.[17]

Maurice, the erstwhile black sheep of the family, returned from exile with his fleece very heavily gilded. But a shock awaited him in Geneva: during his absence dishonest persons had absconded with all his Swiss cash assets. However, despite this, he had become, as a result of inheritance and his own labours, the richest member of the family. Fate in the form of childless unions, intermarriages and the failure of male lines had made him the sole inheritor of by far the greatest portion of the cumulative wealth of the Rothschilds.

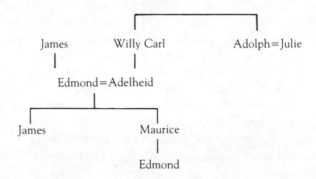

From Adolph had come the residual fortune of the Neapolitan branch. Adelheid had been the co-heiress of her father, the last head of the Frankfurt house. Edmond had inherited a considerable slice of the French fortune. All this immense wealth had come down to James and Maurice, and the younger brother had added to his assets by building a personal fortune in the 1940s. When Maurice returned to Pregny and took up residence once more in that vast, magnificent palace overlooking Lake Geneva, he simply went on adding to his fortune. The château merely replaced his New York residence as the powerhouse of his extensive financial grid. Reclining on a sofa, surrounded by five telephones, he bought and sold on the money markets of the world. He already had a large portfolio of mining shares in such rapidly expanding areas as South Africa, Canada and the Congo and he added to these steadily, partly by borrowing Swiss francs, which he could obtain at a low rate of interest. But this born entrepreneur did not restrict himself to equity dealing. He also turned his knowledge of *beaux-arts* to good account and became a considerable dealer in art and antiques. When he died in 1957 his enormous accumulation of money, equities, property and works of art passed to his only son, Edmond, a young man of thirty-one whom he hardly knew.[18] And Edmond would build a quite new Rothschild banking and commercial empire.

CHAPTER 28
"Le style Rothschild"

In 1960 Baron Guy de Rothschild reopened Ferrières and for a dozen glittering years it became the Mecca of the international jet set. The great château, empty since the beginning of the war, stripped and defaced by the Nazis, and abandoned to two decades of neglect, was in a sorry state. Structural repairs, central heating, clearing and replanting the overgrown gardens, redecoration, refurnishing with superb paintings and fine furniture – all this cost millions. But Baron Guy had no doubt that the restoration was worth every penny. It was symbolic of a double rejuvenation. Three years earlier he had divorced his Jewish wife in order to marry the Catholic Marie-Hélène van Zuylen de Nyevelt, a vivacious blonde eighteen years his junior. This exuberant new love swept him along with her passionate enthusiasms and made him feel young again. But it was not only his own renewal of spirit that Guy was proclaiming. Restoring Ferrières to something of its pre-war splendour was a declaration that the Rothschild fortunes were reborn.

The refurbished château became the venue for a succession of exotic dinners, fancy-dress balls and house parties. Celebrities came from all over the world to be entertained by the Rothschilds – film stars, royalty, jet-setters, artists, politicians. And what entertainment! For example, the eight hundred guests who attended the Surrealist Ball experienced a night of total bewilderment, as Guy himself later proudly recalled:

As the guests went up the main staircase, everything appeared calm, harmonious, grandiose, as usual . . . except that an army of lackeys, lackeys with cats' heads, seemed to have fallen asleep on the steps, the banisters, the landings, in the most grotesque positions.
Then began an interminable voyage through a dim labyrinth, a forest of black ribbons that had to be separated like dense branches, groping in the dark. Now and then some of the liveried cats would suddenly appear, bearing torches: weird phantom animals amid the giant cobwebs . . . The way was so long that finally, shivering with delightful horror, the guests passed through the last portals of this

surrealistic hell with a sigh of relief. They entered the tapestry salon, impassive as ever in its gold, reds and pinks — where Marie-Hélène (with the head of a hind weeping diamond tears) and myself (wearing a head-dress representing still life arrangement on a huge platter) tried to suppress our cries of admiration, and appear to recognize the raving mad (disguised) arrivals. All the while, a concealed pianist was playing music by Satie.

The guests at this extravagant *bal masqué* were only those who had the exuberance, the wit — and the money — to enter into the spirit of the thing. Each had spent hundreds or thousands on costumes which would vie, in imagination and costliness, with the bizarre setting devised by their host and hostess. Nor was the inventiveness of Guy and Marie-Hélène exhausted by the décor. The banquet to which the assembled company sat down was equally sumptuous and exotic:

> On each table, covered by a tablecloth representing the sky, there was a centre-piece inspired by some surrealist painter or poet, designed to be at the same time crazy, incongruous and poetic. For example on the table entitled "Eggs à la Florentine", it was a mound of cooked spinach transpierced by the carcass of a giant bird, garnished with women's breasts . . .
> The warmly applauded climax was a huge platter carried by eight men, with a nude woman reclining on a bed of roses, all made of edible spun sugar to be hacked to pieces. "Dessert of the Barbarians?"

As Guy vividly recalls, "The whirl went on till dawn. Everyone was enchanted with himself, everyone was enchanted to be there . . . in short, everyone was enchanted."[1]

If the 1960s really were "swinging", no one swung with more vigour than the French Rothschilds. Not since the 1920s had they had so much disposable wealth. Not since the end of the last century had they wielded so much power. For, in the expansionist 1960s and early 1970s, when the Rothschilds regained something of their traditional leadership in the worlds of finance and high society, they also experienced a resurgence of political influence. It was, of course, influence of a very different kind to that exercised by their grandfathers. Natty had regarded his duty to government and nation as including applying pressure and giving advice to the policy makers. Alphonse had had frequent confidential meetings with ministers and deputies. Both had held and expressed strong political views. Both had ignored the complaints and innuendoes of opponents and journalists who regarded their influence as sinister and motivated by narrow, sectional interest. But, sixty years on, the world was a very different place. By then there had developed a widespread suspicion of all connections between government and big business. Men and women in public office were obliged by law to declare any commercial interests. Clear guidelines were laid down for lobbying members of parliament and presenting cases to government departments. Politicians, industrialists and financiers who ignored those guidelines ran the real risk of damaging scandal and charges of corruption. Influence, therefore, could only be at a personal level.

From 1962 to 1968 Georges Pompidou was Prime Minister of France and from 1969 to 1974 he was President. And Georges Pompidou was a lifelong friend of the Rothschilds and ex-manager of the Paris bank. The day following the 1962 elections was a field day for the press. Referring to a recent racing triumph of Guy's, one newspaper made the comment "Pompidou of the Rothschild stable, wins the Grand Prix Matignon".* Other headlines and cartoons made the same point. The subjects of these attacks did not let them affect their feelings for each other. For several years Baron Guy and the Prime Minister met once a month for a private lunch and Rothschilds were often on the guest lists of official functions. They shared common views on many issues, particularly the need for government to support the free-market economy and resist Socialist pressures. Pompidou appreciated expert advice on financial matters and the support of his friends during the darker days of his tenure of office, particularly during the wave of student riots, strikes and popular demonstrations that rocked France in 1968. Politically and commercially the Pompidou-Rothschild relationship was a perfectly correct one but it did not endear the banking family to the parties of the Left, and when those parties came to power they were quick to show their displeasure.

But for the time being everything was *couleur de rose*. Guy re-established the Rothschild stud and he and his cousins and nephews were often seen at fashionable race meetings on both sides of the Channel. They had successes with many horses but the finest animal that ever carried the blue and yellow colours was a colt named after Edmund's English estate, Exbury. He seemed to enter into the spirit of Rothschild expansionism, for he won many French and English classics in the mid-1960s.

Marie-Hélène was not the only fabulous Rothschild hostess of that gay era. Baron Edmond's wife, Nadine, presided at Pregny over fêtes scarcely less exotic than those of Ferrières. For her Bal Boldini, she decked out the large riding school in the château grounds in swathes of mauve and violet silk, and hung its walls with large canvases of frivolous women painted by Boldini in *fin-de-siècle* Paris. She installed a dance floor, heating, lighting,

*The Hôtel Matignon is the official residence of the French Prime Minister.

plants and trees in pots and, of course, organised a sumptuous repast. Her five hundred guests, who were instructed to come in late-nineteenth-century costume, included Hélène Rochas, Yul Brynner, Estée Lauder, Teddy Kennedy, Audrey Hepburn, Gina Lollobrigida, Gloria Swanson, Prince Victor Emmanuel of Naples and Gregory Peck. As Nadine, herself, later wrote: " 'Le style Rothschild' is not only a matter of decorating houses with a subtle combination of comfort and exquisite furnishings. 'Le style Rothschild' is also about living and about entertaining carried to perfection." [2]

The story of Edmond and Nadine reads like a modern fairy tale — a combination of Cinderella and Sinbad. On the death of his father, Edmond "inherited a more important fortune than that of any other Rothschild in the world, and few responsibilities". [3] There was enormous irony in this, even a double irony, for the son of the "outcast" of the family was himself something of an outcast. Through no fault of his own the richest Rothschild was also a Rothschild out on a limb. His father had deliberately severed his contact with the bank but Edmond was isolated by a chain of circumstances. He was not of an age with any of his cousins and had been brought up by his mother's family. His formative teenage years had been spent in isolation in Switzerland. After the war, when he might have gone into the bank, the opportunity did not exist because, as he says, "there was no bank to go into". (He did, in 1949, go to America to work for Commerciale Transocéan, a Rothschild subsidiary, but that only lasted a year.) For want of anything better to do, he studied law, but never with any serious intention of practising. [4]

At the age of twenty-four he decided to go into business for himself. With his family background and particularly with his father's example to inspire him, this might have seemed the logical, even inevitable, thing to do but Edmond insists that there was nothing obvious about it. He was not close to his father. Whenever they met, as he says, "My conversation did not exactly elate him." So no tips were forthcoming from that quarter. Nor from relatives on the other side of the family: his grandfather was an army officer and his maternal uncle a dilettante. "I had no financial education at all," he insists. "Before I started in business I had never owned a share or a bond. I had to teach myself to read a balance sheet." However, he did have one advantage enjoyed by few non-Rothschilds: his grandfather had left him a million dollars. With this and later with money borrowed from a banker friend, he began buying and selling anything that looked as though it might turn a profit — real estate, commodities, articles for import and export. By the time he came into his inheritance he had learned the ropes, though he modestly attributes his continuing success to having "good advisers". Property development remained the basis of his

410

business activity but he diversified into specifically financial activities, putting money into projects that looked promising. "I later discovered that this is called venture capital," he told me, with a disarmingly straight face.[5]

Edmond's smart office on the fashionable Faubourg St Honoré became the centre of a rapidly increasing commercial empire. One of the concerns which he backed at an early stage was a small firm that was developing "an interesting new approach to vacations". Edmond took a thirty-five per cent stake in this "small firm" called Club Méditerranée, which boomed over the next decade to become the most successful up-market family holiday organisation in the world. But Edmond de Rothschild did not have the Midas touch. Some of his investments, such as his foray into discount-house merchandising, were disastrous. But gains far outweighed losses, and it became apparent very soon that Paris now had a second Rothschild operation every bit as powerful and prestigious as De Rothschild Frères. When his cousins regrouped their banking operations in 1968, Edmond felt free to do what he had felt inhibited about doing before: he set up his own Banque Privé, with its headquarters in Switzerland.[6]

Despite the evidence of all this success, there were for Edmond more important things in life than making money. He was never the hard-edged businessman of whom N.M. would have approved, prepared to dedicate "heart and soul and body and mind and everything" to his commercial activities. In the 1950s and 1960s the religion and land of his people assumed a place of increasing importance in his life. He had not been brought up to be scrupulous in the observance of Judaism, and when he"discovered" the faith of his ancestors as a young man the impact was the greater. He became a zealous Zionist, so much so that his father and his Uncle Jimmy had to dissuade him from visiting Israel for fear that he would do something there which they would consider stupid. The Suez Crisis of 1956 stirred him deeply. The following year his Uncle Jimmy died. Edmond was now the only direct male Rothschild descendant of the "father of Israel" and he felt a deep sense of personal responsibility.

When he paid his first visit to Israel in 1958 he discovered for the first time what his grandfather really meant to the new nation and he desperately wanted to follow the family tradition of personal involvement. He talked with David Ben-Gurion and that wise statesman, while welcoming the young man's enthusiasm, advised him to leave philanthropy to his Aunt Dorothy and stick to what he knew best — finance. "Use your capital to create business and jobs," he advised. Over the next few years Edmond, therefore, directed much of his enterprise into the vulnerable Jewish state. He built the first pipeline from the Red Sea to the Mediterranean to bring much-needed Iranian oil into Israel. He constructed a chemical plant and he founded the Israel General Bank.[7]

Whatever was the reception of Edmond's activities in Tel Aviv, within his own family they were not universally admired and appreciated. Jimmy's widow was not best pleased with her nephew who, she believed, was cashing in on his grandfather's reputation for his own profit. After her husband's death she had taken the initiative in continuing his work of building up the new nation. She maintained the philanthropic attitude of Edmond and Jimmy while directing it towards different objectives. The need now was not for settlement land but for technical, scientific and cultural projects which would enhance Israeli life and independence. She set up a foundation called Hanadiv which has supplied funds for a wide variety of innovations, including support for the Hebrew University of Jerusalem, the establishment of educational television, the stocking of art galleries, the provision of new hospitals and geriatric care centres, the supplying of aids for the handicapped, the endowing of fellowships and Everyman's University, the presentation of prizes for a variety of technological and scientific achievements, the building of a golf course and an animal breeding centre, and many others. Later, other Rothschilds were also involved in a variety of philanthropic enterprises in Israel. None of them followed Edmond's commercial lead.

Undoubtedly his affair with and subsequent marriage to an actress — who was also a Gentile — did not enhance his image as the devout Diaspora Jew working selflessly for his people. Edmond's first marriage in 1958 was not a success. Perhaps that is not very surprising. This energetic bundle of enthusiasms and ambitions living on his nerves (to this day he chain-smokes) cannot have been easy to live with. His wife was expected to run ten homes, including a house in Paris, a country retreat at Armainvilliers, east of Paris, and the château and estate at Pregny. She had to preside at a table to which her husband brought business associates and politicians from several different nations. She had to be ready to respond at a moment's notice to his ebullient decisions to go sailing, or racing, or to catch a plane for New York, Tel Aviv or Nairobi.

In 1960 Edmond met a young blonde actress and dancer. There could not possibly have been more difference between the multimillionaire and the twenty-eight-year-old Nadine Lhopitalier. She was born the illegitimate daughter of a French labourer in a Paris slum. By the age of fourteen she was working as an unskilled factory hand. Then part-time work as an artist's model led to a much more romantic world — films. She obtained work first as an extra and then as stand-in for major stars in nude scenes. Nadine was shrewd enough to realise that sexiness is a passing attribute and had taken every opportunity to develop her mind as well as her body, learning all she could in her travels about art, fashion and culture — the things smart people talk about. Before she met Edmond she had already been briefly engaged to the son of an English peer. Then, one evening at a society dinner, she caught the attention of Baron de Rothschild. He came across to her, and commented on the splendid necklace she was wearing, "What a beautiful diamond — such a pity it's a fake."[8]

They lived together for three years, during which time Edmond and his wife were divorced. The Baron now had to consider what to do next. He would not ask Nadine to change her religion but the consequences of marrying a Catholic had to be weighed very carefully. Edmond hesitated. And Nadine became pregnant. When he did make up his mind, she was confined to bed because her doctor feared possible complications. So the wedding took place, with just a few friends present, in Nadine's bedroom with the bride sitting on a chair and the groom stooping beside her to recite his vows.

Writing her memoirs, years later, Nadine recalled:

> "You won't last twenty-four hours in the family", a friend predicted at the time of my marriage. Well, now I have been sharing Edmond's life for twenty-four years.
> Twenty-four years of which I have savoured every moment. Twenty-four years during which I have laboured . . . with the enthusiasm which gives one faith in what one has accomplished.[9]

In theory, the cards were stacked against a successful marriage. In fact, the gamble turned out to be one of Edmond's best speculations, largely because his actress wife worked very hard to learn the most demanding rôle of her life.

It was Baron Elie who pointed out that it is often the ladies who marry into the family who become *"plus Rothschild que les Rothschilds"*. He cited his own wife as an example of someone steeped in and fascinated by Rothschild history and tradition.[10] Other examples spring as readily to mind: Mrs James de Rothschild, now the oldest living member of the family and possessing a fund of stories about three generations of her husband's relatives, was the perfect hostess at Waddesdon and an enthusiastic supporter of Rothschild interests in Israel before and after Jimmy's death. Pauline, Baron Philippe's second wife, was the conceptual and organising genius behind the creation of the modern Château Mouton (see pp. 415ff.). Clarice, a quiet Englishwoman before her marriage to Alphonse, not only shared fully the misfortunes of her Austrian in-laws, but worked harder than any of them for the restitution of their property after the war and was more attached to the land and people of Langau than either Louis or Eugène.[11]

There is a certain irony in the fact that, while several Rothschild daughters have had to "escape" from the family in order to do their own thing, several Rothschild wives have found their fulfilment in complete identity with the dynasty. It was certainly so with Nadine Lhopitalier. She became a Rothschild *grande dame* in the best nineteenth-century tradition. At her own wish she converted to Judaism, learned how to be an enthusiastic hostess, a tireless traveller, keenly interested in business and an active philanthropist. Thus, like Guy, Edmond, with money, success and a beautiful young wife, felt that he had much to celebrate in the sixties. "It was," he says, "a wonderful period of our lives and we made the most of it." As well as the parties and visits to exotic locations with Hollywood friends, there were yacht trips, African safaris, skiing holidays and a host of other diversions.[12]

Not content with being an international businessman, a banker and a leader of world Jewry, Edmond decided, in 1972, to enter another traditional Rothschild sphere of activity: he bought a Médoc vineyard. His motives were a genuine enjoyment of fine wine, the love of a new challenge, and a belief that this was a good business venture. In the post-war years wine growers, at least those at the top end of the market, had struggled to show a profit. But then came the swinging sixties. Throughout the western world, wine-drinking was suddenly chic. Wealthy Americans, in particular, developed a taste for claret and those who did not bought it anyway because it was the smart thing to do and because it was becoming a good investment. The opening price of first-growth Médoc wines multiplied tenfold in a single decade. If ever there was a good time to get into wine, this was it. But Edmond had no intention of trying to compete with his cousins at Lafite and Mouton. Even if a top vineyard had been available, its price would doubtless have been highly inflated in that time of great euphoria. The Baron chose instead a *cru bourgeois*, Château Clarke at Listrac, some ten kilometres down the road from Pauillac. His target market was those buyers who appreciated good wine but could not afford — or could rarely afford — the best. This, as he rightly judged, was a rapidly growing category of customers worldwide. His Lafite cousins, with whom he discussed his intentions, certainly agreed with Edmond's assessment for in the following year they bought their own *bourgeois* vineyard, Château La Cardonne.

The new owner of Château Clarke went into the enterprise with typical Rothschild enthusiasm, business acumen and foresight. He rooted out over half of the old vines and replanted. He built an impressive new *cuvier* and *chai*, and bought the most up-to-date equipment. It was a

414

considerable capital investment which would take years to cover but Edmond calculated that it was worth it. Wine had become big business; there could be no hanging on to old buildings and modest methods out of a sentimental regard for tradition.[13]

The "battle of the vineyards" is one of the more persistent features of Rothschild mythology and, as such, it has been much exaggerated. As we have seen, there was rivalry between Mouton and Lafite when Mayer Amschel was still an insignificant ghetto Jew, but it was a rivalry felt more keenly by *régisseurs* and estate workers than by owners. Until Baron Philippe took a personal interest in Mouton no proprietor resided in Pauillac and visits from Paris were rare. The 1855 classification certainly rankled with Nat, the first Rothschild owner of Mouton, but was a matter of indifference to his son and grandson. However, once all that has been said, it remains true that after the Second World War what had been a good-natured competition over the annual selling price escalated into a bitter controversy between the Lafite Rothschilds and the Mouton Rothschilds — or, more accurately, between Elie and Philippe.

Ownership of Lafite was shared by Guy, Alain, Elie and Jimmy and in 1946 they were all concerned about the future of the vineyard. For years it had been operating at a loss and the family could no longer afford this drain on its resources. Twenty-nine-year-old Elie volunteered to take the property in hand. This tall, slim young man with the aquiline features and brusque manner saw Lafite as a challenge. He took firm control, galvanised the staff into greater efficiency and within two years was able to declare a modest dividend to the other shareholders. Elie cared passionately about Château Lafite. And that was the problem. The two neighbouring vineyards now both had proprietors who cared passionately. Moreover, they were completely different in temperament and character, and did not much like each other. Philippe was senior by fifteen years and knew the region and its people. Elie was the new boy, coming in with a mind uncluttered by sentiment. Philippe was a showman; Elie carried himself with patrician reserve. The one characteristic they shared was will-power.

Philippe was a born adman with a flair for theatricality. He was alive to every method of popularising his wine, his vineyard and the Médoc generally. When he returned in 1945 Mouton was in a bad state. Allied bombing had damaged buildings and cratered fields. The Nazis had kept the vineyard in production but they had built ugly gun emplacements, looted the château and, in the later stages of the war, torn up floorboards to use as firewood. If Mouton was ever to become viable again, there were repairs to be set in hand and plans to be laid. Philippe decided that, as far as restoration was concerned, the Germans could make good what the Germans had destroyed. There were hundreds of prisoners of war in local camps and several of these were employed at Mouton, dismantling military installations and tidying up house and grounds.

As to the future, there were markets to re-establish amidst keen rivalry in austerity Europe. One of the ways to single Mouton's wine out from others on the merchants' shelves was the use of an imaginative label. Between the wars Philippe had carried out frequent experiments. Now he commissioned a young artist to design a special commemorative label bearing the famous "V for Victory" legend. The idea worked well. It gave all the bottles of that year a distinctive appearance, and one easily recognised by connoisseurs. So the Baron decided to continue the practice. He persuaded the best contemporary artists to produce exclusive designs and over the following years Château Mouton Rothschild bottles carried paintings by such masters as Braque, Dali, Henry Moore, Chagall, Kandinsky, Andy Warhol and Picasso.

When his father Henri died in 1946, the vineyard was left to all three children but Philippe immediately bought out his brother and sister. This was probably his point of no return. Before the war, despite the innovations he had made at Mouton, Philippe had not spent much of his time there. Even on his return to civilian life he had contemplated going back into film-making or taking up some other occupation. But now he committed himself to the complete refurbishment of the estate. This involved not only bringing the vines back to full production, improving the *chais*, and converting outbuildings into a superb residence known as Grand Mouton, but transforming the château into the principal tourist attraction of the Médoc.

In all this he was helped by his second wife, who matched him in imagination and enthusiasm. Pauline Fairfax Potter, whom Philippe married in 1954, was an American dress designer and socialite. She brought enormous artistic flair to the refurbishment of Mouton. It was she who helped him to realise an even grander idea than usual which came into his head on his fiftieth birthday – he would turn the oldest part of the complex into a museum of wine. The couple scoured the world for paintings, Venetian glass, tapestries, antiquities, Renaissance chalices, Chinese ceramics, pottery figures from Latin America, Roman mosaics – anything of worth and beauty connected with the making and enjoyment of wine. Back at Mouton, old cellars were converted into six galleries, where the unique collection could be displayed to maximum theatrical effect. The museum was opened in 1966 and immediately took its place as one of the finest museums in the world. A visit there remains an unforgettable experience. The old *chais* form a brilliantly simple setting for a collection of spectacular artefacts spanning over four thousand years – yet another example of "le style Rothschild".[14]

All this activity did not go unnoticed "next door", where Baron Elie was rebuilding the reputation of Lafite, though in more conventional ways. He shunned "gimmicks" and turned, instead, to that old hallmark of excellence, the 1855 classification. The best Médoc vineyards had been graded in that year and Lafite had come out on top, always regarding itself as the *premier des premiers*, even if the three other châteaux which shared the accolade did not agree. It was only natural that the new regime at Lafite, working hard to achieve commercial success, should stress the distinction conferred in 1855 for all it was worth. Now, back in the 1920s Philippe had formed the Association des *Premiers Crus*, comprising representatives of Latour, Margaux, Haut Brion and Lafite (the *premier cru* vineyards) – and Mouton. It had been a cheeky thing to do but it had worked because business was bad and Baron Philippe's ideas were good. But the association's continuance was a perpetual challenge to the 1855 classification. In 1952 Elie called a meeting of the *premier cru* proprietors and they re-formed the organisation – as the Association of Four.

When Philippe had simmered down, he planned his counter offensive. He decided to organise as many growers as he could behind a campaign to abolish the century-old grading and replace it with a new one. Naturally, the scheme split the Médoc wine men into two camps. Those who thought they would benefit from a reclassification were all for it. Those who suspected that they would be demoted in any new batting order opposed it. Even when he had sufficient support, Philippe had to fight his way through layers of bureaucracy. By this time the conflict had become acrimonious. The cousins were barely on speaking terms. Insults appeared in the press. Catty stories went the rounds of Médocain society.

The battle continued, on and off, for twenty years. Philippe's case went up to the Ministry of Agriculture – and was referred all the way back down to the Bordeaux Chamber of Commerce. By this time the issue was academic. The one fact which had emerged clearly was that there was no method of reclassification which would win universal acceptance. Anyway, in the then buoyant state of the market it scarcely mattered. All the proprietors were prospering. Why tinker with a system which, with all its faults, was working perfectly well? But pride was at stake, the protagonists were dug in, honour had to be satisfied. Eventually, in 1973, the affair ended where it had begun, in a meeting of the Association of Four. Baron Elie, who was, in any case, on the point of resigning his position to his nephew Eric, was persuaded to remove his opposition to Château Mouton Rothschild being included among the *premiers crus*.

417

Philippe and his vineyard workers celebrated with a jeroboam of Mouton '24 and a new version of the old jingle was coined:

Premier je puis,
Second je fus,
Mouton ne change.*[15]

But there was a spectre at the feast. Pauline was seriously ill with a heart condition. The years 1970-6 were taken up with treatments and visits to doctors all over the world but each diagnosis only brought the terrible truth further into the open — there was no cure. She died in California in March 1976. For the first time in his long life (he was now seventy-four) Philippe was completely crushed. When the immediate impact of his grief had passed, he turned to the other loves of his life to fill the empty space in his thoughts and emotions — Philippine, poetry and Mouton. His daughter had married an actor, Jacques Sereys, but she and her father remained very close and in 1981 she began to take on those aspects of the work that were now too much for Philippe. She became a roving ambassador for Mouton: organising a touring exhibition, lecturing, giving press and television interviews.

Totally bilingual and highly cultured, Philippe had a deep love for both French and English literature. He wrote and published a volume of his own poems and, in 1950, he wrote the lyrics for Darius Milhaud's *Vendange*. But it was his translations of English verse which won him the greatest acclaim. In 1960 he brought out a French version of the works of Christopher Fry. About the same time he began on a collection of the Elizabethan poets and, in the 1970s, he published translations of Marlowe's *Dr Faustus* and *Tamburlaine*.

Philippe's plans for Mouton were not yet complete. There was always work to be done — extending and improving the facilities, carrying into effect the plans that he and Pauline had made. But there was another new, completely original project that Philippe had in mind. For many years they had been making wine in California. To most Frenchmen, even if they had ever heard of it, the idea of California wine was a joke. But by the late 1960s connoisseurs were realising that some of the vintages coming out of America were very good. Philippe reasoned that with the expertise of his staff they could be better and that with the prestige of the Rothschild name they could be made highly marketable. Ideas and opportunities took a long time to come together but, in 1978, Philippe sent an invitation to Robert Mondavi, one of the leading growers in Napa Valley, a hundred miles north of San Francisco.

*"First I am/Second I was,/Mouton does not change."

418

Bob Mondavi and his wife travelled to Mouton and the bluff American was bowled over by the luxury, the food, the wine, the sheer "style" of it all. Philippe, he said, looked "every bit a baron, but still, you know, like an old shoe — so easy to talk to".[16] The vital meeting took place one morning in Philippe's bedroom. The old man always spent the mornings working in bed, surrounded by telephones and files and his golden retriever sprawled on the coverlet. "You think better with your legs up than with your legs dangling down," he insisted. After three hours of hard but amiable bargaining they reached agreement on the basis of an exciting new operation — new vineyards, a new winery and a product benefiting from their joint expertise. Since that would take time, they decided to go right ahead producing their first wine using Bob's existing vines and a team drawn from Napa and Pauillac. In April 1980, at press conferences in Paris and San Francisco, the new deal was announced. It was unique. French wine growers had bought property in California before but no one had conceived the idea of bringing together two skilled and dedicated teams to produce a new and distinctive wine. At seventy-eight years of age Philippe de Rothschild was still innovating.

CHAPTER 29

"We must never remain static"

There have always been marked differences of life style between the British and French Rothschilds. Members of the English family placed a higher premium on privacy than their cousins. They took their pleasures more quietly, more discreetly. Evelyn's principal relaxation was polo, often played with members of the royal family. Edmund enjoyed fishing and Jacob tennis. Leopold, when he was not adding to his excellent collections of porcelain and English school portraits, derived great pleasure from sailing. It is largely a question of temperament, but differences of personal wealth also play their part. When Jimmy died in 1957 his estate was encumbered with enormous death duties. He had already made arrangements for Waddesdon Manor and its estate to be given to the National Trust. None of the younger Rothschilds could or would wish to live in such splendour. Bequeathing it to the nation was the only way of preserving the house, its superb collections and its lovely parkland, and of disproving Baron Ferdinand's gloomy prognostication:

> A future generation may reap the chief benefit of a work which to me has been a labour of love, though I fear Waddesdon will share the fate of most properties whose owners have no descendants, and fall into decay. May the day yet be distant when weeds will spread over the garden, the terraces crumble into dust, the pictures and cabinets cross the Channel or the Atlantic, and the melancholy cry of the night-jar sound from the deserted towers.[1]

Exbury House, too, fell empty and silent. After the war Edmund and his mother took the estate in hand but they preferred to live in a smaller and altogether more practicable house nearby. Restoring the gardens was a costly and difficult enough task without maintaining the mansion as well. Stoically, they set about the task of fighting back the undergrowth, reclaiming lawns and walks, replacing dead or overgrown plants. When the work was complete Exbury Gardens went on show once more, but not to royalty and small groups of privileged guests. Now it was the public who were encouraged to come for a day out and, with their entrance fees, help pay for the upkeep of the estate. As is the way with popular attractions, an increasing number of facilities were added over the years: guidebooks, postcards, helpful signposts, a restaurant and a garden shop selling potted plants, peat and tools. The greenhouses were turned over to commercial production. As well as providing new stock for Exbury, they supplied nurseries and municipal authorities with the famous hybrids perfected by Mr Lionel. Exbury remained in the forefront of horticultural development, experimenting with such new techniques as asexual propagation.

Lord Rothschild spent the post-war years refusing to be stereotyped. His active mind, ever seeking new avenues to explore, his need to be "useful", his desire to be at the centre of things took him into a succession of new enterprises. In 1958 he left Cambridge because he believed his research was not leading anywhere "creative" and because the awful spectre of boredom had begun to haunt him. He moved into industry and a job with Royal Dutch Shell, eventually becoming overall research co-ordinator. That lasted until 1970.

These activities by no means exhausted his formidable mental energies. He served on various government and semi-government commissions. His unofficial activities were also multifarious. He enjoyed the confidence of many British and foreign statesmen and politicians, who often turned to him for advice. Though no longer a member of MI5, he was sometimes consulted on security matters and was occasionally able, through his own international contacts, to serve the national interest.[2] Once more a Rothschild was moving freely among the denizens of Westminster, Whitehall and Downing Street. But this position of influence was not without its difficulties.

The 1950s and 1960s also bought their share of personal problems; some of which stemmed from those intellectually intense Cambridge days many years before. Lord Rothschild had maintained no close contact with any of his Cambridge contemporaries other than Anthony Blunt, who also had joined the security service. Although the two men were involved in quite different work, they inevitably had friends and colleagues in common, particularly Guy Liddell, who rose to be deputy director-general of MI5, 1946-51. Liddell was, for a time, friendly with Guy Burgess and inevitably came under suspicion later. His subsequent career was adversely affected by quite unfair speculation and Victor has gone on record as saying, "If I am sure that anyone was loyal to his or her country, it was Guy Liddell."[3]

Burgess had joined the Foreign Office in 1940. Donald Maclean had gone there straight from university. They were both part of a cell organised by Blunt which passed secrets to Moscow. In 1951 the great spy scandal broke. Maclean came under suspicion of passing information to the Russians. Blunt organised his escape and the traitor fled to Moscow in

421

the nick of time, accompanied by Burgess. This sent a shock wave through the British security service. Several other men came under suspicion, but never Blunt. He had risen high in the establishment. He was a Knight Commander of the Royal Victorian Order and a member of the Legion of Honour. He held several honorary degrees and had filled with distinction various academic positions. In 1945 he had been appointed to a palace office when he became Surveyor of the King's Pictures (and subsequently of the Queen's Pictures). Such men are considered to be above reproach. They have to be; if distinguished citizens like Blunt are unmasked as traitors, who can be trusted? Someone who *was* vetted was Kim Philby, another member of the Blunt network, then working for MI6. He was cleared but, the following year, thought it prudent to leave the service and take up a career in journalism. By this time Lord Rothschild's friendship with Blunt had cooled; they had, in fact, drifted apart in 1950.[4]

Unfortunately, over a decade later, in 1963, Blunt's name was once more to hit the headlines. Philby's cover had been blown the year before and he had fled to Moscow. It rapidly became clear just how active Soviet agents had been at Cambridge in the 1930s. Scores of students had obviously been recruited. Some had since turned their back on youthful enthusiasms. Some had become active spies. A few had reached senior positions where they handled top-secret information. So, thirty years later, the arc light of suspicion had a wide area to cover. It was in America that the next exposure was made. A year after Philby's defection, Michael Straight, a US citizen, confessed to having been sucked into the Soviet spy ring while studying at Cambridge. His recruiting officer, he revealed, had been Anthony Blunt. Confronted with this evidence, Blunt admitted his treason. It was the signal for the establishment to go into a flat spin. Publication of the facts would start a press witch-hunt. The Conservative administration could be threatened. The whole sordid affair had to be hushed up. The government offered Blunt immunity in return for full details of his network.

It is evidence of the complete trust placed in him that, although very few people indeed were made privy to the facts about Blunt, Victor Rothschild was one of them. He was appalled by the disclosure. It was, he later wrote, a blow which seemed "devastating, crushing and beyond belief . . . But there was no doubt; and why should 'they' wish to play a cruel and meaningless practical joke on me? What might I be stimulated to confess in return? The short answer was: nothing. As 'they' knew, I was not a Soviet agent."[5] Victor, like other Cambridge graduates of the period, had been investigated and cleared. There, he might have hoped, the matter would rest. It did not. It would rise up again in the years to come.

*   *   *

It was in 1971 that Lord Rothschild's period of greatest influence began. The Prime Minister, Edward Heath, resolved to set up a new and unique government body to be known as the Central Policy Review Staff, or, more popularly, the "Think Tank". He invited Victor to lead it. So unusual was the concept that Heath found difficulty explaining just what he wanted the new unit to do, as Lord Rothschild later recalled.

> *Mr Heath* "It's funny we have never met before." Then there was a sort of row of dots. I could not think what to say; after a while, I said, rather desperately: "Prime Minister, do you not think it would be better to have an economist in charge of this Unit?"
> *Mr Heath* "I did economics at Oxford." Another row of dots. Again after a while, I said rather desperately: "Prime Minister, could you give me an example of the type of problem you want the Unit to tackle?"
> *Mr Heath* "Concorde." At that moment I thought, perhaps wrongly, that I detected some anguished vibrations emanating from Sir Burke Trend and Sir William Armstrong, as they then were, who were hovering in the background. There was some justification for their anguish, if I did not imagine it, because an hour beforehand they had told me it was precisely things like Concorde that the Government Think Tank would *not* be expected to study.[6]

What the Prime Minister, in fact, required was an apolitical group of intelligent and informed academics and professionals who could bridge the gap between the cabinet and the complex world of science and technology; a body which could do some of government's basic thinking, digest information and present it in an easily assimilable form, look at knotty problems and suggest solutions. Victor, with his commitment to the invincibility of logic, his aura of authority and his impatience with red tape, was the right man for the job. He gathered a team of young, enthusiastic people and immensely enjoyed working with them. It was stimulating, it was important — it was new! Over the next three and a half years the Think Tank produced scores of reports for government ministers on subjects as diverse as race relations, the British computer industry, nuclear reactors and population trends. It acted as a funnel. Highly complex, specialised information was poured in at one end. Succinct statements and policy recommendations came out at the other.

Head of the Central Policy Review Staff was a remarkably privileged position. Lord Rothschild had access to all manner of leaders and experts. He was responsible only to the Prime Minister and answerable neither to the electorate nor the civil service chiefs — indeed, he became very critical of the way Whitehall and Westminster were run. And not a few ministers and top civil servants were critical of Victor Rothschild. They were worried by his ill-defined powers and his seemingly unrestricted access to departmental records.

In 1973 the Labour party, under Harold Wilson, was returned to power and the following year Lord Rothschild resigned from the Think Tank. This move was not, he explained, motivated by any dislike for the new Prime Minister, but because he needed a change: "I was worn out. And I'd begun to worry. I became too involved in the questions as opposed to being cerebral about them. When that happens you'd better get out."[7] Matters had actually come to a head during the closing stages of the previous administration when he had made a speech in which he warned that current attitudes and policies, if not reversed, would carry Britain along a path of inexorable economic decline. Edward Heath was unlikely to have been pleased with the speech.[8]

Victor had now reached the age at which most men retire and devote themselves wholeheartedly to the hobbies from which earning a living has hitherto distracted them. But Lord Rothschild was looking for new challenges. So far from throwing himself into his private pastimes he actually changed them. He gave up book collecting and presented to his Cambridge college all his first editions and his unique assemblage of Swift manuscripts. "I had got all the things I wanted or they were impossible to get," he said.[9] He took up the study of mathematical statistics and was tutored by one of Cambridge's leading academics.

But he needed a public career. This need was partly filled by his appointment as chairman of a Royal Commission on Gambling. He also decided to rejoin the family firm. He did not return to New Court as a banker in the strict sense of the word. His distaste for "moving sums of money from Point A, where it is, to Point B where it is needed" had never diminished. He was still, essentially, a scientist and wanted to do everything possible to help emerging technologies. So he became head of Biotechnology Investments Limited (later renamed N. M. Rothschild Asset Management Limited) a separate company, financially advised by NMR, which channelled money into a wide variety of scientific and technological projects. It partly fulfilled his need for an endless succession of fresh challenges.

Dr Miriam Rothschild delights in the title bestowed on her by one journalist, "Queen of the Fleas". After the war she continued her career of private scholarly enterprise. She wrote articles, books and papers on a wide variety of scientific topics. One piece of research, carried out in collaboration with other scientists, led to the discovery of the mechanism

424

of the flea's jump and excited considerable interest. As well as being reported in America it was featured in popular Soviet newspapers. She showed that this remarkable insect, with the aid of a rubber-like substance in its hip joint, develops an acceleration of 149g — twenty times that of a moon rocket re-entering the earth's atmosphere. She considers, however, that it was really the cataloguing of her father's flea collection, in collaboration with a retired civil servant, Harry Hopkins, which earned her the regal title. This mammoth task was undertaken primarily to fulfil her mother's earnest desire that Charles's great pioneering work in this field should be recognised, and this monograph constituted a fitting memorial to his industry and scientific acumen. Miriam describes the job as "a hairshirt willingly worn". Furthermore, writing a quarter of a million words and checking and labelling seven thousand drawings, fitted in well with rearing a young family since it could all be done in the evenings after bedtime. The family was always given priority. "I got a lot more fun out of my children," she says , "than I ever had out of describing the backsides of fleas." [10]

In 1952 the catalogue received official recognition, for the citation which accompanied Miriam's CBE medal ran " . . . for services to taxonomy". "Yes, it's a formidable record," she once remarked in reply to a reporter's question. "I have written more boring words than any other Rothschild!" That is typical of the amused detachment mingled with real pride with which she views public recognition. For example, the photographs and official documents which catalogue the esteem in which she is held are used to decorate her private mini-kitchen. Among the various honorary doctorates, medals and certificates — for prize Jersey cows, gooseberries and wild flowers, as well as scientific achievements — pride of place is awarded to the scroll electing her an honorary member of 351st Bomb Group Association of the 8th US Air Force.

In the 1970s she began to devote more time to conservation than to research. "Staring down a brass tube for fifty years is enough," she says, and she has put *finis* to microscopy with the publication of a book on insect histology. One morning she woke up and realised that it was too late to pursue conservation only along the lines advocated by her father. Modern feats of chemistry and engineering had successfully bulldozed, drained, dragged and sprayed the flowers out of the fields and hedgerows. Our beautiful flora was vanishing beneath a grain mountain somewhere in Europe. The time had come to coax the dwindling flowers back again — by way of parks, gardens, waste ground, road verges and hayfields. [11]

It was the right moment to launch such a campaign, for there were still enough people alive to recall with nostalgia fields golden with buttercups and ditches lined with white violets. Largely as a result of her energetic campaigning, wild-flower cultivation suddenly became the "in" thing, displays of cowslips and oxeye daisies appeared at the Chelsea Flower Show, packets of wild flowers were available on the National Trust stalls and in garden centres, and official conservation bodies began researching into their cultivation. Wild flowers were grown on urban dumps, and the owners of stately homes suddenly realised their aesthetic potential. A new era of conservation had been initiated – the era of *re-creation* of habitats and reserves. The "Queen of the Fleas" had become the "Wild-Flower Lady" – a fitting tribute to her energy, persistence and enthusiasm.[12]

The 1960s and 1970s saw further important developments at New Court and Rue Laffitte. By 1963 Edmund had been joined in The Room by his brother, Leopold, his cousin, Evelyn – and his other cousin, Jacob. Jacob's academic career had already shown him to be a high-flyer. He broke completely with family tradition. Most English Rothschilds had gone through Harrow and Cambridge. Jacob went to Eton and Oxford. His father and grandfather had been scientists. Jacob studied History. Charles had been a reluctant banker; Victor had tried the City and rejected it. But Jacob entered New Court with enthusiasm. There had been a suggestion, after he attained his excellent first-class degree, that he might become a fellow of All Souls but, with a little family pressure, he turned his back on an academic career and applied his very considerable talents to the challenge of giving NMR a more dynamic image.

Jacob spent two or three years in different City firms and at Morgan Stanley in New York, learning about accountancy, broking and other aspects of the financial world before taking up his job at the bank in 1963. Very soon the slim young man with the long face and the quick, agile mind earned the respect if not always the admiration of rivals throughout the world. He was involved in a series of brilliant deals. Some of them came off; others did not. But competitors suddenly realised that Rothschild's had woken up with a vengeance. In an interview he gave in 1967, Jacob expressed his philosophy succinctly: "We must try and make ourselves as much a bank of brains as of money . . . We must be the catalyst who helps the development of trade. We must never remain static, always attempting to maintain our initiative."[13]

Retain their initiative they certainly did. No longer diffident about going into the market-place and touting for business, they took a leading rôle in the new, aggressive commercial world of takeovers and mergers, multi-national companies and supranational organisations, like the European Coal and Steel Community (for which NMR helped raise finance).

426

Increasing activity at New Court meant more staff. The bank overflowed its premises and took over a building on the other side of St Swithin's Lane. But the Rothschilds realised that the "dear old bank" was simply an uneconomic and inefficient use of space. In 1966 the bulldozers razed Nathan Rothschild's building to the ground. In its place there appeared a modern office block, all concrete and glass. Less picturesque, less "romantic", but altogether more in keeping with the needs of a twentieth-century merchant bank. The large portrait of N. M. and his family now graces a foyer where tradition is very little in evidence; where visitors sit on functional chairs, while functionally blue-suited messengers call secretaries on functional telephones to tell them that their next appointment is waiting.

Three years after their English cousins moved into new banking premises the French Rothschilds set in motion the rebuilding of Rue Laffitte. Work began in 1968 and was completed two years later. The structure which now amazed the Parisian business community was quite unlike the headquarters of any other commercial organisation. Set back from the adjoining Second Empire façades, it confronted the street with a front of white stone and glass, broken by terraces set with shrubs and magnolias. As Baron Guy affirms, "Great care was taken in the decoration of the offices as well as of the public rooms, with an eye to aesthetics as well as comfort."[14] It was an attitude that had marked every project the French family had inaugurated from their own country mansions to the HBMs. Nothing demonstrates more clearly the difference in style between the French and English families than the modern offices at Rue Laffitte and New Court.

But the reason underlying both new buildings was identical: the need for expansion. Banque Rothschild with sixty-five per cent of its assets in non-banking operations was a major industrial conglomerate. For example, so big and powerful had IMETAL become that, in 1975, its acquisition of the American company Copperweld was challenged in the federal court, on the basis that the proposed takeover was an infringement of the Anti-Trust laws. The hearing in Pittsburgh caused quite a sensation. There were union demonstrations and adverse press comments about European commercial giants swallowing up honest little American companies (an interesting reversal of current trends) but eventually the decision went in favour of IMETAL. In the nation dedicated above all others to free enterprise, where success is the ultimate justification and big is beautiful, it was difficult for the Rothschilds' enemies to sustain their case.

But times were changing, and the years ahead had some very nasty shocks in store for the family. The euphoric sixties merged into the seventies — the decade of the oil crisis, spiralling inflation, industrial unrest, rising unemployment and a slump in popular morale throughout the western world. The Rothschilds were not immune to the drastic change of atmosphere. There were no more extravagant parties, but not because the Rothschilds could no longer afford them. Guy gave the reason very simply: "they were no longer appropriate".[15] Edmond, perhaps rather more perceptively, told me, "Our son Benjamin and his generation were more serious, not interested in a showy life style; so we said goodbye to that chapter of our lives."[16]

In 1975 the head of the French house removed all his treasures from the Château de Ferrières and gave the building, with 340 acres, to the University of Paris. When the doors closed on the empty palace, an era closed with them. The canvases, the *fauteuils* and the great panels of painted leather found a new, splendid home in Guy's new house, the Hôtel Lambert on the Ile St Louis, in the heart of Paris; but nothing could conceal the fact that a symbolic link with the past had been severed. The extravagant dream that Guy and Marie-Hélène had created at Ferrières had proved to be just that — a dream, a reverberation of the 1920s or the 1890s that jarred in the modern world.

At the turn of the next decade the banks were rocked by two crises. The one that shattered the even tenor of the London house was internal but publicity was to make it an international event. As chairman of the executive committee from 1975, Jacob was very much the man holding the centre of the New Court stage but his cousin Evelyn was now the major shareholder. For some years Evelyn had, apparently, been content to allow the younger man to pursue his flamboyant and largely successful career. Much of his energies had been devoted to his domestic life and his many other interests. In 1966 he had married Jeannette Bishop, a radiantly beautiful fashion model nine years his junior. It was a love match and for a time they were very happy. But their backgrounds were very different and Jeannette was a prey to bouts of depression. Probably the discovery that Mrs de Rothschild could not have children was the worst blow of all. In 1971 the couple were amicably divorced and remained friends.[17] Two years later Evelyn remarried. By 1978 his new wife, Victoria, had provided him with a daughter and two sons. At the same time changes in the economic climate strewed obstacles in the path of Jacob's banking strategy. Evelyn decided to take a more active rôle at the bank — to be, in fact, master in his own house.

What happened over the next few years is clear enough but, naturally, there are differences of opinion about why it happened and the motivation of the principal actors. Evelyn believes that it was differences over financial policy which lay at the root of the conflict. It occurred at a time of rapid change in the financial services industry, a change largely brought about by the increasing use of computers and satellite technology. From the mid-1970s money men had had to accustom themselves to a situation in which information circled the earth in seconds, markets became more volatile, and agents in different continents could conclude deals of great sophistication by running their fingers over rattling keyboards. In the City, financial activity was still divided among specialists – bankers, brokers, jobbers, insurance dealers, investment companies, etc. At the same time world money markets were dominated by American and Japanese conglomerates which combined all or most aspects of financial business. Jacob wanted to transform and enlarge NMR, using public money, into a major concern capable of competing with the giants. Evelyn wanted to maintain the bank as a private business, achieving growth cautiously and remaining competitive within a more restricted field.[18]

As the two cousins continued to pursue divergent policies, a showdown became inevitable. It happened in 1980. A deep disagreement over major decisions had to be resolved quickly. Lord Rothschild was brought in to act as mediator. Victor considers that he remained above the conflict.[19] Jacob felt that he did not receive the support he might have expected from his father. In fact, the outcome was inevitable. As Jacob ruefully admitted, "You can't win against someone who has effective voting control." But the stance his father took hurt him deeply.[20] What happened immediately was that an arrangement was patched up making it possible for Jacob to withdraw gracefully. But it was obvious that he had, in fact, been dismissed.

It was a difficult time for everyone concerned. Evelyn could certainly have done without the tragedy which intruded itself into his life shortly afterwards and kept his name before the public for several months. In November 1980 his friend and first wife, Jeannette, disappeared with a lady friend while on a visit to the Marche area of central Italy. Her car was found abandoned on a lonely mountain road. The incident inevitably attracted much public interest. Had the two women fallen a prey to kidnappers? Jeannette, although remarried, still carried the name Rothschild on her passport and had, indeed, filled in the register of her hotel at Sarnano "Rothschild, Dorothy Jeannette Ellen". Someone with such obviously wealthy connections, defenceless and travelling with only a female companion in wild country, would be a prime target for Sicilian gangs, long active in the region. The *carabinieri* questioned Evelyn. Had he received a ransom demand? He had not. Police investigations brought no results. Only because Jeannette's husband kept the case alive and eventually offered a reward for information did another macabre chapter

429

in the story unfold. In January 1982 the remains of the two women were discovered in a steep forest five miles from Jeannette's abandoned car. More sensational press coverage. The official verdict of the Italian authorities was "death by misadventure": the two women had been cut off by a snowstorm and, after taking temporary refuge in an uninhabited cottage, had set out on foot with tragic but almost inevitable results.

That was not good enough for the press. The "mystery" was kept alive for months by journalists whose investigations revealed, or purported to reveal, a story of police incompetence, official cover-up and peasants too terrified of local criminals to reveal what they really knew about what was, they believed, a murder. Whatever the truth, it was a harrowing time for all those close to a beautiful woman who may have died in a kidnap attempt that went wrong — perhaps because she carried a famous name.[21]

The upset in the English bank was as nothing compared with the disaster which shortly afterwards fell upon Rue Laffitte. In May 1981 François Mitterrand was elected President of the French Republic, pledged to rescue the country from economic depression by means of a programme of out-and-out Socialism. Within a year he had nationalised the private banking sector. The splendid building on the Rue Laffitte had a new name over the door, "Européenne de Banque". After 165 years the axe fell suddenly and unexpectedly. Guy and Alain were very bitter. They felt the blow personally. Guy relieved some of his feelings in a long article for Le Monde. The Rothschilds have acquired a unique image, he asserted:

> They have become the proverbial symbol of wealth, a wealth which is evidenced with no pretence of guilt in their life-style. Furthermore, the succession of one generation after another at the head of their business has created the appearance of a dynasty — which is merely a fantasy. In business, they are noted for a certain competence and scrupulous behaviour, but in identifying them with the hypertrophy of private capitalism, they have been turned into "untouchables". One would think they are the only capitalists in France! In other societies, the attitude is different — in America, the idea of such long-standing success creates a favourable prejudice; in England, their proven professional ability, their celebrity, are recognized and encouraged as one of the national financial assets.

Multitudes of citizens, he suggested:

> appreciate the number of hospitals, schools, homes for children, for convalescents, for the elderly, the number of dispensaries, sana-

toriums, social buildings of all kinds that the Rothschild family has built, furnished and maintained; the number of works of art it has donated to museums; the number of artists, scientists, doctors, writers, the family has been fortunate in being able to aid at one time or another.

Nevertheless, the politicians, conscious of the jealousy of wealth which is characteristic of the French, wish to keep them at arm's length.

And he ended with the words:

A Jew under Pétain, a pariah under Mitterrand – for me it's enough.
To rebuild on ruins twice in a lifetime is too much.
Forced into retirement, I have decided to strike. [22]

What hurt most was being obliged to say goodbye to so many old and faithful employees. There were emotional farewells before Guy went off to live in America and Elie took up residence in London (he also assumed chairmanship of Rothschilds' Zürich bank). Alain died two years later.

But there were still Rothschilds in Paris. Alain's son, Eric, and Guy's son, David, were still young enough and resilient enough to realise that this was only a re-run of a crisis that the family had faced several times before. Speaking to a journalist in 1982, David remarked, "In ten years' time you will see what has become of Européenne de Banque – and what has become of Rothschild." [23]

Arrows Up and Down

In the last few years the Rothschilds have come out into the open. Or, at least, some of them have. A few members of the family have tunnelled out from the bastion of secrecy whose walls have been so solidly built by the ancestral document-burners. Some earlier Rothschilds, like Ferdinand, did keep journals or write their reminiscences, but these were definitely *not* for publication. Even among Henri's extensive *œuvres* there are only two pieces of real autobiography and they are restricted to a description of his childhood and youth. How fascinating a first-person account by N.M. or Betty or Baron Lionel would be, and a mid-nineteenth-century world view from the Great Baron's own pen would be an historical document of considerable importance. Alas, such remarkable men and women lacked either the time or the inclination to record their thoughts for posterity. The only exception to this reticence was Constance Battersea, whose *Reminiscences*, published in 1922, was an immediate sellout. Otherwise, the Rothschilds have kept themselves to themselves to a quite remarkable degree.

That makes all the more interesting the veritable "explosion" of self-publicity which occurred in the early 1980s. In 1983 two remarkable biographies and one autobiography appeared: Anka Muhlstein wrote an account of her great-great-grandfather, Baron James; Dr Miriam Rothschild described the life and work of her eccentric Uncle Walter and Baron Guy launched the book he had been brooding over since the nationalisation of his bank. Miriam's brother, Lord Rothschild, had already published a collection of semi-autobiographical essays in 1977 and another volume followed in 1984. The same year saw Baron Philippe's memoirs in print and also Baronne Nadine's account of her life with Edmond. These events were all part of a change of attitude which had been steadily overtaking the family. Just as the banks could no longer wait for business to come to them, so private individuals felt unable to maintain a patrician aloofness to newspaper comment and public criticism. They wanted to explain themselves, to make their point of view known. There are, of course, still members of the family, such as Evelyn and

Victor, who guard their privacy jealously, but more and more of the Rothschilds realise that large areas of their lives are public domain. As well as going into print themselves, they are open to journalists and television interviewers to an extent which would have been unthinkable a few years ago.

Sometimes, like all celebrities, they find media probing painful. Jacob certainly resented the publicity attracted by his breach with Evelyn. Thereafter his name was seldom out of the headlines. Ever since that traumatic day in 1980 when he left NMR for good, Jacob's career has been watched closely by the financial columnists. It has certainly been worth watching. In the space of four years, this tall, disarmingly quiet-spoken businessman accomplished what no other Rothschild had accomplished since the days of great-great-grandfather Nathan. Indeed, there is a marked parallelism between the career of Jacob Rothschild and that of N.M., the man who left the family business to set up on his own because "there was not room enough for all of us in Frankfurt". The energetic immigrant took the English financial establishment by storm. So did Jacob. Nathan galloped his way in a few years to a spectacular success that left observers breathless. So did Jacob. The founder of the London house attracted the attention of journalists and cartoonists. So did Jacob. The new man's ascent to the financial heights was so rapid that some cute copy-writer coined the expression "Jacob's ladder" and the metaphor was worked to death over the ensuing years.

When he left New Court, Jacob was angry and determined to prove that his ideas — ideas rejected by the bank — were sound. But it was not merely personal pique that fired the boiler of his runaway success. He had made a careful assessment of the changing financial scene and he planned accordingly. Although professional services were traditionally contained within watertight compartments, the bulkheads were leaking badly and the more radical City men prophesied a shift to a very different situation. Jacob Rothschild was one of them. He believed even more firmly than before that the future lay with large, multifaceted institutions. Addressing a conference of financiers in October 1983 he observed:

> We can expect the emergence of a number of financial conglomerates with interests straddling disciplines which have been traditionally distinct. I believe it is important that one or two concerns in the UK show themselves willing to jump in with both feet, and to play an active part in the redefinition of the financial sector's competitive boundaries.[1]

He had already begun suiting action to words. In 1980 he had taken with him the small part of the family's financial holdings for which he had been particularly responsible. This was Rothschild Investment Trust, a small public company with a good reputation for investing shareholders' money wisely in a portfolio of expanding firms. Since New Court refused to let him use the name "Rothschild" in his future financial dealings, Jacob changed the trust's name to RIT. He now set about expanding this company (whose assets were £99,400,000) into a major financial services business. On the lookout for extra capitalisation and the best financial brains available, he merged with another trust company, Northern, in May 1982. Before the year was out RITN had taken a major stake in a London stockbroking firm. They acquired holdings in companies specialising in factoring, office equipment, leasing and assurance-linked trust funds. In August 1983 they moved into Wall Street with a fifty per cent share in a New York merchant bank. Two months later money markets were buzzing with news of a colossal merger between RITN and the Charterhouse banking group. By the end of 1983 the world had a new Rothschild bank, Charterhouse J.Rothschild, and with a £400,000,000 capitalisation it was one of the largest merchant banks in the City. But Jacob had not finished. He had for some time been interested in Hambro Life, a leading insurance company with big plans for expansion into other areas. Hitherto, Jacob's enterprise had been too small to offer an attractive proposition to Mark Weinberg of Hambro. Now, it was Weinberg who took the initiative and suggested a get-together.

This was the point at which Jacob's express train came to a sudden and unscheduled halt. After several months' negotiation the Hambro deal, which would have resulted in a multi-billion pound conglomerate, was called off. The result was a serious setback for Jacob's whole strategy. He had wanted, as he told shareholders, to create an organisation "capable of competing on level terms with the great financial multi-service corporations of the United States".[2] Instead, he was left with a variegated clutch of companies many of which, like cuckoos' eggs, were in the wrong nest. On the other hand, several of these companies were very attractive propositions to other financial empire-builders. Over the next year Jacob sold off most of his major holdings, at a considerable profit.

The result of what he calls his "retreat from Moscow" was the emergence of J. Rothschild Holdings, a much slimmed-down operation but one commanding assets (in March 1986) of £603,500,000. It was, once again, a trust company but one with much more financial muscle than the old RIT. It could intervene in major takeovers and mergers by acquiring short-term or medium-term stakes in target companies whose value seemed likely to increase as a result of forthcoming negotiations. This new commercial power game called "arbitrage" has become one of the most significant developments in modern international finance. It is a game in which some of the toughest players have won fortunes. Jacob and his shareholders have done well from the game and he intends to remain at the tables for a long time to come.

Part of the slimming-down process involved relinquishing bronzed steel premises in St James, which have been likened to a Star Wars command module, and moving to more modest accommodation just along the road. But although there is nothing ostentatious about his present offices, the hanging sign above the door claims a proud ancestry and cocks a permanent snook at New Court. It depicts a sheaf of five arrows. Shortly after leaving NMR Jacob discovered that the symbol which the bank has always used had never been registered as a trademark. So he appropriated it and registered it himself. The outcast Rothschild using the symbol of Rothschild unity and harmony — what delicious irony!

As if such hectic activity were not enough, Jacob became, like Alfred a century before, a trustee of the National Gallery. Having inherited an appreciation of fine art as well as business acumen, Rothschild was doubtless seen as an ideal overseer of the gallery's fortunes in an age of intense international competition for masterpieces. In 1985 he was appointed chairman of the trustees and was immediately in the limelight over such controversial issues as the design for a gallery extension (the first choice having been described by Prince Charles as "a monstrous carbuncle") and the appointment of a new director with no previous experience as a curator. Talking with Jacob Rothschild is rather like participating in a college tutorial. He is donnishly genial and relaxed but let fall the loose statement or ill-considered judgement and there is a whiplash response. He is a man who expects precision thinking, and only colleagues who can match his intellectual stature survive in his team.

Jacob is the first to admit that Evelyn has made a great success of his leadership of NMR. At a difficult time for traditional merchant banks, when massive American conglomerates like Citibank were establishing themselves in London and competition for business reached an un-precedented intensity, New Court attracted more new corporate clients than its rivals. By 1986 its trust management department alone was handling four and a half billion pounds for clients, five times the 1981 figure. But increased business was not achieved by rushing into mergers and takeovers. Evelyn, with what many saw as a reference to his cousin's activities, commented in mid-1986: "There is considerable concern in the City, which I share, at the speed with which some new financial service groupings have been put together. We have already seen some of the neg-ative consequences."[3] NMR, therefore, made no attempt to buy up firms specialising in other types of financial expertise. They took up modest hold-ings in a jobber and a broker and waited to see what the market would do.

435

Tradition still haunts the modern rabbit warren of New Court. Every member of staff still receives a Christmas turkey and an annual bonus. The firm still does not employ union labour. There still seems to be a real feeling among employees that "Rothschilds look after their people". The bank's refinery still makes gold bars and NMR is still the most important bullion dealer in the country. Perhaps the most curious contact with the past is the ritual that takes place daily in the Gold Fixing Room. The leading London dealers sit round a table to agree the price of gold. Each one has a telephone and a small Union Jack in front of him. The flags are turned down and dealing begins. All verbal agreements must be honoured. But if a member wants to call his office for instructions or simply buy a few minutes to think he raises his emblem, calling out "Flags up!" and everything comes to a halt. Eventually the Rothschild representative in the chair asks "Figures please!" and the dealers make their offers which are phoned through to the Bank of England. This routine is as much an unchanging feature of the City of London as the nightly ceremony of the Queen's keys along the road at the Tower.

Evelyn is very much a traditionalist. It is hard to escape the past completely if you are a Rothschild, and even more so if you are running a bank still situated in the place where your great-great-grandfather began business 180 years before. Evelyn believes passionately in keeping NMR a private bank, maintaining family control and concentrating on those things Rothschilds have learned to do well. "There are, today, four hundred and eighty banks in the City," he says. "If we are to stay ahead of the field, we have to give a quality service."[4] There are few who do not respect his firm way of doing business. And the head of NMR can disdain criticism on two counts. The first is the status "Rothschild's" enjoys in the world of international finance. NMR, as the only one of the original banks to have enjoyed an unbroken succession, has inherited the mystique and kudos of a great name. As a pure family bank it has outlived almost every one of its City competitors. Only Baring's still have a descendant of their founder at the helm and Baring's is now a considerably smaller organisation than N.M. Rothschild and Sons. Evelyn is chairman of the Accepting Houses Committee, the élite of the City, representing sixteen banks which have a special relationship with the Old Lady of Threadneedle Street, a relationship which gives them a very privileged credit status. This position means that Evelyn, personally, is second only to the Governor of the Bank of England in the unofficial hierarchy of the City.

The other reason for Evelyn's confidence is the continuing expansion of his bank's business. He heads a group of subsidiary and associated companies which has offices in Guernsey, Zurich, New York, Hong Kong,

436

Singapore, Sydney and Melbourne. Through these offices and through agents Rothschild's provides banking and investment services in every major financial centre in the world. Nick McAndrew, one of the banking group's four managing directors, says that NMR is more active internationally than ever before: "The group advises government and multinationals and multi-millionaires, insurance giants across the Atlantic to buy Rothschild bond and currency market skills, mining magnates count on the group's engineers to scout out promising gold and silver prospects — the group's banking division plays a key role in global precious metal trading — and stacks a few bullion bars in its vaults."[5] The bank has advised on all aspects of commercial activity from mergers to Eurobonds, from the organisation of export finance to the privatisation of British Gas.

Evelyn has firmly resisted any suggestion of going public and affirms strongly that Rothschilds can still, as they have in the past, raise private capital whenever necessary. In mid-1986 Rothschilds Continuation successfully launched a thirty-million-dollar issue of primary capital undated guaranteed floating rate notes, which seems to prove his point.

Evelyn may be a traditionalist but he is also a realist. He accepts, for example, that in matters of executive control as opposed to ownership the dynastic principle may have to be abandoned. There are two other Rothschilds at New Court — Edmund's brother, Leopold, and son, Lionel — and Evelyn's young sons may one day follow him in the firm, but the chairman has gone on record as saying, "every business should be run as efficiently as possible. The advancement of family members by right is totally wrong."[6] Whoever succeeds Evelyn will have to be a real professional prepared to subordinate his other enthusiasms to finance. Not that Evelyn's is a one-track mind; far from it. As well as running a merchant bank, he manages to find time to be chairman of the medical school of St Mary's Hospital, chairman of *The Economist*, and chairman of United Racecourses.

Thus, the two rivals of 1980 have both demonstrated in their different ways that in world money markets Rothschild is not just a legendary name. The financial genes are as evident in the family as ever they were.

While all this was happening their French cousins were also proving dramatically that Rothschilds cannot be written off. A curious feature of the Rothschild symbol is that in England the arrows point downwards and in France they point upwards. NMR adapted its emblem from the baronial coat of arms which has, as two of its quarters, "azure, an arm embowed proper, grasping five arrows points to the base argent". The French,

perhaps feeling that having the sharp ends uppermost indicated a more forthright and optimistic outlook, turned their shafts upside down.* Their remarkable recovery since 1981 certainly reflects a bold spirit with no trace of defeatism.

The chairman of the Paris-Orléans holding company at the time of nationalisation was Baron Eric, a quietly determined, deceptively casual man of forty-one. A childhood spent in America, followed by years in an English prep school and a university course in engineering at Zürich had turned him into a modern, cosmopolitan businessman. He had worked his way up in the corporation, starting in one of the Rothschild transport subsidiaries, and had developed a minute understanding of corporate structures and a deep sense of responsibility for Rothschild employees. Now, with his cousin, David, he set about collecting together what was left of the commercial empire and using it as a basis for expansion.

They had a hundred million francs which the family had received as its share of compensation from the government. They had their vineyards. They had their stake in the international Rothschild group. And they had Paris-Orléans. This one-time railway network was now a holding company for a ragbag of relatively small Rothschild commercial activities, ranging from oil refining to cold storage. Eric and David combined all these resources and set aside some of the capital for the formation of a new private bank. Unlike the older members of the family, who felt nationalisation personally, the two young men decided to regard it as an opportunity. "This is a very exciting time for a new bank," Eric told me, "especially one which is part of a strong international group."

Looking back on the events of 1981, he said, "Mitterrand thought his

*Jacob Rothschild has also upended the arrows in his trademark.

strong potion would finish the family off. Instead it gave us a shot in the arm . . ."[7] The old Banque Rothschild was an industrial conglomerate with sixty-five per cent of its assets devoted to non-financial activity. Furthermore, thanks to falling world prices, its heavy involvement in the mining and processing of nonferrous metals was becoming something of a liability. State confiscation enabled the Rothschilds to slim down their operation and concentrate on the things they did best. Immediately after nationalisation they set up Paris-Orléans Gestion as a vehicle for their expertise in financial consultancy and investment management. Several of their staff followed the two Rothschilds into their new enterprise and many of their old clients remained loyal. Within months they applied for permission to open a new bank.

It was a challenge to the Socialist government and they saw it as such. Guy's celebrated *Le Monde* article had already provoked considerable support and Mitterrand was widely suspected of anti-Semitism. This popular backlash helped to create the climate in which David scored a personal triumph in January 1985. He had had the audacity to apply for membership of the Jockey Club. Since Edmond's strongly opposed election in 1868, this exclusive body had become even more the preserve of Gentile aristocrats. In fact, despite their enthusiastic support for horse-racing, no Rothschild had gained the coveted accolade for almost a century. David's nomination, therefore, aroused enormous interest. Pro- and anti-factions lobbied furiously and sponsors wrote hundreds of letters pointing out David's services to the sport since he had taken over the management of the Rothschild stud. A record number of members travelled to Paris for the secret voting. To David's supporters this seemed to be a bad sign but, in the event, their man was successful, though the margin of his victory was, in accordance with club rules, not revealed.[8]

Meanwhile the more important application was encountering equally determined opposition. It was impossible for the government to agree to the re-emergence of the Rothschilds as a force in French banking without losing face. What made matters worse was that its policies were running into difficulties. In particular, many of the nationalised banks, including L'Européenne de Banque, were in the red. Baron Guy's autobiography — published in 1983, as we have seen — added to the armoury of the government's critics. In it he scornfully dismissed his political opponents with the words, "the encyclopaedic ignorance of the Left on matters of economics is a constant of French political life".[9] It is hardly surprising, therefore, that David and Eric were locked into over two years of tough bargaining with officials. They wanted to revert to the old name of De Rothschild Frères for their new operation but the government would not hear of it. There was to be no question of the family name being used. At last, they granted a licence to an enterprise to be known as "P.O. [Paris-Orléans] Banque". The new Paris house opened its doors in July 1984. The Rothschilds were back in business.

The forbidden name did not appear on the notepaper of the latest Rothschild bank but prospective clients were left in no doubt as to its origins. Under the familiar family symbol the prospectus explained:

> The five arrows of the Rothschild family symbolise the five sons of Mayer Amschel who left Frankfurt at the end of the eighteenth century to found an international network of banking houses.
> James de Rothschild set up in Paris in 1817 and rapidly established a reputation as an eminent financier.
> His descendants participated in the expansion and industrialisation of France and invested in those sectors which dominated progress such as mining, electricity and transport, notably the company which developed the Paris-Orléans railway system. P.O. became a financial holding company and from it P.O. Banque takes its name. P.O. Banque marks the return of the Rothschild family to the banking scene after an interruption of two years (1982-84).

To reach the nerve-centre of the Rothschilds' French operation in the Rue Rabelais, close to the Avenue des Champs Elysées, you have to pass a barrier guarded by a gendarme. This is not for the protection of the Rothschilds: the building next door houses the Israeli embassy. When you ascend to the discreet first-floor offices of the bank you come to a foyer where walls and chairs are in restful green and a large portrait of the Great Baron gazes down at you with an expression of calm assurance. And here you may meet several of his descendants, for these offices house the Rothschilds' private secretariat as well as the bank.

Baron Guy puts in several hours a day here, though he may slip out to walk his black poodle or to lunch at his favourite restaurant just along the street. The resurgence of Rothschild financial activities has helped to assuage the anger he felt in 1981. He has returned to Paris from his self-imposed American exile and taken up residence once more in his palatial home on the Ile St Louis. Having worked the bitterness out of his system he now, once more, looks to the future. He is proud of what his son and nephew are building and admits that, even without the interference of M. Mitterrand, the old bank was overdue for a change. "The building in Rue Laffitte was too big and our holdings needed pruning," he told me. "David and Eric are now choosing new investments. They're much more flexible." But the recent past has left its scars. The amazingly bright blue eyes cloud over when he talks of the "old bank", and the staff who no longer work for Rothschild's. Even today he cannot bring himself to drive down Rue Laffitte.[10]

Baron Elie also bases himself in Rue Rabelais when he is in Paris. Although he lives most of the time in London, he keeps a beautiful town house in the French capital. There, over an extremely elegant private luncheon served by a white-gloved major-domo who has been with him for years, Elie shared with me his enthusiasms and his feelings about the family: "You could say that, whatever we do, we are all professionals." My host, slim, grey-haired, alert and distinguished, has "done" many things in his sixty-eight years and talked easily about his varied life as banker, Nazi prisoner of war, polo player, art collector (he specialises in modern paintings) and vineyard proprietor. Like the true professional, he was dedicated and well informed. For my benefit, he spoke fluent English only lapsing occasionally into his native tongue for greater expressiveness. The ornate Louis Quinze dining room which would have accommodated a modest banquet, the exquisite food and the wine — Château Lafite, of course — were all impressive, but not so impressive as Elie's enthusiasm and strongly expressed opinions. He became most animated, not over matters financial or vinicultural, but on the subject of his family's charitable institutions.[11] Elie is not alone in being proud of 130 years of achievement in the fields of social and medical care. Eric, now chairman of Fondations Rothschild, travels widely to keep himself up to date with the latest knowledge and technology, and David speaks for them all when he says, "Life isn't just about work and play. We also have to have civic responsibilities. That's why the Fondation has become second nature to us."[12]

Some of the hospitals, research centres and homes have been wholly or partially incorporated within the national welfare system but the Rothschilds are still actively involved, even on the committees of state-owned institutions. And they are still taking new initiatives. In 1975 the most technically advanced unit for treating mentally handicapped infants was added to a psychiatric centre founded by Alain in the 13th *arrondissement* of Paris in 1960. In 1976 Nadine donated an operating theatre to the cardiac unit at l'Hôpital Broussais. And in 1985 Edmond and the Fondations Rothschild provided it with one of the most advanced diagnostic units in France, equipped with a nuclear magnetic resonance scanner.

Yet, there is no doubt that the institution on the Rue Picpus holds a special place in the family's affections. It was here that James opened a Jewish hospital which was the first of all the other major Rothschild benefactions. Today it still operates, but as a centre for geriatric care without any sectarian bias. The establishment on Rue Picpus is not, in any conventional sense, an old people's home. Children play in the gardens and chatter with the residents who watch from their benches beneath the trees. Women drink coffee and talk with visitors in the bistro. Men play cards or pool with their grandchildren, for friends and relatives are free to come and go at will. For the sick and dying, there is the very best in hospice care. The individual rooms would not disgrace a luxury hotel and the overall décor is modern and imaginative. For the five hundred people who live there, the centre is a community within which they have all the privacy they want, all the freedom they can cope with and all the care they need. Above all it is a community open to the wider community.

And the French Rothschilds are completely involved in its maintenance, management and improvement. This kind of activity never makes the headlines but as much care and concentration goes into it as is expended on nurturing the vines at Lafite and Mouton, arranging a multimillion-dollar business deal or appraising a fine painting to be added to one of the collections.

The creation of the new bank brought the Rothschilds a greater degree of professional unity than they have experienced for over sixty years. Among the shareholders of P.O. Banque were NMR and Baron Edmond. The new institution proclaimed itself as *une banque d'affaires privée et internationale*, offering the full range of merchant-banking services and largely capitalised from within the family. David believes that participation in the worldwide Rothschild group is a great attraction for clients and that remaining private makes planned growth simpler "because it's easier to follow a policy of retaining earnings in the early years".[13] The first two years suggest that his analysis may well be correct. While state-owned competitors were going through a difficult patch, the Paris-Orléans holding company trebled its share value and the bank reported a return on capital after tax of twenty-five per cent. In that period also, the Rothschilds once again outlasted their political enemies. The conservatives returned to power, pledged to privatisation. Some of the confiscated Rothschild industrial assets may soon be repossessed. But what is even more significant is the fact that the name "Rothschild" is now back on the door. In 1986 P.O. Banque became Rothschild et Associés.

One of the cornerstones of the late twentieth-century Rothschild banking edifice is their New York office. In 1981-2 the American operation was completely revamped. Under the personal supervision of Guy and Evelyn, the Paris and London houses took firmer control, replaced New Court Securities with a new company, Rothschild Incorporated, and set about making it a major force in US finance. That was the plan.

It proved very difficult to accomplish. Part of the problem was internal discord. Edmond — by now, as we have seen, the wealthiest individual member of the family — declined to be involved. The president of New Court Securities disliked the new corporate structure and resigned. And in 1984 another Rothschild member of the board, Elie's son, Nathaniel, left to join Jacob in London. But the real reason for the new bank's sluggish beginning lies in history. Modern Rothschilds are paying the price for their ancestors' lack of personal involvement in the USA. They may have had a modest presence in New York since the last war but, for the insular Americans, the Rothschilds are still foreigners and their name exercises less magic there than in any other centre of international finance. The new institution will have to fight hard for every inch of ground it may gain in the New World.

The early signs are that Rothschild Inc. is developing the aggressive strategy necessary for success. The first step was to appoint an outstanding chief executive. Their choice fell on a commercial lawyer, Bob Pirie. Pirie is very much in the Belmont mould: a tough businessman who moves in Long Island society, is well connected and active politically, a Harvard graduate, an intimate of several titled people in Britain and Europe. He collects rare books, has a country estate, hunts in Massachusetts and sails his yacht off the coast of Maine. Under his presidency the firm has begun to make an impact in the field of arbitrage and corporate deals, specialising in the financial fisticuffs of takeovers and mergers. But it also offers a wide range of merchant bank services to clients. Unlike Belmont, Pirie seems to have the complete backing of his principals and David de Rothschild has gone on record as saying, "We want to grow from a small firm, to become a bit more visible. How the firm accomplishes that is more or less left to Bob." [14] And one of the ways Bob responds is by promoting the Rothschild image, bringing home to Americans, or at least the ones that matter, the achievements of the family in the fields of art, science and fine wine, as well as banking. If any one man can transplant the mystique of the Rothschild name to an alien soil, that man is Robert S. Pirie.

In France, the vineyards, which began as a hobby, are now an integral part of the family's commercial operation. Eric continues the modest empire building begun by Elie. The company now not only owns Lafite, the neighbouring Duhart-Milon (a *quatrième cru*) and La Cordonne, but acquired a leading Sauternes vineyard, Château Rieussec, in 1984. An enterprise which was for eighty years in the financial doldrums is now making excellent headway. "The big annual question now is no longer whether we'll make a loss or a profit," Eric told me with his schoolboyish grin, "but how big the profit will be." [15] And, as Baron Edmond, who has a one-sixth share in the vineyard, says, "Lafite is not sold, it's bought."[16] With recent vintages retailing at four to five hundred pounds a case, in bond, drinking Château Lafite is, more than ever, a rich man's indulgence. However, when a bottle of 1787 Lafite sold for a staggering £105,000 at a Christie's auction in December 1985, it was beyond what even a Rothschild was prepared to pay. Eric, clad in the black velvet garment − a cross between a dressing-gown and a Victorian frock coat − that he likes to relax in during evenings at the château, told me that he had been interested in acquiring the bottle for the unique *Vinothèque*, the "library" of wines arranged, year by year, in Lafite's prestigious cellar, but that he had not even entered the bidding. I asked him about the old rivalry with Mouton. "When the classification battle was over that died out," he said. "Philippe pursues a different policy; he is a *négociant* who owns a vineyard. We stick to farming and are building up a group of vineyards." With a high stake in the Haut Médoc, which must be the richest 150 square miles of arable in the world, the Rothschilds are certainly not just "farmers". With their spread of vineyards they are no longer restricted to prestige labels but aim to produce Bordeaux wines across the whole price range. Their latest venture is the creation of Savour Club, a mail-order wine service operating in France, West Germany and Belgium.[17]

Baron Philippe, in his mid-eighties, was afflicted by poor health and died in January 1988. But, in the last years, the ideas which flowed from his alert mind were as clear and robust as the wine sold under his prestigious labels. From his canopied bed he organised and planned. Frequently he travelled. Part of every year was spent in his homes in Paris and London. In February 1984 he was in the Napa Valley for the first sale of Opus One, an event eagerly awaited in the wine world which had been kept on its toes by skilful publicity. For example, the first bottles ever to be sold had created a US wine record. That was in June 1981 when a case was auctioned, and knocked down after vigorous bidding for twenty-four thousand dollars. The release to the trade three years later was at a more modest price, but Opus One achieved its objective of being a prestige wine, an undeclared *premier cru* of the Napa Valley. Back home, Philippe, assisted by his equally ebullient daughter, continued to improve Mouton. The modern visitor to Mouton passes many châteaux on his journey through the Médoc which are intrinsically more impressive as historic buildings but they only serve to point up the achievement of Mouton Rothschild. The dazzling white gravel driveways are raked daily. The lawns and shrubs are kept immaculate and form the perfect setting for the fine-blended old and new buildings in cream-coloured stone. The stunning simplicity of the museum and its priceless exhibits attract an increasing number of visitors every year to a region which makes surprisingly few concessions to the tourist industry.

The "new boy" among the Rothschild wine growers, Baron Edmond, is making a considerable success at Château Clarke. It will be some time before he has recouped the enormous cost of replanting and building but the very name "Rothschild" adds several francs to the price of a bottle and Edmond's wines regularly open at fifty francs, which is very high for a *cru bourgeois*. Like Philippe, Edmond has visited the Napa Valley and has learned much from Californian methods. This greatest of all living Rothschild entrepreneurs is very much impressed with American professionalism and has streamlined the administration of his Médoc estate.

Clarke lacks the theatricality of Mouton and the old world gentility of Lafite. Everything is geared to the efficient production and selling of wine, from the computer-monitored stainless-steel vats to the calculation of the precise sector of the market at which the product is targeted. The house Edmond has converted from old garages for his rare visits to Listrac is modest by Rothschild standards. It is in the separate suite of rooms reserved for entertaining that the unmistakable *style* takes over. Here, Edmond has a banqueting hall, served by its own kitchen, and a library containing almost every available book on the wines of Bordeaux. The Baron's adjoining study is panelled in mellowed oak richly inlaid with other woods. It is much travelled. Edmond brought it here from Paris, where it once graced his town house. A century before Adolph had conveyed it thither from Italy where it originally formed part of the décor of a Renaissance prince's palace. It still bears the date of its construction – 1497. His latest venture, however, has taken him many miles from Bordeaux. From the Caribbean island of St Kitts he launched a new drink – Cane Spirit Rothschild.

The magnificent Château de Pregny, last of the great Rothschild mansions, is still Edmond's principal residence. He spends a couple of months every year there and tries to get to it whenever possible at weekends. Yet, ironically, it is the one house that does not belong to him. "When I was a young man," he explained, "I casually and rather foolishly remarked to my father one day that this place would make a good hotel. I think he remembered that, because he gave it to the city of Geneva, in case I decided to act on the idea."[18] In fact, the Baron has done a deal with the local authorities which allows him and, after him, his son, Benjamin, to continue living at Pregny. Edmond and Nadine make full use of the château's dozens of rooms. Benjamin (now in his twenties) has his own extensive quarters and the rest is frequently occupied by visiting friends and business colleagues.

The Baron, himself, moves in a very "ungrand" way among the splendours

445

of Pregny. He finds the title of "baron" rather absurd and is at pains to put people at ease. Calling on a multimillionaire who lives in royal splendour is not exactly a relaxing prospect, especially if your taxi arrives before the sweeping steps of the château's façade just as a convoy of black limousines is leaving. Such was my experience at our first meeting and I fully expected to be ushered into a sumptuous waiting room to take my turn among a succession of more important guests. A butler descended the steps to open the car door for me but I had scarcely extricated myself when a stocky, bustling man with crinkly, greying hair shook my hand warmly and introduced himself as Edmond de Rothschild. "A bunch of international bankers," he explained, with a wave of his hand towards the disappearing motorcade. He took the steps two at a time and preceded me across a large marble hall to a comfortable study with expansive views across the lake. "Now, if you're taking notes perhaps you'd like to sit in my chair." He indicated the leather, executive swivel seat behind the almost inevitable Louis Seize desk.

The interview continued as informally as it had begun. Edmond talked frankly and seemingly with equal enthusiasm about both successes and failures. Early in 1984, by what turned out to be a great stroke of luck, he had been forced to sell his thirty per cent holding in the Bank of California to Mitsubishi. Months later the bank had run into difficulties. But in 1985, his toy business — the biggest in France — had almost been wiped out because he did not anticipate the switch of children's interests to electronic and computer games. As a result company turnover fell from sixty million to ten million dollars. But at the same time his activities were expanding in other directions. Cigarette after cigarette burned down in his holder, as Edmond told me about his new ventures. Like Jacob, he saw clearly the opportunities inherent in his reorganisation of financial services (greatly enhanced by deregulation of the City of London in 1986). In 1984 he obtained Bank of England approval to establish an institution dealing in securities and bonds. From modest offices just along the road from Cousin Jacob, he established a small private bank, one of the many diverse operations run under the umbrella of his Geneva holding company. Small it may be, but this third Rothschild financial organisation in London is poised to expand into various branches of the service and investment industry. With this project scarcely off the ground, Edmond took a major stake in Italian banking. In the spring of 1985 he acquired a twenty-seven per cent share in Banca Tiburtina and runs it conjointly with Banca de Lavorno, Italy's largest state-controlled financial institution. These banks, added to his interests in France, Switzerland, USA and Israel, and his share of P.O. Banque, show Edmond to be a Rothschild fully imbued with the spirit of the Frankfurt Five.

The similarity extends also to his religious life. When he speaks of Israel he speaks with passion. The memory of the Six Day War, in 1967, is still vivid for him. When the outbreak of the conflict was announced over French radio on the morning of 5 June Edmond was in his bath. He immediately dressed and telephoned Alain, the lay head of French Jewry. Within hours the two cousins were on a plane for Tel Aviv and the next day Nadine flew out to join them. They were among the first civilians to enter, amidst scenes of great emotion, the Old City after the Jordanians had been driven out of the West Bank. Edmond's own eyes were moist as he recalled how he had prayed with Ben-Gurion at the Wailing Wall, restored to Jewish ownership after nearly nineteen hundred years. Six years later Israel was, once again, fighting her Arab neighbours in the Yom Kippur War. This time, Edmond was travelling to a dinner in Lugano when the news reached him. "I was sick with worry, yet I had to sit and make small talk for several hours. It was one of the worst evenings of my life," he told me.

Edmond believes he has been a failure in Israel and that depresses him − much more than any commercial setback. He would like to have exercised a strong political influence, as his friend Henry Kissinger had done, but that was not possible. He feels frustrated because he believes that the new state has lost its direction and that he has been powerless to prevent it. He is highly critical of the current leadership and its rôle in Middle East squabbles. He worries about the moral and religious line of the nation and what he calls its "Levantisation". The spirit of that other Edmond broods heavily over his grandson. "I'm proud of what we're doing at the hospital and the institute of molecular biology that my grandfather founded but in Israel I have let him down. I've achieved nothing." He seemed to be talking to himself, rather than me. "My relationship with Israel is like a marriage which hasn't lived up to expectations − I'm bitterly disappointed but still emotionally involved." He came out of his reverie. "Of course the whole family − French and English − is more involved in Israel than ever."[19]

That is certainly true. Apart from their various individual interests in the Jewish state, many of them are involved with L'Institut Alain de Rothschild, set up after Alain's death in 1983 to cater for the needs of French Jewry. It would be true to say that, from a religious point of view, most Rothschilds today are non-practising, or, at least, only occasional in their devotions. But their support for Israel − a place where they still have no desire to settle − has never been stronger. The events of 1948, para-doxically, enabled them to merge their Zionism and their assimilationism. They remain Jews of the Dispersion − the Diaspora − but they feel that the triumph of their co-religionists in Palestine has also vicariously

447

liberated them. That, at least, is how Guy sees it:

> We, the Jews of the Diaspora, are proud of the Israelis, of their courage and military valour. After centuries of humiliation, Jewish honour and dignity have been proven to the world. We are now less vulnerable to hostility, to doubts concerning our acceptance by others, to the fear of still another tragedy befalling us. Israel is not our country, its flag is not our flag; but Israel is the liberator of part of our inner ego.[20]

One thing Edmond has certainly achieved is the closing of the gap with his cousins which had opened up in the previous two generations. Now, he is fully involved with their various professional and philanthropic activities. He has contributed considerably to the re-establishment of *concordia* which is such a marked feature of the family today.

In 1980 the ghosts of the past once again returned to haunt Lord Rothschild. The previous year Anthony Blunt had died and the government had revealed his treachery. Naturally there was a press outcry, not only about the appalling record of the Cambridge Four – Blunt, Burgess, Maclean and Philby – but also about the way that Blunt's complicity had been concealed since its discovery sixteen years before. There was a fresh spate of speculation concerning possible spies in high places. What other reputations were being protected by an embarrassed government? There was talk of a "fifth man" in the Blunt circle and of moles in the security service. Sir Roger Hollis, a former director-general of MI5, came under suspicion. Mrs Thatcher ordered an internal inquiry and Hollis's name was cleared. But sections of the press and some MPs were not satisfied. Questions were asked about what constitutes "national interest" and how the relationships between British Intelligence, other civil service departments, government, parliament and Fleet Street should be regulated. Throughout the eighties such matters would be seldom out of the headlines.

Lord Rothschild, of course, knew that *he* was innocent. He had been thoroughly vetted before his appointment as head of the Think Tank. MI5 knew all about his wartime record and had no reason to doubt his loyalty. But Victor knew that in security matters there was no such thing as one hundred per cent clearance. Writing about the Blunt affair, he said, "You never get over a blow of this sort. What about John, Peter, Thomas and so forth, one asks oneself? The Intelligence Services ask the same questions and, of course, many more. In their world the file is never closed."[21]

Lord Rothschild also knew that he could not publicly clear his name: he was still bound by the Official Secrets Act. This, reinforced by his own patriotism and loyalty to friends, prevented him coming out into the open. He maintained an outward stoical disdain and remained silent.

Then, in 1980, came news that another former MI5 officer was planning to break *omertà*. Peter Wright, a scientist, had joined the security service in 1955. On leaving he had taken up farming but soon discovered that retirement was not what he had hoped for. He felt cheated. He was galled by the realisation that, had he made deliberate use of his contacts and knowledge, he could have ended his days a richer man. Eventually he packed his bags and went off to Australia. There, beyond the reach of the British courts, he eventually decided to publish his memoirs. The result was *Spycatcher: the Candid Autobiography of a Senior Intelligence Officer*. The book was altogether too candid for the British government which, in 1985, gained an injunction preventing publication. They were determined to make an example of Wright to prevent other retired officers breaching the Official Secrets Act and making damaging allegations.

Wright's attempt to have *Spycatcher* published in Australia led to a long and highly publicised court case, leaks of sections of the book in the British press, untrammelled publication in the USA and the widespread circulation elsewhere of "smuggled" copies. After the government had failed to prevent Wright's memoirs coming out in Australia, they maintained a campaign through British and some foreign courts to prevent newspapers printing extracts from *Spycatcher*, thereby protracting publicity for many months.

It was particularly unwelcome publicity for Lord Rothschild. His name figured in Wright's memoirs and in the press coverage of the trial as someone influential in Intelligence circles, yet none of the supposed revelations provoked him into making public comment. But something else did. This was the bringing out and dusting down of the old "fifth man" speculation. Several newspapers published colourful versions of Victor's past in the hope of luring this very private man into leaving his shell. Lord Rothschild was deeply wounded by it all. On 3 December 1986 he responded unexpectedly, succinctly and passionately by sending a letter to *The Daily Telegraph*. It was published on the next day's front page.

Dear Editor and Readers,
Since at least 1980 up to the present time there have been innuendoes in the Press to the effect that I am "the 5th man", in other words a Soviet agent.
    The Director-General of MI5 should state publicly that it has unequivocal, repeat unequivocal, evidence that I am not, and never

have been, a Soviet agent. If the "regulations" prevent him making such a statement which, in the present climate I doubt, let him do so through his legal adviser or through any other recognizably authoritative source.

I am constrained by the Official Secrets Act but I write this letter lest it be thought that silence would be an indication of anything other than complete innocence.

I shall not make any other public statement to the Press until further notice.
Yours truly
Rothschild[22]

The Prime Minister responded promptly:

10 DOWNING STREET

Press Notice

LORD ROTHSCHILD'S LETTER TO THE DAILY TELEGRAPH
OF 4 DECEMBER 1986

STATEMENT BY THE PRIME MINISTER

I have now considered more fully Lord Rothschild's letter in the Daily Telegraph yesterday, in which he referred to innuendoes that he had been a Soviet agent.

I consider it important to maintain the practice of successive governments of not commenting on security matters. But I am willing to make an exception on the matter raised in Lord Rothschild's letter.

I am advised that we have no evidence that he was ever a Soviet agent.

5 December 1986

No mention was made of Lord Rothschild's distinguished service to his country and, although pressed in parliament, Mrs Thatcher refused to add anything of substance to her statement. Not even the fact that Victor had played a major rôle in unmasking Philby earned him more generous

450

treatment. The government knew then, what Philby himself later public-ally acknowledged, that it was Lord Rothschild who, in 1962, alerted MI5 to suspicions concerning Philby voiced by Mrs Flora Solomon. It was this information which led directly to the discovery of the fourth man.[23]

Perhaps what emerges most clearly from this story is a paradox: Rothschild influence may be as formidable as it was a century ago; yet the British public is not prepared to tolerate that influence. Who but a Rothschild could, throughout thirty-five years, during most of which he occupied no government or civil service post, have held such sway in high places? His public record was impressive but no more so than that of several other prominent citizens. He was not unique in intellectual accomplishment nor in experience as an intelligence officer. The mystic operations of the old boy network are inadequate to explain Victor's unofficial eminence. It is the kind of phenomenon that causes cranks and fanatics to indulge in the conspiracy theory of history. There is no need to go to such lengths. Victor grew up with the conviction − perhaps conscious, perhaps not − that the head of the Rothschild family held a particular responsibility to his country. Seemingly, this view was shared by some others at the top.

Yet, in the last quarter of the twentieth century, the British press and people do not take kindly to what some would describe as the "overmighty subject". When Natty manipulated politicians, indulged in secret negotiations, and influenced the course of national and international affairs, the common man loved him for it. But that was a hundred years ago. Victor could not take a leaf from his ancestor's book without arousing jealousy, suspicion and resentment. The owl is mobbed by the sparrows because he is out of place in their daylight world. The paradox is only capable of resolution if we insist that none of the normal rules apply to the Rothschilds. It is an arguable hypothesis.

Within the family there is certainly a consciousness that being a Rothschild is something special. The unity Mayer Amschel set so much store by is still maintained, despite the present-day dispersion and diversity of the family. Perhaps "community" would be a better word than "unity". Every modern Rothschild, whether he or she finds the common heritage inspiring or boring, has a sense of belonging to something important. There are certainly strong centripetal forces at work which tend to fling members of the family off into their highly individualistic lives. Marriage is one such influence. Resentment of the public Rothschild image is another.

Undeniably the most potent such force is sheer talent. "The Rothschilds are all so interesting," as Anne, Edmund's second wife, remarked during a walk among the rhododendrons at Exbury. She should know; she has been closely connected with the family most of her life. She met Eddy in 1940 and married a friend to whom he introduced her after the war. She and Eddy both had happy marriages and were widowed within six months of each other. They were wed in 1982. Exbury is the centre of their life – not just making it pay, important though that is – but helping other people to enjoy it.

Their enthusiasm is certainly infectious, as I discovered when they took me on a tour of the estate. Edmund, jovial and avuncular, strode among the trees and cascading blossoms, talking about and *to* his beloved plants, for he is a great believer in encouraging and cajoling his rhododendrons and azaleas to give of their best. "You really are a beautiful thing," he assured one of his favourite Rothschild hybrids, "Idealist", whose elegant blossoms, shading from pink to greenish yellow, preened themselves amidst a grove of shrubs and trees. "You see that pair of *Cupressus sempervirens?*" He pointed out two pillars of green, towering over the neighbouring foliage. "Grown from cuttings of a wreath which fell from the Duke of Wellington's bier at his funeral in 1852." He marched on through the woods, scattering stories and anecdotes like a seasoned and experienced guide. "George Forrest was one of the most amazing plant collectors who worked for my father. Braved incredible hardships and dangers to find rare species in the wild. Once he was staying at Father Dubenard's mission station in Tibet when it was attacked by some of the local monks. Forrest escaped with twelve men and was hunted for eight days. At last the enemy caught up with him and faced him across a narrow river. He was cornered. Then he saw Dubenard with them and assumed he had been brought along as a captive. The old priest motioned to him to move away down river. He did so, and found a track which enabled him to escape." Edmund stood suddenly still and faced his audience, pausing for maximum theatrical effect. "Only later did Forrest learn that Father Dubenard had been killed several days before their encounter at the river." Our tour came to an end when we found a bemused elderly visitor, hopelessly lost in the Exbury acreage. "You stay there," he said to the old man. Then he dashed off to find his car, pick up the wanderer and restore him to the rest of his party.

As we drove back to her house to lunch off a fine salmon caught by her husband, Anne explained that looking after – and tidying up after – Joe Public was one of their major activities. She recalled with amusement how one visitor, seeing her scoop up discarded cigarette cartons and crisp packets, came up to her and said, "I hope you get paid for that; the Rothschilds can certainly afford it." The truth of the matter is that they cannot. They have to work hard at both the tourist side of the business and its commercial horticulture. Only recently has it proved possible to modernise and reoccupy Exbury House, which had stood empty since the war. But it is not only a large estate that Anne has to cope with. There are also her grown-up stepchildren, all of whom lead interesting lives. One is a banker, another runs his own film and television production company. A third is a concert soprano.

Outstanding ability is, by definition, rare. Most families can boast only a few exceptional members. With the Rothschilds, high talent seems to be the norm. "One of our characteristics is that we are all keenly *interested* in things. My father, for instance, in addition to all his scientific work, wrote some very interesting papers about coinage," Miriam explained, during one of my visits to her home near Peterborough. Finding Ashton Wold is rather like stepping into the story of Sleeping Beauty. It involves leaving human habitation behind and driving for almost two miles along a suspension-bruising, unmade track through tangled woods. The lane dwindles to a narrow drive, rounds a bend and deposits you in a courtyard bordered by overgrown flowerbeds. The house, too, is literally overgrown; so covered with creepers that it seems to be an integral part of the forest, a rambling, hidden, secret place. Inside, the house is comfortable and spacious. Untamed nature obviously stops at the door although vases are filled with wild flowers, rather than cultivated blooms, and the household seems to be ruled by a pack of small, temperamental collie dogs. In this rather unlikely location, Miriam dispenses hospitality à la Rothschild to distinguished guests — mostly naturalists and scientists — from all over the world. From here she corresponds with her fellow scientists, studies butterflies and writes a succession of articles and papers about them. Eight years younger than the century, her memory is long, her mind sharp and her sense of humour keen. She tells vivid, and sometimes wicked, stories and loves to slip challenging and outrageous comments into conversation to keep people on their toes.

Miriam attributes her own energy to the family trait of being insatiably "interested and curious". When, in 1981, she was elected a Fellow of the Royal Society another Rothschild "first" was notched up. Victor had become an FRS thirty-three years before. They are now the only brother and sister ever to have enjoyed this honour simultaneously.

Miriam, as both a Rothschild and a student of nature, also finds certain of the characteristics of her own family interesting. "So many of the younger generation, unlike the previous one, excel academically," she explained. Of the surviving children of Victor and his sisters, several won scholarships and collected "firsts" or fellowships at university, and went on to pursue successful literary, artistic and scientific careers. Among their contemporaries in the French family are a painter, a writer and a leading paediatrician — all of them are making their own way in widely diverse occupations.

But just as strong as the impulsion which drives members of each generation into new activities is the centrifugal force which holds the family together. Meeting the Rothschilds leaves one with a strong sense that *plus ça change plus c'est la même chose*. Some of their magnificent settings have gone. Ferrières stands empty. Mentmore was, some years ago, stripped of its magnificent treasures in one of the greatest auction sales of the century. Waddesdon belongs to the nation, as does Ascott, although Evelyn and his family continue to live in it. But the Rothschilds are still *here*. They continue to occupy their traditional rôles — bankers, wine growers, collectors, stockbreeders, art experts, men of influence, public figures. And the sense of family remains almost as strong as ever. Lord Rothschild has compiled a detailed and accurate genealogical tree and every name on it is identified by a number. Most of his relatives have a copy and they keep Victor informed about all births, marriages and deaths so that new up-to-date editions can be produced every few years. The Rothschilds I met were genuinely interested in each other's activities. Lionel de Rothschild, who gave me enormous help in my researches, once went through with me a list of every living family member — dozens of them. And he was able to provide a quick verbal sketch of each one. The mutual fascination still exists. Members of the family I spoke with were as eager to hear odd facts that my researches had unearthed as they were to share their memories with me.

For me it was all symbolised one summer Sunday afternoon when I attended a charity recital in "the Temple", a neo-classical building in the grounds of Gunnersbury House. It was a warm day. The small room was crowded; not the most ideal conditions. But for two hours we were held spellbound as Charlotte de Rothschild recreated for us the kind of entertainment that might have been offered at Gunnersbury or Aston Clinton or Ferrières a century or so ago. She interspersed her songs with anecdotes about N.M. and Alfred and the Great Baron and Connie. She sang pieces by Chopin and Rossini, Liszt, Sullivan, and, of course, Mathilde de Rothschild, whose works she has been collecting and preparing for performance. It was a programme put together by a young, very modern, member of the family inspired by interest, by affection and by a genuine pride in her heritage. Above all, inspired by a fascination with the extraordinary, persistent Rothschild phenomenon.

Various members of the family view that phenomenon differently. Philippe regarded the whole Rothschild thing as a "myth", and Lord Rothschild once told a journalist that the family was "a remnant of the past". For Evelyn the bank is everything. In his view, the Rothschilds would be nothing without their financial base. Baron Elie, on the other hand, is convinced that success in so many spheres stems from an inbred professionalism. Miriam told me, "the real secret of the Rothschilds is their incredible industry". Lionel, who explained how hard he had to work at Cambridge to get a first, because anything less was unthinkable, believes that part of the Rothschild inheritance is a commitment to the highest standards. Nadine regards the key to the family's success as "its ability to adapt to every situation with realism and far-sightedness".

About one fact there can be no debate: there is magic in the name. Edmond impressed upon me the intense importance of that one word "Rothschild" in the family's recovery after the Second World War. Batsheva admitted, philosophically, that it opens doors for her dance company that would otherwise be closed. Its appearance on a label adds several francs to the price of a bottle of wine. There can be no other name carried by such a bizarre variety of objects, from a French hospital to an African giraffe. There is even a Viennese finger-shaped chocolate confection which glories in the title Rothschildbiscotte. It is, of course, the reputation built by talented and forceful individuals which has made the name so formidable, but undeniably the name helps to create and sustain reputations.

Genetics, mythology, deliberate training, the opportunities provided by wealth and connections — all have played their part in producing one of the most remarkable families (perhaps *the* most remarkable family) of recent history. Few dynasties, with the exception of hereditary monarchies preserved from oblivion by the right of primogeniture, have maintained their influence in the world for seven generations. The Rothschilds have achieved this feat by constantly producing men and women of outstanding ability. How long this remarkable process continues will be something for later historians to record.

NOTES

1. "A CIVILISED LIFE AMIDST BARBARISM"

1. Most of the Judengasse was dismantled in the 1890s, by which time the ghetto itself had ceased to exist, but the street plan remained unaltered for another half century. The bombs of 1944 virtually flattened the centre of Frankfurt and in the post-war rebuilding Jew Street disappeared.
2. Quoted in the Historisches Museum, Frankfurt, *Historical Documentation Guide*, 1979, p.267.
3. *Ibid.*
4. I. Kant (ed. F. Cross), *Vermischte Schriften*, Leipzig, 1921, pp.389-90; J.G. Fichte, *Beiträge zür Berichtigung der Urteile über die französische Revolution*, 1793. Cf. L. Poliakov (trans. M. Kochan), *The History of Anti-Semitism*, III, 1975, p.180.
5. Alexander Weill, *Pensées*, Paris, 1875, p.65.
6. G.H. Berghoeffer, *Mayer Amschel Rothschild: der Grunder des Rothschildschen Bankhauses*, Frankfurt, 1922, p.3.
7. A distinction must be made between Yiddish, a mixture of words of German, Hebrew and Slav origin, and Judendeutsch, a transliteration of German words into Hebrew script. It was the latter that was commonly used in the private correspondence between Mayer Amschel and his five sons. The distinction may seem a small one but it does provide one more indication that the Rothschilds were a cut above their Judengasse neighbours.
8. M. Mendelssohn (ed. A. Jospe), *Jerusalem and Other Jewish Writings*, 1969, pp.74-5.
9. E. Corti, *The Rise of the House of Rothschild* (trans. Brian and Beatrix Lunn), I, 1928, p.64. Cf. also B. Gille, *Histoire de la Maison Rothschild*, I, 1965-7, pp.7f.

2. "THERE WAS NOT ROOM ENOUGH FOR ALL OF US IN FRANKFURT"

1. For a full discussion of Mayer Amschel's improving fortunes see B. Gille, *op. cit.*, I, p.39 and E. Corti, *op. cit.*, I, pp.36-7. He was taxed on property valuation of two thousand florins in 1773 and on a valuation of fifteen thousand florins in 1796. When his eldest daughter, Jeanette, married he was able to provide an impressive dowry of five thousand florins.
2. This skirmish is recorded in the city annals as a famous victory and a

456

memorial, the Hessendenkmal, was erected to commemorate the fifty-six
German soldiers who died in the action.

3. Loan transactions handled by Rothschild were:

1796-7	Frankfurt	100,000 fl*	@	4%
1799	Wittgenstein	23,000 fl	@	4%
1801	Denmark	180,000 fl	@	4½%
1802	Denmark	200,000 fl	@	4½%
1802	Denmark	120,000 fl	@	4½%
1802	Bavaria	500,000 fl	@	4% and 4½%
1803	Denmark	200,000 th**	@	4½%
1804	Hesse-Darmstadt	200,000 th	@	4½%
1804	Denmark	200,000 th	@	4½%
1804	Baden	700,000 fl		
1805	Denmark	200,000 th	@	4½%
1806	Denmark	200,000 th	@	4½%
1806	Denmark	1,305,000 th	@	4½%
1806	Hesse-Darmstadt	111,000 fl	@	5%

This information was culled from Hesse-Kassel archives by J. Sauer in
*Finanzgeschäfte der Landgrafen von Hesse-Kassel. Ein Beitrag zur Geschichte des
Kurhenischen Haus und Staatschätzen und zür Entwicklungsgeschichte des
Hauses Rothschild*, Fulda, 1930, pp.145-7.
* fl=florins **th=thalers

4. C. Buxton (ed.), *Memoirs of Sir Thomas Fowell Buxton, Bart.*, 1872, p.343.
5. Quoted in Lord Rothschild, "The Shadow of a Great Man", *Random
Variables*, 1984, p.111.
6. Quoted in R. Davis, *The English Rothschilds, 1799-1915*, 1983, p.38.
7. Unpublished memoirs of Baron George de Worms, by kind permission of
Mrs Sylvia Anderson.
8. Cf. R.D. Barnett, 'Anglo Jewry in the Eighteenth Century' in V.D. Lipman
(ed.), *Three Centuries of Anglo-Jewish History*, 1961, p.61.
9. S.D. Chapman, *The Foundation of the English Rothschilds: N.M. Rothschild as
a Textile Merchant, 1799-1811*, 1977, p.5.
10. C. Buxton (ed.), *op.cit.*, pp.343-4.
11. Cf. S.D. Chapman, *op.cit., passim.*
12. Quoted in *ibid*, p.15.
13. *Ibid.*, p.16.
14. S. Austin (ed.), *A Tour in Germany, Holland and England in the Years 1826,
1827 and 1828 . . . by a German Prince*, III, 1832, pp.167, 380.

3. "GOD, HOW THINGS HAVE CHANGED"

1. Berlin Decree, 21 November 1806.
2. Quoted in E. Corti, *op.cit.*, I, p.59.
3. *The Morning Herald*, 5 August 1836.
4. C. Buxton (ed.)., *op.cit.*, p.161.
5. E. Corti, *op.cit.*, I, p.65.
6. *Ibid.*, I, p.70.
7. Chapman in his study of Nathan suggests that James was the intended

partner for Nathan. It seems unlikely, however, that a boy of sixteen (as James was in 1808 when these plans were being mooted) could have been entrusted with the organisation of the Rothschild's blockade-running activities. James was only a year short of his majority when he eventually settled in Paris in 1812.

8. Cf. J. Demachy (ed.), *Les Rothschild, une famille de financiers juifs au XIX siècle*, Paris, 1896, I, p.139.
9. Buderus to the Elector, 2 November 1810, quoted in E. Corti, *op. cit.*, p.106.
10. As already mentioned, Nathan had no financial involvement in M.A. Rothschild and Sons. This interpretation runs counter to those of Corti and Gille. Corti states (I, pp.102-3): "In point of fact, however, Mayer Amschel was holding the twelve-fiftieths destined for Nathan; but for the sake of public opinion, on account of the French domination, the connection with Nathan, who was living in England, had to be kept secret. We may assume that there was a secret subsidy agreement with Nathan, accurately defining the latter's relation to the company." Gille's assertion is even briefer and more forthright (I, p.44): "Nathan was not mentioned in the contract, but his share was undoubtedly set aside." Neither authority, it will be observed, offers evidence or reason for Nathan's supposed inclusion as a partner in the firm. It seems much more likely that Nathan was his father's *associate*, not his partner. The capital of the newly established Frankfurt business did not include any contribution from Nathan. Why then should it be assumed that a share of the profits was reserved for him? We must conclude that N.M.'s companies were, at this stage, separate Rothschild operations.

4. "THE KURFURST MADE OUR FORTUNE"

1. Quoted in R. Davis, *op. cit.*, p.28.
2. Quoted in E. Corti, *op. cit.*, I, p.105.
3. *Ibid.*, I, pp.107-8.
4. *Ibid.*, I, p.112.
5. Quoted in R. Davis, *op. cit.*, p.37.
6. R. Stead, *Bygone Kent*, 1892, pp.225-7.
7. I am greatly indebted to Mr M.B. Cullen for providing details and documents concerning his family history.

5. "EMPLOY THAT GENTLEMAN IN THE MOST SECRET AND CONFIDENTIAL MANNER"

1. Cf. E. Corti, *op.cit.*, I, pp.133-4; B. Gille, *op.cit.*, I, pp.46ff.; R. Davis, *op.cit.*, p.30; and A. Muhlstein, *Baron James: The Rise of the French Rothschilds*, 1983, pp.46-7. These sources do not all agree about Rothschild activities at this crucial time. The interpretation of events is mine.
2. L. Loewe (ed.), *Diaries of Sir Moses and Lady Montefiore*, 1983, p.19.
3. Cf. B. Gille, *op.cit.*, I, p.42.
4. *Ibid.*, I, pp.46-7.
5. Cf., for example, A. Muhlstein, *op.cit.*, pp.37-8.
6. Mayer Amschel's will is in the Historisches Museum Archive, Frankfurt, and published in G.H. Berghoeffer, *op.cit.*, pp.201ff.

7. Quoted in Lord Rothschild, "The Shadow of a Great Man", *Random Variables*, 1984, pp.124-57.
8. Quoted in R. Davis, *op.cit.*, p.30.
9. *Ibid.*, p.33.
10. Unpublished memoirs of Baron George de Worms.
11. *The Graphic*, 13 August 1885.
12. Cf. E.Corti, *op.cit.*, I, p.176.
13. Lord Rothschild, *op.cit.*, p.223.
14. For a full investigation of these stories see Lord Rothschild, *op.cit.*, pp.127ff.
15. *Ibid.*

6. "THE RICHEST PEOPLE IN EUROPE"

1. Quoted in A. Muhlstein, *op.cit.*, pp.73-4.
2. Quoted in *Transactions of the Jewish Historical Society of England*, XIII, p.339.
3. Friedrich von Gentz to Adam Muller, December 1818, quoted in E. Corti, *op.cit.*, I, p.228.
4. *La Renommée*, Paris, 3 September 1819.
5. Quoted in Lord Rothschild, "Gutle, 1753-1849", *Random Variables*, 1984, pp.101–2.
6. Constance (Lady) Battersea, *Reminiscences*, 1922, p.2.
7. Staatsarchiv, Vienna, Box 231, f.17 Anm 113, 3 November 1821.
8. Quoted in E. Corti, *op.cit.*, pp. 193-4.
9. *Ibid.*, p.197.
10. C. Buxton (ed.), *op.cit.*, p.160.
11. *The Gentleman's Magazine*, 229, November 1871, pp.733-4.
12. Quoted in E. Corti, *op.cit.*, I, p.206.
13. S. Austin (ed.), *op.cit.*, III, pp.62ff.
14. *Ibid.*, III, pp.165-7.
15. *Ibid.*, IV, pp.37-8.
16. *Ibid.*, III, pp.66-7.
17. F. Brennan (ed. and trans.), *Pückler's Progress*, 1987, p.194.
18. C.G. Leland (trans.), *The Works of Heinrich Heine*, III, 1891, pp.174-5.
19. A. Muhlstein, *op.cit.*, p.55.
20. *Ibid.*, p.49.
21. *Ibid.*, p.55.
22. *Ibid.*, p.59.
23. I am obliged to Baron Elie de Rothschild for this anecdote.
24. E. Corti, *op.cit.*, I, p.458.
25. *The Gentleman's Magazine*, I, 1810, p.610.
26. E. Corti, *op.cit.*, I, p.214.
27. Quoted in Lord Rothschild, "The Shadow of a Great Man", *Random Variables*, p.113.
28. I. Balla, *The Romance of the Rothschilds*, 1913, pp.155-6.
29. C.G. Leland (trans.), *op.cit.*, III, p.176.

7. "LORD AND MASTER OF THE MONEY-MARKET OF THE WORLD"

1. Quoted in E. Corti, *op.cit.*, I, pp.292-3.
2. Lady Battersea, *op.cit.*, pp.66-7.

3. F.L. Gower, *Letters of Harriet Countess Granville, 1810-1845*, II, 1894, p.156.
4. D. de Girardin, *Lettres Parisiennes*, Paris, 1861, p.283.
5. *The Morning Herald*, 5 August 1836.
6. F. Niecks, *Frédéric Chopin as a Man and Musician*, II, 1902, p.165.
7. G. Karpeles (ed.), *Heinrich Heine's Memoirs*, II, 1910, p.114.
8. *Ibid.*, II, pp.133-4.
9. *The Times*, 23 November 1825.
10. For a full account of this episode, see Lord Rothschild, "The Shadow of a Great Man", *Random Variables*, pp.144ff.
11. Unpublished memoirs of Baron George de Worms.
12. Baron Ferdinand de Rothschild, unpublished reminiscences, 1897; quoted by Mrs James de Rothschild in *The Rothschilds at Waddesdon Manor*, 1979, pp.10-11.
13. Unpublished memoirs of Baron George de Worms.

8. "TO MAKE OURSELVES ABSOLUTE MASTERS"

1. Quoted in E. Corti, *op.cit.*, I, pp.235-6.
2. In 1836 Frankfurt acknowledged the inevitable and joined the Zollverein. Her recovery and the decline of Offenbach were, thereafter, equally rapid. But Frankfurt bought her economic prosperity at the price of dependence on Prussia.
3. Quoted in E. Corti, *op.cit.*, II, p.292.
4. Cf. L. Geiger, *Die deutsche Literatur und die Juden*, Berlin, 1910, pp.94-5.
5. A. Muhlstein, *op.cit.*, p.76.
6. C. Roth, *History of the Great Synagogue*, 1950, p.236.
7. *The Times*, 19 February 1828.
8. Quoted in E. Corti, *op.cit.*, I, p.403.
9. *Le Moniteur universel*, 3 August 1830.
10. Quoted in A. Muhlstein, *op.cit.*, p.102.
11. *Ibid.*, p.103.
12. *Ibid.*
13. E. Corti, *op.cit.*, I, p.433.
14. Staatsarchiv, Vienna, R8 Land 82, Apponyi to Metternich, Paris, 24 June 1835.
15. Quoted in A. Muhlstein, *op.cit.*, p.141.
16. Cf. H. Weinstock, *Rossini, a Biography*, 1968, pp.191-2.
17. *The Times*, 3 August 1836.
18. *Ibid.*
19. B. Disraeli, *Conningsby, or The New Generation*, 1844 (Penguin Edition 1983), pp.235-6.

9. "THE GREAT BARON"

1. Ernest Feydeau, *Mémoires d'un coulissier*, Paris, 1837, p.125.
2. *Ibid.*, p.138.
3. G. Karpeles (ed.), *op.cit.*, II, p.79.
4. Quoted in A. Muhlstein, *op.cit.*, p.152.

5. *Ibid.*, p.172.
6. The real owner, for whom Scott acted, was a French aristocrat, Aimé-Eugène Vanderberghe, whose financial affairs were extremely complex. Cf. C. Ray, *Lafite — The Story of Château Lafite-Rothschild*, 1985, pp.40-1.
7. Lady Battersea, *op.cit.*, p.54.
8. L. Cohen, *Lady de Rothschild and her Daughters, 1821-1931*, 1935, p.147.
9. André Maurois, *Lélia, the Life of George Sand*, 1953, p.279.
10. A. Muhlstein, *op.cit.*, p.154.
11. G. Karpeles (ed.), *op.cit.*, II, p.115.
12. Cf. H. Weinstock, *op.cit.*, p.460.
13. Quoted in R. Davis, *op.cit.*, p.60.
14. Quoted in A. Muhlstein, *op.cit.*, p.157.
15. Quoted in R. Davis, *op.cit.*, p.60.
16. I. Epstein, *Judaism*, 1959, pp.290-1.
17. Karl Marx, *New York Daily Tribune*, 4 January 1856.
18. M. Hess, *Rome and Jerusalem*, 1862, p.12.
19. L. Cohen, *op.cit.*, pp.11-12.
20. L. Cohen, *op.cit.*, p.15.
21. *Ibid.*, pp.17-18.
22. Quoted in R. Davis, *op.cit.*, p.26.
23. *Ibid.*, p.63.
24. L. Cohen, *op.cit.*, pp.38-9.
25. BM.Add.Mss.47948, Anthony to Louisa, 17 November 1842.
26. Cf. B. Gavoty, *Frédéric Chopin*, New York, 1977, p.307.
27. Lady Battersea, *op.cit.*, p.66.

10. "YOU REMAIN UNMOVED"

1. A. Muhlstein, *op.cit.*, pp.203-4.
2. A. Zamoyski, *Chopin, a Biography*, 1979, p.259.
3. C. Woodham-Smith, *The Great Hunger*, 1962, p.164.
4. *Ibid.*, p.165.
5. *Ibid.*
6. Staatsarchiv, Vienna, R.245, 15 November 1843.
7. Lady Battersea, *op.cit.*, pp.62-3.
8. Ernest Feydeau, *op.cit.*, pp.160-1.
9. Quoted in A. Muhlstein, *op.cit.*, p.181.
10. L. Cohen, *op.cit.*, p.50.
11. *Ibid.*, p.53.
12. Unpublished memoirs of Baron George de Worms.
13. *Ibid.*
14. Quoted in A. Muhlstein, *op.cit.*, p.181.
15. *Ibid.*, pp.184-5.
16. *Ibid.*, p.187.
17. *Ibid.*, p.162.
18. Quoted in E. Corti, *op.cit.*, II, pp.270-1.

461

11. "IF THEY ADMITTED JEWS, WHERE WOULD THEY STOP?"

1. A.P. Stanley, *The Life and Correspondence of Thomas Arnold D.D.*, I, 1877, p.28. For a fuller detailed study of the whole issue see A. Gillam, *The Emancipation of the Jews in England, 1830-1860*, New York, 1982.
2. Quoted in R. Davis, *op.cit.*, p.70.
3. Quoted in L. Wolf, *The Queen's Jewry*, 1923, p.47.
4. Quoted in R. Davis, *op.cit.*, p.71.
5. *Ibid.*
6. *Ibid.*, p.78.
7. *Ibid.*
8. *Ibid.*
9. *The Gentleman's Magazine*, 229, November 1871, p.734.
10. Quoted in R. Davis, *op.cit.*, p.75.
11. *Ibid.*, p.77.
12. *Punch*, 10 April 1847.
13. Quoted in R. Davis, *op.cit.*, pp.75-6.
14. A. Gillam, *op.cit.*, p.100.
15. *Ibid.*
16. L. Cohen, *op.cit.*, p.42.
17. *Punch*, 1851.
18. Tomcul, Mayer to Thomas Cullen, April 1859. Letter in the possession of Mr. M.B. Cullen.
19. *Folkestone Gazette*, undated.
20. T. Pinnery (ed.), *Letters of Thomas Babington Macaulay*, 1981, pp.227-8.
21. L. Cohen, *op.cit.*, p.44.
22. *Ibid.*, p.47.

12. "IT IS ABSOLUTELY VITAL THAT YOU FREE YOURSELF FROM THE TUTELAGE OF THE ROTHSCHILDS"

1. L. Cohen, *op.cit.*, p.31.
2. Lady Battersea, *op.cit.*, p.233.
3. L. Cohen, *op.cit.*, pp.47-9.
4. *Ibid*, p.73.
5. *Illustrated London News*, 7 March 1857.
6. R. Davis, *op.cit.*, p.64.
7. Quoted in C. Ray, *op.cit.*, p.29.
8. *Ibid.*, p.28.
9. Quoted in J. Bouvier, *Les Rothschild*, Paris, 1967, p.159.
10. Cf. B. Gille, *op.cit.*, II, p.98.
11. Ernest Feydeau, *op.cit.*, pp.149-150.
12. Guy de Rothschild, *The Whims of Fortune*, 1985, pp.8-9.
13. A. Muhlstein, *op.cit.*, pp.208-9.
14. Quoted in E. Corti, *op.cit.*, II, p.316.
15. J. Bouvier and R. Cameron, "Une Lettre inédite de Presigny à Napoléon III (1855)" in *Revue historique*, Paris, July-September 1963.
16. Cf. E. März, *Österreichische Industrie- und Bankpolitik in der Zeit Franz Josephus I*, Vienna, 1968.

13. "THERE IS NOT A PEOPLE OR GOVERNMENT IN CHRISTENDOM IN WHICH THE PAWS ... OF THE ROTHSCHILDS ARE NOT PLUNGED TO THE VERY HEART OF THE TREASURY"

1.   Unpublished memoirs of Baron George de Worms.
2.   My authority for this and for most of the details of Belmont's career is I. Katz, *August Belmont: A Political Biography*, New York, 1968.
3.   When Salomon, Baron James's son, visited New York in 1861 he made several sarcastic observations about American society as seen from the "superior" vantage point of a Parisian sophisticate, but he confessed admiration for Belmont's style of entertaining: "The season of parties has begun, but New York has not been particularly brilliant. Still, Belmont has given a magnificent ball which will mark an epoch in the annals of New York society. The flowers, the ladies and the clothes competed in beauty and brilliance and I confess the spectacle was charming." S. Diamond (ed.), *A Casual View of America: The Home Letters of Salomon de Rothschild, 1859-1861*, New York, 1962, p.90.
4.   Cf. B. Gille, *op.cit.*, II, p.582.
5.   *Ibid.*, p.581.
6.   *Ibid.*
7.   *Ibid.*
8.   *Ibid.*, p.584.
9.   *Ibid.*, pp.582-3.
10.   *Ibid.*, p.586.
11.   Lady Battersea, *op.cit.*, pp.77, 84, 87.
12.   S. Diamond (ed.), *op.cit.*, p.66.
13.   *Ibid.*
14.   *Ibid.*, pp.70-1.
15.   *Ibid.*, p.90.
16.   I. Katz, *op.cit.*, pp.144-5.
17.   Lady Battersea, *op.cit.*, p.87.

14. "A VERY SERIOUS AND DANGEROUS SITUATION"

1.   I am indebted to Professor E. März for this information, which is only partly covered in his history of the Creditanstalt, already cited.
2.   Quoted in F. Stern, *Gold and Iron: Bismarck, Bleichröder and the Building of the German Empire*, 1977, p.114.
3.   *Ibid.*, p.73.
4.   Lady Battersea, *op.cit.*, pp.45-6.
5.   L. Cohen, *op.cit.*, p.126. There seems to have been a rumour in the family that Evy may have been affected by some injury sustained in a slight railway accident during her pregnancy (cf. Mrs James de Rothschild, *The Rothschilds at Waddesdon Manor*, p.13) but I have been able to find no contemporary reference to such a theory. The immense shock which Evy's death caused suggests that it was totally unexpected.
6.   Cf. J.P.T. Bury, "The Identity of 'C. de B.' ", in *French Historical Studies*, III, No.4, 1964, pp.538-41; also R. Henrey, *Letters from Paris 1870-1875, Written by C. de B., a Political Informant to the Head of the London House of Rothschild*, 1942.

7. R. Henrey, *op.cit.*, pp.19-20, reports dated 2 August, 21 September and 29 July 1867.
8. Quoted in R. Davis, *op.cit.*, p.146.
9. Quoted in B. Gille, *op.cit.*, II, p.604.
10. H. Weinstock, *op.cit.*, p.322.
11. Quoted in A. Muhlstein, *op.cit.*, p.210.
12. C. Ray, *op.cit.*, p.42.
13. Quoted in A. Muhlstein, *op.cit.*, p.211.
14. *Ibid.*, p.211.
15. *The Gentleman's Magazine*, 229, November 1871, p.735.

15. "WAR AND WARLIKE TALK THE ORDER OF THE DAY"

1. A. Ramm (ed.), *The Political Correspondence of Mr Gladstone and Lord Granville, 1868-1876*, Camden Society, 3rd Series, lxxxii, 1952, I, 113.
2. *Ibid.*, II, 881.
3. *Ibid.*, I, 250.
4. L. Cohen, *op.cit.*, pp.144-5.
5. Letter of F. Bergman to Leonora, 1 January 1871, cited by Baron Guy de Rothschild, *op.cit.*, pp.12-13.
6. *Ibid.*
7. *Ibid.*
8. *Ibid.*
9. H. Salingré, *Im grossen Hauptquartier 1870-1*, Berlin, 1910, p.144.
10. R. Henrey, *op.cit.*, p.34.
11. *Ibid.*, p.77.
12. *Ibid.*, p.110.
13. *Ibid.*, pp.166-7.
14. Lady Battersea, *op.cit.*, p.75.
15. R. Henrey, *op.cit.*, p.111.
16. E. Corti, *op.cit.*, II, p.421.
17. Letter of a director of the Crédit Lyonnais, 4 March 1871, quoted in J. Bouvier, *op.cit.*, p.214. For details of the financial negotiations and indemnity payments cf. F. Stern, *Gold and Iron*, 1977, pp.145ff.
18. R. Henrey, *op.cit.*, pp.133-4.
19. Quoted in B. Gille, *op.cit.*, II, p.603.
20. *Ibid.*, II, p.595.
21. A.J.P. Taylor, *The Struggle for Mastery in Europe, 1848-1918*, 1954, p.211.
22. A Ramm (ed.), *op.cit.*, I, pp.297, 314.
23. *Ibid.*, I, pp.483, 484.

16. "WE WERE VERY JOLLY"

1. Lady Battersea, *op.cit.*, p.160.
2. *Ibid.*, p.9.
3. L. Cohen, *op.cit.*, p.130.
4. *Ibid.*, p.131.
5. *Ibid.*, p.134.
6. *Ibid.*, p.135.

7. *Ibid.*, p.37.
8. *Ibid.*, pp.35-6.
9. Lady Battersea, *op.cit.*, pp.60, 61.
10. *Ibid.*, pp.156-7.
11. L. Cohen, *op.cit.*, pp.138-9.
12. *Ibid.*, pp.153-4.
13. *Ibid.*, p.154.
14. BM. Add.Mss. 47948, 168, Alfred to Louisa, 2 November 1872.
15. BM. Add.Mss. 47948, 173, Charlotte to Louisa, 8 November 1872.
16. L. Cohen, *op.cit.*, p.158.
17. BM. Add.Mss. 47848, 174, Queen Victoria to Louisa, 9 November 1872.
18. BM. Add.Mss. 47848, 178, Lord Stanley to Louisa, 26 November 1872.
19. BM. Add.Mss. 47848, 170, G. Samuel to Anthony, undated.
20. BM. Add.Mss. 47848, 172, Betty to Louisa, 4 November 1872.
21. Cf. Lady Brassey, *The Voyage of the Sunbeam*, 1878.
22. Lady Battersea, *op.cit.*, p.153.
23. *Ibid.*, p.52.
24. Ferdinand de Rothschild's unpublished reminiscences quoted by Mrs James de Rothschild, *op.cit.*, pp.24-5.
25. *The Graphic*, 17 May 1890.
26. J. Vincent (ed.), *The Crawford Papers*, 1984, p.49.
27. A. Ponsonby, *Henry Ponsonby, Queen Victoria's Private Secretary. His Life from His Letters*, 1942, p.261.
28. Mrs J. de Rothschild, *op.cit.*, p.73.
29. J. Vincent (ed), *op.cit.*, pp.49, 600.
30. *Aylesbury Plus*, 28 May 1986.
31. L. Cohen, *op.cit.*, p.259.

17. "A CLOSE ACQUAINTANCE WITH THE COURSE OF PUBLIC AFFAIRS"

1. L. Cohen, *op.cit.*, p.73.
2. Lady Battersea, *op.cit.*, pp.26-7.
3. This incident is one of those about which many romantic legends have gathered. In his monograph, *You Have It, Madam*, published in 1980 and reproduced in *Random Variables*, 1984, Lord Rothschild has used bank and state archives to re-create a "blow by blow" account of the transaction. This work is thus a concise but authoritative study and forms the basis of my treatment of the subject.
4. Quoted in Lord Rothschild, *You Have It, Madam*, pp.15-16.
5. *Ibid.*, p.27.
6. *Ibid.*, p.20.
7. A. Ramm (ed.), *op.cit.*, II, 1020.
8. Lord Rothschild, *You Have It, Madam*, p.22.
9. A. Ramm (ed.), *op.cit.*, II, 1052.
10. A.J.P. Taylor, *op.cit.*, p.250.
11. For more detail on this diplomatic activity and the Rothschilds' part in it cf. G.A. Knight, "The Rothschild-Bleichröder Axis in Action, An Anglo-

German Co-operative 1877-1878" in *The Leo Baeck Year Book*, 1983, pp.43-57. For an excellent study in the interchange of politics and finance in this period (in which considerable reference is made to Rothschild activity) cf. F. Stern, *op.cit.*

12. Not all obituary comment was so fulsome. A colleague of Bleichröder's reported to him, "few people genuinely mourned because Lionel did not know how to make himself liked and did next to nothing for the poor". F. Stern, *op.cit.*, p.479.

18. "WE ARE ALL PROFESSIONALS"

1. *The Graphic*, 14 February 1874.
2. *Ibid.*
3. L. Cohen, *op.cit.*, p.97.
4. Quoted in Mrs James de Rothschild, *op.cit.*, p.12.
5. J. Vincent (ed.), *op.cit.*, p.599.
6. "Le Baron Alphonse de Rothschild" in *Librairie de L'Art*, Paris, 1905, p.14. I am indebted to Baron Elie de Rothschild for providing me with a copy of this little known, lavishly illustrated monograph.
7. *Ibid.*, p.28.
8. Unpublished memoirs of Baron George de Worms.
9. J. Hurst, *Enquéte sur la question sociale en Europe*, Paris, 1879, p.370.
10. J. Halévy, *Trois diners avec Gambetta*, Paris, 1929, pp.25-6.
11. Quoted in J. Bouvier, *op.cit.*, p.216.

19. "OH, ... THE SENSE OF LAVISH WEALTH, THRUST UP YOUR NOSE"

1. Letter of Balfour to Lady Wemyss, quoted in B.E.C. Dugdale, *Arthur James Balfour, First Earl of Balfour*, II, 1936, p.35. Cf. also Miriam Rothschild, *Dear Lord Rothschild: Birds, Butterflies and History*, 1983, p.38. Dr Rothschild provides a fuller biographical sketch of Natty in Chapter 5, as does R. Davis in *op.cit.*, Chapter 9.
2. BM. Add.Mss. 47193, ff.76-7.
3. Dr Miriam Rothschild in conversation with the author.
4. For a fuller treatment of this subject see A.E. Adam, *Beechwoods and Bayonets, The Book of Halton*, 1983, pp.19-23.
5. Dr Miriam Rothschild in conversation with the author.
6. J. Vincent (ed.), *op.cit.*, p.600.
7. Miriam Rothschild, *Dear Lord Rothschild.*, p.11n.
8. *Vanity Fair*, 13 May 1884.
9. Cf. A.E. Adam, *op.cit.*, pp.28ff.
10. Miriam Rothschild, *Dear Lord Rothschild.*, p.11n.
11. The Earl of Carnarvon, *No Regrets*, 1976, p.6.
12. *Ibid.*, p.10.
13. *Ibid.*, pp.13-14.
14. Lady Battersea, *op.cit.*, p.48.
15. Lady Battersea, *op.cit.*, p.186.
16. L. Cohen, *op.cit.*, pp.240-1.
17. Lady Battersea, *op.cit.*, p.409.

18. *Ibid.*, pp.415-16.
19. Lady Battersea, *op.cit.*, p.430.
20. Henri de Rothschild (under the pseudonym "André' Pascal"), *Croisière autour de mes souvenirs*, Paris, 1933, p.151.
21. *Ibid.*, pp.152-3.
22. J. Littlewood, *Milady Vine: The Autobiography of Philippe de Rothschild*, 1984, p.6.
23. Henri de Rothschild, *op.cit.*, p.161.
24. *Ibid.*, pp.238-40.
25. Mrs Bettina Looram in conversation with the author.
26. Valentine grew into a clever young woman, despite her handicap. She studied history and became very accomplished in the subject. One of her favourite pastimes was going to the silent pictures, which she enjoyed more than the rest of the audience because she knew — by lip-reading — what the romantic heroes and heroines were *really* saying to each other.
27. Mrs Bettina Looram in conversation with the author.

20. "IF THY BROTHER BE WAXEN POOR ... THOU SHALT UPHOLD HIM"

1. For James's letters to Salomon and a discussion of their significance, cf. N. Gelber, "Oesterreich und die Damascusaffaire im Jahr 1840, nach bisher unveröffentlichen Akten" in *Jahrbuch der Jüdisch-Literarischen Gesellschaft*, XVIII, 1926, pp.21-64.
2. Lady Battersea, *op.cit.*, p.409.
3. Quoted in R. Davis, *op.cit.*, p.198.
4. Quoted in J. White, *Rothschild Buildings: Life in an East End Tenement Block, 1887-1920*, 1980, p.17.
5. *Ibid.*, p.20.
6. *Ibid.*, pp.24, 31, 258. White's book is an excellent study of life in the buildings but contains no detailed assessment of the motivation of Lord Rothschild and his colleagues.
7. Quoted in R. Davis, *op.cit.*, p.299.
8. *Ibid.*, p.228.
9. Quoted by L. Finestein in V.D. Lipman (ed.), *Three Centuries of Anglo-Jewish History*, 1961, p.113.
10. E. Drumont, *La France juive*, Paris, 1943 edition, I, p.322.
11. A Toussenel, *Les Juifs, rois de l'époque*, Paris, 1888, I, p.xi.
12. E. Newman, *The Life of Richard Wagner*, IV, 1933-47, pp.638-9.
13. F. Stern, *op.cit.*, p.521.
14. J. Vincent (ed.), *op.cit.*, p.62.
15. Quoted in R.S. Wistrich, *Socialism and the Jews: The Dilemmas of Assimilation in Germany and Austria-Hungary*, 1982, pp.34-5.
16. P. Proudhon, *Césarisme et christianisme*, Paris, I, 1883, p.139.
17. *Une Page d'amour de Ferdinand Lassalle: Récit: Corréspondance: Confessions*, Leipzig, 1878, pp.49-50.
18. Precise figures are impossible to discover. Estimates of the population around 1880 vary from 13,920 to 35,000. Cf. S. Schama, *Two Rothschilds and the Land of Israel*, 1978, p.58. I have relied heavily on Schama's work for

the material in this section. I have also been much helped by Mrs James de Rothschild whose memories of Baron Edmond, her father-in-law, are very vivid, and supply a necessary corrective to some of Schama's conclusions.

19. I. Margalith, *Le Baron Edmond de Rothschild et la colonisation juive en Palestine, 1882-1899*, Paris, 1957, p.171.
20. Quoted in S. Schama, *op.cit.*, p.71.
21. Quoted in S. Schama, *op.cit.*, p.75.
22. This story is told in D. Druck (trans. L. Glassman), *Baron Edmond de Rothschild: The Story of a Practical Idealist*, New York, 1928, pp.101-3, but the author cites no authority for it.
23. S. Schama, *op.cit.*, p.94.
24. T. Herzl (trans. A. Hertzberg), "Der Judenstaat", in *The Zionist Idea*, New York, 1959, p.209.
25. R. Palai (ed.), *The Complete Diaries of Theodor Herzl*, I, New York, 1960, pp.248, 426.

21. "HAVE A GO AT THE GRAND OLD MAN ON HIS OWN DUNGHILL"

1. Quoted in R. Davis, *op.cit.*, p.185. Davis's account should be read as a valuable summary of the Egyptian crisis from the point of view of the English Rothschilds.
2. *Ibid.*, p.195.
3. *Ibid.*, pp.196-7.
4. From this time other changes of title took place within the English family. The senior branch dropped the "de" from their name. Thus Natty's elder son was known as the Honourable Walter Rothschild. The other branches of the family retained the "de" but no longer used the foreign title of "Baron". So Natty's brother was henceforth Alfred de Rothschild or "Mr Alfred" but never "Baron Alfred".
5. R. Davis, *op.cit.*, p.197.
6. *Ibid.*, pp.197-8.
7. Quoted in André Maurois, *Cecil Rhodes*, 1953, p.44.
8. R. Davis, *op.cit.*, p.215.
9. R.B. Haldane, *An Autobiography*, 1929, p.144.
10. Quoted in R. Davis, *op.cit.*, p.205. For a full assessment of the Rothschild rôle in British politics at this time, cf. *ibid*, pp.160-220.
11. *Ibid.*
12. J. Vincent (ed.), *op.cit.*, pp.92-3.
13. Miriam Rothschild, *Dear Lord Rothschild*, p.296.
14. *Ibid.*, p.301.
15. R.R. James, *Lord Randolph Churchill*, 1959, pp.227-8.
16. Lord Rosebery's Diary, quoted in R. Davis, *op.cit.*, pp.171-2.
17. *Ibid.*, p.172.
18. J. Vincent (ed.), *op.cit.*, p.600.
19. BM. Add.Mss. 47963, ff.160, Annie to Constance, 4 October 1893.
20. It was Dr Miriam Rothschild who told me of Natty's pride in his achievement and she had the information from her father. Cf. E.S. Purcell,

Life of Cardinal Manning, II, 1973, pp.662ff., for an account of how the strike was settled.

22. "TOO MUCH LORD ROTHSCHILD"

1. Miriam Rothschild, *Dear Lord Rothschild.*, p.57. Dr Rothschild's detailed and entertaining book presents a lively picture of her Uncle Walter and considerable hitherto unpublished information about many members of her family.
2. *Ibid.*, p.68.
3. *Ibid.*, p.70.
4. *Ibid.*, pp.64-5.
5. J. Vincent (ed.), *op.cit.*, p.105.
6. I am indebted to Dr Miriam Rothschild for much of the information about her father.
7. Miriam Rothschild, *Nathaniel Charles Rothschild, 1877-1923*, 1979, published privately, p.8.
8. Dr Miriam Rothschild in conversation with the author.
9. R. Palin, *Rothschild Relish*, 1970, p.42.
10. *Ibid.*, pp.140-1.
11. Miriam Rothschild, *Dear Lord Rothschild*, p.85.
12. *Ibid.*, p.46.
13. *Ibid.*, pp.41-2. Dr Rothschild argues (pp.42-4) that this caricatures her grandfather, who was not purely negative but put forward several alternative suggestions for reform measures.
14. *Neue Freie Presse*, 19 July 1932.
15. *Ibid.*
16. M.J. Dumont, "La Fondation Rothschild et les premières habitations à bon marché de Paris" 1900-1914, Sorbonne doctoral thesis, Paris, 1981, p.101.

23. "HIS MAJESTY'S GOVERNMENT VIEW WITH FAVOUR"

1. P. Rowland, *Lloyd George*, 1975, p.285.
2. Miriam Rothschild, *Dear Lord Rothschild*, p.45.
3. *Ibid.*
4. Dr Miriam Rothschild in conversation with the author.
5. R.B. Haldane, *op.cit.*, p.163.
6. Miriam Rothschild, *Dear Lord Rothschild*, caption 23c.
7. *Ibid.*, p.288.
8. *Encephalitis lethargica* is widely thought to have been carried by the influenza virus and a severe outbreak of the disease coincided with the 1918 epidemic. However, a connection has never been proved and is unlikely to be so since this strain of *encephalitis* died out in the 1920s. Miriam Rothschild, *Nathaniel Charles Rothschild, 1877-1923*, p.5. Other details from Dr Miriam Rothschild in conversation with the author.
9. Alfred to von Bülow, via Baron von Eckardstein, 20 February 1892, quoted in E. Corti, *op.cit.*, II, pp.454-7.
10. A.E. Adam, *op.cit.*, p.60.
11. *Aylesbury Plus*, 28 May 1986.

12. J. Littlewood, *op.cit.*, p.15.
13. A. Mackintosh (ed.), *Asquith, H.H. Memories and Reflections, 1852-1927*, II, 1928, p.65.
14. Statement recollected by Chaim Weizmann in *Letters and Papers*, VI, 1974, p.117.
15. Cf. Miriam Rothschild, *Dear Lord Rothschild*, pp.264-5.
16. This is a necessarily brief account of the developments leading up to the issuing of the Balfour Declaration. Various Zionist groups were at work and not infrequently falling out among themselves. For full details cf. L. Stein, *The Balfour Declaration*, 1961. For Walter Rothschild's contribution cf. Miriam Rothschild, *Dear Lord Rothschild*. Dr Rothschild uses family papers and personal reminiscences to correct previous views about her uncle's participation in the Zionist movement.
17. Quoted in S. Schama, *op.cit.*, p.209.
18. Quoted in L. Stein, *op.cit.*, p.565.
19. For greater detail on the Halton sale cf. A.E. Adam, *op.cit.*, pp.65ff.

24. "CAUGHT BETWEEN TWO PHILOSOPHIES"

1. Baron Guy de Rothschild, *op.cit.*, pp.57-9.
2. Siegfried Loewy in *Neues Wiener Journal*, 29 August 1927.
3. Mme Batsheva de Rothschild in conversation with the author.
4. Baron Guy de Rothschild in conversation with the author.
5. Mr Edmund de Rothschild in conversation with the author.
6. I am indebted to Professor Eduard März for much information about the Austrian banking situation.
7. Mrs Bettina Looram in conversation with the author.
8. Professor Edouard März in conversation with the author.
9. E. März, *Austrian Banking and Financial Policy: Creditanstalt at a Turning Point, 1913-1923*, 1984, p.550.
10. E. März in *International Business in Central Europe, 1918-1939*, Leicester, 1983, p.434. I discussed the question of the responsibility for the Creditanstalt crisis at some length with Professor März, the historian of the bank, and with Dr Dieter Stiefel of the Institut für Wirtschafts und Sozialgeschichte Wirtschaftsuniversität, Vienna. The problem is lack of evidence. Austria's political leaders were, in Stiefel's words "small men out of their depth in international politics". If they saw what was happening to the leading banks their natural inclination would have been to cover it up and keep Rothschild in ignorance so that he would go on using his influence to attract foreign investment and, hopefully, stave off disaster. If Louis at some stage got wise to what was happening no record of his enlightenment has become available.
11. Mrs Bettina Looram in conversation with the author.
12. Ditto.
13. Dr Miriam Rothschild in conversation with the author.
14. Quoted by D. Stiefel, "The Reconstruction of the Credit-Anstalt" in *International Business in Central Europe, 1918-1939*, Leicester, 1983, p.420.

15. For a full study of the work of the Austrian Creditanstalt International Committee cf. D. Stiefel, *op.cit.*, pp.415-36.
16. Mr Edmund de Rothschild in conversation with the author.

25. "ONE CONTINUAL PARTY"

1. Miriam Rothschild, *Dear Lord Rothschild*, pp.xxii-xxiii.
2. Mme Batsheva de Rothschild in conversation with the author.
3. Miriam Rothschild, *Dear Lord Rothschild*, p.74.
4. *Ibid.*, pp.290-291.
5. *Ibid.*, p.92.
6. *Ibid.*, p.288.
7. J. Bakewell, "Lord Rothschild" in *The Observer*, January 1978.
8. Miriam Rothschild, *Dear Lord Rothschild*, p.304.
9. Dr Miriam Rothschild in conversation with the author.
10. The story is related in R. Palin, *op.cit.*, pp.118-19. Palin was an eyewitness of this event. He also relates another incident which he did not personally observe. Lionel's son, Edmund, assures me that it is apocryphal but it is such a good story that, perhaps, I may be forgiven for perpetuating it. Lionel was asked to address the City Horticultural Society and on the evening in question dozens of office workers gathered to hear what advice the great gardener had to give them about the cultivation of their suburban plots. Mr de Rothschild was duly introduced and opened his remarks with the words, "No garden, however small, should contain less than two acres of woodland." *Op.cit.*, p.118.
11. I am indebted to Mr Edmund de Rothschild for this information about his father.
12. Mrs James de Rothschild, *op.cit.*, p.110.
13. I am indebted to Baron Edmond de Rothschild for this information about his father.
14. Baron Guy de Rothschild, *op.cit.*, p.66.
15. Dr Miriam Rothschild in conversation with the author.
16. *Wiener Sozialdemocratische Bucherei: Hochverräter der Wirtschaft und der Republik*, Vienna, pp.5-7.
17. Mrs Bettina Looram in conversation with the author.
18. Dr Miriam Rothschild in conversation with the author.

26. "GROWING INTO REALITY"

1. Mme Batsheva de Rothschild in conversation with the author.
2. Ditto.
3. Baron Eric de Rothschild in conversation with the author.
4. Ditto.
5. This story — not, I believe, hitherto recorded in the chronicles of World War II — was told me by Maurice's son, Baron Edmond de Rothschild.
6. Baron Edmond de Rothschild in conversation with the author.
7. Mrs Bettina Looram in conversation with the author.
8. Baronne Philippine de Rothschild in conversation with the author.
9. Details of Victor's early life from Lord Rothschild, *Meditations of a*

Broomstick, 1977. Also J. Bakewell, "Lord Rothschild" in *The Observer*, January 1978; "The Autocrat who Lost His Way" in *The Observer*, 29 March 1987.

10. Lord Rothschild, "The File Is Never Closed", *Random Variables*, pp.203-4.
11. *Ibid.*
12. J. Colville, *The Fringes of Power*, 1985, p.597.
13. Chapman Pincher in *The Sunday Express*, 7 December 1986.
14. Lord Rothschild, *Meditations of a Broomstick*, p.26.
15. *Ibid.*
16. Chapman Pincher, *op.cit.*
17. J. Colville, *op.cit.*, p.471.
18. J. Bakewell, "Lord Rothschild" in *The Observer*, January 1978.
19. Malcolm Muggeridge quoted in "Profile", *The Observer*, 29 March 1987.
20. Based on a written account of her wartime experiences given to the author by Dr Miriam Rothschild.
21. Mr Edmund de Rothschild in conversation with the author.
22. J. Colville, *op.cit.*, p.44.
23. *Ibid.*, p.580.

27. "THE ROTHSCHILDS SHOULD MAINTAIN THEIR TRADITIONAL ROLE"

1. Mr Edmund de Rothschild in conversation with the author.
2. R. Palin, *op.cit.*, p.187.
3. The Hon. Jacob Rothschild in conversation with the author.
4. Mr Evelyn de Rothschild in conversation with the author.
5. The Hon. J. Smallwood, "Churchill Falls" in *The Atlantic Advocate*, July 1967, p.9.
6. P. Smith, *Brinco: The Story of Churchill Falls*, Toronto, 1975, pp.12-13.
7. J. Smallwood, *I Chose Canada*, Toronto, 1973, p.470.
8. I am indebted to Mr Edmund de Rothschild for information concerning the post-war activities of NMR.
9. Baron Guy de Rothschild, *op.cit.*, pp.155-7.
10. Baron Guy de Rothschild in conversation with the author.
11. I am indebted to Mrs Bettina Looram for most of the details concerning the post-war history of the Austrian family.
12. Lionel de Rothschild in conversation with the author.
13. Mrs Bettina Looram in conversation with the author.
14. Mme Batsheva de Rothschild in conversation with the author.
15. Ditto.
16. Ditto.
17. Ditto.
18. Baron Edmond de Rothschild in conversation with the author.

28. "LE STYLE ROTHSCHILD"

1. Baron Guy de Rothschild, *op.cit.*, pp.234–6.
2. Nadine de Rothschild, with G. de Sarigné, *La Baronne rentre à cinq heures*, Paris, 1984, p.141.
3. *Ibid.*, p.88.

4. Baron Edmond de Rothschild in conversation with the author.
5. Ditto.
6. Ditto.
7. Ditto.
8. Nadine de Rothschild, *op.cit.*, p.255.
9. *Ibid.*, p.255.
10. Baron Elie de Rothschild in conversation with the author.
11. Mrs Bettina Looram in conversation with the author.
12. Baron Edmond de Rothschild in conversation with the author.
13. Ditto.
14. J. Littlewood, *op.cit.*, pp.217ff. Cf. also *Mouton Rothschild, Paintings for the Labels, 1945-1981*, Boston, 1983, pp.106-15.
15. J. Littlewood, *op.cit.*, pp.218ff.
16. C. Ray, *Robert Mondavi of the Napa Valley*, 1984, p.115.

29. "WE MUST NEVER REMAIN STATIC"

1. Mrs James de Rothschild, *op.cit.*, p.31.
2. C. Pincher in *The Sunday Express*, 7 December 1986.
3. Lord Rothschild, *Random Variables*, 1984, p.204.
4. Lord Rothschild, *ibid.*, p.204.
5. Lord Rothschild, *ibid.*, 1984, p.203.
6. Lord Rothschild, *ibid.*, 1984, p.75.
7. J. Bakewell, "Lord Rothschild" in *The Observer*, January 1978.
8. J. Fallon, *M. Magazine*, October 1986, p.133.
9. *Ibid.*
10. Dr Miriam Rothschild in conversation with the author.
11. Ditto.
12. Ditto.
13. J. Wechsberg, *The Merchant Bankers*, 1967, p.357.
14. Baron Guy de Rothschild, *op.cit.*, p.158.
15. Baron Guy de Rothschild in conversation with the author.
16. Baron Edmond de Rothschild in conversation with the author.
17. P. Knightley, "Murder on a Mountain" in *The Sunday Times Magazine*, 21 November 1982.
18. Mr Evelyn de Rothschild in conversation with the author.
19. Lord Rothschild in correspondence with the author.
20. The Hon. Jacob Rothschild in conversation with the author.
21. P. Knightley, *cit.* at note 17 above.
22. Baron Guy de Rothschild, *op.cit.*, p.272.
23. *The Banker*, August 1982, p.108.

EPILOGUE: ARROWS UP AND DOWN

1. R. Lambert, "Jacob Rothschild Spreads His Wings", in *Financial Times*, 4 November 1983.
2. J. Rothschild Holdings plc, *Annual Report 1985*, p.3.
3. D. Lascelles, "Endangered Species", in *Financial Times*, 27 June 1986.
4. Mr Evelyn de Rothschild in conversation with the author.
5. N. McAndrew, "The Rothschild Influence" in *Personal Investor*, April 1986.
6. D. Lascelles, *op.cit.*
7. Baron Eric de Rothschild in conversation with the author.
8. The *Evening Standard*, 21 January 1983.
9. Baron Guy de Rothschild, *op.cit.*, p.268.
10. Baron Guy de Rothschild in conversation with the author.
11. Baron Elie de Rothschild in conversation with the author.
12. C. Clerc, *Fondations Rothschild, 130 ans de solidarité*, Paris, 1982, p.41.
13. Paul Lewis, "Awaiting a Restoration in France" in *International Herald Tribune*, 6 March 1986.
14. E. Ipsen, "The High Roller at Rothschild Inc." in *Institutional Investor*, March 1986, p.131.
15. Baron Eric de Rothschild in conversation with the author.
16. Baron Edmond de Rothschild in conversation with the author.
17. Baron Eric de Rothschild in conversation with the author.
18. Baron Edmond de Rothschild in conversation with the author.
19. Ditto.
20. Baron Guy de Rothschild, *op.cit.*, p.261.
21. *The Daily Telegraph*, 4 December 1986.
22. *Ibid.*, 6 December 1986.
23. Philip Knightley, "Philby: How I got away", *The Sunday Times*, 30 March 1988.

BIBLIOGRAPHY

Place of publication is London unless otherwise stated.

(i) PRIMARY SOURCES

(a) UNPUBLISHED
Archives nationales, Paris.
British Library, London. The Battersea Papers.
Historisches Museum, Frankfurt.
Letters in the possession of Mr M.B. Cullen.
Museen der Stadt, Vienna.
Nationalbibliothek, Vienna.
Österreichisches Finanzarchiv, Vienna.
Staatsarchiv, Vienna.
Worms, George de (Baron), unpublished memoirs, in the possession of Mrs S. Anderson.

(b) PUBLISHED
Austin, S. (ed.), *A Tour in Germany, Holland and England in the Years 1826, 1827 and 1828 ... by a German Prince*, 4 vols, 1832.
Battersea, Constance (Lady), *Reminiscences*, 1922.
Brennan, F. (ed. and trans.), *Pückler's Progress*, 1987.
Buxton, C. (ed.), *Memoirs of Sir Thomas Fowell Buxton, Bart.*, 1872.
Carnarvon, Henry (Earl), *Ermine Tales*, 1980.
—— *No Regrets*, 1976.
Churchill, Winston, *Great Contemporaries*, 1937.
Cohen, Lucy, *Lady de Rothschild and her Daughters, 1821-1931*, 1935.
Colville, J., *The Fringes of Power*, 1985.
Diamond, S. (ed.), *A Casual View of America: The Home Letters of Salomon de Rothschild, 1859-1861*, New York, 1962.
Drumont, E., *La France juive*, Paris, 1943.
Feydeau, Ernest, *Mémoires d'un coulissier*, Paris, 1837.
Girardin, D. de, *Lettres Parisiennes*, Paris, 1861.
Gower, F.L., *Letters of Harriet Countess Granville, 1810-1845*, 2 vols, 1894.
Haldane, R.B., *An Autobiography*, 1929.
Halévy, J., *Trois diners avec Gambetta*, Paris, 1929.

475

Henrey, R., *Letters from Paris, 1870-1875, Written by C. de B., a Political Informant to the Head of the London House of Rothschild*, 1942.

Herzl, T. (trans. A. Hertzberg), *The Zionist Idea*, New York, 1959.

Hess, M., *Rome and Jerusalem*, 1862.

Karpeles, G. (ed.), *Heinrich Heine's Memoirs*, 3 vols, 1910.

Leland, C.G. (trans.), *The Works of Heinrich Heine*, 3 vols, 1891.

Loewe, L. (ed.), *Diaries of Sir Moses and Lady Montefiore*, 1983.

Mackintosh, A. (ed.), *Asquith H.H. Memories and Reflections, 1852-1927*, 2 vols, 1928.

Mendelssohn, M. (ed. A. Jospe), *Jerusalem and Other Jewish Writings*, 1969.

Palai. R. (ed.), *The Complete Diaries of Theodor Herzl*, 2 vols, New York, 1960.

Pinnery, T. (ed.), *Letters of Thomas Babington Macaulay*, 1981.

Ponsonby, Arthur (Baron), *Henry Ponsonby, Queen Victoria's Private Secretary. His Life from His Letters*, 1942.

Pope-Hennessy, J. (ed.), *Baron Ferdinand de Rothschild's Livre d'Or*, Roxburghe Club, Cambridge, 1957.

Proudhon, P., *Césarisme et christianisme*, Paris, 1883.

Pückler-Muskau, Hermann von (Prince), *Briefe Eines Verstorbenen*, 4 vols, 1830.

Ramm, A. (ed.), *The Political Correspondence of Mr Gladstone and Lord Granville, 1868-1876*, Camden Society, 3rd series, lxxxii, 1952.

Rothschild, Arthur de (Baron), *Histoire de la poste aux lettres depuis ses origines les plus anciennes jusqu'à nos jours*, Paris, 1873.

Rothschild, Ferdinand de (Baron), unpublished reminiscences, quoted extensively in Rothschild, Mrs James de, *The Rothschilds at Waddesdon Manor*, 1979.

Rothschild, Guy de (Baron), *The Whims of Fortune*, 1985.

Rothschild, Henri de (Baron), *Exposé des travaux scientifiques*, Paris, 1906.

——, *Les Timbres-poste et leurs amis*, Paris, 1938.

——, *Cent ans de Bibliophilie, 1839-1939. La bibliothèque James de Rothschild*, Paris, 1939.

——, *Un Bibliophile d'autrefois, le Baron James-Edouard de Rothschild*, Paris, 1934.

——, (under the pseudonym "André Pascal"), *Croisière autour de mes souvenirs*, Paris, 1933.

Rothschild, James Edward de (Baron), *Catalogue des livres composant la bibliothèque de feu M. le Baron J. de Rothschild*, 5 vols, Paris, 1884-1920.

Rothschild, Nadine de (Baronne), with Sarigné, G. de, *La Baronne rentre à cinq heures*, Paris, 1984.

Rothschild, Victor (Lord), *Meditations of a Broomstick*, 1977.

——, *Random Variables*, 1984.

——, *Rothschild Family Tree, 1450-1973*, 1973.

Rothschild, Walter (Hon.), *The Avifauna of Laysan and the Neighbouring Islands*, 1893.

——, *Extinct Birds*, 1907.

Rothschild, Willy de (Baronne), *30 Mélodies de la Baronne Willy de Rothschild*, Paris (n.d.).

Stanley, A.P., *The Life and Correspondence of Thomas Arnold D.D*, 2 vols, 1877.

Toussenel, A., *Les Juifs, rois de l'époque*, Paris, 1888.

Vincent, J. (ed.), *The Crawford Papers*, 1984.

Vincent, J.R. (ed.), *Disraeli, Derby and the Conservative Party: The Political Journals of Lord Stanley, 1849-1869*, 1978.

Weizmann, C., *Trial and Error, The Autobiography of Chaim Weizmann*, 1949.

(ii) SECONDARY SOURCES

The more important works, based upon original material, are marked with an asterisk.

(a) UNPUBLISHED

*Dumont, M.-J., "La Fondation Rothschild et les premières habitations à bon marché de Paris, 1900-1914", Sorbonne doctoral thesis, Paris, 1981.

(b) PUBLISHED BOOKS

Adam, A.E., *Beechwoods and Bayonets, The Book of Halton*, 1983.

Ayer, J., *Century of Finance, 1804-1904: The London House of Rothschild*, 1905.

Balla, I., *The Romance of the Rothschilds*, 1913.

Berghoeffer, G.H., *Mayer Amschel Rothschild: der Grunder des Rothschildschen Bankhauses*, Frankfurt, 1922.

Blake, R., *Disraeli*, 1966.

*Bouvier, J., *Les Rothschild*, Paris, 1967.

Buckle, G. and Monypenny, W.F., *The Life of Benjamin Disraeli, Earl of Beaconsfield*, 6 vols, 1910-20.

Chadwick, G.F., *The Works of Sir Joseph Paxton*, 1961.

*Chapman, S.D., *The Foundation of the English Rothschilds: N.M. Rothschild as a Textile Merchant, 1799-1811*, 1977.

*Corti, E.C. (Count) (trans. Brian and Beatrix Lunn), *The Rise of the House of Rothschild*, 1928.

—— *(trans. Brian and Beatrix Lunn), *The Reign of the House of Rothschild*, 1928.

—— and Gong, W., *Die Rothschilds*, Frankfurt, 1962.

Cowen, A. and R., *Victorian Jews through British Eyes*, Oxford, 1986.

Cowles, V., *The Rothschilds: A Family of Fortune*, 1973.

*Davis, R.W., *The English Rothschilds, 1799-1915*, 1983.

Demachy, J. (ed.), *Les Rothschild, une famille de financiers juifs au XIX siècle*, Paris, 1896.

Disraeli, Benjamin, *Conningsby, or The New Generation*, 1844 (Penguin Edition 1983).

Druck, D. (trans. L. Glassman), *Baron Edmond Rothschild: The Story of a Practical Idealist*, New York, 1928.

Dugdale, B.E.C., *Arthur James Balfour, First Earl of Balfour*, 2 vols, 1936.

Egremont, M., *Balfour: A Life of Arthur James Balfour*, 1980.

Emanuel, C.H.L., *A Century and a Half of Jewish History*, 1910.

Epstein, I., *Judaism*, 1959.

Flint, J., *Cecil Rhodes*, 1976.

Foster, R.F., *Lord Randolph Churchill*, Oxford, 1981.

Gardiner, A.G., *The Life of Sir William Harcourt*, 2 vols, 1923.

Gavoty, B., *Frédéric Chopin*, New York, 1977.

Geiger, L., *Die deutsche Literatur und die Juden*, Berlin, 1910.

*Gillam, A., *The Emancipation of the Jews in England, 1830-1860*, New York, 1982.

*Gille, B., *Histoire de la Maison Rothschild* (to 1870), 2 vols, 1965-7.

Grigg, J., *Lloyd George: The People's Champion, 1902-1911*, 1978.

Holland, A.J. and Rothschild, Edmund de, *Our Exbury*, Southampton, 1982.

Holmes, C., *Anti-Semitism in British Society, 1876-1939*, 1979.

Hurst, J., *Enquête sur la question sociale en Europe*, Paris, 1879.

James, R.R., *Lord Randolph Churchill*, 1959.

Katz, I., *August Belmont: A Political Biography*, New York, 1968.

*Lipman, V.D. (ed.), *Three Centuries of Anglo-Jewish History*, 1961.

Littlewood, J., *Milady Vine: The Autobiography of Philippe de Rothschild*, 1984.

Margalith, I., *Le Baron Edmond de Rothschild et la colonisation juive en Palestine, 1882-1899*, Paris, 1957.

*März, E., *Österreichische Industrie- und Bankpolitik in der Zeit Franz Josephus I*, Vienna, 1968.

*——, *Austrian Banking and Financial Policy: Creditanstalt at a Turning Point, 1913-23*, 1984.

Maurois, André, *Cecil Rhodes*, 1953.

——, *Disraeli, A Picture of the Victorian Age*, 1927.

——, *Lélia, the Life of George Sand*, 1953.

Morton, F., *The Rothschilds: A Family Portrait*, 1962.

*Muhlstein, A., *Baron James: The Rise of the French Rothschilds*, 1983.

Newman, E., *The Life of Richard Wagner*, 4 vols, 1933-47.

Niecks, F., *Frédéric Chopin as a Man and Musician*, 2 vols, 1902.

Palin, R., *Rothschild Relish*, 1970.

Phillips, C.E. and Barber, P.N., *The Rothschild Rhododendrons: A Record of the Gardens at Exbury*, 1967.

Poliakov, L. (trans. M. Kochan), *The History of Anti-Semitism*, III, 1975.

Ray, C., *Lafite – The Story of Château Lafite-Rothschild*, 1985.

——, *Robert Mondavi of the Napa Valley*, 1984.

Read, C.H., *The Waddesdon Bequest, The Collection of Jewels, Plate and Other Works of Art, Bequeathed to the British Museum by Baron Ferdinand Rothschild*, 1899.

——, *The Waddesdon Bequest, Catalogue of the Works of Art Bequeathed to the British Museum by Baron Ferdinand Rothschild*, 1902.

Rhodes, James R., *Rosebery*, 1963.

Roth, C., *History of the Great Synagogue*, 1950.

——, *The Magnificent Rothschilds*, 1939.

*Rothschild, Mrs James de, *The Rothschilds at Waddesdon Manor*, 1979.

*Rothschild, Miriam, *Dear Lord Rothschild: Birds, Butterflies and History*, 1983.

——, *Nathaniel Charles Rothschild, 1877-1923*, 1979.

*Rothschild, Victor (Lord), *"You Have It, Madam": The Purchase, in 1875, of Suez Canal Shares by Disraeli and Baron Lionel de Rothschild*, 1980.

*——, *The Shadow of a Great Man*, 1982.

Rowland, P., *Lloyd George*, 1975.

Salingré, H., *Im grossen Hauptquartier, 1870-1*, Berlin, 1910.

*Schama, S., *Two Rothschilds and the Land of Israel*, 1978.

Smallwood, J. (Hon.), *I Chose Canada*, Toronto, 1973.

Smith, P., *Brinco: The Story of Churchill Falls*, Toronto, 1975.

Stead, R., *Bygone Kent*, 1892.

Stein, L., *The Balfour Declaration*, 1961.

*Stern, F., *Gold and Iron: Bismarck, Bleichröder and the Building of the German Empire*, 1977.

Taylor, A.J.P., *The Struggle for Mastery in Europe, 1848-1918*, 1954.

Wechsberg, J., *The Merchant Bankers*, 1967.

Weill, Alexander, *Pensées*, Paris, 1875.

Weinstock, H., *Rossini, a Biography*, 1968.

*White, J., *Rothschild Buildings: Life in an East End Tenement Block, 1887-1920*, 1980.

Wistrich, R.S., *Socialism and the Jews: The Dilemmas of Assimilation in Germany and Austria-Hungary*, 1982.

Wolf, L., *Essays in Jewish History*, Jewish Historical Society of England, 1934.

——, *The Queen's Jewry*, 1923.

Woodham-Smith, C., *The Great Hunger*, 1962.

Zamoyski, A., *Chopin, a Biography*, 1979.

(c) ARTICLES, CATALOGUES, ETC.

Bouvier, J. and Cameron, R., "Une Lettre inédite de Presigny à Napoléon III (1855) à propos de la rivalité Rothschild—Péreire" in *Revue historique*, Paris, July-September 1963.

Bury, J.P.T., "The Identity of 'C. de B.'" in *French Historical Studies*, III, No. 4, 1964.

Clerc, C., *Fondations Rothschild, 130 ans de solidarité*, Paris, 1982.

Dairnvaell, G., *Histoire édifiante et curieuse de Rothschild Ier, Roi des Juifs par Satan*, Paris, 1846.

Davis, C., *A Description of the Works of Art forming the Collection of Alfred de Rothschild*, 2 vols, 1884.

Eriksen, S., *Waddesdon Manor*, 1982.

Gelber, N., "Öesterreich und die Damascusaffaire im Jahr 1840, nach bisher unveröffentlichen Akten" in *Jahrbuch der Jüdisch-Literarischen Gesellschaft*, XVIII, 1926.

Historisches Museum, Frankfurt, *Historical Documentation Guide*, Frankfurt, 1979.

"The House of Rothschild" in *The Gentleman's Magazine*, 229, November 1871.

Knight, G.A., "The Rothschild-Bleichröder Axis in Action, An Anglo-German Co-operative 1877-1878" in *The Leo Baeck Year Book*, 1983.

"Le Baron Alphonse de Rothschild" in *Librairie de L'Art*, Paris, 1905.

Mouton Rothschild, Paintings for the Labels, 1945-1981, Boston, 1983.

"Notable collections: the collection of Mr Alfred de Rothschild in Seamore Place by Mrs Steuart Erskine" in *Connoisseur*, III, No. 10, June 1902.

Novitates Zoologicae. A Journal of Zoology. Vols 1-40, ed. Walter Rothschild,

Ernst Hartert and K. Jordan, 1894-1938. Vol. 41, ed. Miriam Rothschild and K. Jordan, 1938-9, Tring, Herts.

Ramm, A., "Great Britain and France in Egypt 1876-1882" in *France and Britain in Africa*, 1971.

Rosebery, Hannah, *Catalogue of Mentmore and its Contents*, 2 vols, Edinburgh, 1884.

Rothschild, Carl von (Baron and Baroness), *Catalogue of Baron and Baroness Carl von Rothschild's Art Collection at Günthersburg and Untermainquai*, No. 15, 5 parts, Frankfurt, 1895.

Rothschild, Henri de, *Trois cent autographes de la donation Henri de Rothschild*, Paris, 1933.

——, *Lettres, autographes et manuscrits de la collection Henri de Rothschild. T.I. Moyen Age — XVI siècle, Paris, 1924.*

Rothschild, Victor (Lord), *The Rothschild Library. A Catalogue of the Collection of Eighteenth-century Printed Books and Manuscripts Formed by Lord Rothschild*, 2 vols, Cambridge, 1954.

Rubens, A., "The Rothschilds in Caricature", in *Transactions of the Jewish Historical Society of England*, XX, 1968-9.

Smallwood, J. (Hon.), "Churchill Falls" in *The Atlantic Advocate*, July 1967.

Sotheby & Co. *Catalogue of the Celebrated Collection of German, Dutch and other Continental Silver and Silver-Gilt of the 15th, 16th, 17th and 18th Centuries. Mainly inherited from the late Baron Carl von Rothschild of Frankfurt; also collected by the Baron Lionel de Rothschild and by the first Lord and Lady Rothschild. Also massive English silver and silver-gilt of the 18th and early 19th centuries. Removed from 148 Piccadilly, W.1. Sold by order of Victor Rothschild.* London, 1937.

Stiefel, D., "The Reconstruction of the Credit-Anstalt", in *International Business and Central Europe, 1918-1938*, Leicester, 1983.

Wolf, L., "Lord Rothschild: an appreciation", *Daily Chronicle*, 1 April 1915.

——, "The Rothschilds", *Jewish Chronicle Supplement*, No. 88, April 1928.

——, "The political problems of the Rothschilds", *Jewish Chronicle Supplement*, No. 103, July 1929.

480

INDEX

Rothschild Family Index

Gutle) (m. S. Beyfus) 18
battle of the vineyards 415-19, 444
Benjamin (son of Edmond/ Nadine)
428, 445
Bethsabée (Batsheva) (daughter of
Edouard/ Germaine) 350, 360,
375-6, 379, 403-5, 455
Bettina (daughter of Alphonse/
Leonora) (m. Salomon Albert) 275
Bettina (daughter of Alphonse/
Clarice) (m. M. Looram) 355-6,
370, 379, 403
Betty (daughter of Salomon/
Caroline) (m. James) 70, 80-1,
83-4, 111-12, 135, 149, 166, 200,
211, 224, 270, 292

caricatures/cartoons of 60, 92, 95, 97,
102, 124, 127, 409
Carl (son of Mayer Amschel/ Gutle)
(m. Adelheid Hertz) 18-20, 73, 95,
125, 171
ennobled by Austria 66, 77
establishes Neapolitan business
79-80
and William of Hesse-Kassel 32-4,
38, 40
Caroline (Stern) (m. Salomon) 49, 76
charitable activities 95-6, 125-7, 187,
195, 231-2, 248, 256, 265-70, 274,
279-80, 320-2, 324-5, 328, 441-2
Charles (son of Natty/Emma) (m. R.
v.Wertheimstein) 256, 317-20,
328-30, 340, 361, 388, 425, 426,
453
Charlotte (daughter of James/Betty)
(m. Nathaniel) 84, 89, 111, 113,
119, 135, 223, 267
Charlotte (daughter of Nathan/
Hannah) (m. Anselm) 88-9, 120-1,
142
Charlotte (daughter of Carl/
Adelheid) (m. Lionel) 101, 120,
155, 158-9, 160, 193, 279, 282

Charlotte (daughter of Edmund/
Elizabeth) 454
Clarice (Sebag-Montefiore) (m.
Alphonse) 370, 378-9, 402-3,
413-14
coat of arms 66, 77-8, 132, 437-8
collecting mania 8-9, 88, 109-10,
241, 244-8, 269, 270, 291, 383
communications system 10-11, 25,
43-4, 57-8, 197, 209-10, 238-9
Constance (daughter of Anthony/
Louisa) (m. C. Flower) 81-2, 193-5,
207, 217-26, 230, 232, 242, 255,
264-7, 279-80, 309, 344, 432

David (son of Guy/Alix) 431, 438-43
division of capital/shares 36-7, 50-1,
72
Dorothy (Pinto) (m. James) 335, 340,
364-5, 391-2, 411-13

Edmond (son of James/Betty) (m.
Adelheid) 111, 135, 211, 322-4
and Palestine 291-8, 338-40, 404,
406
Edmond (son of Maurice/Noémie) (m.
Nadine Lhopitalier) 366, 378, 406,
410-15, 441-8, 455
Edmund (son of Lionel/Marie Louise)
(m. E. Lentner, A. Harrison) 357,
384-6, 391, 394-9, 420-1, 451-2
Edouard (son of Alphonse/Leonora)
(m. Germaine Halphen) 350-1,
365-6, 371, 375-6, 378, 400
Elie (son of Robert/Gabrielle) (m. L
Fould-Springer) 375-7, 400, 413,
415-18, 431, 441, 443, 454
Elisabeth de Chambure (Lili) (m.
Philippe) 380-1
Emma (daughter of Mayer
Carl/Louise) (m. Natty) 191, 255-6,
259, 267, 344, 349, 360
endogamy 81-3, 313

The Rothschilds
c. 1550-1985

Based on Rothschild, Victor, *Rothschild Family Tree*, 1450–1973 (Cambridge University Library) and information supplied by members of the family

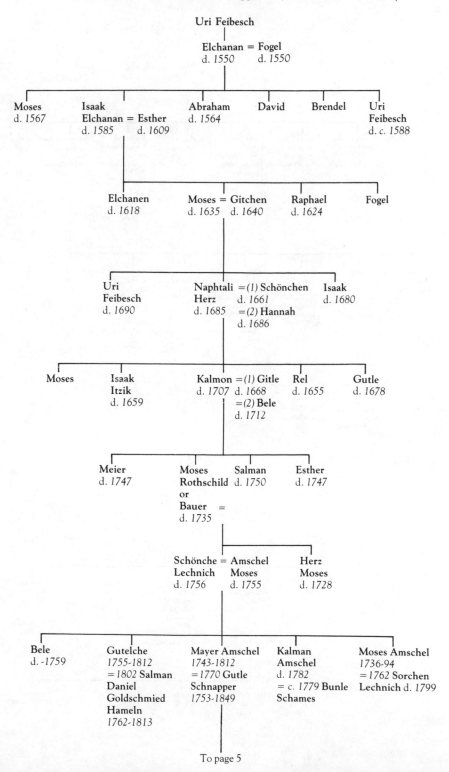

Uri Feibesch

Elchanan = Fogel
d. 1550   d. 1550

Moses d. 1567 — Isaak Elchanan = Esther (d. 1585 / d. 1609) — Abraham d. 1564 — David — Brendel — Uri Feibesch d. c. 1588

Elchanen d. 1618 — Moses = Gitchen (d. 1635 / d. 1640) — Raphael d. 1624 — Fogel

Uri Feibesch d. 1690 — Naphtali Herz d. 1685 =(1) Schönchen d. 1661 =(2) Hannah d. 1686 — Isaak d. 1680

Moses — Isaak Itzik d. 1659 — Kalmon d. 1707 =(1) Gitle d. 1668 =(2) Bele d. 1712 — Rel d. 1655 — Gutle d. 1678

Meier d. 1747 — Moses Rothschild or Bauer d. 1735 = / Salman d. 1750 — Esther d. 1747

Schönche Lechnich d. 1756 = Amschel Moses d. 1755 — Herz Moses d. 1728

Bele d. -1759 — Gutelche 1755-1812 =1802 Salman Daniel Goldschmied Hameln 1762-1813 — Mayer Amschel 1743-1812 =1770 Gutle Schnapper 1753-1849 — Kalman Amschel d. 1782 = c. 1779 Bunle Schames — Moses Amschel 1736-94 =1762 Sorchen Lechnich d. 1799

To page 5

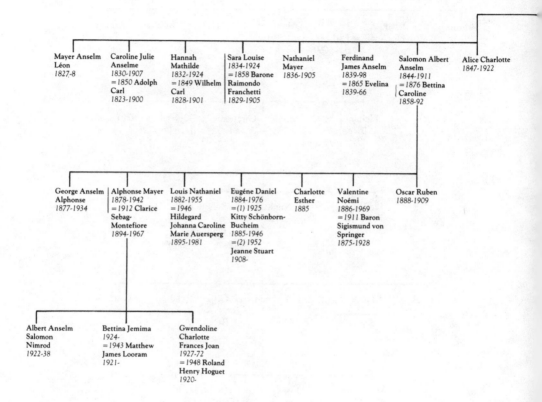

Mayer Anselm
Léon
1827-8

Caroline Julie
Anselme
1830-1907
=1850 Adolph
Carl
1823-1900

Hannah
Mathilde
1832-1924
=1849 Wilhelm
Carl
1828-1901

Sara Louise
1834-1924
=1858 Barone
Raimondo
Franchetti
1829-1905

Nathaniel
Mayer
1836-1905

Ferdinand
James Anselm
1839-98
=1865 Evelina
1839-66

Salomon Albert
Anselm
1844-1911
=1876 Bettina
Caroline
1858-92

Alice Charlotte
1847-1922

George Anselm
Alphonse
1877-1934

Alphonse Mayer
1878-1942
=1912 Clarice
Sebag-
Montefiore
1894-1967

Louis Nathaniel
1882-1955
=1946
Hildegard
Johanna Caroline
Marie Auersperg
1895-1981

Eugéne Daniel
1884-1976
=(1) 1925
Kitty Schönborn-
Bucheim
1885-1946
=(2) 1952
Jeanne Stuart
1908-

Charlotte
Esther
1885

Valentine
Noémi
1886-1969
=1911 Baron
Sigismund von
Springer
1875-1928

Oscar Ruben
1888-1909

Albert Anselm
Salomon
Nimrod
1922-38

Bettina Jemima
1924-
=1943 Matthew
James Looram
1921-

Gwendoline
Charlotte
Frances Joan
1927-72
=1948 Roland
Henry Hoguet
1920-

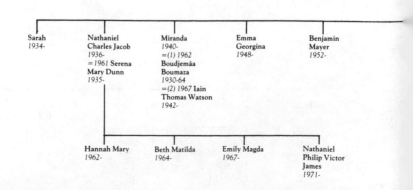

Sarah
1934-

Nathaniel
Charles Jacob
1936-
=1961 Serena
Mary Dunn
1935-

Miranda
1940-
=(1) 1962
Boudjemâa
Boumaza
1930-64
=(2) 1967 Iain
Thomas Watson
1942-

Emma
Georgina
1948-

Benjamin
Mayer
1952-

Hannah Mary
1962-

Beth Matilda
1964-

Emily Magda
1967-

Nathaniel
Philip Victor
James
1971-

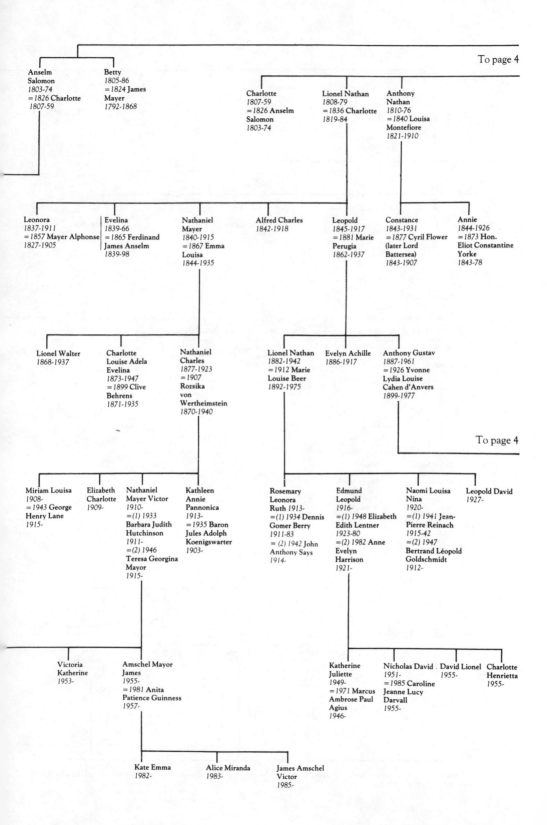

To page 4

Anselm
Salomon
1803-74
=1826 Charlotte
1807-59

Betty
1805-86
=1824 James
Mayer
1792-1868

Charlotte
1807-59
=1826 Anselm
Salomon
1803-74

Lionel Nathan
1808-79
=1836 Charlotte
1819-84

Anthony
Nathan
1810-76
=1840 Louisa
Montefiore
1821-1910

Leonora
1837-1911
=1857 Mayer Alphonse
1827-1905

Evelina
1839-66
=1865 Ferdinand
James Anselm
1839-98

Nathaniel
Mayer
1840-1915
=1867 Emma
Louisa
1844-1935

Alfred Charles
1842-1918

Leopold
1845-1917
=1881 Marie
Perugia
1862-1937

Constance
1843-1931
=1877 Cyril Flower
(later Lord
Battersea)
1843-1907

Annie
1844-1926
=1873 Hon.
Eliot Constantine
Yorke
1843-78

Lionel Walter
1868-1937

Charlotte
Louise Adela
Evelina
1873-1947
=1899 Clive
Behrens
1871-1935

Nathaniel
Charles
1877-1923
=1907
Rozsika
von
Wertheimstein
1870-1940

Lionel Nathan
1882-1942
=1912 Marie
Louise Beer
1892-1975

Evelyn Achille
1886-1917

Anthony Gustav
1887-1961
=1926 Yvonne
Lydia Louise
Cahen d'Anvers
1899-1977

To page 4

Miriam Louisa
1908-
=1943 George
Henry Lane
1915-

Elizabeth
Charlotte
1909-

Nathaniel
Mayer Victor
1910-
=(1) 1933
Barbara Judith
Hutchinson
1911-
=(2) 1946
Teresa Georgina
Mayor
1915-

Kathleen
Annie
Pannonica
1913-
=1935 Baron
Jules Adolph
Koenigswarter
1903-

Rosemary
Leonora
Ruth 1913-
=(1) 1934 Dennis
Gomer Berry
1911-83
= (2) 1942 John
Anthony Says
1914-

Edmund
Leopold
1916-
=(1) 1948 Elizabeth
Edith Lentner
1923-80
=(2) 1982 Anne
Evelyn
Harrison
1921-

Naomi Louisa
Nina
1920-
=(1) 1941 Jean-
Pierre Reinach
1915-42
=(2) 1947
Bertrand Léopold
Goldschmidt
1912-

Leopold David
1927-

Victoria
Katherine
1953-

Amschel Mayor
James
1955-
=1981 Anita
Patience Guinness
1957-

Katherine
Juliette
1949-
=1971 Marcus
Ambrose Paul
Agius
1946-

Nicholas David
1951-
=1985 Caroline
Jeanne Lucy
Darvall
1955-

David Lionel
1955-

Charlotte
Henrietta
1955-

Kate Emma
1982-

Alice Miranda
1983-

James Amschel
Victor
1985-

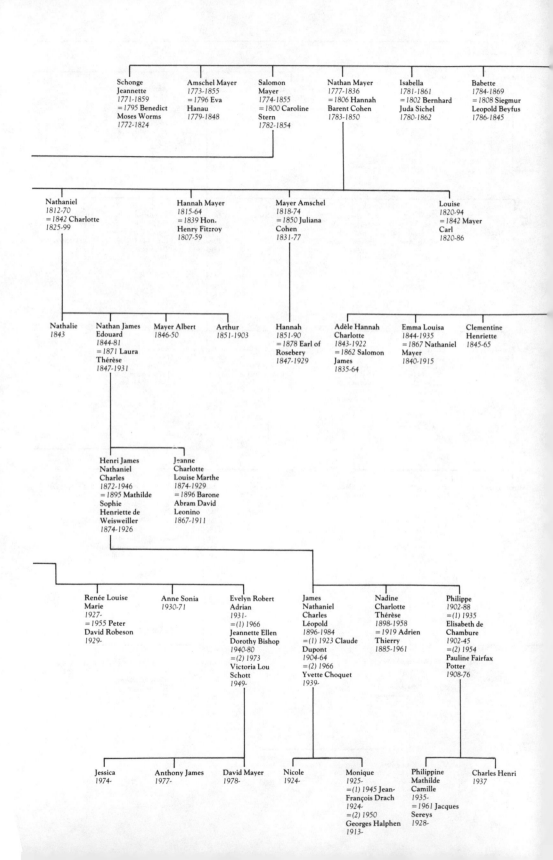

Schonge Jeannette 1771-1859 =1795 Benedict Moses Worms 1772-1824

Amschel Mayer 1773-1855 =1796 Eva Hanau 1779-1848

Salomon Mayer 1774-1855 =1800 Caroline Stern 1782-1854

Nathan Mayer 1777-1836 =1806 Hannah Barent Cohen 1783-1850

Isabella 1781-1861 =1802 Bernhard Juda Sichel 1780-1862

Babette 1784-1869 =1808 Siegmur Leopold Beyfus 1786-1845

Nathaniel 1812-70 =1842 Charlotte 1825-99

Hannah Mayer 1815-64 =1839 Hon. Henry Fitzroy 1807-59

Mayer Amschel 1818-74 =1850 Juliana Cohen 1831-77

Louise 1820-94 =1842 Mayer Carl 1820-86

Nathalie 1843

Nathan James Edouard 1844-81 =1871 Laura Thérèse 1847-1931

Mayer Albert 1846-50

Arthur 1851-1903

Hannah 1851-90 =1878 Earl of Rosebery 1847-1929

Adèle Hannah Charlotte 1843-1922 =1862 Salomon James 1835-64

Emma Louisa 1844-1935 =1867 Nathaniel Mayer 1840-1915

Clementine Henriette 1845-65

Henri James Nathaniel Charles 1872-1946 =1895 Mathilde Sophie Henriette de Weisweiller 1874-1926

Jeanne Charlotte Louise Marthe 1874-1929 =1896 Barone Abram David Leonino 1867-1911

Renée Louise Marie 1927- =1955 Peter David Robeson 1929-

Anne Sonia 1930-71

Evelyn Robert Adrian 1931- =(1) 1966 Jeannette Ellen Dorothy Bishop 1940-80 =(2) 1973 Victoria Lou Schott 1949-

James Nathaniel Charles Léopold 1896-1984 =(1) 1923 Claude Dupont 1904-64 =(2) 1966 Yvette Choquet 1939-

Nadine Charlotte Thérèse 1898-1958 =1919 Adrien Thierry 1885-1961

Philippe 1902-88 =(1) 1935 Elisabeth de Chambure 1902-45 =(2) 1954 Pauline Fairfax Potter 1908-76

Jessica 1974-

Anthony James 1977-

David Mayer 1978-

Nicole 1924-

Monique 1925- =(1) 1945 Jean-François Drach 1924- =(2) 1950 Georges Halphen 1913-

Philippine Mathilde Camille 1935- =1961 Jacques Sereys 1928-

Charles Henri 1937

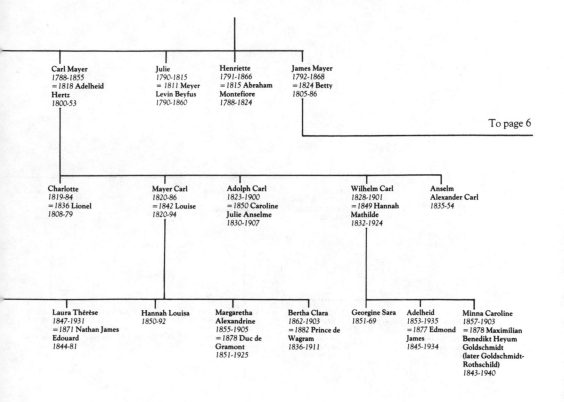

Carl Mayer
1788-1855
=1818 Adelheid
Hertz
1800-53

Julie
1790-1815
= 1811 Meyer
Levin Beyfus
1790-1860

Henriette
1791-1866
=1815 Abraham
Montefiore
1788-1824

James Mayer
1792-1868
=1824 Betty
1805-86

To page 6

Charlotte
1819-84
=1836 Lionel
1808-79

Mayer Carl
1820-86
=1842 Louise
1820-94

Adolph Carl
1823-1900
=1850 Caroline
Julie Anselme
1830-1907

Wilhelm Carl
1828-1901
=1849 Hannah
Mathilde
1832-1924

Anselm
Alexander Carl
1835-54

Laura Thérèse
1847-1931
=1871 Nathan James
Edouard
1844-81

Hannah Louisa
1850-92

Margaretha
Alexandrine
1855-1905
=1878 Duc de
Gramont
1851-1925

Bertha Clara
1862-1903
=1882 Prince de
Wagram
1836-1911

Georgine Sara
1851-69

Adelheid
1853-1935
=1877 Edmond
James
1845-1934

Minna Caroline
1857-1903
=1878 Maximilian
Benedikt Heyum
Goldschmidt
(later Goldschmidt-
Rothschild)
1843-1940

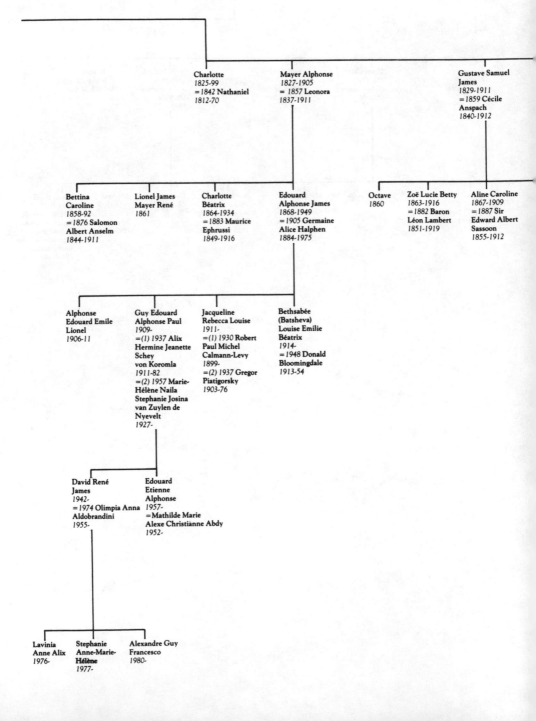

Charlotte
1825-99
= 1842 Nathaniel
1812-70

Mayer Alphonse
1827-1905
= 1857 Leonora
1837-1911

Gustave Samuel
James
1829-1911
= 1859 Cécile
Anspach
1840-1912

Bettina
Caroline
1858-92
= 1876 Salomon
Albert Anselm
1844-1911

Lionel James
Mayer René
1861

Charlotte
Béatrix
1864-1934
= 1883 Maurice
Ephrussi
1849-1916

Edouard
Alphonse James
1868-1949
= 1905 Germaine
Alice Halphen
1884-1975

Octave
1860

Zoë Lucie Betty
1863-1916
= 1882 Baron
Léon Lambert
1851-1919

Aline Caroline
1867-1909
= 1887 Sir
Edward Albert
Sassoon
1855-1912

Alphonse
Edouard Emile
Lionel
1906-11

Guy Edouard
Alphonse Paul
1909-
=(1) 1937 Alix
Hermine Jeanette
Schey
von Koromla
1911-82
=(2) 1957 Marie-
Hélène Naila
Stephanie Josina
van Zuylen de
Nyevelt
1927-

Jacqueline
Rebecca Louise
1911-
=(1) 1930 Robert
Paul Michel
Calmann-Levy
1899-
=(2) 1937 Gregor
Piatigorsky
1903-76

Bethsabée
(Batsheva)
Louise Emilie
Béatrix
1914-
= 1948 Donald
Bloomingdale
1913-54

David René
James
1942-
= 1974 Olimpia Anna
Aldobrandini
1955-

Edouard
Etienne
Alphonse
1957-
=Mathilde Marie
Alexe Christiànne Abdy
1952-

Lavinia
Anne Alix
1976-

Stephanie
Anne-Marie-
Hélène
1977-

Alexandre Guy
Francesco
1980-

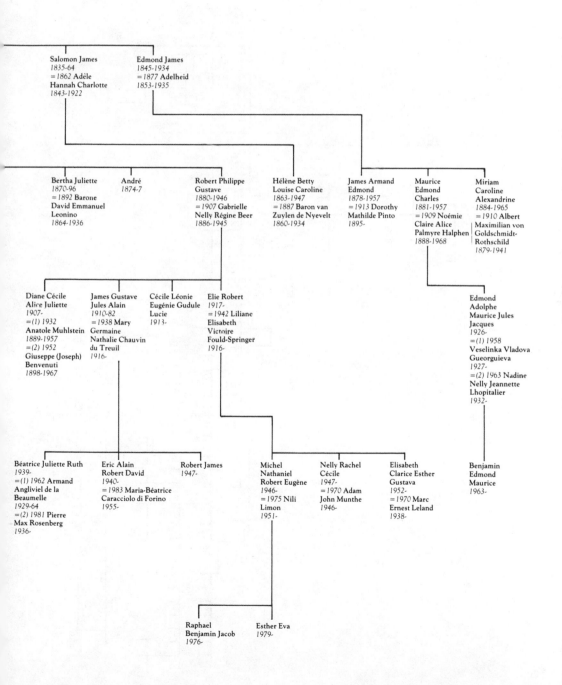

Salomon James
1835-64
= 1862 Adèle
Hannah Charlotte
1843-1922

Edmond James
1845-1934
= 1877 Adelheid
1853-1935

Bertha Juliette
1870-96
= 1892 Barone
David Emmanuel
Leonino
1864-1936

André
1874-7

Robert Philippe
Gustave
1880-1946
= 1907 Gabrielle
Nelly Régine Beer
1886-1945

Hélène Betty
Louise Caroline
1863-1947
= 1887 Baron van
Zuylen de Nyevelt
1860-1934

James Armand
Edmond
1878-1957
= 1913 Dorothy
Mathilde Pinto
1895-

Maurice
Edmond
Charles
1881-1957
= 1909 Noémie
Claire Alice
Palmyre Halphen
1888-1968

Miriam
Caroline
Alexandrine
1884-1965
= 1910 Albert
Maximilian von
Goldschmidt-
Rothschild
1879-1941

Diane Cécile
Alice Juliette
1907-
= (1) 1932
Anatole Muhlstein
1889-1957
= (2) 1952
Giuseppe (Joseph)
Benvenuti
1898-1967

James Gustave
Jules Alain
1910-82
= 1938 Mary
Germaine
Nathalie Chauvin
du Treuil
1916-

Cécile Léonie
Eugénie Gudule
Lucie
1913-

Elie Robert
1917-
= 1942 Liliane
Elisabeth
Victoire
Fould-Springer
1916-

Edmond
Adolphe
Maurice Jules
Jacques
1926-
= (1) 1958
Veselinka Vladova
Gueorguieva
1927-
= (2) 1963 Nadine
Nelly Jeannette
Lhopitalier
1932-

Béatrice Juliette Ruth
1939-
= (1) 1962 Armand
Angliviel de la
Beaumelle
1929-64
= (2) 1981 Pierre
Max Rosenberg
1936-

Eric Alain
Robert David
1940-
= 1983 Maria-Béatrice
Caracciolo di Forino
1955-

Robert James
1947-

Michel
Nathaniel
Robert Eugène
1946-
= 1975 Nili
Limon
1951-

Nelly Rachel
Cécile
1947-
= 1970 Adam
John Munthe
1946-

Elisabeth
Clarice Esther
Gustava
1952-
= 1970 Marc
Ernest Leland
1938-

Benjamin
Edmond
Maurice
1963-

Raphael
Benjamin Jacob
1976-

Esther Eva
1979-

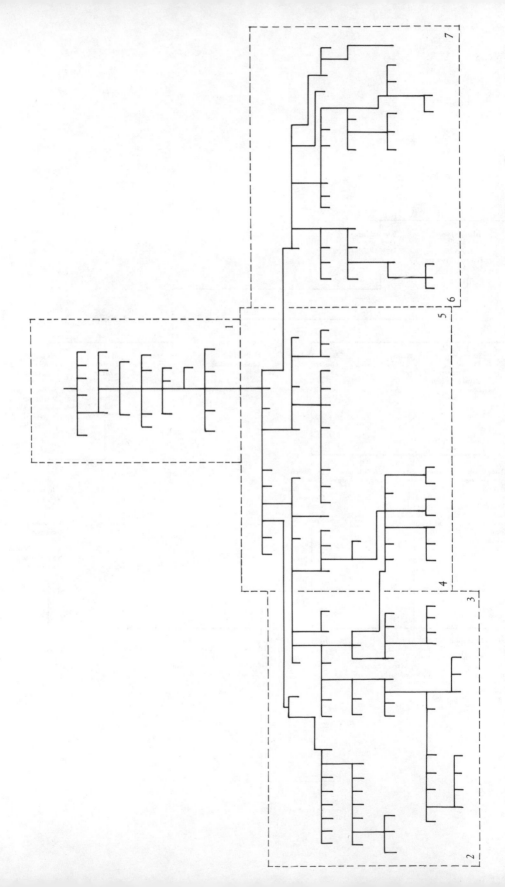